THE SPLINTERED EMPIRES

Dedication

To Lisa

The Splintered Empires

THE EASTERN FRONT 1917–21

Prit Buttar

Osprey Publishing
c/o Bloomsbury Publishing Plc
PO Box 883, Oxford, OX1 9PL, UK
or
c/o Bloomsbury Publishing Plc
1385 Broadway, 5th Floor, New York, NY 10018, USA
E-mail: info@ospreypublishing.com

www.ospreypublishing.com

OSPREY is a trademark of Osprey Publishing, a division of Bloomsbury Publishing Plc.

First published in Great Britain in 2017

A CIP catalogue record for this book is available from the British Library.

Prit Buttar has asserted his right under the Copyright, Designs and Patents Act, 1988, to be identified as the Author of this Work.

ISBN: HB: 9781472819857
ePub: 9781472819871
ePDF: 9781472819864
XML: 9781472826022

17 18 19 20 21 10 9 8 7 6 5 4 3 2 1

Index by Zoe Ross
Typeset in Adobe Garamond Pro, Trajan and Times New Roman
Originated by PDQ Digital Media Solutions, Bungay, UK
Printed and bound in Great Britain by CPI (Group) UK Ltd, Croydon CR0 4YY

Front cover: Russian prisoners of war being marched into captivity by their German captors, circa 1916. The prisoners include a 15-year-old boy, who claimed he volunteered in order to avoid starvation after his father joined the army and his mother fled their home. (Photo by FPG / Hulton Archive / Getty Images)

Osprey Publishing supports the Woodland Trust, the UK's leading woodland conservation charity. Between 2014 and 2018 our donations are being spent on their Centenary Woods project in the UK.

To find out more about our authors and books visit **www.ospreypublishing.com**. Here you will find extracts, author interviews, details of forthcoming events and the option to sign up for our newsletter.

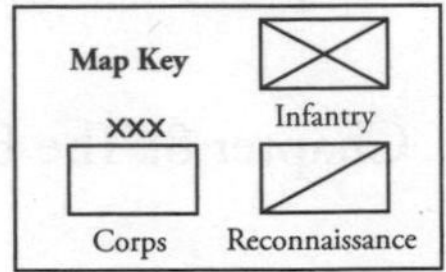

CONTENTS

LIST OF ILLUSTRATIONS

A Red Army armoured train.
Red Army artillery.
Red Army infantry.
Troops of the First Cavalry Army.
White Russian troops on a recruitment drive.
Troops of the Russian Red Army entering the city of Riga, Latvia, in 1919.
German troops fighting the Red Guard during the Finnish Civil War, circa April 1918.

LIST OF MAPS

AUTHOR'S NOTE

This is the fourth volume of a series that describes the First World War on the Eastern Front. After the huge battles and bloodshed of the preceding years, 1917 saw comparatively little fighting as Russia became embroiled in its revolutions and the Germans took advantage of this to concentrate their energies elsewhere. Compared to the first three volumes, this work therefore contains less about purely military matters and more about the politics that shaped events. Unlike the Western Front, there was no tidy end to the war in Eastern Europe, and conflicts dragged on into the 1920s, shaping the nations that were born from the splinters of the great empires. Ultimately, the imperfections in borders and other matters would lead to a second conflict barely two decades later, and an understanding of the end of the First World War in the east, particularly with regard to its legacy, therefore requires an account of events after the armistice in the west in November 1918.

CHRONOLOGY

1917

22 January	Mass demonstrations in Petrograd to commemorate the Bloody Sunday massacre
29 January	Beginning of meetings between Prince Sixtus and representatives of Austria-Hungary to discuss possible peace terms
27 February	Strikes begin in Petrograd
7 March	Cossacks and other troops deployed on the streets to prevent looting
8 March	First clashes between strikers and police; Cossacks side with the people against the authorities
9 March	Troops of the Petrograd garrison begin to mutiny
10–11 March	Mutineers and workers release prisoners from Petrograd's prisons and police stations
13 March	Ivanov dispatched from Mogilev to suppress dissent in Petrograd. Soviet of Workers' Deputies and Provisional Committee of Duma Members formed. Tsar leaves Mogilev to travel to Tsarskoe Selo
15 March	Tsar abdicates. Provisional Government formed
22 March	Tsar arrives in Tsarskoe Selo and he and his family are placed under arrest
23 March	Prince Sixtus and Emperor Karl have a secret meeting outside Vienna
27 March	Lenin leaves Zurich
4 April	German attack to eliminate the Toboly bridgehead on the River Stochod
6 April	USA declares war on Germany
16 April	Lenin arrives in Petrograd
3 May	Austro-Hungarian diplomats suggest to Germany that peace might be possible in return for ceding Alsace-Lorraine
12 May	Central Powers commanders transmit radio message to Russian commanders calling for ceasefire

30 June	Beginning of Kerensky Offensive
7 July	Kornilov's Southwest Front and Denikin's West Front attack
14 July	Litzmann launches counterattacks against Southwest Front
	Estonian National Council or *Maapäev* convenes
16 July	Further unrest in Petrograd; mutinous troops and Red Guards demand that the Soviet takes power
18 July	Troops loyal to Provisional Government restore order in Petrograd
19 July	Central Powers launch counteroffensive against Russians in eastern Galicia; Kerensky replaces Prince Lvov as Russian head of state
	Reichstag declaration calling for peace without annexations or reparations; dismissal of Bethmann-Hollweg
23 July	Romanian Army attacks in Moldova
24 July	Meeting of Entente Powers in Paris to discuss separate peace with Austria-Hungary
6 August	Germans begin counteroffensive in Moldova
24 August	Kornilov orders troops to move closer to Petrograd
1 September	Germans begin attack to capture Riga
3 September	German troops occupy Riga
4 September	Vladimir Lvov informs Kerensky of military plot to overthrow him
9 September	Kerensky dismisses Kornilov as commander-in-chief; Kerensky orders troops to advance on Petrograd
11 September	Kerensky appoints himself commander-in-chief
13 September	Kornilov arrested
18 September	Creation of the Vilnius Conference
10 October	Beginning of *Albion*, the German campaign to capture the Estonian islands
17 October	*Slava* sunk by German warships
6 November	Kerensky tries to take steps against the Bolsheviks
7 November	Bolsheviks begin to occupy key buildings around Petrograd; Kerensky leaves in search of loyalist troops
8 November	Bolsheviks seize the Winter Palace
10 November	Kerensky and Krasnov occupy Tsarskoe Selo
12 November	Red Guards defeat the attempt by Krasnov to attack towards Petrograd
19 November	Dukhonin releases Kornilov and other prisoners
2 December	Soviet delegation leaves Petrograd to meet Germans for peace talks
3 December	Brest-Litovsk conference begins
7 December	Romanian delegation travels to Focşani for peace talks

11 December	Vilnius Council accepts German offer of limited independence
15 December	Armistice terms for Eastern Front agreed at Brest-Litovsk
28 December	Brest-Litovsk conference is adjourned

1918

8 January	Brest-Litovsk conference resumes
28 January	Finnish Reds try to secure control of Finland
8 February	Peace treaty signed between the Ukraine and Central Powers
16 February	Brest-Litovsk conference collapses
	Vilnius Council issues declaration of full independence
18 February	Central Powers commence advance into Russian territory
26 February	German troops occupy Tallinn
3 March	Brest-Litovsk Treaty signed
15 March	Mannerheim commences White Finnish attack to capture Tampere
21 March	Germans launch their last major offensive on the Western Front
3 April	German troops land in Hanko in southern Finland
12 April	Declaration of the creation of the *Baltische Staat*
13 April	German troops capture Helsinki
6 April	Mannerheim's troops capture Tampere
18 April	Mannerheim's troops capture Viborg
7 May	Bucharest Treaty signed
2 October	Emperor Karl announces reorganisation of the Austro-Hungarian Empire along federal lines
4 October	German and Austro-Hungarian governments send first messages to USA to seek peace
26 October	Kaiser Wilhelm accepts Ludendorff's resignation
29 October	Naval mutinies begin in German ports
10 November	Kaiser Wilhelm goes into exile in the Netherlands
4 November	Armistice declared on the Italian Front
8 November	Piłsudski is released from captivity in Magdeburg and returns to Warsaw
10 November	Romania formally rejects Bucharest Treaty and resumes hostilities
11 November	Armistice declared on the Western Front
	Emperor Karl abdicates
	Creation of *Baltische Landeswehr*
	Piłsudski becomes Polish head of state and commander-in-chief
13 November	Russia renounces the Treaty of Brest-Litovsk
22 November	British 6th Light Cruiser Squadron leaves for Estonia
25 November	Red Army invades Estonia

28 November	Bolsheviks capture Narva
24 November	Bolsheviks capture Tartu
5 December	HMS *Cassandra* sinks after hitting a mine in the eastern Baltic
7 December	British warships reach Tallinn
8 December	Declaration of Provisional Lithuanian Revolutionary Government
17 December	Declaration of Latvian Soviet Socialist Republic
25 December	Red Army reaches Koeru in northern Estonia
26 December	Naval action in Tallinn Bay; Russian destroyer *Spartak* captured
27 December	Russian destroyer *Avtroil* captured

1919

1 January	Polish *Samoobrona* drives communists from Vilnius
4 January	Red Army captures Riga
5 January	Bolshevik troops reach Vilnius
25 January	Red Army takes Telšiai
19 January	Estonian forces retake Narva
1 February	Goltz arrives in Latvia
7 February	Red Army attacks towards Kaunas
14 February	Final Bolshevik attacks towards Kaunas defeated Polish and Russian forces clash at Bereza Kartuska
18 February	Red Army attacks Narva again
27 February	Soviet Socialist Republics of Lithuania and Belarus merge to create Lithuanian-Belarusian Soviet Socialist Republic or 'Lit-Bel'
3 March	German and Latvian forces commence attacks to recapture Latvia
16 April	Polish forces commence advance towards Vilnius
19 April	Polish troops enter Vilnius
26 April	First clashes between Polish and Lithuanian forces
13 May	Northern Corps of the White Russian forces attacks from Narva into Russian territory
22 May	*Freikorps* units attack towards Riga
23 May	Riga falls to *Freikorps* and *Baltische Landeswehr*
29 May	*Freikorps* and *Baltische Landeswehr* advance into northeast Latvia
5 June	Beginning of Battle of Cēsis
17 June	Agar attacks the Bolshevik warships in Kronstadt, sinking *Oleg*
22 June	Estonian forces advance and drive the Germans back from Cēsis
24 June	Estonian forces move closer to Riga
3 July	Ceasefire between Estonian and German forces in Latvia
5 July	Latvian forces take control of Riga
18 July	French propose new border between Poland and Lithuania

2 August	Polish Army attacks towards Minsk
8 August	Polish troops capture Minsk
10 August	First peace offer to Estonia by Russia
18 August	British torpedo boats attack Kronstadt again, sinking *Pamiat Azova* and damaging *Andrei Pervozvanni* and *Petropavlovsk*
28 August	Attempted pro-Polish coup in Lithuania
8 October	Bermontians attack towards Riga
10 October	Northern Corps launches major attack towards Petrograd
14 October	Goltz leaves Latvia
20 October	White Russians capture Tsarskoe Selo
21 October	Bolshevik counterattack drives back leading elements of Northern Corps
3 November	Latvians launch counterattacks to drive back Bermontian forces near Riga
26 November	Latvia declares war on Germany
30 November	Last German forces driven from Latvia
5 December	Peace talks between Estonia and Russia open in Tartu

1920

3 January	Ceasefire between Russia and Estonia
25 April	Polish forces attack Bolsheviks in Ukraine
7 May	Polish troops occupy Kiev
27 May	Russian First Cavalry Army commences attacks on Poles in Ukraine
4 July	Red Army attacks towards Minsk
10 July	Polish troops pull back from Kiev
11 July	Red Army recaptures Minsk
14 July	Russian cavalry capture Vilnius
15 July	Peace treaty between Latvia and Germany
11 August	Peace treaty between Latvia and Bolshevik Russia
12 August	Red Army attacks towards Warsaw and captures Radzymin
16 August	Polish Army launches its counterattack in the Battle of Warsaw
9 October	Polish troops re-enter Vilnius
12 October	Peace treaty between Poland and Bolshevik Russia

DRAMATIS PERSONAE

Austria-Hungary

Arz von Straussenberg, Arthur – chief of general staff
Aust, Albrecht – commander, 15th Infantry Division
Burián, Stephan – foreign minister, replaced by Czernin
Conrad von Hötzendorf, Franz – commander of *k.u.k.* forces on the Italian Front
Csanády von Békes, Friedrich – commander XXVI Corps
Czernin von und zu Chudenitz, Ottokar – foreign minister
Edler von Schenk, Alfred – commander XIII Corps
Hadfy, Emmerich – commander XXVI Corps, replaced by Csanády
Kövesz, Hermann von – commander Seventh Army
Kritek, Karl – commander Third Army
Rohr von Denta, Franz Freiherr – commander First Army
Tersztyánsky von Nadas, Karl – commander Third Army, replaced by Kritek

Estonia

Kuperjanov, Julius – freedom fighter
Laidoner, Johan – first head of the Estonian Army
Päts, Konstantin – first head of state

Finland

Aaltonen, Ali – commander Red forces
Lehtimäki, Verner – commander Red garrison in Tampere

Mannerheim, Carl Gustaf Emil – commander White forces
Salmela, Hugo – commander Red garrison in Tampere, succeeded by Lehtimäki
Svinhufvud, Pehr Evind – chair of Finnish senate
Thesleff, Vilhelm – commander Finnish Jägers

Germany

Bethmann-Hollweg, Theobald von – chancellor of Germany, replaced first by Michaelis, then Hertling
Bischoff, Josef – commander of Iron Brigade/Iron Division
Brandenstein, Otto Freiherr von – commander mobile column in Finland
Bruchmüller, Georg – German artillery officer, nicknamed 'Durchbruchmüller' ('durchbruch' = 'breakthrough')
Eben, Johannes von – commander Ninth Army
Eberhardt, Walter von – general and later *Freikorps* commander
Ebert, Friedrich – chair of Social Democrats, later German president
Erzberger, Matthias – Centrist member of Reichstag
Estorff, Ludwig von – commander 42nd Infantry Division
Falkenhayn, Erich von – former chief of general staff
Fletcher, Alfred – commander of *Baltische Landeswehr*
Goltz, Rüdiger von der – commander of German forces deployed in Finland and the Baltic States
Hertling, Georg Graf von – chancellor of Germany after Michaelis, replaced by Prince Max von Baden
Hindenburg, Paul von – chief of general staff
Hoffmann, Max – chief of staff, *Ober Ost*
Hutier, Oskar von – commander Eighth Army
Kühlmann, Richard von – foreign minister
Liebknecht, Karl – Social Democrat member of Reichstag
Linsingen, Alexander von – commander of eponymous army group
Litzmann, Karl – deputy commander *k.u.k.* Third Army
Ludendorff, Erich – quartermaster-general
Mackensen, August von – military governor of Romania, commander of forces of the Central Powers on the Romanian Front
Max von Baden (Prince) – chancellor of Germany
Morgen, Curt von – commander I Reserve Corps
Noske, Gustav – Social Democrat member of Reichstag, later defence minister

Riemann, Julius – commander VI Corps
Scheidemann, Philipp – co-chair of Social Democrats
Winckler, Alfred von – commander I Corps

LATVIA

Kalpaks, Oskars – first commander of Latvian Army
Manteuffel, Hans von – prominent member of Baltic German community
Niedra, Andrievs – pro-German politician and former pastor
Stryk, Heinrich von – prominent member of Baltic German community
Ulmanis, Kārlis – first prime minister
Zemitāns, Jorģis – commander North Latvian Brigade

LITHUANIA

Mickevičius-Kapsukas, Vincas – leader of Lithuanian communists and head of state of Lit-Bel
Sleževičius, Mykolas – prime minister
Smetona, Antanas – first Lithuanian president
Voldemaras, Augustinas – first prime minister

POLAND

Belina-Prazmowski, Wladyslaw – Polish cavalry commander
Haller, Józef – Polish army commander
Piłsudski, Józef – commander Polish Legion, later head of state of Poland
Rydz-Śmygły, Edward – Polish army commander
Sikorski, Władysław – Polish army commander
Szeptycki, Stanisław – commander of Polish forces in capture of Minsk
Wasilewski, Leon – colleague of Piłsudski
Żeligowski, Lucjan – Polish army commander, head of state of Republic of Central Lithuania

ROMANIA

Averescu, Alexander – commander Second Army, later prime minister (replaced by Marghiloman)
Brătianu, Ion – prime minister of Romania, replaced by Averescu
Marghiloman, Alexandru – prime minister of Romania

RUSSIA

Alexeyev, Mikhail Vasiliyevich – chief of general staff, replaced Tsar Nicholas II as commander-in-chief, replaced by Brusilov
Bachirev, Mikhail Koronatovich – commander Baltic Fleet during fighting for Estonian archipelago
Baluev, Petr Semenovich – commander Special Army, then commander Eleventh Army, commander West Front from August 1917
Beliaev, Mikhail Alexeyevich – war minister
Benckendorff, Pavel Constantinovich – Grand Marshal of the Imperial Court
Bermont-Avalov, Pavel – White Russian commander of West Russian Volunteer Army
Bizenko, Anastasia Alexandrovna – member of Bolshevik delegation at Brest-Litovsk
Boldyrev, Vasily Georgiyevich – commander XLIII Corps
Brusilov, Alexei Alexeyevich – commander Southwest Front, later commander-in-chief
Budyonny, Semyon Mikhailovich – commander First Cavalry Army
Byelkovich, Leonid Nikolayevich – commander Seventh Army
Cheremisov, Vladimir Andreyevich – commander Eighth Army, later commander Northern Front
Chkheidze, Nikolai Semionovich – chairman of the Soviet of Workers' Deputies and member of the Provisional Government
Denikin, Anton Ivanovich – chief of general staff (replaced by Lukomsky), then commander West Front, then commander Southwest Front
Dragomirov, Abram Mikhailovich – commander Northern Front
Dukhonin, Nikolai Nikolayevich – quartermaster general Southwest Front, then chief of general staff
Erdeli, Ivan Georgevich – commander Eleventh Army, replaced by Baluev
Fedotov, Ivan Ivanovich – commander Eleventh Army, replaced by Erdeli

Frederiks, Vladimir Borisovich – minister of the imperial household
Gapon, Georgi – priest and leading figure in 1905 protests
Golitsyn, Nikolai Dmitrievich – prime minister
Guchkov, Alexander Ivanovich – Duma member, war minister in Provisional Government
Gurko, Vasily Iosifovich – acting chief of general staff, then commander West Front
Gutor, Alexei Evgeneyevich – commander Eleventh Army (replaced by Fedotov), then commander Southwest Front
Ivanov, Nikolai Iudevich – former commander of Southwest Front, dispatched to Petrograd to suppress the February Revolution
Joffe, Adolf Abramovich – leader of first Bolshevik delegation at Brest-Litovsk
Kelchevsky, Anatoly Kiprianovich – commander Ninth Army
Kerensky, Alexander Fyodorovich – socialist deputy in the Duma, later war minister, then prime minister
Khabalov, Sergei Semenovich – commander Petrograd Military District, replaced by Kornilov after February Revolution
Kiselevsky, Nikolai Mikhailovich – commander Tenth Army
Klembovsky, Vladislav Napoleonovich – chief of general staff after February Revolution, replaced by Denikin, later commander Northern Front
Kornilov, Lavr Georgeyevich – commander Petrograd Military District, then commander Eighth Army (replaced by Cheremisov), then commander Southwest Front, then commander-in-chief
Kvyetinsky, Mikhail Fedorovich – commander Third Army
Lenin, Vladimir Ilyich – leader of the Bolsheviks
Lesh, Leonid Vilgelmovich – commander Third Army, replaced by Kvyetinsky
Lukomsky, Alexander Sergeyevich – chief of general staff
Lvov, Prince Georgi Yevgenyevich – leader of the Union of Zemstvos, then 1st Minister-Chairman (prime minister) of Provisional Government
Lvov, Vladimir Nikolayevich – member of the Duma, Procurator of the Holy Synod
Mikhail Alexandrovich (Grand Duke) – brother of Tsar Nicholas II, proposed as regent
Miliukov, Pavel Nikolayevich – founder and leader of Kadets, foreign minister, replaced by Tereshchenko
Nadozhny, Dmitri Nikolayevich – commander III Corps
Parsky, Dmitri Pavlovich – commander Twelfth Army
Protopopov, Alexander Dmitrievich – interior minister

Raskolnikov, Fyodor Fyodorovich – commissar of the Baltic Fleet
Rodzianko, Mikhail Vladimirovich – chairman of the Duma
Rodzianko, Alexander Pavlovich – commander of White Russian Northern Corps
Ruzsky, Nikolai Vladimirovich – commander Northern Front, replaced by Dragomirov
Savinkov, Boris Viktorovich – commissar Southwest Front, then deputy war minister
Shcherbachev, Dmitri Gregorovich – advisor to King of Romania
Shulgin, Vasily Vitalyevich – right-wing member of the Duma
Snesarev, Andrei Yevgenyevich – commander Western Army
Stashkov, Roman Ilarionovich – peasant member of Bolshevik delegation at Brest-Litovsk
Sukhovnin, Mikhail Alexeyevich – commander First Army after February Revolution
Sveshnivov, Dmitri Alexandrovich – commander of Estonian islands
Tereshchenko, Mikhail Ivanovich – foreign minister after April Crisis
Trotsky, Leon (born Lev Davidovich Bronstein) – leading Bolshevik, leader of delegation at Brest-Litovsk after Joffe
Tsereteli, Irakli – leading Menshevik, later interior minister
Tukhachevsky, Mikhail Nikolayevich – commander Bolshevik forces at Battle of Warsaw
Vesilovsky, Antonii Andreyevich – commander Second Army
Yanushevsky, Grigory Yefimovich – commander III Corps, replaced by Nadozhny
Yudenich, Nikolai Nikolaevich – commander White Russian forces in the Baltic region

Miscellaneous

Alexander-Sinclair, Edwin (Britain) – commander 6th Cruiser Squadron
Buchanan, George (Britain) – ambassador in Petrograd
Cichowski, Kazimierz – chairman of Communist Party of Lit-Bel
Knox, Alfred (Britain) – military attaché in Russia
Nezerov, Stefan (Bulgaria) – commander Third Army
Paléologue, Maurice (France) – ambassador in Petrograd
Poincaré, Raymond (France) – president of France

INTRODUCTION

The war that engulfed Europe in the last months of 1914 had been dreaded for years, but there were many in every country who welcomed its coming. Their reasons for doing so were varied, but the failure of the three great European empires – Germany, Austria-Hungary, and Russia – to anticipate the nature of war in the industrial age ultimately led to their destruction.

Much has been made of the widespread expectation in 1914 of swift victory, but there were many who suspected that however desirable such an outcome might be, reality would be different. German planning evolved from preliminary proposals drawn up by Alfred von Schlieffen, chief of the German general staff from 1891 to 1906, and intended to deliver a killing blow against France within weeks of the onset of hostilities. In the meantime, minimal forces would be able to hold off the Russians before the victorious forces in France moved east to destroy any threat to Germany. It is clear that from an early stage, Helmuth von Moltke – Schlieffen's successor as chief of the general staff and nephew of the Moltke who had masterminded the German Wars of Unification – doubted that a future war would be either swift or easy to win, but all of his planning appears to have been based upon delivering a quick victory.[1] Nevertheless, he gave Kaiser Wilhelm II a very clear warning in 1905:

> It will become a war between peoples which is not to be concluded with a single battle, but which will be a long, weary struggle with a country that will not acknowledge defeat until the whole strength of its people is broken; a war that even if we should be the victors will push our people, too, to the limits of exhaustion.[2]

The motivation for war in the three empires varied. In all nations, there was a sense that the war would bring some form of spiritual renewal. Writing shortly after the outbreak of the war, Thomas Mann asked:

> Is not peace an element of civil corruption, and war a purification, a liberation, an enormous hope?[3]

He was not alone in such sentiments. Rupert Brooke, the British poet, also welcomed the coming of war:

> Now, God be thanked Who has matched us with His hour,
> And caught our youth, and wakened us from sleeping,
> With hand made sure, clear eye, and sharpened power,
> To turn, as swimmers into cleanness leaping,
> Glad from a world grown old and cold and weary,
> Leave the sick hearts that honour could not move,
> And half-men, and their dirty songs and dreary,
> And all the little emptiness of love!
>
> Oh! we who have known shame, we have found release there,
> Where there's no ill, no grief, but sleep has mending,
> Nought broken save this body, lost but breath;
> Nothing to shake the laughing heart's long peace there
> But only agony, and that has ending;
> And the worst friend and enemy is but Death.[4]

Similarly, Tsarina Alexandra echoed a widely held view in Russia when she wrote to her husband, Tsar Nicholas II:

> I read such a lovely article in an English newspaper – they hold our soldiers in such high regard and say that their deep religious belief and their respect for their peace-loving monarch will help them fight bravely for such a holy cause …
>
> With God's help, all will go well for us and come to a glorious end. The war has raised spirits, has cleared so many reluctant minds, has brought unity to our feelings and in the moral sense is a 'good war'. … Such a war must renew the soul.[5]

There were more practical reasons for war. For the Germans, there was the constant threat that France would seek revenge for the defeats of 1871, and in particular would not rest until the lost provinces of Alsace and Lorraine were returned to French rule. There was steadily growing evidence that France was helping Russia rebuild its forces after the disaster of the Russo-Japanese War of

1904–1905, and this led to the widespread belief in Germany that the longer a future European war was delayed, the less the chances of Germany emerging victorious. Consequently, even if Moltke and others believed that any future war carried great risk and may prove to be prolonged, it was essential to bring about this conflict while there remained any chance of victory.

For the Russians, war with Germany was something that was widely feared. The Russian military establishment had respect bordering on awe for the power of the German Army, and there was considerable doubt that Russia would be able to prevail. In 1904, Russia found itself in a war with Japan, and contrary to the expectations of almost everyone apart from the Japanese, was soundly beaten both at sea and on land. The unrest caused by this defeat triggered a wave of revolutionary unrest across Russia, but the root causes of the unrest existed before the disastrous war. Bungled land reforms, aimed at turning Russia's peasants into a class of landowners, left much of the countryside unable to function efficiently, leading to widespread rural food shortages. This in turn created financial hardship, both at the level of the peasants and the government, which was deprived of millions of roubles of unpaid taxes. Like other European countries, Russia had experienced a considerable population increase in the second half of the 19th century, but although the amount of land under agricultural production had increased, productivity was lower than before.[6] Matters weren't much better in urban centres, which had undergone a wave of industrialisation in the closing decade of the old century. This resulted in large slums where factory workers lived in extremely poor conditions, struggling to make ends meet on low incomes. Many of these workers remained closely linked to the rural communities from which they had come, resulting in strong contacts between those who lived in squalor in Russia's industrialised cities and those who struggled in the countryside.[7] In addition, there were growing tensions in the non-Russian parts of the tsar's empire, particularly Finland, the Baltic region, and Poland; heavy-handed attempts to impose Orthodox Christianity in Lithuania, for example, were completely unsuccessful and led to huge resentment. The increase in higher education, too, proved to be a source of unrest, with large numbers of radicalised students from poorer backgrounds – denied access to higher paid jobs because they lacked the appropriate family connections – demanding change in the autocratic state.

The first signs of trouble came as early as 9 January 1905, a day that became known as 'Bloody Sunday'. Led by a priest, Georgi Gapon, tens of thousands of workers in St Petersburg converged on the Winter Palace with the intention of presenting the tsar – Russia's 'Little Father' and earthly representative of the

Great Father in heaven – with a 'Humble and Loyal Address', asking for the tsar to intervene on their behalf and to address their grievances about poor housing, low wages and inadequate food supplies. The tone of the petition was respectful and powerful:

> Sire. We the workers and inhabitants of St Petersburg, of various estates, our wives, our children, and our aged, helpless parents, come to Thee, O Sire to seek justice and protection. We are impoverished; we are oppressed, overburdened with excessive toil, contemptuously treated … We are suffocating in despotism and lawlessness. O Sire we have no strength left, and our endurance is at an end. We have reached that frightful moment when death is better than the prolongation of our unbearable sufferings …[8]

After reminding Nicholas of his obligations to his people, it concluded with the words:

> And if Thou dost not so order and dost not respond to our pleas we will die here in this square before Thy palace.[9]

There was a tradition dating back more than two hundred years for making such requests, but the workers who took part had little doubt that there were considerable risks involved. Father Gapon sent a copy of the petition to the authorities in advance, to leave them in no doubt what to expect. Nicholas was advised by his counsellors to remain in St Petersburg; instead, he left for Tsarskoe Selo, a short distance to the southeast, the day before the expected demonstration.

Carrying icons and other religious items and singing hymns and patriotic songs, including 'God Save the Tsar', the workers began to gather outside the Winter Palace before dawn, unaware that the 'Little Father' had already left. As other groups attempted to reach Admiralty Square, outside the Winter Palace, troops intervened in an often-haphazard manner. Father Gapon's group came under fire, leaving 40 dead or wounded.[10] There were incidents elsewhere, leaving dozens more dead, but the worst occurred during the afternoon when workers – many of them unaware of the killings earlier in the day – mingled with passers-by along Nevsky Prospekt, the broad avenue leading to the Winter Palace and Admiralty Square. Troops drew up in ranks, and, after the briefest of warnings, opened fire with rifles and even artillery. In total, perhaps a thousand workers and ordinary citizens were killed or wounded during the day. One elderly protester grabbed a shocked youth and shouted at him:

> Remember, son, remember and swear to repay the tsar. You saw how much blood he spilled. Did you see? Then swear, son, swear![11]

It was a terrible moment, born as much from incompetence and miscalculation as deliberate brutality. The result was an eruption of strikes that spread through Russia as the year progressed. Eventually, the tsar was forced to concede to some of the demands of his opponents, granting a degree of suffrage and the establishment of the Duma as Russia's parliament, but by the end of the year the country was paralysed by a general strike. Workers took control of large parts of Moscow, and Nicholas resorted to brutal suppression and further violence. By the time that the unrest had been suppressed, an estimated 20,000 people had been killed or wounded in fighting. Another 15,000 had been executed after being arrested, and 45,000 exiled beyond the Russian Empire or sent to Siberia.

The modest political reforms were inadequate to satisfy the critics of the regime and many remained dissatisfied, ensuring that thoughts of revolutionary change continued to circulate. The events of Bloody Sunday created a fatal rift between the ordinary people of Russia and the tsar, and many of those who were arrested during the year of revolution remarked that, even within the government's prisons, many officials seemed sympathetic and discipline was generally far looser than had been the case in the past.[12] Critically, the survival of the Romanovs as Russia's rulers was due to the loyalty of most of the army and its commanders; this latter group was dominated by a small number of families, many of them Baltic Germans in origin. In combination with Russia's aristocracy, the generals rallied around the tsar, aware that their own privileged position depended on the continuation of the status quo. If there were to be any future unrest, Tsar Nicholas would have to retain the support of these men and the soldiers they commanded.

If the officer corps was still dominated by traditionalist senior figures, there was still a growing group of commanders from other walks of life. These were largely men who had come up through the system of military schools established after the Crimean War of 1853–1856, and unlike the aristocrats and other traditionalists they were increasingly vocal and impatient for genuine reform. They deplored the continuing obsession with cavalry, and rightly recognised that the training of the rank and file remained far below the standards of Russia's potential or likely enemies. For the moment though, they remained unable to exert influence, but the failure of the tsar to address their concerns was the start of a process that would drive a widening wedge between the throne and the army upon which it ultimately depended.

The ordinary soldiers of the army in 1905 were largely drawn from the peasantry, or the new urban poor. They therefore already felt close kinship with those who were now being branded as revolutionaries, and matters were worsened by the fact that, with increasing frequency, the army had been required to help the police restore order in the past few years – over 1,500 times in the preceding two decades.[13] The shock of the Bloody Sunday killings had spread throughout Russia by the end of the year, and, when ordered to help suppress the ongoing strikes and demonstrations, many soldiers refused, and there were over 400 mutinies.[14] The damage done to internal discipline and morale was immense, and would take years to repair. In times of trouble, the tsars had often turned to the Cossacks to help them deal with dissent, and 1905 was no exception. Raised from Cossack populations who had been granted land on the southern and eastern borders of European Russia, the Cossack formations of the army retained a degree of ethnic distinction from the rest of the troops, but whilst this allowed the Cossacks to be directed against non-Cossack populations with little fear of refusal, it also led to increasing demands by Cossack communities for political concessions in return for their service. The future reliability of the Cossacks would depend on the degree to which the tsar could satisfy the increasing nationalist demands of their home regions.

Calm returned to Russia as the unrest was forcibly crushed, but nothing would ever be the same again. The belief that the tsar, the 'Little Father', would always look after his people and would act as the ultimate arbiter in any dispute was destroyed by the violence of Bloody Sunday. All of society grew more polarised. Many landowners and businessmen had been minded to support the calls for reform in 1905, but the violence suffered by some – particularly in the countryside where many buildings were set ablaze by rioting peasants, and some landowners and their families were killed – led to opinions hardening. Previously progressive groups now became increasingly conservative, working almost entirely to protect the property and rights of the landowners, and many of the idealistic students who had joined the revolution with passion and energy turned their backs upon the ordinary people. Their views were summarised neatly by Mikhail Gershenzon, who had edited popular liberally minded journals before and immediately after the revolution. Despite the absurd restrictions that he personally faced under the tsarist regime – as a Jew, he could not be employed in any official academic position, and was forbidden from marrying his Orthodox Christian partner Maria Goldenweizer – he called on fellow intellectuals to support the government:

> The intelligentsia should stop dreaming about the liberation of the people – we should fear the people more than all the executions carried out by the government, and hail this government which alone, with its bayonets and its prisons, still protects us from the fury of the masses.[15]

Peasants and workers were left increasingly aware that they could not rely on the middle classes to improve their lot in life; any change would have to be forced by themselves, and Lenin particularly took this view – the reactionary shift of the intelligentsia and the liberal bourgeoisie effectively eliminated them as future allies of the Bolsheviks. Nevertheless, the power of the workers and peasantry had shaken the empire to its core, and if the circumstances were right – for example, if the nationalist movements of the western parts of the Russian Empire were to weaken the power of the government – the workers might succeed in a future revolution, even without the help of the intelligentsia. Indeed, such was the sense of betrayal amongst revolutionary groups like the Bolsheviks after the end of the 1905 Revolution that for them, the only way to guarantee success would be to rely upon nobody but themselves. This fitted firmly within the ideology of Marxism, which taught that over time, one section of the bourgeoisie might enlist the support of the proletariat to overthrow those in power – but the outcome was always that, while the rulers and their opponents changed places, the proletariat remained oppressed.

The rearmament programme of the opening years of the 20th century repaired much of the damage suffered by the Russian Army as a result of the Russo-Japanese War and the 1905 Revolution, not least through substantial investment by France, but few believed that the Russian Army would triumph against Germany without considerable help. Nevertheless, if the Germans were forced to commit their forces against France, there would be an opportunity for Russia to strike in the east, and there was optimistic talk of the 'Russian Steamroller' crushing East Prussia, and even continuing over the Vistula into Pomerania and thence towards Berlin. But although Germany was regarded as the main enemy of the Franco-Russian Entente, rather more prominent in Russian thinking was the question of the Austro-Hungarian Empire. For over half a century, the Russians had regarded the Habsburg territories as ripe for conquest, particularly in the Balkans, and several developments appear to have featured strongly in Russian thinking.

The first was the legacy of the Romantic Movement that dominated the first half of the 19th century. Growing partly from the German *Sturm und Drang* ('Storm and Stress') movement and partly as a conscious repudiation of the rational values of the Enlightenment and the Industrial Revolution, Romanticism placed great value on traditional culture, resulting in a widespread growth of nationalist sentiment. This led both to the creation of an empire – through Bismarck's wars of German unification – and to the placing of great strain on some parts of other European empires. Another product of Romanticism was the growth of Pan-Slavism in the second half of the 19th century, with Slavic intellectuals promoting the concept of all Slavs being unified in a single state. Inevitably, Russia – as the largest Slav state – saw itself as the obvious means by which such unity might be achieved, and, with the Austro-Hungarian Empire showing increasing internal divisions, many in Russia perceived opportunities for Russian expansion into the Habsburg Empire's Slav lands. In this context, the failure of Russia to intervene on behalf of Balkan Slavs in 1908, when the Austro-Hungarian Empire annexed Bosnia-Herzegovina, was widely deplored in Russian society.

The second area of interest for Russia was actually a territory that lay outside the Austro-Hungarian Empire. There had long been a desire in Russia for control of the Bosporus and the gates of the Black Sea, but Russia would be able to gain control of Istanbul from the decaying Ottoman Empire only if the Balkan region were to come under Russian hegemony, if not outright annexation. Bulgaria, Romania and Serbia had broken away from Turkish rule, but these Slav states could surely be brought under the control of the tsar, or at least form part of Russia's sphere of influence, allowing for the vital Black Sea exit at Istanbul to be occupied. Again, the cultural consequences of Romanticism featured in Russian thinking; much of the region was Orthodox Christian, and, as the largest Orthodox nation on the planet, Russia felt that it had an automatic right to the allegiance of others of similar faiths. However, such an expansion of Russian influence into the Balkans would require a marked weakening of the Austro-Hungarian Empire and, in the opening years of the 20th century, this was regarded in Russia as a major objective in any future war. However, there was also widespread consensus that war should be postponed for the moment. The rearmament and modernisation of the Russian Army would not be complete until 1917, and a conflict before then would leave Russia facing an adverse balance of power on the battlefield. In particular, some were concerned that Russia could find itself committed to a long-drawn-out war that would prove catastrophic. Pyotr Durnovo, an eminent Russian politician, wrote to the tsar in February 1914, warning him in prophetic terms of what was likely to occur. He regarded an Anglo-German conflict as inevitable, and believed that Russia would find itself fighting for the interests of other powers:

> The main burden of the war will undoubtedly fall on us, since England is hardly capable of taking a considerable part in a continental war, while France, poor in manpower, will probably adhere to strictly defensive tactics, in view of the enormous losses by which war will be attended under present conditions of

> military technique. The part of a battering ram, making a breach in the very thickness of the German defence, will be ours, with many factors against us to which we shall have to devote great effort and attention.
>
> … Are we prepared for so stubborn a war as the future war of the European nations will undoubtedly become? This question we must answer, without evasion, in the negative. That much has been done for our defence since the Japanese war, I am the last person to deny, but even so, it is quite inadequate considering the unprecedented scale on which a future war will inevitably be fought.
>
> … In the event of defeat, the possibility of which in a struggle with a foe like Germany cannot be overlooked, social revolution in its most extreme form is inevitable.
>
> As has already been said, the trouble will start with the blaming of the Government for all disasters. In the legislative institutions a bitter campaign against the Government will begin, followed by revolutionary agitations throughout the country … The defeated army, having lost its most dependable men, and carried away by the tide of primitive peasant desire for land, will find itself too demoralised to serve as a bulwark of law and order. The legislative institutions and the intellectual opposition parties, lacking real authority in the eyes of the people, will be powerless to stem the popular tide, aroused by themselves, and Russia will be flung into hopeless anarchy, the issue of which cannot be foreseen.[16]

Like tsarist Russia, the Austro-Hungarian Empire was a troubled institution in 1914. Born from the weakened Austrian Empire in 1867, the institution was also known as the Dual Monarchy in recognition of the fact that, in addition to being Emperor of Austria, its ruler was also King of Hungary. This in turn reflected the special status of Hungary within the empire, with its own parliament and electoral rules; its authority excluded military and foreign matters, with the result that there was constant friction between Vienna and Budapest. The former felt that many of the actions of the Hungarian parliament, particularly in obstructing greater military expenditure, went against the spirit of the great compromise of 1867, while the Hungarians constantly sought greater autonomy. This triggered growing resentment in other parts of the empire, which – influenced by the sentiments of Romanticism – felt increasingly strongly about their own ethnic identities and wished for greater self-determination, if not outright independence. To an extent, the empire played upon these tensions for internal reasons. For example, the limited electoral franchise in both Vienna and Budapest was dominated by traditional landowning families, and, in an attempt to prevent the rising power of the urban bourgeoisie from destabilising matters, Eduard von Taaffe, the Austrian prime minister from 1879 to 1893, allowed the Czech language equal status alongside German in Prague. This was intended to create a counterbalance to the German industrialists, but, as was the case with Hungarian devolution, it merely served to stimulate greater demands for autonomy from the Czechs. Prior to this reform, they had expressed their dissent by mass abstention from elections, and, perceiving Taaffe's move as a sign of weakness, they pressed for further concessions. Other ethnicities also demanded linguistic recognition, with the result that the empire officially recognised a multitude of languages by the end of the 19th century, including German, Hungarian, Czech, Serbo-Croat, Polish, and Ruthenian (Ukrainian).

A direct consequence of the multilingual nature of the Austro-Hungarian Empire was the structure of the *k.u.k.* ('*kaiserlich und königlich*' or 'Imperial and Royal', reflecting the nature of the Dual Monarchy) Army. Its regiments had strong regional backgrounds, and although German was the official language for all military documents and orders, officers were expected to be able to speak the same language as their men. Whilst such an arrangement was possible in peacetime, the system would inevitably come under great strain in any prolonged war, and, in an attempt to address this, a regionally based system of replacements was created. The intention was that each part of the empire would raise 'march battalions' that would be sent to the regiments in the front line, preserving internal ethnic coherence, but this broke down almost immediately. Some regiments suffered far higher losses than others, but the march battalion system could not accommodate this, resulting in many regiments accumulating large numbers of battalions while others shrank below their establishment strength. As a result, some of the surplus troops were then assigned from the over-strength regiments to weaker ones, but it was impossible to ensure that this would occur only between regiments of the same ethnicity. In peacetime, officers had gone to great lengths to learn the languages and customs of their men, but few of those brought in as wartime replacements had the time or inclination to do so, and in any case the increasingly jumbled ethnic structure of regiments made this almost impossible.

For the Austro-Hungarian Empire, the outbreak of the war was of course in the context of the Sarajevo assassinations that triggered the conflict. Franz Ferdinand, the recognised heir to the throne, had made no secret of his intention to try to ease the tensions within the empire by extending the privileges granted to Hungary to other regions, such as Bohemia, southern Poland and into the

Balkans. However intriguing it might be to speculate how Europe might have developed had he survived, his assassination led to a brief surge of pro-Imperial sentiment throughout the Dual Monarchy. All parts of the empire responded to mobilisation orders and the *k.u.k.* Army went off to war, confident that it would be able to hold off the Russians whilst simultaneously striking against Serbia. In the same spirit, the Russians mobilised and marched west, expecting to prevail against the Central Powers, while Germany embarked upon the gamble of a huge strike against France before turning east in strength.

By the first winter of the war, all of these hopes and ambitions were in tatters. Despite most of the German Army being deployed in the west, the Russians failed to strike a decisive blow in the east and the great Russian Steamroller, widely predicted to roll irresistibly across East Prussia and the parts of Poland that were in German control, ran out of momentum as a result of the inescapable logic of supply lines; armies in the early 20th century required huge quantities of munitions, food and other supplies, and motorised transport – and the roads on which it depended – was too primitive and unreliable to sustain troops who pushed forward beyond the reach of railway networks. Fearful of a German invasion, the Russians had been reluctant to modernise their western railways too much, as the Germans might have used these to good effect. They now found that the limitations of those lines, and the huge inefficiencies of the Russian railway service, effectively limited their own ability to project power to the west. As 1914 came to an end, the Russians pulled back from the western parts of the old Polish kingdom, unaware that this marked the high-tide mark of their involvement in the war.

The following two years saw further widespread fighting. Russia was driven from Poland and part of the Baltic region, and although its resurgent army shook the Central Powers – particularly Austria-Hungary – in the summer of 1916, success proved to be transient. The Balkan region was brought under the control of Germany and Austria-Hungary, but every attempt to bring the war to a successful conclusion proved to be a mirage. Increasingly exhausted by the conflict, the three great European empires looked to 1917 with little hope.

Given the internal ethnic strains of the Austro-Hungarian Empire, it is little surprise that the Dual Monarchy as a whole, and the *k.u.k.* Army in particular, were the first to show signs of tension as the war unfolded. The surge in pro-Habsburg feeling brought about by the Sarajevo assassinations proved to be short-lived, and there was increasingly vocal dissent in Prague by the first winter about the war. A small number of Czech units had surrendered en masse to the Russians, resulting in widespread suspicion of other Czech formations, even though the majority fought loyally for the empire. Civilians in Bohemia spoke with increasing confidence about the coming of the Russians as liberators – at the time, the Russian Army was only a short distance to the east of Krakow, about 300 miles (480km) from Prague. This led to a crackdown on dissent, and some Czech activists were executed for treason.[17] The victory that might have welded together the growingly disparate parts of the Austro-Hungarian Empire proved to be a mirage, and, as the next two years of the war progressed, it became increasingly clear to those in high office that, even if the Central Powers were to emerge triumphant at the end of the war, the true winner would be Germany; the Austro-Hungarian Empire would be reduced to little more than a client state.

Tensions were rising elsewhere, too. The Russians had made no preparations for prolonged war, and what plans existed were reliant on buying supplies from other countries. In a world where all of Europe was at war and all nations were scrambling to use the resources of neutral nations like the United States, it was almost impossible to secure timely supplies from overseas, and geography was also against Russia; prior to the war, more than 50 per cent of Russia's imports had come through its western borders. By the first winter there were severe shortages of everything – ammunition, rifles, clothing, boots, food and medical supplies. New recruits barely saw rifles during training, and were often expected to go into battle unarmed and to pick up the rifles of men killed in preceding attacks. Belatedly, the war ministry discovered that in all of Russia, there was only one large factory that could produce tanning extract for leather, and almost all of its supplies of tannin before the war had come from Germany. Unlike previous wars, this occurred in an age in which, even in Russia with its relatively poor communications and low levels of literacy, many soldiers were able to write home about their misfortunes. During the first winter, families in villages, towns and cities across Russia learned with horror about the appalling conditions in which their men were fighting for the tsar. They also learned of the tendency of officials to try to give Nicholas and other senior figures as rosy an impression as possible, regardless of the reality on the ground:

> For the tsar's inspection [of a regiment in the front line], they prepared one company and collected all the best uniforms from the other regiments for it to wear, leaving the rest of the men in the trenches without boots, knapsacks, bandoliers, trousers, uniforms, hats, or anything else.[18]

The unprecedentedly high casualty rate brought changes to all armies. It disjointed the delicate ethnic structure of the *k.u.k.* Army, and the loss of so many officers from the traditional class backgrounds was greatly disruptive for both the Germans and the Russians. Men from Prussian *Junker* families, steeped in spartan discipline and a strong sense of duty to their men, the kaiser and Germany, were replaced by men from middle-class backgrounds; this might have been expected to narrow class divides between officers and men, but in many cases it led to widespread unhappiness – the new generation of officers was less likely to place such a high value on the welfare of lower ranks. But while the German Army could fall back upon its pool of highly trained NCOs, the class from which these men were drawn was almost non-existent in Russia. Replacement junior officers in the Russian Army were largely created by promotion of men from the front line, who owed more loyalty to their fellow soldiers than to the military hierarchy above them.

In Germany, the economic pressure of isolation began to take a toll on the civilian population, resulting in food riots that spread to the Austro-Hungarian Empire. In Russia, the pressures that led to the 1905 risings remained as strong as ever, and although they diminished briefly as the tsar's empire experienced the same wave of patriotic fervour that swept most of Europe in 1914, the ever-growing casualty lists, the rampant mismanagement of the war, and enormous domestic hardships brought matters to a head. By the end of 1916, it was no longer a question of whether Russia would undergo a revolution, merely one of when it would occur.

All three empires entered the war with little understanding about the military realities of prolonged fighting in the industrial age, despite the warnings of those like Durnovo. Although they all managed, with varying degrees of success, to rise to the challenges of maintaining such immense forces in the field for far longer than anyone had imagined would be required, it was at a huge social price. In this respect, their lack of preparedness for the changes that the war brought was even greater than their lack of military preparedness. Just as the war galvanised industrialists and engineers to innovate at a speed that far exceeded the rate of development during peacetime, so the pressures of war stimulated social changes, building on and amplifying the pressures that were already present. By the beginning of 1917, these changes were beginning to break up the internal cohesion of the empires, and would prove to be irresistible pressures that would change the map of Europe forever. The only question was which empire would be the first to collapse.

CHAPTER 1

THE ROAD TO FEBRUARY

After the crushing disappointments of 1914, all sides struggled to find a way to achieve victory. The Germans had planned to win the conflict in two stages, first with triumph in the west against France, and then with a victorious march in the east to hurl back the Russians, but the French survived and in combination with the British – and a small number of Belgian troops – continued to tie down the great bulk of the German Army in a bloody stalemate that stretched from the English Channel to the Alps. Troops were sent to the east, even during the height of the preparations for the Battle of the Marne, but these arrived in stages rather than the triumphant tide that German planners had anticipated. The first reinforcements allowed the Germans to drive the Russians from East Prussia in 1914; they were followed by further contingents that were used in the victories at Łódź and Masuria, but they were too few to achieve a decisive victory over Russia.

If the Germans emerged from 1914 with disappointment, the mood in the Austro-Hungarian Empire was closer to one of almost catastrophic foreboding for the future. The primary role of the *k.u.k.* Army had been to tie down as many Russian troops as possible until Germany was able to transfer its forces east, though it is remarkable that the two Central Powers had made no detailed plans for coordinating their efforts against Russia. Led by the chief of the Austro-Hungarian general staff, Franz Conrad von Hötzendorff, the armies of Austria-Hungary suffered crippling losses in Galicia and were ultimately driven back to the line of the Carpathian Mountains. Conrad was, more than any other individual in the war, responsible for the army that his nation deployed; he had written most of its doctrine and training manuals, and had been hugely involved in the training of its officers. The scale of the mistakes that he made – concentrating on the merits of offensive warfare, not placing sufficient importance on firepower and the use of cover, and disdaining the value of taking a defensive posture – resulted in a huge cost for the *k.u.k.* Army. By the end of 1914, it had lost nearly a million men on the Russian Front, with a further 274,000 squandered in two appallingly bungled invasions of Serbia. In a desperate attempt to prevent total collapse, age limits for conscription were relaxed and the training period for new recruits was shortened, but the result was that the poorly trained replacements rapidly perished in the grim battlefields of the east. Individual trains frequently brought several march battalions from different parts of the empire to the front together, and rather than distribute these formations to their parent regiments, hard-pressed corps and army commanders frequently cobbled them together into ad hoc units; the lack of common language and a desperate shortage of officers, combined with limited quantities of weapons and ammunition, ensured that these units were almost always ineffective in battle.

Whatever the weaknesses of the *k.u.k.* Army, the most damaging factor was beyond doubt the direction of the war by Conrad. From his base in Teschen (now Cieszyn), he attempted to conduct battles without ever visiting the front, ordering the movements of flags on his maps with no regard to the terrain, the weather, supply issues, or the fact that almost every formation was far below its establishment strength. The fighting of 1914 had left a substantial garrison encircled in the fortress of Przemyśl in southern Poland, and although the siege was briefly lifted in the autumn, no attempt was made to evacuate the troops. Instead, they were left in place in the expectation that their presence in the rear of the Russian forces would hinder their progress. Any hope of such a strategy succeeding effectively disappeared as supplies ran short; indeed, when they briefly lifted the siege in the autumn, the relieving troops helped themselves to the stores of food and ammunition in the fortress, thus reducing its ability to endure a second encirclement. Conrad now attempted to reach Przemyśl again, choosing to attack through the Carpathians early in 1915. Although this was the closest point to the besieged city, it was a singularly bad choice – the roads and railway lines along which supplies would have to be brought for the relief effort were completely inadequate, and the challenges of mounting a major offensive through such rough terrain in the middle of winter would have taxed a far more efficient army than that of the Austro-Hungarian Empire. To make matters worse, the Russians attempted an offensive in the opposite direction at the same time, trying to break out of the mountains into Hungary. Casualties were terrible on both sides, and the front lines barely moved. Przemyśl was forced to surrender, adding the loss of another 120,000 men to the price that the *k.u.k.* Army continued to pay for Conrad's incompetence.

Aware that something needed to be done on the Eastern Front to prevent the complete collapse of their allies, the Germans considered their options. Decision-making was complicated by internal feuding within the German Army; in the northern part of the Eastern Front, Paul von Hindenburg and Erich Ludendorff were in command, and there was a widespread belief that they should be promoted to overall command of Germany's war effort. The chief of the general staff, Erich von Falkenhayn, was determined to resist such suggestions and ignored proposals that a new offensive in the east should be led by Hindenburg and Ludendorff. To a point, he was correct – a German offensive in the northeast would do little to reduce pressure upon Austria-Hungary, and the logical place to attack was in southern Poland, advancing east parallel to the line of the Carpathians. However, there had been plenty of occasions in 1914 when senior officers – including both Hindenburg and Ludendorff – were switched from one part of the Eastern Front to another, and had relations between the two sides been better, such a policy might have been adopted again.

Instead, Falkenhayn chose to put his faith in August von Mackensen, who after a shaky start to the war had shown great skill and fortitude. Starting in early May 1915, Mackensen began a remorseless advance that saw the front line move steadily east, reaching and passing Przemyśl in a month; the city had been in Russian hands for only 67 days. From here, the victorious troops of the Central Powers pushed on to the city of Lemberg (now Lviv), the capital of the Austro-Hungarian province of Galicia, and then turned north. Every attempt by the Russians to establish a new front line that would hold were in vain, and the great offensive, originally intended just to relieve pressure upon the *k.u.k.* Army, developed progressively into an advance that threatened to knock Russia out of the war entirely. First, the territories that had been seized from the Austro-Hungarian Empire were recaptured; then, the Russians were forced out of the parts of Poland that had been held by the tsars since the end of the 18th century, followed by much of Lithuania and even parts of western Russia. Already demoralised by their experiences in the winter and then during the long retreat, the rank and file of the Russian Army now had to endure the spectacle of Russian peasants streaming to the east to escape the advancing enemy. While the soldiers and civilians struggled along choked roads, the few available wagons overloaded with the wounded, the sick, and the meagre possessions of the peasants, trains carried the Russian Army's senior officers together with their baggage, servants and mistresses to safety.[19] Only the advent of winter, and a final disastrous intervention by Conrad, brought the long series of setbacks to an end.[20] After losing so much territory and so many men, the army was hugely weakened in terms of manpower, equipment, and just as importantly discipline. Defeatism was widespread, as was talk of betrayal. Tsarina Alexandra had never been popular with ordinary Russians, and her crippling shyness and social awkwardness was often misinterpreted as arrogance and contempt; coming from a German background, she became the centre of dark rumours of enemy spies and sympathisers at the highest levels.

Such a disastrous string of defeats inevitably resulted in changes in the high command. Vladimir Sukhomlinov, the Russian minister of war who had presided over the rebuilding of Russia's armies after the disasters of 1905, had also used his post to build his own political faction in the upper echelons of the army, and his enemies used the parlous state of affairs to strike. He was sacked in June 1915, and replaced by Alexei Polivanov. The universal choice as commander-in-chief of the army at the beginning of the war had been Grand Duke Nikolai, cousin of the tsar, but he proved to be ineffective at imposing his will upon his often-unruly subordinates. But while there was considerable dissatisfaction with his performance, there were no obvious candidates to replace him, particularly as it was difficult to imagine anyone other than a high-ranking aristocrat or a member of the imperial family being appointed to the post, and he remained personally very popular. Nevertheless, there was almost universal dismay when the tsar announced that he would personally take command of Russia's armies.

Tsar Nicholas was a man of little practical experience in any field. His entire reign was littered with poor judgement, and this occasion was no exception. Grand Duke Nikolai had previously held high command in the army, but once the war began he showed no ability to learn the realities of modern war; the tsar started with almost no military knowledge at all. Given the rising dissatisfaction in the Russian Empire, any involvement of the tsar in military command carried considerable risk in that setbacks on the battlefield would directly impact upon the personal standing and prestige of the imperial family. The only faction that showed any enthusiasm for his decision was centred on Tsarina Alexandra, whose belief in the tsar's destiny in saving Russia bordered on religious fervour. She offered her support to Nicholas, writing to him that 'It will be a glorious page in your reign and in Russian history.' Significantly, she added: 'Our Friend's prayers arise night and day for you to Heaven, and God will hear them.'[21]

The friend in question was of course Grigory Rasputin, the self-styled holy man who had such a great influence on Alexandra. Compounding the poor decision to take command of the army, Nicholas appointed Alexandra as his regent in Petrograd while he was absent at the front. If his fitness for command was poor, her ability to oversee the civil administration of Russia was non-existent, particularly given the fact that she was almost entirely dependent upon Rasputin for counsel.

Without naming Alexandra directly, Yuri Danilov, who was quartermaster-general of the Russian Army at the time, later wrote:

> I will not examine in detail the reasons that persuaded Tsar Nicholas II to assume command of the active army in the situation that prevailed. These reasons are of too complex an order and can only be considered with great caution. At the time, I was convinced that the principal reason was the sovereign's mystic belief in his own abilities, his tendency to dwell on the great history of Russia, which had perhaps been presented to him in a false light; although certain human weaknesses may have played a role. But what I do not understand at all is how persons in his entourage, those in his confidence, could have sought deliberately to strengthen his conviction of the necessity and the opportunity to pursue this idea instead of dissuading him. How blind were they; could they not see the grave events that were developing and did they not understand that they risked compromising the already shaky authority of the head of state?[22]

With no military aptitude and a history of poor civil rule behind him, Nicholas was perhaps the worst choice to lead Russia's armies in the wake of the disasters of 1915. His reign had been marked by revolution and political dissent, and perhaps because of this he placed far more importance on personal loyalty than military skill. His chief of staff was Mikhail Vasiliyevich Alexeyev, who would probably have been an excellent man in the post with a good commander-in-chief, but his obsessive attention to detail, flooding his subordinates with huge amounts of paperwork, merely added to the problems of the army. The first test of the new team came almost immediately as Conrad attempted to capitalise on the victories of the Central Powers by pushing forward in Volhynia; as with almost every operation in which it operated without close German support, the *k.u.k.* Army soon ran into trouble, suffering heavy casualties and further denting its confidence. As some of the Russian Army's supply problems began to ease, not least because the retreating forces were now much closer to their heartland, a modicum of confidence began to return. Through his detailed staff work, Alexeyev restored order to the army, while the tsar spent much of his time responding to endless requests from Alexandra to appoint members of families from her inner circle of flatterers to command of regiments, brigades and divisions. Unfortunately for Russia, many of those who were granted appointments had already been found wanting in the past, and large numbers of incompetent officers took up posts in the first months of the tsar's time as commander-in-chief.

The fears of many – that the tsar would personally become associated with the military setbacks suffered by the army – rapidly became reality. There were widespread (and completely unfounded) rumours that the tsarina was at the heart of a group of pro-German traitors, but such allegations, as well as lurid and equally unfounded ones related to sexual misconduct, further damaged the standing of the imperial family. The popular view that opposition to the imperial establishment was consistent with patriotic pro-Russian sentiment added further to the growing sense of political crisis. The 'betrayal' of the workers by the bourgeoisie after the 1905 Revolution had not been forgotten by either side; the ordinary people felt strongly that they couldn't rely on the Duma to initiate significant change, while the radical elements in the Duma were fearful that, if they did not take a lead, events might accelerate beyond their ability to control them. Many politicians – with varying degrees of reluctance – came over to the view that evolutionary change was unlikely to be sufficient. Prince Georgi Yevgenyevich Lvov, a prominent politician who was a member of the Constitutional Democrat Party (on account of their abbreviation, known as the 'Kadets'), wrote at the end of 1916:

> Abandon all further attempts at constructive collaboration with the present government, they are all doomed to failure and are only an impediment to our aim. Do not indulge in illusion; turn away from ghosts. There is no longer a government we can recognise.[23]

Even by the end of 1915, such views were widespread.

The ranks of its depleted armies were slowly restored, though even the immense human resources of Russia could not replace the losses of 1915: over 2.5 million men had been lost, and even though the prodigious Russian replacement system produced 2.25 million men, this still represented a very substantial shortfall.[24] To overcome this, Polivanov and Alexeyev had to break commitments given in the past to older men and certain groups of the population who had been spared front-line service. This led to widespread protests, with many simply deserting before they reached the front. Nevertheless, enough arrived to bring the front-line formations close to their full strength. In particular, Alexeyev's painstaking efforts ensured that the recruits received a higher level of training than their predecessors, and in a remarkably short time the Russian Army had been transformed from a badly beaten force, close to collapse, into something that once more was a force to be reckoned with.

After reaching Brest-Litovsk, Falkenhayn decided that there was little point in advancing further into Russia. There were no critical objectives within easy reach, and he judged the Russian Army to be broken beyond immediate repair. There was therefore an opportunity to deal with other issues, in particular in the Balkans, and significant numbers of troops were transferred from the Eastern Front to the southern borders of the Austro-Hungarian Empire in preparation for an attack on Serbia. When the attack came, it was a great success: Serbia was overrun and Bulgaria brought into the war on the side of the Central Powers. Land communications with Turkey were established, but the indirect cost was that Alexeyev and Polivanov had time to repair their armies. Almost as rapidly as they had crumbled away, they were restored to something approaching strength, and there was a feeling that, having survived 1915, the army could look forward to better times. It is arguable that Falkenhayn missed a key opportunity to knock Russia out of the war completely in 1915, but even if he had been minded to continue offensive operations in the east, it is not immediately obvious how such a killing blow could have been landed. The German forces operating in Russia were at the end of a long supply line, and in need of rest. Perhaps the only major objective within reasonable reach was the series of railway lines running south from Petrograd towards Moscow and other central Russian locations, but even if these lines had been reached, the German forces making the attack would have been badly exposed. Autumn weather was expected to make campaigning increasingly difficult, and for Falkenhayn, Russia had always been a subordinate area of interest. For him, the war could be won or lost only in the west. The sooner he could turn his back on Russia with a modicum of safety, the better.

If there was a glimmer of light for Russia in the autumn, it soon disappeared. The southern armies launched an assault on the Austro-Hungarian lines during the winter of 1915–1916 and were badly beaten, gaining almost no ground at all before being crushed by artillery fire. A few weeks later, as the Germans began their assault on Verdun, the French appealed to the Russians to attack in order to divert German forces from the west. During the previous year, Russian appeals to the French and British for major attacks to try to alleviate the pressure of Mackensen's great advance resulted in only modest attacks, by the French in Champagne and the British at Loos, but the Russians responded to the French appeal with greater alacrity. To an extent, this was driven by self-interest; if Russia had struggled to survive in 1915 when the bulk of German forces were tied down in the west, it was inconceivable that anything better could be expected if the French were to suffer a major defeat. Similarly, with the Germans clearly devoting more of their efforts to their great offensive at Verdun, some senior Russian figures such as Alexei Evert, commander of the West Front, believed it was possible that there would be opportunities to exploit weaknesses in the east.[25] It would also be of great benefit to Russia to be seen to have come to the aid of France – if the Germans were to resume their attacks that had seen them advance so far in 1915, Russia would be in a far stronger moral position to demand reciprocal aid from France. It was a common belief in Russia that the Russian Army had thrown itself against Germany in 1914 before it had completed mobilisation purely for the benefit of the French, and had saved France by sacrificing so many of its men. Consequently, there was considerable resentment at the failure of the Western Powers to come to Russia's aid by launching relieving attacks in 1915, and anything that made a repetition of this less likely in future was to be welcomed.

The French appeal for help, made at the beginning of March, came at a particularly bad time. It would take several weeks for the Russian Army to prepare for a major attack, which would mean that any assault would take part when the great winter freeze was coming to an end. The ground, firmed by hard frosts, would rapidly turn to mud, making all movements almost impossible – not only by attacking troops, but equally critically by their support services. There was also the question of where an attack should fall. The failed winter attacks had deliberately been directed against the Austro-Hungarian forces in the south in the expectation that they would prove to be easier to defeat than the Germans, but if pressure on France was to be relieved, it was essential that the new attack should be on German positions. In any case, the troops of Southwest Front had not recovered from their losses and were in no state to launch fresh assaults. After some discussions with his front commanders, Alexeyev decided that the attack should be close to the junction between Northern and West Fronts. Despite the unfavourable time of year and the choice of the region around Lake Naroch – prone to flooding at the best of times – as the point of main effort, there were grounds for hope. The Russians enjoyed a numerical superiority of about 2:1 in terms of infantry and cavalry, and had the prerogative of attackers to concentrate at a point of their choosing. Nevertheless, the orders that were issued, effectively outlining a major breakthrough with the subsequent collapse of the German positions along the entire front line, were optimistic in the extreme.

After the disastrous winter attacks in the south, Dmitri Gregorovich Shcherbachev, the commander of the Russian Seventh Army which had suffered badly in the fighting, wrote a lengthy report assessing the reasons for the failure. It was almost traditional for Russian officers to complain about inadequate quantities of artillery ammunition and heavy guns, but, after making these points, Shcherbachev offered some more pertinent observations. Compared to the Germans, the Russians lacked good coordination between their artillery and infantry, resulting in too many occasions when the gunners inadvertently shelled their own troops as they tried to press home their attacks or failed to provide timely supporting fire. Commanders at every level had lacked initiative and had remained too far to the rear to intervene when attacks did not unfold as expected. Instead, they had simply reiterated the same orders, regardless of the reasons for failure.[26] Although the report was widely circulated, senior commanders did what they have done on so many occasions through history – they embraced the parts that reinforced their own beliefs and ignored the rest. In particular, they reiterated the importance of large quantities of heavy artillery; once the guns had blasted a route through the German lines, they believed, the infantry would simply march through and occupy uncontested positions.

When the attack came on 18 March, it was a disaster. Russian artillery fire might have been heavier than in previous attacks, but its efficacy was minimal and the advancing infantry died in their thousands in the face of machine-gun and artillery fire. Repeated attempts to penetrate the German defences ended on 29 March when Alexeyev called a halt. Casualties had been appalling, even by the standards of the First World War, exceeding 120,000 dead or wounded; by contrast, the Germans lost barely 20,000, and the maximum advance was only 2 miles.[27] Despite Shcherbachev's report, the same mistakes were repeated: no real coordination between infantry and artillery; haphazard bombardments that achieved little, often because the wrong guns were directed at specific targets; commanders who attempted to run matters from the rear areas and ignored the physical realities on the ground; and, as an additional factor, the obstruction of rear areas by thousands of mounted troops who had been gathered in expectation of a breakthrough, but instead simply blocked roads and consumed supplies needed for the infantry.

While the senior officers indulged in wholesale blame-passing and obstructed an official enquiry to protect their own reputations, the morale of those in the front line plummeted. On occasion, they attacked across ground that was thawing, only to freeze shortly after, leaving wounded men locked in the earth, where they died in large numbers. The Germans recorded finding over 5,000 Russian corpses hanging from the barbed wire entanglements – obstacles that should have been blasted away by the Russian artillery bombardment. The men who had been dispatched to the front line by Polivanov, despite being given reassurances that they would be spared such duty – the *Polivanovtsy*, as they became known – and their families were already resentful of the authorities, and this resentment grew even stronger. The only senior military figure to lose his post was Polivanov, the war minister, whose involvement in events was peripheral at most; he had fallen out of favour with Tsarina Alexandra when he challenged a clumsy attempt by Boris Stürmer, the prime minister, to misappropriate funds for his personal use. Stürmer was a close ally of Rasputin, who prevailed upon Alexandra to demand Polivanov's dismissal. As on so many occasions, Tsar Nicholas listened only to those who affirmed his opinions, regarding anyone who took a different view as being disloyal to the Romanovs, and Polivanov was replaced by Dmitri Shuvayev, a man with a good reputation as a logistician but with little else to recommend him.

The results of the disastrous attacks of the winter were multiple. Firstly, the Germans and their Austro-Hungarian allies were left with the strong feeling that the Russian Army was a spent force – it might still be able to gather impressive numbers of men together for an attack, but the attacks themselves were poorly conceived and executed. Secondly, morale in Russia took a further plunge. It was one thing to endure hardships, both at the front and in Russia's interior, if there was a prospect of victory; it was quite another when the news from the war was unremittingly bad, and a steady stream of broken and maimed men returned to the main population centres with stories of mismanagement, poor logistics, and incompetence. Politically, Prime Minister Stürmer consolidated his hold on power, surrounding himself with favourites and cronies. This created further discontent, but for the moment there did not appear to be any opportunity to express this in a meaningful way. The result was a sense of calm, but it was deceptive.[28]

It was at this stage that Alexei Alexeyevich Brusilov was appointed to take command of Southwest Front from Ivanov, who had singularly failed to impress throughout the war to date and owed his survival largely to his unquestioned loyalty to the tsar. Brusilov had led his Eighth Army with distinction in the opening phases of the war, and when Alexeyev called a conference on 14 April to plan the summer campaign, Brusilov volunteered to launch attacks with his front. Alexeyev had already decided on broadly repeating the catastrophic attempts to break the German lines at Lake Naroch, and advised Brusilov that, if he wished to attack, he would have to do so with his own resources – no further troops or supplies would be allocated to him. Brusilov was undaunted; he had already implemented training programmes to put right some of the mistakes made in the winter attacks against the *k.u.k.* Army, and he was confident that he could succeed. Moreover, he told the conference, it was his duty to attack, even if this was only as a subsidiary attack to draw enemy troops away from the north and thus facilitate the progress of the main planned attack. After securing the grudging support of Alexeyev and his fellow front commanders, Brusilov had to convince his subordinates, the commanders of Southwest Front's armies, that they could succeed. Patiently, he brought them around to his point of view. A victory was perfectly possible, but only if the attack was made in a manner that differed markedly from previous attempts.

With varying degrees of enthusiasm, the armies of Southwest Front began to prepare for Brusilov's offensive. The team of staff officers working with Brusilov had absorbed fully the lessons outlined in Shcherbachev's winter report, reinforced by the failure at Lake Naroch. Great attention was paid to artillery preparation, which would be more carefully planned than before. Gunners and infantrymen trained together, experiencing the difficulties of their rival arm at first hand and devising means by which they could cooperate more flexibly. Aware that he would be unable to hide preparations for his attack, Brusilov told his men to make preparations everywhere; hardened shelters were constructed where the assault troops could wait in safety for the gunners to do their work, and although the Austro-Hungarian observers could see the bunkers being built, they were so numerous and widespread that they gave no clue about where the points of main effort would be. As the moment for the attack approached, the Russians began to dig sap trenches towards the Austro-Hungarian lines.

After its successful defence in the winter battles, the *k.u.k.* Army was remarkably complacent in the face of Brusilov's preparations. Many of the experienced troops and much of the artillery that had played such an important part in the defence had been transferred from the Eastern Front to take part in Conrad's planned offensive against Italy, but the belief that the Russians were incapable of launching an effective attack appears to have been so strong that only half-hearted attempts were made to harass Brusilov's troops in their preparations; there were very few raids to stop the digging of sap trenches, and the defenders lacked sufficient artillery and ammunition to bombard known concentrations of Russian troops.

Until now, attacks had been made in large waves, and defensive gunfire simply cut them down in swathes. Brusilov planned for his attacking infantry to function in small groups, often with specialised roles; heavily armed formations would be tasked with destroying individual strongpoints, while following waves penetrated swiftly into secondary positions. This required extensive training, and simulations of Austro-Hungarian positions were constructed, on which infantry and artillery trained repeatedly, perfecting their tactics and coordination. After perhaps the most detailed preparations of any offensive in the entire war, Brusilov's troops began their artillery bombardment on 22 May. The assault on the lines of the *k.u.k.* Army at either end of Southwest Front succeeded almost immediately; in the north, Lutsk was swiftly captured, and in the south the Russians began an advance that would sweep a considerable distance across Galicia immediately north of the Carpathians. Hundreds of thousands of Austro-Hungarian troops were captured, many surrendering without firing a shot.

The main summer offensive by the Russian Army, farther to the north, was a complete failure; unlike Brusilov, Alexei Evert had made little attempt to modify the failed tactics of previous attacks. Nevertheless, Brusilov's gains created a huge crisis for the Central Powers. With German troops heavily committed at Verdun and in anticipation of the Anglo-French attack on the Somme and Austro-Hungarian troops bogged down in northern Italy, there was little scope to send reinforcements to replace the troops that were lost in May and June. This was in fact the intended policy of the Entente Powers; they had agreed the previous winter to launch simultaneous attacks to achieve this very end, in the expectation that, at some point, the lines of the Central Powers would collapse. For a few weeks, it seemed as if this point would be in the east, where units of the *k.u.k.* Army repeatedly demonstrated an alarming fragility when they came under Russian pressure. But despite their successes, the Russian attacks were not without heavy casualties, and, once the highly trained initial wave of troops had been exhausted, attacks tended to revert to traditional massed waves. Nor was there sufficient time for the careful reconnaissance needed to ensure that preliminary artillery bombardments were as successful as those of late May. By the end of the summer, the Russian attacks were petering out; after their rapid initial gains, the Russians made only modest progress, but lost huge numbers of men.

Morale throughout Russia rose on the news of Brusilov's initial successes. As the offensive of Evert's West Front failed and attempts to continue the advance of Southwest Front foundered, the mood darkened again. Critically, the divisions of the Russian Guards had been gathered together into a united force, first the Guards Army, later renamed the Special Army after non-guards formations were added to it, and were thrown into the attack. The Guards had suffered heavy losses in 1915 and had been withdrawn from the front line to recuperate and retrain; unfortunately, they were trained according to the old tactics of massed attacks, and were cut to pieces as they advanced. By this stage, the Germans had positioned increasing numbers of their own troops throughout the front line, and although the Austro-Hungarian units continued to be prone to moments of fragility, their German equivalents held firm. The importance of the setback for the Russian Guards was that these regiments had traditionally been the most loyal to the Romanovs, and had played a key role in suppressing the 1905

Revolution. After the slaughter of the summer of 1916, it was questionable whether their loyalty remained as strong.

There were growing signs of disillusionment everywhere in Russia in 1915 as the tsar's armies were driven east in growing disarray, and this mood – lifted briefly by the initial success of the Brusilov Offensive – returned with a vengeance towards the end of 1916. Alfred Knox, the British military attaché in Petrograd, recorded:

> I hear whispers that the Russian infantry has lost heart and that anti-war propaganda is rife in the ranks. It is little wonder that they are downhearted after being driven to the slaughter over the same ground seven times in about a month, and every time taking trenches where their guns could not keep them. However, I do not attach importance to this, for they will be fresh again next spring.[29]

Knox was usually a sharp and accurate observer of Russian affairs, and his closing sentiment is curious. Whilst it is possible that he genuinely believed that morale would rise again after the winter, other entries in his diaries record his growing awareness of the political strains within Russia. He must surely have known that tensions were accumulating and were unlikely to ease without major changes. Maurice Paléologue, the French ambassador in Petrograd, clearly took a less optimistic view than Knox when he described an incident in the capital that gave a hint at the trouble that lay ahead:

> About the end of last October [1916] a very significant incident occurred in Petrograd … A strike broke out in the Viborg quarter and as the police were very roughly handled by the workmen, two regiments which were in barracks in the vicinity were sent for. These two regiments fired on the police. A division of Cossacks had to be hastily called in to bring the mutineers to their senses. So in case of a rising the authorities cannot count on the army. My conclusion is that time is no longer working for us, at any rate in Russia, and that we must henceforth take the defection of our ally into our calculations and draw all inferences involved.[30]

George Buchanan, the British ambassador, was also aware of the darkening mood. He wrote on 18 October about a viewpoint that was apparently gaining support throughout Russian society:

> 'It is Great Britain,' they keep on repeating, 'that is forcing Russia to continue the war and forbidding her to accept the favourable peace terms which Germany is

ready to offer, and it is Great Britain, therefore, that is responsible for the privations and sufferings of her people ...'

The losses which Russia has suffered are so colossal that the whole country is in mourning. So many lives have been uselessly sacrificed in the recent unsuccessful attacks at Kovel and other places, that the impression is gaining ground that it is useless continuing the struggle, and that Russia, unlike Great Britain, has nothing to gain by prolonging the war. This insidious campaign is much more difficult to meet than the old lies about our former inaction.[31]

Buchanan was inclined to blame this on German propaganda, and whilst there can be no doubt that the Germans were agitating in this manner, the view in Russia that the Western Powers had left the tsar's armies to bear the brunt of the load was widespread and required little encouragement from Germany. Throughout 1915, the Russians had appealed in vain to the British and French for them to launch relieving attacks to draw away German troops – by contrast, the Russians had thrown their incompletely mobilised armies into action in 1914 in an attempt to prevent France from being overwhelmed in Germany's opening campaign, and again in early 1916 had attacked at Lake Naroch to provide relief as the crisis around Verdun developed. This attitude ignored the substantial material benefit provided by the British and French in terms of guns, ammunition and other supplies, but even this had been on financial terms that were very unfavourable to Russia. By the end of 1916, Britain and France were reeling from their appalling casualties on the Western Front, and in the context of the losses of the Somme and Verdun, it is understandable that warnings about growing Russian resentment were not heeded.

Political developments in Russia continued through the winter. Stürmer, who owed his position as both prime minister and foreign minister to Tsarina Alexandra's patronage, was dismissed by the tsar in late November 1916. He had been strongly criticised in the Duma, and Alexandra tried in vain to persuade Nicholas to change his mind, though she prevented Nicholas from using the dismissal of Stürmer explicitly as a step towards appeasing the Duma. The relationship between Nicholas and Alexandra was neatly summarised by Buchanan:

Her Majesty, unfortunately, was under the impression that it was her mission to save Russia. She believed – and, in principle, as subsequent events have shown, she was not altogether wrong – that the autocracy was the only regime that could hold the empire together. The tsar, she knew, was weak, and she therefore preached firmness. He must, she repeatedly told him, be an autocrat in deed as well as in

> name. In her desire to help him and to relieve him of some of the burden of his double role of autocrat and commander-in-chief, she assumed an active part in the government of the country, and in advocating, as she did, a policy of 'thorough[ness]' she was honestly convinced that she was acting in Russia's best interests. She was so obsessed with the idea that there must be no weakening of the autocracy that she was opposed to all concessions, while she encouraged the tsar to choose his ministers more out of regard for their political opinions than for their qualifications for office.
>
> The weaker will yield to the stronger, and the tsar was entirely under her influence. But woefully mistaken as she was, the tsarina was throughout inspired by the best of motives – love of her husband and love of her adopted country. The same cannot, however, be said of the little band of unscrupulous and self-serving adventurers who, in their turn, influenced Her Majesty, using her as their unconscious agent to further their own political ends and ambitions. It was to Rasputin more especially that she looked for guidance before tendering advice to the tsar; and as her health failed her – for, what with the strain of the war, anxiety about her son, and the overtaxing of her strength in hospital work, she had fallen into a nervous neurotic state – she came more and more under his baneful influence.[32]

Grigory Rasputin, whom Buchanan and many others regarded with some justification as a 'baneful influence', was assassinated in almost comic circumstances at the end of 1916: the conspirators lured him to the Yusupov Palace in Petrograd where they tried unsuccessfully to poison him, and then shot him before throwing him into the River Neva. Despite their clear anger and shock that someone that they regarded as their inner circle had been killed without the assassins making much of an effort to conceal their involvement, Nicholas and Alexandra could do little. Vladimir Purishkevich was a right-wing member of the Duma and could not be arrested under Russian law; the rest of the conspirators were members of the aristocracy, who could be detained only under the direct orders of the tsar. Although Alexandra demanded summary executions of those involved, Nicholas rather characteristically shied away from such strong action, choosing instead to send the aristocratic members of the conspiracy into a form of internal exile. A petition from other aristocrats calling for the exiles to be pardoned was ignored, alienating many who might otherwise have supported the Romanovs. Despite this, Nicholas felt that he had to do more to assuage Alexandra's anger at Rasputin's death. The deeply unpopular Stürmer had been replaced by Alexander Trepov, who found himself at loggerheads with

Interior Minister Alexander Dmitrievich Protopopov, another of Buchanan's 'little band of unscrupulous and self-serving adventurers'. It speaks much about the extraordinary world inhabited by the tsarina that Protopopov successfully curried favour with her by claiming to receive nightly visitations from Rasputin's ghost and passing on messages from the dead monk to Alexandra. Partly in an attempt to appease the tsarina, partly to put in place men he regarded as personally more loyal to himself, Nicholas dismissed Trepov and also War Minister Shuvaev, replacing them with the elderly Nikolai Dmitrievich Golitsyn (who begged in vain not to be appointed) and General Mikhail Alexeyevich Beliaev respectively. The two dismissed men were widely regarded as amongst the last politicians who were both loyal to the old regime and had sufficient respect in the Duma to hold dissent in check; their dismissal therefore edged Russia closer than ever to revolution. As Buchanan wrote a month after Rasputin's assassination:

> Revolution was in the air, and the only moot point was whether it would come from above or from below. A palace revolution was openly spoken of, and at a dinner at the embassy a Russian friend of mine, who had occupied a high position in the government, declared that it was a mere question whether both the tsar and tsarina or only the latter would be killed. On the other hand, a popular outbreak, provoked by the prevailing food shortage, might occur at any moment.[33]

Buchanan appealed personally to the tsar, begging him to break down the barriers that separated him from his people and to regain their confidence. Nicholas' reply must have been utterly disheartening; rather than seeking to regain the confidence of the people, Nicholas said, the people should seek to regain the tsar's confidence. The interview left Buchanan in little doubt that his best efforts had been in vain, and that disaster lay ahead:

> Whatever momentary impression I may have made was not strong enough to counterbalance the adverse influence of the Tsarina, whose displeasure I had already incurred on account of the language which I had held in previous audiences. So much was this the case that, according to a current report, the question of asking for my recall was seriously considered.[34]

Speeches in the Duma became increasingly strident. Pavel Nikolayevich Miliukov, a founder member of the Kadets with strong links to western diplomats, listed the mistakes and corrupt practices of the government, asking rhetorically after each point: 'Is this stupidity, or is it treason?' It was the first time that the word 'treason' had been used in the Duma with regard to the government. Accounts of his speech were banned, but copies circulated as a result of numerous presses run by pro-revolutionary groups. Miliukov remained cautious and wished to avoid a revolution, and told a meeting of his party:

> It will be our task not to destroy the government, which would only aid anarchy, but to instil in it a completely different content, that is, to build a genuinely constitutional order. That is why, in our struggle with the government, despite everything, we must retain a sense of proportion … To support anarchy in the name of the struggle with the government would be to risk all the political conquests we have made since 1905.[35]

The fact that Miliukov still believed that the gains made after the 1905 Revolution were worth saving shows the gulf that had grown between progressive parties like the Kadets and the increasingly restive workers. Alexander Fyodorovich Kerensky, a prominent member of the Trudovik ('Labour') Party, dismissed the position of those like Miliukov as being further evidence that the liberals wished to remain firmly seated in their comfortable armchairs rather than taking action. Vasily Yevgenyevich Shulgin, who had served in the army and been wounded in 1915 before becoming a member of the Progressive Bloc in the Duma, was equally clear about what lay ahead, even though he remained a committed monarchist: 'Nobody believes in words any longer.'[36]

Whilst 1916 brought Russia close to the brink of revolution, it was also a year of great disappointment for her allies. Both the Entente and Central Powers had entered the year with clear plans for how the war would be won – or at least, how big steps towards victory would be achieved. The Entente Powers intended to wear down Germany and Austria-Hungary by a deliberate campaign of attrition, culminating in simultaneous offensives in the west, in Italy and in Russia during the summer. These would leave the Germans unable to shuffle forces from one front to another, and would eventually trigger a collapse on one front or other. Although the strategy failed, there were desperate moments, particularly as the fragility of the *k.u.k.* Army necessitated the dispatch of German reinforcements to the east. An extraordinary degree of importance was placed by the Entente Powers in enticing Romania into the war, not because of any great expectation that its relatively primitive army would prove to be a war-winning asset, but because Romanian entry against Austria-Hungary would greatly increase the length of front line that the Central Powers would have to defend. When Bucharest finally agreed to enter the conflict, it was too late; Brusilov's offensive had lost impetus and was winding down, and this allowed the Central Powers to concentrate sufficient forces in Transylvania, first to stop the Romanian advance, and then to invade and overrun most of the country. Far from being a positive asset, Romania proved to be a negative one – it was the Entente, exhausted by the terrible casualties suffered on all fronts, that found itself having to find troops to defend an unwelcome new segment of front line, as well as supplying weapons, ammunition and other equipment to resupply and reorganise the Romanian Army.

But if it had been a year of disappointment for the Entente, the same was true for Germany and Austria-Hungary. Like the Entente, both nations had drawn up plans for how they would make substantial progress towards victory, but crucially they did so without any attempt at coordination. Relations between Conrad, chief of the Austro-Hungarian general staff, and Falkenhayn, his German opposite number, had never been good. Falkenhayn made little attempt to hide his opinion that firstly, the critical front was in the west, and secondly, the performance of the *k.u.k.* Army was so poor that it would have lost the war without the support of Germany. Whilst Conrad could not deny the second point, he repeatedly drew attention to the fact that his armies had effectively drawn upon themselves the weight of Russia's initial assault in 1914 in the hope that the Germans would win a quick victory against France. Although it had been clear for several years that a European war would see the two central empires fighting against their encircling enemies, there were few attempts at anything more than the most rudimentary collective planning for the conduct of such a war, and this continued even after hostilities had started. By the end of 1915, relations between the two chiefs of staff had broken down completely – at the end of the conquest of Serbia, Falkenhayn wanted Austro-Hungarian troops to be sent east so that more German troops could be spared for the Western Front, but instead Conrad authorised the invasion of Montenegro. In the winter that followed, Falkenhayn drew up his plans for the trap that he had devised at Verdun – the French Army would be forced to defend a location that was exposed to German artillery, and would be bled white over the following weeks – while Conrad concentrated on his intention to deliver a knock-out blow against Italy. His personal antipathy for the conduct of the Italian government, which had started the war as an ally of the Central Powers, seems to have clouded his judgement on more than one occasion, and he drew up a plan of campaign that would see his forces advance out of the Alps and onto the north Italian plain. After breaking through, his troops would wheel to the east, surrounding and isolating a large part of the Italian Army in and around Venice.

Both plans had their flaws. Falkenhayn's operation at Verdun failed to secure the vital high ground from which German artillery could then crush the French Army, and instead drew the Germans into a huge slaughter that cost them at least as dearly as the French. The *Strafexpedition* ('Punishment expedition') against Italy fared even worse. Devised entirely from the safety of Conrad's headquarters without any visit to the front line to assess the terrain, Conrad's plan started with an initial success but rapidly ran out of steam as the Austro-Hungarian forces found it almost impossible to bring up supplies through the mountains in adequate quantities. Even before the Brusilov Offensive forced Conrad to divert troops to the east, the drive to knock Italy out of the war had effectively ground to a halt. The disasters that followed on the Eastern Front effectively reduced the *k.u.k.* Army to little more than a militia. In return for bailing out their ally, the Germans insisted upon German officers being inserted into positions throughout the Austro-Hungarian command structure. The forces of the Dual Monarchy effectively became subordinate to the control of the German Army, and there could be little doubt that, even before the Central Powers had achieved final victory, the Austro-Hungarian Empire was being reduced to little more than a vassal state of Germany.

By the end of 1916, the two chiefs of staff had both been dismissed. Hindenburg and his chief of staff Ludendorff had been hailed as the saviours of East Prussia in 1914 when they won a remarkable victory over the Russians at Tannenberg, and then oversaw the expulsion of the Russians from the areas of East Prussia they had occupied, as well as overrunning parts of Russian Poland. Thereafter, their supporters agitated for them to be granted greater power, openly suggesting that Falkenhayn should be replaced by Hindenburg. The rivalry between the two camps was a constant source of tension within the German military throughout 1915 and 1916, and grew more severe as Falkenhayn's master plan – to bleed the French Army to death at Verdun – foundered. Finally, it was the declaration of war by Romania that triggered Falkenhayn's fall. Despite plentiful evidence to the contrary, Falkenhayn had repeatedly advised the kaiser that Romania would not enter the war until after the harvest season, dismissing warnings from Austro-Hungarian sources as attempts to secure the use of larger numbers of German troops in the east. On 28 August 1916, he was advised that the kaiser had summoned Hindenburg to discuss the changed situation now that Romania had entered the war. Falkenhayn responded that this demonstrated that the kaiser must have lost confidence in the chief of his general staff if he chose to discuss matters with a subordinate without first speaking to the chief of staff, and asked to be relieved of his post. He was dismissed the following day, and Hindenburg was appointed as his successor. Ludendorff became quartermaster-general, effectively the second most powerful person in the German military hierarchy.

Falkenhayn's strategy for winning the war had been first to weaken Russia to a point where the tsar would either be forced to sue for peace or the Russian Army would be too impotent to intervene further, and then to turn against France, as only the decisive defeat of the French would ensure a lasting, favourable peace. Despite this, he was not greatly in favour of major annexations of territory, though the wish-list of those in high office in Germany grew steadily – for them, the sacrifices made by the German people required huge compensation, and any post-war settlement had to ensure that Germany was safe for the foreseeable future. The Russians rejected the tentative proposals for peace that the Germans offered in late 1915, and recovered remarkably despite the further setbacks of early 1916 to shake the defences of the Central Powers in the Brusilov Offensive, while the operation to wear down the French at Verdun turned into a stalemate that threatened to bleed both armies to death. Falkenhayn had inherited command in the failure of his predecessor, Helmuth von Moltke, to knock out the French in the opening months of the war and without any clear path to follow; his departure left his successor in a similar position. It had been difficult for Falkenhayn to devise a new strategy while Germany geared up for a prolonged war, and it was no less difficult for Hindenburg, with a nation showing increasing strain at every level. Despite rationing, there were widespread food shortages, resulting in riots in some towns and cities. The endless casualty lists had left almost no families untouched, and many were pressing for any peace that did not humiliate Germany. Woodrow Wilson, the president of the United States, had offered to mediate in peace talks, and despite the demands of the German right wing for major territorial gains, peace along the lines of the American suggestions seemed to many to be preferable to the endless losses, the growing food shortages, and the sense that Germany's enemies were growing steadily stronger.

By the end of 1916, Germany found itself involved in two contradictory developments. On the one hand, there was a strong desire for peace; on the other hand, the privations of ordinary Germans led to growing support for unrestricted submarine warfare in the hope that this would starve Britain into defeat in the same manner that the British blockade was trying to grind down the German population. The initial American peace proposals were not particularly favourable to Germany, calling for the return of Alsace and Lorraine to France, and Russian naval access to the Bosporus and Dardanelles, without offering the Central

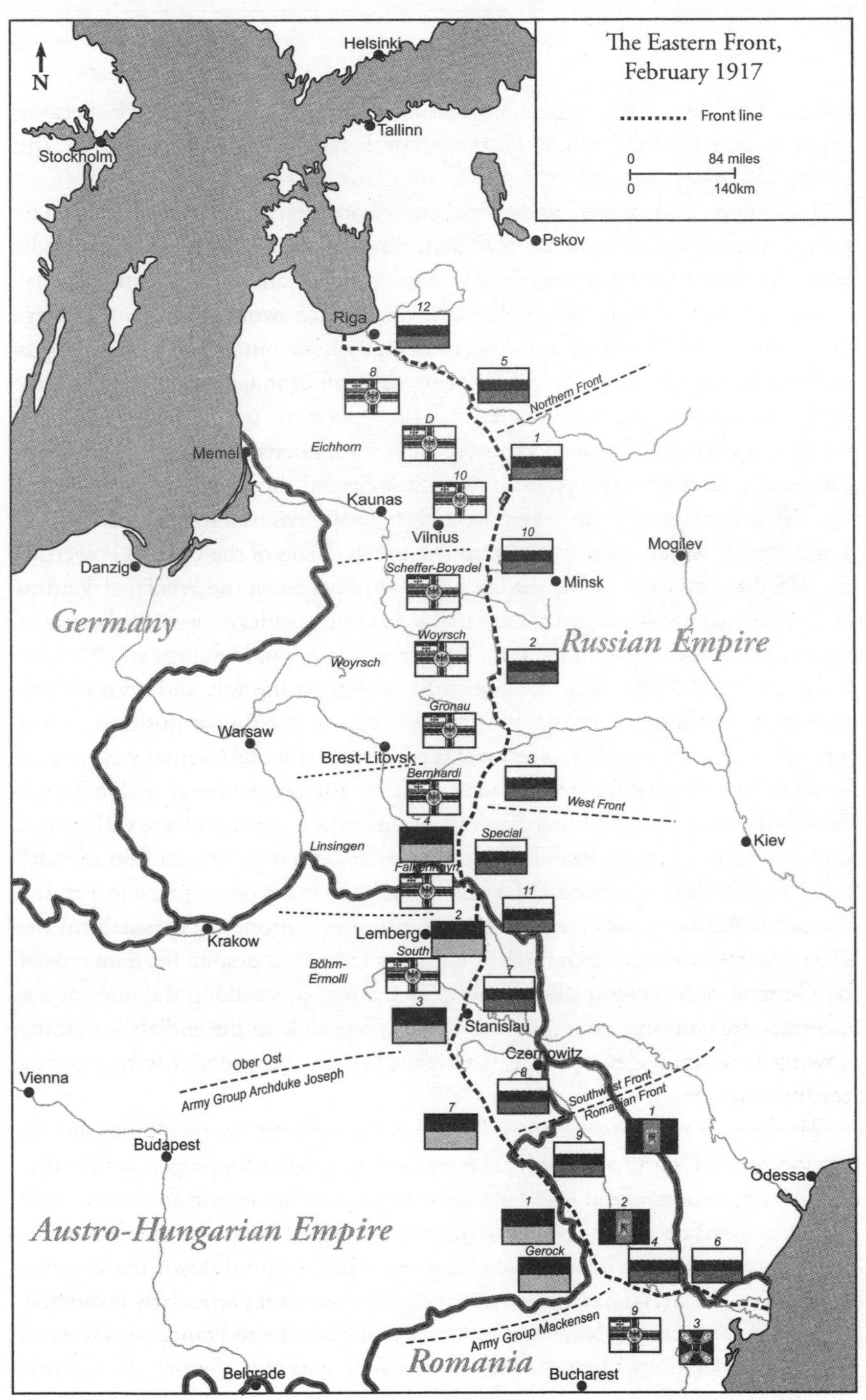
The Eastern Front, February 1917
Front line
0 84 miles
0 140km
N
Helsinki
Tallinn
Stockholm
Pskov
Riga
Memel
Kaunas
Vilnius
Danzig
Mogilev
Minsk
Germany
Russian Empire
Warsaw
Brest-Litovsk
Kiev
Krakow
Lemberg
Stanislau
Czernowitz
Vienna
Budapest
Odessa
Austro-Hungarian Empire
Romania
Belgrade
Bucharest
Northern Front
West Front
Southwest Front
Romanian Front
Ober Ost
Army Group Archduke Joseph
Army Group Mackensen
Eichhorn
Scheffer-Boyadel
Woyrsch
Gronau
Bernhardi
Linsingen
Special
South
Böhm-Ermolli
Gerock

Powers anything in return, but Stephan Burián, the Austro-Hungarian foreign minister, and Theobald von Bethmann Hollweg, the German chancellor, tried to engage the Americans in further discussions. Instead of accepting the American preconditions or proposing their own, the Central Powers suggested that these matters should be discussed in a conference that would be held in Europe. At the same time, in an attempt to create a favourable situation on the ground, the Central Powers announced the creation of an independent Polish nation in November 1916 – it was calculated that the Americans would find it very difficult to oppose this and return parts of Poland to Russian rule against the wishes of the indigenous population.

At the same time, Admiral Henning von Holtzendorff, the chief of staff of the German Navy, submitted a proposal to end the war by military means. Arguing that the British were strongly dependent upon imported wheat, he suggested that it would bring Britain to the brink of starvation if German U-boats could sink a minimum of 600,000 tons of shipping per month.[37] This would be achieved by resorting to unrestricted submarine warfare, a policy that had been dropped in the face of American protests earlier in the war. The proposal was optimistic on many levels – Germany simply lacked the U-boats to sustain such a campaign, and Holtzendorff's plan contained large numbers of assumptions with little evidence to support them. The two paths – the proposal for a peace conference and the suggestion of waging unrestricted submarine warfare – developed in parallel without any attempt to coordinate them, and the announcement in early 1916 that Germany was about to unleash its submarines effectively killed any further talk of peace. The United States broke off diplomatic relations with Germany, and began to prepare for war.[38]

Hindenburg and Ludendorff also instigated plans to improve the fighting power of the German Army. Production of key weapons such as machine-guns, trench mortars and flamethrowers would be increased, and there would be major changes to the way that German industry worked. Ludendorff described how the German *Oberste Heeresleitung* ('Army High Command' or *OHL*) wished to take complete control of matters:

> The war obliged us to call on the last reserves of manpower and to make them available. Whether it was for combat or for other service in the home army and in the civil service was all the same. An individual man could only serve the homeland in one place, but his strength must be put to use. The civil service was another matter. Overall, relative importance in general between the army, navy and the homeland was assessed by *OHL* in consultation with the homeland administrations. Only *OHL* could oversee these approximations.[39]

The new plan, widely known as the Hindenburg Programme, proved to be a failure. General Wilhelm Groener, an eminent railways logistician, was appointed to head a new *Kriegsamt* ('War Office') that would coordinate increased production as part of the war ministry, but ran into difficulties on many levels. There were some examples of outright obstruction by vested interests, such as Hermann von Stein, the war minister, who resented Groener's powers, but the main problem was that the plans took little account of the complexity of increasing production. To date, the war ministry had slowly increased production of munitions in line with increases in the availability of raw materials, and the sudden demand for increased output rapidly used up the modest stockpiles that were available. As a result, production of some items actually fell after an initial surge. Consequently, there was little prospect of the German Army being transformed into a machine that would be able to win the war before the intervention of the United States. Much would depend upon the submarine campaign, or other events that were beyond the control of Germany.

Conrad, too, came to the end of his term of office as chief of staff. Despite presiding over an almost unbroken series of military disasters, he had survived because he retained the personal support of Emperor Franz Joseph, and because there was no obvious alternative. On 21 November 1916, the venerable ruler of the Austro-Hungarian Empire died after a short illness, and was succeeded by his grand-nephew Karl, who also appointed himself commander-in-chief of the army in place of Archduke Frederick. Despite Conrad's protests, the location of *AOK* (*Armee Oberkommando* or 'Army High Command') was moved from Teschen, where it had been based for almost the entire war, to the town of Baden to the south of Vienna. At the end of February 1917, Conrad was told that he was no longer chief of the general staff. Increasingly disheartened by a war that had not developed as he had expected and hoped, he asked for permission to retire, but was persuaded to take over command of all Austro-Hungarian forces on the Italian Front. His replacement at *AOK* was Arthur Arz von Straussenberg, who had performed well on the Eastern Front and crucially had the confidence of the Germans.

Like Germany, the Austro-Hungarian Empire faced increasing food shortages, but these were at least partly due to internal problems. Hungary refused to allow exports of food to Austria in sufficient quantities to alleviate shortages, and attempts to regulate matters and introduce rationing were as bureaucratic and chaotic as almost every such intervention by Austro-Hungarian authorities. The death of the old emperor brought mixed feelings; on the one hand, there was a widespread sense that the entire institution of the Dual Monarchy was so closely associated with Franz Joseph that it was difficult to conceive of one continuing without the other, but on the other hand there was also hope that a new, young emperor would use the opportunity offered by his accession to power to bring about major changes. What these changes would be was something that caused huge disagreement – many regions of the empire were increasingly vociferous in demanding increased autonomy, while almost everyone was desperate for peace. There was certainly no prospect of the Austro-Hungarian Empire being able to make a decisive unilateral contribution to a victory by the Central Powers; the strength and morale of the *k.u.k.* Army had been dealt irreparable blows in 1916. At best, Austria-Hungary could expect to help an increasingly dominant German partner to achieve victory.

All three empires thus endured a grim winter at the end of 1916. For all of them, victory seemed as far away as ever. All faced increasing internal strains, many of which had been developing for years but had been exacerbated by the exigencies of war. There was a widespread sense of instability – only small additional changes would be needed to precipitate uncontrollable events.

CHAPTER 2

THE FALL OF THE ROMANOVS

There had been major fighting on the Eastern Front in the first two winters of the war; in early 1915, Hindenburg and Ludendorff expelled the Russians from the eastern parts of East Prussia, but failed to deliver the major blow that they expected to land on the northern flank of the Russian Army, and, in early 1916, the Russians launched their calamitous attacks first against the *k.u.k.* Army, and then against the Germans at Lake Naroch just as the ground began to thaw. By contrast, there was little military activity in early 1917. After surviving the Brusilov Offensive, the Central Powers were content to sit in their fortified positions, and the Russians were too exhausted to try to force them out. Apart from local raids and occasional harassing fire by the artillery, the long Eastern Front settled down to endure the winter. But if the front line was relatively quiet, momentous events were developing elsewhere.

Buchanan had speculated whether there would be some form of *coup d'état* before a spontaneous popular rising took place in Petrograd. Had such a coup occurred, it is questionable whether it would have been enough to prevent the people from taking matters into their own hands, so great was the level of frustration throughout the Russian population. There were several conspiracies afoot for just such a coup. Alexander Ivanovich Guchkov, chair of Russia's Central War Industry Committee, was part of a group that looked at various options. After considering and rejecting a direct seizure of the entire imperial family in the Alexander Palace at Tsarskoe Selo by troops commanded by Kossikovsky, a cavalry officer who was part of the conspiracy, they opted for waylaying the imperial train as it travelled between *Stavka*, the headquarters of the army in Mogilev, and Tsarskoe Selo. They intended to demand that the tsar abdicated in favour of his son Alexei with Grand Duke Mikhail Alexandrovich, Nicholas' brother, as regent. At the same time, a new government would be appointed in the hope that this would forestall a popular revolution. Plans for this coup, which would have taken place in early March, were overtaken by events.[40] Another scheme was considered by Prince Lvov in discussions with Alexeyev, the chief of the general staff; they intended to arrest Tsarina Alexandra and force Nicholas to abdicate in favour of Grand Duke Nikolai. Prince Lvov would become the premier of the government. When Nikolai refused to take part in the plot, it was abandoned.[41]

Food shortages had grown increasingly frequent in Russia throughout the war, and, given the demands that the war effort placed upon Russian food production and its railway network, it was almost inevitable that there would be severe shortages in the winter of 1916–1917. The crisis was particularly severe in Petrograd and Moscow, both of which were hugely dependent upon supplies from the countryside to feed their populations, which were swollen by the combination of expansion of war industries and the steady flood of refugees from western Russia. The dismissal of Trepov alienated the few remaining allies that the tsar had in the Duma, and Alexandra's attempts to arrest the aristocratic members of the Rasputin conspiracy angered the one remaining part of Russian society that might have supported the Romanovs. Whatever the rights and wrongs of Rasputin's murder, the contempt and hatred for him amongst the aristocracy – who resented hugely the influence that he had over the tsarina – was so great that it overcame all other concerns. Grand Duke Andrei Vladimirovich was not alone in protesting about the attempts to detain the assassins:

> This means open revolt. Here we have the war, with the enemy threatening us from all sides, and we have to deal with this sort of nonsense. How can they not be ashamed to stir up all this fuss over the murder of such a filthy good-for-nothing![42]

Andrei Vladimirovich's mother, Grand Duchess Maria Pavlovna, was known as 'the grandest of the grand duchesses' and deliberately attempted to outshine the imperial family's social life by hosting extravagant balls in the Vladimir Palace on the Neva embankment. Her antipathy for Tsarina Alexandra was well known, and late in 1916 she told Mikhail Vladimirovich Rodzianko, the president of the Duma, that Alexandra should be 'annihilated'.[43] With her son now joining the vociferous criticism of the imperial family, Nicholas summoned Maria Pavlovna and ordered her to leave Petrograd with her family.[44] They left in stages, reaching the Caucasus as events gathered pace in the Russian capital. Others who had also spoken out in favour of the assassins were also expelled, or left voluntarily. But despite these attempts by the tsar to remove those in high places who might conspire against him, there was continuing speculation that a coup was imminent. Another of the grand dukes, Alexander Mikhailovich, issued his childhood friend the tsar with a further warning:

> This cannot go on for long. Discontent is mounting rapidly and, the further it goes, the more the abyss deepens between you and your people … It is the government which is preparing the way for revolution. We are watching a play with an unheard-of plot: we are looking on while revolution comes from above, not from below.[45]

Nicholas chose once more to ignore the advice that he was offered, rejecting any suggestion that there would be some sort of coup to remove him. He was correct – the revolution would come from the bottom, not the top. Conditions for Petrograd's workers had deteriorated steadily throughout the war; coal prices had quadrupled through 1915 and 1916, and the cost of a meal in the sort of cheap café frequented by workers had increased sevenfold. In 1917, the inflation rate worsened dramatically, with food prices increasing by about 5 per cent every week.[46] Contrary to the fears of the grand dukes, the agents of the *Okhrana*, the state security police established in 1881 after the assassination of Tsar Alexander II, accurately assessed where the real danger lay:

> Children are starving in the most literal sense of the word. A revolution, if it takes place, will be spontaneous, quite likely a hunger riot.[47]

Matters were worsened by the weather. With its sources of food tens or hundreds of miles away, Petrograd was completely dependent upon the railway network, and heavy snow reduced the already inadequate supply. By mid-February, Protopopov could only rage impotently that 60,000 freight cars filled with food, fuel and fodder were stranded across the countryside.[48] In a final, despairing attempt to persuade the tsar to take drastic action, Rodzianko prepared a substantial report for Nicholas, listing all of the shortages: no raw materials for war production; no fuel; and no bread. He concluded with ominous words:

> The final hour is beginning to strike. The time is very near when any appeal to the masses' reason will be too late and useless.[49]

Nicholas' reaction was as predictable as it was disappointing; as had been the case with all such warnings; he impatiently cut Rodzianko short, insisting that his personal information contradicted the Duma president.

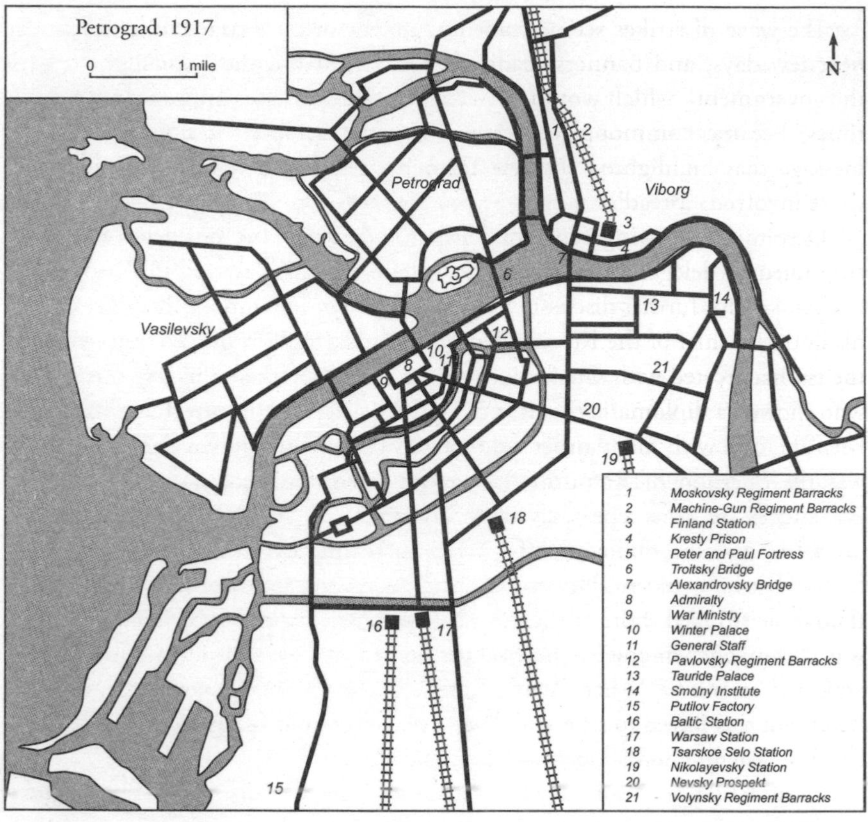

The ordinary people were about to take matters into their own hands. On 22 January, nearly 150,000 workers across the city joined demonstrations to mark the twelfth anniversary of the Bloody Sunday massacre.* The slogans shouted by the strikers rapidly encompassed not only the deaths of 1905, but also protests against the war, inflation, wage cuts, and food shortages. There were similar protests in other Russian cities, and there was little attempt by the police or the army to intervene. Emboldened by this, agitators organised more strikes for 27 February; on this occasion, a detachment of Cossacks was sent to deal with a group of protesters at the Izhora factory in Kolpino, to the southeast of Petrograd, but police reports worriedly described the action of the troops as half-hearted.[50]

* Throughout this account, dates are in the modern calendar, rather than the old calendar that was in use in Russia at the time, unless quoting directly from a contemporary source.

The wave of strikes seemed unstoppable. More stoppages followed in the next few days, and banners reading 'Down with the war!' and 'Down with the government!' which would have triggered immediate suppression in earlier times, became commonplace. Other banners displayed a simple one-word message that highlighted the one factor that dominated the thoughts of all those involved: 'Bread!'[51]

Despite the growing sense of tension and dread, the business of the war continued. A delegation from France, Britain and Italy arrived in Petrograd in late January for further discussions. Alexeyev had been temporarily excused from his duties as chief of the Russian general staff due to illness, a development that the tsarina greeted with satisfaction. At first, she had taken a liking to Alexeyev, who showed a diplomatic touch in his dealings with the imperial family. As had been the case with many other competent figures, both military and civilian, it was the question of Rasputin that led to Alexeyev becoming the subject of Alexandra's ire. She repeatedly suggested in 1916 that Rasputin should visit *Stavka* to give the military staff the benefit of his advice, and finally Alexeyev found that he could no longer duck the issue and had to issue a clear refusal, though he stopped short of the position taken by Grand Duke Nikolai when he was commander-in-chief – he had threatened to have Rasputin hanged if he appeared at *Stavka*. When Alexeyev became ill, the tsarina wrote to Nicholas: 'God sent this illness to save you from a man who was losing his way and doing harm by listening to bad letters and people.'[52]

In his absence, Vasily Iosifovich Gurko, one of Russia's more successful generals, was acting chief of staff. He advised the conference in Petrograd that, since mobilisation, Russia had lost a staggering two million dead or wounded, and a further two million taken prisoner. Despite this, the Russian Army still fielded 7.5 million troops, with a further 2.5 million reservists and under training. However, he did not feel that the army was in any shape to launch major offensives. Its divisions were undergoing reorganisation into smaller formations, with the troops that were thus freed being used to create another 60 divisions – until these were ready, fully equipped and properly trained, it would be folly to attack in strength. Instead, the best that could be expected was that the army would make local, limited attacks to tie down German units. The French delegation pressed for more aggressive action, but the conference drifted on without any clear resolution; the French took solace from the fact that the tsar reaffirmed his support for the return of Alsace and Lorraine to France, together with the annexation of German territories on the west bank of the Rhine. Repeated French calls for a Russian offensive in April were turned down, with

Gurko insisting that his armies would not be ready at least until May, and even then only if the other Entente Powers supplied Russia with huge quantities of weapons and ammunition. The conference dispersed without reaching any clear conclusions.[53]

Civil unrest had eased during the conference, but now resumed. There was no sign of an end to the crippling food shortages. On 7 March, after Tsar Nicholas had left his palace at Tsarskoe Selo and returned to Mogilev, the location of *Stavka*, women from fabric factories in the Viborg district went on strike demanding bread. The slogans rapidly grew to include denunciations of the government and the war. During the afternoon, the strikers were reported to be looting food shops and the police intervened to restore order, which they achieved with little violence. Although there was little sign of trouble as darkness fell, General Sergei Semenovich Khabalov, commander of the Petrograd Military District, ordered that the Cossacks at his disposal should be issued with knouts – the heavy whips used on so many occasions to crush dissent. After discussions with his subordinates, he deployed troops at key locations around the city, and as a token measure to reduce unrest, he ordered a modest amount of flour to be made available to the city's bakeries.[54]

Throughout the night, strike organisers laboured to prepare further protests. The following morning, as Petrograd enjoyed a brief period of warmer weather, over 40,000 strikers marched from the Viborg district to the Alexandrovsky Bridge, linking the industrial area north of the Neva with the administrative centre of Petrograd. The northern approaches to the bridge were defended by about 500 soldiers, Cossacks and mounted police, and at first there was a stand-off between the two sides. The deadlock was broken by women workers who stepped forward and approached the soldiers. They pleaded with them, reminding them that the soldiers too had mothers, wives, sisters and children who were hungry – 'We are only asking for bread and an end to the war!'[55] The Cossacks exchanged glances amongst themselves, then grinned at the workers and winked at them, some telling the workers that they had nothing to fear. With growing confidence, the strikers surged past the Cossacks, who simply sat their horses at attention.

The mounted police were less accommodating and attacked the strikers without mercy, but thousands of other strikers were converging on the city centre from all directions. By the end of the day, over 160,000 workers were on strike, many of them in the streets, others occupying their places of work. A day later the protesters marched down Nevsky Prospekt in the centre of the city, stopping in the west when they reached the Kazan Cathedral, barely half a mile from the

Winter Palace, the Admiralty, and other key buildings on the Neva embankment. At the eastern end of the great thoroughfare, they were confronted by a body of Cossacks. The workers cheered; the Cossacks bowed in reply. Throughout the day, strikers made angry speeches against the government, and neither the police nor the army tried to stop them.

Worried government officials met that night. Khabalov summoned military reinforcements in the form of several units of Guards cavalry that were stationed nearby in Novgorod, and the *Okhrana* was ordered to detain all known revolutionaries and agitators. Troops were to confront strikers and demonstrators; mounted units would disperse small gatherings, while troops would fire on larger gatherings after issuing warnings. Characteristically, Protopopov was absent from the meeting; Rodzianko, the foreign minister, later recalled that the reason for his absence was that he was attempting to get advice from the ghost of Rasputin.[56]

It was too late to stop the unrest with a wave of arrests. Striking workers held meetings in the factories they had occupied over the next few days, where agitators made rousing speeches, safe from arrest. Women workers confronted soldiers in the streets, begging them to join the workers. Only the police continued to attempt to disperse the crowds. There was another confrontation on the Alexandrovsky Bridge on 9 March, and the leader of the police detachment, Mikhail Shalfeev, led his mounted men in a charge against the protesters; a crowd of strikers engulfed him and pulled him from his horse, punching and kicking him and beating him with an iron rod. Then, one of the strikers managed to seize his pistol and shoot him. At the same moment, the industrial workers in the Putilov factories in the southwest of the city, who had been locked out of their place of work, stormed the factory gates. Here, they set up the first provisional revolutionary committee, tasked with leading the struggle and organising armed units. The unrest of hungry workers had become a revolution.

There was an even more significant development the same day at the eastern end of Nevsky Prospekt. The striking workers were now waving placards proclaiming 'Down with the tsar!' and the police attempted to disperse them, riding into their ranks and lashing out with their heavy whips. Many of the workers had inserted padding under their coats for just such an eventuality, but there then occurred an incident that would shake any regime to the core. A detachment of Cossacks was standing ready to support the police, and workers ran to them, pleading to them to help. The Cossacks promptly rode into the fray. There are differing accounts of what happened next – some described how a police officer struck a Cossack, and the latter retaliated, while others claimed that the Cossacks cut down several policemen. Regardless of the details, the Cossacks killed the leader of the police detachment, and the broader message was clear: in this location at least, the Cossacks had sided with the people against the police. The workers began to construct barricades across the streets.[57]

The defection of men from the Cossack formations who had been so reliable in suppressing dissent in tsarist Russia was a deeply ominous moment, but from the point of view of the tsar's regime, worse was to come. Later the same day, strikers found themselves facing soldiers at a junction on Nevsky Prospekt, close to the Kazan Cathedral. The workers approached the troops and called on them to join the strikers; most of the soldiers shouldered their rifles and joined the crowd to loud cheers. Other groups of soldiers opened fire on protesters, killing several, but a key moment had been passed, though the true magnitude of it was not immediately obvious to some.

Throughout 10 March, workers continued to confront the police and troops. Units of the Guards opened fire on several groups, killing and wounding dozens. Some troops deliberately fired into the air over the heads of protesters, but others – including machine-gunners – showed no such restraint. During the afternoon, a company of the Pavlovsky Guards, left to guard the regiment's barracks, received news that their comrades were firing on civilians and took it upon themselves to intervene. They encountered a mounted police that attempted to stop them; the soldiers promptly opened fire.

There had been a stream of reports to *Stavka* about events in Petrograd, and, despite Khabalov's attempts to play down the crisis, there could be little doubt in Mogilev that matters were getting out of hand in the capital. Nicholas sent a brief telegram to Khabalov: 'I order you to bring all of these disorders in the capital to a halt as of tomorrow. These cannot be permitted in this difficult time of war with Germany and Austria.'[58]

Desperately, the authorities tried to keep the news of the mutiny by the Pavlovsky Guards secret. Several mutineers were confined to barracks, while others were arrested and sent to the Peter and Paul Fortress, a traditional prison for political prisoners. An *Okhrana* report neatly summed up the state of affairs:

> At the moment, everything depends on the conduct of the military units. If they do not go over to the side of the proletariat, then the disorders will recede rapidly. If the troops turn against the government, then nothing can be done to save the country from revolutionary upheavals.[59]

In the circumstances, with so much depending upon the loyalty of the army, it is astonishing that the *Okhrana* had made no attempt to determine the mood and allegiances of the troops in the capital. Their ranks were full of middle-aged reservists and men who had been deemed unfit for front-line service as a result of wounds and injuries, groups amongst whom dissent was greatest. Yet Khabalov continued to reassure Protopopov that the garrison could reliably be ordered into action against the people.

Rodzianko sent an urgent message to Nicholas: 'There is anarchy in the capital. The government is paralysed … There is disorderly firing in the streets. A person trusted by the country must be charged immediately to form a ministry. There must be no delay.'[60]

Nicholas' response was further proof, if any were needed, of the gulf between the tsar and what was unfolding in Petrograd. Speaking to the elderly Count Vladimir Borisovich Frederiks, the Minister of the Imperial Household, he grumbled: 'Again, this fat Rodzianko has written to me lots of nonsense, to which I shall not even deign to reply.'[61]

Many of the soldiers had already made up their minds, regardless of the attempts of the authorities to stop other units learning of the events at the Pavlovsky Guards' barracks. There were meetings in barracks throughout the city that night in which some spoke openly about refusing to fire on the people. Sergei Kirpichnikov was a sergeant in the Volynsky Guards Regiment and had been present at the eastern end of Nevsky Prospekt in some of the demonstrations. He now addressed his men:

> It would be better to die with honour than to obey any further orders to shoot into the crowds. Fathers, mothers, sisters, brothers, even brides, are begging for bread. Should we strike them down? Have you seen the blood running in the streets? I propose that we not march against them again tomorrow. I personally don't want to.[62]

When the officers of the Volynsky Regiment learned of the mutiny, they left the barracks. The soldiers were aware that they had irrevocably crossed a line; several of them opened fire on the fleeing officers, killing their commander. Kirpichnikov and his comrades sped to other barracks within reach, and were soon joined by men from the Preobrazhensky and Lithuanian Guards and a detachment of military engineers. Led by the band of the engineers, the soldiers seized the Liteinyi Arsenal; the soldiers and strikers now had access to tens of thousands of rifles and pistols, and several hundred machine-guns. Until now, the government forces – even the police alone, if the army had simply refused to intervene – comfortably outgunned the protesters. Now, the balance shifted decisively. Other weapons stores were also seized, and there was the first exchange of fire between armed workers and soldiers still loyal to the government on the Alexandrovsky Bridge. The government force was swiftly driven off, and the workers linked up with the mutinous soldiers. The next targets were the prisons, and in swift time the Kresty, Military, and Women's Transit Prisons, as well as several police stations, had been captured and the inmates set free.

Alfred Knox, the British military attaché in Petrograd, was in the Artillery Department building in the city:

> We went to the window … Outside there was evident excitement, but no sound came to us through the thick double windows. Groups were standing at the corners gesticulating and pointing down the street. Officers were hurrying away, and motor-cars, my own amongst the number, were taking refuge in the courtyards of neighbouring houses.
>
> It seemed that we waited at least ten minutes before the mutineers arrived. Craning our necks, we first saw two soldiers – a sort of advanced guard – who strode along the middle of the street, pointing their rifles at loiterers to clear the road. One of them fired two shots at an unfortunate chauffeur. Then came a great disorderly mass of soldiery, stretching right across the wide street and both pavements. They were led by a diminutive but immensely dignified student. There were no officers. All were armed, and many had red flags fastened to their bayonets. They came slowly and finally gathered in a compact mass in front of the Department. They looked up at the windows, which were now crowded with officers and clerks, but showed no sign of hostility …
>
> Soon we heard the windows and the door on the ground floor being broken in, and the sounds of shots reached us …
>
> An excited orderly rushed in: 'Your High Excellency! They are forcing their way into the building. Shall we barricade your door?' But Manikovsky [the head of the Artillery Department] had kept his nerve, and said: 'No. Open all the doors. Why should we hinder them?' …
>
> Hypatiev [a general with expertise in chemicals] and I went to the staircase and looked over the banisters. Down on the ground floor, soldiers were taking the officers' swords, and a few hooligans were going through the pockets of coats left in the vestibule. I went down and found an NCO of the Preobrajenskis [one of the Guards regiments], who was ordering his men to take only the swords and to steal nothing. I told him who I was, and he helped me on with my coat …
>
> A party of soldiers was almost timidly breaking the glass of one of the arm-stands to take out the rifles – specimens of the armament of other nations, that

> were without ammunition and would be of no use to them. As they went off, proud of their capture, an officer caught the arm of one of them – a young soldier with a straight, honest face – and remonstrated with him, and I heard the boy reply: 'I could not help it. They forced me.'[63]

By the end of 12 March, large numbers of soldiers had gone over to the side of the revolutionaries. The violence of the initial stages of demonstrations and strikes had been limited to clashes with the police and loyalist troops, but matters were slowly becoming more violent through a mixture of factors. The raids on police stations and prisons released numerous common criminals in addition to detained dissidents, strikers and soldiers, and large numbers of weapons were now in the hands of individuals with little or no training in their use. Alcohol, forbidden since early in the war, circulated freely, increasing the level of disorder. Stinton Jones, a British engineer who was in Petrograd at the time, described the scenes on the streets:

> The mobs presented a strange, almost grotesque appearance. Soldiers, workmen, students, hooligans and freed criminals wandered aimlessly about in detached companies, all armed, but with a strange variety of weapons. Here would be a hooligan with an officer's sword fastened over his overcoat, a rifle in one hand and a revolver in the other; there a small boy with a large butcher's knife on his shoulder. Close by a workman would be seen awkwardly holding an officer's sword in one hand and a bayonet in the other. One man had two revolvers, another a rifle in one hand and a tramline cleaner in the other. A student with two rifles and a belt of machine-gun bullets round his waist was walking beside another with a bayonet tied to the end of a stick. A drunken soldier had only the barrel of a rifle remaining, the stock having been broken off in forcing an entry into some shop. A steady, quiet businessman grasped a large rifle and a formidable belt of cartridges.
>
> Singing, shouting, roaring, firing off their weapons into the air regardless of whom the bullets might hit, these mobs would wander along without leaders, apparently without purpose. Suddenly machine-guns served by the police would rattle and begin to spit their leaden venom from adjoining roofs. There would be a momentary hush, followed by the cries of the wounded and a general scurry for cover. As the streets cleared, little heaps, some very still, others writhing in agony, told of the toll of the machine-guns. From the doubtful protection of doorways and arches the mob would send a spatter of bullets in the direction from which it was thought the leaden hail came. Then a few of the braver spirits would form

themselves into a patrol and force their way to the roofs of the buildings and hunt out the police at their guns.

This was not so dangerous a proceeding as it might appear, as owing to their cramped positions the police could not put up a very serious hand-to-hand fight. In many cases the police were simply thrown over the parapets into the roadway below. In cases where policemen were wounded, no medical assistance was allowed them, but they were dispatched out of hand. The people of Petrograd had much to avenge.[64]

The authorities were in complete disarray, and Khabalov sent a despairing telegram to the tsar:

I beg to inform His Imperial Highness that I am not able to carry out his instructions about the restoration of order in the capital. The majority of army units, one after another, have betrayed their oaths, refusing to fire upon the rebels. Other units have joined with the insurgents and have turned their weapons against the troops still remaining loyal to His Highness.[65]

This was followed by another unequivocal plea from Rodzianko for the tsar to act before it was too late, and Grand Duke Mikhail Alexandrovich joined the chorus. Alexeyev presented all of the telegrams to the tsar, who remained obdurate. There would be no concessions. Instead, Nicholas decided that he needed to send someone he could trust to crush the uprising. In this desperate moment, he turned to Nikolai Iudevich Ivanov, who had been dismissed as commander of Southwest Front after the disasters of the first few months of 1916. After his dismissal, Ivanov was a forlorn figure, lingering in or near *Stavka* in the hope that he would be recalled; eventually, Nicholas granted him a post as an advisor in his headquarters. Now, he instructed him to take command of a selected force and march to Petrograd; the troops would assemble at Tsarskoe Selo, where Ivanov would join them. Initially conceived as a force of perhaps four infantry regiments, four cavalry regiments, four batteries of artillery and two machine-gun battalions, further troops were added, increasing the strength of Ivanov's command by another six battalions.

Ivanov set off from Mogilev on 13 March. In Petrograd, events continued to unfold at rapid pace. The revolutionaries formed the Soviet of Workers' Deputies, which held its first meeting in the Tauride Palace – home of the Duma – that evening. The tsar had prorogued the Duma, and the deputies met to discuss their options – defying the tsar's instruction would mean open rebellion. Terrified of a possible descent into anarchy, the moderate and right-wing members of the Duma tried to find legal pretexts to avoid a total break with the tsar, suggesting instead that it would be better to send a telegram to Nicholas asking for permission to form a new government of their choosing. After much wrangling, 12 deputies declared that they were forming a 'Provisional Committee of Duma Members for the Restoration of Order in the Capital and the Establishment of Relations with Individuals and Institutions'. By the end of the day, as news arrived of growing disorder and the steps that the Soviet was taking to organise itself, the Provisional Committee had assumed power. It included Nikolai Semionovich Chkheidze and Kerensky, both members of the Soviet. This new committee was explicitly answerable only to the Duma, not to the tsar. It was, in some respects, the 'revolution from above' that many had expected, except that it came in response to a far larger, and increasingly difficult to control, revolution from below. It was the sort of ministry that Rodzianko had repeatedly urged the tsar to establish; now, the Duma had done so unilaterally.

Within days, other urban centres joined the ranks of the revolution. Moscow and the industrial centres of the Baltic region declared themselves in support of the revolution, and Alexeyev and Ivanov tried in vain to persuade Tsar Nicholas to follow the advice that Rodzianko had been offering him for months. In any case, it was too late – it is highly likely that even had it wished to do so, the Provisional Committee would not have felt permitted to recognise any appointment of the tsar – but Nicholas refused anyway. He decided that at this critical moment, his place was at the side of his family. It was almost certainly too late for him to have taken any action that could have saved his throne, and he ignored the protests of Alexeyev, who reminded him in vain that he remained commander-in-chief and would be too far away in Tsarskoe Selo to exert any influence in Mogilev, especially given the growing chaos. He set out by train, but found that the line was blocked by the actions of revolutionaries. Eventually, after two days of travelling back and forth, he ended up in Pskov, little more than half way from Mogilev to Petrograd.

Pavel Constantinovich Benckendorff, the Grand Marshal of the Court, was in Tsarskoe Selo with Tsarina Alexandra and her family throughout these tumultuous days. Since the tsar had left to rejoin *Stavka*, the most pressing issue in the palace had been an outbreak of measles amongst the imperial children. Benckendorff followed events by telephone, receiving first reassurances, then calls for help from Khabalov. Tsar Nicholas had contacted him to inform him that he was coming to Tsarskoe Selo and that the family should prepare for departure, though it was not clear where they would be going. On 13 March,

Benckendorff received first-hand news of what was happening in Petrograd, only 15 miles (24km) from Tsarskoe Selo:

> At 9 o'clock in the morning, Apraksin [a fellow courtier], whom I had told to come to Tsarskoe the night before, telephoned me that he had arrived at the station on foot and that the town was entirely in the hands of the revolutionaries.
>
> The tsarina received us at 10 o'clock in the morning. After we had informed Her Majesty of what had happened on the eve and had told her that the whole town was in the hands of the rebels, and that the tsar had left Mogilev and expected to be at Tsarskoe the next morning at 6 o'clock, the tsarina told us that in no case would she consent to leave by herself, and that owing to the state of her children's health, especially that of the Heir-Apparent, departure with them was completely out of the question. Consequently, it was decided that they should not start, but await the arrival of the tsar.
>
> Towards 11 o'clock, Apraksin arrived and had luncheon with us and told us what had happened in the city during the last days. At 1130 Grooten [assistant commandant of the palace] came to tell us that the managers of the railways had informed him that in two hours all the railway lines would be cut, and that if there was any idea of starting, it should be done at once. As it was impossible to start so hurriedly, we decided not even to make the proposal.
>
> The day ... was spent quietly at Tsarskoe. Many motorcars, however, arrived from Petrograd carrying soldiers, evidently with the object of making propaganda in the garrison.
>
> After dinner, towards 8 o'clock, they came to tell us that rifle shots and even salvoes had been heard in the barracks and garrison. Later we heard music and songs. I cross questioned Putyatin [another aide] as to what was happening, and he told me that a contingent of the regiment of the Guards, which had refused to surrender to the rebels, had arrived in the barracks, that quarrels and brawls had arisen; but since they had received orders to start for Gatchina he thought that order would be restored afterwards. Shortly afterwards we heard that the whole garrison had left the barracks armed, without their officers, and that the Tsar's escort, the combined regiment, and all the troops who were under the Commandant of the Palace, had been mobilised and assembled in the courtyard of the Alexander Palace.[66]

The Alexander Palace garrison consisted of three infantry battalions, two squadrons of Cossacks, and an artillery battery. Whilst the force was fairly strong numerically, its morale was low, and when the tsarina visited a group of them, they responded without the expected degree of deference and formality. Some of the troops later shot their officers and headed for Petrograd to join the revolutionaries. Inside the palace, the tsarina, her family and their entourage waited in fear. Telephone lines had been cut, and they had little firm news of what was happening, either in Petrograd or with regard to the tsar's journey.

Unable to speak to the tsar during his travels, Alexeyev contacted General Nikolai Vladimirovich Ruzsky, commander of the Northern Front – the sector of the front line closest to the capital – and enlisted his support in persuading the tsar to see reason, even though he must have known from the steady flow of reports that it was probably too late to arrest the slide towards widespread revolution. Ruzsky had been appointed and replaced several times during the war, failing singularly to impress in any command he held but resurfacing each time because the Russian Army was hardly full of viable alternatives. His headquarters was in Pskov, and he greeted the tsar on his arrival. It was not an encounter that Ruzsky approached with any enthusiasm, and he started by offering frank opinions on a variety of individuals, civilian and military, in a manner that he would not have dared adopt in earlier times. When he broached the subject of acceding to Rodzianko's advice, Nicholas calmly refused. He insisted that he remained responsible to God and to Russia for everything that had happened and was still happening, and that his post did not allow him to grant a ministry responsible to the Duma rather than to himself.

At this stage, a telegram arrived from Alexeyev, advising the tsar that the Duma was still – just – in control of events, but the opportunities to exert influence were diminishing by the hour. Finally, Nicholas agreed to appoint a government answerable to the Duma and not to himself. The relevant proclamation was dispatched to Petrograd, but late that night, Rodzianko contacted Ruzsky using Northern Front's Hughes apparatus, a very early form of teleprinter. After Ruzsky had told Rodzianko that the tsar had finally granted the ministry that the Duma president had been asking for, he was stunned when Rodzianko responded that it was too late, and that the Provisional Committee was now in control. Rodzianko went on to say that there was widespread talk in Petrograd that Nicholas must abdicate. Although he distanced himself from this suggestion, Rodzianko added a bitter attack on the imperial family and how they and their supporters – the 'little band of unscrupulous and self-serving adventurers' that Buchanan had described – had made a mockery of the terrible sacrifices made by the Russian Army and the Russian people.

Ruzsky now contacted Alexeyev to advise him that the revolutionaries were demanding the abdication of the tsar. As chief of the general staff, Alexeyev regarded his prime duty as being to the army, and he knew only too well how fragile morale was throughout the forces that had suffered so much. He contacted all of the front commanders:

> The dynastic question has been posed point-blank, and … the war can continue to a victorious end only with the fulfilment of the demands that have been set forth for an abdication from the throne in favour of his son under a regency of Mikhail Alexandrovich [the brother of the tsar]. [It is] essential to preserve the field army from disintegration, continue the struggle against the foreign enemy to the end, and save Russia's independence. I therefore ask each of you to let me have your views as soon as possible. I repeat every minute that is lost can be fatal for the existence of Russia … Among the chief commanders of the field army, there must be established a unity of thought and purpose in order to save the army.[67]

At the same time, Alexeyev issued orders to stop the assembly of the troops that had been intended for Ivanov to use to re-establish order in Petrograd. In many respects, it was too late for such a venture to succeed without major loss of life, and even if it had succeeded, the news of trouble in other cities meant that the same battles might have to be repeated in Moscow, Kiev, Riga and elsewhere. Equally important in his calculations was the state of the army at the front, where there were growing signs of unrest; if the army was used to suppress the revolution, Alexeyev feared that this unrest would turn to open mutiny, which would be disastrous in the middle of a war.

At the headquarters of Southwest Front, Alexei Brusilov had spent the winter more concerned with the welfare of his men than the developments in distant Petrograd. He later wrote that, for the first time in the war, he could supply his troops with plentiful winter clothing, but boots were in short supply. When he made enquiries with the war ministry, he was advised that there was insufficient leather, and attempts were being made to source more from the United States. Brusilov wryly noted that at the time much of the population of Russia appeared to be wearing army boots – many recruits sold their footwear almost as soon as it was issued to them. Clothing, too, was frequently sold, but at least Brusilov was able to replace much of that. But just as was the case in the Russian interior, it was the shortage of food that caused the most concern. Supplies of meat and bread had been reduced, and when that proved to be insufficient, Brusilov was obliged to impose two meatless days per week, leading to considerable unrest:

> All this began to cause serious dissatisfaction among the soldiers, and I received a lot of anonymous abusive letters, as if responsibility for supplying the troops with

food was entirely mine. I began to receive letters – in most cases, anonymous – which stated that the troops were tired, no longer willing to fight.[68]

Nevertheless, Brusilov could not help but be aware of the increasing chaos in the Russian capital, and took advantage of an encounter with Grand Duke Mikhail Alexandrovich, the tsar's brother, to urge him to use his influence with Nicholas to initiate reforms that would bring order before it was too late. Writing after the war, he described how he regarded the February Revolution as an inevitable consequence of the unfinished business of 1905 – the lack of any meaningful reform meant that the pressures that led to the uprisings in the wake of the Russo-Japanese War remained, and would only grow worse as the strains of a long war added to them. Whilst it is not clear how strongly he felt this at the time, there is no question that his most pressing priority was to ensure that his armies remained disciplined and strong. He was aware of the consequences of past failures, and how brittle that discipline was:

Let me just say that in 1916, my armies showed unbelievable bravery and selfless devotion to duty and to Russia, and experienced a lamentable end to their combat operations, which they attributed to the indecision and lack of ability of the Supreme Command. In the ranks of the army, especially in the minds of the soldiers, there was certainty that the war could never be won under such command … A direct consequence of this belief was the question of why they should sacrifice their lives and would it not be better to save themselves for the future? We must not forget that during almost three years of war, the best soldiers had been killed, wounded and maimed, the army was weak, the *Opolchenie* [reservist militia, who were dispatched to the front and became the *Polivanovtsy*] had the worst discipline and training, and discontent and criticism of the state of affairs started to develop unconsciously in the minds of men, and often at random.

… By February 1917 the whole army – more in one front, less in another – was prepared for the revolution. The officer corps at this time was also hesitant and, in general, was extremely dissatisfied with the state of affairs.[69]

It was at this moment that Alexeyev's telegram arrived, asking for Brusilov's views on whether the tsar should abdicate. Rodzianko had also contacted Brusilov, and the commander of Southwest Front was unequivocal in his response to Alexeyev:

At the present moment, the only way out that can save the situation and make it possible to fight on against the foreign enemy … is to renounce the throne in

> favour of the Sovereign Heir the Tsarevich under a regency of Grand Duke Mikhail Alexandrovich.[70]

All other front commanders made similar replies.

While Alexeyev gathered the views of his subordinates, Ruzsky continued his discussions with the tsar, informing him for the first time that the question of his abdication was being discussed. After a pause, Nicholas told Ruzsky that he believed that he had been born for unhappiness, and had brought great unhappiness to Russia. Never a man for great displays of emotion, the tsar calmly stated that he would readily abdicate if such an act were required for the welfare of Russia. Aware that Alexeyev was asking the front commanders for their opinions, Nicholas asked Ruzsky for his views. Throughout his time in the army, Ruzsky had been notorious for his indecision, and this occasion proved to be no exception when he replied: 'The matter is so important and so terrible that I beg Your Highness' permission to think about this dispatch before I answer. Let's see what the front commanders say. Then the situation will be clearer.'[71]

Alexeyev's summary arrived shortly afterwards. For the moment, the army remained intact, but unless urgent action was taken there was no guarantee that it would be spared from the turmoil that had swept through the cities and garrisons of Russia. After considering all of the requests for his abdication, Nicholas informed Ruzsky and two aides who were present that he had decided to abdicate. He drafted two telegrams – one for Alexeyev, the second for Rodzianko – informing them of his decision to renounce the throne in favour of his son Alexei, who would become tsar under the regency of Grand Duke Mikhail Alexandrovich, but then hesitated when he learned that a delegation from the Duma's Provisional Committee was travelling to Pskov to meet him. After a brief pause, he decided that further prevarication was pointless and sent the telegrams.

By the time that the Duma's delegation reached Pskov, the decision had therefore already been made. Nicholas now informed Vasily Shulgin and Alexander Guchkov, the representatives of the Provisional Committee, that after further consideration, he had concluded that it would not be appropriate for Tsarevich Alexei to become tsar, on account of his poor health, and that Nicholas was therefore abdicating on behalf of both himself and his son, in favour of Mikhail Alexandrovich. The final declaration was then drawn up, though the timing of the document was set at 3pm on 15 March, to make it seem that the Duma's delegation had extracted the abdication, rather than finding it already in place when they arrived:

> In these days of the great struggle against the foreign enemies who for nearly three years have tried to enslave our fatherland, the Lord God has seen fit to send down on Russia a new heavy trial.
>
> Internal popular disturbances threaten to have a disastrous effect on the future conduct of this unrelenting war. The destiny of Russia, the honour of our heroic army, the welfare of the people and the whole future of our dear fatherland demand that the war should be brought to a victorious conclusion whatever the cost.
>
> The cruel enemy is making his last efforts, and already the hour approaches when our glorious army together with our gallant allies will crush him. In these decisive days in the life of Russia, Our conscience imposes upon us the duty to draw all the forces of Our people into the closest union possible for the speedy attainment of victory.
>
> In agreement with the Imperial Duma We have decided that it is necessary to renounce the throne of the Russian Empire and to lay down the supreme power. As We do not wish to part from Our beloved son, We transmit the succession to Our brother, the Grand Duke Michael Alexandrovich, and give Him Our blessing to mount the throne of the Russian Empire.
>
> … In the name of Our dearly beloved homeland, We call on Our faithful sons of the fatherland to fulfil their sacred duty to the fatherland, to obey the tsar in the heavy moment of national crisis, and to help Him, together with the representatives of the people, to guide the Russian Empire on the road to victory, prosperity, and glory.
>
> May the Lord God help Russia![72]

Throughout these meetings, Nicholas maintained a dignified calm. He recorded his true feelings in his diary that night:

> At 1am I have left Pskov with a heart that is heavy over what has happened. All around me there is nothing but treason, cowardice, and deceit![73]

A week later, Nicholas was finally permitted to join his family in the Alexander Palace in Tsarskoe Selo.

When the Great Powers planned for war at the beginning of the century, they thought in terms of potentially great changes in the existing balance of power – Germany wished to eliminate any future threat from France, Russia wanted to secure the gates to the Black Sea, and Austria-Hungary merely wanted to prevent its own dissolution – but few thought in terms of replacing the rulers of their opponents. There was certainly no expectation on the part of the Central Powers that the tsar would be forced from his throne, yet suddenly, Nicholas was gone. The pressures within Russia might have been festering and building since 1905, but the speed at which they swept away the tsar was utterly unexpected, and events showed no sign of slowing. When he learned that the tsar had named him as the next ruler of Russia, Grand Duke Mikhail Alexandrovich rapidly issued his own proclamation the following day:

> A heavy burden has been laid on me by my brother's will in transferring to me the imperial throne of All Russia at a time of unprecedented war and unrest among the people.
>
> Inspired by the thought common to the whole nation, that the well-being of our homeland comes above all, I have taken the hard decision to accept supreme power only in the event that it shall be the will of our great people, who in nationwide voting must elect their representatives to a Constituent Assembly, establish a new form of government and new fundamental laws for the Russian State.
>
> Therefore, calling on God's blessing, I ask all citizens of the Russian State to obey the provisional government which has been formed and been invested with complete power on the initiative of the State Duma, until a Constituent Assembly, to be convened in the shortest possible time on the basis of general, direct, equal, secret ballot, expresses the will of the people in its decision on a form of government.[74]

Mikhail Alexandrovich must have known that there was no possibility of a future government granting him supreme power. It was effectively as final an abdication as that of Nicholas. In barely a day, Russia had ceased to be one of the most autocratic hereditary monarchies in the world; however, there was no clear idea of what form of government it would now have.

The first priority for the Provisional Committee was to try to restore order. Over 1,400 people had been killed in Petrograd alone and thousands more injured in the unrest to date, and several steps were taken to try to bring the violence to an end. Ministers of the former government were arrested – some surrendered voluntarily to the Provisional Committee out of fear of falling into the hands of the restive crowds – and many were dispatched to imprisonment in the Peter and Paul Fortress, where the tsars had traditionally imprisoned those who plotted against them. The soldiers were ordered to return to their barracks, but many were reluctant to do so, fearing that they would be punished for their mutinous actions. Indeed, many had also killed their officers. They did not trust the Provisional Committee, seeing Rodzianko, who was its head, as a figure who had in the past been closely associated with the tsar. Seeking guarantees to protect themselves from any punishment, the soldiers turned to the Soviet for help. The result was Order Number One, a document of profound importance.

The order, issued by the Soviet, called upon military units to elect representatives who would attend the Soviet on 15 March. Crucially, Order Number One declared:

> All orders issued by the Military Commission of the State Duma shall be carried out, except those which run counter to the orders and decrees issued by the Soviet of Workers' and Soldiers' Deputies.[75]

In other words, orders would only be carried out with the approval of the Soviet. At about the same time, the Russian Socialist Democratic Labour Party, a grouping that included the communists, issued a proclamation calling on soldiers to be entitled to elect their own officers. In combination with Order Number One, this effectively destroyed the basis of army discipline.

Inevitably, the momentous events in the interior of Russia had a profound effect on the Russian armies in the front line. Brusilov cannot have been surprised by the effect of Order Number One on his troops:

> Corps officers knew nothing about politics because it was strictly forbidden for soldiers on duty, and the officers [who tried to intervene] had little impact, as those who were sent to the Soviet of Soldiers' and Workers' Deputies to urge for peace 'without annexations or reparations' were led by various agents and emissaries of the socialist parties. The soldiers did not want to fight any more, and felt that if the world war could be concluded without annexations or reparations and if the principal right of the people to self-determination could be promoted, further senseless bloodshed was unacceptable. It was, so to speak, the same basis as the slogan: 'Down with the war, immediate peace at all costs, and immediate land transfers from the landlord', on the grounds that the landowners were amassing the wealth of centuries on the backs of the peasants and [it was right to] take this illegally acquired wealth from them. The officer immediately became the enemy in the minds of the soldiers, for he demanded the continuation of the war and was in the eyes of the soldiers a type of gentleman in uniform.[76]

As everyone, both in the front line and throughout Russia, scrambled to catch up with events, Nicholas was permitted to travel to Tsarskoe Selo where his family awaited. The news of the abdication had reached the Alexander Palace a day after the event:

> On the afternoon of 3 March [old calendar, 16 March in the new calendar] the rumour of the abdication of the Tsar, which was vague at first, began to circulate. Towards 4 o'clock the rumours became so substantial that I thought it my duty to inform the tsarina of them. The tsarina could not imagine that the tsar could have taken so momentous a step so hurriedly, especially since he knew that the Heir-Apparent was so ill. About 5 o'clock we received in the palace sheets which had been printed hastily in the city, announcing the abdication of the tsar in favour of his brother, Grand Duke Mikhail, the renunciation of the latter of the throne, until such a time as the Constitution Assembly should have elected him, and the definite establishment of a Provisional Government. Some moments later Grand Duke Pavel [uncle of the tsar] reached the Palace to announce this terrible event to the tsarina. He was greatly moved … and he communicated the news to Her Majesty as delicately as possible. When he left her, he told me that all was lost, that Russia was in the hands of the worst revolutionaries, and that the tsar and tsarina should try to leave as soon as possible for abroad. Consternation was general. The officers had tears in their eyes. After dinner, towards 9 o'clock, Baroness Buxhoeveden, Count Apraksin and myself reported to the Tsarina. She was very brave and said that the tsar had preferred to abdicate the crown rather than to break the oath which he had made at his coronation to maintain and to transfer to his heir the autocracy such as he had inherited it from his father … As we went out, I saw that she sat down at the table and burst into tears.[77]

Lili Dehn – a descendant of Mikhail Kutusov, the victor over Napoleon in 1812 – was a close friend of the tsarina and was also present:

> Her face was distorted with agony, her eyes were full of tears. She tottered rather than walked, and I rushed forward and supported her until she reached the writing table between the windows. She leant heavily on it and, taking my hand in hers, she said brokenly, 'Abdicated!' I could not believe my ears. I waited for her next words. They were hardly audible. As last, 'The poor dear … All alone out there … Oh, my God, what has he gone through! And I was not there to console him.'[78]

Before Nicholas reached Tsarskoe Selo, newssheets arrived from Petrograd announcing that the imperial family was to be arrested. The commander of the garrison of Tsarskoe Selo informed the imperial court that he would execute the order, but would then send his 'prisoners' to Murmansk, where they would board a British warship. General Lavr Georgeyevich Kornilov, who was something of a hero for his exploits in the war – he had been taken prisoner by the *k.u.k.* Army in early 1915 but escaped and made his way back to Russia – had been appointed as commander of the Petrograd military district by the Provisional Committee and outlined this plan personally to the tsarina, but the men now in charge of Russia had no intention of allowing the Romanovs to escape into exile, and in any case there was no British cruiser waiting in Murmansk. The garrison of the Alexander Palace had been replaced by troops sent from Petrograd:

> The soldiers of the new Guard were horrible to look at; untidy, noisy, quarrelling with everybody; the officers, who were afraid of them, had the greatest difficulty in preventing them from roaming about the Palace and entering every room. These officers, all of them subalterns, had joined for the war, and there was among them not one single officer of the old army. The first one to come on guard made a bad impression on us. They were all impregnated with new ideas, and they spared us nothing in order to show that they were the masters. There were many quarrels between them and the household staff, whom they reproached for wearing livery and for the attentions they paid to the royal family. This day and this first night were very painful for all of us. We heard shots in the garden. We afterwards learned that these were fired by the sentries on the half-tame deer which were in the park, and that three of them were killed ... One could never have believed that in so short a space of time, thanks to the unfortunate 'Order Number One', so great a change could have come about in the outward appearance as well as in the spirit of the troops.[79]

Nicholas arrived at the Alexander Palace on 22 March. Benckendorff described the moment:

> The officers of the Guard were all at the first entrance, where many soldiers with their caps on their heads, smoking and extremely slovenly, were walking about in spite of the efforts made by the officers to send them away. The Commandant of the Guard had given orders that the gates of the palace should be locked and that he should be informed by telephone if anybody wished to enter. The gate is about a hundred yards from the palace. Towards 1115, the Emperor's motorcar arrived in front of the gate and was stopped by the sentry, who asked who was in it. After having received the answer of the chauffeur, he made the prearranged signal to the Commandant. The Commandant went down the steps and asked in a loud voice

who was there. The sentry cried out, 'Nicholas Romanov.' 'Let him pass,' said the officer.[80]

The imperial couple were under arrest. The last act of Nicholas before he formally stepped down as commander-in-chief of the army was to issue an emotive order of the day to the troops:

> I address you for the last time, you soldiers who are so dear to my heart. Since I renounced the throne of Russia for myself and my son, power has been transferred to the Provisional Government which has been set up on the initiative of the Imperial Duma.
>
> May God help that government to lead Russia to glory and prosperity! And may God also help you, my brave soldiers, to defend your country against a cruel foe! For more than two years and a half you have continuously borne the hardships of an arduous service; much blood has been spilt, enormous efforts have been made and already the hour is at hand in which Russia and her glorious allies will break down the enemy's last desperate resistance in one mighty common effort.
>
> This unprecedented war must be carried through to final victory. He who thinks of peace at the present moment is a traitor to Russia.
>
> I am firmly convinced that the boundless love you bear our beautiful Fatherland is not dead in your hearts. May God bless you and St George, the great martyr, lead you to victory![81]

Inevitably, the new government refused to publish this last message from Nicholas to his troops.

That afternoon, Benckendorff spoke to the former tsar at length. Nicholas showed him the telegrams received from the front commanders calling on him to abdicate, and blamed Ruzsky for arguing with him incessantly and leaving him no room for reflection. Benckendorff concluded that the behaviour of the army's senior officers amounted to treason – the only reason he could see for their unanimity was that they or their staff officers must have conspired in advance. The thought that Nicholas' mismanagement of affairs had left them with no doubt about the need for him to abdicate clearly did not occur to the Grand Marshal of the Court.[82]

Fate was not kind to Nicholas and his family. In August 1917, they were moved from Tsarskoe Selo to Tobolsk, about 2,600 miles (4,200km) east of Petrograd, with the intention that they should leave for Japan the following year – a combination of Russia's withdrawal from the war and concern that the presence of the Romanovs might be a focus for left-wing agitation meant that the other Entente Powers showed no interest in offering them a home. At first, the family lived in considerable comfort in the governor's mansion but conditions became more spartan following the October Revolution. In March 1918, the Bolsheviks imposed soldiers' rations on the Romanovs and most of their servants were dismissed; a month later, they were moved to Yekaterinburg in the Ural Mountains. On 17 July 1918, with anti-Bolshevik forces approaching the city, Yakov Mikhailovich Yurovsky and a group of fellow Bolsheviks entered the house where the former tsar and his family were being held and abruptly told them that they had been sentenced to death by the Ural Soviet of Workers' Deputies. They were shot without further ceremony and their bodies were thrown into a disused mine; shortly after, they were recovered and buried beside a small road just outside the city. They remained there until they were rediscovered in 1979. They were formally identified in 1998 and were re-interred in the Peter and Paul Cathedral in St Petersburg.

Inevitably, a great deal of mythology has grown up around the events of early 1917. Far from being a glorious event in which the workers prevailed over the old regime with the minimum of bloodshed, it was a chaotic and confused affair, with a mixture of grandeur, passion, and opportunistic crime – Knox described how, under the pretext of rooting out policemen loyal to the regime, mutineers and civilians looted the houses of ordinary people, sometimes even killing the occupants if they showed the slightest attempt to resist. He gave a characteristically blunt summary:

> The mutiny … would never have developed into a revolution if the government, by its gross stupidity, had not previously succeeded in alienating every class of the population … What was wanted in the interests of Russia and of her allies was an orderly transition to constitutional government. The tragedy of the position lay in the fact that the educated patriots of the country, upon whose initiative only such a transition might have been possible, had in sheer patriotism and loyalty to their allies tried to defer revolution till the end of the war. They had hardened their hearts to bear temporarily with whatever evil the government might impose, lest in the probable disorder of a change of government Russia's pressure on the enemy might be weakened.[83]

It has been argued that the Bolsheviks worked from the outset to undermine the Provisional Committee in order to create the conditions for their own revolution later in the year, and whilst this certainly became their policy as the year continued, the leadership of the Bolsheviks – like the leadership of every political grouping in Russia – was completely taken by surprise by the pace of events. The future of Russia would depend on which party reacted fastest to events and managed to come up with a formula that would deal with the three most pressing problems: the continuing war; the demands of the ordinary people; and the political vacuum created by the collapse of the Romanov regime.

CHAPTER 3

THE WAVERING ALLY

Slowly, a degree of order returned to Petrograd. For a frenzied few days after the fall of the *ancien régime*, ill-organised bands of troops and civilians raced around the city ostensibly dealing with the last of the tsarist police, who continued to open fire from their vantage points on rooftops. Most motorcars in the city had been commandeered for this task, as Stinton Jones, the British engineer, described:

> At this time the crowds commenced to commandeer every automobile in the city, no matter to whom it might belong. These automobiles they filled with armed men, with at least two soldiers lying on the mudguards with loaded rifles and fixed bayonets. These formidable units then rushed all over the city shooting wildly, but with the chief object of hunting down the police, especially those in the outlying districts who had not yet become aware of the true state of affairs in the city itself, but who, having heard the intense firing, believed that their programme [i.e. the suppression of the revolution] was being carried out …
>
> It was a terrifying sight to see a private limousine tearing down the road filled with armed men and a machine-gun mounted on its roof. The gun was of very little use, as it was with the greatest difficulty that the men themselves could keep in position, let alone the gun, which wobbled about perilously. Upon the motor-lorries machine-guns were mounted in such a way as to command the front edge of the house roofs from the roadway. When those in charge were certain of a particular building from which the police were firing, the lorry would draw up and return the fire.
>
> With such indiscriminate shooting the casualties were extremely heavy. They would have been much more so had the police arranged their machine-guns on a

> level with the roadway instead of on the roofs of the buildings. Situated as they were the machine-guns could only command a narrow strip of road, whereas on the ground level they could have commanded a whole street.
>
> The Head Office of the Secret Police [*Okhrana*] was situated in a large block of buildings on the Fontanka Canal, where was also situated the flat of the Minister of the Interior. The mob broke in and, to avoid destroying the property of their fellow citizens, brought out every article of furniture from the Minister's flat and the Secret Service Offices, together with every document, book and scrap of paper they could find. These were made into huge bonfires in the streets. Thus in a few moments were destroyed thousands of documents containing details and general particulars of every criminal and political and religious suspect throughout the empire, to say nothing of the vast volumes of information relating to enemy spies.
>
> That the incriminating evidence relating to the political and religious prisoners and suspects should be burnt was entirely just, but it was certainly deplorable that documents containing particulars of criminals and spies were destroyed. By the destruction of these documents all evidence of such characters was lost, and the duties of the militia, which was formed later, were rendered more difficult in rounding up such prisoners.[84]

In addition to rooting out the last loyalist police officers, the new rulers of Petrograd had to deal with the last pockets of military resistance. Several officers and their families had taken refuge in the Astoria Hotel, and many people were killed when revolutionary troops opened fire on the building.

Late on 14 March, representatives of the Soldiers' and Workers' Soviet met their opposite numbers from the Duma. Power was effectively shared between the two bodies, and they approached the meeting with trepidation and distrust; somewhat to the surprise of everyone, they found that they had much in common. Whilst some in the Duma wished to retain the monarchy with diminished powers, the Soviet representatives were adamant that this was not acceptable, and it was agreed to leave the decision to a future date. The meeting concluded with a declaration of amnesty to all political prisoners, lifting of restrictions on freedom of speech and assembly, the abolition of restrictions based on class, religion and nationality, the replacement of the police by a people's militia, and guarantees that soldiers who had mutinied would not be sent to the front. In addition, there would be preparations for a new assembly, but the two key areas where there was no agreement were not mentioned. The Marxists wanted an immediate end to the war and mass redistribution of land, whereas the Duma members broadly remained committed to their obligations to the Entente and were nervous about the disruption to agricultural production that would inevitably occur if traditional landowners handed over their land to the peasants; after the abolition of serfdom, there had been some compulsory transfers of land ownership, and the result had been a substantial drop in productivity. A day later, the new government was announced. Prince Lvov was the prime minister, Guchkov the minister for war, Miliukov the new foreign minister, and Kerensky – who was both a member of the Duma and of the Soviet, the latter of which had resolved not to take part in the new government – became minister of justice. Rodzianko, who had played such an important role in the abdication of the tsar, was an unacceptable figure to the more militant soldiers and workers, and stepped down from office.

The two ambassadors from the western members of the Entente, Buchanan and Paléologue, were anxious to ensure that the new Russian government would remain loyal to their alliance. Miliukov met Buchanan on 18 March to ask if the British were ready to recognise the new Russian government; Buchanan replied that he needed assurances that Russia would not seek a separate peace with Germany. Miliukov replied that the new government was firmly committed to the war, but had to tread carefully in view of the anti-war sentiments of the left-wing members. Accompanied by Paléologue and Andrea Carlotti, the Italian ambassador, Buchanan was received by the new government on 22 March. He read out an address to the new ministers in French:

> In this solemn hour when a new era of progress and glory opens up before Russia, it is more important than ever not to turn one's eyes from Germany, because Germany's victory will subsequently destroy this fine monument to liberty that the Russian people are about to erect. Great Britain extends its hand to the [Provisional] Government, sure that true to the commitments made by its predecessors, the latter will do all it can to conduct the war to a victorious outcome, ensuring especially the maintenance of order and national unity, the reprise of normal work in the factories, and the training and discipline of the army. Yes, *Messieures les Ministres*, if today I have the honour of sending you the salutations of a friendly and allied nation, it is because my government believes that, under your high command, the new Russia will not shrink from any sacrifice and in solidarity with its allies it will not stand down its armies before the great principles of right and justice, liberty and nationality, that we have defended, are finally established and sustained.[85]

The other two ambassadors made similar addresses, and received in return the assurances of the new government that it would stay true to its Entente obligations.

The Germans, whom Buchanan urged the Russians to watch closely, were as much taken by surprise by the February Revolution as everyone else. After an eventful few months at the beginning of the war, first at Liège and then in East Prussia, Ludendorff had spent some considerable time fretting impatiently as chief of staff at *Ober Ost** while Falkenhayn sidelined his rivals in the east. Now, he was busy in his role as effective second-in-command of the German war effort, but naturally continued to monitor events in the east. In his memoirs, he speculated whether the tsar had grown weary of the war and was therefore deposed through the machinations of the other Entente Powers. Regardless, Ludendorff greeted the news positively:

> The outbreak of revolution cast a glaring spotlight on the situation in Russia; the people and the army were rotten, otherwise it would not have been possible. As with us, the army was a part of the people; there, too, the army and people were the same. How often had I hoped that a revolution in Russia would ease our military situation, but it had always remained a pipe dream; now it was there, but nevertheless unexpected. I felt a heavy burden lifted from my heart. I could not have believed at that time that it would also engulf us.
>
> It was not possible in any way to see in what manner there would be an easing of the situation in the east; we had to count on further attacks, but nevertheless the revolution inevitably meant that as there would be a substantial weakening in the war capability of Russia, there would be a considerable diminution of the Entente and a substantial easing of our extremely difficult situation. This easing first manifested itself to *OHL* in that it was possible to spare troops and munitions from the east. This allowed us to replace fought-out divisions in the west with better ones from the east on a broad scale.
>
> … The outbreak of the Russian Revolution was one of those events that no field commander could have taken into account with certainty in his calculations. Now, it was no longer a hope, but a certainty with which I as a soldier could work.[86]

Ludendorff's replacement at *Ober Ost* was Max Hoffmann, an inveterate plotter on behalf of the Hindenburg-Ludendorff camp. He spent much of the winter

* *Ober Ost* was an abbreviation for *Oberbefehlshaber der gesamten Deutschen Streitkräfte im Ost* ('Supreme Commander for All German Armed Forces in the East') and referred to the military headquarters in the region, the man appointed as its head, and the territory it controlled.

dealing with matters such as setting up a new administration to run Lithuania and the Vilna-Suvalki region from the city of Vilna – the creation of 'Greater Lithuania', in his words. This was a conscious attempt to limit the territorial size of any Polish nation that might emerge from the war; Polish nationalists were already demanding that the territories that had previously belonged to the great Polish-Lithuanian federation, including all of Lithuania and the Courland Peninsula, should be part of the new Poland. As early as 21 February, Hoffmann commented in his diary that reports from the Russian interior suggested that Germany's eastern foe was unlikely to remain in the field for another year.

The previous year had seen bitter fighting along the line of the River Stochod to the south of the great Pripet Marshes, and all that the Russians had gained were two limited bridgeheads. One was eliminated by the Germans before the end of 1916, but the other, around the village of Toboly, remained in Russian hands. It was connected to the east by four bridges over the river, and if it were left in Russian hands, there was a good probability that it would be used as the start-line for a new offensive in the summer towards Kovel. General Alexander von Linsingen, who commanded the army group in this sector, had planned to reduce the bridgehead during the winter, but renewed fighting at the northern end of the Eastern Front near Riga resulted in the designated troops being moved away. As fighting in Latvia died down, the Germans decided to destroy the Russian bridgehead when the spring thaw would flood much of the adjoining land, making it almost impossible for the Russians to bring up reinforcements. At the end of February, the onset of warmer weather appeared to create ideal conditions for a successful attack, and General Leopold Freiherr von Hauer, the commander of the eponymous corps holding the line in this sector, made preparations for an assault on 4 March. However, the weather almost immediately turned cold again, freezing the ground solid, and the attack was postponed.

Aware that the Germans were planning an attack, the Russians launched an artillery bombardment on the lines of 1st *Landwehr* Division with explosive and gas shells on 27 March. By this stage of the war, the troops were accustomed to donning gasmasks at the first sign of trouble, and the impact of the bombardment was minimal; when the Russian infantry from Lieutenant General Grigory Yefimovich Yanushevsky's III Corps probed forward, it was beaten off with ease. Again, Hauer issued orders for an advance that was to begin on 29 March, but again there was a delay – on this occasion, the floodwater on which the Germans were relying to hinder Russian movements worked against them, pouring into the trenches of 1st *Landwehr* Division and rendering them unusable. Tentatively, the start date for the assault was moved to 4 April.

Yanushevsky was confident that he would be able to hold his bridgehead, though the commander of the Russian Third Army, Leonid Vilgelmovich Lesh, had his doubts and considered evacuating the defenders back across the Stochod. Before dawn on 4 April, the waters of the river rose high enough to sweep away one of the bridges, and the artillery bombardment that began at first light rapidly suppressed III Corps' artillery as well as damaging the dykes that the Russians had built to hold back the waters of the Stochod. Substantial firepower had been gathered for this operation under the command of Oberst Georg Bruchmüller, a renowned artillery expert, and he once more demonstrated his skills. After enduring a six-hour bombardment in muddy trenches that were rapidly filling with bitterly cold water from the river, the Russians faced the German assault. Due to the limited resources available, the attack was initially launched only on the southern side of the bridgehead, with the intention of moving to the northern perimeter in the following days, but the initial assault went so well that the infantry of 1st *Landwehr* Division rapidly overran the entire bridgehead, and Yanushevsky's troops flooded back in growing disarray under heavy fire. Bavarian cavalry pursued them into the floodwaters of the Stochod by the light of the rising moon.[87]

Curiously, Hoffman's diary, published after the war, gives the date of the attack as 4 March, when it was originally scheduled to take place. He was pleased with the outcome:

> Our small operation yesterday on the Stochod went well. 9,000 prisoners including four regimental commanders, 15 field guns, 200 machine-guns and mortars constitute quite a good haul. I had reckoned on at most 3,000 [prisoners]. The Russian Army is deteriorating.
>
> The Russian Revolution is a great stroke of good fortune for us.[88]

Whilst the success was gratifying, Hoffmann's assessment that it represented a substantial deterioration in the Russian Army is surely incorrect. Once Yanushevsky had made the decision to defend an isolated bridgehead in conditions where communications with rear areas could so easily be disrupted, the outcome was never in doubt, particularly as the bridgehead extended along the Stochod for perhaps 5 miles (around 8km) and was barely 2 miles (around 3 km) deep – attacks in the First World War were usually capable of making the limited progress required to destroy this particular bridgehead. The placement of this account in the wrong point of his diary is probably not accidental. Hoffmann wished to create a narrative that the disintegration of the Russian Army represented an opportunity for exploitation that was largely ignored by Ludendorff and Hindenburg.

Yanushevsky was dismissed from command of what remained of III Corps. His replacement was Major-General Dmitri Nikolayevich Nadozhny. Following on from the successful destruction of the Toboly bridgehead, there was some consideration of exploiting the apparent weakness of the Russian Army, but *Ober Ost* lacked the men and reserves of ammunition required for a sustained operation. Nor was Chancellor Bethmann-Hollweg keen on such an assault; he hoped that the growing collapse throughout Russia would lead to early peace negotiations, and did not wish to launch any assault that was not guaranteed to achieve a decisive strategic success for fear of stiffening the resolve of the Russians to continue fighting.

Throughout March, Hoffmann observed events in Russia with mixed feelings; clearly the disruption to Russian factories and railways would hinder the stockpiling of munitions, but beyond that it was not clear what the consequences would be. On 18 March, he was less optimistic when he learned that Grand Duke Nikolai had been nominated to become commander-in-chief again – as the grand duke had made no secret of his dislike of Germany in the past, his appointment could not be expected to lead to any early peace. Nevertheless, he would have to deal with both Russia's enemies and the revolutionaries. Whatever his other concerns were, Hoffmann need not have worried about the return of the grand duke.

Grand Duke Nikolai had not shown the determination and assertiveness required to bring order to Russia's armies when he was in command in the first year of the war, and since his dismissal in 1915 he had been in command of the Caucasus Front against Turkey. When he arrived, he found that the troops were under the able command of Nikolai Nikolaevich Yudenich and had the wisdom to leave military matters in his subordinate's hands, concentrating on administrative and civil matters. It was a strategy that worked well and the Russians penetrated into northeast Turkey, capturing Erzurum and Trabzon before a Turkish counteroffensive brought the advance to a halt. Believing that his drive had been hindered by supply shortages, Nikolai ordered the construction of a railway line through the Caucasus with the intention of renewing the drive in 1917, but events in Petrograd intervened. Even as he stepped down, Tsar Nicholas appointed the grand duke as his replacement as commander-in-chief and Nikolai immediately set off for Mogilev, leaving Yudenich to manage affairs against Turkey.

Despite his poor performance during his previous term as commander-in-chief, Nikolai was greeted with enthusiasm when he arrived at *Stavka*. Regardless of his failings, he was popular with the men who formed the senior staff of the army, but the new commander-in-chief remained in post for barely a day. Almost immediately, a message arrived from Petrograd and the Provisional Government: it was unacceptable for a member of the imperial family to be commander-in-chief of the army. Alexeyev, chief of the general staff, would become commander-in-chief, a role that he had effectively filled during the tsar's term. Vladislav Napoleonovich Klembovsky, who had been his deputy, became chief of the general staff.

Meanwhile, Miliukov continued to give what assurances he could to the British, French and Italian ambassadors. On 25 March, Knox recorded in his diary his observations of a meeting with the Provisional Government:

> Paléologue ... said that he believed in the patriotism of the [foreign] ministry and in its loyalty to the alliance; he was also told that all the Russians were patriotic, 'though appearances were against it'. ...
>
> Miliukov replied with a declaration that Russia would fight till the last drop of blood. I have no doubt that Miliukov would, but can he answer for Russia?
>
> When this was over and the groups broke up and mingled, I attacked General Manikovsky [Guchkov's deputy in the war ministry] ... I said that these were merely diplomatic words, but what of the situation at Dvinsk [now Daugavpils in Latvia], where Neilson had told me that the men were streaming back from the trenches with the officers powerless to control. I said the same thing to Kerensky. He said that the great preoccupation of the government was to restore discipline in the army, and more especially in the navy. He spoke of the proclamations issued ... But what is the good of proclamations? It seems to me that we are moving straight to anarchy and a separate peace.[89]

Lavr Kornilov, who had been appointed as Petrograd's military governor, had at first been optimistic that things would turn out for the better, but Knox noted a change in him as he struggled to restore some semblance of discipline to the troops of the garrison:

> Kornilov gradually gave up his former optimism. On 6 April he was called to attend a meeting of the cabinet, and said afterwards that its members showed great weakness.
>
> He was a man, at all events, and feared no one. One day a man of the Pavlovsky battalion asked him sneeringly when he proposed to have a parade, and he replied: 'Parade! How do you imagine I should show rubbish like you to the Russian people? As soon as you have established order I will have a parade.'

> To a man in one of the machine-gun regiments he said: 'I suppose you think that the troops at the front regard you as heroes? Well, I will tell you that they don't; they think you are merely cowards that don't want to fight.'
>
> ... The 176th Depot Regiment had come in from Krasnoe Selo 'to demonstrate', and finding Petrograd more interesting, wished to remain here. Kornilov ordered Lieutenant-Colonel Vilhaminov, who had been elected to the command by the men, to move his regiment back to Krasnoe Selo. Vilhaminov said that the men objected to the barracks there as unhealthy. Kornilov summoned the commandant of Krasnoe Selo, and in the presence of Vilhaminov arranged for the allotment of new quarters. Vilhaminov then said that he did not know whether the regiment would go or not. Kornilov gave him a direct order to move the regiment to Krasnoe Selo.
>
> The regimental committee passed a strongly worded resolution, condemning 'the action of the commander-in-chief, Kornilov, who in spite of the protests of its colonel had ordered the regiment back to Krasnoe Selo. It wished to remind General Kornilov that it was a revolutionary wave that had elevated him to his high estate, and a similar wave might throw him down again.'
>
> ... Kornilov sent for the deputation and for the colonel. He said that he would hand over the latter to be tried by court-martial. To the men he said: 'You are wrong when you say that I was raised to my present position by the Revolution. I took no part in the Revolution and I never will. I came here because I was ordered, and any advancement I have got has been solely owing to the bravery of the soldiers of the 46th Division and of XXV Corps [his former commands]. I did not want to come to Petrograd, and as soon as order is restored here I will go back to my XXV Corps on the front, and no one will be gladder than I.'
>
> The deputation left the office somewhat depressed.[90]

While Kornilov wrestled with the difficulties of bringing order back to Petrograd's garrisons, Guchkov and Alexeyev made changes in the command of the army in the front. Ruzsky remained commander of Northern Front, but Litvinov, commander of First Army, was dismissed and replaced by Lieutenant-General Mikhail Alexeyevich Sukhovnin. Alexei Evert, commander of West Front, had been entrusted with huge resources in 1916 for a major attack and had made almost no impact on the forces opposing him; like Litvinov, he was pensioned off and replaced by Gurko. His subordinate armies also received new commanders: Third Army was now led by Mikhail Fedorovich Kvyetinsky; Tenth Army was commanded by Nikolai Mikhailovich Kiselevsky; and Second Army received Antonii Andreyevich Vesilovsky. Brusilov continued to command

Southwest Front, but Gurko was replaced as commander of the Special Army by Petr Semenovich Baluev. Alexei Evgeneyevich Gutor took command of Eleventh Army, and Leonid Nikolayevich Byelkovich replaced Shcherbachev as commander of Seventh Army. Shcherbachev became assistant to the King of Romania and therefore effectively commander of the Romanian Front. It remained to be seen whether these new commanders would be any better than their predecessors, and of course all would depend upon the state of the troops that they commanded.

Whilst the authorities in Petrograd attempted to make sense of events, others too were coming to terms with what had happened. Prior to the revolution, many of the leading proponents of revolution in the tsar's empire had been imprisoned or driven into exile. Perhaps the most famous of them was Vladimir Ilyich Lenin, who was in Switzerland. His path to radicalisation began with the execution of his older brother Alexander for involvement in a plot to assassinate Tsar Alexander III, and developed further when he studied law in Kazan University. He was already in trouble with the authorities at this stage but did not acquire a criminal record until ten years later, in 1897, when he was arrested and dispatched to Siberia for three years for distributing seditious literature. He then moved to Western Europe, and was a key participant in the conference of the Russian Social Democratic Workers' Party in London in 1903, where he and others who favoured strong centralised leadership of the party – the 'majoritarians' or *Bolsheviki* – argued bitterly with the 'minoritarians' or *Mensheviki* who favoured greater independence.

In 1905, Lenin urged violent insurrection in response to the massacre of workers on Bloody Sunday, and even before the revolution had been suppressed – and long before the liberal intelligentsia stepped back from supporting the revolutionaries – he prophesied that Russia's liberals would regard the creation of a constitutional monarchy a sufficient success, and could not therefore be regarded as the allies of the workers. He returned to Russia at the end of the revolution but fled again in 1907 when the *Okhrana* began a new wave of arrests. He continued to quarrel bitterly with other Russian socialists, Mensheviks and Bolsheviks alike, and the outbreak of the First World War found him in Austro-Hungarian Galicia, where he was briefly arrested as a Russian national. Thereafter, he lived in Zurich, where news reached him of the fall of Tsar Nicholas.

From the outset, Lenin regarded the war as the product of imperialism, which in turn was in his opinion the ultimate exposition of capitalism, and he was appalled by the manner in which socialist parties rushed to support their governments, insisting that they were betraying and destroying the international socialist movement. But when the strains of war began to affect civil society in every country, he grew more optimistic:

> The conflagration is spreading; the political foundations of Europe are being shaken more and more; the sufferings of the masses are appalling, the efforts of governments, the bourgeoisie and the opportunists to hush up these sufferings proving ever more futile. The war profits being obtained by certain groups of capitalists are monstrously high, and contradictions are growing extremely acute. The smouldering indignation of the masses, the vague yearning of society's downtrodden and ignorant strata for a kindly ('democratic') peace, the beginning of discontent among the 'lower classes' – all these are facts. The longer the war drags on and the more acute it becomes, the more governments themselves foster – and must foster – the activity of the masses, whom they call upon to make extraordinary effort and self-sacrifice.[91]

Nevertheless, Lenin was astonished when a young fellow communist rushed into his apartment while he was having lunch and told him that Petrograd was gripped by revolution. With only incomplete information, he spent the next two days trying to determine what was happening. He was desperate to return to Russia at this crucial moment, but he faced arrest if he entered the territory of any of the combatants. Finally, after extensive negotiations, he left Zurich on 27 March with a group of other Bolsheviks aboard a train organised by the Swiss Social Democrats. The train would travel through Germany, which was keen to return to Russian territory someone who would further destabilise matters, but in order to prevent any 'contamination' the Bolsheviks were kept in a separate railway carriage and forbidden any contact with any Germans. A ferry then carried the Bolsheviks across the Baltic Sea to Sweden, from where they journeyed on through Finland by train.

Lenin and his comrades reached Petrograd's Finland Station on 16 April to a tumultuous if contrived welcome, hastily arranged by his fellow Bolsheviks; most of those who gathered in and around the station had never seen Lenin, as he had been out of the country for 14 years, and it took the promise of liberal quantities of beer to ensure the presence of an enthusiastic crowd. Throughout his political life, Lenin had been a divisive figure, rejecting cooperation and compromise with other factions in favour of rigid adherence to his own views, and this day was no different. The reception committee was headed by Nikolai Chkeidze, the chairman of the Soldiers' and Workers' Soviet, who gave a cautious speech of welcome, stressing that the Soviet believed that it was vital to defend the revolution from external or internal encroachments, and that this would best be achieved by unity and a closing of ranks. He concluded with the hope that Lenin would be able to work with him, but Lenin clearly had other ideas, as he made clear in the speech he gave from the roof of an armoured car to the honour guard of sailors:

> I greet you without knowing whether or not you have believed in all the promises of the Provisional Government. But I am convinced that when they talk to you sweetly, when they promise you a lot, they are deceiving you and the whole Russian people. The people need peace; the people need bread; the people need land. And they give you war, hunger, no bread – they leave the landlords still on the land ... We must fight for social revolution, fight to the end, until the complete victory of the proletariat. Long live the worldwide socialist revolution!'[92]

Many of the Bolsheviks who had not been driven into exile hoped that it would be possible to achieve a rapprochement with the Mensheviks, who dominated the Soviet. The day after his return, Lenin demonstrated – once again – that any such thought was anathema. The first of what became known as the 'April Theses' categorically placed Lenin in opposition to the fragile cooperation of the Soviet and the Provisional Government, and gave a sign of future plans that would undermine the ability of Russia to continue in the war:

> In our attitude towards the war, which under the new government of Lvov and Co. unquestionably remains on Russia's part a predatory imperialist war owing to the capitalist nature of the government, not the slightest concession to 'revolutionary defencism' is permissible.
>
> ... In view of the undoubted honesty of those broad sections of the mass believers in revolutionary defencism who accept the war only as a necessity, and not as a means of conquest, in view of the fact that they are being deceived by the bourgeoisie, it is necessary with particular thoroughness, persistence and patience to explain their error to them, to explain the inseparable connection existing between capital and the imperialist war, and to prove that without overthrowing capital *it is impossible* to end the war by a truly democratic peace, a peace not imposed by violence.
>
> The most widespread campaign for this view must be organised in the army at the front.
>
> ... [We must offer] no support for the Provisional Government; the utter falsity of all its promises should be made clear, particularly of those relating to the renunciation of annexations.

> … [We must recognise] the fact that in most of the Soviets of Workers' Deputies our Party is in a minority, so far a small minority, as against a bloc of all the petty-bourgeois opportunist elements … who have yielded to the influence of the bourgeoisie and spread that influence among the proletariat.[93]

Revolutionary defencism, which attracted Lenin's ire in this particular publication, was the invention of Irakli Tsereteli, a Georgian Menshevik who had returned from exile in Siberia in the closing days of the February Revolution. His closely argued contributions to debates in the Soviet gradually brought his colleagues to face up to reality: if the revolution was to succeed, they had to cooperate with the Provisional Government. But perhaps the epitome of what Lenin opposed was Kerensky, who was simultaneously justice minister and vice-president of the Soviet. His rise to power was predicated upon his eloquence and energy, and he continued to put this to good use. Repeatedly, he made impassioned, persuasive speeches to soldiers, workers, and his fellow politicians, but never gave any details of what he intended. He promised a great future, but many who heard his speeches remembered more of their style and passion than their content. Trotsky summed up the views of many:

> He expressed more completely than anyone else the first epoch of the revolution, its 'national' formlessness, the idealism of its hopes and expectations.[94]

Leon Trotsky, born Lev Davidovich Bronstein, was the fifth child of a Ukrainian Jewish family. He was involved in revolutionary politics from a young age and was arrested and exiled to Siberia. He escaped in 1902, changing his name to Trotsky, and lived for some years in London. Trotsky clashed repeatedly with Lenin, largely because it was in the character of Trotsky to seek unity with the various factions within the revolutionaries, whereas Lenin exploited such differences. He returned to Russia in 1905 but was arrested the following year and once more dispatched to Siberia; he escaped again and fled first to London, then to Vienna. When war broke out he moved to Switzerland and then Paris, from where he was expelled for promoting anti-war activities. When the tsar was overthrown, he was living in New York and immediately tried to return to Russia, but his ship was intercepted by the British and he was interned for several weeks in Nova Scotia before being allowed to travel to Petrograd in May 1917. Immediately, he threw himself into the activities of the Soviet, making up for his lack of experience and knowledge by reading and consulting widely.

For the moment, Kerensky's views prevailed over those of Lenin. The great majority of socialists condemned Lenin's divisive views, and even *Pravda*, the Bolshevik newspaper, assured its readers that the April Theses merely reflected Lenin's personal views rather than those of the party. However, Lenin continued to give speeches, rapidly finding a ready audience amongst the ordinary workers and soldiers who felt that the revolution that they had created was not following the path that they wished.

Meanwhile, the news of the events in Petrograd had a profound effect on the field army. Nahum Sabsay was an infantryman in a regiment that had been sent to the Romanian section of the front line in late 1916. The Russian soldiers found that the locals, who did not speak Romanian, treated them with suspicion, but the area they occupied had not repeatedly changed hands, and the roads and villages were in relatively good condition, and the troops devised activities to keep themselves occupied during the winter lull in fighting. He later described a moment about six weeks after their deployment in Romania:

> I was with the captain in his dugout, both of us seated at a makeshift table, lighted by a single candle, our greatcoats on, working on a problem of arithmetic as he and I had been doing whenever we had a chance. But this time our minds were not on the problem. For the last couple of days we had been hearing rumours about food and fuel riots in Petrograd and a number of other cities. No one knew where the rumours had started, and no one dared to talk about them except with the closest friends. I didn't even dare speak of them to the captain or ask him if he had heard anything.
>
> We were still going through the motions of working on a problem when we heard a strangely excited voice outside the dugout asking permission to come in.
>
> 'Come in,' the captain replied.
>
> The soldier, one of our telephone men on duty, entered and, standing at attention, the fingers of his right hand touching the lower rim of his headgear, blurted out excitedly, 'Permit me to report, sir!'
>
> 'Go ahead,' the captain said.
>
> 'Somebody just passed word over all the regimental and divisional telephone lines that the tsar has abdicated. They told us to pass it on to all battalion and company commanders.
>
> The captain and I were on our feet at the same time.
>
> 'Did the tsar abdicate on his own?' the captain asked, his voice catching.
>
> 'No, sir. He was made to abdicate. He's now under arrest,' the soldier continued, still standing at attention, his hand still touching his headgear. 'It will

> be in this evening's order of the day, sir,' he added.
>
> 'All right, you can go,' the captain dismissed him.
>
> … The captain and I remained silent, looking at one another.
>
> I knew that he was torn between two feelings: one of joy and one of dismay. As to me, no other news, not even that proclaiming the sudden end of the war, could have brought me greater happiness.[95]

Vasily Gurko, who had taken over the duties of chief of the general staff during Alexeyev's illness in December and January, had returned to his headquarters in Lutsk to resume command of the Special Army when the revolution took place and he summoned his corps commanders to relay to them the news of the abdication. Problems arose when two further orders were passed on. The first required troops to remove the tsar's initials from their shoulder insignia, and an infantry regiment of the Guards refused to do so. The second related to a new oath that the soldiers had to take; many refused to take an oath while standing in front of regimental flags that still bore imperial insignia, or took exception to the wording – in particular, they objected to the word *Gosudarstvo* being used for the Russian national state, as it was derived from the word *Gosudar*, meaning monarch. Gurko reflected that this merely exemplified the degree to which state and monarchy were so deeply intertwined in Russia, but in both cases, he allowed soldiers to proceed as they wished – those who wanted to retain the imperial shoulder insignia were allowed to do so, and those who did not wish to take the new oath did not need to do so. After a variable period of time, Gurko wrote, the dissenters fell in with the majority; Nicholas' initials gradually disappeared, and eventually nearly all the troops took the new oath.[96]

When the details of Order Number One reached the front line, there was at first little reaction in Gurko's command, and the wily commander of the Special Army did what he could to keep some control of events:

> Later was received the explanation from the new Minister of War, Guchkov, wherein he stated that this order appertained only to the Petrograd garrison. But as time went on agitators were found amongst the troops who explained the injustice of such a partially distributed order to the soldiers – an order which only affected the soldiers who had never smelled powder and lived quietly in the capital. The simultaneous publication, by both the Provisional Government and the Petrograd Soviet, of the gift to the whole of Russia of every possible freedom also produced its active effect … Amongst the Lutsk garrison, composed mainly of rear organisations, meetings began to be called by people chosen for this

> purpose from amongst these organisations. Gradually these were added to by those chosen from neighbouring fighting units. It remained for us to send soldiers and officers to take part so as to lead the meetings on a straight course, and, so far as possible, to endeavour to manoeuvre some clever and modest people into the circle of those who would be authorised to prepare the rules by which such meetings would be directed.[97]

Brusilov's Southwest Front experienced considerable turmoil. At first, the officers appeared to support moderate groups such as the Octobrists who were part of the Provisional Government, but the soldiers were more inclined to back the Soviet. Herein lay the biggest problem for Russia after the revolution; power was effectively shared between the two bodies, each of which drew its support from a different part of the population, and the failure to resolve the resultant tensions would ultimately lead to further unrest. Brusilov noted that while the Bolsheviks preached about international communism, the ordinary soldiers were interested in only two factors: an end to the war, and redistribution of land. In such a situation, it was inevitable that distrust would grow between soldiers and their officers, who tried in vain to retain control of events:

> At that time, the typical officer was a very sorry figure, for in this maelstrom of emotions he was poorly equipped to determine what to do. His speeches were disrupted by anyone who knew how to read and had studied some socialist brochures. In these topics, the officer was completely unversed and did not understand what counter-propaganda he could use. The soldiers would not listen. In some cases it had reached the point where the soldiers expelled their commanders and chose their own, and then announced that they were going home because they were no longer willing to fight … There were also those cases, mostly on the Northern Front, where the commanders were killed.[98]

Discipline within the front-line units began to collapse. For the moment, the commanders of the Central Powers were happy to leave their opponents to fall apart rather than to attack them; German officers actively encouraged men in the front line to fraternise with the Russians and to encourage further disintegration. All sides in the war had attempted to bombard the other side with leaflets at various stages, with little or no effect, but the new campaign of propaganda by the Germans proved far more effective. The German foreign ministry played a leading role in choosing subject material, concentrating repeatedly on the theme that whilst Germany wanted peace, it did not need peace, whereas Russia now clearly needed an end to the war in order to concentrate on its domestic problems. Russian-speaking officers were assigned to front-line units to encourage closer fraternisation, particularly over the Easter period, and the Germans also produced Russian-language newspapers that looked completely authentic but were designed to demoralise and to disrupt discipline. With so many conflicting rumours from the hinterland reaching the Russian field army largely by word of mouth, these German-produced newspapers circulated widely and were largely taken as being the authoritative truth.[99]

Increasingly worried about Russia's ability to continue to play a full part in the war, Buchanan raised the matter with Kerensky when the two men dined together:

> In a long conversation I told him quite frankly why my confidence in the army, and even in the Provisional Government, was shaken. He admitted the accuracy of the facts which I cited, but said that he knew his people and that he only hoped that the Germans would not delay taking the offensive, as, when the fighting began, the army would pull itself together ... He saw no danger of the Provisional Government being overthrown, as only a small minority of the troops were on the side of the Soviet.[100]

The German encouragement of disorder amongst the ranks of the Russian Army was clearly very effective, but it was a dangerous weapon. The soldiers of the German Army were also wearying of the war, and the Soviet repeatedly called on proletarians in the nations of Russia's enemies to rise up against the war. For the moment, German discipline remained strong, not least because the troops themselves felt that they had – on the Eastern Front, at least – the upper hand in military terms.

In a letter to his father, a young Russian officer concisely summed up the state of affairs in many regiments:

> Between us and the soldiers there is an abyss that one cannot cross. Whatever they might think of us as individuals, we in their eyes remain no more than *barins* ['masters']. When we talk of 'the people' we have in mind the nation as a whole, but they mean only the common people. In their view what has taken place is not a political but a social revolution, of which we are the losers and they are the winners. They think that things should get better for them and that they should get worse for us. They do not believe us when we talk of our devotion to the soldiers. They say that we were the *barins* in the past, and that now it is their turn to be the *barins* over us. It is their revenge for the long centuries of servitude.[101]

The signs of disorder in the Russian forces were everywhere. Paléologue described a particularly unpleasant episode in Helsinki, the administrative centre of Russian-administered Finland:

> A funeral service was being held for Lieutenant-Commander Polivanov, who was murdered by his crew during the recent disorders. The coffin was open as the orthodox rite prescribes. Suddenly a mob of workmen and sailors burst into the church. The whole lot marched past the catafalque in single file and spat in the dead man's face. The stricken and weeping widow wiped the sullied features with her handkerchief and implored the brutes to cease their infamous behaviour.
>
> But, thrusting her roughly aside, they seized the coffin, turned it upside down, emptied out the corpse, the candles and the wreaths, and left the church bawling the *Marseillaise*.[102]

Knox visited several units in the front line closest to Petrograd and heard stories of officers being dismissed by soldiers' committees simply because they attempted to impose fairly unremarkable levels of discipline and order. He despaired at the attitude of many of the troops:

> There was a general illogical mistrust of the Command, and the credulity of the men was fantastic. An NCO of 144th Regiment told me that he had himself counted 14,000 head of cattle that were driven to the front by order of the old government in order that they might fall into the hands of the Germans when Vilna was evacuated in September 1915. The men of 138th Division expelled the commander, the chief of staff and two out of the four regiment commanders, the objection to two of them being that they had German names – and yet these very soldiers were ready to fraternise freely with the Germans.[103]

Like most senior army officers, Alexeyev regarded the activities of soldiers' committees as unacceptable interference in military affairs. He sent a series of telegrams to Petrograd, insisting that Guchkov should stop the Soviet from its meddling. In doing so, he mistakenly believed that the Provisional Government – of which Guchkov was a part – was actually in complete control. The reply that he received from Guchkov was as depressing as it was honest:

> The Provisional Government has no real power whatsoever, and its authority exists only to the extent that the Soviet of Workers' and Soldiers' Deputies, which holds all the most important elements of real power – the army, the railroads,

> post, and telegraph – in its hands, permits it. I can tell you very frankly that the Provisional Government can continue to exist only so long as the Soviet of Workers' and Soldiers' Deputies allows it to do so.[104]

Whilst Russia's socialists wished to bring the war that they perceived as being the product of capitalist imperialism to an end, the conflict was spreading. On 6 April, the United States declared war on Germany, an event that had been anticipated ever since the resumption of unrestricted submarine warfare. For the moment, this would make little material difference, as the factories of the United States, already fully committed to producing munitions for the Entente Powers, would now devote their energies to arming the new armies that would ultimately be sent to Europe. The Germans had calculated that by the time the US Army was ready for action, Britain would have been starved into defeat, and the same U-boats could then be used to interdict any attempt to transport American troops across the Atlantic. The same reasons why unrestricted submarine warfare would fail to bring Britain to its knees – over-optimistic assessments of the efficacy of the U-boat weapon and underestimates of the ability of Germany's enemies to defeat U-boats by extensive use of convoys – would apply to any hope of preventing the United States from moving its troops to Europe.

Many who marched on the streets of Petrograd in February and March carried placards demanding an end to the war, yet the Provisional Government remained committed to its alliance obligations. Miliukov, the foreign minister, repeatedly spoke of the need for Russia to 'fight to the last drop of her blood' in order to achieve victory – completion of the aims of the revolution would be impossible unless the war were first brought to a successful conclusion.[105] The opponents of this policy provided Lenin with a ready audience, and fuel was added to the fire when news emerged that Miliukov had written a new declaration of Russia's war aims. In this, he stated that Russia did not seek domination over other peoples or annexation of foreign territory, and favoured a peace established on the basis of national self-determination. However, Russia had to insist on securing its vital interests, particularly control over the gates of the Black Sea. The wording of the declaration could not hide the internal contradiction of Miliukov's position, and a covering note that reassured Russia's allies that Russia would not seek a separate peace and would pursue the war to decisive victory further undermined the commitment to peace without annexations or indemnities that was an absolute requirement of the Soviet.

The assurance to Russia's Entente partners – and particularly the covering note – was seen as hugely inflammatory by the Soviet, and most of its supporters.

If the revolution wasn't about bringing the war to an end, what had been the point? Lenin now called for protests to force Miliukov and the other 'bourgeois ministers' to resign. The first demonstrations began on 3 May, and were followed the next day by larger crowds when the Soldiers' and Workers' Soviet joined the call. The workers from the Vyborg district who had been in the vanguard of the February Revolution once more led the way, streaming south into the city centre where they mingled with over 20,000 troops from the Petrograd garrison, all demanding Miliukov's resignation. The angry shouts of a worker summed up the views of many of those present:

> I spent two years in the trenches and I know what war is. If the bourgeoisie wants it, then let them go and fight it. We've had enough. We've already spilled enough blood for them. Take your fat belly, go there, see how you like it. Then you can go around shouting 'Long live the war!'[106]

At the same time, supporters of Miliukov were on the streets, and for a while there was the very real possibility of civil strife – there were even some clashes and loss of life, largely because many of the armed workers had only the most rudimentary understanding of how firearms worked and even less of how to use the weapons accurately. Fearful that events were sliding out of control, Prince Lvov immediately went to the Soviet to inform them that his government was prepared to resign, as it was clear that it no longer had the support of the Soviet. This put the members of the Soviet in a difficult position. They were acutely aware that it was far easier to function as a critical body of opposition than as the actual government, and both sides desperately tried to find a way out of what became known as the April Crisis. This led to further intensive talks between the Soviet and the Provisional Government, largely over two points.

Firstly, both sides tried to come up with a form of words regarding Russia's war aims that would satisfy both the Provisional Government and the Soviet. Miliukov continued to press for Russia to commit itself to unconditional victory, but he was increasingly isolated. Practically none of the other members of the Provisional Government or the Soviet were still interested in war aims such as the annexation of Constantinople, and even Miliukov had to accept that this would be a very unlikely outcome; he confided in Buchanan that the declaration of Constantinople as an open city, giving Russian warships free passage through the Bosporus, was all that could realistically be expected. Paléologue grew increasingly exasperated, not least because a delegation of French socialists was visiting Petrograd and, he felt, undermining his determination to hold Russia to its commitments. From his point of view, the growing demands of Russia's socialists for a peace without indemnities or annexations might endanger France's demands for the return of Alsace and Lorraine from Germany. On 5 May, the Soviet and the Provisional Government agreed the draft of a joint declaration that condemned Miliukov's note to Russia's Entente partners, but the Soviet still refused to form a coalition with the Provisional Government.

The second issue was the insistence of the Soviet that it had the right of veto over any instructions issued to the army. Knox wrote at length to Buchanan, and therefore indirectly to London, about the disintegration of the army as a direct consequence of political agitation:

> Units have been turned into political debating societies; the infantry refuses to allow the guns to shoot at the enemy; parleying in betrayal of the Allies and of the best interests of Russia takes place daily with the enemy, who laughs at the credulity of the Russian peasant soldier. Many senior officers complained that the government, to which every army has a right to look for support, had left all the burden of dealing with agitation to the army.
>
> In Petrograd things are growing worse daily. The tens of thousands of able-bodied men in uniform who saunter about the streets without a thought of going to the front or of working to prepare themselves for war, when every able-bodied man and most of the women in England and France are straining every nerve to beat the common enemy, will be a disgrace for all time to the Russian people and its government.
>
> … The movement of German troops to the western theatre which you foretold to Prince Lvov on 14 April has commenced.
>
> … It is necessary for us to arrive at some conclusion as to whether the Russian army will fight. No army in the history of the world has ever fought with such anti-war agitation in rear as is now permitted in Petrograd by the government.[107]

Guchkov, the war minister, declared that it was impossible for him to fulfil his duties in view of the veto that the Soviet exercised and he resigned, followed by Kornilov, the military governor of Petrograd. To a large extent, these resignations triggered the final phase of the April Crisis. Prince Lvov and Kerensky concluded that the current power-sharing arrangement between the Provisional Government and the Soviet was unsustainable. To date, Kerensky was the only member of the Soviet who had taken part in the government, but Lvov insisted that the Soviet had to show greater responsibility and commitment. He indicated to Tsereteli that he would be prepared to remove Miliukov if the Soviets would take part in government, but the embattled foreign minister continued to walk a difficult line between sticking to Russia's existing commitments and softening its previous position regarding annexations and reparations. Almost alone in the government, he argued that, given a choice of allowing the Soviet greater representation and facing down this rival source of power, the only hope for Russia lay in the latter.[108]

There were difficult negotiations between the Soviet and the Provisional Government in the three days after the resignation of Guchkov. Finally, Kerensky announced the shape of the new government to all those concerned; there had been bitter arguments over many of the posts, and in some cases no conclusion had been reached, but Kerensky's decisive attitude seemed to bring the exhausted men to the end of the process. Kerensky became the new war minister in place of Guchkov. Miliukov, who had tried to keep Russia to its existing commitments, was left with no option but to resign. His replacement was Mikhail Ivanovich Tereshchenko, who had previously been finance minister and had no experience whatever of foreign affairs.

Given the difficulties that both the Soviet and the Provisional Government had faced to date, and the very real threat of civil strife, the compromise was greeted with enthusiasm and relief. Ultimately though, it sowed the seeds of future conflict. Until now, those who stood to lose most from the revolution – the aristocracy, the landowners, and the industrialists – had been left with nobody to represent their interests, as those who might have been partisan to their cause had been keen to embrace the new spirit of the revolution. Now, Miliukov and the other members of the Kadets took a position of opposition to the new Provisional Government, championing the cause of those who would lose land, money, and status. For the first time, the spectre of counter-revolution began to grow.

The new government faced almost insurmountable problems. It needed to work on the framework for a future republic, and ultimately its failure to do so in a timely manner would doom it to failure. In the meantime, the legacy that it inherited was itself an impossible burden. As Kerensky later described, 'a terrible war, an acute food shortage, a paralysed transport system, an empty treasury, and a population in a state of furious discontent and anarchic disintegration' would have taxed the most capable and established system of government.[109] Nevertheless, Kerensky threw himself into the task with characteristic enthusiasm and fine words, but also characteristically without clear ideas. When a group of senior army officers who had gathered to discuss Guchkov's resignation expressed pessimism at the future prospects for the army, he responded: 'Is it really possible that Free Russia is only a country of mutinous slaves? I grieve that I did not die … in the first hour of the revolution.'[110]

Kerensky did as much as he believed he could to restore army discipline. The elected committees set up in response to Order Number One and the corresponding proclamation of the Soviet had effectively destroyed the normal chain of command, meeting to discuss and debate any orders that were received, and Kerensky limited the power of the committees, allowing commanders to appoint and remove subordinate officers without first securing the approval of their committee. Commissars were assigned to each field army, charged with restoring morale and acting as mediators between army commanders and the soldiers' committees. Naturally, the Bolsheviks regarded these developments as backward steps and continued to agitate against them, further damaging trust and morale. In an attempt to bypass the numerous interests vying for influence in the minds of the soldiers, Kerensky visited the front himself, speaking to gatherings of soldiers whenever he could. In one address, he harangued his audience:

> You are the freest soldiers in the world. Must you not show the world that the system on which the army is now based is the best system? … Our army under the monarchy accomplished heroic deeds; will it be a flock of sheep under the republic? … I summon you forward, to the struggle for freedom, not to a feast, but to death. We, revolutionaries, have the right to death.[111]

Whilst such speeches seemed to have the desired effect on their audiences, the benefit was very transient. As soon as Kerensky moved on, Bolshevik (and other) agitators resumed their work, and any temporary improvement in morale and discipline soon evaporated.

By the beginning of 1917, every army in the First World War was showing signs of strain as a result of the terrible conflict, but it is noteworthy that two armies fared worse than the rest: the *k.u.k.* Army of the Austro-Hungarian Empire, and the Russian Army. The reasons for this were broadly similar. In France, Germany and Britain, the disillusionment brought about by the enormous casualties that had been suffered for so little gain was offset by strong patriotic sentiments, and such sentiments – born out of a strong sense of national identity – were markedly lacking in both the Dual Monarchy and the tsar's Russia. Few, if any, of the troops in the *k.u.k.* Army saw themselves as citizens of a unified empire – instead, their self-identity was more strongly based upon ethnic divisions within the empire. Similarly, Russian soldiers had little sense of loyalty to any concept of a Russian state. When they joined the army, they gave an oath of loyalty to the tsar, and that tsar was now under arrest. With no notion of national pride to drive them to continue the conflict, ordinary Russian soldiers found the ideas of the Bolsheviks – that the war was largely a product of capitalism and would do nothing to improve the lives of ordinary people – both persuasive and attractive. It was a straightforward step to adopt other Bolshevik ideas, such as forming soldiers' committees that would debate and vote on whether or not to obey orders, as these allowed the soldiers to opt out of a war that for them had lost whatever little meaning it might once have had. Kerensky's urging that soldiers should continue to fight for Russia's welfare and glory might have some resonance amongst the traditional officer classes, but these were the groups that had suffered disproportionately high casualties in the war, and the replacement officers were far closer to ordinary soldiers in their mindset. Knox summarised the problem neatly: 'To the average Russian peasant, his country was the hovel on the Volga, or perhaps in the Urals, where he happened to have been born, and to which he thought the Germans would never penetrate.'[112]

Knox and a fellow British officer visited many of the garrisons around Petrograd, trying both to assess the mood of the troops and to exert a little influence over them:

> The Ismailovsky Battalion had expelled its old colonel, who was 'strict', and three or four of the officers. The colonel at the time of our visit … told us that he had established a 'regimental university' in which he delivered lectures himself on the 'psychology of the masses', while his second in command discoursed on the 'military law of various nations'. I ventured to remark that the subject he had chosen seemed rather recondite, but he said, on the contrary, it was of extraordinary interest. It is easy to imagine how futile such an attempt must have been to occupy and amuse the men, three quarters of whom were illiterate. This poor fellow somewhat later commenced writing the regimental orders in verse, and was removed from his command by the district staff.
>
> In this battalion a private soldier, who had been an actor in civil life, proved very talkative. I had asked the men to forbear from 'experiments' at such a time, and pointed out that the experiment of electing officers had only been made once, as far as I knew – in the great French Revolution – and the result had been Napoleon. The ex-actor said: 'With the "broad Russian nature" experiments are possible that could not be tried in western countries. Russia will find a Dostoyevsky, and not a Napoleon!'
>
> The 'broad Russian nature' was always the excuse for every extravagance. What was wanted was a little narrow common sense.[113]

After centuries of autocratic rule, Russians both at home and at the front struggled to deal with their newly granted freedom. Topics that had been forbidden during the rule of the tsars were now discussed widely, even interminably. Paléologue described a typical impromptu gathering in Petrograd:

> I found 'meetings' in progress everywhere, held in the open air, or perhaps I should say open gale. The groups were small: twenty or thirty people at the outside, and comprising soldiers, peasants, working men and students. One of the company mounts a stone, or a bench, or a heap of snow and talks his head off, gesticulating wildly. The audience gazes fixedly at the orator and listens in a kind of rapt absorption. As soon as he stops another takes his place and immediately gets the same fervent, silent and concentrated attention.
>
> What an artless and affecting sight it is when one remembers that the Russian nation has been waiting centuries for the right of speech![114]

The revolution had been triggered by food shortages and, despite all the tumultuous events, the shortages remained as severe as ever. Inflation had vastly reduced the purchasing power of ordinary people, and factory workers asserted their new freedoms to demand huge increases in their wages. As the food they wished to buy remained in short supply, this merely fed the spiral of inflation. At the same time, demands for shorter working hours became so strong that the concept of the eight-hour working day became almost universal. Workers routinely took to leaving their workplaces after working eight hours, though a few employers found ways of circumventing this; for example, the workforce of the Petrograd Cartridge Works agreed that the eight-hour day had been established as a fundamental principle, but were prepared to work longer hours in the interests of supplying the soldiers in the front with sufficient ammunition.[115] At the same time, peasants in the countryside took the revolution as permission to take all matters into their own hands, looting and burning many country estates. Demands for land redistribution ignored simple arithmetic realities – in the Orel province, an agrarian expert pointed out in vain that even if all the land in the great estates was handed over to the peasants, this would amount to barely a third of an acre for each peasant, nowhere near enough to bring prosperity, and the dislocation that would result would surely reduce production and exacerbate the existing food shortages.[116] As peasants started to seize parcels of land without any formal process, word slowly reached their sons and brothers in the front line; fearful that they might miss out on securing new land, soldiers began to desert and head for their homes.

As Russia moved towards the end of the muddy spring season, thoughts turned once more to the war. Nicholas had ordered a new offensive during the spring and the army command continued to plan for a major attack by Southwest Front, with subsidiary attacks farther north – given the fragility of the *k.u.k.* Army, it was felt that it would be more profitable to direct an attack against its divisions rather than against the Germans. Many doubted that the army was capable of mounting any such attack, but some thought that an offensive was not only a political requirement of Russia's obligations to its allies, but was also the only means by which the army might be saved. At the end of March, Alexeyev wrote to Guchko:

> If we fail to go onto the offensive, we will not escape having to fight, but will merely condemn ourselves to fighting at a time and place of the enemy's choosing. And if we fail to cooperate with our allies, we cannot expect them to come to our aid when we need them. Disorder in the army will have just as great an effect on defensive ability as on offensive power. Even if we are not fully confident of success, we should mount an offensive. The consequences of an unsuccessful defence are more undesirable than those of an unsuccessful offensive … The faster we throw our troops into action, the faster their interest in politics will dissipate … It can be said that the less steady the troops, the less successful defence will be, hence making it more desirable to mount active [i.e. offensive] operations.[117]

At his headquarters in Minsk, Gurko concluded somewhat hopefully that some of his formations, notably I Siberian Corps, remained strong and disciplined, and in many other cases much of the pernicious disorder of the revolutionary period seemed to be waning. In the past, he had limited personal inspections to small sections of the front line, relying on soldiers spreading the word that he had shown an interest, but now he felt the need for more extensive visits, particularly to rear areas where he could address large gatherings of soldiers. In order to avoid any suspicion, he chose to drop his pre-revolutionary practice of having a separate conference with the officers of whichever unit he was visiting, instead addressing them at the same time as their men.[118] But if the troops of Gurko's command were showing signs of returning to something approaching normal attitudes, matters were very different elsewhere, with widespread fraternising with the German and Austro-Hungarian troops on the other side of the front line. Investigators sent by the Duma to ascertain the scale of the problem returned with disheartening reports about attempts by officers to stop fraternisation by ordering their artillery to open fire on the enemy lines, and the lengths to which the soldiers were prepared to go to prevent this:

> Infantrymen often cut the telephone lines between artillery batteries and their forward observers [and] warn the artillery that if it begins to fire upon the enemy, they will hoist its gunners on their bayonets.[119]

Brusilov, too, felt that morale and discipline was continuing to deteriorate:

> By May, the troops on all fronts were completely out of hand, and the impact of any measures taken was negligible … For example, VII Siberian Corps, which was moved away from the front line position for rest in a rear area, refused to return to the front and informed the corps commander, Boris Savinkov, that the combat troops wished to have a prolonged further stay in Kiev, and no amount of persuasion or threats by Savinkov helped. There were many such cases on all fronts.[120]

At first, many of those who were sent to the Soviet as delegates by the front-line troops had called upon the Soviet to support the men facing the enemy, and there were incidents where these delegates blamed workers in Petrograd and elsewhere for the shortages that had crippled the army. However, contact with the workers gradually changed their minds, and as they learned of crippling shortages of coal and raw materials, they came to regard the war as something that had been mismanaged at the highest levels.

As the army continued to disintegrate, a commission was created under the control of General Alexei Polivanov, who had been the war minister in 1915–1916, to try to bring some order to affairs. The commission was to create a set of rules by which the army was to be run, including matters of discipline, but its initial proposals angered Gurko so much that he replied that, if implemented, these proposals would destroy any hope of restoring discipline. Alexeyev now summoned the front commanders to *Stavka* in Mogilev to discuss matters, and Gurko proposed that they should all submit their resignations together if the government attempted to implement the new rules of conduct. In a final attempt to persuade the politicians to change their minds, the front commanders proceeded to Petrograd, arriving shortly after Kerensky had taken up his post as war minister. They met the government in Prince Lvov's house, and in turn, Alexeyev, Brusilov, Abram Mikhailovich Dragomirov (who had replaced Ruzsky as commander of Northern Front), Shcherbachev and Gurko addressed the politicians, giving repeated examples of indiscipline and interference in military affairs. After describing the actions of an agitator, sanctioned by the Soviet, whose activities resulted in a division refusing to take part in preparations for the coming offensive, Gurko continued:

> I said that the general watchword remained 'The revolution continues'. My advice was ... either the Revolution must be stopped, or at least discontinued until the end of the war, or else there was the grave risk of throwing Russia herself into an abyss and, together with her, the revolution itself and all its conquests. Unless the leaders of political life in Russia changed their tactics, they would find that in the near future the same democracy for which they now fought would curse their names and their memory ...
>
> I reminded them that there had been a time when the tsar ... was accused of playing the game of the Germans, in regard to internal politics. So a time would come when those who sat there would be accused of just the same things and with much more foundation should they not change their own political views. I also declared that, if the proposals of army changes were carried out as they were projected, I saw no possibility of fulfilling the duties which the Provisional Government had entrusted to me ... and the eventual result would be much bloodshed, especially of the democracy itself. If the [Provisional Government] cared to take upon themselves the responsibility of this blood, that was for their own conscience, but I for one would not take the responsibility of it upon myself ... I finished ... by saying ... that the country was on the verge of ruin, and that they were pushing her to it.[121]

Alexeyev directed his address at the government ministers who had been appointed by the Soviet, telling them that their deeds and words had disorganised the army and that it was irresponsible to give rights to the people without at the same time explaining their duties. Gurko recorded that Tsereteli responded by protesting at the sharpness of the accusations of the generals, saying that it was difficult for anyone to control the direction of the revolution. Anton Ivanovich Denikin, who had been appointed chief of the general staff, recorded that Tsereteli told the generals:

> The masses of the soldiery do not wish to go on with the war. They are wrong, and I cannot believe that they are prompted by cowardice. It is the result of distrust. Discipline should remain. But if the soldiers realise that you are not fighting against democracy, they will trust you. By this means the army may yet be saved. By this means the authority of the Soviet will be strengthened. There is only one way of salvation, the way of confidence and of the democratisation of the country and of the army.[122]

Whatever Tsereteli might have meant by this, it was of no comfort to the generals who were trying to prepare for an offensive with an army that was increasingly disinclined to obey any orders. After a few more contributions from the politicians, none of whom impressed the soldiers, Gurko highlighted the fundamental differences between the two sides:

> We are discussing the matter from different angles. Discipline is the fundamental condition of the existence of the army. The percentage of losses which a unit may suffer without losing its fighting capacity is the measure of its endurance. I have spent eight months in the South African Republics and have seen regiments of two different kinds: small and disciplined, and volunteers and undisciplined. The former continued to fight and did not lose their fighting power when their losses amounted to 50 percent. The latter, although they were volunteers who knew what they were fighting for, left the ranks and fled from the battlefield after losing ten percent. No force on earth could induce them to fight. That is the difference between disciplined and undisciplined troops. We demand discipline. We do all we can to persuade. But your authoritative voice must be heard. We must remember that if the enemy advances, we shall fall to pieces like a pack of cards. If you will not cease to revolutionise the army – you must assume power yourselves.[123]

This last comment was directed squarely at the members of the Soviet, but had as little effect as the other speeches. The generals returned to their headquarters, aware that their views had not prevailed. To a large extent, their failure reflected the degree to which they had misunderstood the position of the Soviet. For Tsereteli and his colleagues, the February Revolution was merely the first step. They had tried to stay out of government as they saw the current state as merely the overthrow of the tsar by the bourgeoisie – they expected that there would be a further revolution at a later date in which the proletariat would finally come to power. Furthermore, their view of the future was one in which there would be no nation states, and the workers of the world would overthrow the governments that they believed were responsible for wars and strife. For the Bolsheviks, a military victory over the German Army was meaningless; true victory would come in the form of spreading the revolution to Germany and the rest of Europe. There was a degree of hard-nosed financial realism behind this, too. Russia was hugely in debt as a result of the war, and its long-term recovery would depend on revolutionary governments elsewhere cancelling its debts. The threats to the revolution therefore came not only from the danger of counter-revolution by reactionary elements in the army, but also from foreign powers that might, as had been the case after the French Revolution, seek to restore the old regime.

Having effectively removed the ability of the army's commanders to impose discipline upon the army, the Provisional Government now moved to remove any option for the army's leadership to distance itself from the increasing chaos. Shortly after the abortive conferences in Mogilev and Petrograd, Kerensky issued an order or *Ukaze* stating that senior officers could no longer resign or ask to be dismissed. As soon as he heard of this, Gurko took action:

> I at once wrote a report … in which I stated that the *Ukaze* of the Minister of War deprived me of my right to ask for my dismissal from my post, and that was why I left the Provisional Government to judge for itself whether I could remain under these conditions, without the means of carrying on the task entrusted to me. I also declared that I discarded the moral responsibility, the responsibility of my conscience, for all that might happen in the future in directing the troops at the front … I had to wait rather a long time for the answer. In reality the Provisional Government signed the order for my dismissal on 5 June, at the same time as that of General Alexeyev.[124]

There was a further series of changes of appointments to reflect the departures of Gurko and Alexeyev. Denikin took command of West Front, and was replaced in turn as chief of the general staff by Alexander Sergeyevich Lukomsky, who had led troops with distinction during the Brusilov Offensive of 1916 and as quartermaster-general had been drawing up preparations for the coming campaign season. As a replacement for Alexeyev as commander-in-chief, Kerensky turned to Russia's most successful commander: Alexei Brusilov. Fearing that it was already too late to save the army and bring the war to anything other than a disastrous conclusion, Brusilov accepted the appointment with little enthusiasm. Knox, who was no admirer of Brusilov, felt that he had acquired his reputation for success more through luck than good judgement, and that many of his subordinates regarded him as an insincere opportunist; it was therefore no surprise, in Knox's opinion, that he now accepted supreme command.[125] His replacement at Southwest Front was Alexei Gutor, who had been commanding Eleventh Army through the preceding weeks of turmoil; control of Eleventh Army now passed to Ivan Ivanovich Fedotov.

Thoughts began to turn in earnest to the coming campaign season. To date, the Germans had deliberately left the Russians alone, for a mixture of reasons. Firstly, they had used the turmoil of the revolution to move troops west. Secondly, they deliberately encouraged fraternisation in the expectation that it would accelerate the collapse of the Russian Army and reduce further its will to fight.

Thirdly, some military circles were concerned that if the Germans were to launch attacks, this might bring about a resurgence in Russian resistance, and prove counter-productive. Finally, there were hopes that the new Russian government might be willing to seek a separate peace. Writing after the war, Max Hoffmann felt that this was a lost opportunity:

> The idea naturally occurred that it would be a good thing to accelerate the collapse of the Russian Army by a few strong thrusts …
>
> Now, when it is possible to examine the conditions more clearly, one is obliged to regret that [the proposal to attack] was not adopted, and already in the first days of the Revolution, when the Russian soldier was inclined to draw, what for his understanding, were the natural consequences of the Revolution, that is to say, to lay down his arms and go home, that we did not attempt by a general attack on the whole of the front to cause the Russian soldiers to waver. If we had succeeded in this, no power on earth would have been able to stop the process of disintegration that would then have set in, or to bring the masses again into order.[126]

This assessment, like many of Hoffmann's assessments, is largely self-serving and benefits from the advantages of hindsight. The reality was that Germany would have struggled to assemble sufficient forces to strike a decisive blow, especially given that there were no obvious objectives within easy reach. At best, the Russians could have been left badly weakened, but one of the lessons that the Germans had learned in the Franco-Prussian War was that it was necessary to have a government with which to negotiate in order to bring a war to a tidy end. Given the ongoing bloodletting in northern France, the only satisfactory conclusion on the Eastern Front for Germany would have been one that allowed the army to disengage and be brought west in strength. Such an endpoint would have been very unlikely in the chaos of the revolution, and whilst it was reasonable to take advantage of the Russian turmoil to concentrate attention and resources elsewhere, it was almost inevitable that the onset of the summer campaign season would lead to a resumption of hostilities.

CHAPTER 4

AUSTRIA-HUNGARY'S PEACE INITIATIVE

While the Russians were causing concerns in Entente circles about their commitment to the war, the same was true of the Austro-Hungarian Empire and its willingness – and even its ability – to continue alongside Germany.

During the half-hearted attempts of Germany to open negotiations towards securing a peace in the winter of 1916–1917, the diplomats of the Dual Monarchy were particularly keen to bring hostilities to an end. By the end of 1915, the *k.u.k.* Army had been reduced to little more than an armed militia; recruits were sent to the front with only the most rudimentary training, and showed little ability or inclination to fight. As was the case in every army, the officer corps had suffered disproportionate losses and replacement officers were not even up to the standard of those with which the Austro-Hungarian Empire went to war, let alone the far higher standard that was needed in an era of industrialised warfare. German officers like Hermann Balck, who commanded armoured forces with great distinction in a later war, were struck by the contrast between the German Army, where officers remained committed to the welfare of their men, and their equivalents in the *k.u.k.* Army:

> They replaced their officers constantly and the constant refrain we heard was 'We do not know why we are fighting this war. It is only for Germany anyway.' ... We were horrified to hear the continual mutterings such as: 'Better an end with terror than this terror without an end.'
>
> ... One of their supply units had been in bivouac for three or four weeks behind one of mine. Every night their soldiers sat around the fires and got drunk

> until they just passed out. The officers, on the other hand, established a mess, where they were fed cooked meat twice a day. They had pastries, candy, cigarettes, and every night plenty of women.
>
> Meanwhile, their soldiers were running around hungry as dogs. Almost daily one of them came into my area asking for bread. I saw Bosnian soldiers ... picking up corn kernels off the road that washed up in the thaw. I thought they were collecting them for the horses, but one of them who spoke a little German explained that they were making their polenta with what they managed to scrounge.[127]

There were widespread food shortages throughout the western parts of the empire, though Hungary was to an extent spared the worst effects of the shortages, largely because István Tisza, the Hungarian prime minister, refused to allow exports of food from Hungary to the Austrian parts of the Dual Monarchy.

The relationship between Vienna and Budapest had never been easy. Tisza consistently followed a policy of narrow self-interest, acting primarily for the benefit of Hungary, and more specifically for the small population of wealthy landowners that had been granted suffrage and therefore controlled the Budapest parliament. Ottokar Czernin von und zu Chudenitz had been the Austro-Hungarian ambassador in Bucharest before Romania declared war on the Central Powers, and became the empire's foreign minister shortly after the Emperor Karl ascended to the throne. His observations of Tisza were an accurate summary:

> He often told me that he knew no patriotism save the Hungarian, but that it was in the interests of Hungary to keep together with Austria; therefore he saw things with a crooked vision. Never would he have ceded one square metre of Hungarian territory; but he raised no objection to the projected cession of Galicia [which was a 'crown land' of Austria]. He would rather have let the whole world be ruined than give up Transylvania; but he took no interest whatever in the Tyrol.
>
> ... He opposed any expansion of the Monarchy, as it might weaken Hungary's influence. All his life he was an opponent of the Austro-Polish solution, and a mortal enemy of the tripartist project [the suggestion that the Dual Monarchy should evolve into a Triple Monarchy of Austria, Hungary and Poland]; he intended that Poland at most should rank as an Austrian province, but would prefer to make her over to Germany. He did not even wish Romania to be joined with Hungary, as that would weaken the Magyar influence in Hungary. He looked upon it as out of the question to grant the Serbians access to the sea, because he wanted the Serbian agricultural products when he was in need of

> them; nor would be leave an open door for the Serbian pigs, as he did not wish the price of the Hungarian to be lowered.
>
> ... [However,] the Magyar-Central standpoint was not a specialty of Tisza's; all Magyar politicians upheld it. Secondly, Tisza had one great point in his favour: he had no wish to prolong the war for the purpose of conquest; he wished for a rectification of the Romanian frontier and nothing beyond that. If it had come to peace negotiations, he would have supported me in taking as a basis the *status quo ante*. His support – and that was the third reason – was of great value, for he was a man who knew how to fight ...
>
> For many years Hungary and Tisza were one. Tisza was a man whose brave and manly character, stern and resolute nature, fearlessness and integrity, raised him above the average man. He was a thorough man, with brilliant qualities and grave faults; a man whose like is rare in Europe, in spite of those faults.[128]

Never an enthusiast for the war, Czernin became intimately involved in the attempts to start peace negotiations at the end of 1916, leading ultimately to what became known as the Sixtus Affair. A detailed account of this sheds an interesting light on the degree to which both sides were prepared in private to deviate from their stated policies; in particular, the manner in which French claims on German territory escalated are in stark contrast to general condemnations of German territorial greed and the importance of self-determination for the peoples of Europe.

In his memoirs, Czernin recorded that, late in February 1917, he was approached by an individual from a neutral country with documentation that confirmed that he was accredited to speak on behalf of one of Austria-Hungary's enemies. This person advised Czernin that this enemy nation was ready to conclude a separate peace. However, the proposals had to be kept secret, and would be repudiated if made public. Czernin responded cautiously but favourably, asking for a meeting of representatives on neutral ground, but heard no more. A week later, he learned of the tsar's abdication.

Czernin was convinced that the tentative peace overtures came from Russia, and after the revolution he waited in vain for fresh approaches. Meanwhile, there had also been developments in the west, where Prince Sixtus of Bourbon-Parma, the brother-in-law of the Emperor Karl, was serving as a junior officer in the Belgian Army. Aware of his close links with the Austro-Hungarian ruler, French diplomats had – according to Sixtus' account of the event – already been in contact, tentatively exploring whether it might be possible to detach war-weary Austria-Hungary from the increasingly militant and militaristic Germany.[129]

During the winter in which Germany and Austria-Hungary appeared to be edging towards peace talks whilst Germany was simultaneously preparing for unrestricted submarine warfare, Sixtus received a letter from his mother, who was living in Switzerland, asking him to visit her. He left his regiment and travelled via Paris to Switzerland, arriving on 28 January, as he described in a letter that he later wrote to President Raymond Poincaré of France:

> Accompanied by my sister Maria Antonia, my mother had already arrived there two days before, travelling strictly incognito. She told us of the wish of the emperor [Karl] to see us to hold direct talks with us about peace. Everything had already been arranged for us to travel to Vienna in strict secrecy … If however, this was not possible for us, the emperor was ready to send to us in Switzerland someone in his confidence to inform us of his views. We concluded that this second option was the only one possible and furthermore we could not let it take place without first having notified Paris.[130]

Sixtus further informed Poincaré that he outlined what he believed to be the minimum position of France: restoration of Alsace and Lorraine to French rule; an independent Belgium; an independent Serbia; and Russian control of Constantinople.[131] Given his frequent contacts with French diplomats in the preceding months, he would have been in a position of some knowledge regarding this.

From Switzerland, Sixtus travelled to Paris, where he informed Poincaré of Karl's tentative overtures. When he returned to Switzerland in early February, he met Thomas Erdödy, a lifelong friend of the new emperor, who gave him further details. Karl wished for an armistice with Russia in the first instance, followed by the return of Alsace and Lorraine to France and the restoration of Belgian independence. Finally, Serbia would be permitted to combine with Bosnia-Herzegovina, Albania, and Montenegro; this state would have an Austrian archduke as its nominal head, and would remain part of the Austro-Hungarian Empire, though with considerable autonomy. There was no mention of the status of Constantinople.

Sixtus was of course aware that, with the possible exception of the Balkan rearrangement, none of this was within the power of Emperor Charles to deliver, and he asked Erdödy to obtain further information on how these terms were to be achieved. He informed Erdödy that Karl had two options. The preferable one was to present the Germans with a fait accompli by agreeing terms with the Entente Powers; the alternative was to enter negotiations for peace, which would be a more drawn-out process with no guaranteed outcome. Erdödy returned to Vienna and then travelled back to Switzerland with a variety of documents, including letters from Karl, Czernin, the Empress Zita (Sixtus' sister), and Sixtus' mother:

> The emperor repeatedly stated how much he desired peace, not as an imperious and urgent demand from a military point of view, but from his duty before God for his people and for all the belligerents. He repeated his sympathies for 'la belle France' and the valour of her armies and for the spirit of sacrifice and devotion to duty in all nations. I was beseeched to act in complete secrecy. Only Count Czernin had been brought into the confidence of the sovereign couple.[132]

Czernin's note was the first contribution to the process by a professional diplomat, and a list of points distanced him from Karl's original proposals, effectively killing any prospect of the Austro-Hungarian Empire being enticed to abandon Germany at this stage of the process. He declared that the alliance between Austria-Hungary, Germany, Turkey and Bulgaria was absolutely indissoluble and there was no question of any of them agreeing a separate peace. Whilst Austria-Hungary had no intention of annexing Serbia or Romania, it would be necessary to establish appropriate guarantees to prevent 'political acts such as those that led to the murder in Sarajevo', and Romania would have to give up its claims to Transylvania, which was part of the Kingdom of Hungary. He agreed that Belgium should be restored to its pre-war state and compensated for the damage it had suffered, but with regard to the question of Alsace and Lorraine, he merely stated that if Germany wished to renounce its claims to the two disputed states, Austria-Hungary would raise no objections. He also attempted to head off the growing clamour in the Entente Powers for greater recognition and self-determination of nationalities within the Austro-Hungarian Empire; he declared that all nationalities already enjoyed the same rights and status. And in a clever move to try to undermine the unity of the Entente, he commented that there was no question of Austria-Hungary being politically subservient to Germany, whereas there was a widespread opinion within the empire that France was acting in accordance with British interests.[133]

Czernin's letter was accompanied by a note from the Emperor Karl. Sixtus read and destroyed this document, but later reproduced its contents from memory – it is impossible to know how accurate this later version was. Adding to Czernin's points, Karl wrote that he would support France with all the means at his disposal and would seek to influence Germany on the question of Alsace and Lorraine, and that he felt the greatest sympathy for the Belgians, who had been wronged by what had happened, and should receive restitution from all the combatants.[134]

It is noteworthy that, despite their repeated declarations of Entente unity and the fears that Paléologue expressed about post-revolutionary Russia seeking a separate peace, the minimum French preconditions that Sixtus listed – presumably with the approval of Poincaré, who was aware of these developments – made no mention of Italy's claims on Austro-Hungarian territory. In further discussions with Sixtus, Poincaré clarified France's position with regard to Italy: France has promised to help Italy secure Trieste, but had not guaranteed that this would happen – in other words, Italy would be supported in holding onto any gains that it might make during the war, but France was not prepared to spill the blood of its soldiers in pursuit of Italian objectives.

In any case, none of these proposals paid the slightest attention to the declared war aims of Germany, and failing to address this would have ultimately doomed the process to failure, regardless of other developments. The industrial scale of the war, and in particular the British blockade of Germany – which in some cases crossed the boundaries of legality when it came to interference with neutral shipping heading for the Netherlands or Denmark – had left the Germans desperate to ensure that they would not face such a predicament in a future war. There was a range of opinions in Berlin on what would constitute an acceptable outcome to the war, ranging from socialist members of the Reichstag who were increasingly strident in supporting a 'peace without annexations or indemnities', through Bethmann-Hollweg who wished for substantial gains but was prepared to be flexible in order to secure peace, to Hindenburg, Ludendorff and their supporters who demanded major territorial adjustments and financial penalties on Germany's enemies. As 1917 unfolded, Bethmann-Hollweg saw the turmoil in Russia as an opportunity for a separate peace, and was prepared to reduce his demands considerably in order to secure a settlement, but the militarists were of a completely different opinion, insisting that this was the moment to exploit Russia's weakness to secure the greatest possible concessions. In April, their will prevailed, and Bethmann-Hollweg was forced to agree their military priorities – for example, the annexation of Liège and southeast Belgium and the occupation of the Belgian coast – over economic considerations. Furthermore, at the prompting of Hindenburg and Ludendorff, Kaiser Wilhelm ordered Bethmann-Hollweg to draw up a formal list of minimum and maximum war aims.[135] The outcome was an expansion of previous proposals. Belgium would remain under German military control until it was politically and militarily ready to join

Germany in an alliance. Luxembourg would become a German federal state, and the French coal region of Longwy-Briey would be annexed. Courland – the western half of Latvia – and all of Lithuania, already administered by *Ober Ost*, would become permanent parts of the German Empire. Poland would have to agree substantial buffer zones gained from its territory to protect Germany, with these border zones being settled by German army veterans after the war – this was in some respects a forerunner of German policy in Eastern Europe in the Second World War. Also, there would be adjustments in the Balkans in favour of Austria-Hungary. The only crumb of comfort that Bethmann-Hollweg could secure was that he was permitted to add a minute to the final document stating that he refused to be bound by these aims if he were to conduct negotiations.[136]

The French president consulted the rest of the French government, and it was agreed to continue discussions with the Emperor Karl with a view to securing complete acceptance of the initial four points that Sixtus had described. Given that Romania and Italy wished territorial gains at the expense of the Dual Monarchy, Poincaré suggested that Karl should be offered parts of Silesia and Bavaria by way of compensation – an additional benefit of this would be the weakening of a post-war Germany. In the context of the repeated assertions by the Entente Powers that any post-war settlement should recognise the nationalist ambitions of groups such as the Czechs, Balkan Slavs and Poles, it is remarkable that when it came to the territory of the German Empire, no such concerns seemed to apply. The same was true of Alsace and Lorraine. Contrary to the view both at the time and since, the unequivocally French nature of these provinces was not as clear-cut as the French portrayed. Although much of Alsace became French territory in 1648 after the Treaty of Westphalia, complete occupation by France only occurred after the French Revolution. Fewer than 50 per cent of its inhabitants spoke French as their first language at the time of the Franco-Prussian War, and fewer than 10 per cent of the population chose to leave after 1871. At no stage, from the German annexation of the region in 1871 to the Treaty of Versailles in 1919, did any side attempt to determine the preferences of the people of Alsace and Lorraine. At the time of the Franco-Prussian War, the forces of the North German Confederation expected to be greeted as liberators and were surprised at the ambivalence of the population. Heinrich von Treitschke, a German politician and historian, writing in 1871, expressed the views of many:

> We Germans who know Germany and France know better what is good for the Alsatians than the unfortunates themselves … we will give them back their own identity against their will.[137]

During the years that the region was under German control, there were repeated occasions when the Germans behaved badly towards the population, particularly the Saverne Affair of late 1913, when a young Prussian officer insulted Alsatians and received only a token punishment; civil protests were met with military force. Nevertheless, many in Alsace and Lorraine did not feel particularly warm towards France, and at the end of the war there was a short-lived movement that attempted to establish an independent state of Alsace-Lorraine; the French rapidly suppressed it, again without any attempt to consult the population.

Towards the end of March, Prince Sixtus wrote to Emperor Karl, stressing that the basic minimum Entente requirements that he had outlined at the outset remained the basis for any armistice. He advised his brother-in-law that the Entente would support Italy in annexing Austro-Hungarian territory, but only if it had succeeded in capturing it. Stressing that time was of the essence, he urged Karl to accept the four points – the return of Alsace and Lorraine to France, the restoration of independence for Belgium and Serbia, and Russian control of Constantinople – in writing and without qualifications. He added that while an opportunity for peace existed, the people of France remained committed to the war. As an additional warning, he stated that if Germany were to arrange peace terms, Berlin would probably ensure that any concessions by the Central Powers were made by Turkey and Austria-Hungary:

> God protect you from falling victim to such calculations about Galicia, Bukovina, Transylvania, and in the south. All of this [would be] to preserve Prussian Poland or the left bank of the Rhine …
>
> Soon the entire world will be aligned against Germany and it will be impossible to conclude an acceptable peace while [your] fate is tied to that of Germany, if only because the greater the number of allies, the harder it will be to secure peace because of the number of interests that will have to be satisfied.[138]

These comments were calculated to play upon the awareness in the Austro-Hungarian Empire that, even in the event of a victory by the Central Powers, Germany would become the dominant power in Europe and the Dual Monarchy would be reduced to a subservient status. The failures of the *k.u.k.* Army and the dependence upon Germany for munitions, fuel and all manner of other materiel had already made this clear – Austro-Hungarian officials were acutely aware that many Germans, including Ludendorff, regarded their alliance with Vienna as being shackled to a corpse. It also seems ironic, even cynical, that Sixtus suggested that, to avoid the risk of Germany purchasing peace at the expense of Austria-

Hungary, Karl should purchase peace at the expense of Germany's territorial claims to Alsace and Lorraine.

On 19 March, Sixtus met Erdödy in Geneva, from where they travelled together in great secrecy to Vienna. They met Karl at Laxenburg Palace, a short distance outside Vienna, on 23 March. Sixtus later wrote the words that the emperor spoke to him:

> It is absolutely necessary to make peace, and I wish it at any price. The moment is completely propitious, as we have all experienced successes and reverses: there is an approximate equilibrium of force at the moment.[139]

He went on to add that, in his opinion, the best peace was often not achieved by great military victories, and used the oppressive settlement imposed upon France by Germany in 1871 as an example. Despite the insistence of Berlin on pressing on to achieve total victory, Karl told Sixtus that he would do all in his power to persuade the Germans to accept peace, but if this proved impossible, he would be obliged to seek a separate peace for his empire. Sixtus informed Karl that the French demands for the recovery of Alsace and Lorraine actually extended farther than the territories seized by Germany in 1871; the French wanted all of the left bank of the Rhine, or at the very least the removal of any German military presence from the area. With regard to Constantinople, Karl expressed doubt that the current government in Petrograd would survive, and that any question about the gates of the Black Sea should therefore be deferred. Sixtus was inclined to agree, suggesting that guaranteed access for Russian shipping might suffice to satisfy this requirement. Admittedly, by this stage in Petrograd only the embattled Miliukov continued to hold out hope of securing Constantinople for Russia, but Sixtus can have offered this solution only with the awareness and consent of the French government. Given the insistence of French and British diplomats that Russia should continue to honour all its obligations to the Entente, the failure of France to press for the demands that Russia had already made – and the revolutionary government had not withdrawn – is noteworthy. When the discussion moved to Italy, Karl reminded Sixtus that – from the point of view of Vienna – Italy had entered the war purely to gain territory, and that his army had fought heroically to hold back the Italians along the Isonzo. However, he was prepared to offer small territorial concessions, provided that these were acceptable to Austrian public opinion.

Czernin joined the party for a brief interval, during which the atmosphere was notably cooler; Sixtus found it hard to determine the reserved foreign minister's position. Czernin advised that he could see no circumstances in which Germany would agree to concede Alsace and Lorraine, and asked why France wanted to go farther in securing the entire left bank of the Rhine; Sixtus replied that this merely recognised the full extent of Alsace and Lorraine before the territory was reduced at the Congress of Vienna in 1815, conveniently ignoring the fact that this included territory that had become part of France only in 1798, having been independent German city states under the aegis of the Holy Roman Empire before then.

There was a further meeting the following day at Erdödy's residence between Sixtus and Czernin. The foreign minister insisted that Austria-Hungary would continue to stand by its ally Germany, until and unless Germany conclusively made it possible for Vienna to achieve a 'reasonable' peace settlement, which represented a shift from his previous position that the Central Powers would never make peace separately. During the evening, Karl met Sixtus in Laxenburg and gave him a letter confirming his acceptance of French demands regarding Alsace and Lorraine, and agreement to restore independence to Belgium and Serbia, though the latter was contingent upon the Serbs ceasing their support for any groups attempting to undermine the Dual Monarchy. The matter of Constantinople was deferred until the outcome of the Russian Revolution became clear. It was a perilous moment: unlike the previous letter that Sixtus destroyed, this was intended to be passed to the French, concrete evidence that Austria-Hungary was exploring peace talks without consulting its powerful ally. All would be well if the desired outcome was achieved; if not, it represented a dangerous hostage to fortune.

Sixtus returned to Paris and met the French president, who in turn sent an envoy to meet David Lloyd George, the British prime minister, in Folkestone. Lloyd George was informed of the developments and asked to keep them strictly secret. Both during the Folkestone meeting and at a subsequent discussion in Paris, the question of when, or whether, to inform the Italians was discussed. The British and French were concerned that Italy had been the source of serious leaks in the past, and that Germany had to be kept in the dark about the issue for as long as possible. There was also the risk that even if the Italians did not leak information to the Germans, they might do so to the Russians – and if the Russians were to learn that Britain and France were contemplating a separate peace with Austria-Hungary, then Russia might be tempted to secure a separate peace with Germany. More importantly, Poincaré made clear that, regardless of the intentions of Karl and Czernin to put pressure on Germany to accept reasonable peace terms, the French position was that there was no question of peace with Germany: only the complete defeat of France's enemy was acceptable. In addition to the territories that had been demanded, including those lost in 1815, France intended to press for substantial financial reparations. Aware that the turmoil in Russia would allow the Central Powers the opportunity to send substantial forces west, Poincaré was in favour of pushing Emperor Karl as hard as possible to try to isolate Germany, and concluded by stressing once more:

> It is certain that for us, the French and English, there can be no question of peace with Germany; the sole purpose of the current negotiations is to isolate Germany so that it can then be completely smashed.[140]

Unaware that the French had no intention of agreeing peace with Germany, Czernin persuaded Karl that the time was right to approach the Germans to open discussions. Inevitably, the issue of Alsace and Lorraine immediately raised the hackles of the Germans; Bethmann-Hollweg protested angrily that the Dual Monarchy had steadfastly refused to concede territory to Italy to prevent the Italians from entering the war, and even now was not prepared to offer more than minimal concessions, whereas Germany was being asked to concede all of Alsace and Lorraine, and the additional territories on the left bank of the Rhine.[141] Anticipating this, Czernin had prepared a fallback position. If Germany would agree to concede the territories demanded by the French, Austria would allow its Galician territory to be included in the new Polish state, which in turn would be 'attached to Germany' in some binding manner while still remaining independent. Czernin noted that the offer was neither rejected nor accepted, and that Kaiser Wilhelm and Bethmann-Hollweg asked for time to consider the proposal.[142]

Czernin now drew up a most prescient summary of the situation for Emperor Karl, with the expectation that it would be handed on to the kaiser, thus putting pressure on him to accept the proposals:

> It is quite obvious that our military strength is coming to an end …
>
> I allude … to the decrease in raw materials for the production of munitions, to the thoroughly exhausted human material, and, above all, to the dull despair that pervades all classes owing to under-nourishment and renders impossible any further endurance of the sufferings from the war.
>
> Though I trust we shall succeed in holding out during the next few months and carry out a successful defence, I am nevertheless quite convinced that another winter campaign would be absolutely out of the question; in other words, that in the late summer or in the autumn an end must be put to the war at all costs.

Without a doubt, it will be most important to begin peace negotiations at a moment when the enemy has not yet grasped the fact of our waning strength …

I cannot here ignore the subject on which lies the crux of the whole argument. That is, the danger of revolution which is rising on the horizon of all Europe … Five monarchs have been dethroned in this war, and the amazing facility with which the strongest monarchy in the world was overthrown may help to make us feel anxious … Let it not be said that in Germany or Austria-Hungary the conditions are different; let it not be contested that the firmly rooted monarchist tendencies in Berlin and Vienna exclude the possibility of such an event. This war has opened a new era in the history of the world. It is without example and without precedent. The world is no longer what it was three years ago …

Your Majesty has seen the secret reports from the governor of the town. Two things are obvious. The Russian Revolution affects our Slavs more than it does the Germans, and the responsibility for the continuation of the war is a far greater one for the monarch whose country is united only through the dynasty than for the one where the people themselves are fighting for their national independence. Your Majesty knows that the burden laid upon the population has assumed proportions that are unbearable; your Majesty knows that the bow is strained to such a point that any day it may be expected to snap. But should serious disturbances occur, either here or in Germany, it will be impossible to conceal the fact from the Entente, and from that moment all further efforts to secure peace will be defeated.

I do not think the internal situation in Germany is widely different from what it is here. I am only afraid that the military circles in Berlin are deceiving themselves in certain matters …

I am firmly persuaded that, if Germany were to attempt to embark on another winter campaign, there would be an upheaval in the interior of the country … If the monarchs of the Central Powers are not able to conclude peace within the next few months, it will be done for them by their people, and then will the tide of revolution sweep away all that for which our sons and brothers fought and died …

Germany places great hopes on the U-boat warfare. I consider such hopes are deceptive. I do not for a moment disparage the fabulous deeds of the German sea heroes; I admit admiringly that the tonnage sunk per month is phenomenal, but I assert that the success anticipated and predicted by the Germans has not been achieved …

Your Majesty … owes it to God and to your peoples to make every effort to avert the catastrophe of a collapse of the Monarchy; it is your sacred duty to God and to your peoples to defend those peoples … and your throne with all the means in your power and to your very last breath.[143]

Czernin was not alone in questioning the success of unrestricted submarine warfare. He had received reports from the ambassador in Madrid that Spanish officers returning home from London reported food shortages in the wake of the German U-boat campaign, and other reports suggesting that the French public was losing hope of victory, but he was careful to keep a sense of perspective:

> During a war every Minister of Foreign Affairs must attach an important and adequately estimated significance to confidential reports. The hermetic isolation which during the World War divided Europe into two separate worlds made this doubly urgent. But it is inevitable in regard to confidential reports that they must be accepted, for various reasons, with a certain amount of scepticism. Those persons who write and talk … are apt to be deceived … France was tired of war, but how far the leading statesmen were influenced by that condition, not to be compared with our own war-weariness, was not proved.
>
> … After the beginning of the unrestricted U-boat warfare … many grave fears were entertained in England … But it was a question of fears, not deeds. A person who knew how matters stood, and who came to me from a neutral country in the summer of 1917, said: 'If the half only of the fears in England be realised, then the war will be over in the autumn.' But a wide difference existed between London's fears and Berlin's hopes, on the one hand, and subsequent events, on the other.[144]

Despite his scepticism about the German attempts to starve Britain to defeat, Czernin knew that many in Berlin clung to their belief in the U-boat campaign, with the tenacity of men who know that they have few other ways of achieving success. Consequently, after Czernin's summary was passed to the Germans, the response from Bethmann-Hollweg in early May cannot have been a surprise to the Austro-Hungarian foreign minister. The German chancellor commented with satisfaction that, despite being outnumbered, the German Army had repulsed major attacks by the British and French. At the same time, the disarray of the Russian Army had allowed the transfer of substantial forces to the west, and should there be further pressure from Britain, France or Italy, there was scope for further troop reductions on the Eastern Front. Bethmann-Hollweg dismissed Czernin's concerns about raw materials and food shortages, stating that the seizure of Romania in particular would do much to alleviate the problems that had brought Germany and Austria-Hungary to such a low state at the end of 1916. He described the progress of the U-boat campaign in glowing colours, and concluded that whilst he wished to secure a just peace, too hasty an attempt to secure it might be interpreted by the Entente Powers as a sign of weakness.

Given the widespread disdain – even contempt – within German circles with regard to Austria-Hungary, news of Karl's attempts to secure peace can have done nothing to improve matters. The apparent lack of outrage in Berlin can be interpreted in a number of ways. There would have been concern at openly showing the world that the Central Powers were not speaking with one voice, but there was also a view that Austria-Hungary was increasingly irrelevant. After all, there could be no peace until the differences between France and Germany were addressed, and regardless of Karl's views about the justice of the French claims on Alsace and Lorraine, Berlin had no intention whatever of handing over the territories. A far stronger reaction would come the following year, when the entire Sixtus Affair resurfaced. For the moment, after the rebuff from Berlin, Vienna might have abandoned its attempts to negotiate with the Entente, but instead Karl chose to continue. Nevertheless, it would be better to proceed cautiously.

As if to reinforce this, just a few days later Czernin received a letter from Tisza, which seems to have persuaded him to back off from Emperor Karl's previous desire to make haste:

> The varied information received from the enemy countries leaves no doubt that the war is drawing to a close. It is now above all essential to keep a steady nerve and play the game to the end with *sang froid*. Let there be no signs of weakness. It is not from a love of humanity in general that our enemies have become more peacefully inclined, but because they realise that we cannot be crushed.
>
> I beg you no longer to give vent to the sentiments in your report of April 11. A pessimistic tendency evinced now by the leader of our foreign affairs would ruin everything. I know that you are prudent, but I beg you to use your influence so that both His Majesty and his entourage may show a confident front to the world.[145]

The minimum and irreconcilable positions of France and Germany ensured that, ultimately, Karl's peace initiative was doomed. The leadership of both nations had reached the point where the losses suffered by their nations were so great, only the complete defeat of the enemy would make sense of the casualties. Both intended to press for crippling reparations that would leave the other incapable of going to war ever again, and there was no question of any compromise peace. Writing in January 1917, Kaiser Wilhelm informed an American correspondent that he regarded the war as a struggle between two completely incompatible ways of life, characterising the German way as one of 'loyalty, faith, truth and real freedom' and the Entente way as the pursuit of financial gain, lies, and treason. He concluded: 'One must win, the other must perish!'[146] The zero-sum nature of the conflict between France and Germany was therefore sufficient to ensure that the war would continue to the bitter end, but the Italians now added further obstacles to the tentative attempts towards peace. Cautiously, French diplomats had sounded out their Italian counterparts on the question of whether there might be any interest in securing peace with Austria-Hungary, and in mid-April Sydney Sonnino, the Italian foreign minister, stated flatly that there was no possibility of any such peace unless Italy's war aims – the annexation of Trentino and Trieste – were secured; he added that any Italian government that agreed to anything less would survive less than 48 hours before being thrown out of office. With varying degrees of reluctance, the British and French agreed to add Italy's demands to their minimum list of requirements. Lloyd George felt that if Vienna would agree to a separate peace and would make some concessions to Italy, it might be possible to negotiate a reduction in the amount of territory that the Italians were demanding. The French thought otherwise. Sonnino showed not the slightest sign of flexibility, and in such circumstances, it seemed impossible to reach a solution that would be acceptable to Vienna.

On 22 April, Jules Cambon, the French foreign minister, met Sixtus for further talks. He told him:

> No peace proposals can be considered with Austria without taking complete account of the views of the Italian government … conversations in Saint-Jean-de-Maurienne [close to France's border with Italy] have shown that the Italian government is not inclined to abandon any of the conditions that it declared when it entered the war. In such circumstances, there is no room for engaging in any discussion that will not end in certain failure. If at the current moment … the Austrian government calculates that new efforts could be made with a view to a separate peace, it would be appropriate for it to take account of Italian aspirations for Trieste as much as for Trentino.[147]

The nature of the offer to Austria-Hungary was thus shifted considerably. The subject of a separate peace was now explicitly part of what was being discussed, and even this would require sacrifices with regard to Italy that the French must have known would be impossible for Vienna. Sixtus was aware of Lloyd George's view that it might be possible to satisfy Italy with lesser concessions, but when he asked about this, Cambon expressed astonishment; it is inconceivable that the French foreign minister was not aware of the British position, not least because he had been present when Lloyd George made that position clear. The best he could suggest was that if Austria were prepared to accept Italy's demands, the

Entente would compensate Austria by assigning it Silesia from Germany in a post-war settlement. In vain, Sixtus protested about the change in France's position, which previously had been merely to support Italy in holding onto any gains that it had made on the battlefield. He lamented the ongoing loss of life, adding: 'But we cannot sacrifice the entire world in this manner because the Italians are incapable of taking what they wish to have.'[148]

Nevertheless, Sixtus wrote to Emperor Karl to update him on the state of negotiations, pointing out with regard to Italy that, given that France, Britain and Italy now appeared to be of a united position, their views would prevail sooner or later, but circumstances might change. This last hint was probably based upon the difference of views regarding Italy between the French and British, but he must have known that such platitudes could not hide the fact that, whilst it had always been most unlikely that the Entente minimum position would be acceptable to Germany, it was now becoming unacceptable to Austria-Hungary too, due to the position of Italy.

The rival claims to Trentino were in some respects not dissimilar to the dispute over Alsace and Lorraine. Although it had been part of the so-called Kingdom of Italy during the medieval era, the region enjoyed considerable autonomy, variously coming under the control of the French, Spanish and Austrians. It became part of Austria after the Napoleonic Wars, and although some Italian nationalists agitated against Austrian rule as part of the Italian Irredentist Movement of the 19th century, such sentiments were largely limited to urban intellectuals and had little support from the predominantly rural population, most of whom spoke the local German dialect as their first language. By 1917, over 60,000 men from Trentino had been called into the *k.u.k.* Army, fighting with distinction on several fronts and showing no signs of the fragility that bedevilled formations from the Slav parts of the empire. There was widespread doubt whether the entire province would support union with Italy, particularly away from the southern third where a larger percentage spoke Italian; predictably, none of the Entente Powers had the slightest intention of offering any sort of plebiscite, despite their protestations that self-determination should form the cornerstone of any future peace.

The slow pace of diplomacy continued, while men continued to die. April saw the start of a new Entente offensive on the Western Front – British forces attacked at Arras while French forces attempted to break through farther south. Both achieved limited objectives at huge cost, and the failure of the French attacks – known as the Nivelle Offensive – resulted in the dismissal of Henri Nivelle, the French supreme commander, and his replacement by Philippe

Pétain, the 'Lion of Verdun'. Although the Germans succeeded in holding off both assaults, the cost was heavy. The Entente lost over half a million men, the Germans a little less. More seriously, the slaughter of French troops precipitated a series of mutinies amongst front-line units. The strains of the war were showing even amongst the French.

Only on the Eastern Front was there relative calm, though even here there were periodic bombardments; in a further meeting with Sixtus, Erdödy described how the *k.u.k.* Army only made any serious effort if senior officers were visiting the sector, whereas the Germans still put down heavy fire from time to time.

Meanwhile, the exchanges between Sixtus and Erdödy and a subsequent further trip by Sixtus to meet Emperor Karl in early May revealed another surprising fact: the Austro-Hungarians informed Sixtus that an envoy sent from Luigi Cadorna, the Italian commander-in-chief, had approached the German legation in Switzerland, offering peace in exchange for only the Italian-speaking parts of Trentino. The Germans had passed the details on to Vienna. This suggestion, it seemed, had the support of King Victor Emmanuel III, but was made without reference to the Italian government – it was questionable whether it could be enforced. Nevertheless, it indicated growing war-weariness in Italy and concerns that what had happened in Russia might trigger similar events elsewhere, and it seemed to provide a possible – perhaps the only – way of keeping the tentative peace initiative moving. In addition to the possibility of offering Silesia to Austria-Hungary as compensation, there were even speculative suggestions that Italy might be prepared to concede its African colonies of Eritrea and Ethiopia to the Dual Monarchy in return for Trentino and Trieste.

Czernin continued to be peripherally involved in the negotiations. On this occasion, his first contribution was to insist that, if Austria-Hungary was to be offered consolation, it should be by Italy – in the form of its African colonies – rather than a third party. Before he left, he suggested that it was high time for a formal meeting between himself and a diplomat from the Entente so that negotiations could begin in earnest. It was agreed that Karl would write a letter stating the empire's case with regard to Italy, and on receipt of an acceptable reply, both sides would send plenipotentiaries to a formal meeting in Switzerland. This meeting concluded with Karl pledging that, if Germany were not prepared to accept the terms on offer, Austria-Hungary would be obliged to proceed alone. All parties agreed that, were this to happen, Bulgaria and Turkey would almost certainly abandon their alliance with Germany, not least because all land contact between Germany and its remaining allies would be lost.[149]

Despite the public declarations on both sides about their determination not to make peace in isolation, there was now clear evidence everywhere that several combatants – Austria-Hungary, Italy, and Russia – were prepared to do precisely that. Worried that their unity might splinter, the leading Entente Powers – France and Britain – began to feel a sense of urgency; unless they could secure a separate peace with Austria-Hungary, thus isolating Germany, there was a danger that Russia would leave the war entirely and Italy might agree its own terms with the Central Powers. If this were to happen, the outcome would be far less desirable – far from being isolated, Germany would find itself with its alliances intact and would be able to concentrate its strength against the French. In Paris, there was growing concern that several notable politicians in London, including Andrew Bonar Law, the leader of the Conservative Party and Chancellor of the Exchequer in Lloyd George's coalition government, were publicly calling for a peace without annexations or reparations; by this stage, France was determined to extract major financial compensation from Germany as well as securing control of the left bank of the Rhine, both aims of course being contrary to the principle of peace without annexations or reparations.

There was also growing uneasiness at the relationship between London and Paris on the one hand and Rome on the other. The senior Entente Powers were aware that they were effectively dealing with Austria-Hungary without the knowledge of their ally, and were even making tentative decisions about Italy's possible war gains in a somewhat high-handed manner; they had also learned from Erdödy that at least some elements of the Italian leadership had made an independent approach to the Central Powers to explore possible peace terms. In a belated attempt to bring their affairs into order, Lloyd George proposed a conference consisting of the heads of state of the three powers – King George V, President Poincaré and King Victor Emmanuel III – who would be accompanied by their prime ministers. At such a conference, all parties would be invited to 'come clean' and to state their positions clearly.

On 1 June, Sixtus spoke again to Lloyd George, who advised him that he had sent a telegram to Sonnino suggesting a meeting, but the Italian prime minister had replied 'evasively', claiming that he could see no reason for such a meeting.[150] The reasons for this were not clear, but it is likely that the different factions within Italy had become aware of each other's positions, and until these different positions had been resolved, they were not prepared to commit to a meeting in which they might need to make definitive statements. To the alarm of Sixtus and those with whom he continued to discuss possibilities in London and Paris, the Italian government issued a declaration that effectively increased its war aims: Rome now demanded that in addition to seizing many of the islands along the east coast of the Adriatic Sea, Albania should become an Italian protectorate, effectively turning the sea into an Italian lake. There had already been discussions with Austria about including Albanian territory in a future Serb state – needless to say, without any attempt to consider the preferences of the Albanians – and there was also the question of the effect that Italian control of Albania would have upon the attitude of Greece.

It was not until 24 July that the British, French and Italian heads of state met in Paris; Russia was represented by its ambassador. In the meantime, Czernin had sent the diplomat Nikolaus Graf Revertera von Salandra to the Austro-Hungarian diplomatic mission in Berne to try to facilitate negotiations. He repeatedly requested clarification from the Entente Powers about their position, largely in vain. The problem for the British and French was that they had made extensive promises to Italy in the secret Treaty of London in 1915, which was the basis for Italian involvement in the war: large parts of the Tyrol and the Adriatic, including Trieste; the reduction of Albania to an Italian protectorate; parts of German colonies in Asia and Africa; and, should the Ottoman Empire be broken up, Italy would gain a segment of the south coast of Turkey.[151] All of these commitments predated the initiative started by the United States towards a peace without annexations or reparations, and the Italians regarded it as completely binding – much as the French and Germans regarded compromises as dishonouring the memories of the millions of men they had lost, the same applied to the Italians, whose casualties in their futile assaults along the River Isonzo were just as heavy.

Karl's desire for peace was driven by a combination of a sense of hopelessness about the war – victory seemed to be out of reach, and even if it were achieved, the Austro-Hungarian Empire would be left as Germany's inferior – and a desire to allow attention to be concentrated upon the empire's internal ethnic problems before they tore it apart. Germany had no such internal separatist concerns, but despite the unrestricted submarine campaign there were widespread doubts that victory could be achieved. The Social Democratic Party split after the mainstream tried to muzzle the left wing of the party by colluding with the authorities and having much of the left-wing leadership conscripted into the army; until now, German political parties had respected the kaiser's calls at the beginning of the war for internal unity, but the new left-wing grouping, the *Unabhängige Sozialdemokratische Partei Deutschlands* ('Independent Social Democratic Party of Germany' or USPD), the extreme left of which included the revolutionaries who called themselves the Spartakists, overtly turned its back on the war. As the Russian Revolution broke out, this new group rapidly attracted membership, and the party played a major role in widespread strikes in Germany in April 1917 over bread shortages. This and other strikes left the military authorities increasingly angry and minded to use force to suppress dissent; they interpreted the unrest as signs of agitation by foreign agents or internal traitors, rather than signs of growing strains within Germany itself, as a document circulated in the Prussian Interior Ministry during the summer suggested:

> Simultaneous downing of tools in industrial complexes far removed from each other, sometimes on a particular signal, streams of demonstrators coming together at a clearly pre-arranged point, the putting forward almost everywhere of identical demands, in the case of threatened police intervention almost everywhere women, youths and children to the fore … points to uniform intentions.
>
> All these circumstances leave little doubt that we have faced demonstrations and riots painstakingly spread through arrangement passed from mouth to mouth. They were not simply spontaneous expressions of uproar … but in part are to be attributed to the secret agitation of unscrupulous rabble-rousers, possibly to be found in the ranks of the supporters of radical Social Democracy, or possibly agents in the pay of our enemy or their henchmen.[152]

In July 1917, a loose grouping of the Social Democrats and others who were tiring of the war resulted in the Reichstag passing a resolution calling for peace without annexation or reparations:

> The Reichstag strives for a peace of understanding and lasting reconciliation between nations. Forcible annexations and political, economic or financial sanctions are not compatible with such a peace. The Reichstag rejects all plans that create economic barriers or turn nations into enemies after the war … Only the freedom to trade will prepare the way for peaceful cooperation between nations.[153]

The military – and the kaiser – had no intention whatever of acting on this resolution, but it gave Hindenburg and Ludendorff the opportunity to demand the removal of Chancellor Bethmann-Hollweg, on the grounds that he was no longer able to control the Reichstag. The chancellor was forced to resign, and, at the instigation of the military leadership, Kaiser Wilhelm appointed Georg Michaelis, who had been head of the Prussian *Reichsgetreidestelle* ('Reich Grain Office') since 1915; he was widely regarded as little more than an administrator, firmly under the influence of Hindenburg and Ludendorff. His tenure of office proved to be short-lived, and the Reichstag successfully demanded his resignation in the autumn of 1917. His successor, the Bavarian Georg Graf von Hertling, had in fact been offered the post when Bethmann-Hollweg was dismissed; he too was a firm adherent to the military 'victory at all costs' movement, and showed even greater subservience to Hindenburg and Ludendorff than Michaelis.

Whatever the differences of the Entente Powers and the internal pressures within both Austria-Hungary and Germany for peace, any possibility of securing a negotiated peace, or of a separate peace that would have broken up the Central Powers, disappeared as the summer of 1917 wore on. Due to their prior promises to Italy – made without any reference to the people in the regions involved – the Entente Powers were unable to agree a set of terms that would be acceptable to Austria-Hungary, and for the moment the German military leadership was too strong for any peace movement to prevail.

It is difficult to assess the sincerity of all parties in the tentative attempts to start peace negotiations. There can be little doubt that Emperor Karl believed that he was acting in the best interests of his empire, and that he tried to maintain a principled position with regard to Germany – he would consider a separate peace only if Germany proved to be intransigent. The French seem to have increased their requirements with regard to Alsace, Lorraine and the rest of the left bank of the Rhine during Sixtus' shuttle diplomacy, but this may merely reflect increasing clarity of their intentions. The biggest problem for the Entente was that Italy had clearly been promised a great deal in return for entering the war, and Rome had no intention of accepting anything less, even though its armies had failed to make the expected conquests. Just as the French demands were far beyond anything that Germany might be prepared to consider, so the Italian demands ensured that Vienna could not accept what was going to be offered. Ribot, the French foreign minister, attempted to claim that the refusal of Austria-Hungary to agree terms that would satisfy Italy guaranteed the collapse of the tentative peace process, but this ignores the fact that the initial demands submitted via Sixtus made no mention of Italy, and that at that time, Vienna was not aware of the detailed promises made by Britain and France to Italy in the Treaty of Rome.[154] Czernin's summary is as accurate as any:

> Taking it all together, the real historical truth concerning the peace movement is that, in general, neither the Entente nor the ruling, all-powerful military party in Germany wished for a peace of understanding. They both wished to be victorious and to enforce a peace of violence on the defeated adversary. The leading men in

> Germany – Ludendorff above all – never had a genuine intention of releasing Belgium in an economic and political sense; neither would they agree to any sacrifices. They wished to conquer in the east and the west, and their arbitrary tendencies counteracted the pacifist leaning of the Entente as soon as there were the slightest inclinations of it. On the other hand, the leading men in the Entente – Clemenceau from the first and Lloyd George later – were firmly resolved to crush Germany, and therefore profited by the continuous German threats to suppress all pacifist movements in their own countries, always ready to prove that a peace of understanding with Berlin would be a 'pact between the fox and the geese'.
>
> Thanks to the attitude of the leading ministers in Germany, the Entente was fully persuaded that an understanding with Germany was quite out of the question, and insisted obstinately on peace terms which could not be affected by a Germany still unbeaten. This closes the *circulus vitiosus* which paralysed all negotiating activities.
>
> *We* were wedged in between these two movements and unable to strike out for ourselves, because the Entente, bound by its promises to its allies, had already disposed of us by the Treaty of London and the undertakings to Romania and Serbia. We therefore *could* not exercise extreme pressure on Germany, as we were unable to effect the annulment of these treaties.[155]

Instead all parties turned back to the war. The Germans continued to cling to their hopes of bringing the war to an early finish via the U-boat campaign, before the industrial and numerical power of the United States irrevocably turned the tide in favour of the Entente; the British and French were prepared to wait for their ally to train its new armies and bring them to Europe; and Austria-Hungary was forced to accept that, despite Karl's honest desire to achieve an honourable peace for his empire, such a peace was unattainable. The stalemate in the west continued, and it was only on the Eastern Front that any significant change seemed possible in the immediate future.

CHAPTER 5

KERENSKY'S OFFENSIVE BEGINS

At the beginning of the year, the Russians had informed their Entente partners that they would attack in strength in May. If the momentous events of February and March had not taken place, the army might have been ready for another bloody assault that would have left tens of thousands dead for little or no gain; instead, Russia and its army went through the huge turmoil of the revolution and its aftermath. In many parts of the front, a combination of war-weariness, revolutionary agitation, and clever German propaganda effectively destroyed the cohesion and will to fight of the Russian formations in the front line, and as the summer campaign season approached, it was highly questionable whether the army would be able to make the huge effort and sacrifice that a major assault entailed.

The task of restoring morale fell to Kerensky, who toured the front line energetically with a view to launching a major attack in midsummer. All of the skills that had made him such a potent orator in Petrograd were now put to use, and soldiers everywhere listened to him with rapt attention. Even had he been alone in seeking to influence the rank and file, it is barely conceivable that order could have been restored, and the army might have been motivated to make the huge efforts that were needed. Unfortunately, the liberties announced in Petrograd – compounded by the untidy and imprecise division of power between the Provisional Government and the Soviet – ensured that the same influences that had wrecked cohesion during the weeks after the revolution repeatedly undermined Kerensky's efforts, as Denikin later described:

> [There was] a torrent of newspapers, appeals, resolutions, orders, from some unknown authority, and with them a whole series of new ideas, which the soldier

masses were unable to digest and assimilate. New people appeared, with a new speech, so fascinating and promising, liberating the soldiers from obedience and inspiring hope that they would be saved from deadly danger immediately. When one regimental commander naively enquired whether these people might not be tried by field court-martial and shot, his telegram, after passing through all official stages, called forth the reply from Petrograd that these people were inviolable, and had been sent by the Soviet to the troops for the very purpose of explaining to them the true meaning of current events.

... True, the officers strove to persuade the men not to believe the 'new word' and to do their duty. But from the very beginning the Soviets had declared the officers to be the foes of the Revolution; in many towns they had been subjected to cruel torture and death, and this with impunity.

... Perhaps, however, it might have been possible to combat all this verbal ocean of lies and hypocrisy which flowed from Petrograd and from the local Soviets and was echoed by the local demagogues had it not been for a circumstance which paralysed all the efforts of the commanders – the animal feeling of self-preservation which had flooded the whole mass of the soldiers. This feeling had always existed. But it had been kept under and restrained by examples of duty fulfilled, by flashes of national self-consciousness, by shame, fear and pressure. When all these elements had disappeared, when for the soothing of a drowsy conscience there was a whole arsenal of new conceptions, which justified the care for one's own hide and furnished it with an ideal basis, then the army could exist no longer.[156]

To some extent, Kerensky had only himself to blame. In May, shortly after becoming minister for war, he issued Order Number Eight, entitled 'The Declaration of Soldiers' Rights'. This proclaimed that all servicemen enjoyed the rights of citizens, though it obliged every soldier 'to guide his conduct strictly according to the demands of military duty and military discipline'. Saluting was abolished, and men in the military were granted freedom to belong to any political, national or religious organisation they chose, and could express their views openly when off duty.[157] Whilst some of this – particularly the abolition of restrictions on certain religious groups – was eminently sensible, much was simply incompatible with maintaining order and discipline in the army during wartime. Shortly after, the Soviet issued its own proclamation:

Comrade Soldiers!

For two months we have been waiting for this day when the rights which we attained by revolutionary means have received the force of law ...

> The revolution has made everyone equal: now, by law, the soldier has become a citizen.
>
> … The 12th point of The Declaration of Soldiers' Rights says that the old requirement of giving a salute no longer exists.
>
> Henceforth the soldier-citizen has freed himself of servile salutation and, as an equal, can freely greet whomever he pleases.
>
> Long live the free, conscious citizen-soldier. May the united and strong free people's army live and grow stronger.
>
> The discipline of the revolutionary army will exist through popular enthusiasm and through the awareness of duty to a free country, and not through compulsory salutes.
>
> We, soldiers, will be able to prove that the free army of citizen-soldiers is much stronger than the army of the old regime.[158]

This proclamation came in response to a direct request from Kerensky; it had been his hope that the Soviet would advise soldiers to continue to salute officers voluntarily, but the Soviet stopped far short of that. Emboldened by the revolutionary literature that now flooded the front-line formations, many men now took advantage of the new rules allowing freedom of expression when off duty to undermine the exhortations of Kerensky and others to prepare once again for combat, as Brusilov described in his memoirs: 'The rank and file welcomed him enthusiastically, promised him everything he could have wanted, and then broke every one of their promises.'[159]

Regardless of the agitation of revolutionaries, the entire Russian nation – military and civilian – was sick of war. Towns and villages hundreds of miles from the frontier with Germany and the Austro-Hungarian Empire were mourning their dead, and the plight of those who laboured so hard in the industrial centres like Petrograd, Moscow and Riga had swept away the Romanov regime. It was perhaps a little unrealistic to believe that people who had endured so much suffering and so much mismanagement could be inspired merely by a few fiery speeches to resume their will to fight. In an empire with little sense of national consciousness, ordinary people who had come from impoverished backgrounds, and were suddenly promised freedom and equality with the hated landowners and aristocrats of the past, were bound to ask: why were they still being asked to spill their blood in a war that seemed increasingly meaningless?

The Germans had been active in undermining the will of the Russian soldiers to continue the struggle, as Denikin described:

> In a large, open field, as far as the eye can see, run endless lines of trenches, sometimes coming close up to each other, interlacing their barbed wire fences, sometimes running far off and vanishing behind a verdant crest. The sun has risen long ago, but it is still as death in the field. The first to rise are the Germans. In one place and another their figures look out from the trenches; a few come out onto the parapet to hang their clothes, damp after the night, in the sun. A sentry in our front trench opens his sleepy eyes, lazily stretches himself, after looking indifferently at the enemy trenches. A soldier in a dirty shirt, bare-footed with coat slung over his shoulders, cringing under the morning cold, comes out of his trench and plods towards the German positions, where between the lines stands a 'post-box', it contains a new number of the German paper, *The Russian Messenger*, and proposals for barter.
>
> All is still. Not a single gun is to be heard. Last week the Regimental Committee issued a resolution against firing, even against distance firing … When yesterday the commander of a field battery began firing at a new enemy trench, our infantry opened rifle fire on our [artillery] observation post and wounded the telephone operator …
>
> The first company gradually begins to awaken. The trenches are incredibly defiled; in the narrow communication trenches and those of the second line the air is thick and close. The parapet is crumbling away. No one troubles to repair it; no one feels inclined to do so, and there are not enough men in the company. There is a large number of deserters; more than 50 have been allowed to go. Old soldiers have been demobilised, others have gone on leave with the arbitrary permission of the committee …
>
> In the trenches the hours pass slowly and wearily, in dullness and idleness. In one corner men are playing cards, in another a soldier returned from leave is lazily and listlessly telling a story; the air is full of obscene swearing. Someone reads aloud from *The Russian Messenger* the following:
>
> 'The English want the Russians to shed the last drop of their blood for the greater glory of England, who seeks her profit in everything … Dear soldiers, you must know that Russia would have concluded peace long ago had not England prevented her … We must turn away from her – the Russian people demand it; such is their sacred will.'[160]

Denikin went on to describe the attempts of the company commander to get the men to do routine tasks such as repair the parapet; the troops listened to him patiently and without rancour, but refused to do the work that he asked of them – their committee had voted against making any attacks, and anything that improved their positions was interpreted as preparing for such an attack.

Desertion was a huge problem for many formations. Some men who were allowed home on leave, or who were convalescing from wounds, chose not to return to their units, while others simply left the front line and began to make their way home. Nikolai Nikolayevich Sukhanov, a Menshevik politician, described what had become a daily occurrence:

> A huge flood of soldiers took off for home without any sort of permission whatsoever. They clogged all the railroads, terrorised the authorities, threw passengers off the trains, threatened the entire transport system, and, in general, created a civic disaster.[161]

Alfred Knox travelled to Southwest Front at the end of May to witness at first hand the preparations for the coming assault, and made similar observations:

> Appearances at Kiev and on the railway did not promise well for the coming offensive. The station at Kiev was constantly full of men who should have been at the front. Permission had been given for 5% of the rank and file up to 40 years of age and for 15% of men of 40 to 43 to go on leave every three weeks. Very many more than the percentage allowed left the front, and few returned. The roofs of carriages as far as Kiev were crowded with soldiers, but when we turned west from Kiev the train was comparatively empty.[162]

But while much of the army was utterly disaffected, some showed a remarkable sense of patriotism. Maria Leontievna Bochkareva was a Siberian woman who had volunteered for front-line service, finally persuading the authorities to allow her to join V Corps in 1915. She fought with distinction and was wounded several times, and was in Petrograd when the revolution erupted. She appealed personally to the Duma for it to restore discipline in the army, and she suggested the creation of *Batalanov Smerti Zhenshchin*, or 'Women's Battalions of Death'. These units would then be deployed alongside the men and would shame them into performing better:

> I was told that my idea was sound, but that I needed to report to the supreme commander, Brusilov, and should consult him. Along with Rodzianko, I went to Brusilov's *Stavka* … In his office, he told me that my hope was to create the first women's battalion in the world. Would it not risk disgracing Russian women? I told Brusilov that … if he gave me full authority, I would vouch that my battalion

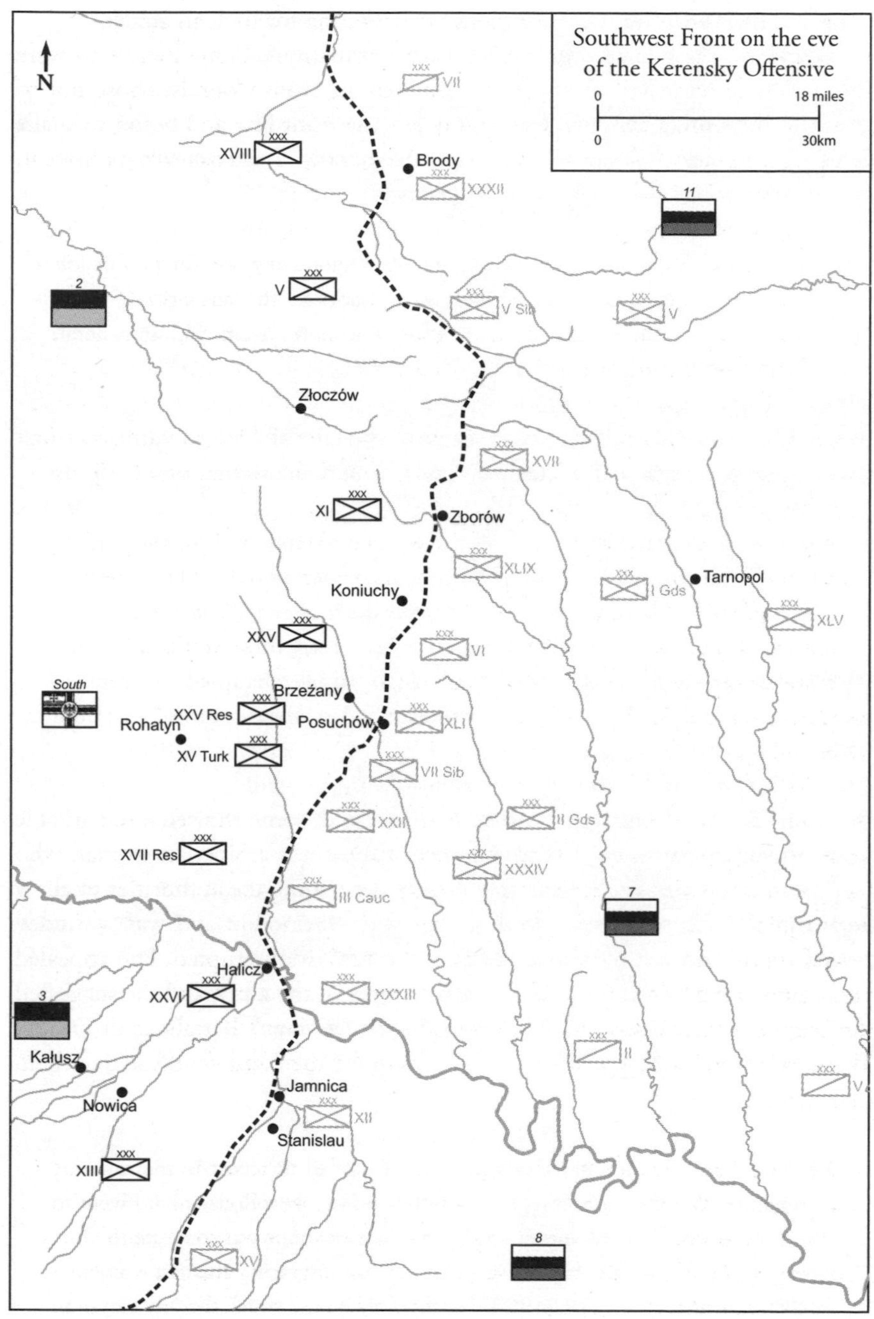
Southwest Front on the eve
of the Kerensky Offensive
0
18 miles
0
30km
N
XVIII
Brody
XXXII
VII
11
2
V
V Sib
V
Złoczów
XVII
XI
Zborów
XLIX
Koniuchy
Tarnopol
I Gds
XLV
XXV
VI
South
Brzeżany
XXV Res
Rohatyn
Posuchów
XLI
XV Turk
VII Sib
XXII
II Gds
XVII Res
XXXIV
III Cauc
7
Halicz
XXVI
XXXIII
3
Kałusz
II
Nowica
Jamnica
XII
V
Stanislau
XIII
XV
8

> would not shame Russia ... Brusilov told me that he trusted me and would do his best to try to help in the formation of a female volunteer battalion.[163]

After the showdown between senior army figures and the politicians in Petrograd, Brusilov had been appointed supreme commander. With some reservations, Brusilov approved the creation of Bochkareva's Battalion of Death and it duly entered front-line service in July. He also created special shock battalions from other groups of volunteers, including many from the garrisons of cities like Moscow and Petrograd that had been active in the revolution, though it remained to be seen whether their enthusiasm would survive the reality of life in the front line. Rather prosaically, many of these Battalions of Death were deployed first not against the enemy, but to round up stragglers and deserters. On occasion, the numbers of men that they rounded up were spectacular; one battalion detained 12,000 – almost sufficient to create an infantry battalion – on a single night near Volochisk in the western part of the Ukraine, simply by blocking a major road running east from the front line.[164] Their efforts were sorely needed. According to Nikolai Nikolayevich Dukhonin, the chief of staff of Southwest Front, the front-line formations of his armies were 200,000 men short of their establishment strength, and replacement formations numbered only 60,000; by contrast, the great offensive of 1916 had seen the front-line forces start at establishment strength, with 200,000 reserves in waiting.[165] Inevitably, this meant that any offensive could not be sustained for long in a war in which casualties exceeding 100,000 in just a few days were commonplace on all fronts.

The most southern formation of Southwest Front was Eighth Army, now commanded by Kornilov. Perhaps because of the distance from Petrograd, there had been less disruption of discipline by visiting politicians, but the effect of newspapers such as *Pravda* continued to undermine the authority of army commanders. Knox noted that literacy amongst the rank and file was barely 20 per cent, and having grown up in an era of strict censorship, those who could read tended to regard everything they read as being true. The acerbic Knox wrote in his diary on 14 June:

> What can the Russian soldier know of 'Peace without annexations and without contributions' – the formula produced in Berlin for his special misleading? Many of them think that 'Anneksiya' and 'Contributsiya' are two towns, and one of them, when asked if he understood the motto, said that he did not know where 'Anneksiya' was, but that 'Contributsiya' was 'somewhere in Turkey!' He thought of Constantinople![166]

Knox must have known that 'peace without annexations or reparations' was not an invention of Germany, even though German propaganda had made extensive use of the phrase.

Even while the army struggled to prepare itself for the coming offensive, changes continued in command. Brusilov's appointment as commander-in-chief in place of Alexeyev was announced a day after Kerensky had met Alexeyev, when no mention of the imminent change had been made. When he learned of his dismissal, Alexeyev bitterly said to Denikin, 'The cads! They have dismissed me like a servant without notice!'[167] Like Knox, Denikin had little time for Brusilov, and had in any case learned that he too was about to be moved from his post as chief of the general staff; his replacement was Alexander Sergeyevich Lukomsky. Gurko had been appointed commander of West Front, but his outspoken criticism of the Provisional Government, and in particular the telegram that he sent to Petrograd stating that he could not be responsible for his armies after Kerensky's declaration of rights for soldiers led to his dismissal from this post on 8 June. Gurko had no intention of going quietly, and made a forthright attack on the Provisional Government in his parting words to his staff:

> I said that I was accused of the sharp manner in which I expressed my opinion to the Provisional Government; when I wanted to resign, I drew attention to the fact that I never had two languages, one for my subordinates and another for my chiefs, as also I did not have two languages, one for gentlemen – I pointed to those present – and another for lackeys – pointing afar. I did not, I said, belong to the class of invertebrate beings; that I never bent my back before the tsars, so naturally I would not bend before these new autocrats. Never before had I addressed such an attentive audience, or one which so eagerly listened to every word. A great effort of will was required to continue my speech calmly to the end. It was the cry of the troubled soul, into it penetrated the whole bitterness of what was passing in the land, in it one could hear the anxiety for the near future.
>
> ... It was not the usual farewell before taking a new post, which had happened to me more than once, but it was a farewell to all the past, to all that was dear to me, to all to which I had given over 30 years of my life and service. It was a farewell with the possibility, at least in the near future, of giving active help to my country in the moment when she needed every conscientious worker.[168]

Denikin regarded two of his three subordinate armies as effectively useless, due to the influence of soldiers' committees and the weakness of the army commanders.

When he toured the front line, he saw for himself how much the army had disintegrated:

> Most of the units … were more akin to a devastated ants' nest than to an organised unit, although they had retained a semblance of discipline and drill. After the review I walked down the ranks and spoke to the soldiers. I was deeply depressed by their new mental attitude. Their speeches were nought but endless complaints, suspicions and grievances against everyone and everything … I witnessed scenes which I shall not forget till my last hour. In one of the army corps I asked to be shown the worst unit … We drove up to a huge crowd of unarmed men who were standing, sitting, wandering about the plain behind the village. Having sold their clothes for cash or for drink, they were dressed in rags, bare-footed, ragged, unkempt, and seemed to have reached the utmost limit of physical degradation. I was met by the divisional commander, whose lower lip trembled, and by a regimental commander who had the face of a condemned man. Nobody gave the order 'Attention!' and none of the soldiers rose. The nearest ranks moved towards our motorcars. My first impulse was to curse the regiment and turn back. But that might have been interpreted as cowardice, so I went into the thick of the crowd. I stayed there for about an hour … They were like men possessed, their brain dimmed, their speech stubborn and completely lacking logic or common-sense … We tried to speak, but the replies were angry and stupid. I remember that my feelings of indignation as an old soldier receded to the background and I merely felt infinitely sorry for these uncouth, illiterate Russians to whom little was given and of whom little will, therefore, be asked.
>
> … One of the army corps commanders led his troops with a firm hand, but experienced strong pressure from the army organisations; another was afraid to visit his troops. I found the third in a state of complete collapse and in tears because someone had passed a vote of censure upon him: 'And this after forty years' service! I loved the men and they loved me, but now they have dishonoured me, and I cannot serve any longer!' I had to allow him to retire. In the next room a young divisional commander was already in secret consultations with members of the committee, who immediately requested me, in a most peremptory fashion, to appoint the young general to the command of the army corps.[169]

Having spent the first weeks of the post-revolutionary period putting their propaganda strategy to work, the Central Powers considered what further steps they should take. Arthur Arz, the chief of the Austro-Hungarian general staff, wished to move from local arrangements to a formal ceasefire along the entire front; once this had been in force for 48 hours, negotiations could commence on a formal end to hostilities. Hindenburg's response was lukewarm at best; he was not convinced that the terms of a ceasefire could be agreed between Germany, Austria-Hungary, Bulgaria and Turkey, and he added that Germany would not accept any attempt by Russia to insist on both sides freezing troop movements during peace negotiations. In the meantime, worn-out formations from the Western and Italian Fronts were transferred to the Eastern Front, and the comparatively strong formations they replaced were sent west.

On 12 May, the three commanders of the armies of the Central Powers on the Eastern Front – Prince Leopold of Bavaria at *Ober Ost*, Archduke Joseph, and August von Mackensen in Romania – sent a radio message to their Russian counterparts calling for a ceasefire. Numerous small groups were sent across the front line in an attempt to create local ceasefires; whilst some were greeted cordially and with enthusiasm, others came under fire, and some were taken prisoner. One such emissary was allowed to proceed to the headquarters of the Russian Ninth Army and spoke briefly to Georgi Vladimirovich Stupin, the commander. He reported back to his superiors that Stupin had turned down the suggestion of a local ceasefire, on the grounds that such a decision rested with higher authorities rather than with local officers and soldiers.[170] Overall, the outcomes were largely as might have been expected: the farther north the contact, the more likely the Russians were to agree a ceasefire. Nearly all of Mackensen's emissaries came under fire, but a total of 160 of Russia's 240 divisions were contacted. Of these, 38 assured their visitors that they had decided never to attack again.[171]

Local commanders did what they could to prevent fraternisation, sometimes ordering their artillery to fire on sectors where they believed Russian and German soldiers were meeting in no man's land.[172] Kerensky and Prince Lvov repeatedly denounced fraternisation, but their attempts were undermined by contradictory messages emerging from Bolshevik circles. Writing in *Pravda* in April, Lenin gave a different message to that of the Provisional Government:

> The capitalists either poke fun at fraternisation, or wrathfully attack it with lies and calumny, reducing it all to 'deception' practised by the Germans upon the Russians …
>
> … It is obvious that fraternisation is a road to peace. It is obvious that this road leads not to the capitalist governments, not to harmony with them, but, on the contrary, it leads against them. It is obvious that this road develops, strengthens, consolidates the feeling of brotherly confidence among the workers of various

countries. It is obvious that this road is beginning to undermine the damnable discipline of the barrack prisons, the discipline requiring the absolute submission of soldiers to 'their' officers and generals, to their capitalists (for officers and generals are for the most part either members of the capitalist class or defenders of its interests). It is obvious that fraternisation is the revolutionary initiative of the *masses*, that it is the awakening of the conscience, the mind, the courage of the oppressed classes...

Long live fraternisation![173]

Whilst Lenin and other Bolsheviks might have regarded fraternisation as a means of undermining the traditional loyalties of armies of all nations, the reality was that any modest impact on the armies of the Central Powers was dwarfed by the impact on the Russian Army. Other voices within the Soviet spoke against the position of the Bolsheviks through the pages of *Izvestia* and other publications:

Remember, comrades, that at the front, in the trenches, you are now standing guard over Russian freedom. It is not the tsar, or the Protopopovs and the Rasputins, or the rich landowners and capitalists, that you are now staunchly defending. You are defending the Russian Revolution, you are defending your workers and peasants. Then let this defence be worthy of the great cause and the great sacrifices which you have already endured ...

Remember this, comrade soldiers. Having pledged yourselves to defend freedom, do not refuse to take the offensive if the tactical situation should so demand. Russia's freedom and happiness are in your hands.

In defending this freedom, beware of provocation, beware of traps. The fraternisation which is becoming widespread at the front can easily turn into such a trap. Revolutionary troops may fraternise – but with whom? With an army that is equally revolutionary, that is equally determined to die for peace and freedom. But the German and Austro-Hungarian Army is not such an army yet, regardless of how many conscious and aware individuals it may contain. There is still no revolution over there. There the army still follows Wilhelm and Karl, the landowners and the capitalists, and it aims at seizures of foreign territories, at pillage and violence ...

When you go to fraternise, you go with an open heart, but you are met by an officer ... who comes out of the enemy trenches, dressed in a soldier's uniform.

When you talk sincerely to the enemy, his superiors are photographing the locality. When you stop firing in order to fraternise, artillery is being shifted from one place to another behind the enemy trenches, fortifications are erected and troops are being transferred.

> Comrade soldiers! It is not through fraternisation that you will achieve peace, or through the silent agreements which are concluded at the front by individual companies, battalions, or regiments ... People who are assuring you that fraternisation is the road to peace are leading both you and Russian freedom to destruction. Do not believe them.
>
> ... Sweep aside everything that may bring disintegration into the army or a fall in morale. Your fighting strength serves the cause of peace ...
>
> Comrade soldiers! Workers and peasants of Russia and of the whole world are looking to you with confidence and hope. Soldiers of the revolution, you will prove worthy of this confidence knowing that your combat work serves the cause of peace!
>
> In the name of the happiness and freedom of revolutionary Russia, in the name of the forthcoming brotherhood of nations, you will perform your military duty with unflinching determination.[174]

For the men of Russia's armies, many of whom were illiterate and dependent upon the reading of documents by their more fortunate comrades, the impact of these contradictory messages can be imagined. Faced with a choice between answering the call for further bloodshed and fighting and following Lenin's path to peace through fraternisation, it is unsurprising that so many who had already endured years of war and loss chose the latter. Nevertheless, the hopes of the Central Powers that Russia's front-line armies would either melt away entirely or would initiate a comprehensive ceasefire did not come to fruition. Despite the best efforts of those involved in the propaganda campaign, it became clear that further efforts were not going to yield results. Slowly, as the Russian Army prepared to renew hostilities, fraternisation along the front line died down, even if the willingness of the Russian troops to fight remained questionable.

Nevertheless, an offensive would have to be attempted to satisfy the demands of Russia's Entente partners, though many observers, both within and outside Russia, had concluded that the offensive was likely to fail, and thereafter nothing more could be expected of Russia. Many in Russia hoped that a success similar to that achieved the previous summer by Brusilov might give Russia's armies renewed hope and optimism, and sweep away the defeatist and pacifist influences that were threatening the nation's forces with complete dissolution. There was also a sense of inevitability about where the effort would be made. Given the greater disarray in the armies in the northern half of the Eastern Front, there were good reasons for preferring to make the effort in the south. Even if that had not been the case, it was in the south that the Russians had repeatedly enjoyed their biggest successes, against the armies of the Austro-Hungarian

Empire. The fragility of the *k.u.k.* Army had brought the entire defensive line of the Central Powers close to disaster on more than one occasion, and the only solution had been to stiffen their ranks by inserting German units amongst them in order to prevent wholesale retreats. The troops of the Dual Monarchy had started 1916 at least numerically in good shape: compared to the beginning of the war, the *k.u.k.* Army had an additional 150 infantry battalions, three times as many machine-guns, and twice as much artillery.[175] By the end of the year, the huge losses suffered on the Eastern Front left the army more dependent than ever upon poorly trained replacement drafts, hastily dispatched to face the Russians.

At first, there was huge resentment in the high command of the *k.u.k.* Army about the increasingly overt German dominance in all matters, but by the end of 1916 there could be little doubt of the success of this policy. With varying degrees of enthusiasm, the troops of the Dual Monarchy adopted German training methods, in particular creating *Kampfschulen* ('war schools') near the front line to remedy the poor training of new recruits. Officers and NCOs received training in the new techniques of small-scale 'storm troops', first used with such marked success by Brusilov's troops in their drive towards Lutsk in the summer of 1916. The use of gas and defensive measures in the face of a gas attack were also addressed for the first time, and in an attempt to address the delays with which artillery responded to calls for support from the infantry, light-gun sections were established in every infantry formation, equipped with a mixture of mortars and 37mm guns. Whilst these guns were welcome, they were actually of little use; they lacked the power to destroy established, reinforced defensive positions, and there were constant complaints from the front line about their ineffectiveness, poor design and lack of ammunition. Mortars, too, were a source of contention. For much of 1916, the troops of the *k.u.k.* Army were equipped with small numbers of light mortars with a maximum range of perhaps 650 yards (600m), compared to the heavier weapons of the Russians that had twice the range. Plans were made for the supply of large numbers of light, medium and heavy mortars to improve matters, but it took most of 1916 for production to be increased to an adequate level. Furthermore, priority was given to supplying troops on the Italian Front, leaving those facing the Russians to wait, and when the weapons finally arrived, ammunition supplies were poor. Nevertheless, the result of this process was, in the words of the Austrian official history of the war, a gradual transformation of the 'queen of the battlefield' into a set of small units equipped with a variety of weapons, rather than large formations that specialised in artillery, machine-guns etc. Throughout the winter, these new units were put to use on small-scale operations to give the officers and men experience and confidence in their use; initial reports were promising, with low casualties and modest successes.[176]

At least partly owing to the relative lack of fighting in early 1917, most divisions had raised their strength to between 8,000 and 10,000 men, compared to their establishment of about 12,000. But just as the civil population struggled with constant shortages, there were also worrying deficiencies in the supply of fuel and other materiel – to date, the army had been able to ensure that its food supplies took priority over those of the homeland, but even despite this priority, 1917 saw the beginning of cutbacks. It was clear to all that whilst the *k.u.k.* Army could continue the war deep into 1917, the empire as a whole was approaching the end of its strength.

The great Brusilov Offensive of 1916 had achieved important breakthroughs at Lutsk in the north and Czernowitz in the south, but these came as a result of pressure along a huge stretch of the Eastern Front – crucially, the modest reserves available to the *k.u.k.* Army were directed first one way, then another as the Russian blows fell over several days, and were frequently unable to intervene effectively at either their original locations or at other points as crises arose. As a result of the weakening of the army by the revolution and a catastrophic fall in output from Russia's munitions factories, the new offensive planned for the summer of 1917 would have to be more limited. The objective would be the city of Lemberg (now Lviv), the capital of Austro-Hungarian Galicia and a vital rail hub. The Russian Army had occupied the city in 1914 before Mackensen's great rolling offensive of 1915 recaptured it, and if the Russians could once more secure it, the *k.u.k.* Army would find it difficult to maintain communications and supplies for a significant portion of the Eastern Front. Even such a limited objective would challenge the Russian Army: Lemberg was about 58 miles (93km) to the west of the front line, and the attacking forces would therefore have to advance farther than Brusilov's armies had managed the previous year in far more favourable circumstances.

General Lukomsky, who before he became chief of the general staff was quartermaster-general at *Stavka* and Director of Military Operations, wrote a memorandum in April painting a bleak picture of the state of the Russian Army. There was inadequate food for daily consumption, let alone sufficient to rebuild stockpiles, and consequently the army would have to reduce its manpower and horses, or reduce rations. In any event, it was proving impossible to requisition enough horses to serve the needs of the army. Disruption of the supply of raw materials and the ongoing industrial unrest meant that the supply of both weapons and ammunition was falling, and the chaotic state of the railways prevented the movement both of supplies and troops. The Baltic Fleet had been particularly disrupted by the revolution, with the sailors in Kronstadt briefly declaring their own republic after killing many of their officers; the ships of the fleet could not be expected to defend against any German foray into the Gulf of Finland.[177] At least two months' work would be required before the troops could be expected to carry out any meaningful offensive.

Brusilov had started drawing up plans for the proposed operation while he was still in command of Southwest Front. He intended for the southern flank of Eleventh Army to provide the main thrust, while the northern flank of the same army attempted to advance along the Brody–Lemberg railway on a converging axis. The Special Army to the north, which had borne the brunt of the attempts to rekindle the offensive in the late summer of 1916, would also attack, but with the intention of tying down enemy forces to prevent their redeployment farther south. To the south of Eleventh Army, Seventh and Eighth Armies would also attack, partly to pin down local forces and partly to exploit weaknesses in the Austro-Hungarian defences. This was the policy that had yielded such striking victories the previous summer, but others in the Russian military establishment preferred concentration on narrower axes. Throughout the war, the Russian Army had been hindered by the lack of any clear overall central authority strong enough to exert his will on the various front commanders, and this remained the case after the fall of Tsar Nicholas; even though the intention was to attack in the south, Nikolai Ruzsky, commander of Northern Front until the end of April 1917, demanded substantial reinforcements in case the Germans launched a drive towards Petrograd. Numerically, the forces available to Northern Front were perfectly adequate to beat off any German attack – Ruzsky had 420,000 men compared to 200,000 deployed by the Germans – but this was the sector that had suffered the worst turmoil after the revolution, and it was clear that the true fighting strength of the front-line formations was far below their numerical strength. Consequently, XLII Corps and additional forces from the Caucasian Front were sent to the north, troops that might have made important contributions to the coming offensive towards Lemberg. In addition, I Corps was withdrawn from its position near Lutsk and also dispatched to Northern Front; together with the other reinforcements, it was used to create a new First Army to cover the approaches to Petrograd. There were further reorganisational measures, none of which did anything to improve the fighting power of the Russian Army. Lesh was dismissed from command of Third Army, ostensibly because of the loss of the Toboly bridgehead. His army was disbanded and assigned to Second Army to the north and the Special Army to the south. A new Third Army was created, again in the north, to cover the German lines to the east of Riga.[178]

On 16 June, Gutor issued revised orders for the forthcoming offensive to the armies of Southwest Front. The main effort would be made by Eleventh and Seventh Armies, which would attempt to drive west towards Lemberg. Much in keeping with Brusilov's original plans, the Special Army would try to tie down the enemy by attacking towards Kovel, over ground where so much blood had been spilled for no gain the previous summer, while the forces to the south of the main effort put pressure on the enemy defences to the north of the Carpathian Mountains. The start date for the operation was set as 29 June. Given the tight timetable, there was insufficient time to alter Brusilov's original proposals very much. From his new post as commander-in-chief, Brusilov added attacks by the other fronts to the overall plan. West Front would attack on 16 July, followed two days later by Northern Front; the forces on the Romanian Front would then advance on 22 July. This strategy was aimed to ensure that any reserves that the Central Powers had available would – it was hoped – be transferred from one location to another, only to find a crisis erupting in the very sector they had left. At the same time, Brusilov warned Kerensky that there was no enthusiasm amongst the troops in the front line for an attack. A great deal of work needed to be done if there was to be any hope of success. Kerensky continued his visits to formations both in and behind the front line, exhorting the troops to fight heroically in defence of the revolution, which he told them was threatened by German militarism. When he spoke to the men of II Guards Corps, he was heckled by shouts of 'Bourgeois! Down with the war! Down with everything!'[179]

The offensive plans of the Russians were of course entirely predictable, and their preparations were rapidly detected through a mixture of aerial reconnaissance, wireless intercepts, and information gained from the numerous deserters who continued to cross the front. The reserves available to the German and Austro-Hungarian forces were minimal, largely made up of formations that had suffered heavy losses in the west and had been sent to the quiet Eastern Front for a period of rest and recovery; on the eve of the Russian offensive, the German South Army, commanded by the Bavarian General Felix von Bothmer, had six German and three Austro-Hungarian divisions and a solitary Turkish division with which to defend a front line of 39 miles (65km).

Bothmer's army was one of three armies collectively under the command of the Austro-Hungarian General Eduard von Böhm-Ermolli. In the south was the *k.u.k.* Third Army under the command of Karl Tersztyánsky von Nadas, with XIII and XXVI Corps at its disposal. Next came Bothmer's South Army, consisting of the German XVII Reserve Corps, the Turkish XV Corps, and the *k.u.k.* XXV Corps, and in the north was the *k.u.k.* Second Army under

Böhm-Ermolli's personal command, with XI, V and XVIII Corps. On the eve of the Russian offensive, Bothmer received welcome reinforcements in the form of the German XXV Reserve Corps. The opposing Russian forces were numerically superior, though nobody could be sure how well they would fight. But the forces of the Central Powers did not intend merely to defend against the coming assault. They had already laid plans for a counterthrust into the northern flank of any Russian attack; the greater the initial Russian advance, the better the prospects for this counterthrust. Much of the artillery that would be required for this was currently deployed in Flanders against an expected British attack; it would not reach the Eastern Front until mid-July. However, the German and Austro-Hungarian high commands knew with some certainty when the Russians would attack, and the timing of the arrival of artillery from the west would be perfect, as it would coincide with the end of the first phase of the Russian assault.[180]

Gutor assembled the forces of Southwest Front in their start positions. Numerically, they were strong, but their willingness to fight would be the decisive factor. On a front similar to that defended by Bothmer's South Army with its ten divisions, he had a total of 31 divisions. They had at their disposal some 800 light, 158 medium and 370 heavy guns, though many of these were effectively unserviceable – perhaps a more realistic estimate was 693 light and 337 medium and heavy guns.[181] Eleventh Army's main assault would be led by XVII, XLIX and VI Corps, with I Guards Corps in reserve; additional troops would arrive later in the campaign. Seventh Army's assault was spearheaded by XLI Corps, VII Siberian Corps, XXXIV Corps and the Finnish XXII Corps, with II Guards Corps and II and V Cavalry Corps in reserve. Both armies included new formations made up of men who had been captured from the Central Powers in earlier battles; Eleventh Army had a 'Czechoslovakian Brigade' and Seventh Army had a Polish Division. In a move calculated to create disarray in the ranks of the defenders, the Czechoslovakian Brigade would be attacking men of the *k.u.k.* 19th Infantry Division who were themselves Czechs.[182]

Eleventh Army's artillery preparation began on 29 June. During the day, Austro-Hungarian reconnaissance flights, patrolling almost untroubled over the front, reported that the assembly areas behind the Russian front line were empty – troops had clearly moved forward in preparation for an attack. Slightly to the surprise of the defenders, the only infantry attack of the day came late in the day; a brief probing attack attempted to push into the positions of the *k.u.k.* 54th Infantry Division, but was beaten off with relative ease.

During the following night, men in the front line laboured to repair the damage done by the bombardment. The following morning, the Russian gunners resumed their efforts. Brusilov's great offensive successes of 1916 were preceded by careful reconnaissance and equally careful artillery bombardment that made the most of that reconnaissance; in 1917, preparations were less thorough, though the sheer weight of shelling made a lasting impression on soldiers of both sides. Although many of the artillery positions of the defenders came under fire, it was rarely sustained, and gas attacks proved to be relatively ineffective. The defensive lines of the infantry to the east of Brzeźany were shelled intensely, and defensive artillery added to the thunder and destruction – in contrast to the Russians, aerial reconnaissance by German and Austro-Hungarian pilots had identified the main concentration points for Russian infantry preparing to attack, and these areas came under heavy bombardment. In 1916, numerous shelters had been built for the attacking infantry to gather in comparative safety, but a year later the Russian soldiers had little protection. At least one Russian attack on the German XXV Reserve Corps south of Brzeźany was so badly disrupted by artillery fire that it was abandoned before it even began. Elsewhere, Russian infantry advanced on the defences of the Turkish 20th Infantry Division and the German 16th and 24th Reserve Infantry Divisions. At many locations, they fought their way into the first defensive line, which had been generally reduced from a series of carefully constructed positions to little more than a mass of shell craters. When they attempted to advance farther, they ran into concentrated machine-gun fire and were driven to cover; determined counterattacks then drove them back to their start line.

To the northeast of Brzeźany, the Russians made two attempts to break into the defensive positions, using dense smokescreens for cover. In places the massed infantry managed to force its way through the three lines of trenches that formed the primary position of the defenders and then turned north in an attempt to roll up the front line, penetrating into the village of Posuchów where they were finally brought to a halt. Slightly to the north, the Russians managed to capture part of the front line immediately northeast of Posuchów, triggering furious counterattacks; the fighting raged all afternoon without either side able to gain an advantage.

The Russian Eleventh Army was now commanded by General Ivan Georgevich Erdeli. He started the year as commander of 64th Infantry Division before being appointed to command XVIII Corps in the first wave of reassignments that followed the February Revolution. At the beginning of June, he found himself elevated to commanding Eleventh Army, and his men now attempted to force the seam between Bothmer's South Army and Böhm-Ermolli's Second Army, immediately to the north. The most southerly formation of Eleventh Army was VI Corps; Alfred Knox described its mixed progress.

> VI Corps took the enemy's first three lines of trench in 20 minutes, practically without loss. The village of Koniuchy was occupied by 2nd Finnish Infantry Division, but as liquor was found there, the other divisions of the corps were held back [ostensibly because there were reports that the Austrians intended to leave poisoned alcohol in their trenches, more likely because the Russians did not intend to take any chances with exposing their men to alcohol, poisoned or otherwise]. General Maimayevsky, commander of 4th [Finnish] Infantry Division, marched to the attack at its head.
>
> Progress was, however, much interfered with by the indiscipline and stupidity of the men. The left regiment of 16th Infantry Division had been allotted a passive task. While the artillery preparation was in progress, the division commander was informed by the regimental committee that the men refused to move because only two passages had been prepared for them through the wire, while eight passages had been prepared for the neighbouring regiment. To destroy the wire that worried these men much shell had to be wasted that would have been otherwise used against the enemy's trenches. The extra passages were not required, and the enemy's trenches being insufficiently destroyed the regiment that had raised the objection suffered more heavily than it need have done in the attack.
>
> Further to the right in XLIX Corps, 24th Regiment of 6th Finnish Infantry Division refused to attack, and so exposed 6th and 8th Regiments of 2nd Finnish Infantry Division to heavy counterattacks.[183]

Knox's account is not entirely accurate. There was considerable fighting in the first line of trenches, with the initial Russian attacks being repulsed at first. It was only when the Russians penetrated into Koniuchy and from there turned north and south that the defences were unlocked; as other Russian forces pressed on west from the village, defensive artillery batteries either withdrew or in some locations were blown up to prevent them from falling into Russian hands. Consequently, the heavy defensive artillery fire that had pinned down much of the Russian infantry in their jumping-off positions began to slacken, allowing more Russians to advance. To make matters worse, a 'Ukrainian Legion' and an associated battalion of newly trained storm-troops had been committed in a local counterattack to try to hold back the Russians; the surrender of most of this group suddenly created a gap in the defences that was nearly a mile wide.

These Russian successes occurred at the precise junction of the northern flank of the *k.u.k.* XXV Corps, the most northerly point of Bothmer's South Army, and the southern flank of the *k.u.k.* IX Corps, the most southerly point of Böhm-Ermolli's Second Army. Both corps commanders struggled to bring up their modest reserves to restore the situation, but for IX Corps the movement of troops towards its southern flank proved to be an error. Contrary to Knox's account, 6th Finnish Infantry Division – or at least parts of it – succeeded in penetrating into the defences of the *k.u.k.* 19th Infantry Division, and the forces sent south were hastily recalled. Although the troops who had been driven out of Koniuchy were able to stop the Russians driving farther west, they were too weak on their own to mount a counterattack to recapture the village; they would have to await the arrival of higher-level reinforcements.

These reserves – two regiments of German infantry – struggled forward along dusty roads in the midday heat towards the fighting. Meanwhile, the reinforcements that had spent much of the day marching back and forth returned to 19th Infantry Division's sector during the afternoon, where the defenders were now being levered out of their second line of defences. Gradually, fighting died down with the defensive lines still intact, though badly stretched. As 1 July drew to a close, the Russians could look back with some satisfaction. Contrary to the pessimistic opinions of many, the army could still fight effectively. The attacks by Seventh Army might have failed, but those farther north by Eleventh Army had achieved as much as could have been expected on the first day. In recognition of this, Kerensky telegraphed Prince Lvov from the headquarters of Seventh Army:

> Today has furnished the reply once and for all to the malicious and slanderous attacks on the organisation of the Russian Army, based on democratic principles. I earnestly beg you to sanction urgently, in the name of the free people, my presentation of red revolutionary standards to the regiments which took part in the battle of 1 July.[184]

In reality, Seventh Army's troops had achieved little, with the successes coming farther north. Knox was also accompanying Gutor's forces, and commented that the command post was overcrowded with representatives of the various soldiers' committees who insisted on being present. His account was in stark contradiction to Kerensky's triumphant telegram:

> The watch of the artillery colonel in my observation post was eight minutes slow, and he continued firing at the enemy's trenches after ten o'clock, till notified by one of the batteries that the trenches were already occupied by the Russian infantry.
>
> About 2pm I went back to the headquarters of Seventh Army …
>
> The 74th Infantry Division [immediately to the southeast of Brzeźany] was making no progress and complained of heavy gunfire from its left. The commander

telephoned that many men of this division were streaming to the rear, and ordered that all available delegates [the representatives of the soldiers' committees] were to be sent to hearten the waverers. No doubt Kerensky had suggested the delegates, his universal panacea. He was to see how ineffective they were to stop a panic as compared with the officers whose prestige he had allowed to be undermined.

... General Skoropadsky, commander of XXXIV Corps [to the south of 74th Infantry Division and the forces trying to break into Brzeźany] soon began to call for help. 'Two regiments of 19th Siberian Division had reached the second line of German trench, but the other two regiments could not be brought up owing to the enemy's barrage. The 23rd Infantry Division had three regiments already in line and was suffering much from the German fire. He feared a counterattack. The 153rd Infantry Division had so many men down with the scurvy [more likely dysentery] that only 40 rifles per company were left.' At 4pm he telephoned that he had two German divisions against him, as he had taken prisoners from both the 15th and 24th Reserve Divisions. As a matter of fact, these two German divisions were not only holding up Skoropadsky's four divisions, but also the two divisions of VII Siberian Corps and one division of XLI Corps!

General Skoropadsky proposed that his corps should be relieved that night by II Guards Corps, and the army staff recommended this course on the ground that it was necessary to restore confidence at the outset of the operation.

By 5.30pm XXXIV Corps had retired to its original trenches.

XXII Corps on the left shared the same fate. At first light all three divisions made good progress, and especially 1st Finnish in the centre. The 5th Finnish Division on the right captured two lines of Turkish trench, but retired owing to a counterattack and the other two divisions followed its example.

... Most of the infantry behaved badly. The men were some of them impressed by a supporting artillery fire to which they had been little accustomed, and they went as far as the enemy's trench had been destroyed. They had lost many of their officers and had no incentive to further effort; in fact, they knew that further progress would be attended by risk and they knew they could retire without fear of being punished. To dig themselves in where they were was too much trouble, so they went back to their old ready-made defences. As a Russian artillery general expressed it, 'They felt lonely in front and went back to their dug-outs to sleep.'

Many of the officers behaved heroically. One officer, after fruitless efforts to induce his men to advance, tore off his shoulder-straps and swore he would 'never again try to lead such swine', then he took a rifle and went over the top like a man. Another – a machine-gunner – was seen three times to go forward and each time to return to appeal to his men to follow, but without result.[185]

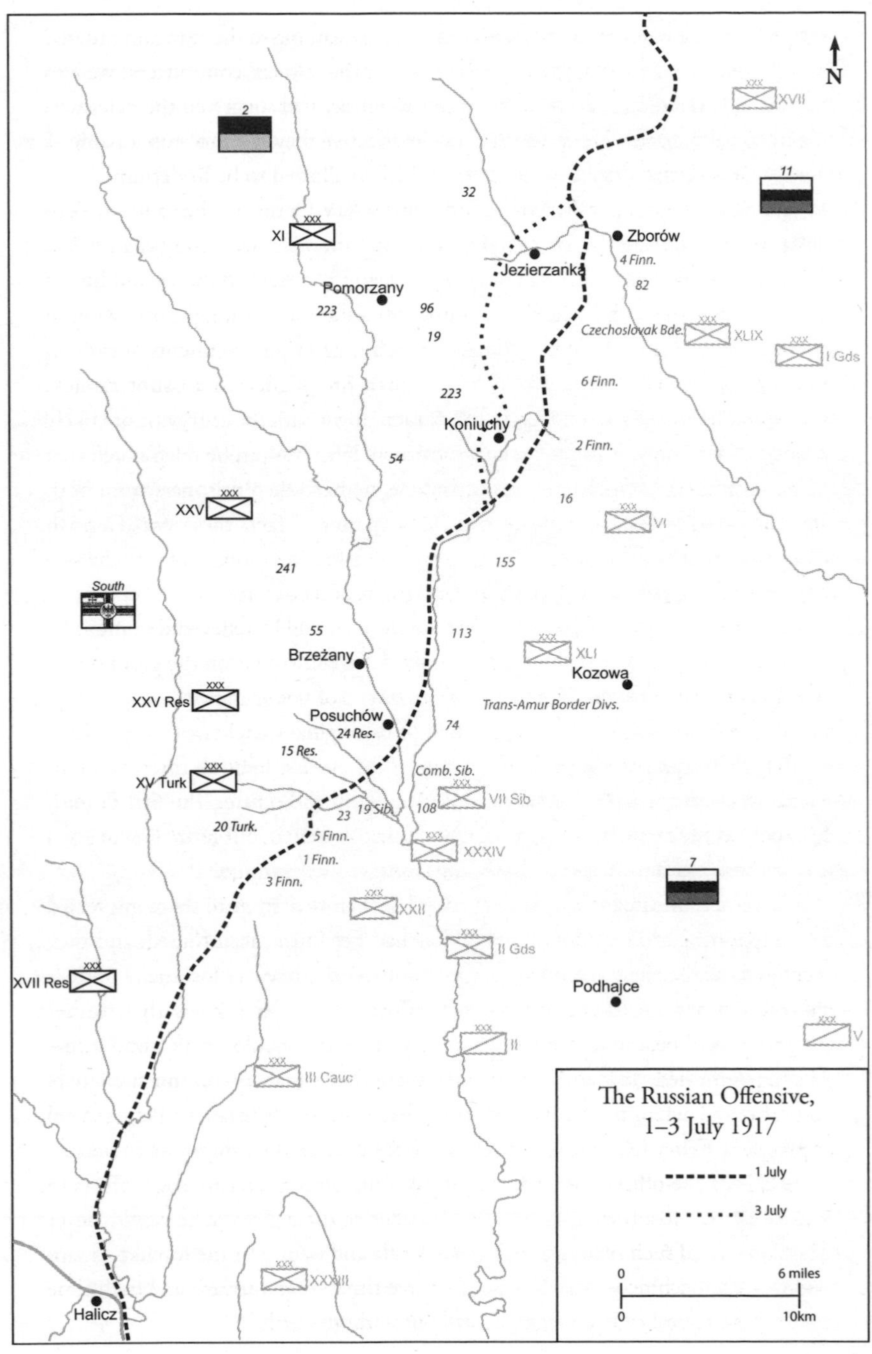

The Russian Offensive, 1–3 July 1917

Kerensky was deeply unhappy with Knox's dispatches and sent a telegram to Miliukov, the foreign minister, demanding that the British military attaché be recalled.[186] Although Knox's memoirs make no mention of this demand, he returned to Petrograd shortly after. The yield of prisoners on the first day of the offensive was modest – Eleventh Army had captured nearly 8,500 and Seventh Army about 2,000, but Seventh Army alone reported over 17,000 of its men were dead, wounded or missing. As the next few days passed, many of those 'missing' returned to the ranks – inevitably, with discipline being so weak, dozens of men simply lay low until the fighting was over. The chief of military communications in Southwest Front later told Knox that he saw a train carrying 850 wounded men; of these, only 15 were actually wounded, and the remainder had minor wounds mainly of their left hands. Prior to the revolution, such self-wounding would have been punishable by death, but Kerensky had abolished the death penalty in the army for any crime, and few medical personnel were prepared to risk the wrath of the soldiers' committees by reporting these attempts to evade front-line service.[187]

During the night of 1/2 July, II Guards Corps moved forward to replace Skoropadsky's XXXIV Corps. Its deployment was tardy, making it impossible to develop any momentum south of Brzeźany, and local counterattacks by mainly German units drove the Russians out of some of the areas where they had gained a foothold in South Army's trenches the previous day. Elsewhere on 2 July the Russian guns began a new preparatory bombardment, every bit as heavy as the one that had preceded the first day's attacks. With the defenders pushed back in places to secondary positions, the gunfire was expected to have more effect – these positions were not as hardened as those in the original front line. At first light, Russian infantry began to move forward from Koniuchy against the lines of the German 223rd Infantry Division, but repeated attacks throughout the morning failed to make any impression. However, farther north the *k.u.k.* 32nd and 19th Infantry Divisions began to give way. The Russian Army attacked at the seam between the divisions with the Czechoslovakian Brigade, and although the southern flank of 32nd Infantry Division – made up of Hungarian troops – was able to hold firm, the predominantly Czech troops on the northern flank of 19th Infantry Division put up far less resistance. Some surrendered, some fled, and those who fought on were swiftly overwhelmed.[188] The minimal reserves behind the front line were swept away in the rout, and by early afternoon the entire division was streaming back in defeat. Russian reinforcements moved forward to drive in the exposed southern flank of 32nd Infantry Division, and this formation too was driven back with heavy losses. The reinforcements intended to launch a restorative counterattack had to be used instead to shore up the disintegrating front line. By the end of 2 July, the *k.u.k.* IX Corps had been reduced to fewer than 7,000 combatants, having started the previous day with 16,000. The two shattered Austro-Hungarian divisions were pulled out of line and replaced by the few German troops available.

At the headquarters of *Ober Ost*, Hoffmann, the chief of staff, had earnestly hoped that the Russians would attack in strength, so that the planned counteroffensive could then proceed against them. On 2 July, he wrote in his diary:

> The Russians are actually a remarkable people. My most heartfelt concern was that they would not launch an attack in Galicia, and consequently a very effective counterstroke by us would not be possible. Instead of which, they have attacked for two days with a fury and concentration of forces such as we have never before seen in the east; against one of our divisions there are seven or eight Russian divisions. That's even more than I wished for … In any event, the situation is very interesting with us at the moment. I have no concerns, but one must pay sharp attention, as even a small Russian victory will restore public opinion in favour of the war.[189]

Throughout the previous year, the Germans had repeatedly complained about the inability of their allies to stand their ground unless German troops were present, and once more this proved to be the case. The German 223rd, 96th and 237th Infantry Divisions now took control of the endangered sector, but for the moment, the Russian pressure seemed to ease. Gutor would need to reorganise his Seventh Army before a renewed assault could be made, and although Erdeli's Eleventh Army had achieved a considerable success, the losses in his front-line formations required the urgent deployment of his reserve formation, I Guards Corps. Unfortunately for Erdeli, the Guards simply refused to move forward. Unable to rely upon the Guards for support, VI Corps – which had successfully captured Koniuchy on the first day – was forced to hold back one of its divisions as a reserve in the event of a counterattack, thus weakening its own impetus. Before leaving for Petrograd, Knox visited the headquarters of 1st Guards Infantry Division and spoke to its commander, General Nikolai Nikolayevich Ignatiev:

> He took me into his small tent to have a quiet talk. He was very pessimistic, and as he is a man of good digestion, with plenty of robust common sense, his opinion is valuable. He thinks there is no hope.
>
> I put three questions to him, whether Russia would: fight as she fought before

> the revolution; fight as she has fought since the revolution till the general peace; or make a separate peace.
>
> To the first question he said emphatically, 'No.' He was inclined to say 'Yes' to the second, but with hesitation, as he was unable to deny the possibility of a separate peace.
>
> ... He said: 'If you were now to go out on the village square and to proclaim that the war will end at once, but only on one condition – that Nikolai Romanov returns to power, every single man would agree and there would be no more talk of a democratic republic.'
>
> ... [He said] that the mass of the soldiery only wanted an excuse for saving their skins – they were not Bolsheviki or Mensheviki, but simply 'Shkurniki' (fearers for their own skins).[190]

The hard-earned Russian success was largely due to the fragility of the Czech troops of 19th Infantry Division. These men had fought with distinction in earlier battles, and were widely regarded as reliable, but the two regiments that collapsed were largely recruited from urban centres, and these were areas in which there was considerable anti-Habsburg feeling. Supported by Czech accounts, the Austrian official history of the war states that the troops fought well until the attacking Czechoslovakian Brigade was at close quarters – when they realised that they were fighting men who spoke the same language, many of the men of 19th Infantry Division simply surrendered or left the battlefield. In some respects, it was a considerable gamble on the part of the Russians to put foreign troops in the front line – Kerensky had opposed the policy, telling Czech prisoners that rather than asking to fight for Russia, they should return home and start a revolution – but it resulted in a great success. It marked the first occasion that former troops of the Austro-Hungarian Empire were fielded against the empire. Whatever the tactical consequences, the political implications were immense. The insistence of Emperor Karl that all citizens of the empire were equals was eclipsed by calls from the United States and elsewhere for the right of self-determination to be granted to the people of the Dual Monarchy, and whatever confidence the Germans had in the resilience of the *k.u.k.* Army was undermined still further.[191]

After the war, the episode, widely known as the Battle of Zborów, became the subject of a great deal of mythology and propaganda. At best, the battle was a tactical success against the *k.u.k.* Army, but its importance lay in the fact that Czech troops were actively fighting against the forces of the Dual Monarchy. Rudolf Medek, a Czech officer who had been taken prisoner by the Russians in

1915 and had volunteered to join the fledgling Czech Legion a year later, wrote at length on the subject, and this passage is typical of the degree to which this relatively minor episode – from a purely military perspective – was venerated:

> [At Zborów] the Czechoslovak nation stood in direct opposition to the old monarchy. It is significant as a battle that stood for the freedom of our independent state – this manifested itself as a beacon of hope before those who heroically sacrificed their lives for that cause. The national army abroad was the very embodiment of national will, the will for independence of the Czech lands and Slovaks in the great struggle between democracy and German and Prussian aggression … All of that previously shackled strength was suddenly released, unleashing a torrent of national consciousness and belief in a victorious future … Zborów, a lasting testament to legionary brotherhood for the sake of a glorious victory … the source of our courage to defend the state now and in the future.[192]

By 3 July, the Russian Seventh Army had finally managed to move sufficient fresh troops into the front line southeast of Brzeźany to renew its assaults, only to find that the South Army too had brought in fresh men. Bitter fighting raged all day with neither side able to make significant ground, and when darkness and exhaustion brought the fighting to a halt, it was the Russians who felt that they had fared the worst. Two days of fighting had cost Seventh Army over 13,000 dead – after adding the wounded and the large numbers of men who simply melted away to avoid the fighting, some 40,000 men had disappeared in just three days. By comparison, the defenders had lost about 12,500. Over the next few days, there was further close-quarter fighting, but Bothmer deliberately reduced the efforts of his men to launch counterattacks. Instead, they were to preserve their strength in preparation for a much larger counteroffensive.

The opening phase of Kerensky's offensive was over. Compared to the dazzling success achieved by Brusilov the previous year, the gains were modest and bought at huge cost. Although the Russian Army had demonstrated that it still had the ability to mount an offensive, it also showed that its troops – even those of the Guards, described the previous year by Knox as the finest human animals in the world – were unreliable, particularly if prolonged fighting was required. On the other side of the front line, the Germans had demonstrated once again that their formations were tough and reliable, and would prove difficult to dislodge. The Turks acquitted themselves well, but once more the *k.u.k.* Army showed its fragility. Worse was to come as other parts of the Russian Army launched their offensives.

CHAPTER 6

HIGH TIDE FOR REVOLUTIONARY RUSSIA

The assaults of Southwest Front were intended by Brusilov to be the main point of effort for the summer offensive but, as had been the case in 1916, he intended other armies to attack elsewhere. At the very least, these attacks would tie down German and Austro-Hungarian forces, preventing them from being moved to the key battlefields east of Lemberg; at best, these subsidiary attacks might discover and exploit a weakness elsewhere.

Fighting in Eleventh Army's sector rumbled on until 6 July. Even as Erdeli's men paused to recover their breath, the Russian Eighth Army, now commanded by Lavr Kornilov, began to shell the defences of the *k.u.k.* Third Army in front of Stanislau. Kornilov had at his disposal XII Corps with six divisions, supported by two cavalry divisions, and intended to drive forward to Kałusz, a distance of about 13 miles (21km); one attack would be made at Jamnica, to the north of Stanislau, and another immediately to the south. Opposing him was Generaloberst Karl Tersztyánsky von Nadas, who had commanded the *k.u.k.* Fourth Army the previous year. He had been appointed to command that particular formation following its disastrous performance in the opening phases of the Brusilov Offensive, and was selected on account of his abrasive character – Conrad, who was chief of the Austro-Hungarian general staff at the time, wanted to have someone who was robust enough to stand up to German senior officers. Although Fourth Army performed as well as might be expected, given the losses it had suffered at the outset of the campaign, the German General Alexander von Linsingen – who had overall command of the sector – repeatedly demanded Tersztyánsky's dismissal and eventually he was moved to take command of Third Army in Galicia. His army consisted of XXVI Corps in the north and XIII Corps in the south, with a total of four Austro-Hungarian infantry divisions, and an Austro-Hungarian cavalry division reinforced by a regiment of German *Landsturm*.

Like his counterparts farther north, Tersztyánsky had long anticipated the likely axis of a Russian attack. To that end, he had positioned the German 83rd and the *k.u.k.* 16th Infantry Divisions as army reserves behind the two corps; however, the latter formation had arrived recently from the Italian Front where it had suffered heavy losses – it consisted of nine weak battalions without artillery. He was also aware that the main axis of the Russian advance, along the main road from Stanislau towards Kałusz, would be able to take advantage of favourable terrain; the ground to the east, from where the Russians would attack, was higher than the Austro-Hungarian front line, and Russian artillery could enjoy a dominating position. In an attempt to compensate for this, Tersztyánsky ordered the second line of defences to be made deeper than was normally the case, and also intended to pull back the front line to a better position. However, progress on constructing the new position was slow and had not been completed by the beginning of July. Consequently, the local forces – from 15th Infantry Division – had not been able to move back from their exposed positions. Most of the supporting artillery was also positioned close behind the front line, well within range of the Russian guns; if the Russian infantry were able to make quick progress, they would swiftly overrun them.[193]

The terrain over which the fighting would occur was dominated by a series of rivers and streams of varying sizes, running northeast from the foothills of the Carpathian Mountains to the south towards the River Dniester. In theory, the ridges between these waterways, as well as the rivers and streams themselves, should have provided a considerable advantage to the defenders. In practice, the rivers made movement difficult for the *k.u.k.* forces – a deliberate, organised defence along any of the rivers or ridges would require time for troops, guns and supplies to be moved across several bridges. Similarly, the Russians faced a daunting series of obstacles if they were to reach Kałusz. On the basis of their experiences the previous year, they did not expect the Austro-Hungarian forces to put up prolonged resistance, but the challenge would be to move their own supplies forward quickly enough to sustain the advance.

As fighting commenced farther north in the first days of July, Tersztyánsky watched Kornilov's preparations. More troops arrived daily, mainly from the Russian forces farther south, and there was increased aerial reconnaissance activity – unlike in Bothmer's and Böhm-Ermolli's sectors, Tersztyánsky lacked the aircraft to dominate the sky. On 6 July, Kornilov's gunners began their bombardment, and throughout the afternoon there were repeated infantry attacks at a variety of points. Most of these were repulsed with varying degrees of difficulty, and a similar pattern followed on 7 July.

Although Kornilov's troops had made little progress on the ground, their artillery had done a great deal of damage, particularly to the exposed defences of the *k.u.k.* 15th Infantry Division. The repeated infantry attacks and the heavy gunfire had left the defenders exhausted, and on 8 July, after a further heavy bombardment, the Russian XII Corps threw its men forward again in strength, overrunning the village of Jamnica and a substantial strength of the Austro-Hungarian first line. Desperately, the defenders struggled back to the second line; much of 15th Infantry Division's artillery, deployed a short distance to the west of Jamnica, was captured before it could withdraw. The Russians followed close behind the retreating troops and now fought their way into the second defensive line in confused fighting, but were unable to concentrate sufficient forces to sustain their advance – their losses had been heavy, and the terrain made large-scale movements by either side difficult, particularly across ground that had been heavily shelled. Much of the Austro-Hungarian second defensive line lay on more favourable higher ground than the first line, and for the moment the Russian advance stopped.

As news percolated back to his headquarters, Tersztyánsky decided to take a look for himself and met Feldmarschallleutnant Emmerich Hadfy, the commander of XXVI Corps, at the headquarters of 15th Infantry Division, and the two men briefly ascended in a tethered balloon to survey the battlefield. The view to the east must have been impressive, stretching across the low ground where 15th Infantry Division had been forced to fight an ultimately doomed action; in the distance to the east, the Austro-Hungarian officers could see Russian troops being reorganised for a renewal of the assault, while Hadfy's reinforcements would have been visible to the north, where they were gathering for a possible counterattack. This attempt to restore the front started during the afternoon and coincided with a further advance by the Russians; while the two forces struggled for ascendancy, the second Russian attack – a little to the north – broke into the defensive positions, effectively threatening the rear of the Austro-Hungarian counterattacking group, which had no choice but to break off its action.

During the night, Tersztyánsky reshuffled his forces to try to prevent further Russian advances. The loss of most of 15th Infantry Division's artillery was a severe, if entirely predictable blow. His intention was to hold the second defensive

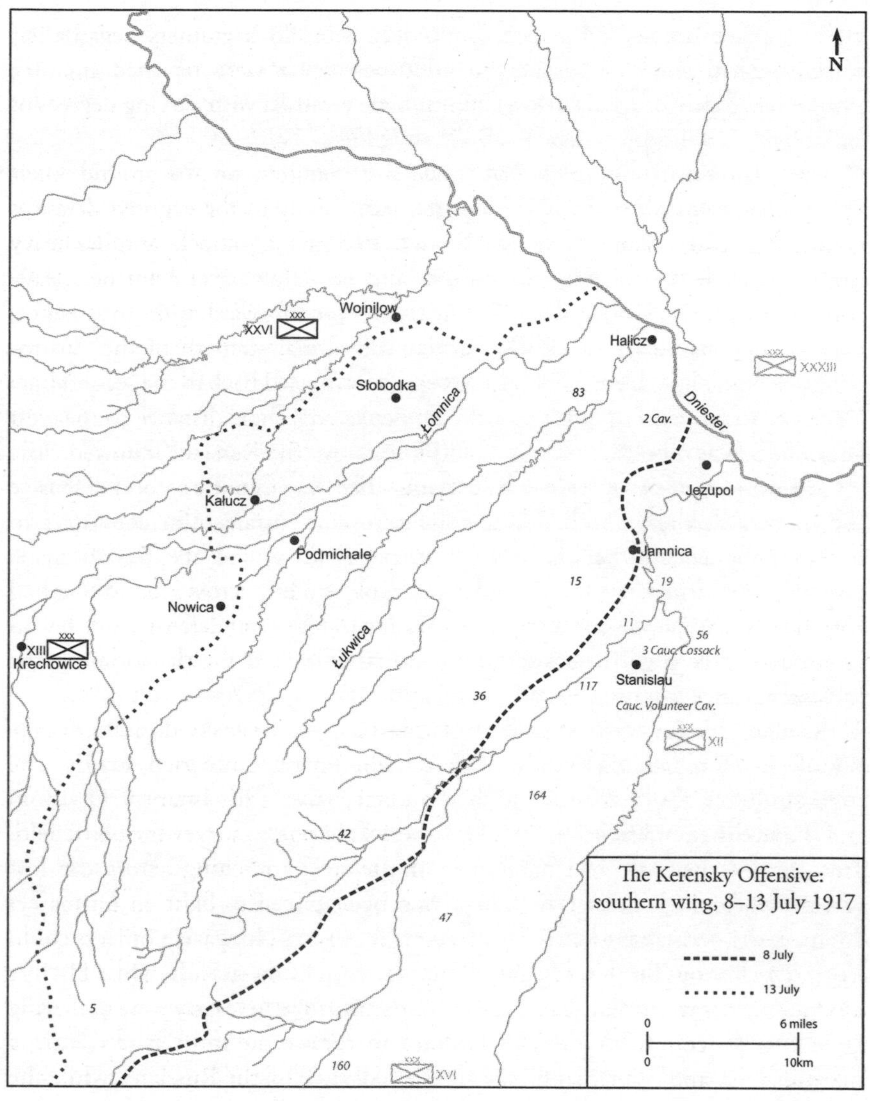

line, but if this failed he would withdraw to the nearest river lines, first to the Łukwica, then to the Łomnica; this latter would place the defences immediately outside Kałusz. Any such withdrawals were to take place only with the express permission of his headquarters. On receiving these orders, XIII Corps to the south reported that it was confident that it could hold its current positions, but

Hadfy replied that XXVI Corps had little power left to resist – just a single day of fighting had reduced it to little more than a screen of demoralised troops. The embattled 15th Infantry Division had suffered catastrophic losses – it started the battle with 7,700 combatants, but by midnight had barely 800 left and had lost 43 guns. In the circumstances, Tersztyánsky contemplated a withdrawal to the line of the Łomnica before a new Russian attack fell, but it was too late. Kornilov opened a new general attack along his entire front on 9 July as well as renewing the assault along the Stanislau–Kałusz road. Instead of withdrawing in an orderly manner, XXVI Corps found itself struggling with the difficult task of pulling back whilst under heavy attack. The Russian XII Corps swiftly overran the second defensive line, and the *k.u.k.* 36th Infantry Division, to the south of 15th Infantry Division, found itself caught up in the growing rout. By the end of the day, the Russians had advanced about 6 miles (10km) from Stanislau to Kałusz.

Hindenburg's low opinion of Germany's ally was shared by many others in the German military, who had little doubt about the unreliability of Czech and other components of the *k.u.k.* Army: 'The wall in Galicia proved to be stone only where Austro-Hungarian troops were stiffened by German … the Austro-Slav wall near Stanislau collapsed under Kerensky's simple tap.'[194]

Tersztyánsky could have done more to strengthen the defences along the anticipated Russian axis of advance; although he correctly identified that 15th Infantry Division's front line was exposed, he failed to build up the second line as planned, claiming that this was due to a shortage of labour battalions. At no point did he instruct corps and division commanders to provide work details – after all, the front had been quiet for much of the year, and it should have been possible to release sufficient manpower to construct the positions. Instead, the division defending the main road from Stanislau to Kałusz was left to suffer the brunt of the Russian onslaught in positions that were completely unfavourable. But even allowing for this, the loss of nearly 90 per cent of its fighting strength in the first day was extraordinary. Even if Tersztyánsky was not minded to allocate troops to prepare good secondary positions, Generalmajor Albrecht Aust as division commander or Hadfy as corps commander should have acted on his own initiative. Instead, as was the case with almost the entire officer corps of the *k.u.k.* Army the previous year, all three senior officers showed deplorable complacency; the rank and file of 15th Infantry Division paid the price of their failure to take adequate measures.

The consequences of Kornilov's success were considerable, far beyond the modest (though encouraging) amount of ground that his men had gained. Troops of the Central Powers were beginning to gather for the planned major counteroffensive in South Army's sector, and some of these – Bavarian 8th Reserve Division and German 16th Reserve Division – had to be diverted as reinforcements for the *k.u.k.* Third Army. Most of their personnel were still en route and would take days to assemble, and given the dire state of Hadfy's XXVI Corps, support was needed far sooner; Bothmer had no choice but to dispatch two German infantry regiments, themselves weakened in the recent fighting, together with several batteries of artillery. Under the blazing summer sun, the men set off on forced marches to intercept the growing crisis south of the Dniester. Given the catastrophic losses suffered by the *k.u.k.* 15th Infantry Division, it was questionable whether they would arrive in time to prevent further Russian gains.

Throughout 10 July, Tersztyánsky and Hadfy struggled to bring order to their battered units; fortunately for them, the Russians had to pause while they brought forward ammunition and artillery to resume their pressure. Although the day passed without further disasters for the *k.u.k.* Army, the damage had been done for the two senior Austro-Hungarian commanders. Both were dismissed from their posts; Tersztyánsky was replaced by Generaloberst Karl Kritek, who had been commander of X Corps, and Hadfy by General Friedrich Csanády von Békes, who had been commanding VI Corps in Transylvania.

Tersztyánsky had spent much of the war being dismissed from formations that he had commanded. In 1915, he fell out with Prime Minister Tisza of Hungary who successfully demanded that he was removed from command of the *k.u.k.* forces preparing to invade Serbia, and when Conrad deliberately selected him in the expectation that an abrasive, tough personality would be required to stand up to the domineering German military hierarchy on the Eastern Front, his clashes with Linsingen led to repeated demands for his dismissal. Aged 62, he had reached the end of his military career. Emperor Karl wished him to take honorary command of the Hungarian Noble Life Guard, but Tersztyánsky declined, writing a long letter to Generaloberst Arthur von Bolfras, head of the military chancellery, listing the multitude of people with whom he had clashed during his career, making it impossible for him to accept a post which would require him to behave with diplomacy and tact. In any case, he advised Bolfras, he didn't speak Hungarian well, which would make a mockery of such a position. Instead, he was appointed to command the Life Guards cavalry squadron in Vienna. He died in the Austrian capital in 1921.

The dismissals of the two commanders were insufficient for the Germans. Given that large numbers of German troops were heading for the sector south of the Dniester, Berlin insisted that a senior German officer should be given a prominent role in the affairs of Third Army. The obvious candidate was Karl Litzmann, who had been moved from the northern part of the front to the central sector the previous year, with a view to his replacing Tersztyánsky as commander of Fourth Army. Despite the insistence of Linsingen, supported by Hindenburg and Ludendorff, Conrad refused to give way, and Litzmann was left to command a predominantly German group of units as part of the *k.u.k.* First Army. His account of his new appointment highlights the continuing tensions between German and Austro-Hungarian commands:

> The *k.u.k.* Third Army found itself as badly shaken, weakened and demoralised as the *k.u.k.* Fourth Army in July in Volhynia, and Prince Leopold, who was well-disposed towards me, wished the army command to be assigned to me as earnestly as Generaloberst von Linsingen had wanted to do at that time. But once again, Austrian jealousy prevented this. For sure, the Slovakian Generaloberst Tersztyánsky was now finally sent home, but replaced as commander of Third Army by the Czech Kritek. I would be able to help, but only under the command of Kritek. As he was junior to me as a General, Emperor Karl promoted him to Generaloberst.[195]

After pausing for breath on the morning of 10 July, Kornilov renewed his advance in the afternoon, largely at the urging of Kerensky; he would have preferred to wait longer while supplies and reinforcements were brought forward. Although all units were ordered to make haste, the reality was that those on the main axis of advance faced the hardest task both in terms of pressing forward and bringing up supplies over cratered terrain, and consequently it was mainly on the flanks that further progess was made. Halicz, on the south bank of the Dniester and part of the second line of defences, fell swiftly to 4th Transamur Infantry Division, while in the southwest the leading Russian elements penetrated into Nowica before being turned back. Throughout the night that followed, Kornilov's staff did all they could to increase the strength of the troops standing in front of Kałusz, with the intention of renewing the main drive the following morning. The defenders were also busy. Whilst the Austro-Hungarian units that had been soundly beaten in the opening phase of the battle might be in little shape for further fighting, the first of the German reinforcements were arriving under the command of Generalleutnant Sieger, whose 16th Reserve Infantry Division was en route. In addition to the leading elements of his division, which had been heavily involved in defeating the Nivelle Offensive in northern France just a few weeks earlier, Sieger also now commanded 83rd Infantry Division and many of the troops sent south piecemeal by Bothmer. In addition, 8th Bavarian Reserve Division was still on its way to the critical sector. Meanwhile, the local Austro-Hungarian commanders attempted to pull the remnants of 15th Infantry Division out of the front line and replace them with 16th Infantry Division, which had been part of Third Army's reserves.

Early on 11 July, the Russian XII Corps renewed its advance. Leading elements of its 164th Infantry Division had taken up positions in the village of Podmichale overnight, and these moved into Kałusz at first light. Breaking with normal practice in the First World War, the Russians pressed on through the town without any preliminary artillery bombardment, taking the defenders completely by surprise. Both sides rushed troops to the town; the Russians concentrated faster, swiftly securing all of Kałusz and the high ground to the north. Several hasty counterattacks followed but the morning belonged to the Russians, who overran and captured several more artillery batteries. Following the departure of Tersztyánsky, Feldmarschalleutnant Alfred Edler von Schenk, commander of the *k.u.k.* XIII Corps, was in command of Third Army until Kritek arrived, and he ordered Sieger to counterattack with as many troops as possible. With only a single battalion at his disposal, Sieger replied that such a counterattack was pointless, particularly as the victorious Russians were threatening to push on to Wojnilow, where Sieger hoped to assemble his forces; consequently, he ordered the sole battalion to remain in Wojnilow to prevent the town from falling into Russian hands. In the meantime, the Russians completed their capture of Kałusz, scattering the survivors of the *k.u.k.* 15th Infantry Division towards the west. For the moment, there was a gap between Sieger's fledgling forces assembling in Wojnilow and the northern flank of the Austro-Hungarian units to the south. If the Russians could assemble sufficient forces, they would surely be able to roll up Sieger and his men before they could be reinforced.

Late on 11 July, Kornilov's troops moved against Wojnilow. Fortunately for Sieger, some of the heavy artillery dispatched by Bothmer had arrived and was able to put down a heavy barrage that broke up the Russian attack at Słobodka, immediately to the south of Wojnilow. At the same time, assorted formations were strung out in a makeshift line to the west of Kałusz under the command of Generalmajor Maximilian Ritter von Jehlin, commander of the Bavarian division. Fortunately for him, the Russians made no attempt to advance farther west for the moment. At the same time, the southern wing of Third Army cautiously withdrew so that its line conformed with the forces driven back at Kałusz; as a result, several battalions and batteries were released from the shortened line and gathered together as a local reserve in Nowica. It was the high tide mark for the armies of Russia.

The capture of Kałusz was the stated objective of Kornilov's army, but only for the opening phase of the campaign. Beyond the town lay Stryj, 30 miles (50km) farther to the west, and if the Russians were to penetrate that far, they would disrupt Austro-Hungarian lines of communication in the entire sector – the defence of all of Galicia south of Lemberg would be badly compromised. As a result, it was vital from the perspective of the Central Powers to stabilise the situation as rapidly as possible, and *Ober Ost* ordered the diversion of 20th Infantry Division, which was one of the formations earmarked for the planned counteroffensive farther north. With so many of the units intended for that counteroffensive already heading south, there was now serious concern whether the counteroffensive should be moved to take place south of the Dniester, or even whether it would be possible to mount it at all. While such doubts circulated in many circles, Bothmer intervened from the headquarters of South Army. Throughout the tense fighting of the summer of 1916, his army had stood firm against repeated attacks, even though it was threatened on both flanks, and even now his troops had successfully repulsed all Russian assaults on their lines. He spoke persuasively against the abandonment or relocation of the counteroffensive. It would be logistically difficult to mount the attack south of the Dniester, as the Russians – just like the Austro-Hungarian forces – would be able to fall back from one river or ridge line to another, and the attackers would rapidly run out of momentum as there were so few roads to bring forward supplies for an offensive heading towards the southwest. Nor was there any clear objective within reach of such a counteroffensive. In any case, he pointed out, the Russian efforts south of the Dniester meant that there would be less resistance in front of South Army, where there were several major towns within striking range. Therefore, he insisted, the offensive should take place as planned, with as many troops as could be spared.

Bothmer was right. The terrain was deeply unfavourable for both sides when it came to advancing or retreating. In 1914, the Russians had moved swiftly through this area because Conrad altered the Austro-Hungarian mobilisation plans, detraining his troops farther west than was originally planned; as a result, when Brusilov, who was then commander of Eighth Army, moved towards Lemberg, he encountered almost no resistance until much farther west. In 1915, when the *k.u.k.* Army retook the region, it did so moving north from the Carpathian passes, i.e. advancing along the numerous river valleys towards the Dniester. Now, despite their success – which was largely due to the crippling fragility of the *k.u.k.* Army by this stage of the war – Kornilov's formations found it difficult to retain any momentum. Rains closer to the Carpathians turned most of the streams into torrents, which overflowed and made the surrounding terrain boggy. Kritek arrived to take command of Third Army on 12 July and concluded that, provided there were no further catastrophic collapses, the Russians would be unable to advance farther; but on the other hand, he lacked the strength to recapture Kałusz until all of the German formations en route for the region had arrived. These troops now also included a Bavarian cavalry division, which was expected imminently.

Linsingen arrived to take up his post – the precise details of which remained vague – a day after Kritek:

> The army commander asked me to consider whether XIII Corps, which at the time was still holding the high ground on the right bank of the Łomnica … shouldn't pull back 'just in case'. I replied that this high ground had to be held at all costs; I would need it as the 'springboard for a future offensive'.
>
> But as it was possible that those heights would be given up by the demoralised troops if I did not intervene personally, I drove with Rotberg [a staff officer] through Dolina as far as Krechowice, the headquarters of the *k.u.k.* XIII Corps. In the cavernous space of the administration building of the Krechowice sawmill I found assembled the entire command, from the corps commander, Feldmarschallleutnant von Schenk and his chief of staff, Oberst Czoban, down to secretaries, telephonists and clerks, talking, issuing instructions, reporting, dictating, using numerous telephones, all at the same time, in utter turmoil. I could not accept this type of operation as fit for purpose, not least when, as was the case here, the nerves of all those involved were badly strained by setbacks, disappointments, and orders and counter-orders. But we repeatedly found the same circumstances amongst *k.u.k.* corps and division staffs.
>
> What I had feared was about to happen: Feldmarschallleutnant von Schenk told me that his *k.u.k.* 36th Infantry Division was going to 'voluntarily evacuate the high ground on the right bank of the Łomnica so that it would not be forced to do so'! Army Group Böhm-Ermolli had also approved the evacuation. Incidentally, one brigade commander with his two Croatian regiments had already withdrawn without authorisation, thereby leaving a great gap in the division's front. They were 'looking for the brigade'.
>
> Filled with chagrin at this weak and pathetic leadership, I ordered in a sharp manner that the abandoned positions were to be reoccupied immediately and held without equivocation. The brigade commander had to be held to account. Feldmarschallleutnant von Schenk was not offended by my abruptness; he assured me that he would do what he could to satisfy me.[196]

Something similar had happened the previous year when the Romanian Army invaded Hungarian Transylvania, and forces were hastily dispatched by both Germany and Austria-Hungary to stop the invasion; Austro-Hungarian commanders showed – from the German point of view – an alarming tendency to abandon positions even before they came under attack.[197] At the beginning of the war, the *k.u.k.* Army had fought as effectively as any other, inflicting stinging defeats on the initial Russian incursions into Galicia, but its performance had deteriorated at an unmatched rate. Its casualties had been no worse than those of all armies in this terrible war; however, the quality of replacement officers and men was clearly far inferior in the Austro-Hungarian Empire than elsewhere. Training was poor, often crossing the line into murderously inadequate, and the fragility of the multi-ethnic and multi-national army was completely exposed by the realities of industrial warfare. The lack of any sense of imperial identity or loyalty, even to the monarchy, meant that as soon as the familiar officers and disciplines of peacetime disappeared, soldiers thought more of their loyalty to their regions than to the empire. To some extent at least, this was a predictable outcome, and senior figures like Conrad, who in particular had been involved in every aspect of training and doctrine, must be regarded as being responsible for the manner in which cohesion, morale and battle-worthiness collapsed so dramatically. It should be added that 36th Infantry Division – particularly the Croatian brigade – had been attacked repeatedly by Russian forces in the previous two days and had suffered substantial losses; but it is difficult to imagine a German division simply abandoning ground like this after such actions.

Litzmann drove immediately to 36th Infantry Division, taking with him Oberleutnant von Frankl, a liaison officer from Schenk's headquarters. Their car had to be abandoned when it became stuck in a muddy road, the consequences of the recent rains and flooding. Finally, after night had fallen, he approached his destination in the middle of another heavy rainstorm in a commandeered horse-drawn wagon:

> Small groups and individual soldiers passed us going in the other direction. I called them over. They were Croats. They didn't understand me, shook their heads and disappeared into the darkness. Nor did Frankl speak Croatian; but we had no doubt that they were from the brigade that had withdrawn. I needed to reach 36th Infantry Division. But now, our road was completely blocked by two intermingled columns of wagons. I sent Frankl ahead to clear the way. He didn't come back, even after a long time had passed. Meanwhile, ever more and larger groups of fleeing Croats passed me, edging sideways and vanishing into the night. I endured a difficult hour.

> Finally, Frankl returned. Up ahead, he had found significant flooding on the Łomnica. He said the water was waist-deep. A horse had drowned before his very eyes; our wagon would not be able to get through.
>
> What to do? It was past midnight, and it rained incessantly. The floods coming down from the mountains would swell further, making the obstacle even greater. It was all the more essential to hold onto the high ground! Would I have to wait here for dawn before finding a way through to 36th Infantry Division?
>
> Then came an unexpected solution to the problem. From the west there approached a long, silent column of riders. In the darkness they seemed unnaturally large: giants with steel helmets and lances on mighty steeds appeared as silhouettes against the night sky. They must be the spearhead of the Bavarian cavalry division. They pressed forward silently towards the Russians next to the road that was choked with wagons. 'Are you Bavarians?' 'Yes!' 'Thank God! Now clear a path forward for me, where the Croats are fleeing.' 'We'll do it!' They had no idea who I was, and why I was delighted at their arrival. Now I could be calm. The Bavarians would 'do it'.[198]

The contrast between the two armies could not be greater. When the first detachment of the Bavarian division arrived, a staff officer reported immediately to XIII Corps headquarters and, learning of the withdrawal of the Croatian brigade, took it upon himself to direct the cavalry squadrons to the abandoned high ground as they arrived. Fortunately, the Russians had not noticed the withdrawal, and the Bavarians were able to hold the former front line until the Croats moved back into their trenches; by the time the Russians became aware of the movements and opened up a bombardment, the crisis had passed. Litzmann returned to XIII Corps headquarters for a brief rest – he had been continuously on the move for over 60 hours – and then set off for 36th Infantry Division early the following morning:

> Discarded backpacks and fully loaded artillery ammunition wagons were strewn around the road, the unmistakable signs of the headless flight during the night. Up ahead, Oberleutnant Graf Apponyi, from the staff of the mounted division, waited for us by the Łomnica. He led us through the flooded area to a rocky scree and along a perilous route …
>
> Together with the commander [of 36th Infantry Division], Generalmajor [Maximilian] Nöhring, we rode towards the high ground we had claimed, left our horses at the edge of the woodland behind the heights, and continued on foot to the positions once more occupied by the Croats. We stayed there a while under

> unpleasant Russian shellfire. The ground was suitable for defence. But fighting trenches still hadn't been dug; one would indeed not have wanted to hold the position. I ordered immediate fortification and determined defence.[199]

Over the next few days, the Russians launched a number of attacks at various points, including the line held by 36th Infantry Division, but were beaten off everywhere. The Russian Eighth Army had suffered serious losses in its attacks – the official Austro-Hungarian history of the war put the figure at 40,000 – and momentum had been lost. Matters weren't helped by a disagreement on what the objectives of the attack should be. Kornilov still wished to press on westwards towards the rail hub of Stryj, but Brusilov wanted the axis of the attack to be turned towards the northwest and aimed at Rohatyn – this might unlock the defensive positions in front of Eighth Army's neighbour to the north. Neither Kornilov nor Gutor were minded to agree with him, but in any case, the limited strength that the Russians had gathered for their summer offensive was effectively spent, and a further major effort was impossible.

Compared to the repeated efforts of previous years, this was a remarkably short offensive. The total losses suffered were also modest, but such was the disintegration of the Russian Army that it was impossible to consider further operations. The initial assault was, understandably, made by formations that were regarded as the most reliable; they therefore suffered the bulk of the losses, and the formations that should have then come forward to renew the attack were the ones that were regarded as less reliable.[200] The sense of crisis that swept through the headquarters of the German and *k.u.k.* Armies dissipated as it became clear that further attacks were unlikely to occur, and preparations continued for the planned counteroffensive.

Litzmann was given command of the central sector of Third Army's front line, and when the Russians launched a local attack against the *k.u.k.* 42nd Infantry Division, he immediately counterattacked with four companies of infantry that were attached to the Bavarian cavalry, swiftly restoring the front line; a second Russian attack later in the day was repulsed in the same manner. The German 16th Reserve Infantry Division had taken up positions to the west of Kałusz shortly after the Russians captured the town with a view to preventing a further Russian advance, and by the middle of the month had concentrated its forces sufficiently to start putting pressure on the Russians. On 15 July, there was bitter fighting on the high ground to the north of the town and, although the Germans made little progress, their intention to press forward was enough to decide the issue; rather than risk being driven back from Kałusz with numerous rivers and streams to hinder a withdrawal under fire, the Russians evacuated the town before dawn on 16 July. Litzmann ordered his troops to move forward to the south of the town, and the fighting that followed was typical of the war, with repeated assaults by both sides adding to the casualty lists with little ground changing hands. However, the damage inflicted by such attritional fighting was greater in the Russian Army than those of its opponents.

There was also fighting in the central and northern sectors of the long Eastern Front. Many had called for these attacks to be made before the main effort by Southwest Front, in order to draw away German troops, but the farther north – and therefore closer to Petrograd – they moved, the worse the state of the Russian armies. As a result, each front was left to make its own plans effectively without any attempt at coordination. Denikin's West Front attacked on 7 July, but the assault was greatly hampered by the unreliability of the troops, even though Denikin deliberately tried to select units that were more reliable. One of the divisions designated to attack took up its positions piecemeal only four hours before the start time of the offensive, with one regiment producing only a little over two rifle companies. Half of one regiment refused to advance, while a neighbouring regiment drifted away piecemeal to the rear areas once fighting began. Inevitably, losses were heaviest amongst the officers, who tried in vain to keep the men moving forward. Even where there were successes, these were not sustained:

> On the sector of 51st Infantry Division the attack began at 0705. The 202nd and 204th Regiments … made a dash across two lines of trenches, bayoneted the enemy, and began to storm the third line at 0730. The break was so rapid and so unexpected that the enemy failed to establish a barrage. The 201st Regiment, which was following the advance troops, approached our first line of trenches, but refused to go any further, so that our troops who had broken through were not reinforced in time. The units of 134th Infantry Division, which followed, could not carry out their orders because the men of 201st Regiment had crowded in the trenches, while the enemy had opened a very strong gun fire. These units therefore partly dispersed and partly lay in our trenches. Seeing that no reinforcements were forthcoming from the rear and from the flanks, the men of 202nd and 204th Regiments lost heart, and some of the companies, in which all the officers had been killed, began to retire. They were followed by the remainder of the troops without, however, any pressure from the Germans, who did not put their batteries and machine-guns into action until the retreat had begun … The units of 29th Infantry Division were late in going into position, because the men advanced reluctantly, as their mood had changed. A quarter of an hour before the appointed

> time the 114th Regiment on the right flank refused to advance … for some unknown reason 113th and 116th Regiments also failed to move … After this failure desertion began to grow, and at dawn became general … The Headquarters of XX Corps sent the following report of the battle: 'The cowardice and lack of discipline in certain units reached such a pitch that the commanding officers were compelled to ask our artillery to cease firing, because the fire of our own guns caused a panic among our soldiers.'[201]

The commander of another of Denikin's corps wrote a similarly dispiriting report after the battle:

> Everything was ready for the advance: the plan had been worked out in detail; we had a powerful and efficient artillery; the weather was favourable because it did not allow the Germans to take advantage of their superiority in aircraft; we had superior numbers, our reserves were drawn up in time, we had plenty of ammunition, and the sector was well chosen for the advance, because we were in a position to conceal strong artillery forces in the close neighbourhood of our trenches. The undulations of ground afforded many hidden approaches to the front; the distance between ourselves and the enemy was small, and there were no natural obstacles between us which would have had to have been forced under fire. Finally, the troops had been prepared by the committees, the commanding officers and the war minister, Kerensky, and their efforts induced the troops to take the first, the most arduous steps. We attained considerable success without suffering appreciable losses. Three fortified lines had been broken through and occupied, and there remained only separate defensive positions. The fighting might soon have reached the phase of bayonet fighting; the enemy artillery was silenced, over 1,400 Germans, many machine-guns and other booty had been captured. Also, our guns had inflicted heavy casualties in killed and wounded upon the enemy, and it may confidently be stated that the forces that were opposing our corps had been temporarily knocked out. Along the entire front of our corps only three or four enemy batteries and occasionally three or four machine-guns were firing, and there were isolated rifle shots. But – night came. Immediately I began to receive anxious reports from officers commanding sectors at the front to the effect that the men were abandoning the unattacked front line en masse, entire companies deserting. It was stated in some of the reports that the firing line in places was only occupied by the commanding officer, his staff, and a few men. The operations ended in an irretrievable and hopeless failure. In one day we had lived through the joy of

> victory, which had been won in spite of the low spirits of the men, as well as the horror of seeing the fruits of victory deliberately cast away by the soldiery ... I realised that we, the commanding officers, are powerless to alter the elemental psychology of the men, and I wept long and bitterly.[202]

West Front suffered over 20,000 wounded, but analysis of their wounds revealed further problems. Only 10 per cent were classed as badly wounded, whereas 30 per cent had suspicious finger and wrist wounds, 40 per cent had light wounds from which the dressings were not even removed – and Denikin suspected that had they been, the medics would have discovered no wounds whatsoever in many cases. West Front started with 184 infantry battalions and 900 guns, opposed by 29 German battalions and 300 guns. Despite this, he was unable to hold any of the modest gains his troops made.[203]

Northern Front was expected to attack with its substantial forces in order to drive the Germans away from the city of Riga, an industrial centre in the tsar's empire. In 1915, prominent Latvian delegates in the Duma, led by Janis Goldmanis, called for the creation of new all-Latvian formations, in the expectation that such national units would feel strongly motivated to protect their homeland from the Germans, who were now entering Latvian territory. Nicholas II authorised the creation of new Latvian infantry brigades in July, and the Latvian Rifles, as they became known, inevitably became a potent symbol of the nationalist aspirations of Latvians, despite estimates that fewer than 70,000 Latvians served at some stage in the formations known as the Latvian Rifles, compared to over 150,000 who served in the rest of the Russian Army.

The Latvian Rifles distinguished themselves in the fighting of 1916, often suffering heavy casualties; on some occasions, for example during especially bitter fighting late in 1916 near Riga, many Latvians believed that their units had been deliberately exposed by the Russian Army in an attempt to bleed away the strength of Latvia, thus weakening the nation's ability to assert its independence at a future point. Drawn from the urban industrial centres of Riga, the Latvian Rifles were far more literate than most Russian Army troops and were natural recruits for the Bolsheviks. Deserters from the Latvian Rifles were numerous in the formations of the new Red Guards, the paramilitary units raised by the Bolsheviks from the industrial workers of Petrograd and other parts of Russia, and when Northern Front launched its contribution to the Kerensky Offensive, the Latvians were prominent amongst the units that refused to take part.[204] The entire attack lasted less than a day before petering out.

Meanwhile, *Ober Ost* had completed its preparations for the great counterstroke. The intention was to mount a powerful thrust into the last part of eastern Galicia that was still in Russian hands, recapturing the city of Tarnopol. In doing so, the strength of the Russian Army would finally and irrevocably be broken. A substantial force was to be concentrated for this operation – the headquarters of XXIII Corps and six divisions would come from the Western Front, and LI Corps from the northern sector of the Eastern Front, together with several cavalry formations and a substantial concentration of artillery, the latter under the expert command of Bruchmüller. The original start date of the counteroffensive was set as 12 July, but it was not possible to get all forces concentrated by that date – some had been diverted elsewhere as already described to shore up the front line, and others were delayed by sudden summer rainstorms that turned the unmetalled roads into rivers of mud. In particular, the diversion of the reinforced Bavarian Cavalry Division was a source of irritation for Prince Leopold, the commander of *Ober Ost*, who was a Bavarian himself and had ensured that the division was substantially reinforced; so far, the performance of cavalry formations in the war had been disappointing, and Leopold had hoped that attaching additional infantry to the Bavarian formation would give it sufficient firepower to make a difference.

Instead of moving to the assembly area for the counteroffensive, LI Corps headquarters was dispatched to help stiffen the line of the wavering *k.u.k.* Third Army, and it was replaced by the *Beskidenkorps*, recalled from the Carpathians. On 14 July, Leopold moved his headquarters from Brest-Litovsk to Złoczów, and was greeted by good news: not only had the attacks by the Russian Eleventh Army died down, there was also evidence that Russian troops were being sent south to reinforce Kornilov. Nevertheless, just as the Russians had been unable to hide their preparations in June, the Germans were unable to achieve complete surprise, and the relatively fresh Russian troops replaced the weakened formations facing the assault group. Leopold wished to attack as soon as possible before Russian preparations were complete, but the weather continued to interfere. Finally, on 19 July, all was ready. Overall control of the counteroffensive would be in the hands of General Arnold von Winckler. At his disposal, he had: Generalleutnant Max Hoffmann's *Beskidenkorps* with 96th and 223rd Infantry Divisions; *Gruppe Wilhelmi* with the reinforced 197th Infantry Division and 237th Infantry Division; General Hugo von Kathen's XXIII Reserve Corps with 1st and 2nd Guards Infantry Divisions; Generalleutnant Albert von Berrer's LI Corps with 5th and 22nd Infantry Divisions; and the German 42nd and 92nd Infantry Divisions and the *k.u.k.* 33rd Infantry Division. Arz, the chief of

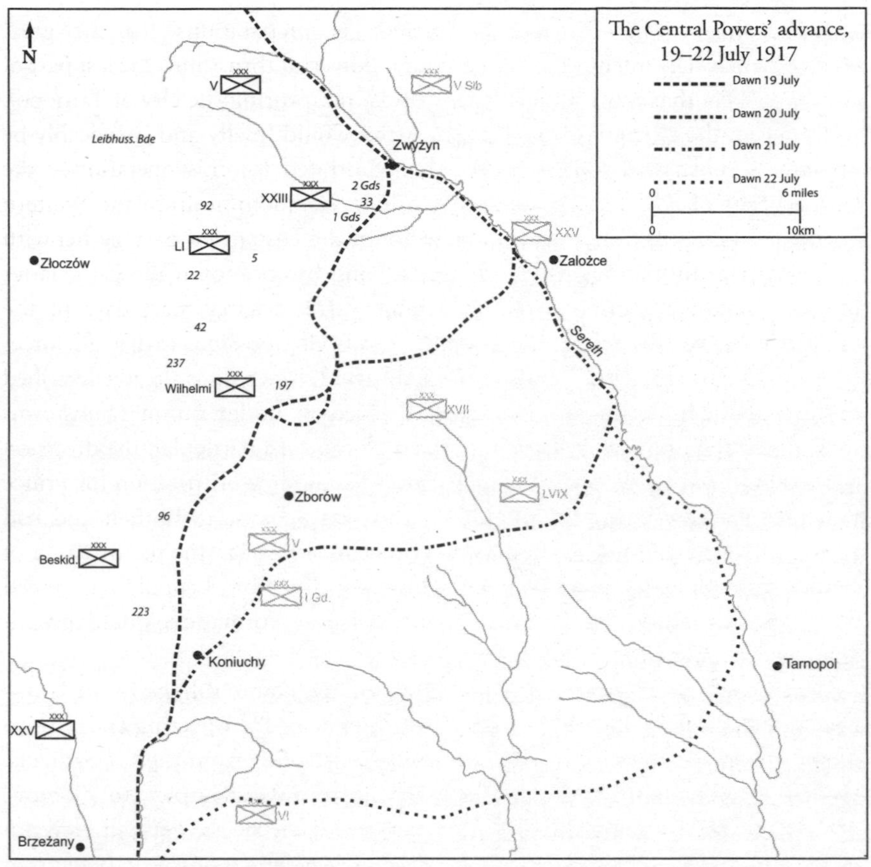

the Austro-Hungarian general staff, protested late in the day that his troops were under-represented in an operation intended to recapture the last parts of Austro-Hungarian territory under Russian control, but given the fragility of his armies, he had limited grounds for complaint. Opposing this substantial force were elements of the Russian V Siberian Corps, and V, VI and XVII Corps. How many of their subordinate formations were actually reliable would be known only once the fighting began.

Supported by aerial reconnaissance, the German and Austro-Hungarian artillery began their preparation on 17 July. Whilst it was impossible to hide preparations from the Russians, there was scope for a degree of deception. There was a local attack by the *k.u.k.* 54th Infantry Division to the south of the sector where the great counteroffensive would take place, and the Russians immediately reinforced that area, diverting units that might have been deployed against the real counteroffensive farther north. Two days later, the intensity of the bombardment suddenly increased shortly before dawn, and a mixture of gas and explosive rounds rained down on the Russians for nearly seven hours. When Kathen's XXIII Reserve Corps attacked in mid-morning, its four divisions found the first line of Russian trenches almost empty. They swiftly pushed on, penetrating into the second line of defences by midday. At first, there was sporadic artillery fire from Russian guns, but this rapidly died down as the gunners began to move away to avoid being overrun. Russian troops had been slipping away from the front line for days in anticipation of the German attack, and now many formations simply evaporated. Some accounts blamed the collapse of the defences on a single regiment from 6th Grenadier Division that retreated without any attempt at coordination with its neighbours, opening a catastrophic breach in the lines of XXV Corps, but whilst this may have been a particularly large-scale incident, the same thing was happening everywhere along the sector that was under attack, allowing the Germans to advance easily.[205]

At the northern end of the sector, the German 2nd Guards Division encountered determined resistance from 6th Siberian Infantry Division at Zwyżyn, which was finally settled at close quarters as the Germans fought their way into the village from the south, while the *k.u.k.* 33rd Infantry Division attacked from the north. Progress everywhere was rapid to the extent that all planned objectives for the first day were secured by mid-afternoon; rather than allow the Russians any breathing space, Kathen ordered his men to push on. The weather turned rainy towards evening, but the advance continued until after dark, overwhelming the few areas where the Russians managed to gather sufficient strength to mount a defence. It had been a hugely successful day, with the leading elements advancing more than 5 miles (8km) on a frontage of 12 miles (20km). Nearly 3,000 prisoners had been taken, but the real damage to the Russian Army was in terms of the mass flight of so many troops.

George Washington is reputed to have said that 'discipline is the soul of an army. It makes small numbers formidable; procures success to the weak, and esteem to all.' By extension, in an army without discipline, even large numbers could not guarantee success. Throughout the day, Russian officers had tried in vain to organise a coordinated defence; on those occasions that their men didn't simply flee en masse, they found that their orders for immediate counterattacks were debated at length by soldiers' committees, which almost always resolved not to obey any such instructions – and on the few occasions when they chose to fight, events had already moved on. During the night that followed the start of the counteroffensive, Brusilov sent an urgent telegram to Gutor. The troops of Eleventh Army had retreated too rapidly, and had to be compelled to fight. He added:

> I order you not only to take all necessary measures to stop the advance of the enemy, but energetically to mount counterattacks to restore the situation. Seventh Army is not permitted to retreat. It is unthinkable that the enemy's advance can be allowed to threaten Tarnopol. Commissar Savenkov, military commissars and soldiers' committees are requested to help officers to encourage the troops to carry out their duties.[206]

It was a measure of how far matters had unravelled that the best that Brusilov could do was to ask the political commissars to encourage the troops to fight. Even if it had been possible to disseminate this instruction in the prevailing chaos, it seems unlikely that the troops would have listened to any such exhortations. On 20 July, *Gruppe Wilhelmi* extended the assault to the south. From the headquarters of the Russian Eleventh Army, Erdeli ordered XLIX Corps, his reserve formation, to intervene, but many of its divisions refused to advance. Those that obeyed the order found themselves caught up in the torrent of fleeing men and were often swept away in disarray; a few small groups of men managed to reach the front line, but broke as soon as they came under German artillery fire. The Russian I Guards Corps was ordered to coordinate its positions with the neighbouring V Corps in and around Zborów; instead, the guardsmen withdrew en masse, leaving V Corps badly exposed and in danger of encirclement. With little or no contact with any other formations, General Vyacheslav Ivanoovich Levitsky, commander of V Corps, ordered his men to pull back to avoid encirclement. They left behind much of their equipment as their withdrawal rapidly turned into a rout. On their northern flank, the Russian XVII Corps effectively ceased to exist as its formations melted away, and the Germans extended their advance to a depth of 13 miles (21km), an astonishingly large gain in the context of a war in which advances were usually of the order of a few hundred yards. Ahead of the German troops, the roads were choked with fleeing Russian troops and rear area units; these now came under machine-gun attack from the air, adding to the confusion and general collapse of any organisation.

The counteroffensive now turned into the pursuit of a beaten army. Further reinforcements arrived from *Ober Ost* in the form of 42nd and 92nd Infantry Divisions. Aware that these formations were en route, Winckler was able to release the *Leibhussar* brigade, which he had been holding back in reserve. The counterattack that Brusilov had demanded was intended to begin on 21 July, with the Russian VI Corps pivoting back its right flank and then attacking from the south, but instead Lieutenant-General Vladimir Vladimirovich Notbek's troops found themselves struggling to hold their lines, particularly as the *k.u.k.* XXV Corps now joined the attack. Farther north, Winckler's formations continued to advance almost unopposed. In barely a day, the Russian XLIX Corps was reduced to little more than a shambles and herded to the south, sweeping away part of VI Corps in the process. The disintegration of the line was now spreading to Seventh Army, despite Brusilov's demands that the breakthrough should be contained and subjected to counterattacks.

The scale of the catastrophe suffered by the Russian Army was unprecedented. Even during the heady days of Mackensen's great offensive of 1915, there had been few occasions when the German and Austro-Hungarian armies had enjoyed such a success; their breakthroughs had been relatively localised, with the Russians rapidly rebuilding their lines. Now, there was little chance of any such reconstruction. With a mixture of pragmatism and desperation, Brusilov advised Kornilov of developments, freeing him to withdraw south of the Dniester if the German and Austro-Hungarian advance should threaten his northern flank. At the same time, West Front was ordered to release X Corps, which would be sent south to try to restore Eleventh Army's positions. Unfortunately, X Corps was one of the formations that Denikin had used in his abortive attacks on the German lines, and its most reliable units had suffered heavy losses; the rest now refused to march south.

The third day of the counteroffensive took the German 6th Infantry Division to the outskirts of Tarnopol, an overall advance of over 20 miles (32km). By dusk, there were further changes in the chain of command. Gutor was dismissed from his post at Southwest Front headquarters and replaced by Kornilov, who was in turn replaced by Lieutenant-General Vladimir Andreyevich Cheremisov as commander of Eighth Army. Erdeli was dismissed as commander of Eleventh Army and replaced by Petr Semenovich Baluev, who had commanded V Corps during the disastrous fighting at Lake Naroch in 1916. Ever since the revolution and the advent of soldiers' committees, Brusilov had consistently tried to deal with matters by persuasion and negotiation, but Kornilov was of a different mindset. He immediately issued orders that, in view of the catastrophic situation, the activities of soldiers' committees were to be suspended immediately; local commanders were authorised to use force, including artillery fire, to disperse any attempts to hold meetings.[207] It was the start of a process that would bring him into direct conflict with the most ardent supporters of the revolution.

The commissars could do nothing to halt the rout. In a report to Kerensky on 22 July, a group of commissars reported: 'The German offensive, which began on 6 July [old Russian calendar] on the front of Eleventh Army, is assuming the character of a disaster which threatens a catastrophe to revolutionary Russia.'[208]

Alarmed by the refusal of X Corps and other units to obey orders, the Soviet sent a delegation to speak to the soldiers of West Front. In the past, such delegations had been received with respect and interest, but the mood had changed. They were heckled and jostled, and one delegate was physically attacked and left with a bloodied head.[209] Until now, the Soviet had exploited its position as representative of the soldiers with some effect, but the assault on its delegates changed the mood markedly. Even those in the Soviet who had supported the abolition of the death penalty and the general relaxation of discipline within the army could see that it was impossible for an army to function in such a state. Some blamed the influence of the Bolsheviks, but most could see that assigning scapegoats was no answer. Discipline had to be restored if disaster was to be averted.

Events on the battlefield did not wait for changes of command to settle down, or for politicians in Petrograd to act. Eleventh Army had effectively disintegrated, and Seventh Army was rapidly following suit. To the south of the Dniester, Eighth Army began to pull back in relatively good order, and from the headquarters of *Ober Ost*, Prince Leopold ordered the forces that had broken through and swept east to Tarnopol to turn south, with a view to rolling up the Russian front line before it could withdraw. The troops of *Gruppe Wilhelmi* and the *Beskidenkorps* continued their rapid advance, hindered less by Russian resistance than by congestion as their line of advance towards the south crossed with elements of South Army trying to advance towards the east. XXV Reserve Corps encountered determined Russian defenders near the line of the River Złota Lipa, but everywhere else progress was relatively smooth. For the German troops who had been transferred from the Western Front to take part in this offensive, the rapid advance must have seemed incredible as the entire Russian Front between the Dniester and the Sereth broke up.

South of the Dniester, Litzmann had anticipated that the Russians would have to withdraw if the counteroffensive north of the Dniester was successful, and had made detailed preparations for as rapid a pursuit as possible through the difficult hilly woodland that lay ahead. The Russians began to withdraw on 23 July, and Litzmann ordered his units to pressure their rearguards as hard as they could. It took most of that day for the Germans to force their way across the Łomnica and through the woods to the east, but there could be no doubt that a great victory was unfolding:

> My staff and I were in high spirits: after 22 months of positional warfare we were finally advancing again. We did not deceive ourselves that there wouldn't be significant problems to overcome. Our opponent lost a lot of men in his attacks. But he had not been decisively broken ... The skill of the Russians in retreating had already been demonstrated to us many times. They understood exactly how to disguise the timing of their withdrawal, to hinder pursuit through destruction of bridges and roads and the erection of roadblocks, to put up tough resistance with rearguards that would then disappear without trace. Also, our troops were unfortunately not fresh, having been worn down and exhausted by their preceding efforts. In all our offensives, we had learned that in the era of rapid-fire weaponry the losses of attackers were very heavy, resulting in the offensive easily faltering. Consequently, we were repeatedly required in eastern Galicia to 'lead', i.e. to keep the troops under firm control, constantly determining points of main effort and concentrating artillery. Nor was it possible in those days to give the individual divisions their own combat corridors and then simply to urge them forwards.[210]

As the rout of Southwest Front continued over the next few days, exhaustion amongst the pursuers was a greater concern than Russian resistance, though there were localised battles every day at one point or other; it was the failure of the Russian Army to convert these into consistent resistance that perpetuated the collapse. Tarnopol was abandoned on 25 July, and Kaiser Wilhelm was present to watch regiments from the Guards Infantry Divisions secure first the high ground to the north and northeast of the city, and then Tarnopol itself. South of the Dniester, towns like Stanislau, captured at such cost the previous year, were abandoned without any significant resistance. The question now was purely of where the advance would stop. On the one hand, the exhilaration of success drove the campaign onwards, but on the other hand, the Germans – they were, after all, dictating events, regardless of the views of their Austro-Hungarian ally – were aware that there were no war-winning objectives within striking range: no capital cities; no vital resources; no geographical goal that could force Russia out of the war, certainly in the southern sector of the Eastern Front. Elsewhere though, there was the possibility of capturing a major objective, as Ludendorff recalled:

> Even during the operations in eastern Galicia, I asked Oberst Hoffmann [chief of staff at *Ober Ost*, a post that Ludendorff had held before he and Hindenburg took control of Germany's war effort] by telephone if he could secure a crossing over the Düna [Western Dvina or Daugava] above Riga. Of course, he would need

troops for this, who were still engaged in Galicia. The Oberst was hooked. *Ober Ost* immediately issued preliminary orders.[211]

Like Litzmann and his staff, Hoffmann was in high spirits; during his visit to the Eastern Front, the kaiser had awarded him the *Pour le Mérite* with oak leaves, Germany's highest award. He recorded acidly that German strength of arms had restored eastern Galicia to the control of the Austro-Hungarian Empire and had not received a word of thanks, but he took pride in the operation that he had helped manage, as he and the rest of *Ober Ost* returned to Brest-Litovsk on 29 July:

Our task down here is effectively over. I never dared hope that the success of the operation would be so great. I know for certain that in the next few days we will succeed in driving the Russians over the frontiers of Galicia and Bukovina. Of course, there will then be a halt, as we are so far from intact railways that we can no longer bring forward supplies. Then something else will have to be considered – if Ludendorff leaves the troops with me. I have already had a very nice idea.[212]

Regardless of whether an attack to isolate and then capture Riga – the largest city in Russia's Baltic possessions, and one of Russia's great industrial centres – came from Ludendorff or Hoffmann, it was an obvious objective. Until preparations could be made, fighting would continue in the south, where a combination of lengthening German and Austro-Hungarian supply lines and good defensive terrain began to slow the advance. Litzmann moved from one location to another, urging his men onwards:

As we travelled on from Stanislau we were met by a crowd of Jews; their faces bore the marks of past terrors. They were inhabitants of Kałusz who had fled and now wished to return home. Cossacks and Circassians had hanged a large number of their people in Kałusz.

There had been much destruction and plundering in Stanislau, and again the Cossacks were the main culprits. A Russian regiment of Uhlans [lancers] recruited in Poland had to go into action against them and had prevented the worst excesses. In front of our hotel on the doorstep a Russian Uhlan officer still lay in a puddle of his own blood; he had been shot in a dispute with the Cossacks. The womenfolk of Kałusz brought me flowers and wanted to kiss our hands in gratitude. Jewesses spoke to us in their unique German: 'May the dear Lord give *Herr General* long life, good health, forever! May he be forever blessed for saving our people from

> great misfortune!' A deputation of citizens asked for permission to bury the corpses of the Uhlans who had been killed in a determined attack on our Bavarians. I readily agreed. An Austrian military band that was in Stanislau would take part in the ceremony.[213]

In 1914, when the Russians first entered this part of Galicia, there were widespread reports of atrocities against the Jews by Cossacks; when the area was taken once more by the Russians in 1916, there was far less misbehaviour, but it was almost inevitable that, following the relaxation of discipline after the revolution, the worst aspects of mistreatment of civilians would once more resurface. Guchkov, the former war minister, was with Eighth Army and witnessed personally the misconduct of Russian soldiers in Kałusz:

> The things that were done in Kałusz baffle description. I arrived there on the eve of the evacuation. It was enough to see the terrified faces of the inhabitants as they peeped from cellars … Eyewitnesses related that forty to fifty men in turn outraged old women of seventy and young girls. The drunken soldiery robbed without pity, and murdered if the inhabitants refused to give them money.[214]

The Jewish community of Czernowitz had suffered considerably in 1914, and it was now the only major urban centre in Galicia that had not been recaptured in the spectacular counteroffensive. As the fighting approached the city, there were further signs of the constant low-level friction between German and Austro-Hungarian units; a Bavarian infantry division complained to Litzmann about the tardy progress of its Austro-Hungarian neighbour, and Litzmann was deeply dissatisfied by a hospital of the *k.u.k.* Army that he visited:

> In the *k.u.k.* field hospital in Horodenka I saw terrible conditions. There was a shortage of suitable large buildings, of care personnel, of adequate supplies for the 1,200 wounded who lay there. Once again we saw that organisational ability, common sense and energy were of the highest importance for medical personnel in the field. In order to help the *k.u.k.* physician, who was deficient in all these factors, I tasked my new munitions and supplies officer, Oberstleutnant Gerhard, with providing straw and liaising with the mayor of Horodenka to arrange for suitable women to be summoned to care for and feed the wounded. The conduct of the wounded was generally impeccable; they endured their pitiable circumstances manfully and patiently.[215]

From the Carpathian Mountains, the *k.u.k.* Seventh Army joined the offensive. Had it done so with energy, significant parts of the Russian Southwest Front might have been squeezed back against the Dniester and destroyed, but the commander of Seventh Army, Hermann von Kövesz, lacked the troops which such an effort would have needed; he had requested two or three fresh infantry divisions, but heavy fighting on the Italian Front prevented *AOK* from agreeing to reinforce him. In the first two days of August, Litzmann's troops penetrated into the high ground to the north of Czernowitz, a region that had seen bitter fighting during the opening phases of the Brusilov Offensive the previous year. There was little prospect of being able to hold the city, and the Russians evacuated it late on 2 August; Litzmann was then obliged to stand aside and allow troops of the *k.u.k.* Army to enter Czernowitz to liberate it from Russian occupation.

Fighting continued for several more days, but the counteroffensive was effectively over. South of the Dniester, the Russians had been driven back over 70 miles (112km) in a little over two weeks – an unprecedented advance in this war of attrition and slaughter. Whilst the gains north of the river were somewhat less, they were still substantial, pushing the front line far to the east of the start-line from where Brusilov had launched his assaults the previous year. But more important than the change of territory was the complete disintegration of the Russian Army. Those killed, wounded or taken prisoner exceeded 400,000; the number of deserters was perhaps just as great.[216] Even as the front moved irresistibly east, Kornilov re-imposed the death penalty for desertion somewhat before the Provisional Government restored the measure across the entire country, and many soldiers were hanged and left on display, bearing placards that declared them to be 'deserters'. He also sent a strongly worded telegram to the Provisional Government, demanding support for his decision:

> I declare that the country is on the verge of collapse and that, although I have not been consulted, I demand that the offensive be stopped on all fronts in order that the army may be saved, preserved and reorganised on the basis of strict discipline, and in order that the lives may not be sacrificed of a few heroes who are entitled to see better days.[217]

He added that unless his demands were met, he would be obliged to resign immediately. On 29 July Kerensky summoned senior commanders to *Stavka* for a conference.

The circumstances of the conference were complicated by the manner in which those present were summoned. Ruzsky and Gurko were in the Caucasus when they received a summons to *Stavka*, and a special train was placed at their disposal. Only a day later, Gurko received a telegram from Lukomsky, the chief of the general staff, asking him not to come to Mogilev. Despite this, and a further telegram from Brusilov himself, Gurko continued to Mogilev. Here, he learned that Brusilov had invited him after being asked to summon the front commanders and others whose presence might be useful, but on learning that Gurko had been invited, the Provisional Government objected. Gurko now decided that he would diplomatically claim that pressing personal business in Petrograd made it impossible to stay in Mogilev. While he waited for his train to depart for the capital, Kerensky's train arrived for the conference. Gurko learned that Kerensky had summoned Brusilov and Lukomsky to meet them at the station, but Brusilov had declined, as he had been meeting those who were attending the conference and was now having lunch with them. Kerensky then sent an unequivocal demand for Brusilov to come to the station immediately.[218]

With his hands full in trying to save his armies, Kornilov was unable to attend the conference, and, according to his own account, Denikin dominated proceedings, speaking at great length about the dismal performance of his West Front in the recent fighting. He concluded:

> The army is falling to pieces. Heroic measures are needed for its salvation. Firstly, the Provisional Government should recognise its mistakes and its guilt, as it has not understood and estimated the noble and sincere impulse of the officers who had greeted the news of the revolution with joy, and had sacrificed innumerable lives for their country. Secondly, Petrograd, entirely detached from the army and ignorant of its life and of the historical foundations of its existence, should cease to enact military regulations. Full power must be given to the supreme commander-in-chief, who should be responsible only to the Provisional Government. Thirdly, politics must disappear from the army. Fourthly, the 'Declaration' [of soldiers' rights] must be rescinded in its fundamentals. Commissars and committees must be abolished, and the functions of the latter must gradually be altered. Fifthly, commanding officers must be restored to power. Discipline and the outward form of order and good conduct must likewise be restored. Sixthly, appointments to prominent posts must be made not only according to the standard of youth and strength, but also of experience in the field and in administration. Seventhly, special law-abiding units of all arms must be placed at the disposal of commanding officers as a bulwark against mutiny, and against the horrors of possible demobilisation. Eighthly, military revolutionary courts must be established and capital punishment introduced in the rear area for the troops and for civilians guilty of the same crimes.[219]

Whilst all officers present agreed that discipline needed to be restored, some doubted that harsh measures could be implemented. Klembovsky pointed out that entire divisions in Northern Front had refused to obey orders – were they all to be executed? If instead they were imprisoned, he warned that half the army would end up in Siberia.[220] The meeting broke up without any clear conclusion about how to restore discipline, but Kerensky had nevertheless made an important decision. Brusilov would be held accountable for the failed offensive, and was to be dismissed.

Kornilov's promotion to command of Southwest Front was largely due to the pressure of Boris Viktorovich Savinkov, the commissar of the front. He had been involved in the assassinations of Vyacheslav von Plehve, the interior minister, in 1905 and Grand Duke Sergei Alexandrovich the following year and escaped captivity while awaiting execution, seeking refuge in France. He fought in the French Army when war broke out, but returned to Russia after the February Revolution. He had urged Kerensky to promote Kornilov to command of Southwest Front, and was present at *Stavka* for the inconclusive conference, representing his commander. In private discussions with Kerensky, he persuaded the war minister that Brusilov was incapable of restoring discipline to the army; Kornilov should be promoted to supreme command. There was a widespread view that a strong man was needed to prevent the slide towards catastrophe, and Kornilov, the charismatic son of a relatively lowly Siberian Cossack, fluent in several central Asian languages – he even wrote poetry in Tadzhik – had been a national hero since his daring escape from captivity in Austria. The fact that he had ignored orders from Brusilov to withdraw his division from its exposed positions in the Carpathians and thus largely had himself to blame for his capture was quietly forgotten. Opinion about his ability and personality was divided; supporters like Denikin described him as 'a fighting general who carried fighting men with him by his courage, coolness and contempt for death'.[221] Alexeyev was less impressed, describing Kornilov as 'a man with a lion's heart and the brains of a sheep', though this latter description seems more than a little unfair in the context of his many accomplishments.[222]

Kornilov was a controversial person to be considered for the role of commander-in-chief, having previously resigned as commander of the Petrograd garrison in protest at indiscipline and at the refusal of the Provisional Government to support his demands for the immediate restoration of discipline. It is a measure of how far Kerensky had travelled in the intervening months, that he now appointed Kornilov to the post of commander-in-chief with the expectation that he would assert the very discipline that had been central to his resignation in Petrograd.

It was effectively the end of Brusilov's career; although Gurko believed that the friction with Kerensky over the latter's arrival at Mogilev for the special conference played a part, it would have been only a minor factor in such an important decision. Brusilov was nearly 64 years old, and until the Kerensky Offensive he had an almost unblemished record as a First World War commander – a unique achievement in the Russian Army. He was not without his critics – Knox, for example, regarded him as lucky rather than skilled, in that he rarely came up against German troops and owed his successes to his opponents being far weaker Austro-Hungarian formations – but there can be no doubt that he was the first senior figure to grasp the need for new tactics, and to implement them with spectacular success in 1916. Given the turmoil of early 1917, the outcome of the Kerensky Offensive would almost certainly have been the same regardless of who was in command, but his preference for negotiation and persuasion in the new revolutionary climate was at odds with the clear need to re-impose discipline. He moved to Moscow, where he was wounded when his house inadvertently came under fire during the October Revolution. In 1920, he issued an appeal to all former officers of the Russian Army to support the Bolsheviks, who he believed were attempting to save Russia from foreign invasions; thereafter, he served in a variety of staff and consultancy roles for the Red Army until 1924. He died two years later.

CHAPTER 7

THE IMPLOSION OF RUSSIA

In Petrograd, events had begun to move forward even before the full scale of the catastrophic military defeats became known. Appalled by the manner in which Soviet delegates had been mistreated by front-line soldiers and suddenly aware that the army was disintegrating, the Provisional Government had already agreed to the restoration of the death penalty, but this provoked further unrest in Petrograd, where much of the garrison remained only nominally under the control of either the Provisional Government or the Soviet. Most of the troops were those who had taken part in the February Revolution and had extracted special concessions, such as guarantees that they would not serve at the front. They regarded it as their duty to stay in Petrograd to safeguard the revolution, claiming that they were defending the gains of February from a reactionary backlash, though there was precious little sign of any practical steps towards counter-revolution. These troops had been joined by some of the more undisciplined troops from the front, who had either travelled to Petrograd under their own volition, or had been sent away by exasperated commanders who wanted to remove their disruptive presence from the front line. Whilst this may have reduced agitation and unrest to a small degree in Russia's field armies, the consequence was a concentration of the most militant soldiers in and around Petrograd.

Aware that there might be trouble, General Peter Alexeyevich Polovtsev, commander of the Petrograd District, had reduced the amount of weaponry available, moving large numbers of machine-guns to the front and reducing stocks of ammunition as part of the preparations for the summer offensive. This in turn triggered further discontent in the garrison, many members of which now feared that, as casualties mounted in the Kerensky Offensive, their exclusion from front-line service might be rescinded. The committees of several formations in and around Petrograd resolved to hold demonstrations to overthrow the government, a move that put the Bolsheviks in a difficult position. On the one hand, many actively supported the move by the soldiers, seeing it as the road to power, but on the other hand, there was concern that the Provisional Government retained considerable support across the country and, if the Bolsheviks were seen to be involved in its overthrow, there would be a major backlash against them. Lenin personally urged caution, drawing on the lessons of the Paris Commune of 1871, which was ultimately suppressed by anti-Communard forces raised in provincial France. But late in June, Lenin left Petrograd to stay in a friend's dacha in Finland and those in favour of an immediate revolution came to dominate the Petrograd Bolsheviks, albeit in a disorganised and somewhat chaotic manner.

On 16 July, the rebellious troops took to the streets backed by pro-Bolshevik workers, largely from the Vyborg district, and large numbers of Red Guards, the armed militia that had been created in the wake of the February Revolution. Barricades were erected and there were sporadic episodes of firing – mostly at random, but some between the troops and right-wing opponents. In one of the worst incidents, a commandeered car with a machine-gun mounted on it drove down Nevsky Prospekt and fired into some of the gathered crowds. Many civilians were killed and wounded, as were about 40 soldiers from the Pavlovsky Regiment; the rest of the regiment returned to its barracks in some disarray.[223]

Many of the soldiers carried banners demanding that the Soviet took power, and condemning the 'capitalist members' of the Provisional Government. They were unaware that the fragile coalition of the Provisional Government had already unravelled, with the Kadets – the 'capitalists' – walking out in protest over concessions that the government had been forced to make to the regional government in Kiev. The departure of the Kadets in turn triggered the resignation of Prince Lvov, but this had not been announced to the public yet. Throughout the night there was constant activity as the soldiers prepared for another day of protests, and various Bolsheviks – with little or no central guidance – continued to agitate. Lenin arrived back in haste from Finland, and apparently spent the night in agonised indecision, repeatedly asking Zinoniev and other senior Bolsheviks if this was the moment to try to seize power. Nobody was prepared to give a clear answer – they were all in completely uncharted territory.

The following day, the troops took to the streets again, joined by a large group of sailors who came ashore from a flotilla that had sailed to Petrograd from the naval base of Kronstadt, a hotbed of mutiny since February. They were led by Fyodor Fyodorovich Raskolnikov, the commissar of the Baltic Fleet. Raskolnikov was, according to some accounts, the illegitimate son of a Russian priest, and had adopted the name of Dostoyevsky's tragic character in place of his surname Ilyin during the February Revolution. Although he told onlookers that the sailors had come to Petrograd to help the garrison in a new revolution, many of the men who accompanied him spent the day promenading along the banks of the Neva accompanied by 'scantily dressed and high-heeled ladies'.[224]

There was growing confusion throughout the day. Whilst pro-Bolshevik soldiers and workers controlled the streets, there was no sign of any overall guiding influence. Alarmed at the turn of events and in particular the demands that it should seize power, the Soviet condemned the armed demonstrations, but at the same time others associated with the Soviet produced leaflets over the signature of the 'Petrograd Federation of Anarchists' that denounced Kerensky as a 'little Napoleon' who had sacrificed hundreds of thousands of Russian soldiers for no gain.[225] A large group gathered outside the Kshesinskaya Mansion, where Lenin had taken up residence, but when he eventually appeared to speak to them from a balcony, Lenin failed to issue a clear order. Had he told the people who had gathered to march on the Provisional Government in the Tauride Palace, there can be little doubt that the Bolsheviks would have been in power by the evening, though whether they could have held on to power is open to question. Instead he spoke briefly, telling the soldiers and sailors that he was confident that the Bolsheviks would soon take charge. In the absence of clear instructions, the large group wandered off to Nevsky Prospekt, joining with other soldiers, sailors and workers. A small group of soldiers approached the residence of Prince Lvov and informed his staff that they were there to arrest him, but when they were invited to send a number of their party into the building to talk to the prince, they lost their nerve and contented themselves with making off with Lvov's car.

Meanwhile, the masses that had gathered in Nevsky Prospekt began looting nearby shops. At about the same time, groups of Cossacks appeared to confront them. The Cossacks had repeatedly been deployed during the days of the tsars to suppress dissent, and they were now sent into action by the Soviet; they charged a group of sailors in the streets near the Neva, killing some and scattering the rest. However, when they attempted to take away their prisoners, other pro-Bolshevik troops intervened, as Knox witnessed from the safety of the British Embassy:

> In a few minutes two Cossacks returned on foot, escorting a prisoner, who appealed to a crowd of idle Pavlovsky men to rescue him. One Cossack dropped him, but the other, a big fellow, held on to him like a man. He was one against 20, and the cowards surged round him and overpowered him. The prisoner got free and at once bolted. A hero of the Pavlovsky drew the Cossack's sword, and

> while the others held back, gave him a swinging blow with it on the head …
>
> The Cossack, however, was only stunned for a moment, and then collected himself and ran off after his squadron. The other man ran in the opposite direction, and the insurgents fired several shots at both, but without hitting either.
>
> A few minutes later there was a stampede of riderless horses down the quay, and some five of them fell on the pavement at the corner in front of the Embassy. We learned later that the squadron had been ambushed and had suffered several casualties from machine-gun fire.
>
> I read in the paper next day that a motor conveying dead and wounded Cossacks across the bridge was stopped by the crowd, all the bodies were thrown out, and the wounded were beaten.[226]

As the day drew to a close, it began to rain, which helped disperse many of those still in the streets. Hundreds had been killed, largely by random fire or when the massed soldiers attacked civilians they regarded as 'bourgeois'. Maxim Gorky was appalled by what he saw during the unrest, as he wrote in a letter to his wife, Yekaterina Peshkova:

> The worst of it all was the crowd, the philistines, the 'worker' and soldier, who is in fact no more than a brute, cowardly and brainless, without an ounce of self-respect and not understanding why he is on the streets, what he is needed for, or who is leading him and where. Whole companies of soldiers threw away their rifles and banners when the shooting began and smashed the shop windows and doors. Is this the revolutionary army of a free people?
>
> It is clear that the crowds on the street had absolutely no idea of what they were doing – it was all a nightmare. Nobody knew the aims of the uprising or its leaders. Were there any leaders at all? I doubt it.[227]

It is surely more than slightly disingenuous to blame the soldiery for being leaderless – it was the responsibility of people like Gorky and Lenin to step into that role. Unless they were prepared to take a strong lead, they should have used their authority over the men to persuade them to return to their barracks; not to do so, and then to complain about their behaviour, highlights more than anything else the unpreparedness of the Bolshevik leadership.

The Provisional Government and the Soviet remained in the Tauride Palace, surrounded by tens of thousands of hostile armed men; only 18 soldiers were assigned to defend the palace, not even enough to man all the guard posts. Kerensky himself had departed by train to visit the front line, and the remnants of his cabinet were ensconced in the magnificent General Staff Building that faced the Winter Palace, protected by a small group of Cossacks. Even without firm leadership, the collapse of the government seemed imminent. When the restive soldiers and sailors penetrated into the Tauride Palace and seized Viktor Mikhailovich Chernov, the agriculture minister, Leon Trotsky – who was at that time a member of the Soviet – confronted them and urged them to release him. It was perhaps the only decisive moment of leadership and authority shown by any senior Bolshevik figure during the entire crisis.

At this stage, an infantry regiment appeared through the heavy rain, marching up from Tsarskoe Selo. The exact purpose for which it had been summoned was not clear to anyone – its small group of officers had been told that they were to march to the Tauride Palace to protect the revolution, though against whom was not specified. If the Bolsheviks were too unsure to seize the moment the same was not true of others; Fyodor Ilyich Dan, a leading Menshevik member of the Soviet, promptly ordered the newly arrived regiment to take up defensive positions around the palace. The moment in which the pro-Bolshevik soldiers might have overthrown the government had passed, and the following day, the remnants of the pro-Bolshevik troops and workers faded away as other military units arrived, this time with clear orders to prevent a Bolshevik seizure of power. Raskolnikov and his sailors from Kronstadt briefly seized the Peter and Paul Fortress, but as preparations began for the pro-government forces to storm it, they agreed to evacuate it on condition that they were allowed to return to their naval base. The unrest was over, at least for the moment.

The orthodox Soviet-era account of this episode describes it as a spontaneous uprising, but some believed that the Bolshevik leadership had intended to seize control; this seems unlikely, as there were several moments when even the most rudimentary instructions to the massed protesters would have resulted in the fall of the government. Instead, their indecision – and the contrasting opportunism of individuals like Dan – prevented such an outcome, though as will be seen later, there was considerable *post facto* rationalisation of their failure to seize the moment. The mood of many of the pro-Bolshevik elements in the garrison changed when the justice ministry published and distributed leaflets alleging that the Germans were financing the Bolsheviks. Whilst this was strictly true – the Bolsheviks received funds from Germany throughout this period – the amount involved was not great, and there was no evidence that the Bolsheviks were shaping their policies to suit the Germans. Nevertheless, it was sufficient to turn the mood against Lenin who was forced to flee, ultimately to Finland. As other Bolsheviks were arrested or turned against their former comrades, it seemed as if the failure of the Bolsheviks to seize the moment might have doomed their movement to oblivion.

For the Soviet, the fallout of the 'July Days' was particularly difficult. On the one hand, the members of the Soviet who had condemned the behaviour of the troops and other protesters were happy to blame the entire episode on the Bolsheviks, but on the other hand, many other members were fearful that suppression of the Bolsheviks would lead to a more widespread right-wing reaction against the revolution – in effect, the very counter-revolution that the rowdy garrison regarded as its duty to prevent. In another letter to his wife, Gorky acknowledged that the Bolsheviks were to blame for the unrest, but added that there was also undoubted evidence of agitation by German agents, and that the Kadets had somehow orchestrated the entire business. Many members of the Soviet felt an instinctive loyalty to their fellow socialists and were reluctant to allow an anti-Bolshevik witch-hunt to develop; they now claimed that right-wing groups were using the events of July as an excuse to try to dismantle the entire revolution. Foremost amongst these right-wing groups were those known as the 'Black Hundreds', who had been in existence since the beginning of the century. With a strong commitment to traditional Russian values, members of the Black Hundreds had been involved in violence against Jews and pro-independence Ukrainians, and had openly expressed their support for the tsar prior to his abdication – Nicholas even produced telegrams from members of the Black Hundreds as proof for Rodzianko that he retained popular support.[228] The Black Hundreds were outlawed after the February Revolution, but they remained a potent symbol against which all Russian socialists could unite.

On 19 July, Kerensky returned to Petrograd, happily accepting credit for having dispatched troops to the capital to prevent a Bolshevik takeover. Following the collapse of the coalition government, he was the only candidate to replace Prince Lvov as prime minister. The prince handed over power with a sense of relief; his hopes of taking Russia peacefully into a new post-tsarist era had always been optimistic, and were now looking ever more unlikely. A few days after officially stepping down, he contacted the writer Tikhon Ivanovich Polner, and told him:

> The only way to save the country now is to suppress the Soviet and fire on the people. I cannot do that. But Kerensky can.[229]

Kerensky's rise had been rapid, and there can be little doubt that he was now far above a level to which his experience and expertise were suited. Despite the disasters of the Kerensky Offensive and the collapse of the governing coalition, he was widely hailed as the man to unite all of the factions of Russia, and the expectations and adulation of so many parts of Russian society removed any personal doubts that he might still have held about his abilities. He moved into the Winter Palace, sleeping in the quarters once used by Tsar Alexander III and adopting many of the trappings of the tsars – guards were changed outside his apartments with pomp and ceremony several times a day, and the flag above the Winter Palace – red, in deference to the revolution – was raised and lowered depending on whether he was in residence. It took him three weeks to assemble a new coalition, which saw the Kadets return to office and effectively sidelined the Soviet; although several members of the new cabinet were members of the Soviet, they were there ostensibly on their own merits rather than as nominees of the Soviet, which was forced to move out of the Tauride Palace to the Smolny Institute a short distance away. Feeling that this represented a betrayal of the arrangements that had existed since the February Revolution, Tsereteli – who was suffering from tuberculosis – refused to be part of the new government.

One of the conditions stipulated by the Kadets for their return to government was the appointment of Kornilov as commander-in-chief of the army. Brusilov's star was already declining, and the increasingly imperious Kerensky was offended when Brusilov did not meet him personally when his train arrived in Mogilev. As a result, the pressure to sack Brusilov and replace him with Kornilov was irresistible. Regardless of those who were lining up behind Kornilov, Kerensky had need of a strong figure to further his own ambitions to run Russia effectively as a dictator, but almost immediately Kornilov placed conditions on his appointment. He wanted the death penalty – recently restored to the front line, and implemented by Kornilov even before it once more became law – to be extended to the rear areas. Furthermore, he told Kerensky that he would act according to his conscience and in the interests of Russia, rather than being subordinate to the Provisional Government. This seems to be because, despite the sidelining of the Soviet, he remained convinced that the government was overly dependent upon compromises made with the Soviet; although he was unable to persuade Kerensky to agree to this demand, further requirements followed, many of them apparently penned by Savinkov, the former terrorist who played a part in Kornilov's meteoric rise and who was now deputy war minister. These included further extensions of the death penalty, the effective elimination of soldiers' committees, the imposition of martial law throughout Russia, and increasingly strict controls over the railways and war-related industries. Many of these would have created something similar to the state of affairs in Germany, where Hindenburg and Ludendorff effectively headed a military dictatorship.

There can be little doubt that Kornilov firmly believed that these demands were vital to prevent Russia from falling under the control of the Soviet – the events of the July Days had shown how easy it would be for the left to seize control of Petrograd. After his experiences in the front line, Kornilov was also acutely aware of the disastrous state of the Russian Army, and as an authoritarian conservative it was not surprising that he believed the only way of restoring discipline in both the army and the nation was through strict discipline. This made him increasingly attractive to those who wished to reverse the revolution, even to restore the tsar to power – the Union of Officers, for example, consisted of current and former middle-to-senior army figures who were plotting a military *coup d'état* in collaboration with right-wing industrialists and members of the Kadets. If there was any coordinating mind behind this group, it was Vasily Zavoyko, who had made considerable money as a property speculator and industrial financier and according to some sources became Kornilov's main political advisor.[230] Shortly after taking up his post as commander-in-chief, Kornilov summoned other senior commanders to *Stavka* for a conference, and spoke privately to Denikin, who had just been transferred to take command of Southwest Front:

> Kornilov … said to me, almost in a whisper: 'It is necessary to struggle, otherwise the country will perish. N. came to see me at the front. He is nursing his scheme of a *coup d'état* and of placing the Grand Duke Dmitri on the throne. He is organising something or other, and has suggested collaboration. I told him flatly that I would take no part in any Romanov adventures. The government itself understands that it can do nothing. They have offered my joining in the government … No, thank you! These gentlemen are far too much entangled with the Soviets, and cannot decide on anything. I have told them that if authority is given me I shall carry on a decisive struggle. We must lead Russia to a constituent assembly, and then let them do what they like. I shall stand aside and not interfere in any way.'[231]

For the moment at least, Kornilov was distancing himself from the plotters. Kerensky and Kornilov were unlikely allies, and there was friction in their relationship from the start, particularly when Kerensky made little if any move to implement Kornilov's demands. In the words of General Yevgeny Ivanovich Martynov, who wrote a biography of Kornilov after the war:

> Kerensky assumed a high-and-mighty tone in his relations with the older generals. A humble hard worker like Alexeyev, or the diplomatically inclined Brusilov,

> could permit this treatment. But such tactics would not go down with the self-complacent and touchy Kornilov, who … for his part looked down on the lawyer, Kerensky.[232]

Savinkov too noted the hostility and mistrust between the two men; he later wrote that he had disagreements with Kerensky almost daily after becoming deputy war minister, and Kerensky repeatedly spoke about removing Kornilov from command.[233]

On 23 August, the commander-in-chief appeared in Petrograd and demanded to meet the government to discuss the lack of progress. A meeting between Kornilov and Kerensky, the latter accompanied by two close political allies, degenerated rapidly into shouting and recrimination, and that evening Kornilov dined with Rodzianko. He told the former prime minister – who was trying with Guchkov to establish a new liberal political party – that unless Kerensky agreed to implement his demands, he would dispatch troops to Petrograd. The following day, he ordered III Cavalry Corps to move to Velikiye Luki, from where the troops could travel rapidly by train to Petrograd if required. The precise reason for this move was at the time not clear; it could be interpreted either as a threat against Kerensky's government, or the deployment of troops who would be available to support it in the event of further pro-Soviet or pro-Bolshevik unrest. Within days though, Kornilov gave explicit orders to the commander of the cavalry corps: in the event of a further Bolshevik uprising in Petrograd, the troops were to move to the capital, arrest the Bolsheviks, and disarm pro-Bolshevik troops and workers.

In an attempt to bring together the increasingly fragmented representatives of Russian politics, Kerensky called a meeting in Moscow commencing on 25 August. He may have been disappointed, but hardly surprised, when it got off to a poor start – the Bolsheviks refused to take part and called out workers on strike paralysing Moscow's trams and closing all cafeterias and restaurants, even those in the Bolshoi Theatre where the conference was taking place. Even within the conference, there were clear signs of disagreement and entrenched positions when delegates from right and left took up seats on the right and left of the theatre, clearly opposed to each other. Kerensky's opening address laid down open challenges to those who might oppose him. When he told the conference that he would suppress any attempt to overthrow the government with blood and iron, he was enthusiastically applauded by many of those present; but when he went on to condemn those who presented him with ultimatums, the right-wing delegates listened in stony silence.[234] But few could deny the realities of what was happening on the front line. Alexeyev condemned the effect of soldiers' committees on discipline and order; he described to the delegates how during the recent disastrous offensive, one regiment's committee refused to obey orders to advance. As a result, the attack was launched by 28 officers, 20 NCOs, and just two soldiers, nearly all of whom were killed while the rest of the regiment watched and took no action.[235]

What was desperately needed was someone who could capture the imagination of all those present, perhaps with a fiery speech or persuasive rhetoric, and with his track record of such speeches in the past, Kerensky must have believed that this was truly his moment to rise up as Russia's saviour. But on the second day of the conference, Kornilov arrived from *Stavka* to a tumultuous reception. Women bombarded him with flowers when he disembarked from his train at the Alexander Station in the west of the city, and a cheering crowd of army officers and right-wing supporters carried him on their shoulders to a waiting motorcade. In a deliberately symbolic gesture, Kornilov drove to the Iversky Shrine near the Kremlin, the traditional destination of all new arrivals in Moscow and most importantly a location that the tsars had always visited when they reached the city. Rather than proceeding to the conference in the Bolshoi Theatre, he returned to his railway carriage where he received a series of visitors, including Miliukov and other members of the Kadets, important financiers, and several generals including Alexeyev and Kaledin. Some of his visitors urged him to take decisive action to arrest the growing chaos, particularly the financiers Putilov and Vishnegradsky, who offered to provide substantial funding. Many of those in Kornilov's entourage openly spoke about overthrowing the Provisional Government; Alexander Ivanovich Verkhovsky, the commander of the military district, was worried by such talk and urged restraint. He left the railway station alarmed that Kornilov's supporters were completely out of touch with the huge spectrum of opinion in Russian society, and commented that 'they seem like people who have just dropped from the moon'.[236]

Kerensky was deeply troubled by the reception that Kornilov was given. The two men were of the same mind that what Russia needed was a strong man; their difference of opinion was that each believed himself to be that strong man. Kornilov was tabled to speak to the delegates at the conference on 27 August, and Kerensky was fearful that, at the very least, the speech would cement the general's position as the man to restore order. He dispatched a personal envoy to meet Kornilov and to urge him to restrict his speech to military affairs; when Kornilov refused to give the envoy any such assurance, Kerensky telephoned him personally to repeat the plea. Kornilov's response – that he would give the speech in his own way – cannot have helped calm Kerensky's nerves.

When the speech was delivered, it proved to be remarkably bland, though it contained a warning that the Germans would attack and capture Riga, potentially opening the way for an advance on Petrograd, unless order was restored in the army. Kornilov was followed by several other speakers who demanded changes that amounted to a counter-revolution, turning back many of the changes since the February Revolution. Perhaps more important was the weakening effect that the exchanges had on Kerensky's personal authority; his personal plea to Kornilov left the general with the strong impression that Kerensky's position was weak. This increased his belief, fed by those on the right wing of Russian society, that it would be Kornilov, not Kerensky, who would be Russia's saviour. To make matters worse, Kerensky's closing address to the conference fell far short of his usual rhetorical flourish and degenerated into a muddled attempt to justify his own position; he appeared to lose the thread of what he was trying to say, and when he paused to collect his thoughts mid-sentence, the delegates brought the conference to an end by standing and applauding. As one of his supporters wrote: 'At the very end of his speech one could hear not only the agony of his power, but also of his personality.'[237]

While the Russians struggled to create a workable and sustainable system of power and command, the Germans made further gains in the front line. Ever since German troops had penetrated into Lithuania in 1915, there had been repeated suggestions from *Ober Ost* for a decisive drive to capture Riga, which ranked alongside Warsaw as an important city outside the strictly Russian parts of the tsar's empire. As will be described later, there had been repeated attempts to 'Russify' the Baltic States with only limited success, and Riga was not only the centre of Latvian nationalist thought, it was also one of the most industrialised cities in the Russian Empire. In August 1915, the Germans mounted a naval operation into the Gulf of Riga as a possible preliminary step to seaborne operations; a force consisting of two dreadnought battleships, two pre-dreadnoughts, three battlecruisers, and a large number of smaller vessels attempted to force their way through Russian minefields with the intention of engaging and destroying elements of the Russian Baltic Fleet. Like so many naval operations of the era, the action was indecisive, with both sides taking damage (the German battlecruiser *Moltke* was torpedoed by a British submarine and narrowly escaped destruction when the British torpedo struck a torpedo store aboard the German warship, but failed to detonate any of the explosives aboard the ship).[238] Even as the successful counteroffensive of 1917 began to wind down, Hoffmann turned his attention once more to this tempting target, just beyond the front line.

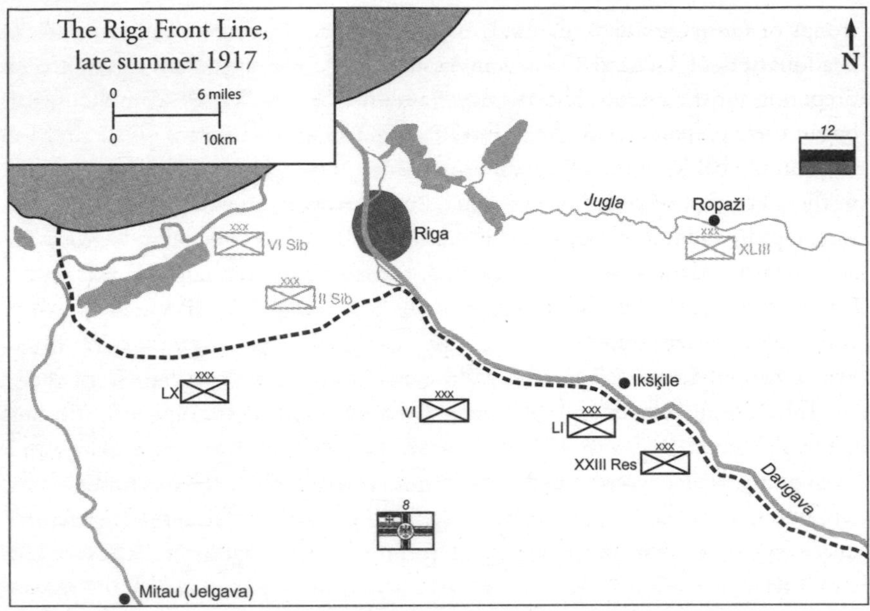

With his job of coordinating the initial artillery bombardment completed in the south, Bruchmüller was summoned to the north to begin preparations. General Otto von Below, the local German army commander, had already identified the best point to force a crossing of the River Daugava. Slowly, forces began to move north from the successful counteroffensive, but throughout the preparatory phase Hoffmann watched anxiously as fighting raged on the Western Front in the Third Battle of Ypres, fearing that Ludendorff would demand that the troops be sent west. On 21 August, he recorded in his diary:

> Early yesterday, Ludendorff telephoned: 'I'm very sorry, I need troops.' So nothing will happen [here]. I dispatched the appropriate orders. During the afternoon, he phoned back: 'Perhaps I will be able to make do!' I cancelled all orders. At midday today there were apparently further counter-orders. I can't accuse Ludendorff of anything, he really would like to allow me to carry out my plans and wants to leave the troops with me. But of course it is more important that the Western Front absolutely holds firm.[239]

Ultimately, Ludendorff was able to give Hoffmann unequivocal permission to proceed. Prince Leopold had made a point of being present personally when the troops of *Ober Ost* attacked, and this was no exception; he travelled first to the headquarters of General Oskar von Hutier's Eighth Army, then to the troops preparing for the assault. Shortly after 9am on 1 September, Bruchmüller's guns began their preparatory fire near Ikšķile, about 18 miles (30km) upstream from Riga on the banks of the Daugava. The balance of firepower was hugely in favour of the Germans, who deployed over 1,100 guns against 66 Russian guns, which were rapidly silenced. Troops from the German 19th Reserve Division and 202nd and 203rd Infantry Divisions crossed the river in small boats, securing a bridgehead against almost no opposition. Engineers immediately set to work constructing three pontoon bridges, which were completed in the early afternoon; Prince Leopold personally led one of the first bodies of men to cross the river.

The Russian defenders in this part of the front line were the men of Lieutenant General Dmitri Pavlovich Parsky's Twelfth Army. Aware that a German attack was coming, Parsky had already started to withdraw his men from Riga and the remaining areas held by the Russians on the west bank of the Daugava. Although his troops were badly affected by the widespread demoralisation in the army, he had little choice but to order a counterattack, and had concentrated four divisions in readiness, together with the 2nd Latvian Rifle Brigade. This group, designated XLIII Corps and commanded by General Vasily Georgiyevich Boldyrev, now began to move against the bridgehead from Ropaži, 11 miles (18km) to the northeast.

By the end of 1 September, the Germans had reached the River Jugla, an advance of about 5 miles (8km), meeting no significant resistance. It was an encouraging start, and German reconnaissance flights brought reports of large numbers of Russian troops withdrawing from Riga and the surrounding area. The operation was rapidly turning into a race – if it was to be entirely successful, the advance had to trap a large number of Russian troops and prevent their withdrawal. To that end, Hutier reorganised his army. Julius Riemann's VI Corps would advance along the east bank of the Daugava towards Riga, Albert von Berrer's LI Corps would drive northeast to intercept the retreating Russians and prevent their withdrawal, and Hugo von Kathen's XXIII Reserve Corps would guard against any Russian attacks from the east.

The almost effortless advance of 1 September might have left the Germans believing that the operation was going to be little more than a rapid march against a fleeing enemy, but this illusion was broken the following day. Parsky decided that the Germans had gained too much ground for his planned counterattack to succeed; the German advance had effectively rendered any defence of Riga impossible, and he ordered the abandonment of the city. Instead of attacking the German bridgehead, XLIII Corps was to stop the German advance for as long as possible in order to allow the rest of Twelfth Army to withdraw towards the northeast. During the night, a front line of sorts was established by the Russians along the Jugla by Boldyrev's troops, and the following morning every attempt by LI Corps and XXIII Reserve Corps to force crossings met with determined resistance, despite further heavy artillery bombardments. Even the use of the newest weaponry – gas shells, aerial attacks and flamethrowers – made little impression and the Russian defenders fought stubbornly, particularly the men of the Latvian Rifles. It took until the afternoon for the Germans to secure bridgeheads.

On the northern flank of the German advance, the German VI Corps advanced relatively smoothly towards Riga and reached the outskirts at dusk, advancing about 10 miles (16km). Riemann issued orders for a formal assault on the city the following day, coordinating with the German LX Corps, which held the line to the west of Riga. The Russian troops in this sector had put up little resistance, and continued to melt away in the night; on the morning of 3 September, German forces entered Riga unopposed. It was a major gain, for a variety of reasons: Riga was a major industrial centre; it was one of the largest cities in the fast-collapsing former Russian Empire with a large non-Russian population; and it moved the front line directly towards Petrograd. When the German Army entered Riga, many of its residents greeted its arrival with enthusiasm, but others – probably the majority – remained silent. For the landowning Baltic German aristocracy, there was hope that the establishment of German rule would preserve the privileged status they had enjoyed under the tsars; for the Latvians, whose nationalist aspirations were growing steadily, it remained to be seen whether the Germans would be better or worse overlords than the Russians.

A little to the southeast, the resistance of the Russian XLIII Corps was coming to an end. Its troops may have been the best available to Parsky, but they were still in poor shape – weak in artillery and ammunition, weak in terms of rear area support – and once the hard core of soldiers who were determined to fight was gone, the corps disintegrated as rapidly as the rest of Twelfth Army. The Latvian Rifle Brigade had suffered particularly, losing more than half its strength, but XLIII Corps had bought enough time for at least the personnel of Twelfth Army to escape. As the Germans advanced, they came across large quantities of military supplies and abandoned guns – much of Parsky's artillery was abandoned by the fleeing troops, and in any case the shortage of fodder for horses, due to the chaotic state of the Russian railways, meant that even if the soldiers had been inclined to take their guns with them, they often lacked the means – but comparatively few prisoners were taken. Hoffmann recorded in his diary:

> The retreat [of Parsky's Twelfth Army] seemed to have become a rout when we walked through the area. Everywhere there were guns, vehicles, field kitchens, and materiel of all types. It was only in prisoners that our gains were unfortunately less than we had hoped for, as the bulk of their troops, which I had hoped to cut off, had already been withdrawn from the bridgehead.
>
> Of course, we would dearly have wished to continue the advance towards Petersburg. Unfortunately, we had to call a halt, as with the best will, Ludendorff could no longer leave the divisions [that had earlier been sent east] with us. They were needed in the west and in Austria; we therefore had to release them.[240]

About 9,000 prisoners were taken, and over 260 guns were captured. German losses in the battle were about 4,200, compared to total Russian losses of over 25,000. Despite Hoffmann's disappointment, it was still a substantial victory, and only the alacrity with which Parsky abandoned the substantial bridgehead to the west of Riga prevented a far greater defeat for the Russian Army. Nevertheless, the loss of Riga was a severe blow to Russian morale and prestige, even if the front line had moved only a modest distance. The newspaper *Novoye Vremya* published an editorial that accurately summarised the situation:

> The loss of Riga was prophesied. The Riga region was abundantly equipped with arms, artillery, military provisions, and a large garrison. Its fortifications were the last word in battlecraft. Under the circumstances one could expect that an attempted assault by the Germans would receive a severe rebuff. And yet experienced military leaders warned that nothing could be achieved unless military discipline was restored in the northern army.
>
> This prediction was correct. Riga surrendered at the first onslaught, after a few hours. Nothing helped – neither the strong defences, nor the powerful artillery, nor the numerous defenders. Everything was in vain because the northern army, devoid of military discipline, was no army at all but a simple collection of armed men. Even if it consisted to the last man of heroes prepared for any sacrifice but not united into a single body of combat responsible to the single will of its commander, it could not have held Riga against the enemy's attack. Acting each at his discretion, the heroes would have been destroyed one by one and their heroism would have been no help.[241]

Whilst almost everyone heaped blame upon the Russian Twelfth Army for its inability to put up sufficient resistance to hold Riga, the 'Executive Committee the Soviet of Soldiers' Deputies of Twelfth Army' sent a telegram of protest to Soviet in Petrograd:

> A section of the press has started a brazen agitation in connection with the retreat on the Riga front. Malicious attacks have been recommenced against the army organisations which are blamed for the nonexistent deterioration of our army. They cast aspersions on the soldiers who are heroically fulfilling their weighty duty. They are blaming them for the absence of moral fortitude in Twelfth Army, they are inflicting treasonable stabs in the back of Twelfth Army at a time when it is sacrificing thousands of lives for the defence of Russia. All the officers and commanders confirm in one voice the amazing staunchness and the dauntless courage of the men in enduring the unprecedented drumfire, who retreated only after suffering enormous losses and failing to receive reinforcements. The frequent counterattacks of our infantry are sufficient confirmation of the complete falseness of the assertion about its demoralisation. In spite of heavy losses our units often rushed into combat, expressing regret when they received the order to retreat. It is criminal to speak of the retreat of our forces as a disorderly flight ... And at this time, when the long-suffering army has every right to expect moral support from the whole country, it is being slandered and attacked ...
>
> On behalf of the entire Twelfth Army, the Executive Committee rises to the defence of the soldier who has been slandered and disgraced by the enemies of the revolution and appeals to all the rear forces of the country ... to uphold the honour and dignity of the truly revolutionary army.[242]

The misrepresentation of events in this telegram is breathtaking in its scale. There was almost no resistance when the Germans secured crossings over the Daugava, and almost no counterattacks at any stage – XLIII Corps fought doggedly for a day to hold up the German advance, but almost no other formation showed any fortitude or determination. In an attempt to resolve the huge disparity between the reports from *Stavka*, which clearly blamed the lack of discipline in the army for the German successes at Tarnopol and Riga, and the protestations of soldiers' committees, the newspaper *Delo Naroda* called for the establishment of a commission of enquiry.[243] Whilst such a commission might be in keeping with the democratic principles of openness that had been established after the February Revolution, it would take time to conduct investigations and report to the government, and even more time for any action to be taken. In the meantime, there was no hiding the fact that the Germans were measurably closer to Petrograd, and there was much agitation that the line of the Daugava, long regarded as one of the strongest positions at which the Germans might be halted, had been breached.

But even if Ludendorff had been able to leave troops in the east, an advance on Petrograd was surely out of the question. There were reasonable roads running through Latvia and Estonia, but if Hoffmann had tried to reach the Russian capital, the forces of *Ober Ost* would have found themselves struggling through swampy terrain between the Estonian city of Narva and Petrograd at a time when the weather would be rapidly deteriorating. The effect of any such attempt on the Russian Army is difficult to measure; on the one hand the northern armies were particularly badly affected by the post-revolutionary turmoil, but on the other hand a direct threat to the cradle of the revolution would have taken events into completely uncharted waters. The combination of Anglo-French pressure in the west and the exigencies of the Italian Front ensured that this potentially ultimate test of revolutionary resolve never came to pass.

Far from the front, after the Moscow conference, Kerensky had little doubt that the future belonged to Kornilov and that his hold on power was slipping away. He told a friend:

> I am a sick man. No, I have died. I am no more. At the conference, I died.[244]

The Bolsheviks appeared to have missed their opportunity to seize power in July, and with Kerensky's star declining as rapidly as it had arisen, it seemed as if it was purely a question of when Kornilov and the right wing would step forward and assert themselves. Denikin's assessment of the situation is a good summary:

> The spectre of the 'General on the White Horse' became more and more clearly visible. And the eyes of many, suffering at the sight of the madness and the shame now engulfing Russia, were again and again turned to this spectre. Honest and dishonest, sincere and insincere, politicians, soldiers and adventurers, all turned to it. And all with one voice cried out, 'Save us!'
>
> He, the stern and straightforward soldier, deeply patriotic, untried in politics, knowing little of men, hypnotised both by truth and flattery, and by the general longing expectation of someone's coming, moved by a fervent desire for deeds of sacrifice – he truly believed in the predestined nature of his appointment. He lived and fought with this belief, and died for it on the banks of the Kuban.
>
> Kornilov became a sign and a rallying point. To some, of counter-revolution; to others, of the salvation of their native land.[245]

At the moment when Kerensky's fortunes appeared to be in terminal decline, there occurred an unlikely intervention by a man named Vladimir Nikolayevich Lvov. First elected to the Duma in 1907, he was appointed chair of a commission looking at the affairs of the Russian Orthodox Church, where he soon clashed with Rasputin and his allies. He became a member of the Provisional Government after the February Revolution and was appointed Procurator of the Holy Synod, and conducted a purge of those identified – with varying degrees of accuracy – as former supporters of Rasputin. He was a man of contradictory opinions; on the one hand, he supported pro-democracy and reformist members of the clergy, but on the other hand he was regarded by many as being autocratic and domineering. Partly due to this, he was dismissed from his post as procurator in July and found himself moving amongst many of those who were now gathering around Kornilov.

On 4 September, Lvov arrived unannounced at Kerensky's offices with a warning that there was a plot in military circles to overthrow him, and offering himself as an intermediary between Kerensky and the plotters. Kerensky's account, written two years later, suggests that the conversation was rather vague:

> I do not now remember the details of the conversation, but the gist of it was that Lvov tried to show that I 'had no support', whereas he had something or somebody behind his back. He kept on repeating; 'We can do this. We can do that.' I asked him who 'we' were, what he could do, in whose name he was speaking. To these questions he replied: 'I have no right to tell you. I am only authorised to ask you whether you are willing to enter into discussion.' … He emphasised the following: 'I am instructed to ask you whether you are willing or not to include new elements in the Provisional Government, and to discuss the question with you.' I replied: 'Before I give you an answer, I must know with whom I am dealing, who are those you represent, and what they want.' 'They are public men.' 'There are various kinds of public men,' said I. At last I said: 'Well, supposing I have no support, what can you offer, what are the actual forces you rely upon? I can imagine of whom your group consists, and who those public men are.' He then hinted that I was mistaken, that 'they' were backed by a *considerable force* which nobody could afford to ignore.
>
> … He asked: 'Will you negotiate if I tell you [who I represent]?' I replied: 'Tell me more definitely what you want to learn from me and why.' He said 'Goodbye' and departed. That was the end of it. Headquarters [*Stavka*] was not even mentioned.[246]

Two days later Lvov appeared in Mogilev and spoke to Kornilov, claiming to be Kerensky's representative. Somewhat oddly, Kornilov did not question this, nor did he ask for any documentary credentials; Savinkov had just left *Stavka* after discussions with Kornilov, and was clearly the person who would be expected to act as an intermediary between Kornilov and Kerensky. Lukomsky, Kornilov's chief of staff, even remarked that it was decidedly odd that Savinkov had made no mention of Lvov before he left – despite which, both Kornilov and Lukomsky acted as if Lvov's role was an official one. However, they interpreted events as a sign that Kerensky was acting in an underhand manner, and agreed to proceed cautiously.[247]

Lvov asked Kornilov what measures might be taken to strengthen the government, and suggested that a dictatorship was required; he added three possibilities, with either Kerensky or Kornilov appointed as dictator or the two men holding the post together. Kornilov told Lvov that he would prefer to take the post himself, but was prepared to act as Kerensky's subordinate if this had widespread support; he concluded the meeting by suggesting that Kerensky should visit *Stavka* to discuss the proposals further. This final suggestion, Kornilov added, was also intended with a view to safeguarding Kerensky against any attempt against his life should the Bolsheviks attempt to seize power. Perhaps it is significant that when he boarded his train at the end of his visit, Lvov was accompanied by Zavoyko, a central figure in military right-wing circles, who stressed to him that he had to remember just three things: Petrograd was to be placed under martial law; Kornilov was to be dictator; and the cabinet was to resign.[248]

When he returned to Petrograd, Lvov informed Kerensky that Kornilov had demanded the post of dictator. He added that Kornilov demanded martial law in Petrograd, the transfer of all civil authority to the army commander-in-chief, and the resignation of all ministers – once he was established as dictator, Kornilov would appoint a new government. It seems that both the suggestion to Kornilov of a military dictatorship and Kornilov's demand to Kerensky were the products of Lvov's imagination, but the messages that Lvov delivered to the two men were broadly in keeping with their own views and expectations, and from their individual perspectives were therefore entirely credible. Lvov's motivations for such a blatant misrepresentation of his conversations were never explicitly stated, but it seems likely that he was strongly influenced by the right-wing circles in which he had moved since being dismissed as procurator, and by the words of Zavoyko when he left Mogilev; acting in the wake of the Moscow conference, he probably believed that Kornilov was the man to bring about the changes that would save Russia, and this motivated him perhaps to try to force Kerensky's hand. His actions were therefore an attempt to bring about the state of affairs that he desired, far from the role of 'honest broker' in which he had cast himself. It is also quite possible that he was manipulated by one of the right-wing factions of which Zavoyko was a member.

Kerensky was stunned by this demand. Since the Moscow conference, he had been increasingly inclined to heed the right-wing agenda for sterner measures to restore order and was indeed planning to take decisive action against the Bolsheviks, but had no desire to allow Kornilov to take the lead in this process. That evening, he used the Hughes apparatus in the war ministry to contact Kornilov. Claiming to be Lvov, he told Kornilov that Kerensky wished for confirmation that the message he had delivered was correct. He did not specify what message had been delivered, and Kornilov replied in the affirmative, repeating the suggestion he had made to Lvov that Kerensky should travel to Mogilev for further talks.

The two men now took further steps based upon their incomplete knowledge of the intentions of the other. Kornilov believed that a dictatorship had been suggested, and all that remained to be settled was its composition; he discussed this at length with Lukomsky, his chief of staff, and speculated on whether Kerensky and Savinkov should be offered ministries in the new government. In Petrograd, Kerensky convened a late-night meeting of his cabinet and presented the demands that Kornilov had allegedly sent via Lvov, together with the teleprinter transcript, in which Kornilov confirmed that he had indeed asked Lvov to deliver a list of proposals. It is arguable that Kerensky genuinely believed that Kornilov was demanding dictatorial powers, but it is equally plausible that he deliberately avoided telephone contact or a more explicit teleprinter exchange purely in order to create an apparent case against Kornilov.

Kerensky placed Lvov under arrest and demanded the authority to move against what he portrayed as a plot against the government, but some members of his cabinet, led by Savinkov, felt that there was at least the possibility of a misunderstanding and suggested direct contact with Kornilov. Even at this late stage the matter might have been resolved, but the majority of the cabinet backed Kerensky, who argued that if he was confronted, Kornilov might appear to withdraw his demands while continuing plans for a *coup d'état*. At the end of the meeting, all ministers resigned and handed their power to Kerensky, thus effectively appointing him dictator. Kerensky then sent a telegram to Kornilov, telling him that he had been dismissed.

The degree to which Kornilov was plotting to overthrow the government is open to more than one interpretation. Denikin later wrote that he received an emissary from *Stavka* about a week before Lvov's fateful intervention, advising him that there was reliable intelligence that the Bolsheviks would attempt to seize power at the end of the month; the emissary added that III Cavalry Corps would move immediately to crush the rising, martial law would be declared, and the army would take control. Denikin was asked to send a number of reliable officers to *Stavka* immediately so that they could take part in the planned thwarting of the Bolsheviks.[249] When the telegram from Kerensky arrived on 9 September announcing that Kornilov was dismissed and that he should hand over power to Lukomsky, there was widespread alarm in *Stavka*. Lukomsky wrote a lengthy response to Kerensky, concluding:

> In the interests of the salvation of Russia you must work with General Kornilov and not dismiss him. The dismissal of General Kornilov will bring upon Russia as yet unheard-of horrors. Personally, I decline to accept any responsibility for the army, even though it be for a short period, and do not consider it possible to take over the command from General Kornilov, as this would occasion an outburst in the army which would cause Russia to perish.[250]

Kornilov rejected his sacking, acting on the basis that Kerensky could not dismiss him personally; his appointment and therefore his dismissal was in the power of the government, not its leader. The telegram dismissing him was signed only by Kerensky, and did not make clear that the cabinet had resigned and handed over power to Kerensky. Assuming that Kerensky was acting illegally – and was perhaps already under the control of the Bolsheviks, who had been rumoured to be making an attempt to seize power at the end of August – Kornilov ordered III Cavalry Corps to proceed to Petrograd to take control. Even at this stage, direct communication between the two men might have averted disaster, but Kerensky believed that he had one last, best chance to strike down the man who was his rival as the figure who would save Russia. He ordered the Petrograd newspapers to publish a special edition condemning Kornilov as a traitor determined to overthrow the government and reverse the gains of the revolution.[251]

Kornilov now turned to the army for support, knowing that he had the backing of many senior officers. Denikin was amongst the first to respond, sending a telegram to Petrograd:

> I am a soldier and am not accustomed to play hide-and-seek. On 16 July, in a conference with members of the Provisional Government, I stated that by a series of military reforms, they had destroyed and debauched the army, and had trampled our battle honours in the mud. My retention as commander-in-chief [of West Front at that time] I explained as being a confession by the Provisional Government of their deadly sins before the Motherland, and of their wish to

> remedy the evil they had wrought. Today I receive information that General Kornilov, who had put forward certain demands capable yet of saving the country and the army, has been removed from the supreme command. Seeing herein a return to the planned destruction of the army, having as its consequence the downfall of our country, I feel it my duty to inform the Provisional Government that I cannot follow their lead in this.[252]

From Northern Front, Klembovsky – who had been in command since June – advised Petrograd that he regarded a change in the supreme command at that moment as 'extremely dangerous', and Baluev, commander of West Front, declared that the overall situation required Kornilov to be retained in power. Shcherbachev, too, the commander of the Romanian Front, warned that Kornilov's dismissal would be fatal to the army. Emboldened by the support he received, Kornilov issued a general proclamation stating that he had not instigated the exchanges in which Lvov took part. Declaring that the Provisional Government was acting in a manner that would destroy Russia, he called for support:

> The solemn certainty of the doom of our country drives me in these terrible times to call upon all Russians to save their dying native land. All in whose breasts a Russian heart still beats, all who believe in God go into the churches, pray to Our Lord for the greatest miracle, the salvation of our dear country.
>
> I, General Kornilov, son of a peasant Cossack, announce to all and everyone that I personally desire nothing save the preservation of our great Russia, and vow to lead the people, through victory over our enemies, to a Constituent Assembly, where they themselves will settle their fate and select the form of our new national life.[253]

Kerensky was also moving to bolster his position. Unable to persuade any general to take Kornilov's place, he appointed himself commander-in-chief on 11 September, with Alexeyev as a reluctant chief of general staff. He also then sent an immediate order to Krymov, commander of III Cavalry Corps, to halt his march on Petrograd. The Soviet had been unsure about whether they should support Kerensky's assumption of dictatorial powers, but the arrival of the leading elements of Krymov's troops in the southern part of Petrograd tipped its members into making a decision. Declaring that the workers and soldiers had to defend the revolution against the forces of reaction, the Soviet called upon its supporters to prepare for battle. Perhaps 40,000 workers were given weapons and the sailors of the Baltic Fleet returned to the capital, this time to protect the Provisional Government that they had intended to overthrow in July.

The power and authority of generals depends upon the fighting power, discipline and loyalty of their men. Despite the attempts of Denikin and others to isolate their men from contact with Petrograd, word spread rapidly that the generals were attempting to overthrow the Provisional Government. In Southwest Front, the head of the soldiers' committee in Berdichev, the location of Southwest Front's headquarters, declared that he was taking authority and ordered the arrest of officers; in some cases, they were executed without any attempt to assess where their loyalties lay:

> The nervous tension increased, the streets were full of noise. The members of the committee became more and more peremptory and exigent in their relations with Markov [Denikin's chief of staff]. Information was received of disorders which had arisen on the Lyssaya Gora [in Berdichev]. The staff sent officers thither to clear up the matter ... One of them ... was attacked by Russian soldiers, one of whom he wounded slightly. This circumstance increased the disturbance still more.
>
> From my window I watched the crowds of soldiers gathering on the Lyssaya Gora, then forming in column, holding a prolonged meeting, which lasted about two hours, and apparently coming to no conclusion. Finally, the column, which consisted of a troop of orderlies (formerly field military police), a reserve *sotnia* [company], and sundry other armed units, marched on the town with a number of red flags and headed by two armoured cars. On the appearance of an armoured car, which threatened to open fire, the Orenburg Cossack *sotnia*, which was on guard next to the staff quarters and the house of the commander-in-chief, scattered and galloped away. We found ourselves completely in the power of the Revolutionary Democracy.[254]

If Kornilov was to have any chance of success, all depended upon Krymov's III Cavalry Corps. Pro-Bolshevik railwaymen disrupted the movement of the troops towards the capital, and deputations from Petrograd hurried to meet the troops. The men of the cavalry corps had been told by Krymov that they were marching on Petrograd to protect the Provisional Government from a Bolshevik *coup d'état*, and when they realised that the Provisional Government was still intact, they began to drift away from their trains with the soldiers who had been sent to meet them. Some mounted a red flag on their trains, others arrested many of their officers. On 12 September, a representative of Kerensky's government arrived in Luga, about 84 miles (135km) south of Petrograd where Krymov's train was stranded. The commander of III Cavalry Corps agreed to go to Petrograd; the following day, he tried in vain to explain to Kerensky that he had been ordered to proceed to the capital to protect the government, not overthrow it. Kerensky dismissed him and told him that he would face a court martial. Krymov went to the home of a friend in the city, a broken man. He told his friend:

> The last card for saving the Fatherland has been beaten – life is no longer worth living.[255]

He then went into a separate room, wrote a letter to Kornilov, and shot himself.

Kornilov was placed under arrest the following day. Together with Denikin and other supporters, he was confined – under fairly lax terms – in the Bykhov Monastery near Mogilev. At the same time, many of the Bolsheviks who had been arrested after the July unrest were released.

Any lingering trust between officers and men in the front-line army evaporated and desertions multiplied at an alarming rate. Many army and front commanders and other senior officers were dismissed. Some were placed under arrest, only to be released shortly afterwards, while others languished in varying degrees of confinement awaiting some form of trial. Vasily Gurko had been placed under arrest in August for a letter that he sent to Tsar Nicholas immediately after the February Revolution, but was once more at liberty during the days of the Kornilov Affair, at the end of which he was again arrested. During his first arrest, he was offered the opportunity of leaving the country for Sweden, but it proved impossible to arrange for him to depart via Russian Finland. After a week or so of renewed captivity after Kornilov's fall, he was allowed to depart for Archangelsk, where he boarded a British warship that took him to England.[256]

The sailors of the Russian Baltic Fleet had been prominent supporters of the Bolsheviks from the days of the February Revolution, and many now stepped up their protests. There was violent unrest in Vyborg, between Petrograd and the Finnish border resulting in the deaths of many officers, as Knox described:

> Poor Neverdovsky [a colonel in the Guards and an old acquaintance of Knox] came to see me at the embassy yesterday [20 October]. He and his wife escaped from Vyborg by the skin of their teeth. The massacre of officers lasted two days, and was organised by sailors who came from Helsingfors [Helsinki] and called the local garrison 'Black Hundred Reactionaries' because they had not shed any officer blood.
>
> At 2pm on the first day a few of his men came to Neverdovsky and asked him to explain Kornilov's movement. When Neverdovsky complied, one man said:

> 'All the officers say that they are for the government, but they are all secretly for Kornilov. They should all be wiped out.' Another man said: 'Come along and don't talk,' and they all went out.
>
> Two hours later he saw some 40 soldiers running with rifles, and soon afterwards he heard that General Oranovsky, the commander of the troops in Finland, General Vasiliev, the general quartermaster, and General Stepanov, the commandant of the fortress, had been arrested. Later a lady came in to say that they had all been murdered. They were thrown over the bridge and shot in the water.
>
> Neverdovsky spent the night in a house with friends. He was about to go to his office in the morning but was implored by his officers to wait while a junior officer spied out the land. This boy soon returned with the news that it had been decided to murder all officers of field rank. Neverdovsky managed to find a hired carriage, which took him for an exorbitant fare to the house of a colonel he knew some 20 miles off. There he hid six days before venturing to escape to Petrograd. The Finnish peasants helped him and gave him a rifle, saying: 'The Russian soldiers are bad men. We will defend you.'
>
> General Marushevsky … told me later that he had warned the government as early as July that this massacre was coming at Vyborg. Twenty-six officers were murdered.[257]

The aftermath of the Kornilov crisis was effectively the end of the army as a fighting force. In addition to the breakdown of trust between officers and men, the rank and file lost any lingering faith in any government to bring the dreadful war to an end and simply decided that they would no longer take part in it. If the Germans were to gather sufficient forces for a further offensive, there could be little doubt that they would advance almost unopposed, and a test of what remained of the fighting power of the Russian Army came not long after.

Ober Ost might not have sufficient troops to mount a major drive, and in any event it was late in the year to be considering a new offensive, but with an eye on a future campaign in the Baltic region, perhaps even with a view to reaching Petrograd, the Germans turned their attention to the archipelago of islands off the coast of Estonia. If the three islands – Saaremaa, Hiiumaa and Muhu (Ösel, Dagö and Moon to the Germans) could be captured, the maritime approaches to Petrograd would be open for the German Navy, and it might be possible to support a drive into Estonia from the sea, both militarily and logistically. To that end, a substantial naval force was dispatched to the eastern Baltic, consisting of the battlecruiser *Moltke*, ten battleships, nine light cruisers, and a large number

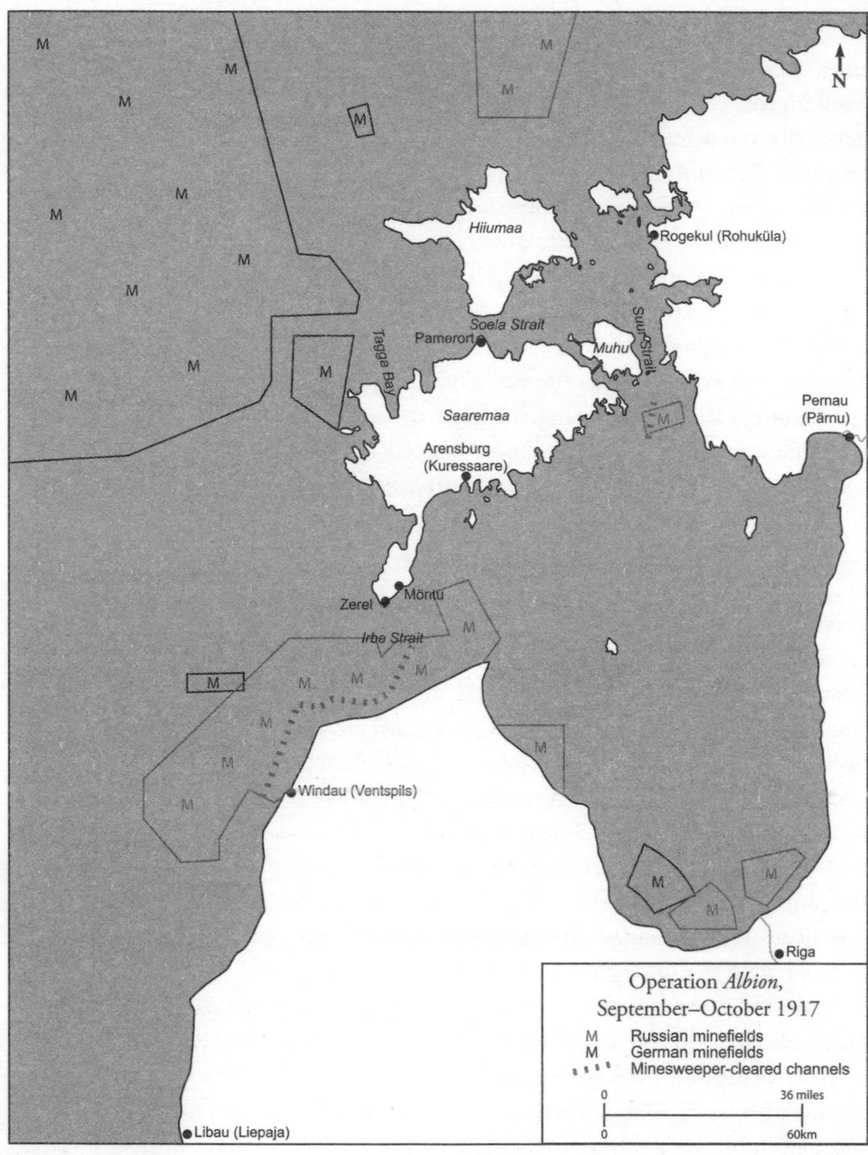

of smaller vessels. Once the warships had secured control of the sea, Lieutenant General Ludwig von Estorff's reinforced 42nd Infantry Division would be landed on the islands.

Even if the Russian forces in the region had not been disintegrating as a consequence first of the February Revolution and then the Kornilov Affair, they would have been hugely outmatched, particularly at sea. The Russian Navy had never recovered from the loss of its Pacific and Baltic Fleets during the Russo-Japanese War, and could deploy only two elderly battleships, three cruisers, and several smaller ships to oppose the German force. The size of the overwhelming naval force deployed by Germany was probably dictated by more than just a desire to ensure military success. There had been considerable unrest in the German Navy during 1917, and it was probably felt that a successful campaign would do much to restore morale and discipline. There was also open resentment in naval circles of repeated criticism from Ludendorff and others, who felt that it was the army that was carrying the burden of war while the navy failed to show any aggressive spirit. The deployment of such a powerful force for the operation, codenamed *Albion*, would bring such criticism to an end.

The Russian garrisons of the islands were at least as numerous as the German troops being sent against them, and consisted primarily of the reinforced 107th Infantry Division. The commander of the garrison of the islands was Rear Admiral Dmitri Alexandrovich Sveshnivov, and his men occupied well-constructed defences. However, the formations were badly under-strength as a result of desertions. Many of the men were more interested in looting the countryside than fighting, resulting in one regiment that had been earmarked for the islands being left in Estonia rather than risking open mutiny if the men were ordered to embark.[258] The coastal batteries, many of which were armed with powerful 6-inch guns, were the most formidable weapons available to Sveshnivov, and at least their crews were fairly reliable.

German preparations for *Albion* were complete by 24 September, with troops and ships gathered in ports on the Latvian coast. In the face of bad weather, the operation was postponed, and preparation was limited to air raids against the coastal batteries. One such raid by army Zeppelins late on 30 September triggered an explosion in the magazine of the battery at Zerel, the southern tip of Saaremaa; the resulting explosion killed more than 110 men and destroyed several guns.[259]

The sea around the islands was heavily mined by both sides, and the success of the operation would require the clearance of suitable channels for the German ships to move into position. Even before the main force set sail, German minesweepers were active, and the dangers that the operation faced were highlighted by the loss of several small vessels and serious damage to the *Cladow*, a larger ship providing logistic support. There was an obvious tension between ensuring that mine-free lanes had been secured before deploying the larger ships and losing any chance of surprise, and this caused major debate amongst the senior officers involved. Ultimately, Admiral Reinhard Scheer, commander of the German Navy, ruled in favour of speed: the longer the delay, the greater the risk of bad weather forcing the abandonment of the entire operation.

Although the Zerel battery in the south of Saaremaa had been badly degraded, the plan was to approach the island from the northwest and put troops ashore in Tagga Bay. At the same time, a second landing would be made farther east at Pamerort; the four infantry regiments of Estorff's infantry division would advance south and southeast to secure the island, while a bicycle-mounted brigade would advance swiftly east to capture the causeway linking Saaremaa with Muhu. The Russians were aware of the suitability of areas like Tagga Bay for landings, but lacked the troops to defend all such positions. Instead, they intended to defend the few roads on the island in order to hold up an invading force as long as possible, until a combination of winter weather and the arrival of reinforcements from the mainland turned the tide in their favour.[260]

Late on 10 October, the German battleships left their anchorage near Danzig and sailed north. The transport ships carrying 42nd Infantry Division joined them as they passed the Latvian coast. In heavy seas, the force laboured on with minesweepers in the lead; eventually, mine-clearing operations had to be suspended. There was a further debate about whether or not to proceed, but Vice-Admiral Ehrhardt Schmidt, aboard the battlecruiser *Moltke*, ordered the ships forward despite the risk. The decision was vindicated – only one small vessel struck a mine, and other ships were able to take off all its crew and the soldiers it was carrying.[261]

Early on 12 October, the German battleships entered the area of water to the north of Tagga Bay. Almost immediately, the fears of those who had wanted more time to clear the minefields seemed justified when *Bayern* and *Grosser Kurfürst* both struck mines. Nevertheless, the gunfire of the ships rapidly silenced the shore batteries and the transport ships were able to begin disembarking their troops in Tagga Bay. Despite being alerted to German preparations for an amphibious operation, the defenders put up little resistance other than some desultory shelling. Originally, Estorff had intended to secure the landing area and bring ashore all of his division's heavy equipment, but when it became clear that the Russian infantry was fleeing from even the most cautious German probes, he ordered his men to proceed into the interior of the island without delay. There were running fights throughout the day, and repeated exchanges of fire between the lighter vessels in the German naval force and Russian destroyers in the shallow waters between Saaremaa and Hiiumaa, but by the end of the day the bicycle brigade had reached and blocked the causeway to Muhu. At this stage, the German naval commanders received reports of several Russian submarines entering the area, and the valuable battleships were ordered to withdraw; *Bayern* was unable to move at speed because of mine damage and dropped anchor in Tagga Bay.

The Russians desperately tried to catch up with events. The garrison of Saaremaa was ordered to withdraw to the Muhu causeway – the leadership was apparently unaware that the German bicycle brigade had already cut off this line of retreat. At the same time, Russian destroyers were to secure the Soela Strait between Saaremaa and Hiiumaa, after which the area would be blocked by sinking the small freighter *Lafviya* and laying mines. Before this operation could begin, disaster struck: the train carrying the mines to the port of Rogekul (now Rohoküla) was derailed in an accident. The resulting explosion destroyed all the mines, as well as causing considerable damage to the surrounding area. The minelayer *Pripyat* was in danger of being engulfed in the resulting inferno and had to set sail hastily. There was widespread suspicion that the train had been derailed by German agents.[262]

On the morning of 13 October, the Russian ships attempted to block the Soela Strait. Before it could reach the location where it was to be sunk, the blockship *Lafviya* ran aground and had to be abandoned, and the crew of the minelayer *Pripyat* – perhaps still unsettled by the explosion of the night before – refused to continue unless their safety could be assured. The escorting eight destroyers pressed on but were twice driven back by gunfire from the German cruiser *Emden*. On Saaremaa, the German advance proceeded at pace; the administrative capital of Arensburg (now Kuressaare) in the south of the island was captured without a fight late in the day. At the Muhu causeway there was chaos as retreating Russian units, often accompanied by rear area formations and even the families of many of the troops, ran into the German forces blocking their line of retreat. Any hope of escape disappeared as the approach road became choked with abandoned vehicles and dead horses. Eventually, the German bicycle brigade pulled back a short distance due to lack of ammunition and some of the Russians were able to escape to Muhu. Here, they encountered Russian reinforcements attempting to move in the opposite direction; the panic and demoralisation of the retreating elements of the Saaremaa garrison swept most of them away.[263]

To date, *Albion* had gone well for the Germans. On 14 October, with most of Saaremaa under their control, the Germans turned their attention elsewhere. Minesweepers were at work clearing the Irbe Strait to the south of Saaremaa, which would allow German shipping to move freely into the Gulf of Riga, and it was decided to carry out landings on Hiiumaa, the most northern island in the archipelago, as soon as possible. Supported by the battleship *Kaiser*, the German cruiser *Emden* moved forward to clear the Soela Strait of Russian warships so that mine-clearing operations could proceed; after a brief firefight, four Russian destroyers were driven off. Once the mines in the Soela Strait had been cleared, German torpedo boats and destroyers moved into the shallow water between the three islands of the archipelago. Once more, the Russian destroyers attempted to intervene, supported by two older armoured vessels. Already damaged earlier in the day by a direct hit from the main armament of the battleship *Kaiser* – fortunately, the shell failed to explode – the Russian destroyer *Grom* was hit repeatedly and lost power. Attempts to tow it to safety failed and the ship was abandoned, sinking later that afternoon.

Finally, German warships were able to start providing fire support for the forces that were still attempting to block the Muhu causeway. A 'battalion of death', raised from volunteers of the Russian Baltic Fleet, had adopted the same title as the women's battalion and proved to be one of the few units capable of fighting energetically but, like its German opponents, a mixture of exhaustion and ammunition shortages brought its activities to an end. With the guns of the German torpedo boats sweeping the causeway, the remaining Russian troops on Saaremaa were definitively isolated.

Throughout the day, German minesweepers dodged shells from the Russian battery at Cape Zerel, clearing several lines of Russian mines. During the afternoon, the battleships *König Albert*, *Kaiserin* and *Friedrich der Grosse* opened fire on the Russian battery. Despite firing over 120 rounds, they scored few hits and did little damage. Nevertheless, many of the gun crews abandoned their posts and headed for the interior of the island – only to find their line of retreat cut by the German forces pressing down from the north. In an attempt to avoid further unnecessary fighting, the Germans called on the Russians to surrender, offering them favourable terms but threatening to fight to the death if the offer was rejected. The Russians made no reply and fierce fighting erupted, supported by the German battleships off the coast. As the hopelessness of their situation became increasingly apparent and rumours of the German offer of surrender spread, many of the Russian troops slipped away to surrender individually.

On 15 October, the Germans planned to overwhelm the Russian forces trapped in the peninsula that stretched down to Cape Zerel. The soldiers' committee of the Russian regiment had issued a radio plea for help the previous night, and in response to this the Russians dispatched a substantial naval force. The leading vessel was the battleship *Grashdanin*, built in France at the turn of the century and completely outclassed by the German battleships. The other vessels, three destroyers and the armoured cruiser *Admiral Makarov*, did little to improve the balance of power. As the Russian group sailed forth, German minesweepers clearing the last of the mine barriers across the Irbe Strait spotted the smoke from the funnels of the leading destroyers. At the same time, German battleships moved to open fire on the Zerel battery, unaware that the Russian troops had abandoned it. Their fire was more accurate than the previous day, not only knocking out several of the remaining guns but also disrupting attempts by Lieutenant Bartinev, a gunnery officer in the battery, to set off demolition charges.

The Russian naval force approached the southeast coast of Saaremaa during the afternoon. Organised resistance was clearly coming to an end, and several ships reached the small fishing port of Möntu, a short distance to the northeast of Cape Zerel. Large numbers of desperate Russian soldiers had gathered here and attempted to board the destroyers in order to escape. After bombarding some of the abandoned positions, the Russian warships withdrew towards the mainland with a few hundred soldiers aboard, leaving the rest to their fate. Overnight, there were further negotiations, and the remaining men surrendered early on 16 October.[264] Throughout the day, the Germans had been pressing down on the Russian forces that had tried in vain to break through to the Muhu causeway; when the Russian warships failed to reach them to lift them to safety, the last of the men surrendered. The whole of Saaremaa was in German hands.

A small bridgehead was established on Hiiumaa on 15 October, but was evacuated when it came under unexpectedly heavy Russian pressure. On 16 October, with fire support from the battleship *Kaiser*, a second landing took place at the southern tip of the island. Despite repeated interventions by Russian warships, the smaller German vessels repeatedly bombarded positions on Muhu and minesweepers finally completed the clearance of the Irbe Strait, allowing the German battleships to move forward, only to encounter yet another line of mines. The warships were forced to drop anchor while they were cleared. Originally, it had been the intention of the German naval commanders to use the battleships to protect transports bringing supplies from Riga to Arensburg, but the ships were now ordered to proceed as fast as possible to the Suur Strait, between Muhu and the mainland, in order to isolate the island. As they advanced, they were spotted by the British submarine *C27*, which fired two torpedoes at the battleship *König*. Both missed, but in a second attack succeeded in hitting the minesweeper support ship *Indianola*, which was towed to safety in Arensburg. By the end of the day, the German warships had reached the southern end of the Suur Strait. From a map that had been found aboard the destroyer *Grom* before it sank, the Germans knew the locations of the Russian minefields in the area and drew up their plans for the following day. The battleships would penetrate the Suur Strait, while the smaller warships would move into the channel between Muhu and Saaremaa.

Preceded by the tireless minesweepers, the German warships moved forward on 17 October. The Russian naval forces were now commanded by Admiral Mikhail Koronatovich Bachirev, and he dispatched *Grashdanin* and the equally elderly *Slava* to stop the German battleships, following a short distance behind aboard the armoured cruiser *Bayan*. The first shots were exchanged not long after dawn; *König* drove off the destroyers that accompanied the Russian battleships, while the Russian warships and coastal batteries opened fire on the German minesweepers. Shortly after, *Slava* opened fire on *König* and *Kronprinz*. It was a decidedly uneven contest, with *Slava* possessing only four elderly 12-inch guns against ten guns on each of the German warships. Nevertheless, *Slava* had been modified to allow her guns to be elevated sufficiently high to out-range the German ships. Despite firing several rounds, no hits were scored, and eventually *Slava* was forced to break off the engagement when her fore turret became jammed.

By mid-morning, the German minesweepers had cleared a large part of the Russian minefield, despite being under almost constant fire, and the two German battleships moved forward in a determined attempt to close to effective firing range. After firing for just four minutes, *König* scored hits on *Slava* below the waterline with the third salvo. Two shells penetrated the Russian ship's armour and exploded, tearing large holes in her hull. The accompanying *Grashdanin* was also hit twice. Moments later *Slava* was hit again, and Bachirev ordered his ships to break off the engagement. The German ships pursued, scoring further hits on *Slava* and *Bayan*, leaving the latter ablaze before breaking off the engagement for fear of running into further mines. *Slava* was unable to keep up with the rest of the Russian ships, and Captain Vladimir Antonov was fearful that, having shipped so much water, his vessel would not be able to pass through the shallow northern part of the Suur Strait. With Bachirev's permission, he decided to sink his ship in the channel in order to block it. Discipline aboard the battleship broke down, preventing Bachirev from manoeuvring his ship into the desired position for it to act as a blockship. A destroyer came alongside to take off the crew, and Antonov was the last to depart. Shortly after, demolition charges in the main magazine exploded; the accompanying destroyers fired six torpedoes at *Slava* to sink her, but only one exploded.[265]

Fighting continued until 20 October to secure Muhu and Hiiumaa, but the Russian position had become impossible. In addition to the loss of the battleship

Slava and destroyer *Grom*, the Russians lost nearly the entire island garrison of 24,000 men. The disintegration of Russian fighting strength was clear from German casualties – only about 200 killed and a similar number wounded. For the German Navy, it was the greatest success of their surface vessels since the destruction of the British 4th Cruiser Squadron at Coronel in 1914. For the Russians, it was a further setback at the end of a calamitous year. There could be no doubt that further attempts to prolong the war would end only in greater disasters. Whatever Kerensky might feel about the need to fulfil his treaty obligations, Russia simply lacked the ability to continue fighting. On 19 October, Hoffmann recorded in his diary:

> At the moment, the Russian Army is in very bad shape – more is the pity that we can't take advantage of it. If I had not had to hand back the divisions [to Ludendorff after the fall of Riga], we would now be on the shores of Lake Peipus.[266]

Nor were Russia's treaty obligations the only matter in which Kerensky's wishes were increasingly irrelevant. He may have succeeded in exploiting Lvov's crass intervention to remove Kornilov, but he was effectively powerless. Just as Kornilov proved to be unable to achieve anything without the support of the army's troops, so Kerensky lacked any means of asserting his will. Even the generals confined to prison in September could not be detained, largely due to the sympathies of their jailers; both Kornilov and Denikin were able to escape and played leading roles in the civil war that broke out shortly after. What remained of the army after its mass desertions was loyal to the Soviet or the Bolsheviks rather than the Provisional Government, as were the armed workers who had prepared to defend Petrograd against III Cavalry Corps. Whilst Kerensky might have removed the figurehead of the right-wing factions in Russia, those factions remained alive and powerful, increasingly convinced that they would have to use force to prevent Russia from falling into the hands of the Bolsheviks; and the Bolsheviks enjoyed a resurgence in power and influence after the setbacks of July, not least because so many leading figures were released from prison. The pieces were in place for civil war – all that was needed was a trigger to ignite the fire.

CHAPTER 8

THE BOLSHEVIKS AND RED OCTOBER

Even before the turmoil of the Kornilov Affair had settled, Russia's allies were showing increasing concern about the ability of their ally to continue the war. In Petrograd, Buchanan attempted to persuade the Italian, French and American ambassadors to join him in presenting a note to Kerensky urging him to take appropriate firm measures to increase factory output, get the trains running efficiently, and restore discipline to the army. The American ambassador responded that he had not received instructions from Washington and could not therefore take part, but, accompanied by the Italian and French ambassadors, Buchanan proceeded to meet Kerensky. The Russian dictator heard them out, and then replied that Russia's predicament owed much to the failures of the tsarist regime, and that it was a shame that Russia's allies had not been more critical at that time. He assured the ambassadors that he was doing all that he could and dismissed them peremptorily. He then ordered the Russian ambassador in London to make a formal protest, and informed Buchanan via Tereshchenko, the Russian foreign minister, that as a further mark of his displeasure, Kerensky had decided not to forward a letter to Prime Minister Lloyd George about the military situation. Buchanan replied that this was a childish act, and added drily that he was confident that Lloyd George would get over his disappointment.[267]

The reality was that Kerensky could do little to achieve the aims demanded by the ambassadors. There had been an escalating series of strikes in all industrial parts of Russia since the Moscow conference as workers demanded higher wages to offset the spiralling inflation rate; without any increase in productivity, their demands merely stoked inflation still further. The railways were suffering from a combination of strikes and desperate shortages of parts, many of which had to be purchased abroad and then shipped to Russia either via Archangel or Vladivostok. The army had passed the point of no return and it is hard to imagine any measures that might have restored order and discipline to its ranks – desertion had reached unprecedented levels as soldiers streamed home, commandeering trains and adding to the chaos of the railways. Many wished to return to their rural homes to take part in the harvest, and there was a great upsurge in rural unrest – reinforced by mutinous armed soldiers, the peasants lost patience with the government and attacked the homes of many landowners, burning them down and claiming the land for themselves.

Kerensky had always portrayed himself as the man who could unite the disparate factions of Russian politics, but after the collapse of Kornilov's supporters, this became as impossible as fulfilling the demands of Buchanan and the other ambassadors. Opinion in Russia polarised enormously, with the centre ground effectively disappearing. Many Bolsheviks who had been arrested as a result of the July unrest had been released when it seemed as if the army might attempt a coup, and local elections to the Soviet in Petrograd – and to its equivalent organisations in Moscow and Kiev – saw the Bolsheviks secure majorities. Lenin had been inclined to seek power through a coalition with the Mensheviks and other socialist groups, but now there was the very real prospect of the Bolsheviks being able to take power without the help of anyone. However, even if the Bolsheviks controlled the Soviets, the Provisional Government still remained the official ruling body in Russia. If Lenin and his comrades were to take power, Kerensky and his government would have to be overthrown.

Lenin appears to have come to the conclusion, sooner than the rest of the Bolsheviks, that the moment for seizing power was fast approaching. The hesitancy he had shown in July was gone; in a letter to the Bolshevik Central Committee and the Petrograd and Moscow committees, he wrote:

> The Bolsheviks, having obtained a majority in the Soviets … of both capitals, can and *must* take state power into their own hands.
>
> They can because the active majority of revolutionary elements in the two chief cities is large enough to carry the people with it, to overcome the opponent's resistance, to smash him, and to gain and retain power. For the Bolsheviks, by immediately proposing a democratic peace, by immediately giving the land to the peasants and by re-establishing the democratic institutions and liberties which

> have been mangled and shattered by Kerensky, will form a government which *nobody* will be able to overthrow.
>
> The majority of the people are on *our side*.[268]

In the same letter, he went on to state that action was imperative because the Provisional Government would surrender Petrograd to the Germans, and this would postpone further the creation of the long-awaited Constituent Assembly, which was intended to make a final decision on Russia's future form of government. Therefore, the Bolsheviks had to create the right circumstances for an armed uprising. But whilst other Bolsheviks might have been more enthusiastic than Lenin about the prospects of seizing power in July, the situation was now completely reversed – the Central Committee was stunned into silence by Lenin's demands. Writing first from his refuge in Finland and then moving to Petrograd where he hid in the apartment of a supporter on the edge of the strongly Bolshevik Vyborg district, Lenin harangued his colleagues for their timidity, and rejected their preference for demanding a transfer of power from the Provisional Government to the All-Russian Congress of Soviets, which was to be convened in Petrograd that autumn. He argued persuasively that the situation had changed since July:

> In July … it could have been argued … that the correct thing to do was to take power … However, to have decided … in favour of taking power at that time would have been wrong, because the objective conditions for the victory of the insurrection did not exist.
>
> 1. We still lacked the support of the class which is the vanguard of the revolution.
>
> We still did not have a majority among the workers and soldiers of Petrograd and Moscow. Now we have a majority in both Soviets. It was created *solely* by the history of July and August, by the experience of the 'ruthless treatment' meted out to the Bolsheviks, and by the experience of the Kornilov revolt.
>
> 2. There was no countrywide revolutionary upsurge at that time. There is now, after the Kornilov revolt; the situation in the provinces and the assumption of power by the Soviets in many localities prove this.
>
> 3. At that time there was no vacillation … among our enemies and among the irresolute petty bourgeoisie. Now the vacillation is enormous. Our main enemy, Allied and world imperialism (for world imperialism is headed by the 'Allies'), has *begun to waver* between a war to a victorious finish and a separate peace directed against Russia …

> We could not have retained power politically in July because before the Kornilov revolt, the army and the provinces could and would have marched against Petrograd.
>
> Now the picture is entirely different.[269]

Trotsky agreed with Lenin that the July turmoil could not have been turned into a successful seizure of power:

> The July demonstrators wanted to turn over power to the Soviets, but for this the Soviets had to agree to take it. Even in the capital, however, where a majority of the workers and the active elements of the garrison were already for the Bolsheviks, a majority in the Soviet – owing to that law of inertia which applies to every representative system – still belonged to those petty bourgeois parties who regarded an attempt against the power of the bourgeoisie as an attempt against themselves.[270]

There was no such rational analysis during the July turmoil – the reluctance of the Bolsheviks to seize that moment was not based upon any careful calculation – but like so many other movements in history, the Bolsheviks did not hesitate to rationalise their past behaviour with the benefit of hindsight. In any case, by October, with the Bolsheviks in control of the Soviets, there was no longer any question of a non-Bolshevik majority in the Soviets.

Just as Russia's allies were constantly fearful that Russia might seek a separate peace, many within Russia feared that the other Entente Powers might find a way of making peace with Germany that left the Germans a free hand to strike at Russia. As the stumbling peace efforts of Emperor Karl had demonstrated, there was no appetite whatsoever in France for any peace other than one that included the defeat of Germany, but Lenin and other Bolsheviks continued to fear otherwise. To what extent they actually believed this, and to what extent they used the threat of this to persuade others to fall in line with their plans, is probably impossible to determine. Isolated from diplomatic contacts, Lenin and his associates could act only on the basis of what they saw happening elsewhere, distorted by their personal perspective.

On 23 October, Lenin ventured out of his hiding place to address the Central Committee in person. Despite the fact that many of those who gathered had been released from captivity during the Kornilov Affair, most wore disguises of varying degrees of efficacy; Lenin had shaved off his trademark beard and wore a curly wig.[271] Beginning in the evening, the arguments continued late into the night for ten hours, with Lenin refusing to accept the qualms of those who felt that the Bolsheviks were not ready for such a step. Eventually, Lenin prevailed, and the committee adopted a resolution – written by an exhausted Lenin with a 'gnawed end of a pencil on a sheet of paper from a child's notebook ruled in squares' to undertake the necessary practical steps for an armed insurrection.[272] Characteristically of Lenin's thinking, the resolution included in the reasons for urgency an assessment that international events were moving towards a more widespread revolution: the Bolshevik seizure of power was merely the first step in a worldwide uprising by the workers of the world against the old order. Only in this manner would a truly 'democratic' peace be achieved.

Agreement was by no means unanimous. Two prominent members of the Bolshevik Central Committee – Grigori Yevseyevich Zinoniev and Lev Borisovich Kamenev – voted against the resolution, and the following day circulated a letter to party members protesting that the committee had 'no right to stake the whole future at the present moment upon the card of armed insurrection'.[273] But Lenin's supporters believed that it was unwise to rely on continuing evolutionary growth of the Bolshevik movement. Far from strengthening their hand, any delay might cost the Bolsheviks support. The workers and soldiers of Russia were already bone-weary of the war, and if another party were to offer them a way out, much of the current enthusiasm for the Bolsheviks would evaporate. An outraged Lenin demanded the expulsion of the two dissenters from the party, but for the moment they remained in place.

If there were to be an armed uprising, the Bolsheviks would have need of fighting men. The garrisons that had been so instrumental in the February Revolution were far less powerful than they had been at the time; they might be prepared to demonstrate on the streets, but whatever real fighting potential they may once have had was long gone. Their refusal to be transferred to the front line, regardless of how dire the war situation was, made them magnets for men who wished at all costs to avoid dangerous duty. Furthermore, many of the more militant parts of the garrison were deliberately weakened after the July unrest, losing much of their stockpile of machine-guns and other weapons. Any Bolshevik seizure of power would run the risk of elements within the army trying to intervene, and a potent fighting force with discipline and resolve would therefore have to be available; it was questionable whether the garrison alone possessed the combat strength that might be needed. Fortunately for Lenin, such a force was readily at hand. During the brief period of panic in Petrograd when Kornilov threatened to march on the capital, thousands of weapons were issued to the workers of Petrograd, who were largely supporters of the Bolsheviks; Trotsky and other leading Bolsheviks now began to convert them into a potent fighting force. In many cases, weapons had been collected again from the workers, but many remained armed and it proved possible to obtain weapons for all those who needed them, as Trotsky, who was now serving as the chairman of the Soviet, later wrote:

> When a delegation from the workers came to me and said they needed weapons, I answered: 'But the arsenals, you see, are not in our hands.' The answered: 'We have been to the Sestroretsk Arms Factory.' 'Well, and what about it?' 'They said that if the Soviet ordered they would deliver.' I gave an order for five thousand rifles, and they got them the same day.[274]

Kerensky attempted at least to remove the garrison from the influence of the Soviet, which was in turn now under the control of the Bolsheviks. The garrison was placed under the authority of Northern Front. In view of the German advance through Riga, Kerensky declared that the Petrograd garrison would have to be deployed to defend the approaches to the capital. Strongly influenced by the committees of the garrison regiments, the Soviet refused to accept this, and the troops stayed in their barracks. Meanwhile, the armed workers – the Red Guards – began to develop into a potent fighting force:

> Concealed rifles came out into the open. The Kornilov insurrection conclusively legalised the Red Guards …
>
> 'Drill in the art of handling a rifle,' says the worker Skorinko, 'formerly carried on in flats and tenements, was now brought out into the light and air, into the parks, the boulevards.' 'The shops were turned into camps,' says another worker, Rakitov … After the whistle [at the end of a working shift] all would draw up in the court for drill. 'Side by side with a bearded worker you would see a boy apprentice, and both of them attentively listening to the instructor.' Thus while the old tsarist army was disintegrating, the foundation of a future Red Army was being laid in the factories.
>
> … In scores of shops and factories of Petrograd an intense military activity was in progress – chiefly rifle practice. By the middle of October the interest in weapons had risen to a new height. In certain factories almost every last man was enrolled in a company.
>
> The workers were more and more impatiently demanding weapons from the Soviet, but the weapons were infinitely fewer than the hands stretched out for them. 'I came to Smolny every day,' relates the engineer, Kozmin, 'and observed how both before and after the sitting of the Soviet, workers and sailors would come up to Trotsky, offering and demanding weapons for the arming of the workers,

> making reports as to how and where these weapons were distributed, and putting the question: "But when does business begin?" The impatience was very great.'[275]

Most of the workers in the Putilov works took their rifles with them, ready to answer a call to arms whenever it might come; men in the Franko-Russkii Factory operated lathes with bandoliers of ammunition over their shoulders.[276] The men were organised into groups of ten, with four such groups being termed a squad. Three squads formed a company, and three companies a battalion; together with its headquarters staff, a battalion numbered over 500 men, and all the battalions of a district – in a few cases, the battalions of one of the huge factories – constituted a division. Whilst there were women who were prepared to fight in the front line of the revolution, most female volunteers took on the role of first aiders. Despite all this activity, Trotsky had little doubt about the rudimentary nature of the Red Guards:

> The organisation of the Red Guard remained, of course, extremely far from complete. Everything was done in haste, in the rough, and not always skilfully. The Red Guard men were in the majority little trained; the communications were badly organised; the supply system was lame; the sanitary corps lagged behind. But the Red Guard, recruited from the most self-sacrificing workers, was burning to carry the job through this time to the end. And that was the decisive thing … Whereas the garrison represented a compulsory assemblage of old soldiers defending themselves against war, the divisions of the Red Guard were newly constructed by individual selection on a new basis with new aims.[277]

Despite the energies of Trotsky and the passionate conviction of Lenin, others remained deeply sceptical about the prospects for success:

> Zinoniev and Kamenev gave warning against an underestimation of the enemy's forces. 'Petrograd will decide, and in Petrograd the enemy has … considerable forces: 5,000 officer cadets, magnificently armed and knowing how to fight, and then the army headquarters, and then the shock troops, and then the Cossacks, and then a considerable part of the garrison, and then a very considerable quantity of artillery spread out fan-wise around Petrograd. Moreover the enemy with the help of the Central Executive Committee [of the Provisional Government] will almost certainly attempt to bring troops from the front.'[278]

But, as Trotsky shrewdly added, an army reflects the society from which it is recruited. Given the divisions in Russian society, it was inconceivable that the entire army could be expected to be loyal to the government, or for that matter loyal to the Bolsheviks. Given the refusal of the rank and file to support Kornilov and his generals, it must have seemed highly unlikely to the majority of the Bolshevik conspirators that Kerensky's government would be able to secure sufficient military support to survive. On paper, the army remained a formidable force – according to Knox, *Stavka* reported that it still fielded over 2.1 million combatants (though *Stavka* itself was unsure of the accuracy of these figures) and nearly 6,000 guns facing the German and Austro-Hungarian forces; furthermore, its ammunition stocks were huge by the standards of previous years, with over 2,000 rounds per artillery piece, compared with barely 300 in the past. But as Knox added:

> It is all too late. If we could only get back to life again the men who died in 1915 through lack of shell![279]

Nor could Kerensky rely on the Cossacks, the traditional enforcers of the Russian government, to support him – many Cossacks regarded the arrests of Kornilov and particularly of Alexei Maximovich Kaledin, a Kornilov supporter and *Ataman* (effectively the supreme commander) of the Cossacks – as unacceptable. However, true to Trotsky's axiom, the Cossacks were as divided as any other part of Russian society. General Alexei Pavlovich Budberg, a cavalry commander, was alarmed when a regiment of Ural Cossacks under his command suddenly demanded that they be relieved of the punitive functions of gendarmerie duties. He added:

> You can't command a flock of hyenas, jackals and sheep by playing on a violin. The only salvation lies in the mass application of the hot iron, a thing which we haven't got and is nowhere to be gotten.[280]

On 5 November, the men of the three regiments of Don Cossacks in Petrograd had a meeting to discuss what they should do. They concluded that they could not support Kerensky, and in any case any attempt by them to suppress the Bolsheviks without infantry support would be doomed to failure. They announced to all sides that they intended to maintain a neutral stance.

Kerensky and the government could do nothing but look on impotently. Everyone knew that a Bolshevik attempt to seize power was coming – the question was purely a matter of 'when' rather than 'if'. Finally, on 6 November – 24 October in Russia's old calendar – the government attempted to act. A shadow of the persuasive orator he had been just a few months before, Kerensky tried to convince his government to take repressive measures against the Bolsheviks, who he proclaimed were preparing to open the way for the Germans to enter Russia; it is ironical that both Kerensky and the Bolsheviks regarded the other side as being determined to allow the Germans to achieve dominance over Russia. Even the Mensheviks, traditional opponents of the Bolsheviks, responded to Kerensky with protests, pointing out that the February Revolution was born out of a longing for peace, bread and land – none of which had been delivered. The Bolsheviks, pointed out Yuli Osipovich Martov, the leader of the Mensheviks, were merely taking advantage of the government's failures. Unable to persuade the government to support him, Kerensky issued instructions on his personal authority for legal proceedings against the Military Revolutionary Committee of the Bolsheviks (Trotsky's group that was organising the Red Guards), and for the suppression of pro-Bolshevik newspapers. Lenin reacted as soon as he heard the news with a letter to the rest of the Bolshevik Central Committee:

> The situation is critical in the extreme. In fact it is now absolutely clear that to delay the uprising would be fatal.
>
> With all my might I urge comrades to realise that everything now hangs by a thread; that we are confronted by problems which are not to be solved by conferences or congresses (even congresses of Soviets), but exclusively by people, by the masses, by the struggle of the armed people.
>
> … We must at all costs, this very evening, this very night, arrest the government, having first disarmed the officer cadets (defeating them if they resist) …
>
> We must not wait! We may lose everything!
>
> … All districts, all regiments, all forces must be mobilised at once … with the insistent demand that under no circumstances should power be left in the hands of Kerensky and Co. until the 25th; not under any circumstances; the matter must be decided without fail this very evening, or this very night.
>
> History will not forgive revolutionaries for procrastinating when they could be victorious today (and they certainly will be victorious today), while they risk losing much tomorrow, in fact, they risk losing everything.
>
> … The government is tottering. It must be given the death blow at all costs.
>
> To delay action is fatal.[281]

Soviet accounts of the days that followed portray the October Revolution as a dramatic, often violent event. The reality was rather more prosaic. From their headquarters in the Smolny Institute – a former school for the daughters of aristocratic families – Bolsheviks set off to secure important locations around the Russian capital. Two men left in haste for the central telegraph office, forgetting their weapons in their agitation; when they entered the building, where almost nobody was a supporter of the Bolsheviks, they announced that they were taking command in the name of Trotsky's Military Revolutionary Committee. They encountered no resistance. There was little or no fighting anywhere, and by the following morning every key location – with the exception of the Winter Palace, where the Provisional Government watched events unfold fearfully – was in Bolshevik hands. Aware that something was afoot, Buchanan contacted Knox and offered him the safety of the British Embassy; Knox declined and remained at home. He described his walk to the embassy on 7 November, the first morning of the new regime:

> The government troops of the night before had disappeared; everywhere were patrols of the local garrison. Trams were running and there was perfect order …
>
> At the Winter Palace bridge a crowd of men of the Preobrajensky Regiment waited on one side, ready at a moment's notice to sweep away the few poor Junkers [officer cadets] on guard near the Hermitage.
>
> Polkovnikov, the commander of the district, pretended to be hopeful. He said that he was certain he would be able to turn the whole situation round in favour of the provisional government. I asked him what he had to go on, and he said that there were 'already certain indications of a reaction'. He was a very brave but rather pathetic optimist!
>
> Poor Bagranuti [an Armenian general] made less concealment. He had not slept for three nights, neither had he shaved, and when an Armenian does not shave it is noticeable. He told me that he had never been in such a position, for he could not depend on any single order being carried out. The troops called in from the front had gone over in the night. The whole town, with the exception of the Palace Square, was in the hands of the Soviets. Some officers had gone to the Winter Palace to offer their services to the Provisional Government. The latter was still sitting and had decided to hold out to the last. Troops were on their way from the front.
>
> The … garrison of the palace was working half-heartedly at the construction of a breastwork of firewood a few yards in advance of the main entrance.[282]

When he returned to the embassy in the afternoon, Knox learned that Kerensky had already left Petrograd. The government cars in the Palace Square had been immobilised by Bolshevik soldiers, and Kerensky was forced to beg the loan of a car from the American Embassy. He left to try to locate pro-government forces, beseeching the Americans to delay recognising a new government in Petrograd for at least five days.

While one head of state left the city in search of his troops, another crossed Petrograd to join his followers. Accompanied by a Finnish bodyguard and wearing his curly wig disguise, Lenin left his hideout and attempted to reach his fellow Bolsheviks. They were stopped by a police patrol near the Tauride Palace; according to the bodyguard's account, they were allowed to pass because the police officers decided that Lenin was a harmless drunkard.[283] The two men then crossed the city to the Smolny Institute, only to find his way barred by the sentries guarding the building. Inevitably, Lenin had no documents with him that identified him. The bodyguard had a moment of inspiration, and blustered his way past the sentries, proclaiming loudly that he was a delegate to the Congress of Soviets, which was due to begin in the Smolny Institute the following day.[284]

The Bolsheviks now moved against the Winter Palace and the Provisional Government. In his film of the revolution, *October: Ten Days That Shook The World*, Sergei Eisenstein portrays the defenders of the palace as a mixture of Cossacks, officer cadets and parts of the 1st Petrograd Women's Battalion; while elements of all of these were present, their numbers were modest. Nor was the final assault as dramatic and violent as portrayed by Eisenstein, who based his scenes on a Soviet re-enactment that took place three years later. After the Provisional Government failed to respond to a demand that it surrender unconditionally, the cruiser *Aurora* famously fired a blank round to signal the beginning of the assault. The guns of the Peter and Paul Fortress a short distance away then fired a brief bombardment. Knox's account of the last moments of Provisional Government rule is probably far more accurate than the scenes from Eisenstein's film:

> The garrison had dwindled owing to desertions, for there were no provisions and it had been practically starved for two days. There was no strong man to take command and to enforce discipline. No one had the stomach for fighting; and some of the ensigns even borrowed greatcoats of soldier pattern from the women to enable them to escape unobserved.
>
> The greater part of the Junkers of the Mikhail Artillery School returned to their school, taking with them four out of their six guns. Then the Cossacks left, declaring themselves opposed to bloodshed! At 10pm a large part of the ensigns left, leaving few defenders except the ensigns of the Engineering School and the company of women.
>
> The government was the whole time in communication with the front, and at midnight was elated by a message that troops were on the march for their relief.

Then a report came that the Fleet Committee was coming to the palace with provisions.

During the bombardment the ministers moved about from room to room. Ragosin [aide de camp to the commander of the Petrograd military district] afterwards related that when he had to report on some subject he found 'the Minister of Marine sitting in a window smoking a pipe and spitting. Other ministers were seated at a table. Tereshchenko walked up and down like a caged tiger. [Alexander Ivanovich] Konovalov [a prominent Kadet politician and minister for trade and industry] sat on a sofa nervously pulling up his trousers until they were finally above his knees' … In reality the plight of this handful of men must have been terrible. Deserted by their leader and surrounded from 6pm on the 7th, refusing to leave their post, though powerless to effect anything, they awaited their fate at the hands of the rabble.

The defence was unorganised and only three of the many entrances were guarded. Parties of the attackers penetrated by side entrances in search of loot. At first these parties were small and were disarmed by the garrison, but they were succeeded by larger bands of sailors and of the Pavlovsky Regiment, in addition to armed workmen, and these turned the tables by disarming the garrison. This was, however, carried out, as an office of the garrison afterwards stated, 'in a domestic manner', with little bloodshed. The garrison fired little and is said to have only lost three Junkers wounded.

… At 2.30am on the 8th the palace was 'taken'. The ministers were arrested and marched through execrating crowds across the Troitsky Bridge to the Fortress of Peter and Paul …

According to Bolshevik accounts the company of women offered the most serious resistance, and a report stated that three of them were stripped and thrown into the Neva. The remainder, 137 in all, were marched to the Pavlovsky barracks, where they were 'searched for bombs in an unnecessary manner'. They were then passed on to the barracks of the Grenadiersky Regiment. These women were volunteers from all classes, but mostly from the intelligentsia. Their real patriotism formed the brightest spot in the general apathy since the Revolution.[285]

Buchanan viewed the palace first-hand the day after it had been taken:

I walked out this afternoon to see the damage that had been done to the Winter Palace by the prolonged bombardment of the previous evening, and to my surprise found that, in spite of the near range [900m], there were on the river side but three marks where the shrapnel had struck. On the town side the walls were riddled with

> thousands of bullets from machine-guns, but not one shot from a field gun that had been fired from the opposite side of the Palace Square [230m] had struck the building. In the interior very considerable damage was done by the soldiers and workmen, who looted or smashed whatever they could lay hands on.[286]

The officers of the Peter and Paul Fortress had been ordered by the Bolshevik Military Revolutionary Committee to bombard the palace, but – reluctant to carry out such a task – the officers informed the committee that five of the six guns facing the palace had not been cleaned and were therefore not ready for action. The lack of military experience amongst the Bolshevik commissars present – largely civilians or men who had only worked with the infantry – was such that they had little experience of artillery, and therefore none suggested the simple expedient of cleaning the guns. Several training guns were dragged into position, but it was then found that there were no shells of that calibre in the fortress. Learning what their officers had told the Bolsheviks, the gunners then suddenly announced that the fortress guns could be made ready with comparative ease.[287] Eventually, they fired a total of 30 or 40 six-inch shells at the palace at a range that should have made the task trivially easy. The fact that only two rounds hit the palace strongly indicates that little attempt was made to inflict serious damage; Trotsky later attributed this to a desire to avoid unnecessary destruction and loss of life.[288]

This was not the only mishap at the Peter and Paul Fortress. It had been agreed that a red lantern would be hoisted onto the flagpole as a signal that all was ready for the assault, but when the moment came, Georgi Ivanovich Blagonravov – the fortress commissar – realised that there was no red lantern at hand. He went off in search of one and fell into a mud bank on the shoreline of the island fortress. Eventually, he extracted himself from the mud and managed to find a lantern – in any case, not red – only to discover that there was no means of attaching it to the flagpole.[289] It is a measure of the utter disarray of Kerensky's government that the Bolsheviks succeeded despite this and other similar incidents.

Most of the soldiers who were meant to be defending the palace and the Provisional Government had fled before the 'assault' took place, while others started looting the extensive wine cellars. As more and more Red Guards and pro-Bolshevik troops entered the palace, they too started to indulge themselves. Vladimir Alexandrovich Antonov-Ovseyenko, one of the Bolshevik commissars who led the attack on the Winter Palace and personally placed the Provisional Government under arrest, later described events with some chagrin:

> The Preobrazhensky Guards Regiment, assigned to guard these cellars, got totally drunk. The Pavlovsky Guards, our revolutionary buttress, also couldn't resist. We sent guards from various other picked units – all got utterly drunk. We posted guards specially chosen from regimental committees – they succumbed as well. We dispatched armoured cars to drive away the crowd. After patrolling up and down a few times, they also began to weave suspiciously. When evening came, a violent bacchanalia overflowed. 'Let's drink the Romanovs' remains!' This happy slogan seized the crowd. We tried sealing up the entrances with brick – the crowd came back through the windows, smashing in the gratings and seizing what remained. We tried flooding the cellars with water – the firemen sent to do the job got drunk instead ... This drunken ecstasy infected the entire city ... The Council of People's Commissars, finally, appointed a special deputy, endowed him with exclusive authority, [and] assigned him a strong detachment to help him carry out his duties. But this person also turned out not to be very reliable.[290]

Comte Louis de Robien, who had replaced Paléologue as the French ambassador earlier in the year, watched aghast:

> There are bottles of Tokay there from the time of Catherine the Great, and it has all been gulped down by these vodka swiggers.[291]

Finally, after many days of riotously drunken behaviour, order was restored only when the new Bolshevik authorities announced that they would blow up the cellars with dynamite without further warning unless the drinking frenzy ceased.

The same day that the Winter Palace fell to the Bolsheviks, Knox visited the General Staff Buildings across the Palace Square from the Winter Palace, and then made his way back to meet the ambassador:

> When I returned to the embassy I found Lady Georgina [Buchanan's wife] in great excitement. Two officer instructors of the Women's Battalion had come with a terrible story to the effect that the 137 women taken in the palace had been beaten and tortured, and were now being outraged in the Grenadiersky barracks.
>
> I borrowed the ambassador's car and drove to the Bolshevik headquarters at the Smolny Institute ... Sentries and others tried to put me off, but I at length penetrated to the third floor, where I saw the Secretary of the Military Revolutionary Committee and demanded that the women should be set free at once. He tried to procrastinate, but I told him that if they were not liberated at once I would set the opinion of the civilised world against the Bolsheviks and all

> their works. He tried to soothe me and begged me to talk French instead of Russian, as the waiting room was crowded and we were attracting attention. He himself talked excellent French and was evidently a man of education and culture. Finally, after two visits to the adjoining room, where he said the Council was sitting, he came back to say that the order for the release would be signed at once.
>
> I drove with the officers to the Grenadiersky barracks and went to see the regimental committee. The commissar, a repulsive individual of Semitic type, refused to release the women without a written order, on the ground that 'they had resisted to the last at the palace, fighting desperately with bombs and revolvers'. He said that they were now under a guard apart from the soldiers, unmolested and quite safe. He refused to let me see them, though I asked twice. It was an extraordinary scene, the officers speaking French, which the commissar probably understood, and urging me not to believe a word he said; the half-dozen soldiers of the regimental committee, not of a bad type, but stolidly indifferent and taking no part in the discussion; the commissar of a race which has been oppressed for centuries now holding all the cards, not arrogant but determined. We tried to telephone to the Smolny to ascertain if the order had been dispatched, but could get no reply. I returned to the embassy and, telephoning through to the Soviet, was told that the order for the release had been sent by special messenger.[292]

The women were released shortly afterwards and left the city for their barracks in Levashovo, immediately to the north of Petrograd. Though many had been beaten, none had suffered rape or torture. Later, they sent a delegation to the British Embassy to thank Knox, and to ask if it would be possible for them to transfer to the British Army. He replied that the British Army did not allow women to bear arms, and berated Russian officers from the women's battalion for allowing women to fight. Elsewhere, despite the exhortations of Lenin, Trotsky and other leading Bolsheviks to show restraint, many soldiers turned on their officers, beating and not infrequently killing them. Knox acidly remarked that in the months since the February Revolution, the sailors of the Baltic Fleet had killed significantly more officers of their own side than they killed German officers in the entire war.

Whilst events in Petrograd unfolded with little significant conflict, the same was not true elsewhere. There was extensive fighting in Moscow; the Bolsheviks were driven from the Kremlin and central parts of the city by forces loyal to the Provisional Government and the retired Brusilov was wounded in his apartment by a hand grenade. In some desperation, the local Bolsheviks arranged a ceasefire. Negotiations began between the two sides, and confident of victory, the pro-Provisional

Emperor Karl and Empress Zita of Austria-Hungary arrive in Debreczin in Hungary, 1918. (Photo by: Universal History Archive/UIG via Getty images)

Franz Conrad von Hötzendorf and General Böhm-Ermolli, left and right forefront. (From the fonds of the RGAKFD in Krasnogorsk via Stavka)

Left to right: Hindenburg, the Kaiser and Ludendorff. (Nik Cornish at Stavka)

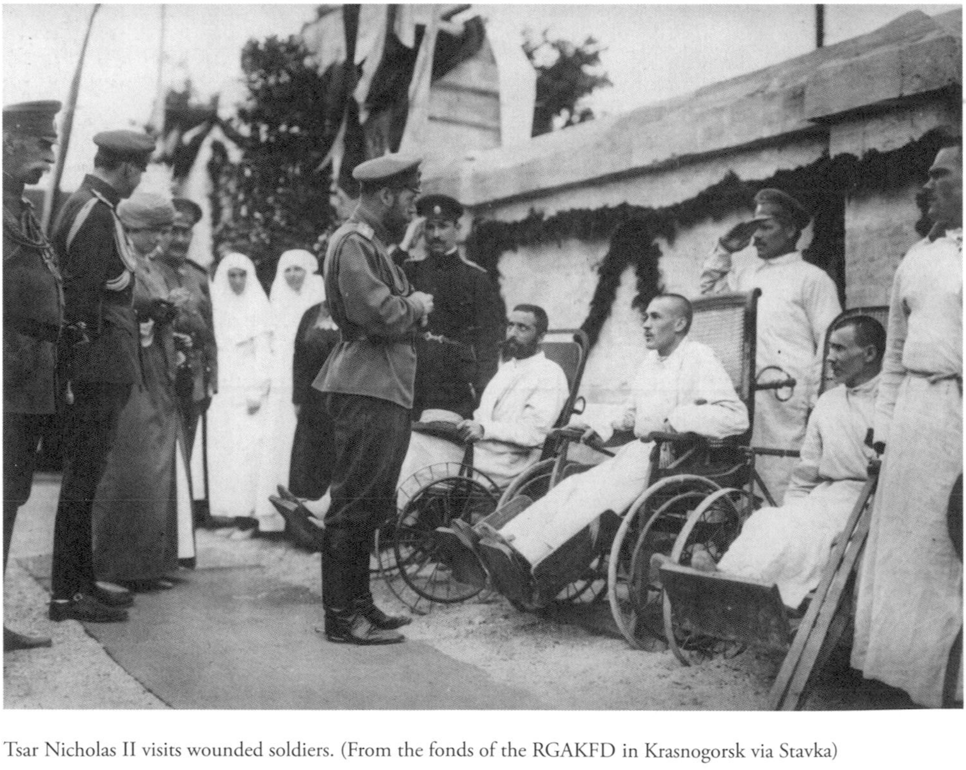

Tsar Nicholas II visits wounded soldiers. (From the fonds of the RGAKFD in Krasnogorsk via Stavka)

The Tsarina and her son Alexis on the steps of the Winter Palace, reviewing troops. (From the fonds of the RGAKFD in Krasnogorsk via Stavka)

Mikhail Alexeyev, commander-in-chief of the Volunteer Army, near Ekaterinodar, Russia, 1918. (Photo by Fine Art Images/Heritage Images/Getty Images)

Alexander Kerensky visits Riga during the build-up to the 1917 summer offensive that came to bear his name. (Nik Cornish at Stavka)

General Lavr Kornilov. He is associated with the Kornilov Affair, an unsuccessful endeavour in August/September 1917 that purported to strengthen Alexander Kerensky's Provisional Government. (Photo by Universal History Archive/Getty Images)

Vladimir Lenin and delegates to the second Comintern congress at the Square of the Victims of the Revolution (Field of Mars), Petrograd, on 19 July 1920. (Photo by Laski Diffusion/Getty Images)

Trotsky (facing camera) at Brest-Litovsk. To his right is A. A. Joffe, and, with his back to the camera, Vice Admiral V. M. Altvater. (Nik Cornish at Stavka)

A Russian wiring party carries out its work. The army was content to undertake defensive tasks such as this shown here. The metal containers at their waists are gas mask containers. (Nik Cornish at Stavka)

Someone from the rear addressing a crowd of front-line troops during spring 1917. So many organisations sent representatives to spread their own messages that the audience grew somewhat jaded with the high-flown phrases on offer and were much more supportive of the simple, direct methods of the Bolsheviks. (From the fonds of the RGAKFD in Krasnogorsk via Stavka)

During the February/March Revolution, a crowd destroys the imperial eagles over the premises of shops and businesses that supplied the Royal Family. (Nik Cornish at Stavka)

Soldiers on the Nevsky Prospekt, Petrograd during the February/March Revolution strike a pose for the camera. (Nik Cornish at Stavka)

Estonian soldiers demonstrate in Petrograd, spring 1917, bearing a banner that demands independence for Estonia. It reads, 'Long live the Russian Federative Republic and autonomous Estonia'. (Courtesy of the Central Museum of the Armed Forces, Moscow via Stavka)

Austro-Hungarian troops fraternise with Russians, Easter 1917. Although it was frowned upon by the Russian high command, the front-line men generally carried on as they felt inclined. (Courtesy of the Central Museum of the Armed Forces, Moscow via Stavka)

Austro-Hungarian delegates cross into Russian territory in Romania to discuss armistice or other terms. (Courtesy of the Central Museum of the Armed Forces, Moscow via Stavka)

A Petrograd workers' demonstration is attacked by police on the orders of the Kerensky Provisional Government, July 1917. (Photo by: Sovfoto/UIG via Getty Images)

Two rows of Red Guards train at a firing range after the July Days, Petrograd, 1917. On July 3rd and 4th, workers and soldiers demanded the Soviet take power. (Photo by Hulton Archive/Getty Images)

Bolshevik soldiers and Red Guards near the Admiralty on Palace Square, Petrograd, during the October/November Revolution, 1917. (Courtesy of the Central Museum of the Armed Forces, Moscow via Stavka)

1st Petrograd Women's Battalion in camp. (From the fonds of the RGAKFD in Krasnogorsk via Stavka)

German troops take part in Operation *Albion*, the invasion of the Estonian islands in September 1917. (Nik Cornish at Stavka)

German and Russian troops fraternising, November/December 1917. (Nik Cornish at Stavka)

Russian troops demobilising in the winter of 1917/18. (Nik Cornish at Stavka)

The Russian delegation arriving at Brest-Litovsk. (Joffe doffing his bowler hat, and Kamenev at the extreme right.) (Nik Cornish at Stavka)

German troops marching into Kiev. (Courtesy of the Central Museum of the Armed Forces, Moscow via Stavka)

Troops of the Polish Legion of the Austro-Hungarian Army. (From the fonds of the RGAKFD in Krasnogorsk via Stavka)

A Red Army armoured train. (Courtesy of the Central Museum of the Armed Forces, Moscow via Stavka)

Red Army artillery, above, and infantry, below. (Courtesy of the Central Museum of the Armed Forces, Moscow via Stavka)

Troops of the First Cavalry Army, a Bolshevik force led by Mikhail Budyonny. (Courtesy of the Central Museum of the Armed Forces, Moscow via Stavka)

White Russian troops marching down street of an occupied city on a recruitment drive to gain more troops for the fight against the Bolsheviks. (Photo by Time Life Pictures/Mansell/The LIFE Picture Collection/Getty Images)

Troops of the Russian Red Army entering the city of Riga, Latvia, in 1919. There were detachments of Latvian riflemen who served in the Red Army, making it easier to secure a quick advance into Latvia. (Photo by Slava Katamidze Collection/Getty Images)

German troops allied with the Finnish White Guard fighting communist forces of the Red Guard during the advance on Helsinki during the Finnish Civil War, circa April 1918. (Photo by Hulton Archive/Getty Images)

Government forces pressed for what would have been a reversal of the revolution.

Meanwhile, Kerensky was searching for troops that would support him. Originally, he intended to travel to the headquarters of Northern Front, but the new commander, General Cheremisov – after some vaccilation – warned him that he intended to remain neutral, and in any event there was little prospect of the troops of Northern Front taking action against the Bolsheviks. Instead, Kerensky travelled to Pskov where he met up with troops under the command of General Petr Nikolayevich Krasnov, who had commanded one of the divisions in III Cavalry Corps during its attempt to reach Petrograd at the height of the Kornilov Affair. At the head of a Cossack division, he had played a prominent part in Brusilov's offensive of 1916, during which he was wounded. Now, ignoring the irony that he was marching on Petrograd in the company of the man against whom he had marched in the same direction just a few weeks earlier, he headed north with 1,000 Cossacks.

As they headed north, Kerensky and Krasnov were joined by other forces, including about 900 officer cadets and an armoured train. Other units refused to obey Kerensky's summons to join him. On 10 November, the force reached and captured Tsarskoe Selo after a short skirmish. Much as had been the case with Krymov's cavalry corps during the days of the Kornilov Affair, his troops melted away as they advanced due to constant agitation by the Bolsheviks. Meanwhile, a substantial force was being organised to oppose them, consisting of elements of the Baltic Fleet, the Red Guards, and the Petrograd garrison troops – in all, a total of over 10,000 men took up positions on the Pulkovo Heights to the south of the city.

Despite being outnumbered, Krasnov – who had been led to believe by Kerensky that further reinforcements were on their way – launched an attack on the centre of the defensive position on 12 November, expecting that his Cossacks would scatter the Red Guards that held that part of the line. His attack was repulsed and followed by a counterattack, forcing Krasnov to pull back to Tsarskoe Selo. Negotiations now began between the two sides, and it became increasingly clear that the Cossacks were not willing to continue fighting. Moving without warning, the Bolsheviks suddenly swarmed into Tsarskoe Selo despite the ceasefire that had been agreed. Krasnov was arrested, but released on condition that he did not fight against the Bolsheviks, despite which he went on to join the White Russians during the Civil War.

Believing that Kerensky and Krasnov were about to enter the city from the south, right-wing elements within Petrograd attempted to seize key installations on 10 November in an abortive uprising, as Knox described:

> The Committee of Public Safety organised the so-called 'Rising of the Junkers'. On Saturday night these boys had seized the Garage [the main motor pool of the garrison], and early on Sunday they occupied without much opposition the Central Telephone Station and the Engineers' Castle. At about 8am the Junkers of the Vladimir Military School overpowered their Bolshevik guard. The school was retaken at 3pm after bombardment by artillery, and many of the Junkers were murdered. The rising was badly organised, and only a handful of the thousands of officers in the town took part. A few of them joined in the defence of the Telephone Station, but very few. While the firing was in progress I met an officer I knew walking in the next street arm in arm with a lady friend. I expressed my astonishment that he took no interest in the fighting, and he said that it had nothing to do with him! By nightfall on Sunday the town was once more in the hands of the Bolsheviks.[293]

To avoid capture, Kerensky fled the scene. He travelled to the Don region where he attempted to persuade Kaledin to support him, but the full legacy of Kerensky's attempts to ensure that he was the saviour of Russia now came back to haunt him, with both right and left factions refusing to deal with him. He eventually left Russia, travelling to Paris. He refused to support either side in the Russian Civil War and left for New York in 1940 when the Germans invaded France. He died there in 1970; the local Russian Orthodox Church refused to allow his burial in their graveyard because he was blamed for the rise of the Bolsheviks and he was a freemason. His body was then flown to London, and interred in Putney.

In Moscow, the ceasefire broke down and the Bolsheviks began to advance back into the city centre; although local Bolsheviks were inclined to be conciliatory in the discussions with their enemies, Lenin had other ideas, and he and Trotsky undermined the Moscow Bolsheviks by every means that they could. Whatever remote remaining chance there might have been of avoiding civil war disappeared in the days that followed, as it became increasingly clear that the Bolshevik leadership had no intention of sharing power with anyone. Indeed, Lenin had no intention even of sharing power with his fellow Bolsheviks. All those who expressed dissent were forced either to accept his control or were driven from the Central Committee. Writing immediately after the 1905 Revolution, Trotsky had warned that the party organisation would one day supplant the party, then the Central Committee would supplant the party organisation, and finally a single figure would rise to supplant the Central Committee.[294] Always inclined to argue with both his opponents and allies, Lenin was clearly on such a path.

Whatever their successes in Petrograd and elsewhere might achieve, this was only a prelude for the Bolsheviks. In order to allow for a genuine 'democratic peace', it was imperative that the workers of other European states also rose up in revolution. In particular, it was vital for Russia to end the war with Germany, and the only means by which a satisfactory peace could be secured was if the Germans overthrew their government. Speaking at the Second Congress of Soviets immediately after the Bolshevik seizure of power, Lenin announced a 'Decree on Peace':

> The workers' and peasants' government, created by the Revolution … calls upon all the belligerent peoples and their governments to start immediate negotiations for a just, democratic peace.
>
> By a just or democratic peace, for which the overwhelming majority of the working class and other working people of all the belligerent countries, exhausted, tormented and racked by the war, are craving – a peace that has been most definitely and insistently demanded by the Russian workers and peasants ever since the overthrow of the tsarist monarchy – by such a peace the [Bolshevik] government means an immediate peace without annexations (i.e. without the seizure of foreign lands, without the forcible incorporation of foreign nations) and without indemnities.
>
> … The government considers it the greatest of crimes against humanity to continue this war over the issue of how to divide among the strong and rich nations the weak nationalities they have conquered, and solemnly announces its determination immediately to sign terms of peace to stop this war on the terms indicated, which are equally just for all nationalities without exception.
>
> At the same time the government declares that it does not regard the above-mentioned peace terms as an ultimatum; in other words, it is prepared to consider any other peace terms, and insists only that they be advanced by any of the belligerent countries as speedily as possible, and that in the peace proposals there should be absolute clarity and the complete absence of all ambiguity and secrecy.[295]

Many in the audience – particularly soldiers – greeted the decree with loud enthusiasm. Russia was desperate for peace; the losses suffered by the army were greater than those of any other combatant, and the near-collapse of industry, agriculture and the railways meant that even without the burdens of a war, the new Bolshevik rulers would struggle to prevent the sort of food shortages that had contributed to the fall of the tsar. There was also the question of consolidating Bolshevik control of Russia. Lenin and Trotsky had no doubt that the right-wing factions would attempt to overthrow them, and it would be impossible to fight a civil war at the same time as one against Germany.

The decree was targeted both at the Russian public and other nations. The Bolsheviks hoped and believed that workers of other nationalities would also rise up, but even if that did not happen, they knew the limitations of trying to secure a separate peace. They cannot have been particularly surprised when the other Entente Powers maintained a stony silence, refusing even to ratify diplomatic links with the *Soviet Narodnykh Kommissarov* ('Council of People's Commissars' or '*Sovnarkom*', the new Petrograd administration). The Bolsheviks did little to endear themselves to Russia's allies – in addition to encouraging revolution, the Bolsheviks announced that they would publish all of the secret treaties that Russia had signed with other powers. Many of those were arrangements for distributing territory after the war, and paid no heed whatsoever to the wishes of the people who lived in those territories. Now that the United States had entered the war and was rapidly developing what would become Woodrow Wilson's Fourteen Points – several of which demanded that the peoples of Europe be given the right to autonomous development – these old agreements, largely drawn up in the style adopted by European powers for several centuries, would look embarrassingly out of date. Nor did Lenin's demands that the people of British and French imperial colonies be given the right to self-determination encourage a friendly attitude in London and Paris. Inevitably therefore, the other Entente Powers ignored invitations to send delegates to a peace conference.

If the other nations refused to engage, the Bolsheviks were perfectly prepared to press on alone. After all, the enormous pressures in Russia demanded that the war be brought to an end as soon as possible. Much in the manner that the Germans had attempted to undermine Russian discipline by the use of propaganda, the Russians now produced a number of anti-war publications in foreign languages, predominantly German, and distributed them as widely as they could. At the same time, *Sovnarkom* made attempts to contact Germany. After the failure of Kerensky's attempt to recapture Petrograd and his flight first into hiding and eventually into exile, *Stavka* came under the control of General Nikolai Nikolayevich Dukhonin, who had been acting as chief of the general staff during part of Kerensky's period as supreme commander. General Mikhail Dmitrievich Bonch-Bruyevich, who had been prominent in Northern Front since the fall of Riga, became chief of the general staff.

Dukhonin had enjoyed – if that is the correct term – a rise that was little short of meteoric. A regimental commander at the beginning of the war, he was assigned to the intelligence staff at Third Army headquarters shortly after, before returning to regimental command in 1915. Promoted that year to major general, he joined the staff of the quartermaster-general of Southwest Front before being transferred to West Front, where he was promoted to lieutenant general in 1917. His field experience was therefore very limited, but given the almost non-existent fighting power of the Russian Army by late 1917, this was perhaps not as great an impediment as it might have been in earlier years.

Already, many right-wing and military factions were gathering around *Stavka* in Mogilev, and the British and French made attempts to communicate with *Stavka* rather than with Petrograd, treating the former military headquarters effectively as the government of Russia. On 20 November, *Sovnarkom* ordered Dukhonin via a telegram to contact the Germans with a proposal for immediate cessation of hostilities prior to opening peace negotiations. Surrounded by right-wing generals and some of the representatives of Britain and France, Dukhonin temporised while he assessed his options, and asked the war ministry in Petrograd to confirm the authenticity of the telegram.

Early on 23 November, Lenin contacted Dukhonin using the Hughes apparatus, the same teleprinter that Kerensky had used in his exchanges with Kornilov. Dukhonin asked for clarification – was he to commence negotiations for peace just with the Germans, or with all Russia's enemies? And what of the Romanian forces under Russian command at the southern end of the Eastern Front – were they to be included in the peace negotiations? And if the negotiations were only to cover Russia and Germany, what was Dukhonin to do with the Romanians? Lenin replied that the instructions had been perfectly clear, and that envoys should be dispatched immediately. Dukhonin countered that such a proposal could only come from a central government that had the full support of the army and the nation at large, clearly implying that *Sovnarkom* lacked this authenticity. Lenin then informed Dukhonin that he was dismissed from command, and would be replaced by Nikolai Vasileyevich Krylenko.

Aged only 32, Krylenko was a man of very limited military experience and almost none of command. He had become a Bolshevik when only a teenager and caught the attention of the authorities during the 1905 Revolution, spending some time under arrest. He studied law and was briefly conscripted into the army before the war; fearing that he was about to be arrested once more, he left Russia in early 1914 and joined other Bolsheviks in Switzerland. He returned to his homeland a year later to start setting up Bolshevik networks but was soon arrested and dispatched to the front line. After the February Revolution he became a prominent member of Eleventh Army's Soldiers' Committee before taking up posts in the central Bolshevik organisation. He now inherited command of what remained of Russia's field armies and set off from Petrograd to take up his new post, while Lenin issued a radio broadcast announcing Dukhonin's dismissal.

The military missions of the other Entente Powers were in Mogilev and were dismayed by this development. The day after Lenin's radio broadcast, they issued a joint note to Dukhonin, reminding him of Russia's treaty obligations not to agree a separate peace or ceasefire. Technically, they presented their note to *Stavka* rather than to Dukhonin, but the reality was that they had no desire to see him replaced by a Bolshevik activist. To date, Dukhonin had been obstructive rather than openly rebellious, but he now sent a signal to Kaledin asking him to dispatch reliable troops to Mogilev as soon as possible in order to be able to beat off any forces that might be sent from Petrograd. The attempt was doomed to failure; Bonch-Bruyevich decided to inform the Mogilev Soviet of the order and the Soviet instructed the largely pro-Bolshevik railway workers to ensure that the troops were diverted elsewhere. Dukhonin was in an impossible situation, and issued orders to the front commanders to try to prevent mass desertion and demobilisation – should their formations start to drift away, they were to fall back to shorter defensive lines while continuing to defend key locations, particularly the industrial and agricultural parts of southern Russia. Wherever possible, these were to be secured by forces that could reliably be expected to oppose the Bolsheviks. He also considered moving *Stavka* to Kiev, but General Mikhail Konsantinovich Diterichs – who had been his superior during his time with Southwest Front – persuaded him to stay in Mogilev and await events.[296] His final act involved the prisoners held at the monastery in Bykhov; he ordered their release. The majority immediately headed south for the Ukraine, where they began to gather anti-Bolshevik elements. The civil war that had increasingly seemed to be inevitable was now becoming imminent.

When they learned of the escape of Kornilov and other generals, many of the more militant Bolsheviks in Mogilev were furious, particularly when they realised that the prisoners had been released on Dukhonin's orders after Lenin had already announced his dismissal. Dukhonin was promptly arrested, and was brought before Krylenko at Mogilev's railway station as soon as he arrived on 20 November. Pavel Efimovich Dybenko was the commander of the small group of Red Guards and Bolshevik troops who accompanied Krylenko; like many who were now thrust into the spotlight, he had a chequered past. He had a long history of arrests for supporting the Bolsheviks and was imprisoned in 1915 after involvement in a naval mutiny before being sent to the front, where he was again arrested. He now led an increasingly aggressive interrogation of Dukhonin, which rapidly turned violent. To the horror of a French officer who was present at the time, Krylenko was unable to intervene – when he tried to step between the increasingly angry soldiers and Dukhonin, he was simply brushed aside.[297] Dukhonin was repeatedly stabbed with bayonets; his body was then dragged away and used for target practice.

Shocked by the murder, Krylenko later contacted Trotsky to request that charges were brought against Dukhonin's killers. Trotsky replied that if any charges were brought, it would be wrong to do so under the pre-revolutionary legal system. The charges would therefore have to be heard by a revolutionary court, which was most unlikely to deliver a guilty verdict.

Krylenko had travelled to Mogilev via Daugavpils, close to the front line in Latvia, where he had issued instructions to envoys who were to cross the front line with proposals for a ceasefire with the Germans. Three men – a cavalry lieutenant, a surgeon, and a volunteer soldier – ventured out across the barbed wire bearing white flags on 26 November, and were immediately seized and blindfolded by the Germans. Within a day, they had been released and sent back to Petrograd bearing the message that the Germans were willing to commence talks at the headquarters of *Ober Ost* in Brest-Litovsk. Trotsky promptly contacted the other Entente Powers and invited them to send delegates to the proposed conference; there was no response. After another appeal went unanswered, *Sovnarkom* dispatched a delegation on 2 December to Daugavpils led by Adolf Abramovich Joffe, a longstanding friend of Trotsky, to commence talks with the Germans. In addition to Joffe, the group included a former tsarist officer, other revolutionaries including Anastasia Alexandrovna Bizenko who had assassinated the military governor of Saratov in 1905, and two sailors from the Baltic Fleet. At the last moment – as they were boarding the train in Petrograd – the delegates realised that they had nobody to represent the peasants of Russia. They saw Roman Ilarionovich Stashkov, a lowly peasant, carrying a rucksack by the side of the road and immediately hailed him, conscripting him into their ranks. This group crossed over to German-held territory and were taken by train to Brest-Litovsk, to commence negotiations to bring the war between Russia and the Central Powers to an end.

CHAPTER 9

RUSSIA'S LOWEST EBB: BREST-LITOVSK

The Russians were not the only ones keen to secure a peace. Germany had gambled everything on the submarine campaign to bring Britain to its knees, and by the end of 1917 it was clear that this had failed. Nor would it be possible for the submarine arm to delay the arrival of hundreds of thousands of fresh American troops in 1918; if Germany was to achieve victory before the advent of the armies of the United States, an offensive would have to be launched in the west in the first months of the coming year, as Ludendorff later recalled:

> The idea of attacking in France in 1918 had occurred already in November [1917] to many commanders in the west, with me amongst the first. I therefore waited with the greatest anticipation the day when the Russians asked us for a ceasefire. Local ceasefires were arranged at various locations on the front in November. The formations that negotiated with us were ever larger, and individual Russian armies had already contacted us with proposals for ending field operations ... it was a confused picture, half of war and half of peace.[298]

There was widespread industrial unrest across the Central Powers, and food shortages remained critical. Another bad winter might trigger in Germany and Austria-Hungary the sort of unrest that had unseated the tsar; but peace in the east might provide access to the agricultural riches of the Ukraine, as well as releasing sufficient troops to allow for an offensive in the west. Much would depend upon the conference in Brest-Litovsk.

When they conceded the city to the Germans in 1915, the retreating Russians set fire to much of Brest-Litovsk and the devastation had barely changed in the intervening years. Large parts of the city consisted of blackened ruins, with the German headquarters in the old citadel. Although Prince Leopold held the post of *Ober Ost*, the negotiating team for the Central Powers was led by Hoffmann, his chief of staff, accompanied by Oberstleutnant Hermann Pokorny from the *k.u.k.* Army, Adjutant General Tsekki Pasha from Turkey, and Colonel Peter Gantchev of the Bulgarian general staff. The contrast between the precise, immaculately dressed officers of the Central Powers and the Russian revolutionaries in their various costumes could not have been greater.

The conference began on 3 December with Joffe and Hoffmann discussing whether the conference was intended to address the entire war or only the Eastern Front; it was agreed that in the absence of representatives of the other Entente Powers, any agreement would apply only to the war in the east, though the Bolsheviks hoped that the agreement would then extend to encompass all nations. The meeting adjourned for the day, and the delegates gathered for dinner together – Hoffmann had offered separate dining arrangements for his Russian guests, but they had expressed a desire to eat alongside the German staff in their dining room:

> We had the opportunity of getting to know what sort of men some of them were. I had, of course, placed those members of the commission who had a vote higher than those who were merely experts, so that the workman, the sailor and the non-commissioned officer sat in higher places than the admiral or the officers. I shall never forget the first dinner we had with the Russians. I sat between Joffe and Sokolnikov … Opposite me was the workman, who was evidently caused much trouble by the various implements that he found on the table. He tried to catch the food on his plate first with one thing and then with another. It was only the fork that he used exclusively as a toothpick. Almost opposite me sat Frau Bizenko next to Prince Hohenlohe who had on his other side the peasant [Stashkov], a typical Russian figure with long grey curls and an enormous untrimmed beard. He caused a smile to appear on the face of the orderly who was serving round the wine, and had asked him if he would take claret or hock, and he inquired which was the stronger, as he would prefer to have that sort.[299]

The following day, Joffe laid out Russia's position. There should be an armistice for six months, with either side committed to giving three days' notice before a resumption of hostilities; the Germans should evacuate the Estonian archipelago that they had seized immediately before the October Revolution; and they should commit not to move troops from the Eastern Front for use against the other Entente Powers. Hoffmann responded that he was happy to agree not to move troops away from the Eastern Front – aside from those who had already received orders – but there was no possibility of Germany evacuating territory that it had gained. With regard to an armistice, he was prepared to agree only to a 28-day ceasefire. Eventually, both sides agreed to this last term, with a notice period of one week for the resumption of hostilities.[300]

Difficulties remained about the coverage of the armistice. The Bolsheviks were anxious for it to include all belligerent powers, but Hoffmann pointed out – perfectly reasonably – that it was not possible to agree anything that involved the other Entente Powers, as they were not present. In order to allow Joffe to seek further instructions, the conference was adjourned for a week, with a ceasefire coming into effect immediately; in practice, this proved easy to implement in the northern parts of the front, where Bolshevik authority was strongest, but harder to agree elsewhere. During this period, Trotsky tried again – in vain – to secure the cooperation of Germany's other enemies in the peace talks, but when the conference resumed in Brest-Litovsk on 12 December – without the symbolic presence of token soldiers, sailors, workers and peasants – there was still no response from the other Entente Powers. Regardless of the disappointment of Britain and France that Russia was seeking to leave the war almost at any price, diplomats within Russia could see that it was unrealistic for the Western Powers to expect Russia to continue fighting. Buchanan wrote to London on 10 December:

> I share the view, already expressed by General Knox, that the situation here has become so desperate that we must reconsider our attitude. In my opinion, the only safe course left to us is to give Russia back her word and to tell her people that, realising how worn out they are by the war and the disorganisation inseparable from a great revolution, we leave it to them to decide whether they will purchase peace on Germany's terms or fight on with the Allies, who are determined not to lay down their arms till binding guarantees for the world's peace have been secured.
>
> It has always been my one aim and object to keep Russia in the war, but one cannot force an exhausted nation to fight against its will.[301]

On 15 December, an armistice was formally agreed. It would continue until 14 January, with automatic extensions of 30 days unless one side or the other gave one week's notice of its cessation. There was a further recess in the talks to allow for consultations before the conference reconvened. The Western Entente looked on with a mixture of resignation and dismay, but the Russians had no choice. Desertions along the front had continued at a steady rate, leaving large sectors of the front almost undefended. One commander commented that in his sector, the front line had become nothing more than a geographical designation.[302] Whilst some of the more romantically inclined Bolsheviks dreamed of the valiant Red Guards marching to victory against the imperialist armies of Russia's foes while the workers of the world rose up in revolution, Lenin had a far more pragmatic view:

> Our tactics ought to rest on the principle of how to ensure that the socialist revolution is best able to consolidate itself and survive in one country until such time as other countries join in.[303]

The Brest-Litovsk talks also involved Germany's allies, and of these the Austro-Hungarian Empire was perhaps in the worst situation. Czernin, the foreign minister, was deeply pessimistic about the future, which he saw as one of a war that stretched on for decades:

> In the autumn of 1917 I had a visit from a subject of a neutral state … He had no faith in the destruction of England, nor had I; but he thought it possible that France and Italy might collapse. The French and Italians could not possibly bear any heavier burdens than already were laid on them; in Paris and Rome, he thought, revolution was not far distant, and a fresh phase of the war would then ensue. England and America would continue to fight on alone, for ten, perhaps 20 years. England was not to be considered just a little island, but comprised Australia, India, Canada and the sea. '*L'Angleterre est imbattable* [England is unbeatable]', he repeated, and America likewise. On the other hand, the German Army was also invincible. The secession of France and Italy [from the Entente] would greatly hinder the cruel blockade, for the resources of those two countries – once they were conquered by the Central Powers – were very vast, and in that case he could not see any end to the war. Finally, the world would collapse from the general state of exhaustion.
>
> … My visitor was astonished by Vienna. The psychology of no other city that he had seen during the war could compare with that of Vienna. An amazing apathy prevailed. In Paris there was a passionate demand for Alsace-Lorraine; in Berlin the contrary was demanded just as eagerly; in England the destruction of Germany was the objective; in Sofia the conquest of the Dobruja; in Rome they clamoured for all possible and impossible things; in Vienna nothing at all was

> demanded. In Krakow they called for a Great Poland; in Budapest for an unmolested Hungary; in Prague for a united Czech state and in Innsbruck the descendants of Andreas Hofer [a Tyrolean civilian who led an anti-French uprising in 1809] were fighting as they did in his day for their sacred land, Tyrol. In Vienna they asked only for peace and quiet.
>
> Old men and children would fight the arch-enemy in Tyrol, but if the Italians were to enter Vienna and bring bread with them they would be received with shouts of enthusiasm.[304]

By the end of 1917, Czernin was deeply disillusioned about the future. His relationship with the Emperor Karl had deteriorated, and sensing that his time in office was drawing to a close, he was desperate to secure peace for the Austro-Hungarian Empire before its internal ethnic tensions tore it apart. However, he was also aware that peace with Russia would accomplish little if the Entente remained determined to dismember the empire – large territories had been promised to Italy and Romania, and there was a clear intention to force Vienna to allow the Czech, Polish and Balkan regions complete independence. If it looked as if Germany was about to lose its main ally, Czernin told the emperor, the Germans would occupy Austria and turn it into another war zone. However, if peace with Russia were to be followed by a successful German offensive in the west, perhaps it might be possible to bring the war-weary nations of the Entente to the negotiating table. He wrote to a friend:

> I believe we could arrive at a tolerable peace of understanding; we should lose something to Italy, and should, of course, gain nothing in exchange. Furthermore, we should have to alter the entire structure of the Monarchy – after the fashion of the *federation Danubienne* proposed to France – and I am certainly rather at a loss to see how this can be done in the face of the Germans and Hungarians. But I hope we may survive the war, and I hope that they will ultimately revise the conditions of the London Conference [which promised large territorial gains to Italy]. Let but old Hindenburg once make his entry into Paris, and then the Entente *must* utter the decisive word that it is willing to treat. But when that moment comes, I am firmly determined to do the utmost possible to appeal directly to the *peoples* of the Central Powers and ask them if they prefer to fight on for conquest or if they will have peace.
>
> To settle with Russia as speedily as possible, then break through the determination of the Entente to exterminate us, and then to make peace – even at a loss – that is my plan and the hope for which I live.

> … So, I hope, we may come out of it at last, albeit rather mauled. But the old days will never return. A new order will be born in throes and convulsions.[305]

Czernin left Vienna for Brest-Litovsk on 19 December accompanied by a substantial delegation that included Feldmarschallleutnant Maximilian Csicserics von Bacsány; on this occasion, the Dual Monarchy would be fully represented. They reached Brest-Litovsk the following day where they met their German counterparts, now led by Richard von Kühlmann, Germany's foreign secretary. Hoffmann, though present, was no longer leading negotiations; he recorded that Czernin looked as if his nerves had been entirely shattered.[306] That evening at dinner, Czernin had his first conversation with Joffe and was left with deep misgivings, as he recorded in his diary:

> They are strange creatures, these Bolsheviks. They talk of freedom and reconciliation of the peoples of the world, of peace and unity, and withal they are said to be the most cruel tyrants history has ever known. They are simply exterminating the bourgeoisie, and their arguments are machine-guns and the gallows. My talk today with Joffe has shown me that these people are not honest, and in falsity surpass all that cunning diplomacy has been accused of, for to oppress decent citizens in this fashion and then talk at the same time of the universal blessing of freedom – it is sheer lying.[307]

When talks began in earnest on 22 December, Joffe outlined once more Russia's main points: there were to be no forcible annexations; populations who had been deprived of their independence during the war were to have it restored; nationalities that had not had freedom before the war would have rights of self-determination; the rights of minorities were to be guaranteed; there would be no indemnities; and colonial issues were to be settled in accordance with these principles.[308] After a further pause for consultations – there were considerable arguments between the German, Austro-Hungarian, Bulgarian and Turkish delegations – the various legations reconvened on Christmas Day, when Czernin stated that the issue of self-determination and the protection of minorities should be responsibilities of individual nations rather than the subject of the peace conference. With regard to overseas colonies, he pointed out that, of the Central Powers, only Germany had such territories, and they had been seized by the Entente Powers; in accordance with the Russian proposals, these would have to be restored to Germany. He added that the native people of these colonies had shown great loyalty to Germany, and their rights to self-determination were an internal matter for the German Empire.

Even with these reservations, the Russians were delighted and felt that real progress had been made. Kühlmann had drawn up a timetable for further discussions and the matters tabled for 26 December – largely about the restoration of trade – were settled rapidly. Czernin spent the afternoon walking through the devastated city and in an encounter with an elderly Jew he gained an insight into the suffering of ordinary people caught up in the war:

> He was sitting in the gutter, weeping bitterly. He did not beg, did not even look at me, only wept and wept, and could not speak at first for sobs. And then he told me his story – Russian, Polish, and German, all mixed together.
>
> Well, he had a store – heaven knows where, but somewhere in the war zone. First came the Cossacks. They took all he had – his goats and his clothes and everything in the place – and then they beat him. Then the Russians returned, beat him again, *en passant* as it were, and then came the Germans. They fired his house with their guns, pulled off his boots, and beat him. Then he entered the service of the Germans, carrying water and wood, and receiving his food and beatings in return. But today he had got into trouble with them in some incomprehensible fashion; no food after that, only the beatings; and was thrown into the street.
>
> The beatings he referred to as something altogether natural. They were to him the natural accompaniment to any sort of action – but he could not live on beatings alone.
>
> I gave him what I had on me – money and cigars – told him the number of my house, and said he could come tomorrow, when I could get him a pass to go off somewhere where there were no Germans and no Russians, and try to get him a place of some sort where he would be fed and not beaten. He took the money and cigars thankfully enough; the story of the railway pass and the place he did not seem to believe. Railway travelling was for soldiers, and an existence without beatings seemed an incredible idea.
>
> … A terrible thing is war. Terrible at all times, but worst of all in one's own country. We at home suffer hunger and cold, but at least we have been spared up to now the presence of the enemy hordes.[309]

That evening, Hoffmann dampened the mood of the Russians. There could be no question of Germany evacuating Lithuania and Latvia until a general peace had been secured, he informed the delegates before dinner; the industrial and agricultural resources of the region were essential for the German war effort. Once there was peace, there could be a vote amongst the people to decide their future, but this would be at a time when the area was still under German occupation. This was repeated the following morning, and it was clear to the Russians that this would probably result in any plebiscite being run with a restricted voting franchise that would ensure that at the very least the area remained under German control, if not formally annexed by Germany. Hoffmann's account describes the reaction of the Russians:

> Joffe looked as if he had received a blow to the head. After lunch we had a conference that lasted several hours. The Russians were represented by Joffe, Kamenev and Pokrovsky – the Germans by the secretary of state [Kühlmann], Czernin and myself. In this conference the Russians gave free vent to their disappointment and indignation. Pokrovsky said, with tears in his eyes, it was impossible to speak of a peace without annexations when about 18 governments [provinces] were torn from the Russian Empire. In the end the Russians threatened to break off the conference and depart. Count Czernin was beside himself.[310]

The difficulties faced by all delegations were immense. Whilst Hoffmann's pronouncement might have been hugely unwelcome both to the Russians and to Czernin, senior German military figures were deeply worried that too much was being conceded. Czernin wrote in his diary:

> Afternoon – matters still getting worse. Furious wire from Hindenburg about 'renunciation' of everything; Ludendorff, telephoning every minute; more furious outbursts. Hoffmann very excited, Kühlmann true to his name and 'cool' as ever. The Russians declare they cannot accept the vague formulae of the Germans with regard to freedom of choice.
>
> I told Kühlmann and Hoffmann I would go as far as possible with them; but should their endeavours fail, then I would enter into separate negotiations with the Russians, since Berlin and Petersburg were really both opposed to an uninfluenced vote. Austria-Hungary, on the other hand, desired nothing but final peace. Kühlmann understands my position, and says he himself would rather *go* [i.e. resign] than let it fail. Asked me to give him my point of view in writing, as it 'would strengthen his position'. Have done so. He has telegraphed it to the kaiser.
>
> Evening – Kühlmann believes matters will be settled – or broken off altogether – by tomorrow.[311]

Hoffmann might have been surrounded by professional diplomats, but he was perhaps a better poker player than any of them, and when Czernin sent Csicserics to persuade him to soften his position with the threat that Austria-Hungary was prepared to pursue a separate peace, his overall assessment of the situation was dispassionate and calculated:

> In my opinion there was no question of the negotiations being broken off by the Russians.
>
> The Russian masses were longing for peace, the army had crumbled away, it consisted now of mere insubordinate armed hordes, and the only possibility for the Bolsheviks to remain in power was by signing a peace. They were obliged to accept the conditions of the Central Powers, however hard they might be.
>
> I therefore answered Feldmarschallleutnant Csicserics' threat of a separate peace very calmly; that I thought this a brilliant idea, as it would free for us the 25 divisions that until then I had been obliged to keep on the Austro-Hungarian front for the support of their army. By a separate peace the right wing of the German Army would automatically be covered by Austria-Hungary, so that the military position of the German Eastern Army would derive special benefit by such a measure.[312]

The legations left Brest-Litovsk for further consultations in their respective capitals. In Petrograd, there could be no doubt that Hoffmann's assessment was correct; peace was desperately needed. However, the formulation devised by the Germans effectively to ensure that the outcome of any plebiscite was favourable to them was a bitter pill to swallow. In vain, Petrograd called upon the other Entente Powers to join the peace talks, but the simultaneous demands by Petrograd that the British and French grant self-determination to their overseas possessions destroyed even the slightest chance of Germany's other enemies joining Russia in its attempts to secure peace. Trotsky repeated the position of the Bolsheviks in calling for the people of the west to overthrow their intransigent rulers:

> If the allied governments, in the blind stubbornness that characterises the declining and dying classes, again refuse to take part in negotations, then the working classes will be confronted by the iron necessity of tearing power from those hands that cannot, or will not, give the people peace.[313]

This was now Russia's last hope; if the governments of the west were unwilling to cooperate with the Bolsheviks, it was vital to gain as much time as possible in the hope that the workers of those nations would take matters into their own hands. Accordingly, when the conference in Brest-Litovsk reconvened, Trotsky replaced Joffe with explicit instructions to delay matters for as long as possible.

On 2 January 1918 in Berlin, the kaiser held a meeting that included Hoffmann, Kühlmann and Ludendorff. Whatever old loyalties might have existed – Hoffmann had been a tireless plotter in the past, trying to ensure that Ludendorff and Hindenburg took overall command of Germany's war effort – the reunion between the two men was less than cordial:

> When I was announced to General Ludendorff I was received very coldly and with the angry question: 'How could you allow such a note [the German terms for peace] to be dispatched?'
>
> I answered that I had supposed, and I was bound to suppose, that the general outline of the negotiations had been discussed and settled between *OHL* and the chancellor of the empire [Hertling] and the secretary of state [Kühlmann] during their conferences in Kreuznach [the current location of *OHL*]. General Ludendorff denied this, but admitted that I had the right to suppose this had been done.
>
> Even now [written in 1924] it is a mystery to me that *OHL* and the leaders of the government had not arrived at an understanding of such a nature during the conference they had had on 18 December. It is impossible to settle the lines for so difficult a task as a treaty of peace by making all sorts of general conversation on both sides.[314]

Discussions turned to the question of Poland, and, in a private conversation with the kaiser, Hoffmann made clear that he took a different position from Ludendorff and Hindenburg, who wished to annex parts of Poland into Germany. Hoffmann preferred to limit the numbers of non-Germans who were absorbed into the kaiser's realm – his proposals for modest changes in the frontier would transfer no more than 100,000 Poles into German territory, as opposed to the plans of Ludendorff and Hindenburg, which would lead to nearer two million Poles becoming a potentially resentful minority in Germany. When the kaiser presented plans broadly in line with Hoffmann's recommendations to the full meeting, there was immediate uproar. Hindenburg and Ludendorff both demanded that no decision be made until *OHL* could present its case in full. In previous decades, it would have been inconceivable for the generals of German (or Prussian) monarchs to make such demands, but on this occasion, Kaiser Wilhelm simply agreed to defer the decision. Inevitably, as Hoffmann wrote, there was personal fallout:

> It was quite clear to me that General Ludendorff would be very much offended with me for differing so completely from them on the Polish question, and I had

> not deceived myself. Already the next day [after he returned to Brest-Litovsk] I was telephoned from Berlin, and informed that Hindenburg and Ludendorff had made a cabinet question of the case. They both threatened to resign and demanded that I should be recalled.
>
> The kaiser gave in on the Polish question but refused to alter the personal one. He protected me.[315]

Czernin returned to Vienna where he briefed the emperor, and then made preparations to return to Brest-Litovsk for the resumption of talks on 3 January. He had no doubts about the difficulties that lay ahead:

> In Vienna I saw, among politicians, Baernreither, Hauser, Wekerle, Siedler, and some few others. The opinion of almost all may be summed up as follows: 'Peace *must* be arranged, but a separate peace without Germany is *impossible*.'
>
> No one has told me how I am to manage it if neither Germany nor Russia will listen to reason.[316]

When he arrived in Brest-Litovsk the following day, he learned from Kühlmann that there had been a suggestion that Ludendorff should join the negotiations, but Ludendorff had eventually decided against this on the grounds that he would only spoil things if he got involved. Czernin wrote in his diary a clearly heartfelt hope that 'heaven grant the man such gleams of insight again and often!' During the recess, the Russians had proposed moving the conference to Stockholm; although both Kühlmann and Czernin were opposed to this, they feared that the Russians might break off talks entirely. To prevent this, the two men decided that they would pursue talks with the Ukrainians in parallel with the main negotiations.

The people of the Ukraine were just as divided when it came to supporting the Bolsheviks as elsewhere in the Russian Empire. An anti-Bolshevik parliament – the *Rada* – had formed in Kiev through a coalition of numerous factions in March 1917, triggering the creation of a rival government in the predominantly Russian city of Kharkov in the eastern Ukraine. Faced with the prospect of political subservience to Petrograd or economic subservience to the Central Powers, it seemed that the Ukrainians were inclined towards the latter, and representatives of the Central Powers had been negotiating in a desultory manner with Ukrainian figures since 1915. As a result, they could see the possibility of isolating the Bolsheviks should matters break down in the main negotiations; whilst peace with the Petrograd government was desirable, access to Ukraine's agricultural riches was fast becoming a necessity for survival. The first talks in Brest-Litovsk with the Ukrainians were held on 6 January:

> The Ukrainians are very different from the Russian delegates. Far less revolutionary, and with far more interest in their own country, less in the progress of socialism generally. They do not really care about Russia at all, but think only of the Ukraine, and their efforts are solely directed toward attaining their own independence as soon as possible. Whether that independence is to be complete and international, or only as within the bounds of a Russian federative state, they do not seem quite to know themselves. Evidently, the very intelligent Ukrainian delegates intended to use us as a springboard from which they themselves could spring upon the Bolsheviks. Their idea was that we should acknowledge their independence, and then, with this as a *fait accompli*, they could face the Bolsheviks and force them to recognise their equal standing and treat with them on that basis. Our line of policy, however, must be either to bring over the Ukrainians to our peace basis, or else drive a wedge between them and the Petersburgers. As to their desire for independence, we declared ourselves willing to recognise this, provided the Ukrainians on their part would agree to the following three points: 1. The negotiations to be concluded at Brest-Litovsk and not at Stockholm. 2. Recognition of the former political frontier between Austria-Hungary and Ukraine. 3. Non-interference of any one state in the internal affairs of another.[317]

This last point was critical for Czernin; the Ruthenian population of eastern Galicia had far more in common with the neighbouring Ukraine than with the rest of the Dual Monarchy, and there had long been fears of this area seceding from the empire. It was therefore vital to prevent pro-Ukrainian agitation.

The Russian delegates delayed their arrival at Brest-Litovsk until 7 January, using the suggestion of moving the venue to Stockholm as an excuse. It was the first stage of the delaying tactics agreed between Lenin and Trotsky. Baron Lamezan, the German officer who had accompanied Trotsky and the others on the train journey from Daugavpils, informed Kühlmann and Czernin that the Russian lines near Daugavpils were almost deserted, and Trotsky's mood had been clearly depressed. Czernin recorded:

> Baron Lamezan had the impression that the Russians were altogether desperate now, having no choice save going back with a bad peace or with no peace at all; in either case with the same result – that they would be swept away. Kühlmann says,

'Ils n'ont que le choix à quelle sauce ils se feront manger [Their only choice is which sauce with which they will be eaten].' I answered, 'Tout comme chez nous [Exactly as is the case with us].'

A wire had just come in reporting demonstrations in Budapest against Germany. The windows of the German Consulate were broken, a clear indication of the state of feeling which would arise if the peace were to be lost through our demands.[318]

Talks between the Russians and the Central Powers commenced the following day, and Trotsky immediately put his formidable powers of rhetoric and argument to use. Small, often irrelevant nuances of language became the subject of intense debate. A session was effectively wasted on the subject of separate representation for the Ukraine; Trotsky objected to a statement that the nations would live in peace and friendship after the treaty on the grounds that friendship was never the outcome of such talks; a suggestion that additional delegates might be required to represent the peoples of Latvia, Lithuania, Poland and Finland led to another adjournment; and there was even a digression while Trotsky delivered what amounted to a lecture on the nature of Marxism. Using all his extraordinary oratorical skills in both Russian and German, Trotsky was undoubtedly the master performer of the conference, aided to a considerable degree by Kühlmann's love of philosophical argument. But time was running out for all the legations. News came from Petrograd that food was desperately short, and Trotsky was only too aware that food shortages had played a major part in the downfall of the tsar earlier in the year. Czernin too received worrying reports from home, which he sent back to the emperor:

I have just received a letter … which justifies all the fears I have constantly repeated to your Majesty, and shows that in the question of food supplies we are on the very verge of a catastrophe. The situation *arising out of the carelessness and incapacity of ministers* is terrible, and I fear it is already too late to check the total collapse which is to be expected in the next few weeks.

… Telegrams arriving show the situation becoming critical for us. Regarding the question of food, we can only avoid collapse on two conditions: first, that Germany helps us temporarily; second, that we use this respite to set in order our machinery of food supply, which is at present beneath contempt, and to gain possession of the stocks still existing in Hungary.[319]

The Germans had little food to spare, and negotiations with the Ukrainians posed huge difficulties; the price of an agreement with Ukraine that would release desperately needed grain for the Austro-Hungarian Empire was the cession of territory in eastern Galicia. The key sticking point was the city of Chełm; the Ukrainians demanded that it form part of the new Ukrainian state, whereas Czernin was deeply worried about Polish hostility should he agree. Hoffmann rejected this – he regarded a completely independent Poland as both undesirable and unachievable – but agreed to act as an intermediary between Austria-Hungary and the Ukraine. The result was that he was able to secure agreement: the Ukraine would accept a separate peace in return for Chełm. Czernin and the Austro-Hungarian Empire were so desperate for peace that they had no choice but to agree, even though Czernin knew in his heart that this would embitter the Poles and make a settlement with them far harder to achieve. But if he was desperate to reach a conclusion and Trotsky was concerned about growing problems within Russia, the Germans too faced their own internal pressures. Every day of delay brought the arrival of American troops closer, and Ludendorff was anxious to commence the redeployment of formations from the Eastern Front for his planned offensive in the west.

On 18 January, Hoffmann presented the Russian delegation with a map showing the areas that Germany regarded as now falling within its hegemony. There was a fierce argument about the manner in which the map had been drawn up: Hoffmann took the position that it merely reflected military reality, while Trotsky accused the Central Powers of intending to strip over 58,000 square miles (150,000km^2) of territory from Russia. This was a matter that would require consultation in Petrograd, he declared, and asked for a further recess. When he reached the Russian capital, he had detailed talks with Lenin and other prominent figures, and proposed that Russia should announce the end of the war and demobilise without signing what he regarded as a hugely unbalanced treaty. This would create pressure within the Central Powers that might trigger the revolutions the Bolsheviks desperately wanted. Lenin disagreed, regarding Trotsky's suggestion as a risky policy; it would be better to accept an unfavourable treaty and safeguard the revolution than to risk matters deteriorating still further. A third option – of declaring a revolutionary war and unleashing the Red Guards against Germany – was popular amongst many Bolsheviks, but utterly unrealistic and was emphatically rejected by those who had even a modicum of military experience. The German Army would crush the Red Guards in battle without even pausing for breath.

The debate raged for several days. There was a vote on 21 January in which 32 were in favour of revolutionary war, 16 in favour of Trotsky's proposal, and only 15 in favour of accepting German terms. In vain, Lenin angrily declared:

> The army is excessively fatigued by the war; the horses are in such a state that in the event of an offensive we shall not be able to move the artillery; the Germans are holding such favourable positions on the islands in the Baltic that if they start an offensive they could take Reval [Tallinn] and Petrograd with their bare hands ... The peace we are now forced to conclude is undoubtedly an ignominious one, but if war begins, our government will be swept away and peace will be concluded by a different government ... We need a breathing space in order to carry out social reforms; we need to consolidate ourselves, and this takes time. We need to complete the crushing of the bourgeoisie, but for this we will need to have both our hands free. Once we have done this, we shall free both our hands, and then we should be able to carry on a revolutionary war against international imperialism.[320]

On this occasion, Lenin failed to prevail. Rather than court disaster with a revolutionary war, he offered to side with Trotsky, though he asked what would happen if the Germans used the opportunity to launch further attacks? Trotsky replied that Russia would then sign a peace treaty under such clear duress that the situation would be clear to the entire world. It was agreed that Trotsky would return to Brest-Litovsk for a further round of delaying tactics, with permission to announce Russia's exit from the war at a propitious moment.

When talks resumed, the issue of the Ukraine became the centre of heated debate. Trotsky was accompanied by two Bolshevik Ukrainians and they demanded the right to represent the Ukraine; there was some justification for this, as the Bolsheviks had been gaining ground and had actually expelled the *Rada* from Kiev, but the Central Powers refused to accept Trotsky's viewpoint. On 3 February, there was another pause and Czernin travelled to Berlin for further discussions, arguing bitterly with Ludendorff: the Austro-Hungarian position was that they were obliged to fight alongside their ally only for Germany's pre-war possessions, while Ludendorff flatly insisted that an end to the war without substantial profit for Germany amounted to a defeat. On 6 February, the full meetings in Brest-Litovsk resumed, and tension grew the following day when the German and Austro-Hungarian delegates learned of an appeal by Lenin to German soldiers for them to overthrow the government and kill the kaiser. Wilhelm immediately sent a telegram to Kühlmann instructing him to demand the entire Baltic littoral without any regard to self-determination, and to break off talks if the Russians did not agree. Kühlmann's response was that this was not the time for such a move and that, if the kaiser insisted, he would need to find himself a new foreign secretary. Never one for standing up to his officials, the kaiser lapsed into a sulking silence.

On 8 February, the peace treaty between the Ukraine and the Central Powers was signed, and two days later Trotsky judged that the moment had come. The speech he gave left his opponents dumbfounded:

> We do not agree to shed any longer the blood of our soldiers … In awaiting the moment – we hope it is near – when all the oppressed working classes of all countries will take in their own hands the authority, as the working people of Russia have already done … we are getting out of this war.
>
> … At the same time, we announce that the conditions of peace set before us by Germany and Austria-Hungary fundamentally work against the interests of all peoples … we cannot inscribe the signature of the Russian Revolution beneath conditions that bring with them oppression, grief, and misfortune to millions of human beings.
>
> … In refusing to sign an annexationist peace, Russia announces that the state of war with Germany, Austria-Hungary, Bulgaria and Turkey is at an end. Orders for general demobilisation have already gone out to the Russian armed forces.[321]

The Central Powers were in completely new territory – never had a war ended in such a manner. The diplomats were in favour of accepting the matter, but Hoffmann argued against them. Trotsky and his fellow Bolsheviks returned to Petrograd, leaving behind a few military figures to liaise with the Central Powers. On 16 February, the sense of accomplishment with which Trotsky had returned to the capital was shattered: the Germans gave the Russians 48 hours' notice of ending the ceasefire. Lenin's fears had come true, and the issue would be settled on the battlefield, at a time when Russia's army had never been so weak.

The town of Bad Homburg, to the north of Frankfurt-am-Main, has a long history of being one of the wealthiest parts of Germany; this was enhanced in 1888 when Wilhelm II adopted the castle as his summer residence, and on 13 February the kaiser chose it as the location of his Crown Council meeting, largely because of its excellent railway connections and proximity to Hindenburg's headquarters at *OHL*. The collapse of the Brest-Litovsk talks was of course the starting point for discussions and consideration on how to proceed. To date, both Kühlmann and Hoffmann had attracted widespread criticism for their comparatively modest aims, and the refusal of the Bolsheviks to agree to their terms – and the imminent resumption of hostilities – led to frenzied discussions for redrawing the map of Europe and indeed much of Asia. The kaiser demanded that Russia should be effectively dismembered: the Ukraine would be allowed independence but within Germany's sphere of influence, and the rest of Russia would be divided into Central Russia, Siberia, and a Union of the Southeast. Poland would become a kingdom under the rule of the House of Württemberg, and a prince of the House of Saxony would rule Lithuania. The rest of the Baltic littoral would belong to the Hohenzollerns, and Finland was at first to be assigned to the kaiser's son Oskar, but later it was agreed that a prince of Hesse would be its ruler. The Bolsheviks were an irrelevance and were to be hunted down and destroyed.[322]

This was a far cry from the treaty that Trotsky had rejected, and had the support of Hindenburg and Ludendorff; the latter suggested further conquests and annexations stretching into the Caucasus, and was backed by financiers and industrialists who looked forward to building new fortunes in the empire that would be created. For the military, this empire would provide an essential counterweight to the British Empire, and would allow Germany to face its enemies in the west forever with impunity. The professional diplomats and politicians who were present – particularly Kühlmann and Chancellor Hertling – were horrified at proposals that owed everything to 19th-century thinking and had no place in the realities of the present. Both men seriously considered resigning rather than agreeing to the plans, and Kühlmann urged moderation; the Bolsheviks did not need to be hunted down, he argued, they could be left to their own devices. Hindenburg suggested that the territorial acquisitions proposed in the Baltic region were of particular importance for future wars in the east, and Kühlmann rejected this notion vigorously, pointing out that Austria-Hungary could not possibly survive another conflict under any circumstances and war without the Habsburg Empire was impossible. His views were brusquely rejected in favour of the expansionist visions of the kaiser and Hindenburg.

After the frustrations of Trotsky's delaying tactics, Hoffmann looked forward to the resumption of hostilities with some relish. On 17 February, he wrote in his diary:

> No other option is possible, as these people will otherwise beat the Ukrainians, Finns and Balts to death while preparing a revolutionary army in peace and unleashing chaos all across Europe. Of course, with only the forces available in the east, I can't mount a rapid campaign of victory as far as Petersburg, but nevertheless I hope to achieve something. I am curious as to whether the Russians will defend themselves at all or will fade away without a fight. The situation in the Ukraine is not encouraging. The Ukrainian troops, like the Russians, are utterly disorganised as a result of revolutionary thoughts and similarly want nothing more than to 'go

> home'. The whole of Russia is nothing more than a whole heap of maggots – everything is foul, everyone swarms about without order.[323]

The Russian Army had been melting away for many months; the introduction of demobilisation merely made it official. Many of the formations that had existed since August 1914 had already been disbanded, and although many divisions, corps and armies still remained, they existed largely on paper. Most lower- and middle-grade officers had been dismissed and replaced by men chosen by election; many of these men had almost no experience of command, much like Nikolai Krylenko, the commander-in-chief, who had never held a rank higher than ensign. He had been tasked with creating a new Red Army, but whilst his oratorical skills were as great as many other Bolsheviks, his organisational abilities were far more limited. In addition to disbanding one army and creating another, he now found himself trying to fend off a sudden offensive by the German Army.

The Russian forces might have effectively disappeared, but their enemies were as formidable as ever. *Ober Ost* had 53 divisions at its disposal, albeit largely composed of *Landwehr*; all had been rested and replenished and were fully equipped, confident and well led. Whilst some divisions had been transferred to the west after the successful Baltic campaign, those that remained were still sufficient to mount a powerful, if limited campaign. Hoffmann's staff officers had commenced planning for such a contingency before the collapse of talks at Brest-Litovsk, and it was now time to execute those plans.

The German advance, codenamed *Faustschlag* ('Punch'), would be along three distinct axes. In the north, 16 divisions would move forward through northern Latvia into Estonia, with the objective of Narva, only 85 miles (137km) from Petrograd. Farther south, Tenth Army – reinforced by XLI Corps – would march on Smolensk, thus threatening Moscow, and in the south the largest group of forces was to drive the Bolsheviks from the Ukraine.

Any concerns that Hoffmann might have had about the willingness of the Russians to fight were dispelled on the first day of the new campaign, 18 February. The town of Daugavpils in Latvia fell with almost no casualties on either side; in the south, Lutsk – captured by Brusilov's Southwest Front at the end of the hugely encouraging first phase of the summer offensive of 1916 – also changed hands without a fight.

Lenin immediately summoned a meeting of the Central Committee to discuss the disastrous situation. Nikolai Ivanovich Bukharin, the leader of the Moscow Soviet and editor of *Pravda*, and his supporters still pressed for a revolutionary war, but Lenin insisted that the only question for discussion was whether or not to accept the German terms for peace. The current situation was an absurdity – Russia was being overrun and her armies were still being demobilised. He railed at his colleagues:

> The peasants do not want war and will not fight. Can we now tell the peasants to fight a revolutionary war? But if that is what we want we should not have demobilised the army … If we are not ready, we must conclude peace. Since we have demobilised the army it is ridiculous to talk of a permanent [revolutionary] war … The peasant will not have a revolutionary war, and will overthrow anyone who openly calls for one. The revolution in Germany has not yet started, and we know that over here, too, our revolution did not win out all at once. It has been said here that they would take Livonia and Estonia; but we can give them up for the sake of the revolution. If they want us to withdraw our troops from Finland, well and good – let them take revolutionary Finland. The revolution will not be lost if we give up Finland, Livonia and Estonia …
>
> I propose a declaration that we are willing to conclude the peace the Germans offered us yesterday; should they add to this non-interference in the affairs of the Ukraine, Finland, Livonia and Estonia, we should unquestionably accept all that as well.[324]

The voting was perilously tight, but Trotsky had assured Lenin that he would vote for him if the policy of 'neither peace nor war' failed, and as a result Trotsky was authorised to send an urgent radio message requesting a meeting so that he could sign the peace treaty that had been proposed:

> The Council of People's Commissars lodges a protest over the German government's movement of troops against the Russian Soviet Republic, which had declared the state of war ended and had started to demobilise its army on all fronts …
>
> The Council … finds itself forced, in the situation that has arisen, to declare its readiness formally to conclude peace on the terms the German government demanded at Brest-Litovsk.[325]

It was too late. The comparatively modest aims of the diplomats and Hoffmann had been surpassed by the new plans for major annexations. The following day, the advance was hindered more by practical problems than resistance, as Hoffmann wrote on 20 February:

> The mess in the Russian Army is much greater than I expected. Nobody wants to fight any more. Yesterday, a single lieutenant and six of our men took 600 Cossacks prisoner. Hundreds of guns, cars, locomotives, wagons, a few thousand prisoners, dozens of division staffs were rounded up, all without any actual fighting.
>
> Acting on orders, I radioed Trotsky yesterday to inform him that his offer had been received here, but that he should submit it in writing to the 'German Commandant of Dünaburg [Daugavpils]'. The answer came back immediately during the night, that the courier was en route with the documents. He seems in a damned hurry – we are not. Unfortunately our advance continues only slowly; there are shortages of horses for supply columns, and the roads are poor. It will be a while before we reach Lake Peipus.[326]

It was no longer in the interests of Germany to settle with Russia immediately; with the Bolsheviks now desperate to secure peace, Hoffmann wanted to push *Faustschlag* as far as he could before his troops were reined in. Even when Trotsky's message appeared in writing, Hoffmann passed it on to the German government for action while continuing his advance. On 21 February, German troops crossed the frozen Baltic from the Estonian archipelago to the mainland while the main forces penetrated ever deeper into Russia, largely along the railway lines; at every station they found stocks of military equipment piled up when the Russian units had demobilised, and after only three days Hoffmann recorded that his troops had captured over 1,500 guns. Desperately aware that the future of Bolshevik rule hung in the balance, the Central Committee published a proclamation calling on Russians to defend their revolution, raising the spectre that in some unfathomable way, the imperial nations – despite being at each other's throats – were trying to destroy Bolshevism:

> Fulfilling the task with which it has been charged by the capitalists of all countries, German militarism wants to strangle the Russian and Ukrainian workers and peasants, to return the land to the landowners, the mills and factories to the bankers, and power to the monarchy. The German generals want to establish their 'order' in Petrograd and Kiev. The Socialist Republic of Soviets is in gravest danger. Until the proletariat of Germany rises and triumphs, it is the sacred duty of the workers and peasants of Russia devotedly to defend the Republic of Soviets against the hordes of bourgeois-imperialist Germany. The Council of People's Commissars resolves: 1) The country's manpower and resources are placed entirely at the service of revolutionary defence. 2) All Soviets and revolutionary

> organisations are ordered to defend every position to the last drop of blood. 3) Railway organisations and the Soviets associated with them must do their utmost to prevent the enemy from availing himself of the transport system; in the event of a retreat, they are to destroy the tracks … 4) All grain and food stocks generally, as well as all valuable property in danger of falling into the enemy's hands, must be unconditionally destroyed … 5) The workers and peasants of Petrograd, Kiev, and of all towns, townships, villages and hamlets along the line of the new front are to mobilise battalions to dig trenches, under the direction of military experts. 6) These battalions are to include all able-bodied members of the bourgeois class, men and women, under the supervision of Red Guards; all those who resist are to be shot. 7) All publications which oppose the cause of revolutionary defence … are to be suppressed … 8) Enemy agents, profiteers, marauders, hooligans, counter-revolutionary agitators and German spies are to be shot on the spot.[327]

As with so many Bolshevik proclamations, the propaganda value of this announcement was as important as its practical content. Lenin would have known that there were effectively no 'military experts' to direct the digging of field positions, and even if they were created, there were no troops with artillery and ammunition to occupy them. Nevertheless, the Bolsheviks had to be seen to be doing something.

Meanwhile, Hoffmann's troops pressed on:

> Our movements continue according to plan. It is the most comical war that I have ever experienced – it is conducted almost entirely on railways and with trucks. One puts a handful of infantry with machine-guns and a field gun on a train and drives to the next station, secures it, rounds up the Bolsheviks, brings up more troops by train, and drives on. In any event, the experience has the attraction of its novelty.[328]

On 23 February, a courier finally brought the German reply to Petrograd. Inevitably, German terms had hardened considerably, and it was clear that the Hindenburg-Ludendorff camp had won whatever internal arguments had remained after the Bad Homburg council. Russia was to lose Finland, the Baltic States, and the Ukraine. There was no longer any commitment to respecting the wishes of whatever proportion of the populations were granted a plebiscite. The ultimatum, dispatched on 22 February, gave the Russians just 48 hours to accept the terms; by the time the courier reached Petrograd, half of this period had elapsed.

There was further bitter argument amongst the members of the Central Committee. Bukharin and three other members continued to demand a revolutionary war, something that Lenin flatly rejected:

> The bitter truth has now revealed itself with such terrible clarity that it is impossible not to see it. The entire bourgeoisie in Russia is rejoicing and gloating over the arrival of the Germans. Only those who are blind or intoxicated by phrases can close their eyes to the fact that the policy of a revolutionary war, without an army, brings grist to the mill of our bourgeoisie …
>
> Let everyone know: he who is against an immediate, even though extremely onerous peace, is endangering Soviet power.
>
> We are compelled to endure an onerous peace. It will not halt the revolution in Germany and in Europe. We shall set about preparing a revolutionary army, not by phrases and exclamations (after the manner of those who … have done nothing even to halt our fleeing troops), but by organisational work, by deeds, by the creation of a proper, powerful army of the whole people.[329]

Trotsky and three other members abstained. Those who voted in favour of accepting the German terms numbered six – the minimum number to make the vote binding. Early on 24 February, a radio message informed the Germans that Russian delegates were en route to sign the treaty.

The leader of the delegation was Grigory Yakovlevich Sokolnikov, who had been in charge of nationalisation of Russia's banks. He reached Brest-Litovsk on 28 February, by which time the German Army had secured all the territory to the west of the River Narva in northeast Estonia and had penetrated far into the Ukraine. It had always been Hoffmann's intention to stop on the Narva, but, with the Ukraine now detached from Russia, the advance continued in the south for several weeks, eventually reaching the line of the River Don. Sokolnikov informed Hoffmann that he had come to sign the treaty and refused to enter into discussions of its clauses; he insisted that they proceed immediately and that hostilities should therefore end. With his military operations not quite complete, Hoffmann was in no hurry. After a few more exchanges, the parties met on 3 March and signed the treaty. With an eye on the future and world opinion, the Russian delegation issued a declaration immediately before the final session of the conference:

> The Workers' and Peasants' Government of the Russian Republic was forced, after the offensive of the German troops against Russia, when the latter had declared

> the war to be at an end and had commenced the demobilisation of its armies, to accept an ultimatum presented by Germany on 24 February. We have been delegated to sign these conditions, which have been forced upon us by violence.
>
> The negotiations … have shown strongly and clearly enough that the 'peace by agreement', as it is termed by the German representatives, is really and definitely an annexationist and imperialistic peace. The Brest-Litovsk conditions at the moment [i.e. the treaty that Russia was now signing] are considerably worse than this. The peace which is being concluded here at Brest-Litovsk is not a peace based upon a free agreement of the peoples of Russia, Germany, Austria-Hungary, and Turkey, but a peace dictated by force of arms. This is a peace which Russia, grinding its teeth, is compelled to accept. This is a peace which, whilst pretending to free Russian border provinces, really transforms them into German provinces and deprives them of the right of free self-determination … This is a peace which, whilst pretending to re-establish order, gives armed support in these regions to exploiting classes against the working classes, and is helping again to put upon them the yoke of oppression which was removed by the Russian Revolution …
>
> We do not doubt for one moment that this triumph of the imperialist and militarist over the international proletarian Revolution is only a temporary and passing one.[330]

The war in the east was officially at an end. For the moment, German and Austro-Hungarian troops would continue to advance across the Ukraine, but the conflict that had consumed millions of men was over. Lenin could concentrate on strengthening his position, both within the Bolsheviks and within Russia as a whole, and the Germans could start the mass movement of troops to the west in preparation for their spring offensive. Shortly after the treaty was signed, Lenin ordered that Russia's capital should move to Moscow, at least partly out of fear that Petrograd was too close to the new frontier with German-occupied Estonia; as will be shown later, he was correct to fear a future German resumption of hostilities.

Germany certainly stood to make a substantial territorial profit from the settlement in the east, and potentially could gain enormous rewards if the offensive in the west proved to be successful; the dreams of *Mitteleuropa*, an empire that would ensure German dominance for the foreseeable future, seemed to be within reach. In 1915, the German occupation of Poland and Lithuania was hailed as the prelude to substantial material gains, but excessive expectations and greedy over-exploitation resulted in those gains being far less than expected, or indeed what might have been achieved. To some extent, the same mistakes were made again. The treaty cost Russia 90 per cent of its coal production, 50 per cent of its industry, and 30 per cent of its population, and the riches of the Ukraine were swiftly divided between the Central Powers: Germany would receive 30 per cent of Ukrainian grain reserves, the Austro-Hungarian Empire 50 per cent, and Turkey 20 per cent. Almost from the start, there were tensions between Germany and Austria-Hungary over the Ukraine.

With the Austro-Hungarian Empire on the brink of starvation, Emperor Karl was desperate to ensure that there was an immediate benefit from the end of the war in the east. He issued orders for the forceful requisition of whatever was available and authorised the use of force if necessary; nor would there be even the most superficial judicial process. Anyone suspected of impeding the acquisitions or spreading pro-Bolshevik propaganda ran the risk of summary execution, and inevitably such behaviour merely hardened the resolve of Ukrainians to resist. There were also differences of practice between the civil authorities, many of which attempted to purchase food rather than merely requisitioning it, and the army, which simply took whatever it could find. The *k.u.k.* Army had always followed a practice of holding onto sufficient food for its own needs before sending supplies home, and this continued; even in 1918, most officers enjoyed a level of food supply that had long been impossible for most people within the Austro-Hungarian Empire.

Some Austro-Hungarian officials proved to be far more astute in dealing with the Ukrainians than others. Archduke Wilhelm had been brought up speaking Polish in the expectation that his family would perhaps head a Polish state within the Austro-Hungarian Empire, but, as the youngest son, Wilhelm proved to be rebellious, identifying strongly with the Ukrainians, whom he saw as rivals to the Poles; rather than oppose his wilful son, Wilhelm's father encouraged him with the hope that, just as he aspired to lead the Poles within the empire, Wilhelm might lead the Ukrainians.[331] Holding the rank of lieutenant, he commanded a Ukrainian regiment, which he led into the southern Ukraine in 1918. Aware that Austria-Hungary faced a future as little more than a vassal state to the German Empire, Vienna explored the possibility of establishing a fully independent Ukraine that would be its ally and a counterweight to German influence – an Austrian intelligence officer wrote at the time:

> We, as the creators of the first Ukrainian military unit, are called upon to enter the Ukraine as leaders – against Germany![332]

Charged with creating the first formations of the new Ukrainian Army, Wilhelm proved to be a popular figure with the local population; he allowed the peasants to keep land that they had seized from rich landowners and intervened to prevent forcible requisitioning of grain, which earned him the ire of both German and Austro-Hungarian officials in Kiev. The Germans repeatedly called for him to be removed from his post, largely because, in keeping with the Bad Homburg conference earlier in the winter, they wished to secure the Ukraine as a German satellite; at the same time, many Ukrainians called for him to be appointed their king. Both requests rested with the Emperor Karl, who decided that he would decline them. Meanwhile, there was considerable unrest throughout the Ukraine, both due to the activities of Bolsheviks – Ukrainian and Russian – and in reaction to the manner in which German and Austro-Hungarian officials outside Wilhelm's area of control seized whatever they wished without regard to the wishes or needs of the population. It was necessary for both the German and *k.u.k.* armies to maintain substantial forces numbering about one million men in the Ukraine, and these troops consumed a very significant proportion of the food that was requisitioned. Exports to the Central Powers amounted to perhaps 10 per cent of what had confidently been expected.[333] Given the behaviour of German occupation authorities in the east earlier in the war, it is striking to note that some German occupation forces expressed frustration that they were required to follow policies of cooperation with the local authorities when it came to acquiring foodstuffs.

In an attempt to improve cooperation between the forces of Germany and Austria-Hungary in Ukraine, a special commission was created, meeting for the first time in Kiev on 11 March. Although demarcation lines had been agreed, the Germans refused to abide by them and demanded a unified command of all Central Powers troops in Ukraine; naturally, under a German officer. Emperor Karl refused, pointing out that the troops were there on occupation duties, not in a war-fighting role. Nevertheless, there were fierce battles as the occupation forces moved east, particularly at Nikolayev and Cherson. Partisans operated in large parts of the countryside, and reluctantly the *k.u.k.* Army was forced to send reinforcements into Ukraine. At the end of March, the commission in Kiev managed to come to an agreement on matters both military and economic, but, even after the arrival of reinforcements, the occupation forces struggled to control the region, continue the advance towards the east, and collect foodstuffs that were desperately needed by the Central Powers.

Whilst the economic gains for the Central Powers were disappointing, the cost was high. *Ober Ost* had calculated that it would be possible to transfer 45 infantry and cavalry divisions from the Eastern Front to northern France in preparation for the spring offensive, but the large amount of territory that was seized, together with the growing resistance to occupation (largely due to heavy-handed occupation policies), limited this to 33. Had another 12 divisions been available in the west, the outcome of Germany's last gamble to secure victory might have been different. It is also likely that the outcome in the east would have been much the same regardless of whether Germany imposed the original terms of the Brest-Litovsk Treaty or the tougher terms drawn up after the resumption of hostilities. If Germany prevailed in the west, its armies would be free to rewrite the map of Europe in any manner that they chose, but defeat in the west ultimately made any settlement in the east irrelevant. It is arguable therefore that greed and a hasty desire to impose as harsh terms as possible on the Bolsheviks effectively eliminated Germany's last chance to win the war. The severe terms imposed upon the defeated French in 1871 guaranteed a future war, and a statesman of high calibre might have learned from this and adopted a more conservative approach in 1918; unfortunately for Germany, control had passed comprehensively from statesmen to the military, and in any case there was nobody of sufficient authority to assert such a view.

The war between Russia and the Central Powers shaped the careers and lives of many of those who held prominent positions. After the victories of 1914, Ludendorff and Hindenburg were hailed as military geniuses and the saviours of Germany, but closer analysis suggests that this was far from the complete story. Others claimed with some merit that the groundwork for the great victory at Tannenberg was already in place before Ludendorff and Hindenburg arrived in the Eastern Front, and the two men did not achieve anything in their later careers that came close to this first triumph. To an extent, this was because Falkenhayn effectively sidelined them for much of 1915 and 1916, but any reputation that Ludendorff established as a great strategic and operational planner must be offset against the manner in which he conducted the 1918 spring offensive in the west. He deliberately chose not to set operational objectives, claiming that the only objective was to create a breakthrough – further objectives would then unfold of their own accord. The spring offensive was widely regarded as Germany's last gamble to win the war, and it is surely not just with the benefit of hindsight that it is clear that leaving troops on occupation duties in the east, and failing to set clear objectives in the west, was not an approach that was likely to succeed. Like all German staff officers, Ludendorff was the heir to the legacy of Helmuth Moltke ('the elder'), the last Prussian and first German chief of the general staff, and Moltke had repeatedly stressed the critical importance of setting clear objectives at every level of command – only in this manner could subordinates be expected to improvise in a manner in keeping with the ultimate objective.

At the moment when the entire future of Germany depended upon his decisions, Ludendorff put aside this principle.

Hoffmann remained chief of staff at *Ober Ost* until the end of the war. His attempts to persuade the kaiser to aim for only modest territorial gains in the east earned him the enmity of Ludendorff and Hindenburg; the former mounted a poisonous press campaign against Hoffmann, describing him as merely the agent of the foreign minister, Kühlmann, and hinted at his wife having unsuitable connections with liberal and Jewish groups. After the war, Hoffmann was briefly involved in proposals for a joint operation by Germany, Britain and France to overthrow Soviet rule in Russia: the so-called 'Hoffmann Plan'.[334] In his memoirs, he wrote – with at least some justification – that he was the architect of the victory at Tannenberg, and was clearly embittered by the manner in which Ludendorff and Hindenburg treated him in 1918, particularly given the leading role he played in plotting on their behalf so that they could replace Falkenhayn at *Ober Ost*. He died in Berlin in 1927.

George Buchanan and Alfred Knox left Petrograd together and returned to England. Buchanan served as ambassador to Rome before retirement, and was criticised for not doing more to save the Romanovs from their eventual murders. This is probably unfair: Buchanan made several requests for Britain to grant Nicholas and his family asylum, but it seems that King George V, who was concerned that the arrival of the Romanovs might trigger pro-Bolshevik unrest in Britain, overruled him. When he published his memoirs, Buchanan was required to redact certain passages under threat of losing his pension, and it is fascinating to speculate on what these passages contained. Knox left the army with the rank of major general and became a conservative politician, serving as MP for Wycombe from 1924 to 1945. He was a lifelong opponent of communism and died in 1964, one of the last survivors of the group who played leading parts in the dramatic events in Petrograd.

CHAPTER 10

ROMANIA

The path that Romania travelled to enter the First World War was a convoluted one. King Carol I, the ruler of the country at the outbreak of the war, was determined not to become embroiled in a conflict that offered his nation very little – he was a member of the Hohenzollern family and Romania had treaty obligations to aid the Central Powers. Whilst the treaty specified that Romania would support Germany in the event of a Russian attack, the Romanian government insisted (as had the Italians in similar circumstances) that the outbreak of the First World War was not a clear-cut attack by Russia on Germany, and therefore Romania was not obliged to help the Central Powers. Moreover, whilst Carol was still inclined to support Germany, public opinion was strongly Francophile and therefore hostile to the Central Powers.

After the death of Carol in September 1914, his nephew Ferdinand became king. Partly through the influence of his British wife, he had little love for Germany. His prime minister, Ion Brătianu, began a prolonged series of negotiations to secure the best possible terms for Romania joining the Entente; whilst his main demand was the annexation of Transylvania from Hungary, he also wished for parts of Russian territory in Moldova and Serbian territory in the west. He refused to enter the war in 1914 when the *k.u.k.* Army was driven from Galicia and suffered humiliating setbacks in Serbia, and the declining fortunes of Russia in 1915 seemed to diminish greatly the chances of success for Romania. However, when Brusilov's armies tore apart the southern part of the Eastern Front in the summer of 1916, Brătianu finally judged that the moment had come. An inveterate schemer, he delayed further in the hope of extracting better terms from the Entente Powers, and when Romania finally entered the war on 27 August 1916 the initial promise of Brusilov's offensive had already turned to stalemate.

At first, Romanian troops made good progress in their long-planned invasion of Transylvania, but largely because of the lack of defenders. Once Austro-Hungarian – and more importantly German – troops began to arrive, the advance rapidly ground to a halt and was reversed in a series of battles. At the same time, Field Marshal August von Mackensen, who had overseen the hugely successful offensive by the Central Powers on the Eastern Front in 1915, led a German-Bulgarian-Turkish force into Dobruja in southern Romania, swiftly destroying all the forces that opposed him. A token force of Russian troops had been sent to support the Romanian Army, but they showed little inclination to stand and fight. By late November, Mackensen had crossed the Danube from Dobruja into Wallachia – the central part of Romania – and had established contact with the German forces advancing south from Transylvania. On 6 December, Mackensen entered Bucharest, and in the days that followed the Romanians and their Russian allies were driven into the eastern parts of Romania.

Having achieved their immediate aims – the rapid conquest of most of Romania and the elimination of any threat to Transylvania – the Germans and their allies were content to let the fighting die down while they concentrated their efforts elsewhere, leaving German officials to make the most of Romania's plentiful agricultural and oil resources. The remnants of the Romanian Army were regarded as too badly degraded to be a significant threat, but the Entente Powers – in particular, the French – had other ideas. Led by the efforts of General Henri Berthelot and his military mission of 1,600 men, the shattered Romanian divisions began to show signs of being capable of action after just a few weeks, though it would take longer for them to learn how to make best use of the impressive quantities of weapons that were now made available to them: 150,000 rifles, nearly 2,000 heavy machine-guns, 2,700 light machine-guns, and 225 field guns and howitzers of various calibres.[335] Much to the relief of Berthelot, the disintegration of morale that struck the Russian Army in early 1917 had almost no effect on the Romanians, who remained strongly motivated to fight to recover their homeland. Nationalist sentiment in Romania was strong, and many men attempted to infiltrate through the front line from German-occupied Romania to join the ranks of the recovering army, despite draconian measures to stop them, as Balck later recalled:

> Posters were plastered everywhere prohibiting such activity. The threatened penalty for such activity was summary execution. Our 2nd Company picked up a number of young Romanians, and our regimental commander ordered their execution. The company commander … reported back in writing that he would

> not follow the order, citing the pertinent paragraph from the military criminal code that to do so would be a war crime. The regiment then obtained a war tribunal legal opinion that was read to us. The bottom line was that the order was not illegal and would have to be executed.[336]

When tentative plans were drawn up for a Russian spring offensive, it was planned that the Romanians would play a subsidiary part, but General Alexander Averescu, commander of the Romanian Second Army, insisted that his troops should have as prominent a role as any other force in the offensive. In any event, the spring offensive never came to fruition, and by the summer the Romanians could field nine infantry and two cavalry divisions, and additional brigades that collectively amounted to perhaps another infantry division. Additional forces were still re-forming in the rear.[337]

The Romanian sector of the Eastern Front had been assigned a 'front' command in keeping with Russian policy elsewhere. The nominal commander of the Romanian Front was King Ferdinand of Romania, who was 'assisted' by a Russian general. At the beginning of 1917, this post was held by General Vladimir Victorovich Sakharov, but he was one of many senior officers to be dismissed after the February Revolution for being a loyalist of the tsar's regime. He was replaced by General Dmitri Gregorovich Shcherbachev, who had commanded the Russian Seventh Army with decidedly mixed results during the Brusilov Offensive of 1916. Numerically, the Romanian Front was far stronger than the opposing forces; it consisted of three Russian armies (Fourth, Sixth and Ninth) with a total of 40 infantry divisions and 12 cavalry divisions, and the Romanian Second Army, which fielded six of Romania's rebuilt infantry divisions and a cavalry division.[338] Early in 1917, further reinforcements took the number of Russian infantry divisions up to 50.

The forces of the Central Powers in the region were under the command of the redoubtable August von Mackensen, one of the most successful generals of any nation in the First World War. Aged 64 when hostilities began, his career almost came to an ignominious end in the Battle of Gumbinnen in August 1914, when his corps was driven from the field in disarray and he was swept along in the rout; had the Russians pursued with resolve, they would have had every chance of capturing him with his men before they could recover. Instead, he pulled his divisions back and restored order as they marched west to play a critical part in the Battle of Tannenberg. Thereafter, almost every operation that he commanded was a success, culminating in 1916 in his swift conquest of Romanian Dobruja and the capture of Bucharest. He now commanded an eponymous army group, consisting of units from several nations. The Bulgarian Third Army was commanded by Major General Stefan Nezerov, who had risen rapidly during the war largely on merit; his army was actually little more than the strength of an infantry corps, consisting of two infantry divisions and a reinforced cavalry division. Alongside his forces was the German Ninth Army, commanded at the beginning of 1917 by General Erich von Falkenhayn, the former chief of the German general staff; in May, he was sent to Turkey to take command of Army Group F in the Middle East, and was replaced first by General Robert Kosch, later by General Johannes von Eben. Much like Mackensen's army group, Ninth Army consisted of a mixture of units from different nations. Much of its strength lay in Kosch's LII Corps, formerly the Danube Army, with three Turkish divisions, a Bulgarian division, an Austro-Hungarian brigade and a German regiment. In addition, the army controlled several other formations. One German infantry division and an Austro-Hungarian cavalry division were grouped as *Gruppe Schaer*, and Generalleutnant Curt von Morgen's I Reserve Corps fielded an additional four German divisions. Finally, Generalleutnant Leo Sontag commanded an eponymous force with an Austro-Hungarian division made up of mountain troops and the German *Alpenkorpsdivision*.[339] It was a measure of Mackensen's multiple talents, both as a commander and as a diplomat, that he managed to make his force – with soldiers from each of the Central Powers – function effectively.

During the first two months of 1917, there were lively exchanges of fire between the two sides, but the spring thaw effectively brought hostilities to a halt. Most of the tough, highly capable troops of the *Alpenkorps* were pulled out of line and sent to the Western Front; in return, Mackensen received the German 217th Infantry Division. After the February Revolution, there was extensive propaganda activity by Mackensen's formations to try to undermine morale in the Romanian Front; the official Austro-Hungarian history of the war merely records that the Romanian soldiers were 'completely unconvinced' by the Central Powers' efforts.[340] Nevertheless, there were plentiful signs of demoralisation and disaffection amongst the Russian forces in the region.

As the moment for Kerensky's summer offensive approached, plans were drawn up for an assault by Romanian Front. The northern part of the front line was held by the Russian Ninth Army, with the Romanian Second Army inserted between it and the Russian Fourth Army. By the summer, the Romanian First Army was also ready for action, and it was in position to the south of the Russian Fourth Army, with the Russian Sixth Army further to the south. The main effort was to be made by the Romanians, particularly First Army, with a thrust towards the town of Râmnicu Sărat, an advance of about 24 miles (40km). The Russian Fourth Army and the Romanian Second Army would actually attack first to try to draw away enemy reserves from the key sector, with the offensive gradually extending along the full width of Romanian Front once the battle was fully under way.

Mackensen's forces were deployed with the German Ninth Army in the north, and the Bulgarian Third Army in the south, and the attack would fall upon the troops of *Gruppe Schaer* (which, due to the appointment of a new commander, would transform into *Gruppe Behr* on the eve of the new battle). The Germans had correctly determined where the Romanian attack would strike, and increasing artillery activity seemed to confirm this in early July 1917. In an attempt to determine more about the intentions of the Romanians and Russians, Mackensen ordered increased aerial reconnaissance; the flights reported that new roads and bridges were being constructed and large numbers of troops were moving up to the front. On 10 July, Mackensen noted in his diary:

> The Russians and Romanians facing my front are beginning to stir themselves and become more hostile by the day. I await their attack. The successes against the Austrians in Galicia [in the opening phase of the Kerensky Offensive] have decisively encouraged them and the agents of the Entente press them with money and lies. I remain confident, as do the troops.[341]

In response to the increasing activity, German troops were transferred to the threatened sector from other areas of Mackensen's command. The Austro-Hungarian forces immediately to the north of Mackensen also became aware that their sector would come under attack, and General Arthur Arz, the chief of the *k.u.k.* general staff, issued orders for the transfer of fresh troops from Archduke Joseph's forces in Galicia to the Carpathians; in return, Joseph would receive two burned-out divisions, which he was required to restore to full strength. When Joseph protested that he had already transferred troops to other sectors, Arz advised him that, if the Italians were to launch further assaults on their front, even more troops would have to be transferred from Joseph's command and sent elsewhere. In other words, things might be even worse.[342] Joseph remained concerned about the weakness of his southern flank, where it met the northern part of Mackensen's command, but Arz remained doubtful that there would be any attack. He advised the archduke that the Russians had actually withdrawn troops from the sector, and the fighting abilities of the Romanians were unlikely to have recovered sufficiently for them to pose much of a threat.

On 22 July, Romanian and Russian artillery opened a heavy fire at several points of the front, reaching an intensity the following day that was far greater than had been experienced previously in the Romanian sector of the Eastern Front.[343] The fire was particularly heavy around Nămoloasa, on the direct axis of any advance towards Râmnicu Sărat, and the defenders bombarded all known preparation areas to disrupt any attack. Somewhat to the surprise of the Germans, no infantry attack followed the intense bombardment. At first, the defenders considered whether their defensive artillery fire had disrupted the imminent attack, but it soon became clear that the growing crisis farther north, with the Central Powers' counteroffensive towards Tarnopol making rapid progress, had persuaded the Russians to withdraw their support – albeit temporarily – for any major operation on the Romanian Front. Shcherbachev was also concerned that several divisions had refused orders to move up to the front, and wished to spend additional time on trying to restore discipline prior to launching an attack.[344]

Farther north, Averescu had no intention of cancelling his attack with the Romanian Second Army. The southern wing of Archduke Joseph's army group consisted of the *k.u.k.* First Army commanded by General Franz Freiherr Rohr von Denta; its southern formation, *Gruppe Gerock*, occupied positions that marked the high-tide mark of the advance by the Central Powers the previous winter. Despite being in these positions for several months, little had been done in some sectors to build strong defences. Whilst the terrain was difficult and there were few roads (and even fewer railways), the Austro-Hungarian commanders appear to have shown little inclination to organise work parties to prepare fortifications or to improve lines of communication, as was the case on many other occasions. This sector too came under heavy Romanian artillery fire from 22 July, supported by Russian guns, and several probing attacks were launched on 23 July. The following day, Averescu's troops attacked at first light, swiftly capturing the village of Mărăști and the high ridge that overlooked it to the west. Much of the artillery of the Austro-Hungarian forces defending the sector was lost before midday, making it almost impossible to mount effective counterattacks, and during the afternoon Averescu's infantry drove through the lines of the weak German 218th Infantry Division, necessitating a wholesale retreat by *Gruppe Gerock*. The northern flank of Mackensen's army group was also forced back, partly due to Romanian pressure but largely to prevent a gap from opening up with *Gruppe Gerock*'s troops. With almost no reserves available, Archduke Joseph and Rohr could do little to support the weakening line. Realising that his confident predictions about the Romanians were faulty, Arz now promised further troops, but they would take several days to arrive.

On 25 July, Averescu moved his reserves forward in preparation for a new assault, but late in the day he was shocked to receive orders from King Ferdinand instructing him to cease offensive operations. The rationale for this was the change of heart of the Russians, but Averescu protested that it would be almost impossible for his troops to set up defensive positions in their current locations, and urged a continuation of the attack to secure the ridges to the west. Reluctantly, Ferdinand's headquarters granted him permission to continue, but made it clear that there would be little or no further help from the Russians. Undaunted, Averescu renewed his assault on 218th Infantry Division on 26 July, forcing it from its rudimentary second line of defences into open ground. Over the next few days, fighting continued, though with decreasing intensity as the difficulty of sustaining operations in mountainous terrain with no roads along the axis of advance hindered the ability of the Romanians to bring up reinforcements and supplies. Ferdinand once more called for a halt on 27 July, but again Averescu refused and continued to attack, and when the fighting finally died down on 2 August, his men had gained about 12 miles (20km) and had captured 70 guns and over 2,500 prisoners for the loss of about 10,000 men.[345] Whilst these losses were modest by the scale of the First World War, and the gains were dwarfed by the catastrophe unfolding for the Russians farther north, the battle nonetheless marked the resurgence of the Romanian Army as a potent fighting force.

As the great counteroffensive by the Central Powers reached and passed Tarnopol, thoughts turned to how this might be exploited into an even greater success. Hindenburg contacted Arz at *AOK* to suggest that a concerted attack along the line of the Carpathians, extending through Mackensen's sector, might collapse the entire southern half of the Eastern Front. The strength of the Romanian advance against *Gruppe Gerock* led to requests from *AOK* for Mackensen to attack sooner rather than later and, in order to deal with the salient that Averescu had created with his advance, Mackensen now changed the axis of the attack that he had been planning. Instead of thrusting towards the northeast, he would angle the assault towards the north, into the rear of Averescu's salient. The starting point of the attack was also shifted about 24 miles (40km) so that it would be launched from Focșani. Farther north, the rest of Archduke Joseph's forces were to launch a convergent attack in order to overrun the last parts of Romanian territory, with the intention of forcing the Romanians to accept peace. Aware of this possibility, Ferdinand ordered troops to be concentrated in northern Moldova to halt any advance by the *k.u.k.* Army; at the same time, preparations were made for the Romanian government to withdraw into Russian territory in the event of the army being driven from its own soil. As Averescu's advance flagged and eventually stopped, Mackensen toyed with reverting to his original plan; but it would take an additional week to move troops back to the originally proposed starting point for the attack, and Hindenburg ruled that the delay was too great.

Artillery preparation for the joint German-Austro-Hungarian attack began on 2 August and increased its intensity steadily. Morgen's troops were to play a leading part, and their commander was worried that he would be moving his divisions on divergent axes; he was expected to push northeast to secure a bridgehead over the River Siret, but also to attack north into the rear of the Romanian salient. Despite his concerns that the northerly advance might leave its eastern flank exposed to enemy fire, Morgen began the German attack against the Russian defences on 6 August after three hours of particularly heavy artillery preparation, with 12th Bavarian Infantry Division on the right, 76th Reserve Infantry Division in the centre, and 89th Infantry Division on the left. The Bavarians rapidly reached the Siret near Ciuslea, but were unable to capture the bridges over the river before the Russians set them ablaze. The men of 76th Reserve Division swiftly overcame the Russian forces in their path, and bridging equipment was brought forward the following night to allow a bridgehead to be secured over the Siret. However, the retreating Russians were replaced by the Romanian 5th Infantry Division, and its artillery on the left bank of the Siret, enjoying the advantages of higher ground than the bank held by the Germans, was in a commanding position. Despite Morgen's confidence that he would nevertheless be able to secure a crossing, he was ordered to call off the attempt and simply advance along the right bank of the river. The Bavarians were to take up defensive positions along the Siret, whilst the rest of Morgen's force pushed on.[346]

Over the following days, the Russian forces in the path of Morgen's attack were progressively replaced by Romanian formations, with the result that resistance steadily strengthened. Nevertheless, by 12 August the German divisions had advanced steadily, though the threat to their eastern flank from the Romanians on the opposite bank of the Siret remained. A bridgehead on the right bank, held by elements of the Romanian 5th Infantry Division, was eliminated on 14 August, and finally the advance halted when 12th Bavarian Infantry Division and 76th Reserve Division captured Marasesti; an advance of about 10 miles (16km). Morgen was content with what his men had achieved; they had taken 15,000 prisoners, mainly Russians, and had captured 29 field guns. Nevertheless, like other observers, he could not fail to be impressed with the determination with which the Romanians had fought, and the losses suffered by his divisions were substantial:

> The August battles resulted in perhaps a local but hardly outstanding success, showing that the Romanians had become respectable opponents. After undergoing six months' training under French guidance behind the front line, they conducted themselves better, were adroitly led, and in particular their artillery and infantry cooperated far better than at the beginning of the Romanian campaign.[347]

Hermann Balck and his soldiers, serving in the *Alpenkorps*, were transferred back to the Romanian Front to take part in the offensive:

> We passed through our own firing batteries, which were emplaced on both sides of the road. Vehicles and formations moved continuously in both directions. All of this was going on under strong Russian artillery fire, which amazingly enough caused little damage. There was nothing you could really do about it. All you could do was quietly march on, hoping that nothing happened.
>
> At noon on 12 August the attack started across the steep and wide Şuşiţa valley. Prussian and Bavarian Jägers descended into the valley. Wave after wave ran across the valley floor and ascended the opposite side. As far as the eye could see the valley was filled with advancing riflemen. The Russian infantry broke and ran. We increased the pace of the advance, but as always, the lead element got through and the follow-on elements got hit. The whole river valley was under Russian interdiction fire. Machine-guns came coughing to life from somewhere, but we had to get through. Wave after wave went through the valley, with the dirt kicking up right and left and in front and behind us. Noise everywhere as we ran on and heard the pinging of bullets around us. And then before we knew it, we were on the other side of the valley.
>
> … [A few days later] I went forward with my machine-guns. We moved ahead swiftly. In Straone the fleeing Russians were everywhere. The houses in the town were packed together so closely it was difficult to see anything. A huge Russian came out of one house screaming, the blood pouring out of his chest like a jet of water. Then he collapsed. From the left we heard the shout, 'Russian counterattack!' Some troops came running back. Then Russians jumped out of the cornfield twenty paces away, bayonets fixed. A really tall one aimed directly at me, but I was faster. Two of my machine-gun crews came running up, gasping for air. 'Assume positions, firing direction towards the open field, half right!' As the ammunition belts were inserted into the feeder tray, a row of Russian riflemen stepped into the open, hesitating as they saw the open field. A young Russian officer jumped ahead of the line, yelled something at them, and swung his sabre. Then the machine-guns opened up. As if hit by a single blow the Russians fell. No one escaped, and the Russian counterattack

> stalled. Right to our front, 50m away in a white house, something was moving. I knelt down to a machine-gun and pointed in the direction, when I was hit in the chest. I fell down and my troops pulled me behind the closest building. Coming from the half right a rifle bullet had hit my left side just above the heart, entered above the ribs, and lodged in my upper left arm.[348]

Balck was evacuated to an aid station, but decided to return to the front line despite the medical staff wishing to send him back to a field hospital. The appearance of a column of Russian prisoners in the area immediately in the rear of the front created a sudden panic with some Germans believing that the Russians had broken through, and many of the *Alpenkorps* troops were left in the trenches to fend for themselves until order was restored. When he reached his men, Balck visited the location where he had been wounded and attempted to find the courageous Russian officer who had tried to lead the counterattack; there was no sign of him, but there was a shallow ditch, and Balck was left to hope that the Russian had been able to crawl back to safety.

At the same time as the fighting in the German sector, Archduke Joseph attempted to press into Moldova farther north, using the revitalised *Gruppe Gerock* as his strike formation. Fighting raged in the mountainous, heavily wooded terrain throughout the second and third weeks of August. Again, the Romanians showed themselves to be far more determined to fight than the Russians; disaffected by the ongoing fallout of the February Revolution, the Russian troops were also fighting on territory that was not Russian, in defence of civilians who regarded the Russians almost as much as enemies as they did the Germans. Eventually, Averescu was forced to abandon almost all of the salient his troops had gained at the beginning of the fighting. The front line was broadly back to where it had started, with tens of thousands dead on both sides. Yet despite this lack of progress and the casualties that had been suffered, the generally gloomy news from the Eastern Front was so bad that British and French newspapers lauded the achievements of the Romanian Army, highlighting its successes in glowing colours.

With pressure increasing in the west – with the British attacking at Ypres and the Italians launching yet another assault on the Isonzo line – there was no prospect of fresh troops being sent to help keep the Central Powers' offensive going, and the *k.u.k.* Army was forced to transfer forces to the Italian Front to shore up their lines. Sensing a weakness in the *k.u.k.* First Army, Averescu made a final attempt to secure a meaningful victory with attacks in mid-September; they all failed in the face of accurate and effective defensive fire. Balck's machine-gun company was involved in repelling one such attack:

> A heavy rain poured down on us. A torrent of water swept us away with all of our equipment, and then the Romanians repeated the same kind of attack … Since we could not observe the impact of our bullets on the wet ground, the Romanians were able to break through our machine-gun fire almost without losses. Then they reached the thicket and the ravines of the Zăbrătău River valley. From there they tried all day long to assault, over and over again. Each time they failed against the iron resolve of our 3rd Company. The dead piled up in front of their positions, sometimes three to four rows deep. I counted forty dead just at one critical point.[349]

As the year wore on, the Russian formations on the Romanian Front continued to disintegrate. After the October Revolution, Mackensen wrote in his diary:

> The situation in Russia grows ever more complex. The army personnel, particularly the officers, find themselves in a situation that becomes more difficult by the day. One notices a dichotomy of emotions in their behaviour on our front. Men and officers talk about a ceasefire, but there are also exceptions. In particular [this refers to] the artillery, which here and there fires the odd shell into the positions of the front line troops. One division behaves completely passively; another enters negotiations; a third fires [on us]; and [the men of] a fourth fight and fire on each other. The Romanians have no idea how to get themselves out of the situation. They cover their helplessness with silence. In their army too the conflicting currents are having an effect. Local politicians are rather exercised that the unfortunate people who embody the Romanian government in Iași may once more miss a favourable opportunity to settle matters with us. We are ready for all eventualities and will remain so, provided I am left with the troops that I currently still have. It would be premature to count on an early peace. One does not know who will hold power in Russia tomorrow.[350]

With Bolshevik Russia seeking a rapid end to the war, the Romanians found themselves caught up in events, unable to continue hostilities without the support of Russia. On 5 December, Shcherbachev transmitted a radio message asking for a ceasefire, and on the same day the Romanians sent an officer, Colonel Rascallu, across the front line at Marasesti to negotiate on behalf of the Romanian Army. Mackensen appointed Curt von Morgen as the officer who would represent the German Army, and the *k.u.k.* Army nominated General Oskar Hranilović von Czvetassin. The Bulgarians and Turks were represented by staff officers of lower rank.

On 7 December, the delegation, led by Russian General Anatoly Kiprianovich Kelchevsky, commander of Ninth Army, and the Romanian delegation, led by General Alexandru Lupescu, crossed the front line and travelled to the town of Focşani. Morgen met them on the steps of the building chosen for negotiations:

> The Russians were as cold as ice, the Romanians somewhat more polite. At first, the Russians did not wish to partake of the breakfast provided for them, but finally sat down at the table. I made the foreign delegates welcome and I expressed the hope that the negotiations would be successful and would be conducted in the spirit of camaraderie that was a common virtue in all our armies. Kelchevsky offered his thanks and drank a toast to democratic camaraderie, which was the right of everyone. This emphasis was made out of consideration for the Russian revolutionaries who were present. He was himself a former Guards artillery officer, his chief of staff a Guards Dragoons officer. General Lupescu also stood up. In making a toast, he made clear that the Romanian delegation was independent [of the Russians].[351]

Somewhat to the surprise of Morgen and his associates, the Russian delegation made clear that they were negotiating specifically on behalf of the Russian Romanian Front, and regarded themselves as independent of any commitments being made at Brest-Litovsk. By the end of the first day's talks, agreement had been reached on all but three points: the status of the lower Danube; the status of the Black Sea (both with regard to whether they would be treated as neutral waters and barred from other combatants); and whether the Central Powers would be permitted to move troops from this sector to other fronts in Italy and the west.

The last point proved to be the most difficult to resolve. The Romanians in particular were anxious not to stir the enmity of the other Entente Powers and therefore wished to retain as many German and Austro-Hungarian troops on their front as possible. In the conflicts of the late 19th century, the Great Powers had imposed territorial adjustments on the Balkans without regard for the wishes of some Balkan states, and naturally there was a fear that if Romania was judged to have been a poor ally, something similar might happen in future, particularly given that Romania had explicitly entered the war seeking substantial territorial gains.

The Russian delegation crossed back to their side of the front line at the end of the first day of talks while the Romanians stayed in Focşani. When the Russians did not return the following day, discussions continued with the Romanians with little progress; but on 9 December Kelchevsky returned and informed Morgen that he had been instructed to secure a ceasefire at all costs. Finally, a ceasefire was signed late that day, giving the Central Powers freedom to move troops who had already been designated for redeployment by 5 December; this released five German divisions for the west.

Morgen later wrote about his impressions from the discussions:

> General Kelchevsky was uncommunicative, but I was able to have a lively conversation with his chief of staff, the youthful and energetic Colonel Baumgarten. He repeatedly said that the situation inside Russia was the fault of the tsar, who had turned a deaf ear to all suggestions of liberalisation. Nor did he speak well of the tsarina. Influenced by Rasputin, she had encouraged the tsar in his resistance to all timely liberal reforms. When leaving, Baumgarten – clearly moved – offered me his hand and parted with the prophetic words: 'I hope that Your Excellency will never see in your homeland and your army the circumstances that now prevail with us.'[352]

The continuing disintegration of the Russian Army began to be felt in the Romanian sector, with increasing numbers of Russian soldiers deserting; many of these plundered the area before trying to make their way home. In any event, it was impossible for Romania to contemplate resuming hostilities with Russia about to leave the war, regardless of the desire of King Ferdinand and his government to avoid offending the Western Powers. The Germans watched on with interest as Romanian and Russian troops repeatedly clashed, as Mackensen recorded in the second half of January:

> The chaos before my front grows ever greater. Russians and Romanians are fighting veritable battles against each other. The Russians want to cross the Prut, the Romanians deny them, demanding that they at least leave their weapons and ammunition in Moldova. Yesterday there was fighting in Galaţi in which even Romanian naval monitors took part. The Russians appear to have been successful as they asked us during the evening to take custody of about 1,000 Romanian prisoners.
>
> … Yesterday 3,200 Russian troops and 20 officers with 47 machine-guns, 22 field guns, 56 loaded ammunition wagons, 52 field kitchens, 363 assorted wagons and about 1,200 horses crossed over to us at Braila, after armed Romanians blocked their withdrawal to Bessarabia. I await further surprises.[353]

The position of Prime Minister Ion Brătianu became impossible; he had been a leading figure in negotiating the terms for Romania's entry into the war, and he stood down in early February 1918. His replacement was Alexandru Averescu, whose reputation was riding high after the fighting earlier in the year. His emotions when he was given his first official duty – to negotiate a peace settlement with the Central Powers, against whom he had fought since August 1916 – can only be guessed.

When peace talks resumed in Brest-Litovsk after the brief resumption of hostilities, Czernin was absent; he was involved in discussions about securing a definitive peace with Romania. At first, the Hungarians were adamant in these discussions that there must be substantial territorial concessions to punish Romania for entering the war against the Central Powers, but Czernin was able to persuade Prime Minister Tisza to moderate his demands. Nevertheless, in a letter to Czernin, the Hungarian leader made clear that he was not prepared to offer any further concessions:

> Our peace terms are so mild that they are as a generous gift offered to vanquished Romania and are *not at all to be made a subject for negotiations.* In no case are these negotiations to assume the character of trading or bargaining. If Romania refuses to conclude peace on the basis laid down by us our answer can only be a resumption of hostilities.
>
> I consider it highly probable that the Romanian government will run that risk to prove her necessity in the eyes of the Western Powers and her own population. But it is just as probable that after breaking off negotiations she will just as quickly turn back and give way before our superior forces.
>
> At the worst a short campaign would result in the total collapse of Romania.
>
> ... It is obvious from the public statements of leading statesmen of the Western Powers that they will not be prevailed upon to agree to an acceptable peace, as they do not believe in our capacity and firm resolve to carry it out. Whatever confirms their views in this respect widens the distance between us and peace; the only way to bring us really nearer to peace is to adopt an attitude that will lead them to think differently.
>
> ... It would certainly be right not to take advantage of Romania's desperate situation, but to grant her reasonable peace terms in accordance with the principles embodied in our statements. But if we do not act with adequate firmness on that reasonable basis we shall encourage the Western Powers in the belief that it is not necessary to conclude a peace with us on the basis of the integrity of our territory and sovereignty, and fierce and bitter fighting may be looked for to teach them otherwise.[354]

Whilst Czernin was able to ensure that the Austro-Hungarian Empire was prepared to offer Romania generous terms, he was also aware that the point of view in Germany was very different. King Ferdinand was a descendant of a branch of the Hohenzollern family, and his act in taking Romania into a war against Germany was regarded as a personal insult by Kaiser Wilhelm, who demanded that there should be no negotiations with Ferdinand. Czernin contacted Kühlmann, the German foreign minister, and advised him that Austria-Hungary had already opened communications with Ferdinand, as was its right as an equal power; there was no requirement for Vienna to seek Berlin's permission in such matters. He added two further reasons:

> From a dynastic point of view, I considered it most unwise to dethrone a foreign king. There was already then a certain fall in the value of kings on the European market, and I was afraid it might develop into a panic if we put more kings on the market. The third reason was that, in order to conclude peace, we must have a competent representative in Romania. If we were to depose the king we should divide Romania into two camps and would, at the best, only be able to conclude an illegitimate peace with that party which accepted the dethronement of the king. A rapid and properly secured peace could only be concluded with the legitimate head in Romania.[355]

Averescu wasted no time, arranging a meeting with Mackensen on 18 January, only five days after assuming office as prime minister. The men had met before and appear to have got on well at a personal level. Nevertheless, Mackensen intended to press for terms that Czernin would have regarded as anything but lenient, as he wrote after the first discussions:

> The outcome of the meetings was my conviction of the firm intention of the general to make peace and to make a complete break with Brătianu's policies, which also means a break with the Entente. He expressed agreement on purely military issues. I remain firm in my demands. I will gladly leave the Romanian Army's honour intact, but it has been defeated, and the regime must accept this. As a soldier I have sympathy for General Averescu and will ensure that there is no personal thoughtlessness.[356]

On 24 February, Averescu returned for further talks, this time meeting Czernin and Kühlmann for the first time. The main area of disagreement was the future fate of Dobruja. Part of this had been Bulgarian until 1913 when Romania seized it in the Second Balkan War, and this section had already been promised to Bulgaria by Austria-Hungary and Germany. The Bulgarians now extended their demands to all of Dobruja as far as the Danube delta, but Averescu informed the foreign ministers of the Central Powers that the cession of Dobruja was unacceptable to Romania. At Czernin's suggestion, King Ferdinand met the Austro-Hungarian foreign minister on 27 February:

> As the king did not begin the conversation, I had to do so, and said that I had not come to sue for peace but purely as the bearer of a message from the Emperor Karl, who, in spite of Romania's treachery, would show indulgence and consideration if King Ferdinand would *at once* conclude peace under the conditions mutually agreed on by the Quadruple Alliance Powers [i.e. Germany, Austria-Hungary, Bulgaria and Turkey].
>
> Should the king not consent, then a continuation of the war would be unavoidable and would put an end to Romania and the dynasty. Our military superiority was already very considerable, and now that our front would be set free from the Baltic to the Black Sea, it would be an easy matter for us, in a very short space of time, to increase our strength still more. We were aware that Romania would very soon have no more munitions and, were hostilities to continue, in six weeks the kingdom and dynasty would have ceased to exist.
>
> The king did not oppose anything, but thought the conditions terribly hard. Without Dobruja, Romania would hardly be able to draw her breath …
>
> I said to the king that if he complained about hard conditions I could only ask what would his conditions have been if his troops had reached Budapest? Meanwhile I was ready to guarantee that Romania would not be cut off from the sea, but would have free access to Constanța.
>
> Here again the king complained of the hard conditions enforced on him, and declared that he would never be able to find a ministry who would accept them.
>
> I rejoined that the forming of a cabinet was Romania's internal business, but my private opinion was that a Marghiloman cabinet, in order to save Romania, would agree to the conditions laid down. I could only repeat that no change could be made in the peace terms laid before the king by the Quadruple Allliance. If the king did not accept them, we should have, in a month's time, a far better peace than the one which the Romanians might consider themselves lucky to get today.
>
> We were ready to give our diplomatic support to Romania that she might obtain Bessarabia [from Russia], and she would, therefore, gain far more than she would lose.
>
> The king replied that Bessarabia was nothing to him, that it was steeped in Bolshevism, and Dobruja could not be given up; anyhow, it was only under the

> very greatest pressure that he had decided to enter into the war against the Central Powers. He began again, however, to speak of the promised access to the sea, which apparently made the cession of Dobruja somewhat easier.
>
> ... Finally I requested that he would give me a clear and decided answer within 48 hours as to whether he would negotiate on the basis of our proposals or not.[357]

Alexandru Marghiloman was a conservative politician who had been in favour of cooperation with Germany rather than war against the Central Powers. When Romania entered the war, Brătianu offered him a cabinet post but he refused. He stayed in Bucharest when the German Army occupied the Romanian capital, acting in his role as president of the Romanian Red Cross and mediating between the occupation authorities and the local population. The Germans tried in vain to persuade him to lead a government that would rival Ferdinand's government in Iași, but Ferdinand now approached him and asked him to replace Averescu, who refused to accept the terms offered by the Central Powers. He was also an old friend of Czernin, and the latter had little difficulty in persuading him that Austria-Hungary had no room for manoeuvre with regard to Dobruja. However, in return for the Romanians accepting the loss of Dobruja, Czernin offered to ameliorate the numerous border adjustments that Tisza had demanded for Hungary's benefit.

The military issues for a peace treaty had largely been settled by Mackensen and Averescu, and Czernin had at least the basis of an agreement on territorial adjustments: Bulgaria would gain the territory in Dobruja that it had lost in 1913, and the rest of the province would be administered by a commission appointed by the Central Powers. Discussions now moved to economic issues, and Czernin faced a far greater challenge. He had disapproved of the rapacious desire of the Germans to extract huge economic benefits from Russia during the discussions in Brest-Litovsk, and he now had to ask Emperor Karl to intervene and write personally to Kaiser Wilhelm, urging the Germans to moderate their demands. Czernin calculated that, as a result of his opposition, German demands were reduced to about half of their original level, but they still remained draconian: Germany would have a 90-year lease on Romanian oil wells; Romania was committed to providing a minimum tonnage of agricultural produce to the Central Powers for several years; and whilst the Central Powers could appoint a number of 'agents' to remain in Romania to ensure that all of the peace terms were enforced, they would leave once general peace was achieved.

To make matters worse, the Turks now demanded a share of the spoils. Their delegates pointed out that two corps of Turkish troops had played a leading role in the conquest of Dobruja and Turkey was therefore entitled to compensation; they demanded that territory to the west of the city of Adrianople (now Edirne) should be returned to Turkey. The city had originally been captured by Bulgarian troops in 1913 at the end of the First Balkan War, only for the Turks to recapture it later the same year in the Second Balkan War. Aware that the Bulgarians were already establishing secret contacts with the Entente Powers and that Turkey's cession from the Central Powers was also a possibility, Czernin and Kühlmann struggled to find a formula that would be acceptable to their own governments, to those of their allies, and would also be the basis of a lasting peace with Romania.

Negotiations dragged on through the spring, but ultimately Romania had no choice but to accept what was offered. On 7 May, Marghiloman signed the Treaty of Bucharest in Buftea, a small town about 12 miles (20km) from Bucharest. The war on the Romanian Front was over, as Mackensen wrote:

> Peace has been secured. Negotiations were successfully concluded yesterday afternoon. During the evening, the outcome was celebrated in our dining house near the front line. Tonight, the peace protocols and all their annexes were drawn up and this morning the signing of the comprehensive documents took place in a final meeting … Consequently, our situation with regard to the Romanians changed completely today, as did my post. Henceforth, we will face each other not as enemies but as friends. We continue to occupy the territory that we previously occupied, but after the signing of the peace treaty we are no longer the ruling authority, rather the supervising authority. I no longer command an operational army, rather one of occupation, and the territorial administration that was until now my responsibility will now be completely handed back into Romanian hands. The Romanian government can make a start at rebuilding national life. But we retain control in many areas of commerce … the half-mobilised Romanian Army remains in the parts of Moldova and Bessarabia that are not occupied by us. Our army of occupation is composed of two thirds German troops and one third Austro-Hungarian troops.[358]

Mackensen looked forward to a formal ratification of the treaty, which he expected would take six weeks (the expected time required for the formation of a new Romanian cabinet), but the ratification never occurred. Ferdinand refused to sign the treaty, and many Romanians remained ready to resume hostilities. Those who had advocated ongoing resistance to the Central Powers had calculated that, ultimately, the Western Powers would prevail over Germany, and it was essential for Romania to remain a member of the Entente to ensure that it gained in full from any future peace treaty. Events would prove their assessment to be correct.

It was Mackensen's last front-line command. At the end of the war, he was detained whilst attempting to lead his men home across Hungary and briefly faced the prospect of a war crimes trial. He was a devout monarchist and at first refused to be involved in political matters after the war, though he soon became a figurehead of the conservative parties. He continued to appear in public wearing the black hussars uniform that he had first donned in 1869, and black uniforms adorned with the *Totenkopf* ('death's head') insignia, traditionally worn by the Prussian hussars, were adopted by the *Panzertruppen* of the Wehrmacht and by the SS in direct emulation of Mackensen. He was deeply worried by the conduct of German troops in the opening campaigns of the Second World War, writing on 4 February 1940 to Field Marshal Walther von Brauchitsch, the commander-in-chief of the army:

> As a man becomes older, he has to watch carefully that age has not reduced his creativity. After reaching the age of 90, I have decided not to involve myself any longer with matters that are not concerned with my private life. However, I am still the most senior German officer. Many turn to me, sometimes with wishes, but more often with their concerns. During these weeks our concern is with the spirit of our unique and successful army. The concern results from the crimes committed in Poland, looting and murder that take place before the eyes of our troops, who appear unable to put an end to them. An apparent indifference has serious consequences for the morale of our soldiers and it is damaging to the esteem of our army and our whole nation. I am sure that you are aware of these events and that you certainly condemn them. These lines intend to convey my daily growing concern at the reports that constantly reach me, and I have to ask you to take up this matter with the highest authority. The messages I receive are so numerous, many come from high ranking persons and from witnesses. As the most senior officer I cannot keep them to myself. In transmitting them to you, I fulfil my duty to the army. The honour of the army and the esteem in which it is held must not be jeopardised by the actions of hired subhumans and criminals.[359]

The Nazis strongly suspected Mackensen of harbouring anti-Nazi sympathies, if not involvement in anti-Nazi activities, but had no proof. Despite Hitler's insistence that there should be no military presence at the funeral of the former Kaiser Wilhelm in Doorn in the Netherlands in 1941, Mackensen – aged 92 – attended in full hussar's uniform. He died in November 1945.

CHAPTER 11

THE PYGMY WARS: FINLAND

During the Second World War, Winston Churchill wrote to President Roosevelt warning that 'When the war of the giants is over the wars of the pygmies will begin.'[360] By 1918, a series of such pygmy wars were already smouldering, and now began to erupt. The involvement of German soldiers led to associations and consequences that helped shape relations between the nations of Europe in the years between the First and Second World Wars, and the transformation of Eastern Europe from large empires into a multitude of independent states requires a clear understanding of these conflicts.

The Grand Duchy of Finland had been part of the Russian Empire since 1809 when it was seized from Sweden. Finland had never been an independent nation, but once it became part of the tsar's domain, nationalist sentiment began to stir. The Fennoman Movement developed and promoted the use of Finnish, which had largely been the language of the peasantry. The motto of the movement – 'svenskar äro vi icke mera, ryssar kunna vi icke bli, derför måste vi vara finnar' (Swedes we are no more, Russians we cannot become, therefore Finns we must be) – could have been applicable to many nationalities that were struggling to assert their identities during this era. There was tension between Fennoman supporters and the Swedish-speaking aristocracy, and the Russians inevitably exploited this to keep control of the Grand Duchy, much in the manner that they used Baltic German landlords to keep control of Estonia and Latvia.

In the wake of the 1905 Revolution, the Finns adopted universal suffrage – including for women – and set up a single-chamber parliament. As he reasserted control over his empire, Tsar Nicholas II effectively made the parliament irrelevant by ignoring its decisions and repeatedly calling new elections. Until this stage, whilst the concept of Finnish identity had gained ground, there had been little genuine support for independence, but frustration with heavy-handed Russian rule and resentment at Nicholas' policy of 'Russification' provided the impetus for independence across all parts of Finnish society – as was the case in the Baltic States, attempts to impose Orthodox Christianity in this largely Lutheran region caused great resentment, as did the compulsory use of Russian in schools.

The southern parts of Finland became industrialised and made an important contribution to Russia's war effort from 1914 onwards. The urban centres became fertile ground for socialist groups, and there was growing tension between them and the Swedish-speaking landowners, whose right-wing Svecoman Movement favoured closer ties with Germany, possibly in preference to outright independence. The fall of the Romanovs in 1917 created a political crisis: the tsar was the Finnish head of state, and in his absence there was little clarity about who or what should replace him. In an attempt to fill this vacuum, the Finnish parliament passed the Power Act which, by stating that it was the highest authority, effectively declared independence, but this was rejected both by Kerensky's Provisional Government and the right-wing groups in Finland; the latter because the left-of-centre Social Democrats had a majority in parliament. By order of Petrograd, parliament was dissolved and in the subsequent election the right-wing parties won a small overall majority; the Social Democrats protested in vain that the dissolution of parliament and subsequent election were both invalid, as the Power Act had removed Petrograd's right to dissolve the Finnish parliament. Many Finnish socialists grew disillusioned with the political system and increasingly believed that the only way that ordinary people's rights could be protected was by revolution.

Even before the Bolsheviks seized power in the October Revolution, right and left groups in Finland had begun to clash violently. Attempts to break up a strike in August resulted in a worker being shot, and a member of the right-wing Civil Guard – an organisation created by the new government to try to maintain order as Russian authority rapidly disintegrated – was killed in early October. When Lenin declared that nationalities within the Russian Empire had the right to determine for themselves the path they would follow, the Finnish parliament declared independence, with the right-wing parties – led by Pehr Evind Svinhufvud – now adopting the principles of the Power Act that they had opposed just a few months before. The Social Democrats demanded the restoration of the parliament that they felt had been dissolved illegally during the summer and, when this was rejected, called a national strike.[361] Urged on by the Bolsheviks, the strikers resolved to seize power from the right-wing government, but abandoned their plans through lack of leadership and expertise.[362]

Whilst they were unable to overthrow the government by force, the Social Democrats resolved to establish their own force – the Workers' Guards – to oppose the Civil Guards. Losing patience with them, Lenin decided to encourage the Finnish Bolsheviks to play a larger role, and a significant proportion of the Workers' Guards owed their loyalty more to the Bolsheviks than the Social Democrats; this faction became known as the Red Guards. There were increasing episodes of violence during the winter of 1917–1918 as the Workers' and Civil Guards clashed. Civil war was becoming as inevitable in Finland as it was in Russia.

As part of the Russian Empire, Finland had provided several divisions of troops for the Russian Army, but several hundred Finns had also travelled to Germany and had volunteered for service against Russia. Largely drawn from university students and the families of Finland's landowners and aristocracy, these men were trained in Germany and organised into the Royal Prussian 27th Jäger Battalion, which was deployed as part of the German Eighth Army in Latvia. The battalion was no longer in the front line by the autumn of 1917; as tensions grew in Finland, Berlin decided to use the Jägers to help the conservative Finns develop the Civil Guards – now known increasingly as the White Guards – into a proper fighting force. The first group of Jägers returned to Finland aboard the steamer *Equity* in September, accompanied by the U-boat *UC-57*, which was carrying armaments. But, just like the rest of Finnish society, the Jägers were divided; several hundred were kept in Germany out of concern for their left-wing loyalties.

The German interest in Finland was due to several considerations. Firstly, although Scandinavia was not involved militarily in the war, it was an essential source of raw materials – without Swedish iron ore, Germany would not be able to continue. It was vitally important that if Finland were to become an independent nation, it was friendly to German interests; a hostile Finland would be able to disrupt the flow of iron ore. Secondly, there was the question of Finland's natural resources. Although Finland imported a considerable amount of grain from Russia, it also exported large quantities of dairy products and meat, and the hungry Central Powers looked at this as a possible solution to their own problems. Thirdly, even before the conclusion of the Brest-Litovsk negotiations, the Germans were looking to the future. They were aware of the degree to which British and French aid – landed in the ports of the White Sea in the frozen north – had helped support the Russian Army. Having Finland as an ally would allow the Germans to threaten the railroad that linked Archangelsk with the rest of Russia. To that end, the German Army created a Baltic Division from a variety of units that were available – three regiments of cavalry, three light infantry battalions, five bicycle-mounted companies, and a mixture of artillery elements – and placed it under the command of Major General Rüdiger von der Goltz.[363] Coming from a family with many men serving in the German Army, Goltz was in many respects a typical Prussian *Junker*: highly patriotic, utterly devoted to the army, and deeply suspicious of Germany's enemies, particularly the British. Before the war, he had served in the foreign section of the general staff and had come to the conclusion that war with Britain was inevitable, given the determination of the British to prevent Germany from securing its rightful place in world trade. After commanding an infantry division of the Prussian Guards in France, he now found himself organising his new division and liaising closely with Finnish conservatives who had travelled to Germany. His own preference was for an early intervention in Finland with his division going ashore in the port of Rauma on the west coast, but he was forced to accept the advice of local naval authorities who pointed out that the Baltic ice was still too thick to attempt a landing on the south coast of Finland. While they waited, the men of the Baltic Division repeatedly rehearsed amphibious operations on the coast of Latvia and around Danzig. Goltz meanwhile developed close links with a liaison officer appointed by the Svinhufvud government, Vilhelm Thesleff. He had been a member of the Russian Army at the beginning of the war before being taken prisoner in Riga at the end of 1917; thereafter he returned to Finland and was appointed commander of the Finnish Jägers before being sent to Germany to try to facilitate a possible intervention.

In addition to the White Guards, the Jägers, and the weapons from Germany, the conservatives had another great asset in the form of Carl Gustaf Emil Mannerheim. The son of a family whose ancestry came from Germany, Sweden and Scotland, he was an unruly child, partly due to the behaviour of his father Carl Robert; suffering from hypomania, he became bankrupt and abandoned his wife and seven children to live in Paris with his mistress. In an attempt to bring the young Gustaf under control, his uncle sent him to the school of the Finnish Cadet Corps, part of the system of military schools that stretched across the Russian Empire. Although he learned to be frugal during his time at the school, he continued to be rebellious and it was not until 1887 – three years later than should have been the case – that he was able to join the army. He had inherited his father's predilection for gambling, and volunteered for service in the Russo-Japanese War to escape his debts. It proved to be a good move, and he returned from the war with his reputation enhanced.[364]

When the First World War broke out, Mannerheim was commander of the Guards Cavalry Brigade and led it with distinction in fighting along the middle Vistula. Shortly after the February Revolution, he was promoted to lieutenant general and given command of VI Cavalry Corps, but there were questions about

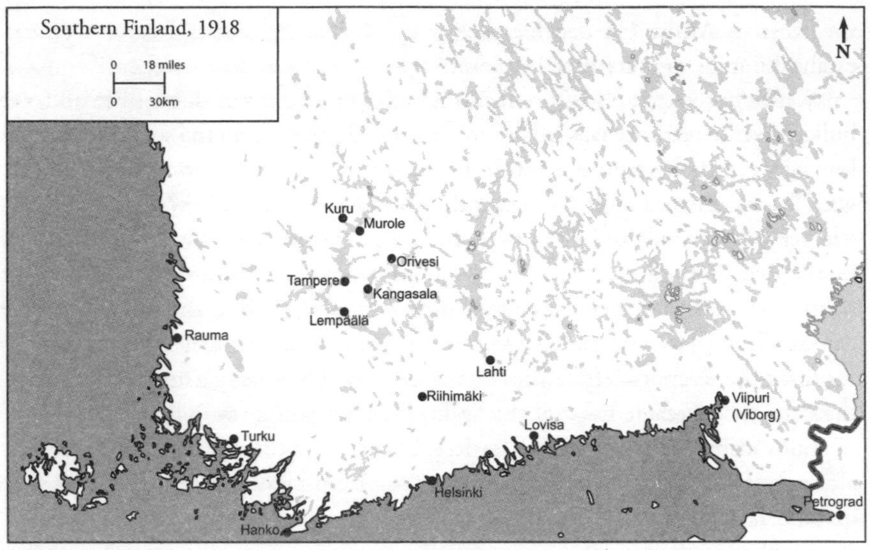

his loyalty to the new regime and he was relieved of his command, returning to Finland. In January, Svinhufvud appointed Mannerheim commander of the new Finnish Army, effectively the White Guards. After several years of service against Germany, Mannerheim was unhappy about the pro-German stance of Svinhufvud's government, and would have preferred closer cooperation with Sweden. However, the Swedish Social Democrats turned down Finnish requests for military assistance and Svinhufvud's faction had no choice but to turn to the Germans. Accepting reality, Mannerheim took up the post that he had been offered. His first task was to start the disarmament of about 42,000 Russian troops in Finland; the weapons gained from them provided the White Guards with valuable firepower. At the same time, the refusal of Sweden's government to help the Whites caused outrage in Swedish right-wing circles, and about 1,000 Swedish men, a mixture of former and serving soldiers in the Swedish Army, volunteered to fight for the White cause and formed a unit under the command of Hjalmar Frisell, a relatively low-ranking officer who had competed in shooting events in the Olympic Games of 1912 in Stockholm. A small number of Swedish staff officers accompanied Frisell's group, giving Mannerheim's headquarters some much-needed professional expertise.[365]

Mannerheim's military experience was a huge asset for the Whites; by contrast, the best leader that the Reds had was Ali Aaltonen, who had been a lieutenant in the Russian Army. He became effectively the leader of the Red movement, establishing his military base in Helsinki.

Whilst both Red and White factions had areas of control all over Finland, the bulk of White territory was in the north while the Reds held the south. The front line between the two groups ran from the port of Pori in the west to the border with Russia between Lake Ladoga and the Baltic; although the Whites controlled a larger area, the bulk of Finland's population was centred on the cities controlled by the Reds in the southwest. There was a small red enclave around Oulu in the northwest, and white enclaves either side of Helsinki and in the southwest near Turku. On 28 January, the Red Guards secured control of Helsinki, where they captured the weapons left behind by the departing Russian garrison. From there, they rapidly overcame most of the White enclaves in the south.

Buoyed by their successes, the Red Guards launched a series of offensives along the front line. They now found their lack of military training and shortage of officers to be a huge disadvantage; without such training and leadership, their cohesion and morale was fragile and vulnerable to relatively minor setbacks. Lenin ordered Russian troops in Finland to assist the Red Guards, but the demoralised, homesick garrisons showed little inclination to fight. The majority simply abandoned or surrendered their weapons and attempted to head home to Russia; perhaps 10,000 chose to fight alongside the Finnish Reds. The terms of the Brest-Litovsk Treaty effectively forbade further Russian involvement, leaving Aaltonen with little support. He was forced to step down and was replaced by a series of would-be military commanders, none of whom had sufficient training or energy to improve matters. But as the momentum of the Red campaign slackened, Mannerheim launched his own offensive. There were two obvious targets – Viipuri (now Viborg), close to the Russian border, which would cut off the Reds from Russia, and Tampere, a major industrial city in the west. The Reds had put the industrial resources of Tampere to good use; its railway workshops produced armoured trains for the coming campaign, which would broadly be along the few railway lines in Finland. Reasoning that the Brest-Litovsk Treaty had already effectively blocked Russian interference and doubting the ability of his White Guards to mount the sort of campaign required to capture Viipuri, Mannerheim decided to target Tampere, which was far closer to the front line. He was also aware that Svinhufvud was negotiating with the Germans, and he wished to achieve a purely Finnish triumph before any foreign intervention.[366]

Aware of the limitations of the White Guards, Mannerheim deliberately kept his campaign plan simple. Some 12,000 men were massed to the north of

Tampere in four groups, which were to launch convergent attacks towards the city. Once the Red Guards had been driven back, Mannerheim intended to encircle the city before completing its capture. The entire operation would require an advance of up to 42 miles (70km), and therefore represented a considerable undertaking. On the one hand, the troop densities were far lower than those seen in the crowded battlefields of the main fronts of the First World War, but, on the other hand, the plentiful waterways of Finland would give the defenders ample opportunity to hold up the advance. Additionally, the White Guards lacked the organised logistic and support services without which a sustained advance was impossible.

On 15 March, Mannerheim launched his attack. The first serious fighting took place in the town of Kuru and lasted all day before the Red Guards pulled back; instead of pursuing closely, the White force paused for two days before beginning a cautious advance and reaching Murole on 19 March. The advance from the northeast sector began well, but when this force pushed on to Orivesi, the White Guards who were meant to be joining it from due north of the town failed to appear – they had not even commenced their attacks. Orivesi changed hands several times before the Red Guards pulled back. Had all gone according to plan, most of this Red force would have been trapped in the town. Instead, it was able to join the forces gathering for the defence of Tampere itself.

After just five days, Mannerheim had to re-evaluate his plans. The White Guards had moved forward about 12 miles (20km), but their lack of training and the almost complete absence of support services made it almost impossible to sustain pressure. Until now, Mannerheim had been reluctant to involve the Germans, but worried that the Bolsheviks would send aid to help the Red Guards and, increasingly aware of how limited the military capabilities of the White forces were, he now bowed to the inevitable. Using the links of the Whites with Sweden, he dispatched a telegram to Thesleff via Stockholm, asking him to expedite German intervention. It would take several days for preparations to be completed – largely due to the need for minesweepers to clear the way for troop-carrying ships – but in the meantime Goltz dispatched aircraft to drop leaflets on Helsinki in an attempt to weaken the resolve of the Reds. Instead of the original plan to land troops in Rauma, where they would be able to link up directly with White forces, the Baltic Division would go ashore at Hanko, on the southern coast to the west of Helsinki. Whilst the Germans would be isolated here, establishing lanes through Russian minefields would take less time, which was now felt to be of the essence. German military intelligence reported – erroneously – that there were several Russian divisions deploying behind the Red front line, and there was growing fear in Berlin that the Bolsheviks would be able to provide aid to the Reds faster than the Germans could support the Whites. Goltz's preference once ashore was to march northeast to cut the railway line between Tampere and Helsinki at Riihimäki, on the grounds that, once the Red forces in the north were cut off from Helsinki, it would be possible to defeat them in detail, after which the capture of the Finnish capital would be comparatively straightforward; he was overruled by Berlin in favour of a direct march against Helsinki from Hanko – supported by the navy operating along the coast.[367] After further debate and delay, it was decided to pursue both objectives at the same time. The main force would attempt to capture Helsinki, but a special mobile force commanded by Generalmajor Otto Freiherr von Brandenstein would move farther north to cut the supply lines of the main Red forces.

With the front line now close to Tampere, Hugo Salmela, the local Red commander, declared a state of war in the city on 19 March. Kangasala, just 9 miles (15km) to the east of Tampere, fell to the Whites on 22 March, and the city came under White artillery fire the following day. The Red lines to the west of Tampere began to give way as the brittle morale of the Red volunteers cracked under pressure, while the White troops that had taken Kangasala now pushed on to Lempäälä, south of Tampere, effectively isolating the Red garrison.[368] For a moment, Mannerheim believed that he would be able to achieve a swift victory, but an attempt to rush the defences on 25 March was repulsed with losses: whilst casualties of 150 men seem trivial compared to the bloodletting elsewhere in the preceding months and years, it still constituted the single worst day of fighting in the Finnish Civil War.[369] Salmela clearly had no intention of giving up without a fight, and had organised the defences sufficiently to put up determined resistance.

Mannerheim sent messages to the encircled Red forces on 25 and 26 March, calling on them to surrender, and whilst some within Tampere were inclined to capitulate, others believed that the Red forces outside the city would be able to march to their assistance. Despite Salmela's orders to hold out to the very end, several hundred Red Guards commandeered an armoured train and attempted to break out to Turku; when the train attempted to cross a bridge immediately south of Tampere, it was brought to a halt by gunfire. After a prolonged firefight, the train pulled back into Tampere. Some 30 Red Guards were dead, many more wounded. Others who attempted to escape west via Nokia, were more successful and managed to slip through the incomplete siege perimeter.[370] But despite repeated attacks on the defences, the White forces were unable to make any headway; any advances they made were rapidly reversed by counterattacks, including one mounted by a battalion of women volunteers.[371]

By 28 March, Mannerheim had managed to assemble artillery near Tampere and subjected the eastern approaches to a heavy bombardment before attempting another advance. Unfortunately for the attackers, the Red front line was far closer to their positions than they had realised with the result that most of the artillery fire fell harmlessly in the rear of the defences. The attacking Whites suffered heavy losses and, though they secured considerable gains, the Reds were able to pull back intact and form a new defensive line.[372] Perhaps more significantly, there was an accidental explosion in the main munitions store of the defenders; amongst those killed was the garrison commander, Hugo Salmela. He was replaced by Verner Lehtimäki. To the south of the city, a column of Red troops repeatedly tried to break through to the besieged city, and the sounds of fighting in Lempäälä, only 7 miles (12km) away, kept the hopes of Lehtimäki's forces alive. Nevertheless, many were in favour of capitulation when Mannerheim transmitted a further ultimatum on 1 April, threatening to bombard Tampere with heavy artillery; the matter was put to a ballot amongst the senior Red officers, and the majority in favour of continuing resistance was a single vote.

After a heavy bombardment that reduced much of Tampere to rubble, the Whites attacked again on 3 April. A small group of Finnish Jägers managed to penetrate into the centre of the city where they captured – and then executed – about 27 defenders before being driven out with heavy losses. About 400 men were killed during the day, which saw the railway station fall to the attackers. Red resistance centred around the town hall, where fighting continued for two days. The last defenders gathered in the western part of Tampere, from where Lehtimäki led a group of perhaps 500 who managed to slip through White lines and escaped to join Red forces farther south. The last Reds, numbering about 11,000, laid down their arms on 6 April. Amongst those captured were about 200 Russians who had either volunteered to fight for the Reds or had been sent by Russia to provide expert help. These men were swiftly separated from the other defenders and executed. A prison camp was established in the Kaelevankangas district of Tampere, but whilst the Finnish Reds escaped immediate execution, they were not safe. Food supplies to the camp were minimal, and all attempts by outsiders to send food packages were blocked, resulting in many deaths from famine and disease. Some of the guards, such as Sakeus Koivunen, acquired a grim reputation for brutality. Hundreds more were rounded up in the days that followed as the Whites conducted a detailed search of Tampere, arresting or killing those who were harbouring fugitives or hiding weapons. There were no official investigations at the time or later into the mistreatment of prisoners, but Koivunen was found dead later that year, having been killed by persons unknown.[373]

Despite accepting the need for German support, Mannerheim had hoped to achieve an important victory before foreign troops intervened in the Finnish Civil War. The German Baltic Division had embarked aboard a fleet of ten large vessels in the Bay of Danzig and, accompanied by the battleships *Rheinland* and *Westfalen*, the cruiser *Kolberg*, and numerous smaller vessels, set off for the Finnish coast. They reached the shoreline near Hanko on 3 April, even as the fighting in Tampere was coming to a climax. Somewhat to their relief, the German troops – largely made up of reservists and new recruits, with a core of battle-hardened veterans – discovered that the Red garrison had already left, and rapidly took control of Hanko without a fight. There had been hopes that, as had been the case in Russia earlier in the year, the Germans would be able to mount a rapid advance along the railway line, but the retreating Reds took the last locomotive in the area with them; the bicycle-mounted elements of the Baltic Division found that their bicycles were useless in the snow that still lay on the ground, and were forced to abandon them and advance on foot. Nevertheless, the vital bridge at Ekenäs – about 20 miles (32km) away, carrying the road from Hanko towards Helsinki – was captured intact on the first day. As the troops filed ashore into the small port, Goltz was delighted to receive a delegation from the Russian warships in Helsinki: the ships would stay neutral during any fighting in the city, the delegation informed Goltz, provided that they were permitted to sail for the Russian naval base at Kronstadt afterwards. Goltz readily agreed.

Three days after their first landings, the Germans had finished debarking and began to move on the Finnish capital. The first serious fighting took place to the northeast of Ekenäs, where the forces deployed to protect the northern flank of the main force came under attack by a mixed force of Red soldiers, supported by an armoured train. Fighting continued for two days before the Reds fell back, and Goltz ordered a pursuit along the railway line to Svartä in order to prevent further Red interference with his main march. Despite supply difficulties – there were no ports east of Ekenäs where supplies could be landed, and the Germans had failed to locate any usable locomotives, instead relying on a few captured railway wagons being pulled by horses – the first German cavalry units reached the outskirts of Helsinki on 11 April. Here, Goltz encountered prepared defences:

> The attack on the intact obstacles was quite difficult everywhere, exposed to flank fire, and impossible in normal circumstances. The position was occupied, as shown by harassing small arms fire that reached us in our overlooking farmhouse and caused casualties. In addition, a few field guns also fired, but very badly.

> There was no time to lose. It was necessary to push through somewhere in confidence of the low combat value of the enemy. The 1st Guards Uhlans were ordered to prepare to attack in woodland to the right of the road, while the artillery would be deployed as it arrived to cover the advance of the Uhlans against frontal and flanking fire. The Carabineers were to hold themselves ready to intervene in the battle on the left of the road. But here, the only cover was further away than on the right of the road. A bold decision. But we had to avoid getting involved in positional warfare. There wasn't enough artillery and ammunition for proper assault bombardment.
>
> Meanwhile Rittmeister Ekström, from the Swedish delegation, tried to persuade the Reds to surrender. He was in contact with us by telephone. I turned down his request to refrain from attacking and urged him to negotiate immediately before it was too late. It worked. At 1pm a truck arrived with a white flag. Ekström and a woman, both serving as interpreters, arrived with two delegates of the Reds.
>
> They asked me an extraordinary question: whether I was waging war on my own initiative or under the orders of my kaiser. As I laughingly confirmed the latter, they asked for my credentials. I explained that every German general was self-evidently a general of the kaiser and therefore required no credentials. They then explained happily that they regarded me as a gentleman and asked for a ceasefire. But I told them that I could not agree to this and merely gave them until 4pm to negotiate. I would attack at that time if they had not surrendered. I actually needed this time to prepare for my attack. I therefore lost no time by giving this ultimatum. I did not call for unconditional surrender, as this might have resulted in desperate resistance against which I could achieve nothing, but rather assured them of their lives, without prejudice to Finnish legal proceedings. Thereafter the negotiators left and drove back to the other side in their truck.[374]

According to Goltz, he later learned that the negotiators had urged the rest of the Red leadership to surrender but had been outvoted. The Germans advanced at 4pm. The Uhlans had sent a patrol ahead and discovered that the farm to their front was not defended; they were able to occupy it, albeit while under increasingly heavy flanking fire. The Carabineers also moved forward swiftly and the first line of defences was overrun with little difficulty. Goltz joined the Uhlans as they advanced; as they entered the suburb of Huopalahti, they were bombarded with garlands of flowers by some of the residents, but came under fire from others. Darkness brought an end to the rapid advance.

The Finnish Reds had perhaps 7,000 combatants in Helsinki. Despite the advantages of being the defenders in a built-up area, they were no match for

Goltz's troops, who attacked again the following day. Fighting continued until late on 13 April, but the outcome was never in doubt. After proclaiming the Red Finnish Revolution, a red lantern had been lit outside the Helsinki Workers' Hall; together with the hall, it was destroyed by accurate German artillery fire. Losses amongst the attackers were remarkably light; the Germans had 60 casualties, with another 23 White casualties. Between 300 and 400 Reds were killed or wounded, and the rest were forced to surrender. Goltz ordered a victory parade for 14 April and the supply of several tons of grain in an attempt to alleviate the food shortages in Helsinki.

During this period, Brandenstein's detachment had been landed separately in Lovisa, 48 miles (77km) east of Helsinki. From there, Brandenstein advanced inland to seize Lahti on 18 April, cutting off the main Red forces from Viipuri and Russia. The Reds made repeated attempts to drive his forces back, but he was able to hold on until Mannerheim's troops reached him from the north. The position of the Reds was now completely untenable. Much of their leadership fled to Russia at the end of April, triggering a collapse of morale. Mannerheim moved against Viborg, capturing the town on 28 April and effectively severing the last links between the Reds and Russia. Most of the remaining Red troops surrendered in the Lahti area in the following few days. Whilst casualties in the fighting had been fairly modest, tens of thousands died in imprisonment in the months that followed, either through illness, malnutrition, or mistreatment.

The fighting in Finland further demonstrated, if any such demonstration was required, that Russia was in no position to achieve any control of events in the western parts of what had been the tsar's empire. On the one hand, Lenin and his associates must have been delighted by the attempt of the Finnish Reds to seize power as the next step in what they still believed would be a wave of pro-Bolshevik revolutions across Europe, but, on the other hand, the speed with which the Red cause collapsed must have been a bitter disappointment. In Finland, the White government announced its intention to create a Kingdom of Finland with the German Prince Friedrich Karl of Hesse as its head of state. Mannerheim had always been ambivalent about German involvement in Finnish affairs and, believing that Germany would ultimately lose the war, he had no desire to be associated with proposals that would be unacceptable to the Entente Powers. Rather than pursue further involvement in events, he resigned from the army and left Finland, ostensibly to visit family in Sweden. Despite his wish to return to the front in France, Goltz remained as commander of the German forces in Finland, tasked with ensuring that the Bolsheviks did not make an attempt to return to power and to help with the transformation of the White Guards into a

Finnish Army. Despite post-war criticism of his role in Finland's internal affairs, he remained unrepentant, later writing:

> [My critics must accept] that Finland enjoyed complete independence in 1918 and the Finnish government, in all its amity with Germany and with me, was fully respected in all its independent rights. If it had been otherwise, if I had actually – as the Swedish newspaper scurrilously claimed – behaved as a Proconsul, that amity would soon have turned into the opposite. It was through its restraint that Germany achieved its position in the hearts of the populace.[375]

Such a viewpoint was entirely understandable. For Goltz and others, the relative ease with which they had triumphed in Finland – and the rapid advance of German and Austro-Hungarian troops across the Ukraine – seemed to herald the realisation of the eastern European empire with which Germany would be able to secure itself forever against its enemies in the west. Provided that the Entente Powers could be forced to accept peace, the huge sacrifices of the German people would not have been in vain.

CHAPTER 12

THE FALL OF THE HOHENZOLLERNS

For Germany, the First World War was a gamble from the outset. As the war continued, the odds against a German victory steadily grew longer, requiring ever-greater risks to be taken.

Faced in the west by the French Army, bent on exacting revenge for the humiliation of the Franco-Prussian War, and in the east by the Russian Army, rapidly modernising and increasing in capability, the German general staff had to hope that Schlieffen's plan to deliver a swift killing blow in the west would deliver results before the slower-mobilising Russians overwhelmed the eastern defences of Germany. The extent of this gamble is shown by Schlieffen's own doubts that the German Army was sufficiently strong to carry out the great outflanking march that he planned; in the event, troops had to be sent east when the Russians threatened to overrun East Prussia, but even if they had been left in the west, it is doubtful that the French and British could have been defeated within six weeks as Schlieffen had envisaged.

Once the great envelopment of the French Army failed and Helmuth von Moltke ('Moltke the Younger') was dismissed, his replacement as chief of the general staff, Erich von Falkenhayn, made one last attempt to force a decision in the west by attacking in strength against the British at Ypres. Victory here would throw the British back to the coast and leave a gap in the north that the French could not repair, but, despite stretching the British Expeditionary Force almost to breaking point, Falkenhayn's armies failed to break through. The two-front war that Germany had feared was now a reality.

The only way that Germany could end the war successfully was by achieving victory in both the east and the west, and of these two fronts the one against the

French and British was always the most important. If Germany could defeat Russia, it was highly likely that the Western Powers would simply continue the war; but if France in particular could be knocked out of the war, the British would be left unable to intervene in mainland Europe and Russia was unlikely to prevail, particularly given the poor performance of Russian armies in 1914. Calculating that he needed to neutralise Russia so that he could concentrate on defeating France, Falkenhayn chose to wage an offensive war in the east in 1915, not least because the Austro-Hungarian Empire seemed perilously close to collapse after just the first winter of the war; but this offensive was not to be pursued until Russia was comprehensively defeated. The intention was purely to achieve a free hand against France. The first part of Falkenhayn's grand strategy – the defeat of the Russian armies in Galicia and Poland – proved to be highly successful, perhaps more so than he had expected; the second part, the defeat of France, was a deliberate attempt to grind down the French by a prolonged battle of attrition at Verdun. Just as Moltke's gamble failed in 1914, so Falkenhayn's gamble came to grief in 1916, and similarly cost him his post.

After earning the thanks of their homeland for defeating Samsonov's Second Army at the Battle of Tannenberg in the opening weeks of the war and thus saving East Prussia from Russian occupation, Hindenburg and Ludendorff were increasingly sidelined in *Ober Ost*, not least due to the personal rivalry between them and Falkenhayn. Many – officers in *Ober Ost*, sympathisers elsewhere, and German industrialists who saw huge profits to be made from developing a German Empire carved from Russian territory – actively plotted the overthrow of Falkenhayn and his replacement by Hindenburg, but until the failure to defeat the French at Verdun and the entry of Romania into the war in late August 1916, Falkenhayn remained secure. His dismissal saw Hindenburg become chief of the general staff and Ludendorff appointed quartermaster-general, effectively Hindenburg's second-in-command. Amongst their first tasks was the requirement to devise a new strategy for Germany to win the war – not in the east, where even as the Brusilov Offensive burned out in the autumn of 1916, there were growing signs of Russian crisis and collapse – but in the west, where the British and French remained obdurately determined to defeat Germany. Just like a gambler who has already bet heavily and lost, the Germans felt that they had to bet even more heavily to try to recover their fortunes. This time, they opted for unrestricted submarine warfare in an attempt to starve Britain to collapse. The evidence for this was weak even at first glance – proponents of the U-boat campaign discounted the shortage of submarines, overstated the likely efficacy of the campaign, totally ignored the ability of the British to adopt countermeasures such as convoys, and made no allowance for Britain increasing domestic agricultural production.[376] Any one of these factors would have made the gamble a risky one; all four effectively ensured that, like the previous gambles, this too would end in failure.

As 1917 progressed and the futility of the submarine campaign became increasingly clear, the fragile political unity that had been achieved in Germany in 1914 began to come under strain. During the heady days of August 1914, a wave of patriotic unity swept the Great Powers, and in Germany the greatest manifestation was the decision of the Social Democratic Party to put aside political disputes for the duration of the war in an act that became known as the *Burgfrieden*, in the expectation that in return for this they would gain political reforms, in particular the end of the current Prussian voting system that greatly advantaged wealthy landowners. At first, only a single Social Democrat member of the Reichstag, Karl Liebknecht, refused to accept this truce, but as the war progressed he was joined by a steady stream of other dissenters. The continuing suffering of the German people was in itself sufficient ultimately to unravel the *Burgfrieden*, but Hindenburg and Ludendorff made its collapse almost inevitable by the imposition of the Hindenburg Programme, in which the military effectively took control of German manpower in an attempt to increase production of war materiel. The publication of the *Vaterländischer Hilfsdienstgesetzt* (Patriotic Auxiliary Service Law) created open dissent, and much to the frustration of Ludendorff it was passed only after major concessions were made to the trade unions; he was left protesting that the ability of the military to impose compulsory labour had been too diluted and the exclusion of women from its terms further reduced its effectiveness.[377] Nevertheless, it was regarded by many in Germany as too onerous.

The fall of the tsar and the growing calls for a 'peace without annexations or reparations' could not fail to have an impact on war-weary Germany during 1917. In March, Philipp Scheidemann, the co-chair of the Social Democrats, published an article in a newspaper warning of the consequences of delaying political reforms. He pointed out that almost the entire world favoured Germany's opponents on the grounds that, to a greater or lesser extent, they were democracies, whereas Germany continued to cling to the Prussian model of government. Russia, formerly the most autocratic nation on earth, had made a fresh start. Only Asiatic despots and Germany continued to cling to their antiquated forms of government, and by doing so Scheidemann believed that they effectively undermined any prospect of transition to constitutional monarchy and were destined to become republics.[378] This and other such warnings – and the entry of the United States of America into the war – had some effect on Chancellor

Bethmann-Hollweg, who tried to introduce electoral changes, but conservative elements succeeded in watering them down and postponed them until the successful conclusion of the war.

Hindenburg remained committed to prosecuting the war to the bitter end, and wrote to the kaiser in early June to warn him of the effect on Germany's enemies of any signs of internal weakness:

> If [our enemies] are nonetheless committed to continuing the war, they calculate that the collapse of Germany and its allies will occur before their own collapse. They hope to achieve this perhaps militarily with a victory on land, but above all else they await economic and internal political developments, i.e. shortages of food and fuel, disunity, discontent and the triumph of radical German social democrats. They base this on the decline of our will to resist, on the growing international unrest, on our food supply situation, and on our unfortunately widely publicised proclamations of our desire for peace.
>
> But reinforcement of our inner strength is the most likely means of convincing them of the futility of continuing the war until the onset of the collapse of their own internal affairs. By contrast, every expression of exhaustion and the desire for peace amongst us and our allies, every word about the alleged impossibility of surviving another winter campaign, will certainly prolong the war.[379]

On 6 July, Matthias Erzberger of the Centre Party made an important speech condemning unrestricted U-boat warfare and calling for a return to the values of 1914, in which Germany had proclaimed that it was entering a war purely to defend its own integrity and independence. This was followed by close cooperation by the Centre Party, the National Liberal Party and the Social Democrats to try to achieve both electoral reform and a declaration of peace without annexations or reparations. Aware of the growing unrest in the Reichstag, Bethmann-Hollweg once more urged the kaiser to embrace reform; Hindenburg and Ludendorff had been seeking his removal for several months, and were now able to prevail upon Wilhelm to dismiss the chancellor.

On 19 July 1917, the Reichstag passed a peace resolution that had been drawn up by Erzberger, Eduard David, Friedrich Ebert and Scheidemann. The resolution stated:

> As was the case on 4 August 1914, on the eve of the fourth year of war the words of the speech from the throne still apply to the German people: 'We are not striving for conquest.' Germany took up arms to defend its freedom and

> independence, and the integrity of its territories. The Reichstag seeks a peace of understanding and reconciliation amongst all nations. Forced annexations and political, economic or financial impositions are incompatible with such a peace. The Reichstag rejects all plans that will lead to trading barriers and hostilities amongst nations after the war. The freedom of the seas must be secured. Only economic peace will prepare the ground for the friendly cooperation of nations. The Reichstag will encourage the creation of international organisations to uphold rights. But so long as foreign governments do not support such a peace, so long as Germany and its allies are threatened with conquest and rape, the German people will stand together as one, persevering steadfastly and fighting until its rights and those of its allies to life and growth is secured. United, the German people are invincible. The Reichstag believes this in unity with the men who defend the Fatherland in heroic combat. The eternal gratitude of the entire population to them is certain.[380]

The wording of the resolution was entirely in keeping with official German pronouncements from earlier years, but many within Germany, in politics, industry and the military, had long passed the point of accepting a peace that did not result in considerable acquisitions. Soldiers and politicians sought safety against future naval blockades in an eastern land empire, while industrialists were lured by the promise of fortunes to be made in developing this empire. For many, the resolution heralded the events that Hindenburg had prophesied in his letter to the kaiser the previous month, and even Erzberger, one of the authors of the resolution, was still in favour of securing territories in the east. Georg Michaelis, who had replaced Bethmann-Hollweg as chancellor, accepted the resolution saying that he would interpret it as he chose. In practical terms, the resolution did nothing to change the course of the German government, though the announcement of the resolution caused considerable consternation amongst German officers. Ludendorff wrote after the war:

> As had clearly been foreseen, it had no political impact on our enemies. The foe saw it as a sign of weakness. Bulgaria and Turkey began to doubt our ultimate victory. Internally, it did not have the effect for which its authors had hoped.[381]

Having lost yet another gamble with unrestricted U-boat warfare, Hindenburg and Ludendorff were left with one last throw of the dice. The Treaty of Brest-Litovsk effectively brought the war in the east to an end, though the territorial ambitions of Germany meant that far fewer troops were available for other fronts than might have been the case if Germany had accepted a more modest peace. Nevertheless, there was sufficient time before the arrival of large numbers of troops from the United States to launch one last attack in the west. In an attempt to maximise the chances of success, Ludendorff reorganised the army into assault divisions, equipped with the best weaponry available, and weaker formations that would be able to hold defensive sections of the front. The assault divisions went through extensive training, were provided with better rations – though still short of the rations available to troops at the beginning of the war – and prepared for what everyone knew would be the last gamble.[382]

There were numerous proposals for offensives in the west, ranging from minor local attacks to more grandiose affairs. Suggestions ranged from a new campaign in the east of France, through a resumption of attacks on Verdun, to an attempt to drive the British back to the coast in the northwest. Ludendorff decided that the latter offered the best hope of success and detailed planning began at the end of 1917. Proposals for the operation – codenamed *Michael* – were presented to Kaiser Wilhelm on 23 January 1918, and detailed orders followed a few weeks later. Over 1.3 million soldiers assembled for the assault, equipped with 14,000 field guns; it was impressive, but the Western Powers actually had even greater firepower available. All would inevitably depend on the execution of the attack.

Somewhat extraordinarily, Ludendorff deliberately did not draw up detailed operational plans beyond the initial assault. It was his intention to exploit whatever successes were gained. Such a policy required excellent flexibility, fast communications, and decisive command if it was to have any chance of success. This flexibility would prove fatal; instead of pursuing a clear objective, Ludendorff and other commanders found themselves diluting their forces in numerous attacks, falling just short of key targets. Ludendorff repeatedly insisted that this was an approach that had served Germany well on the Eastern Front, particularly in 1915 when the limited intentions of the Gorlice-Tarnow Offensive had ultimately led to the Russians being driven far to the east, but this ignored the fact that Mackensen's great offensive was conducted in stages, each of which had a distinct objective. Many of those in the German command structure were deeply critical. Crown Prince Rupprecht of Bavaria, commander of an eponymous army group involved in the fighting, recorded: 'I get the impression as if *OHL* is living from hand to mouth without acknowledging definite operational designs.'[383]

Although the offensive – launched in three phases – achieved considerable success, at no stage did it look like achieving a strategic victory; the reserves of the Western Powers were simply too great. When they looked for reasons for the success of the Germans, many in Britain concentrated on the numbers of troops retained by Lloyd George in the homeland, claiming that the combat strength of the British troops in Flanders was lower than the previous year. There was bitter argument about this in the British press and in the accounts written by many senior officers and officials after the war, but it is clear that there was considerable distrust between Lloyd George and Field Marshal Douglas Haig, commander of British forces in France and Belgium. Haig had promised the British prime minister that he would call off the Ypres offensive in 1917 if it did not show early success, but broke his word and persisted in hugely costly attacks. As a consequence both of Lloyd George's unwillingness to send more reinforcements and the casualties suffered in the second half of the year, the British forces entered 1918 significantly below strength, which undoubtedly added to the success of *Michael*. Haig actually made matters worse by allowing 88,000 men to return to Britain on leave, even when it became clear that a German attack was imminent.[384] Regardless of the causes for the weakness of Haig's armies, Britain was able to send 212,000 men to Flanders as the scale of the crisis became clear in mid-April.[385]

Repeated German attacks continued into the summer, but by then 10,000 American troops were arriving at the front every day. Many German divisions were 2,000 or more below establishment strength, and the failure to achieve victory had a catastrophic effect on the increasingly brittle morale of the army. Exhausted by years of war and slaughter, the men in the front line had steeled themselves for one last effort. As early as 18 April, Rupprecht's chief of staff was warning that the troops appeared to be finished.[386] Germany was approaching the end of its strength; the fighting since March had cost nearly a million casualties, but replacements fell short of this number by 300,000. By contrast, the steady flow of British and American troops tipped the manpower balance increasingly against Germany.

In his memoirs, Hindenburg attempted to put a favourable gloss on events:

> From the military point of view, what we had accomplished in the three great battles completely put in the shade everything that had been done in offensive operations in the west since August 1914. The greatness of the German victories was clearly shown by the extent of the ground gained, the amount of booty, and the bloody losses inflicted on the enemy. We had shaken the structure of the enemy resistance to its very foundation. Our troops had shown themselves in every respect equal to the great demands we had made upon them …
>
> Unfortunately everything we had done had not hitherto been enough to wound our adversaries to death in a military and political sense. There was no sign

> of surrender on the enemy's part. On the contrary, each military defeat seemed only to strengthen the enemy's lust for our destruction. This impression was in no wise diminished by the fact that here and there the voice of moderation was heard in the hostile camp. The dictatorial authority of the political organisms against which we were fighting was on the whole in no way injured. They held the wills and the resources of their nations together as if with iron bands, and by more or less autocratic methods suppressed the capacity for harm of all who dared to think differently from the tyrants in power.[387]

Coming from a man who had effectively established a military dictatorship in Germany that ignored and suppressed all contrary opinion, these comments were remarkable. They also ignored a simple question: given how Hindenburg and the German leadership remained determined to fight a war to the bitter end in the pursuit of total victory at all costs, was it such a surprise that Germany's enemies, who had suffered just as great losses, would do the same?

A disturbing development was the rapid spread of indiscipline. Short of rations, the German infantry repeatedly stopped to loot the plentiful stores of their enemies, and once the habit of helping themselves was established, it spread alarmingly. There were numerous reports of German troops raiding their own army's supply dumps and trains; by May, some supply trains were protected by machine-guns to deter such raids. Several units reported mutinies when exhausted troops were ordered back into the front line, and reinforcements sent from Germany were even worse, with 20 per cent or more simply disappearing from troop trains before they reached the front.[388] Ludendorff blamed the growing signs of disintegration on factors beyond his control:

> The spirit of the troops in the west was now greatly depressed, weakened by influenza and ground down by a monotonous diet. Food supplies in some locations became more varied as a result of the stores that we had captured in our attacks, but now there were potato shortages, even though the German harvest in the previous year had been particularly good.
>
> Amongst the Bavarian troops, a particular mood grew ever stronger. Aspirations tacitly encouraged by the Bavarian government made themselves felt, and were encouraged through the successes of enemy propaganda. Hatred of the Kaiser and the Crown Prince, but also against the Bavarian Royal Family began to bear fruit. The Bavarian troops saw the war as entirely a Prussian affair. They were no longer used as much by the high command as earlier in the war. Only a few divisions conducted themselves as well as before.

> The homeland was completely under the influence of enemy propaganda and the words of enemy statesmen, which were not able to reach us in the front line … All the parties in the Reichstag majority, with the exception of the right wing of the Centrists, consistently believed every word of enemy propaganda and rushed to announce their proposals for reconciliation, understanding and disarmament in a new world order.[389]

The poor behaviour of the new recruits, Ludendorff later claimed, was due to the growing war-weariness at home and the influence of Bolshevism. The reality was more complex. Many training units reported that troops sent to them from the front line to help train new recruits were defeatist and apathetic. Ludendorff might complain that troops returning home on leave were exposed to Bolshevik propaganda left on trains, but such propaganda could have an effect only if the troops were turning their faces from the war. On 8 August, the Western Powers launched a series of powerful attacks at numerous points of the Western Front; the British infantry – supported by numerous tanks and aircraft – moved forward in dense fog near Amiens, penetrating deep into the German positions. Ludendorff described it as the 'black day of the German Army':

> I had division commanders and other officers sent to me from the front to Avesnes to give me their personal impressions. I heard of deeds of outstanding courage, but also of events that I must openly confess I would not have regarded as possible in the German Army: how our men surrendered to individual riders, entire units surrendered to individual tanks! A fresh, brave division moving forward would encounter shouts of 'blackleg' and '*Kriegsverlängerer*' [i.e. one who prolongs the war], words that would be heard again later. The officers in many locations no longer had any influence and allowed themselves to be swept along with the rest.[390]

The degree to which this influenced the outcome of the fighting is difficult to assess. The officers of 11th Bavarian Infantry Division, which repeatedly fought with great distinction both in the west and the east, recorded that, whilst desertion rates rose threefold during 1918, the number absent without leave was still only 71 men.[391] The greatest change was not in the number of desertions or men killed and wounded, but in the number who simply surrendered. During the entire war, the Western Powers took about 712,000 Germans prisoner; of these slightly more than half were captured in just four months in 1918.[392] As was the case with all armies, the German Army had lost proportionately more officers than other ranks, and many of those who remained now saw little point in continuing the slaughter. Some found themselves unable to fight on when their men simply gave up, while others took it upon themselves to negotiate the surrender of the troops under their command. Increasingly, the ratio of officers to other ranks amongst prisoners reflected the ratio in the units involved; men were no longer fighting on until their officers were dead, or abandoning their officers to surrender.

At first, Ludendorff continued to maintain – at least in meetings with the kaiser and government officials – that the army would be able to fight the Western Powers to exhaustion by the end of the year. By mid-July, some officers reported that he was showing signs of nervous strain and depression; Generalleutnant Wilhelm Groener, visiting the Western Front from his duties in the Ukraine, wrote: 'Ludendorff's entourage complained about his indecision and inability to see the larger picture. He really duped himself and, just like Falkenhayn in 1916 at Verdun, was at his wits' end.'[393]

Like many others, Groener's assessment was that Ludendorff simply had not spent enough time in the front line to understand the true nature of the war; his entire combat experience was limited to the siege of Liège in the opening weeks of the conflict. During the Tannenberg campaign, there was a moment when the highly strung Ludendorff appeared to lose his nerve when the critical moment of the battle was at hand, only to be calmed by the massively imperturbable Hindenburg.[394] Now that the last gamble in Germany's quest to achieve decisive victory had clearly failed, he once more was overwhelmed by events. In mid-September, the Salonika Front, long used by both sides to deploy both units and leaders who had failed to impress elsewhere, assumed an unprecedented importance as the Bulgarian Army collapsed. Within two weeks, Bulgaria was out of the war, leaving a hole on the southern flank of the Central Powers that could not be closed. At the end of the month, Ludendorff demanded that the kaiser and the chancellor should seek an immediate ceasefire – in the absence of this, the army would collapse entirely.

This must have come as a thunderclap to those in Berlin. The year had started so encouragingly, with the end of the war in the east and the dreams of a *Mitteleuropa* empire seeming to be close at hand. Ludendorff and Hindenburg had repeatedly sent encouraging reports from the west about the final offensive – and now, suddenly, it seemed as if there was no option but to sue for peace. Richard von Kühlmann, who had negotiated the treaties that took Russia and Romania out of the Entente, was no longer foreign minister having been forced to resign after stating in the Reichstag that the war could not be ended by military means alone. His replacement, Paul von Hintze, was a former naval officer; he warned Hindenburg and Ludendorff that the rapidity of the collapse of Germany's fortunes risked revolution at home, and attempts must be made at least to limit this. He had good reason for believing this. Increasingly, the population of Germany no longer cared for victory – all they wanted was an end to the war. There were now political movements that looked worryingly like those that had overthrown the government of Tsar Nicholas in Russia; one such movement was the Spartacus League, founded by Karl Liebknecht, Rosa Luxemburg and Clara Zetkin in 1915. Even if the censorship of the press had prevented news of setbacks in the west from circulating through German society, soldiers on leave had been very vocal about what was happening. As will be described later, the reappearance of the Sixtus Affair – Austria-Hungary's attempts to secure peace the previous year – had soured relations between Germany and its only European ally, and, without some meaningful prospect of victory, Hintze agreed that Germany had to find a way out of the war.

Ludendorff suggested that those who had deliberately been kept from power, yet whom he regarded as responsible for the current situation – the Social Democrats and others who had not backed his demands for total victory at all costs – should now be awarded ministries and tasked with finding a way out of the mess. Whilst this suggestion was not implemented in full, Prince Max von Baden – a leading liberal who had opposed Hindenburg and Ludendorff on the matter of unrestricted U-boat warfare – was now appointed chancellor specifically with the task of seeking an armistice. Shocked with being thrust into high political office without any prior experience and unwilling to try to enact liberal constitutional reforms in the midst of the war, he took up the post with reluctance, appointing Scheidemann as his secretary of state. He questioned the need to seek an immediate armistice, protesting that such a move would leave him with a very weak negotiating position, but he was persuaded by Ludendorff that the collapse of Bulgaria and the superiority of the armies of the Western Powers, which Ludendorff advised was largely due to their deployment of large numbers of tanks, made it essential to seek an armistice without delay. Every day of postponement brought military collapse closer, he insisted. On 4 October, Max sent a message in conjunction with the Vienna government to President Woodrow Wilson of the United States:

> The German government requests that the President of the United States of America take the initiative in bringing about peace, that he informs all the belligerent states of this request, and that he invites them to send plenipotentiaries for purposes of beginning negotiations. The German government accepts as the

> basis for peace negotiations the programme stated by the President of the United States in his speech to Congress of January 8 1918, and in his subsequent pronouncements, particularly in his speech of September 27.
>
> In order to avoid further bloodshed, the German government requests the immediate conclusion of an armistice on land, at sea, and in the air.[395]

The Western Powers took their time responding to the request. Wilson sent three notes to the Central Powers in reply, the first on 8 October questioning whether Max von Baden's government, appointed by the kaiser, really represented the German people. Whilst Prince Max formulated a reply, there occurred an incident that hardened American attitudes: on 11 October, a U-boat attacked and destroyed a British steamer, killing 450 people, including several Americans. Wilson immediately dispatched a second note to Berlin:

> The President feels it is his duty to say that no arrangement can be accepted by the Government of the United States which does not provide absolutely satisfactory safeguards and guarantees of the maintenance of the present military supremacy of the armies of the United States and of the allies in the fields. He feels confident that he can safely assume that this will also be the judgment and decision of the Allied Governments.
>
> The President feels that it is also his duty to add that … [he] will not consent to consider an armistice so long as the armed forces of Germany continue the illegal and inhumane practices which they still persist in. At the very time that the German Government approaches the Government of the United States with proposals of peace its submarines are engaged in sinking passenger ships at sea, and not the ships alone but the very boats in which their passengers and crews seek to make their way to safety; and in their present enforced withdrawal from Flanders and France the German armies are pursuing a course of wanton destruction which has always been regarded as in direct violation of the rules and practices of civilized warfare … The nations associated against Germany cannot be expected to agree to a cessation of arms while acts of inhumanity, spoliation, and desolation are being continued which they justly look upon with horror and with burning hearts.
>
> It is necessary … that the President should very solemnly call the attention of the Government of Germany to the language and plain intent of one of the terms of peace which the German Government has now accepted. It is contained in the address of the President … on 4 July last. It is as follows: 'The destruction of every arbitrary power anywhere that can separately, secretly, and of its single choice disturb the peace of the world; or, if it cannot be presently destroyed, at least its

> reduction to virtual impotency.' The power which has hitherto controlled the German nation is of the sort here described. It is within the choice of the German nation to alter it.[396]

Ludendorff seemed to be recovering his poise. He now claimed that, provided the German Army could reach the winter intact, it would be possible to fight on and secure better terms in 1919. This was, at best, wishful thinking. Rumours that Germany was seeking an armistice had reached the front line, where many soldiers now demanded peace at any price, or simply surrendered to save their own lives. At the beginning of the month, Ludendorff had been desperate for an armistice while Max von Baden had questioned the need to seek one; now, the roles were completely reversed. Prince Max now approached the kaiser and asked him to call off the U-boat campaign to prevent further inflaming American opinion, and sent a further note to Washington in which he accepted the principle that Germany would evacuate the territories that it had occupied. He protested about Wilson's criticism of illegal and inhumane German behaviour, pointing out that a degree of destruction was inevitable during a retreat, and rejected any suggestion that German U-boats had deliberately attacked lifeboats and assured Wilson that orders had been sent to commanders to avoid attacking passenger vessels, with the caveat that the order might not have reached every U-boat currently deployed. He then turned to the question of the legality of the German government:

> Hitherto the representation of the people in the German Empire has not been endowed with an influence on the formation of the government. The constitution did not provide for a concurrence of the representation of the people, based on the equal, universal, secret, direct franchise. The leaders of the great parties of the Reichstag are members of this government. In future no government can take or continue in office without possessing the confidence of the majority of the Reichstag. The responsibility of the Chancellor of the Empire to the representation of the people is being legally developed and safeguarded …
>
> The question of the President … is therefore answered in a clear and unequivocal manner by the statement that the offer of peace and an armistice has come from a government which, free from arbitrary and irresponsible influence, is supported by the approval of the overwhelming majority of the German people.[397]

Wilson's reply reached Berlin on 23 October. He stated that he would take up the question of an armistice with the allies of the United States, but continued to insist on terms that would make any renewal of hostilities by Germany impossible. The question of the legitimacy of Germany's government continued to cause difficulties:

> It is evident that the German people have no means of commanding the acquiescence of the military authorities of the Empire in the popular will; that the power of the King of Prussia to control the policy of the Empire is unimpaired; that the determining initiative still remains with those who have been the masters of Germany … The President deems it his duty to say, without any attempt to soften what may seem harsh words, that the nations of the world do not and cannot trust the word of those who have hitherto been masters of German policy, and to point out once more that in concluding peace … the Government of the United States cannot deal with any but veritable representatives of the German people who have been assured of a genuine constitutional standing as the real rulers of Germany. If it must deal with the military masters and the monarchical autocrats of Germany now … it must demand, not peace negotiations, but surrender.[398]

Immediately, Hindenburg issued an order of the day to the army:

> Wilson says in his reply that he wishes to suggest to his allies that they enter into ceasefire discussions. But the ceasefire must leave Germany so defenceless that it can no longer take up arms …
>
> Wilson's answer calls for military capitulation. For us soldiers, this is therefore unacceptable. It is proof that our enemies' desire for destruction, which started the war in 1914, remains undiminished. Further, it is proof that our enemies merely speak the words 'a just peace' in order to mislead us and to break our will to resist. Wilson's answer can only prompt us soldiers to continue resisting with all our strength. When the enemy learns that the German front cannot be broken at any price, they will be ready for a peace that secures the future of Germany for its people.[399]

Technically, Hindenburg was the chief of the general staff – he was effectively the military advisor of the commander-in-chief, the kaiser, and therefore exceeded his authority in issuing any such proclamation. Accompanied by Ludendorff, he now travelled to Berlin to demand that the kaiser should dismiss Prince Max and once more return Germany to the path of total war. Perhaps to avoid a difficult conversation, Max claimed to be too unwell to meet the two officers.

The two men who had come to dominate Germany had an inkling of how much things had changed when they attended the Reichstag; they learned that the deputies had roundly condemned their conduct of the war. That evening, Ludendorff held talks with the interior minister, where he received a cold reception:

> [The comments in the Reichstag] worked their effect; I was to be dismissed.
>
> The conversation in the Interior Ministry lasted less than two hours. General von Winterfeldt [the military representative in the ministry] and Oberst von Haeften [in charge of the overseas section of *OHL*] were waiting for me in the hall. Greatly agitated, all I could say to them was:
>
> 'There is no more hope. Germany is lost!' These two gentlemen were equally shocked.
>
> … Early on 26 October, in the same frame of mind as the previous evening I wrote my letter of resignation. I did so in the awareness gained in the previous day's conversation with Vice-Chancellor von Bayer that the government could no longer bring itself to take action. His Majesty, the Fatherland and the Army would thus be placed in an impossible situation. I was now regarded as someone prolonging the war, and for the government and Wilson my departure would perhaps be a relief for Germany. I therefore requested that His Majesty dismiss me with honour.
>
> As usual, the Field Marshal [Hindenburg] came to me at 9am on 26 October. I had put my request to one side as I had decided to let him know after my visit to His Majesty. The Field Marshal … saw the letter. It drew his attention. He asked me not to send it. I should remain in post. I could not yet leave the kaiser and the army. After much internal struggle, I agreed. I came to the conclusion that I must retain my position and suggested to the Field Marshal that he should visit Prince Max again and speak to him. We were unable to do so. He was still ill. While I waited on this decision, Oberst von Haeften reported to me that the government would ask His Majesty to dismiss me as the aforementioned army order of the day prevented any other outcome. I was no longer surprised by anything and had no doubt on my part. During my conversation with Oberst von Haeften I was suddenly summoned to His Majesty at an unusual time of day.
>
> During my drive from the general staff building to Schloss Bellevue I told the Field Marshal what I had just heard. Later I learned that Prince Max had raised the possibility of the cabinet resigning if I were retained.
>
> The kaiser was transformed from the day before, speaking only to me he said that he was opposed to the army order of the day of 24 October. There followed

> some of the bitterest moments of my life. In deferential tones, I said to His Majesty that I had the painful feeling that I no longer had his confidence and therefore requested humbly to be dismissed. His Majesty accepted my request.[400]

In the light of Wilson's naked demands for the removal of the kaiser and Ludendorff's failure to achieve military success in the west, Kaiser Wilhelm could see that the German people were perfectly likely to sacrifice their monarch in order to secure peace; such matters had already been discussed openly in some newspapers. He had been advised that if he were to dismiss the military leadership, this might suffice to save his own position; in any case, Ludendorff's stock had plummeted. Whilst Hindenburg was still widely respected, his deputy was seen by most senior figures in Germany as a spent force, and a man who had singularly failed since taking up high office.

After his dismissal, Ludendorff remained in Berlin. When the armistice was declared, he stayed briefly with his brother, Hans Ludendorff, who was chief astronomer at the Potsdam Observatory. He attempted to hide his identity by wearing spectacles and a false beard, and decided to leave Germany for Scandinavia; although he was recognised in Denmark, he was allowed to travel to Sweden. He remained there a year, writing extensively about his experiences in the war, and inevitably, these accounts cast him in a favourable light and did a great deal to strengthen the myth that Germany was defeated because of the collapse of the home front rather than the defeat of the army. The myth, widely known in Germany as the *Dolchstosslegende* ('stab in the back legend') would become part of Nazi mythology, and simply ignored the reality that by late 1918 Germany was militarily, economically and socially exhausted. The origin of the name *Dolchstosslegende* can be traced back to an encounter with the British Major General Sir Neill Malcolm, who met Ludendorff in 1919. When Ludendorff categorised his list of complaints about the failure of the German homeland to support the army, Malcolm asked, 'Do you mean, General, that you were stabbed in the back?' Ludendorff embraced this imagery with enthusiasm, adopting it as his own view.[401] It was taken up by many senior officers in Germany after the war – it was far more palatable than admitting that they had been outfought on the battlefield.

Ludendorff also became increasingly hostile to the left-wing parties of German politics and strongly anti-Semitic, blaming the Jews for putting profit ahead of duty; this was a shameful distortion of reality, enthusiastically promoted by other right-wing writers such as Alfred Roth. Proportionately, the German Jewish community suffered more casualties than Germany as a whole, at least partly because, being better educated, it produced a larger proportion of officers than non-Jewish parts of society, but without a shred of evidence to support his view, Roth portrayed the Jews who served in the army as being more interested in profit and personal gain than fighting for Germany.[402] After his return from Sweden in 1919, Ludendorff became a member of the Nazi Party and took part in the 'Beer Hall Putsch' of 1923. Although he was subsequently tried, he was acquitted. Despite his repeated disparaging comments about politicians, he served as a right-wing Reichstag deputy from 1924 to 1928, during which he sought election as president of Germany in 1925, but he was heavily defeated by his former commander and now bitter opponent, Hindenburg. He became increasingly eccentric, blaming the woes of the world upon both Christianity and Judaism, and ultimately even the Nazis distanced themselves from him. He died in 1937.

If Kaiser Wilhelm thought that his troubles would be eased by the dismissal of Ludendorff, he was disappointed. The navy was also opposed to the proposals for an armistice; Admiral Reinhard Scheer, chief of the admiralty, had devised a grandiose plan to build 450 U-boats in the coming year.[403] It was an absurd ambition, making no allowances for whether Germany had the shipyards and raw materials to build the new fleet, the crews to man the vessels, or the fuel to propel them. Incensed by the kaiser's decision to suspend unrestricted submarine warfare, Scheer decided – without any formal consultation of the kaiser, the chancellor, or indeed anyone else –that it was essential for the navy to make a last, great gesture before the end of the war. It would sally into the North Sea and seek a final action against the British, regardless of the outcome:

> It is impossible for the fleet to remain inactive in any final battle that may sooner or later precede an armistice. The fleet must be committed. Even if it is not to be expected that this would decisively influence the course of events, it is still, from the moral point of view, a question of honour and existence of the navy to have done its utmost in the last battle.[404]

An operational plan was drawn up by Scheer's chief of staff for the fleet. The intention was to attack British shipping in the southern part of the North Sea in order to provoke a deployment of the Royal Navy, which would first be waylaid by U-boats and then attacked by the German High Seas Fleet. But just as the Russian Baltic Fleet had discovered, prolonged periods confined in warships with little operational deployment proved to be a fertile environment for mutiny and dissent. There had already been a mutiny in 1917; on 2 August, 350 sailors from the battleship *Prinzregent Luitpold* marched through Wilhelmshaven demanding an end to the war. Army and naval personnel rapidly intervened and the protesters returned to their ship, where 75 were arrested. Several were tried and imprisoned, and two were executed by firing squad. Whilst this quashed the mutiny, the result was the radicalisation of many sailors who had not joined the mutiny, and the creation of several sailors' committees in many of the larger warships of the fleet.[405]

When orders were given for the capital ships to prepare for sea, word spread quickly. Many sailors refused to return to their vessels from trips ashore in Kiel, Wilhelmshaven and elsewhere and had to be rounded up by military police. Late on 29 October, several warships anchored off Wilhelmshaven were ordered to weigh anchor in preparation for the suicidal attack, but sailors aboard the battleships of the Third Squadron refused to obey orders and announced that they would passively resist any attempt to go to sea. The network of sailors' committees ensured that news spread rapidly and other ships' crews joined the protest. When threatened by a group of destroyers, the sailors gave up, but it was clearly impossible for the fleet to go into battle and the operation was cancelled. As the ships of the Third Squadron passed through the Kiel Canal, 47 men designated as the ringleaders of the unrest were arrested and dispatched to the nearby military prison. The ships sailed back into Kiel, arriving on 31 October; unable to keep their unruly subordinates in check, ships' officers allowed them to go ashore, where they congregated in the Kiel Union House and commenced a protest, demanding the release of the men who had been arrested. The authorities closed the Union House, but the protesters merely moved to the nearby drill ground, where they were joined by dockyard workers and even elements of the Kiel garrison. By 3 November, there were about 6,000 people gathered on the parade ground. Led by Karl Artelt, a low-ranking engineer who had been a leading figure in establishing sailors' committees, and Lothar Popp, a civilian dockyard worker, they set off towards the military prison to force the release of their comrades who had been arrested. Many armed themselves from the nearby military barracks.

Leutnant zur See Steinhäuser had been sent with an armed patrol to keep an eye on the protesters and ordered his men to fire over the heads of the sailors. When this had no effect, he directed them to fire directly at the protesters and seven were killed and nearly 30 wounded. Some of the protesters who were carrying weapons returned fire, and Steinhäuser was struck in the neck, though he survived. The protesters dispersed, and on 4 November six companies of infantry arrived in Kiel to try to ensure that there would be no further unrest. To the alarm of the authorities, the men of the rifle companies showed little inclination to oppose the protesters, whose numbers were swelling. More committees and councils were created, and rather ominously the sailors and dockyard workers began to address each other as 'comrade Bolsheviks'.[406] As the sailors took control of more of Kiel, the authorities released the men who had been imprisoned.

In conscious emulation of the revolutionaries of Petrograd, Artelt and Popp led their followers in forming a sailors' and workers' council on 4 November. That evening, they published their own 'fourteen points', a list that included freedom of speech and of the press, the release of all political prisoners, and a guarantee that the fleet would not sail. At this stage, there were no political demands, such as the abdication of the kaiser.

The developments in Kiel were watched with growing alarm from Berlin. Gustav Noske was a member of the Social Democrats, but represented the right wing of the party and had played a prominent role in a Reichstag committee investigating excessive profiteering by military contractors. Newly appointed to the team that led the Social Democrats, he was dispatched to Kiel by Prince Max to try to negotiate an end to the mutiny. He was greeted with enthusiasm when he arrived on 5 November and appointed chair of the new council; nevertheless, he was able to restore order and discipline and both the soldiers and dockworkers returned to their duties.[407] But whilst Prince Max and the rest of the government received this news with relief, the mutiny was turning rapidly into a revolution. A deputation of sailors from Kiel travelled to Lübeck on the same day that Noske arrived, and by the end of the day the city was firmly under the control of militant sailors, soldiers and trade unionists. The following day, Hamburg, Bremen and Wilhelmshaven followed suit, spreading rapidly to major cities inland in the next 48 hours. On 8 November, after noisy demonstrations, Kurt Eisner – a Social Democrat who had just been released from imprisonment on charges of inciting strikes amongst munitions workers – declared a socialist republic in Bavaria. To escape what he hoped and expected would be transient turmoil, King Ludwig III of Bavaria had left Munich for the safety of a castle near Salzburg; he would never return as king.

The authorities in Berlin remained determined to limit the spread of the revolution, but their power was fast evaporating. General Wilhelm Groener, Ludendorff's successor as quartermaster-general, urged Prince Max to accept whatever terms were being offered by the Western Powers – the alternative was ongoing fighting at the front while Germany collapsed into chaos. General Alexander von Linsingen, a veteran of the Eastern Front, had been Military Governor of Berlin since the summer and was tasked with protecting the city, but, aware that his troops were hardly any more reliable than the sailors of the German Navy, he had their weapons secured in armouries.

The chairman of the Social Democrats, Friedrich Ebert, was deeply worried that a Bolshevik revolution would become almost irresistible unless something was done to prevent it. Given that military options were limited – Groener had asked nearly 40 senior officers if their men would fight to support the kaiser, and only one had replied unequivocally in the affirmative – it was vital that concessions were made. The influenza outbreak that had appeared to be receding earlier in the year was also returning with a vengeance, and the combination of sickness, desertion, and refusal to obey orders meant that *OHL* could count on barely six infantry divisions on the entire Western Front. In the hope of appeasing the Americans, the German constitution had been extensively altered, increasing the power of the Reichstag substantially and reducing the kaiser to the status of a constitutional monarch, but events were now proceeding too fast for this to be sufficient. On 7 November, Ebert told Prince Max:

> If the kaiser does not abdicate, the social revolution is inevitable. But I do not want it, indeed I hate it like sin.[408]

After receiving a pessimistic and troubling report from the chief of Berlin's police, Kaiser Wilhelm had left the capital on 29 October and travelled west to Spa in Belgium, intentionally placing himself closer to the army so that he could, if necessary – and if possible – return with sufficient forces to restore his place in Germany. Groener informed him that there was no prospect of this occurring – the army would march home in good order under the command of its officers, but would no longer fight either against the enemies of Germany or the enemies of the kaiser.[409] On 10 November, Wilhelm accepted the inevitable and crossed the border into the Netherlands, where he would remain until his death. When the Nazis came to power in the 1930s, he hoped briefly that the monarchy would be restored with his son as kaiser, but he soon came to distrust Hitler. He was genuinely shocked by the anti-Jewish pogroms and the events of *Kristallnacht* in November 1938, though he became increasingly convinced that British opposition to Germany was rooted in a combination of Freemasonry and Jewish influences. He died in 1941.

The day before Wilhelm left Spa for the Netherlands, Scheidemann declared Germany to be a republic and dispatched a delegation to France to negotiate an armistice. President Wilson had sent a final note to Berlin on 5 November, and this formed the basis of the agreement that came into force on 11 November. At the very end, the Germans showed that they had learned from the events in Russia, and Groener and Ebert, the new head of the Provisional Government, agreed that the existing military leadership would remain in control of the army – there would be no widespread purges and resultant disorder. Despite the extraordinary military achievements of the German Army in the east, and despite the immense suffering of German soldiers and civilians, the war between the Central Powers and the Entente was over with Germany forced to accept defeat. A little over two million German soldiers were dead, over five million wounded. But in the east, nothing was settled. The maps of nations, redrawn after Brest-Litovsk, would now be redrawn again as a new series of conflicts erupted.

Whilst conflict continued across much of Eastern Europe, the end of the 'Great War' is an appropriate moment to consider the outcome from the perspective of the nations that entered it with a mixture of trepidation, resolution and ambition. Tsarist Russia had already ceased to exist and the defeat of the Central Powers was a welcome development for the Bolsheviks – two days after the armistice in the west, they renounced the Treaty of Brest-Litovsk and began preparations to reclaim their lost territories. Germany had entered the war determined to weaken Russia before modernisation of Russian forces was complete and to eliminate any future threat from France; as the war progressed, these aims grew to include the protection of Germany from any future blockade. Briefly, the collapse of Russia seemed to offer a tantalising possibility of achieving these aims, but as everyone had always expected, the war would ultimately be decided in the west, and failure to inflict a military defeat on France proved fatal. Such an outcome was probably already unachievable by the end of 1917, if not sooner – as has already been described, the attempt to starve Britain into defeat by unrestricted submarine warfare was never going to succeed, and the entry of the United States into the war tipped the material balance firmly against the Central Powers. Instead of eliminating any threat from France and weakening Russia, Germany's monarchy collapsed and the nation faced an uncertain future, with the military power that had been the bedrock of the original German state the likely target of Entente demands.

Germany's ally, the Austro-Hungarian Empire, was perhaps the Great Power that least wanted a major conflict, even though it was the assassination of Archduke Franz Ferdinand that started the cascade of events that led to war. With no clearly devised plan for military cooperation with Germany, the empire's armies – woefully unprepared for modern warfare – bore the brunt of the initial Russian onslaught, and the terrible losses suffered for no clear war aim revealed fracture lines within Austria-Hungary faster than within any other power. All of the contradictions and weaknesses of the Great Compromise that had created the empire were laid bare, and it is perhaps remarkable that despite this, Habsburg rule survived as long as it did.

Nor was there much cheer for the victorious British and French. The casualties suffered by their armies were immense, as was the cost of industrialised war on an unprecedented scale. Although France achieved its aims of defeating Germany and recovering Alsace and Lorraine, the loss of 1.4 million dead and huge war debts left the nation weakened. Perhaps more than any other nation, France was scarred by its losses and this played a large part in its rapid collapse in the Second World War. For the British, the end of the war found the nation changed almost beyond recognition. The social order that had prevailed before the war had altered markedly and the wealth of the British Empire had been spent on the huge conflict. Social pressures that had largely been contained during the Victorian era and the early 20th century would continue to change the country, as they already had in other parts of Europe.

Hindenburg had remained in *OHL* until the end. Although he played a leading role in persuading the kaiser that he would have to abdicate, he portrayed himself as a royalist and diehard supporter of the monarchy. He announced his immediate retirement from the army and returned to his home, from where he was summoned the following year to appear before a Reichstag commission investigating the matter of the adoption of unrestricted submarine warfare. There was a considerable degree of collusion between Hindenburg and Ludendorff prior to the hearing in Berlin; the former quartermaster-general wrote to Hindenburg advising him that he was writing his memoirs, and the manner in which he portrayed Hindenburg would depend on the testimony that the latter gave to the Reichstag. Ignoring the questions put to him by the commision, Hindenburg used the opportunity to read out a speech prepared by Ludendorff's lawyer, firmly establishing the legend that the army had been stabbed in the back by the collapse of the home front. He reluctantly ran for election as president in 1925 and was successful, at least partly because anti-communist factions united behind his candidacy. He attempted to conduct himself as no more than a figurehead, complaining in private that he wished he had not been persuaded to run for office; those around him manipulated him into using parts of the constitution to oppose and even dismiss the Reichstag. He first met Hitler in 1931, and the two men rapidly came to despise each other. In 1932, beginning to drift into senility, he was persuaded to run for president again, largely to prevent Hitler from winning the position. When the Nazis won a majority in the Reichstag elections of 1932, Hindenburg at first refused to appoint Hitler as chancellor, but early in 1933 he had to concede defeat. The relationship between

Hindenburg and the Nazis continued to be uneasy; when Hitler attempted to pass a law banning Jews from holding posts in the civil service, the president forced him to add a clause excluding Jewish war veterans from the restriction. He was strongly opposed to the political violence of the era, and supported the Nazi suppression of unruly elements of the *Sturmabteilungen* ('assault detachments' or SA, the paramilitary wing of the Nazi Party) in mid-1934, believing erroneously that this would bring order to Germany. He died in August aged 86.

CHAPTER 13

THE FALL OF THE HABSBURGS

The Austro-Hungarian Empire was an institution born out of crisis. As the power of the Austrian Empire waned and conflict erupted in Italy and with Prussia in the 19th century, the Hungarian parts of the empire demanded an increasing degree of independence. There had been popular uprisings throughout the empire in 1848, and the Hungarians remembered with considerable bitterness that it had taken the intervention of Russian troops to restore Austrian control in Budapest; such an achievement had been beyond the power of the Austrians themselves. After the defeat of the Austrian Army by Prussia at Königgrätz in 1866, the empire could no longer claim to speak for the independent German states and that role was now seized by the victorious Prussians; if Austria was to retain its traditional status as one of the world's Great Powers, it needed to deal with the ongoing disagreements with Hungary as a matter of urgency. Out of this came the great Austro-Hungarian Compromise of 1867, by which the empire was transformed into the Dual Monarchy, with Franz Joseph as Emperor of Austria and King of Hungary. The Hungarian parts of the empire were given considerable freedom, but foreign affairs remained a central function. The army adopted the title *kaiserlich und königlich* ('Imperial and Royal') along with the foreign, war and finance ministries.

Whilst the compromise might have saved Habsburg rule, it was – like many compromises – a difficult arrangement. Budapest had sufficient independence to obstruct many initiatives from Vienna, and this was instrumental in preventing the *k.u.k.* Army from expanding as rapidly in the last years of the 19th century as other armies. There was also widespread resentment in other parts of the empire about the special status of Hungary, with other non-German nationalities within the multilingual and multi-ethnic empire demanding similar rights. Such voices were particularly loud in Austro-Hungarian Poland and the Czech lands around Prague, but the lack of strong central authority led to calls from Ruthenia, the Balkans, the Slovak territories, and the Italian territories for greater autonomy. The only unifying force within the empire was the monarchy, specifically the venerable figure of Franz Joseph, and there was a widespread belief in the empire that the Compromise would be unlikely to outlive him. However, it should be pointed out that many – though not all – of the nationalities within the empire might have demanded greater autonomy, but they stopped short of seeking complete independence. As Prince Karl Schwarzenberg pointed out to the Czech nationalist Edward Grégr in 1891:

> What will you do with your country, which is too small to stand alone? Will you give it to Germany, or to Russia, for you have no other choice if you abandon the Austrian union.[410]

Indeed, given the options that Schwarzenberg suggested, most citizens of the Austro-Hungarian Empire were, to a greater or lesser extent, content with the manner in which affairs were run. The constant financial wrangling between Vienna and Budapest may have blocked greater expenditure on the army, but the result was that infrastructure development was better funded, leading to good internal communications and trade. As Karl Kraus, the Austrian author described by one of his contemporaries as 'the master of venomous ridicule' pointed out:

> In Berlin, things are serious but not hopeless. In Vienna, they are hopeless but not serious.[411]

Despite being a strict monarchy with very limited powers granted to the parliaments in Vienna and Budapest, and despite the limited franchise for elections to those two parliaments, the Austro-Hungarian Empire was in many respects a remarkably meritocratic entity. A large proportion of the army's senior officers – greater than in the armies of almost any other belligerent power – came from relatively humble backgrounds. The empire operated a policy of ennoblement for those who gave distinguished service, which may have seemed to outsiders as a mechanism for creating almost Ruritanian names – once ennobled, officers and government officials usually adopted the name of their home towns or the locations where they had earned their promotion – but it provided a means for many to advance far higher than would have been the case in Germany or Russia, or even in Britain.

When war broke out in 1914, the Austro-Hungarian Empire – like all of the belligerent powers – was swept by a wave of popular patriotism, and men of all nationalities obeyed their mobilisation orders. However, as has already been described, the terrible losses suffered by the army in the opening months caused huge damage to the internal structure of the army. In addition, from the very outset the performance of the *k.u.k.* Army proved to be deficient in almost every respect. In truth, no army was ready for the realities of warfare in the industrial age, but the doctrine and practices of the *k.u.k.* Army proved to be particularly unsuited, largely due to the catalogue of errors of Franz Conrad von Hötzendorf, the man who – more than any person of his age – shaped the army of his empire.

One of the consequences of the Treaty of Brest-Litovsk was the return of hundreds of thousands of men who had been taken prisoner by the Russians; as the war progressed and the fighting spirit of the *k.u.k.* Army declined, many formations simply laid down their arms en masse rather than fight. In total, the Russians captured two million Austro-Hungarian soldiers; even if they had wished to provide exemplary care for them, the numbers were far greater than they had ever expected before the war. It was a deliberate policy on the part of the Russians to separate Slav prisoners from others, in the hope that many of them would be willing to fight on the side of the Russian Army, while Austrians, Hungarians and Germans were transported into the depths of Siberia to primitive camps. Many who had been taken prisoner in the first months of the war died in a terrible typhus epidemic that raged through the camps during the first winter, while others were put to work on construction projects. It is estimated that 150,000 Austro-Hungarian prisoners died from their wounds and a further 500,000 died through illness, malnutrition and exposure. After the war, the Austrian authorities calculated that an additional 30,000 were killed by their guards, often without any due process, and a further 11,000 – mainly from the Slav parts of the Austro-Hungarian Empire – fought and died during the Russian Civil War.[412] Far from the centres of authority, many of the camps became hotbeds of Bolshevik propaganda, which intensified after the fall of the tsar. Pro-Bolshevik groups set up committees in the camps; one leading figure was the Hungarian Béla Kun, a former journalist who was taken prisoner in 1916. He was released from captivity in 1918 and immediately joined the left wing of the Bolsheviks, and exhorted Austro-Hungarian soldiers returning home to spread the word that the only path that would avoid total destruction was to foment a revolution.

Despite knowing that hundreds of thousands of soldiers were being held by the Russians and that they would be released once peace was secured, the Austro-Hungarian authorities made little attempt to prepare for the large numbers of men who would return. Camps had to be erected in haste, with haphazard arrangements for food and clothing, and Generaloberst Josef Freiherr Roth von Limanowa-Lapanów was nominated as *Generalinspektor für das Heimkehrerwesen* ('Inspector-General for Returnees'). In the new camps, the former prisoners were deloused and held for a short period. Originally, the intention had been to re-establish military discipline, but the plan foundered through a shortage of food and replacement uniforms: instead of being fed adequately and being re-clothed, the men felt they were treated with suspicion, a feeling that was exacerbated by often clumsy attempts to interrogate them about the circumstances in which they had been taken prisoner. Those suspected of pro-Bolshevik sympathies were meant to be redirected to special camps at Wieselburg and Kenyermezö, but the numbers were too great and many were allowed to continue through the *Heimkehrer* process. When they were finally released and allowed to go home on leave, the former prisoners were shocked by the food shortages and poverty that now prevailed everywhere, strengthening the beliefs of those who looked favourably upon the Bolsheviks. Originally, the intention was to allow the men eight weeks' leave, but this was soon extended to three months. At the end of their leave period, many of the former prisoners simply disappeared, either hiding with their families or joining large bands of deserters who roamed the countryside.

The situation within the empire worsened steadily as the war progressed. Alarmingly, there were already signs of war-weariness by the first winter of the conflict, particularly amongst Czech and Ruthenian citizens, and food shortages brought widespread misery. Hungary placed tight controls on the amount of food that it would allow to be exported to other parts of the empire, and the loss of the fertile lands of Galicia – upon which Austria depended for grain, vegetables and meat – in 1914 proved catastrophic. To make matters worse, the attempts by the authorities to establish rationing were clumsy and incompetent. Even when Galicia was recaptured, the devastation to the infrastructure and the depopulation of large areas made it difficult to re-establish agricultural production, which remained far below peacetime levels until after the war. As was the case in other parts of the Austro-Hungarian Empire, the citizens of Galicia enthusiastically supported the Dual Monarchy at the start of the war, particularly when the Polish Legions were established, but when the Central Powers proclaimed the creation of an independent Poland in 1916, the Polish Legions were transferred to German control. Most of their personnel refused to take an oath of allegiance to the kaiser and were interned, increasing public disillusionment in Galicia and other parts of Poland that were under Austro-Hungarian control. Over time, the legions shrank as men were transferred to other formations, including the Polish Auxiliary Corps, which was under the control of the *k.u.k.* Army.

The Treaty of Brest-Litovsk finally brought the war with Russia to a close, but any 'peace dividend' for the Austro-Hungarian Empire was very limited. Although two thirds of the Ukraine was effectively under German occupation, it was still necessary to keep substantial *k.u.k.* forces in the east, particularly given Emperor Karl's heavy-handed orders regarding food requisitions. Substantial numbers of troops were also tied down on the Salonika Front, and the Italian Front remained as active as ever. There had been some hopes in both Vienna and Berlin that a settlement in the east, with the creation of an independent Poland, might result in the formation of a Polish Army that would fight alongside the Central Powers, but this proved to be illusory. When the terms of the treaty with Ukraine were published and the cession of Chełm became known, the Regency Council in Warsaw – one of the institutions established by the Central Powers to work alongside their appointed military governors – resigned en masse. The *Komitet Wspolny Wszystkich Stronnictw i Grup w Nowym Sączu* ('Joint Committee of All Parties and Groups in Nowy Sacz') published a proclamation denouncing the treaty with Ukraine as amounting to a Fourth Partition of Poland, a betrayal of the Poles who had volunteered to fight in the Polish Legions for the empire against the Russians.[413]

Nor was it only the Polish politicians who were angered by the concessions made to Ukraine. Major General Stanislaus Graf Szeptycki was the son of an aristocratic family in Polish Galicia and had served in the *k.u.k.* Army before being appointed commander of the Polish Legions. He was now governor of Lublin and he too tendered his resignation. Deployed near Czernowitz, the troops of the Polish Auxiliary Corps mutinied in protest at the loss of Chełm; neighbouring units were sent to suppress the revolt, leading to considerable bloodshed.[414] About 1,600 men of the corps, led by General Józef Haller, marched across the frontier into Ukraine where they joined forces with II Polish Corps, a formation raised by the Russians from Poles in Russian-occupied Poland and from Polish men captured from the *k.u.k.* Army; ultimately, the composite force found its way to the Western Front where it served as part of the Blue Army, a force composed of Polish volunteers, including many from the United States of America.

In Galicia, there was a widespread strike in February 1918 when news of the deal with Ukraine was made public and the citizens of Lemberg, including the city's Jews, held religious services supporting the strike. Austro-Hungarian officials – many of whom were ethnically Polish – attended services and meetings in Lemberg, Przemyśl and Krakow. Everywhere, the Habsburg two-headed eagle emblem was torn down and often replaced by the Polish eagle. In Krakow, large crowds attacked the German consulate and the police force was forced to withdraw from the city centre for a while.

The Polish lands of the Austro-Hungarian Empire had a large Jewish population, and many Jews actively supported the cause of Polish nationalism. Throughout the 19th century, when there were several pogroms against Jews in parts of Eastern Europe, particularly those controlled by the Russian Empire, there was remarkably little violence against Jews within the territories controlled by Franz Joseph, and in 1914 the Jewish community enthusiastically supported the empire; three times as many Jews served in the army as might have been expected from the proportion of the population who were Jewish. Although many of Galicia's Jews lived in traditional Jewish communities, many others had integrated themselves fully with urban life, particularly in Krakow, where they formed 20 per cent of the population. In 1898, one of the rare occasions that there was an outbreak of anti-Semitic violence in the Austro-Hungarian Empire, there was no trouble in Krakow. As the hardships of war took hold, the unity between ethnic Poles and Jews began to crumble. Partly due to historical restrictions on the jobs that Jews could hold, they formed a disproportionate number of the city's millers, and some of the protests about food shortages in 1917 were based upon groundless accusations of excessive profiteering by the Jewish community. In early 1918, there were strikes and riots in the city, followed by more unrest when the full details of the Brest-Litovsk talks became known. In April, a large crowd of Polish protesters entered the predominantly Jewish quarter of Kazimierz and looted indiscriminately; police officers did little to intervene. As the violence continued the following day, troops were deployed and managed to restore order, though not before Jewish groups had retaliated by attacking a market in the Christian part of the city. There were exchanges of fire between troops and rioters from both the Christian and Jewish communities and the violence continued in the following weeks, spreading into the countryside. The local military commander sent a warning to Vienna that the population was close to revolution; matters were made worse by large groups of army deserters who roamed through Galicia unchallenged, outnumbering and outgunning the few gendarmerie formations that might have intervened.[415] As food protests and riots broke out across the entire empire, many took an overtly anti-Semitic tinge. The suggestions that Jews had somehow taken advantage of the war for personal profit were almost all false, but much of central European society had been severely brutalised by the war and blaming the Jews for all misfortunes became an everyday part of culture in many societies, with terrible consequences a generation later.

The Poles were not the only nationality within the Austro-Hungarian Empire to demand a clean break. Even as late as 1917, many were still thinking in terms of greater autonomy within the empire; Anton Korošec, a Slovenian politician, called for a unified South Slav within the empire, enjoying the same rights as Hungary, and in a similar manner many within the Czech and Slovak lands demanded similar status.[416] Such demands were anathema to Hungary, which jealously guarded its special status within the empire, and Emperor Karl paid little heed to the Czechs, Slovaks and South Slavs, largely for two reasons. Firstly, he and those who advised him appear to have been genuinely blind to the resentment harboured by the various nationalities of the empire, for example, simply not understanding why the use of German as an official language was such a cause of anger. Secondly, he was careful not to risk offending the Hungarians.[417] Unable to secure support for a more federal empire – something that Franz Ferdinand had favoured before his assassination triggered the cascade of events that led to war in 1914 – the nationalist movements began to demand complete independence.

Throughout the war, there had been suspicion – not entirely misplaced – about the loyalty of Czech regiments, and several had surrendered en masse to the Russians. In 1914, Czech and Slovak émigrés in Russia successfully persuaded the tsar to create an army formation made up of their countrymen, and the first battalion of *Česká Družina* ('Czech Companions') joined the Russian Third Army shortly after.[418] One of their most important roles was to encourage their fellow countrymen to desert, but repeated requests to allow recruitment from those deserters were turned down by the Russian authorities. Nevertheless, the number of men serving with the companions steadily increased, largely because senior officers in the front line ignored rulings from Petrograd about not allowing prisoners of war to be recruited. In 1916, the men were reorganised first into a rifle regiment, then into a brigade of three regiments. The brigade saw action during the Brusilov Offensive of 1916 and again during the Kerensky Offensive, where they performed particularly well – as has already been described, their opponents, Czech soldiers of 19th Infantry Division, fought well initially, but when they realised that their opponents were their fellow countrymen discipline rapidly collapsed. With the fall of the tsar, the ban on recruiting from prisoners of war was abolished and more regiments were raised, first turning the brigade into a four-regiment Czech Division, then raising another four-regiment division which was added to its predecessor, forming the Czechoslovak Legion; eventually numbering some 40,000 men, the legion was predominantly Czech, with less than one tenth of its strength being Slovakian.

The rising tide of Czech and Slovak nationalism caused widespread unrest within the empire, giving rise to the Czechoslovak National Council in 1916, formed from émigrés living outside Habsburg control. Tomáš Masaryk, a leading figure in the council, travelled to Russia in 1918 to negotiate the withdrawal of the Czechoslovak Legion so that it could continue fighting the Central Powers on the Western Front and secured permission for it to withdraw by rail to Vladivostok, from where it would be transported to France by sea. When the talks at Brest-Litovsk broke down and Hoffmann launched his offensive in early 1918, the legion was caught up in heavy fighting against German and Austro-Hungarian troops at Bakhmach in Ukraine, eventually beating off repeated attacks and securing a truce that allowed its personnel to board trains for Siberia. The movement of the legion to the Pacific coast proved to be a drawn-out affair; the Bolsheviks were concerned that it would be used by White Russian commanders against them and insisted that it leave its weapons behind, while the soldiers of the legion were suspicious that the Bolsheviks had signed a secret agreement with the Central Powers to delay or prevent the redeployment of the Czechoslovak Legion. In May, soldiers of the legion intercepted a telegram sent by Trotsky ordering Bolshevik units along the railway to disarm all elements of the legion, using force if required.[419] Elements of the legion clashed in Chelyabinsk with Hungarian prisoners of war being transported west and shot a Hungarian who had thrown stones at their train. In retaliation, local Bolshevik authorities arrested several soldiers of the legion and announced they were to be executed. Incensed by this, the rest of the contingent of the legion stormed the prison and released their comrades, continuing their attacks until they controlled the entire city. As the Czechoslovak troops moved out from Chelyabinsk to capture further key cities along the Trans-Siberian Railway, swiftly securing Tomsk, Omsk and Samara, anti-Bolshevik forces farther east took advantage of the turmoil to rise up, and within weeks the Bolsheviks had lost control of all of Siberia. The Czechoslovak Legion extended its zone of influence as far as Ekaterinburg in the Urals; they captured the town a few weeks after the former tsar and his family had been murdered by the Bolsheviks.

Some – particularly the British – toyed with the idea of using the Czechoslovak Legion to overthrow the Bolsheviks and re-open the Eastern Front against the Central Powers, but the French were particularly adamant that the original plan to transport the men to the Western Front should prevail. Eventually, the French agreed to facilitate discussions between the various anti-Bolshevik factions in Siberia, but talks held during the summer in Chelyabinsk failed to achieve unity. As the Bolsheviks began to recover their poise and made progress in the western parts of Siberia, the factions met again in the autumn, first in Ufa and then in Omsk. During this period, only the two divisions of the Czechoslovak Legion proved to be effective anti-Bolshevik combatants, and when disorder broke out in Omsk and other areas within Siberia, one of the divisions was pulled out of the front and sent east to try to restore order. When White Russian authorities refused permission for the legion to use lethal force in Omsk, the leaders of the legion finally lost patience. By now, they had heard news of the imminent collapse of the Central Powers and the declaration of independence in Prague by Masaryk, and the men of the legion decided it was time to go home. They increasingly refused to take part in the fighting, instead taking control of large stretches of the Trans-Siberian Railway; eventually, they were allowed to evacuate via Vladivostok, the last men leaving Siberia in 1920, two years later than had originally been planned.[420]

In addition to civil unrest within the Austro-Hungarian Empire, there were also mutinies amongst the military. As was the case in Russia and Germany, trouble erupted in the fleet. On 1 February 1918 sailors aboard the cruiser *Sankt Georg* in Cattaro (now Kotor in Montenegro) refused to obey orders and shot and wounded the ship's second-in-command. They hoisted the red flag, and other ships in the port soon followed suit. There was a brisk traffic of small boats between the warships as the mutineers rapidly formed a committee; at first, they demanded better food and conditions, but rapidly escalated their demands to include political reforms, particularly an end to the war. Their list of demands explicitly included the adoption of the Russian principles of peace without annexations or reparations and the adoption of Woodrow Wilson's Fourteen Points, as well as the abolition of different food arrangements for officers and other ranks.

At first, the authorities attempted to negotiate with the mutineers, but on 3 February the arrival of ships from Pola (now Pula in Croatia) and a brief bombardment by shore-based artillery brought the mutiny to an end, with 385 men imprisoned and four suspected ringleaders executed. Almost all of the men who were arrested were pardoned before the end of the war.[421] In May, there was a wave of mutinies throughout the empire, particularly amongst replacement drafts and training formations; these were suppressed, but when new drafts were dispatched to the front line, they proved just as prone as German drafts to desert. Once they reached the front line, discipline was damaged by propaganda from the enemy, aided by worsening food shortages; despite the army ensuring that it had better food supplies than the civilian population, nutrition remained inadequate, and matters were in many respects worsened during late 1917 when German and *k.u.k.* troops advanced rapidly in northeast Italy. When they overran the trenches of the Italians, the soldiers of the Central Powers could see for themselves how well their enemies were supplied.

Just as the Germans gambled on a last offensive in northern France, the *k.u.k.* Army made a final attempt to overcome the Italians. A two-pronged attack was launched along the River Piave in June 1918, with little real confidence of success; within days, the assault was effectively over with little territory gained. Even if a breakthrough to and beyond Venice had been achieved, it is highly unlikely that Italy would have been sufficiently weakened to be knocked out of the war. The losses suffered by both sides were, as ever in the First World War, out of all proportion to the minimal changes in the front line; the *k.u.k.* Army lost 118,000 men killed, wounded or taken prisoner, compared to 43,000 Italian casualties. Warned by deserters of the imminent attack, the Italians bombarded the assault troops before they even left their trenches; those who pressed forward managed to secure a bridgehead across the Piave, but Italian artillery fire made it almost impossible to reinforce them, leaving them to be crushed. But despite the demands of the British and French, the Italians failed to launch a counteroffensive – their own losses had been sufficiently heavy to leave them too weak.

Even without an Italian counteroffensive, the impact of the failed attack was every bit as great as Ludendorff's failure in France. The fragile morale of the *k.u.k.* Army was irrevocably damaged; the various nationalist groups within the Austro-Hungarian Empire, already encouraged by Wilson's Fourteen Points and their insistence on self-determination, were emboldened to stronger action, and those who had the most to lose from the collapse of Habsburg rule became even more disheartened. Remarkably, this latter group included most Hungarians. Despite their constant bickering with Vienna and demand for greater concessions, the Hungarians knew that their best interests were served by remaining part of the empire, not least because they controlled substantial lands that would almost certainly be given independence if Austria-Hungary were to lose the war. István Tisza had been prime minister of Hungary for most of the war and repeatedly intervened in the narrow self-interest of Hungary, for example, over the question of food supplies from Hungary for the rest of the empire, but he remained committed to the continuation of the empire and to retaining the privileged position of the Hungarian elite. He opposed all attempts to increase the voting franchise, which was widely misused by rich Hungarian landowners to ensure that their party remained in power, even opposing demands that war veterans should be given the right to vote on the grounds that such a move would extend the franchise to those who were not ready for such responsibilities.[422] His growing conflict with the reform-minded Emperor Karl led to his resignation in May 1917. His replacements – first Móric Esterházy, then Sándor Wekerle – found that their predecessor retained sufficient influence to prevent reforms from being enacted.

Despite having no military experience, Tisza volunteered for service in the army after resigning as prime minister and served as a colonel in a hussar regiment on the Italian Front. He worked hard to win the loyalty of his men, using his pay to improve their rations and his political and judicial contacts to aid them with their grievances. In September 1918, he travelled through the Balkan region at the request of Emperor Karl to investigate the worsening problems of food supply. In Sarajevo, local representatives asked for his support in their demands for a variety of measures such as the release of political prisoners and compensation for war losses. Still adhering with determination to his opposition to any greater liberties for the South Slavs, Tisza treated them brusquely and dismissively. Shortly after his return to Budapest, as revolution broke out across the Hungarian capital, a group of mutinous soldiers broke into his home and murdered him.

The alliance between Germany and Austria-Hungary was rarely comfortable, and the growing dependence of the latter upon the former caused resentment on both sides. As has already been described, Karl used his accession as an opportunity to explore possible avenues for a negotiated peace, and in his private exchanges with the French via Sixtus, he expressed on more than one occasion the right of France to recover Alsace and Lorraine. Those exchanges now came back to haunt him. After the completion of the Brest-Litovsk negotiations, Karl's foreign minister Czernin made a speech on 2 April in Vienna, attacking the position of Georges Clemenceau, currently serving as France's minister of war:

> Some time before the beginning of the offensive in the west, Clemenceau asked me if I was prepared to negotiate, and on what basis. In agreement with Berlin, I replied immediately that I was ready for this, and with regard to France could see no obstacle to peace other than the French desire for [the return of] Alsace-Lorraine. A response came from Paris that on that basis, it was not possible to negotiate.[423]

Ten days later, Clemenceau retaliated by publishing the first letter that he had received from Sixtus, making clear that Karl recognised the legitimacy of France's claim to its lost provinces. This created a crisis in both Vienna and Berlin; Czernin had not seen the details of the correspondence that Karl had passed to Sixtus, and of course Berlin knew almost nothing of the exchanges. The kaiser and his advisors were both shocked and angry at what they saw as an act of betrayal, and for a while there was a serious possibility of Germany sending its troops into Austria to occupy the country. Such fears were ultimately groundless, not least because the German Army had no troops to spare for such an operation, but relations between the two Central Powers became extremely difficult. In an attempt to placate the Germans, Czernin first denied that he had known anything about the negotiations the previous year, and then persuaded Karl to send a letter to Berlin stating that Sixtus had exceeded his brief, and that Clemenceau was lying about any Austrian assurances about Alsace and Lorraine. He also urged the emperor to consider stepping down from his official duties, if only as a temporary measure; when Karl refused, he submitted his resignation.

Finally, Karl was able to assuage the anger of the Germans by making a personal visit to *OHL* in Spa on 12 May, where he gave Wilhelm every possible assurance of Austria-Hungary's commitment to the alliance. It was the final death of any possible opportunity for Karl to negotiate a separate peace – for better or for worse, the fortunes of his empire were now inextricably bound to those of Germany. Furthermore, it was the end of any independent foreign policy on the part of Vienna. The Germans had long been the dominant partners in military affairs, and now they assumed supremacy in the diplomatic arena too.

The final fallout of the Sixtus Affair had an impact within the empire too. It confirmed the inferior status of Austria-Hungary within the alliance with Germany, and it badly damaged Karl's personal credibility. Until now, the personal authority of the Habsburg monarchy had been the final thread holding the empire together, and this blow to Karl's standing further accelerated the sense that everything was unravelling. The Empress Zita came under growing criticism and suspicion on account of her Franco-Italian origins, in a manner dangerously reminiscent of the treatment of Tsarina Alexandra. But, unlike the situation in Russia immediately before the revolution, there was little direct animosity towards the Habsburgs; the mood was more one of indifference. They were simply becoming irrelevant to the future of the constituent parts of the empire.

As the scale of Ludendorff's failure to achieve a decisive victory in France became clear, the Austro-Hungarian administration tried with increasing desperation to find a way out of the war. On 13 August, Karl travelled to Spa again to meet Wilhelm, and the two men concluded that they would have to adopt a strategy of defensive warfare. Karl made clear to the Germans that there was no prospect of the empire surviving another winter of war and suggested a preliminary conference in neutral Holland to explore possibilities for peace.

Whilst Wilhelm was not averse to this suggestion, Hindenburg urged both rulers to remain strong in the hope that the Entente Powers would finally become too exhausted to continue the war. But it was increasingly clear to both emperors that nothing short of the destruction of the Central Powers would satisfy their enemies; with the prospect of military victory growing stronger, the Entente Powers showed not the slightest signs of the exhaustion for which Hindenburg hoped. It was the last time that Karl and Wilhelm would meet. On his return to Vienna, Karl instructed his ministers to draw up a proposal for the exploratory peace talks, but the Germans now expressed reluctance to proceed until the military situation had at least stabilised. Increasingly desperate, the Austro-Hungarian foreign ministry insisted that further delay would be disastrous; the Germans responded that such a peace initiative would itself be a catastrophic mistake, but in mid-September Karl presented the Germans with a fait accompli, unilaterally sending out a note to the Entente Powers. The response was disheartening in the extreme. Robert Lansing, the American Secretary of State, made a public rejection of the proposal; Clemenceau's response was even brusquer. He simply referred Vienna to a speech he had made in the French Senate in which he had proclaimed: 'On to total victory!'[424] A further sign of the continuing breakdown in relations between the Central Powers can be seen in the manner in which Berlin made its final appeals to Wilson for an armistice, without even informing Vienna.

On 2 October, Karl instructed his prime minister to inform the Austrian parliament that the empire was to be reorganised along federal lines, regardless of the objections of Hungary. A year earlier, such a move might have been effective, but it was now too late. Representatives of the Slovenian, Croatian and Serbian regions of the empire met in Zagreb a few days later and announced that they were the only legitimate representatives of their people, and similar developments in Poland and the Romanian parts of Bukovina followed. There were further discussions in Vienna on how to proceed, and again the Hungarians refused to budge on concessions to the South Slavs – Prime Minister Sándor Wekerle even threatened to cease all food deliveries across the border if Karl attempted to impose his will.

In mid-October, Karl made a further announcement, hoping that while it excluded Hungary, it would go far enough to satisfy Woodrow Wilson's insistence on the rights of people to self-determination:

> Austria will become a federal state in accordance with the will of its peoples; each nationality will create its own administration within the area where it dwells.

> This arrangement will not interfere with the union between Austria's Polish territories and the independent Polish state. The city of Trieste and the surrounding area will receive a special status, consistent with the wishes of the population.
>
> This new arrangement, which in no way will disturb the integrity of the lands of the Holy Crown of Hungary, will guarantee self-determination to each of the individual national states. But it will also protect the common interests, and above all prove its worth in areas where inter-cooperation is a vital necessity for the individual components. In particular all our strength will be exerted to justly and economically address the great challenges posed by the effects of the war.
>
> Until the changes are legally implemented, the current institutions will remain in place to protect common interests … I call upon all the peoples, whose right to self-determination will be the foundation of the new empire, to participate in this great project through national councils to be formed from the *Reichsrat* deputies of each nation; they will regulate the relationships of the peoples with each other and with my government.
>
> Thus our fatherland, fortified by the harmony of the nations of which it is composed, may emerge from the storm of the war as a league of free peoples.[425]

Increasingly, the different nationalities regarded Karl as having no legitimacy to speak on their behalf. The growing independence of regions of the empire further exacerbated the chronic food shortages, as agricultural areas followed the unfortunate example set by Hungary and simply refused to export their surplus, and central imperial authorities found themselves powerless to impose their will. This inability of the imperial government to ensure adequate food supplies for its people was ultimately the decisive demonstration of its impotence and irrelevance. Strikes, particularly in the coalmines, exacerbated the problem by reducing the ability of the railways to function. And a further resurgence of influenza added to the misery of a malnourished population. Unable to ensure the maintenance of order with the police and gendarmerie, the authorities used regular army formations; when these were needed for front-line service, the war ministry refused to release them until they could be replaced by drafts of new recruits. Morale in the army was already low, on account of weariness, poor rations, the endless bad news from the front line, and the impact of Karl's manifesto on reorganising the empire; the use of troops to suppress internal dissent only worsened matters. Mihály Károlyi, who led the Hungarian National Council, was appointed prime minister of Hungary by Karl as the only popular figure who might be able to prevent a descent into revolution, but instead of buttressing the position of the emperor he issued a statement calling on Hungarian soldiers to return home. Whatever unity remained in the army now unravelled further.

In the last week of October, as the Italians launched a major attack that would lead to the complete collapse of the *k.u.k.* Army, people gathered in Wenceslas Square in Prague, where a Czech national committee had taken control of the local grain office. Acting on the announcements of a federal future, the committee took on an increasingly governmental role and imperial officials did nothing to interfere. Careful to ensure that existing laws remained in force in order to prevent a descent into anarchy, local activists and politicians rapidly spread their control over the Czech and Slovak lands. A revolution was avoided, but the price was a degree of unrest that continued for several years.

Even in German-speaking Austria, the remit of the imperial government was fast disappearing. The *Provisorische Nationalversammlung für Deutschösterreich* ('Provisional National Assembly for German Austria') was formed in Vienna. The collapse of the Italian Front, together with the advance of British, French and Serbian troops following the withdrawal of Bulgaria from the war, led to the signing of an armistice, first with Italy on 4 November and then with the rest of the Entente Powers on 11 November. In order to ensure that they were not left out of any post-war settlement, the Romanians rejected the peace treaty signed in Bucharest and resumed hostilities just one day before the end of the war.

On 11 November, Karl issued a final proclamation as king and emperor:

> Since my accession to the throne I have tried incessantly to lead my people from the horrors of the war, in the outbreak of which I had no blame whatever.
>
> I have not hesitated to restore constitutional life and have opened the way for the people to independent development.
>
> As always, full of immutable love for all people, I do not wish my person to stand as an obstacle in their free development.
>
> I accept in advance the decision of German Austria about the future form of its government.
>
> Through their representatives, the people have taken control of the government. I renounce all part in state affairs.
>
> At the same time I relieve all of my Austrian government of their duties.
>
> May the people of German Austria create and establish the new order in harmony and distinction. The happiness of my people was from the outset my greatest wish.
>
> Only inner peace can heal the wounds of this war.[426]

The Provisional Assembly in Vienna formally took power, creating the Republic of German Austria with claims to substantial territories in the Tyrol and Bohemia;

it also incorporated within its constitution a right to seek union with Germany. The Entente Powers had no intention of allowing such a move, and ensured that many of the territories demanded by German Austria were assigned to the new Czechoslovakia. This was contrary to Wilson's Fourteen Points and their insistence on the rights of people to self-determination, and crucially it also left substantial numbers of German-speaking people on the wrong side of the new borders, sowing the seeds for a future conflict.

In Hungary, Károlyi increasingly followed a policy of seeking independence from Vienna. He did not rule out the continuation of Karl as King of Hungary, and in order to prevent a huge diminution of Hungarian territory he proposed the creation of a federal state along similar lines to Karl's suggestions for Austria, with Romanian, Slovakian and South Slav areas being granted a degree of autonomy. As was the case with Karl's plans, it was far too late for such a proposal, which was further undermined by Hungary's long history of refusing to grant any degree of independence to such regions. Inevitably, the Romanians, Slovaks and South Slavs – encouraged by the Entente Powers – preferred to seek a future outside the remit of the Hungarian state, rather than trust the Hungarians to deliver on the promises of their prime minister. On 16 November, Hungary declared itself a republic, hoping that by severing all of its links with Austria it would be spared the wrath of the Entente Powers. It proved to be a vain hope, and, over the following months, territory was cut away and handed to Hungary's neighbours. In March 1919, after the prime minister resigned rather than accept responsibility for the loss of so much land and such a large proportion of Hungary's pre-war population, the communists seized power, establishing the Hungarian Soviet Republic. An attempt by the Hungarian Social Democrats to take power in June 1919 led to wide-scale repression, and the republic found itself at war with the resurgent Romania and Czechoslovakia. Whilst the Hungarians enjoyed a brief period of success against Czechoslovakia, the Romanian Army proved to be far more powerful and the entry of Romanian troops into Budapest on 6 August brought the Soviet Republic to an end. After a new period of violence, in which the communists and their supporters were purged, persecuted and in many cases killed, a new Kingdom of Hungary was established in 1920. There was no prospect of the Entente Powers or Hungary's neighbours allowing Karl to resume as King of Hungary, and Miklós Horthy, who had been the last commander-in-chief of the Austro-Hungarian Navy, became regent.

Farther east, the end of Habsburg rule was more chaotic. Troops in Lemberg took control of the city at the beginning of November and a few days later declared the creation of a new West Ukrainian People's Republic. Immediately, fighting broke out with the Poles, who wished to ensure that the city would be a part of Poland. By the end of the month, the Poles were in control of Lemberg, assigning the city its Polish name of Lvov. The Jewish population, which had tried to remain neutral in the fighting, was subjected to a brutal pogrom.[427]

Karl maintained that his abdication proclamation was effectively forced upon him under duress, and that he did not feel bound by it. He left Vienna for Switzerland in March 1919, announcing that he still claimed his rights as sovereign.[428] A month later, the Austrian government passed a law that placed a permanent ban on the return of the royal couple to Austria, and allowed other Habsburgs to return only if they explicitly renounced all claims to the throne. After attempts to take up the throne of Hungary failed in 1921, Karl and Zita were taken to the city of Baja on the Danube, where they were placed aboard a British warship. They were then taken to Madeira; the following year, Karl developed pneumonia and died, aged 34. He was the last monarch of a great family that claimed to trace its lineage back to Gerard I, Count of Paris, in the 8th century. He was regarded by many as being too weak for the role that was assigned to him, but it is difficult to see how anyone could have prevailed in the dire circumstances of the Austro-Hungarian Empire in 1917–1918. He sincerely tried to secure peace for his people, but the zero-sum aims of both the Germans on the one hand and the Anglo-French politicians on the other left no room whatsoever for any compromise. He was strongly conscious of his duties as the leading monarch of the Roman Catholic world, and recently he has been beatified, an act that many regard as controversial because he authorised the use of poison gas during his brief time as a military commander. Crown Prince Otto, his eldest child, who would have succeeded him to the Habsburg throne, died in July 2011, aged 98.

CHAPTER 14

THE PYGMY WARS: ESTONIA

The most northerly parts of the tsar's empire that faced the Baltic Sea, Finland and Estonia, had longstanding ethnic, linguistic and cultural links. Like Latvia to the south, Estonia was home to Estonians, Russians who had settled in the area, and ethnic Germans – in the main, wealthy landowners, some of whom were descendants of settlers who had moved into the region during the time of the Teutonic and Livonian Knights. These German families had historically been staunch supporters of the tsars, in return for which they were granted considerable privileges, but during the 19th century there was a steady increase in Estonian nationalist feeling. Tsar Nicholas' deliberate policy of Russification caused great resentment, leading to uprisings during the 1905 Revolution, followed by repression when Russian authority was restored.

Following the February Revolution and the fall of the tsar, Estonian leaders demanded greater independence. After some hesitation – due as much to the chaos in Petrograd as to any unwillingness to reduce the degree of control over Estonia – the Russian authorities gave permission in April 1917 for the creation of the Autonomous Governate of Estonia, followed three months later by an elected National Council, or *Maapäev*, led by Konstantin Päts. The degree of independence that would be granted to this new body remained the subject of disagreement, but just a few days before the October Revolution, the Estonian Bolsheviks under Jaan Anvelt seized power in Tallinn. The Bolshevik movement was not strong in Estonia and Anvelt struggled to establish any authority; in any case, his time in office proved to be short-lived, as German troops advanced almost unopposed into Estonia on the northern flank of Hoffmann's offensive following the collapse of the Brest-Litovsk talks, and together with other Bolsheviks he fled to Russia. On 24 February, the *Maapäev* issued a declaration of Estonian independence, assuring full rights to all minorities and ending with a national rallying cry:

> ESTONIA!
>
> You stand on the threshold of a future full of hope in which you shall be free and independent in determining and directing your destiny! Begin building a home of your own, ruled by law and order, in order to be a worthy member of the family of civilised nations! Sons and daughters of our homeland, unite as one in the sacred task of building our homeland! The sweat and blood shed by our ancestors for this country demand this from us; our forthcoming generations oblige us to do this.[429]

For Estonia, it was a unique moment: the nation had never known independence before. On this occasion, it proved to be very short-lived. German troops arrived in Tallinn two days later and refused to recognise the declaration. The *Maapäev* was forced to go into hiding.

The Estonians had started to organise a national army, but the Germans rapidly declared this illegal and arrested several leading Estonian figures, including Päts, who was imprisoned first in Estonia, and ultimately in Grodno in Poland. Despite this, Estonian independence was recognised by the Entente Powers, and, with the tide turning against Germany on the Western Front, many in Estonia looked forward to the future with real hope. The Germans had their own plans for Estonia and tried to create a new political entity combining Estonia with much of Latvia under the control of the Baltic Germans, who were encouraged to declare the creation of the *Baltischer Staat* or Baltic State, with its capital in Riga. The first head of this new state was to be Adolf Friedrich, Duke of Mecklenburg, but the Baltic State would be an autonomous part of the German Empire. Until Adolf Friedrich could take up office, a regency council of ten – four Baltic Germans, three Latvians, and three Estonians – ran the government in Riga under the close watch of *Ober Ost*.

Only Germany recognised the status of the new Baltic administration, and as it became increasingly clear in Berlin that the war would end unfavourably, attempts were made to try to create a government that would be acceptable both to the Estonians and the rest of the world. In October, Prince Max von Bayern sent a telegram to *Ober Ost* with instructions to set up a civilian administration; the intention was to create a series of such governments in the territories overseen by *Ober Ost*, starting in the Baltic region, but time ran out before the policy could even begin.[430] After the end of hostilities in the west, Konstantin Päts was released from captivity and recognised by the new German government as the head of the Estonian government.

As German authority collapsed, Päts struggled to create the institutions that would be vital for the survival of an independent Estonia. In particular, he needed to create an army that could protect the nation from a variety of forces. Ever since the establishment of the *Maapäev*, a paramilitary *Omakaitse* ('Citizen's Defence Organisation') had existed, with Ernst Põdder, a former officer in the Russian Army, as its commander. During the German occupation, the *Omakaitse* was forced to operate clandestinely, but with political control back in the hands of the Estonians, the force was now organised to deal with the multitude of threats that the fledgling nation faced.

There were several military powers operating within Estonia. By far the largest was the German Army, which was in the process of withdrawing and returning home in keeping with the terms of the Armistice. As morale in the army collapsed, many soldiers didn't wait for orders and simply drifted away from their formations, attempting to make their way home, but most continued to obey orders. Päts tried in vain to persuade the Germans to hand over weaponry to the *Omakaitse*, but in the main, the Germans either took their weapons home with them or destroyed them.[431] Fortunately for the Estonians, help was at hand. The newly independent Finland to the north, whose people had a long history of links with the Estonians, provided both weapons and ammunition, though in limited amounts.

In addition to the Germans, there were large numbers of anti-Bolshevik Russian troops in Estonia. These formations had largely been raised from released Russian prisoners of war and anti-Bolshevik Russians who first gathered in Pskov where their officers squabbled ineffectively amongst themselves over questions of precedence. From there, they were forced to flee to Estonia, where General Alexander Pavlovich Rodzianko – the nephew of the former chair of the Duma – managed to organise them into something resembling a military formation that now became known as the White Russian Northern Corps. Whilst Rodzianko remained its commander, the corps was subordinated to General Nikolai Nikolaevich Yudenich, who had commanded the Russian Caucasus Army during the First World War. In some respects, his appearance was deceptive; contemporaries described him 'physically slack and entirely lacking in those inspiring qualities which a political and military leader of his standing should possess'.[432] Despite this, he achieved considerable successes against the Turks during the war, but after the fall of the tsar he was dismissed from his post for insubordination and returned to Petrograd. He was involved in the attempt by Kornilov to oust the Kerensky government in August 1918 and fled to Finland when Kornilov and his associates

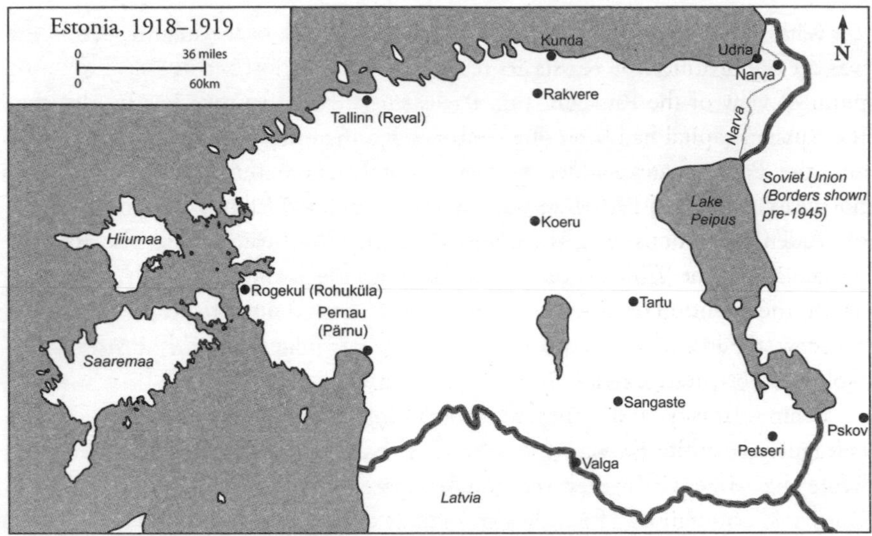

were arrested. In Finland, Yudenich joined the 'Russian Committee', an organisation set up to oppose the Bolsheviks, and was appointed commander of all White Russian forces in the northwest. Like many Russian generals of the tsarist era, he was bound by the prejudices with which he had grown up, and he refused to accept the reality of independent Finland. Rather than try to build an alliance with the strongly anti-Bolshevik Finns, he preferred to relocate to Estonia, where he created the Northern Corps. Whilst this force would be prepared to fight against any Bolshevik intervention, the presence of so many foreign soldiers was nonetheless not entirely welcome to the Estonians.

As the fighting on the Western Front drew to a close, a Bolshevik intervention in the Baltic region grew ever more likely. Lenin had never intended to be bound by the terms of the Treaty of Brest-Litovsk, and the collapse of Germany effectively made the treaty meaningless. The Red Army, successor to the Russian Army of the tsars, was now a far more powerful force than it had been when Hoffmann brushed it aside in early 1918, though it remained very limited in terms of logistic and other support. The disorganised, untrained Red Guards had undergone at least a degree of formal training, and the incorporation of large numbers of soldiers from the Imperial Russian Army further improved the overall level of practical knowledge and ability in the front line. Nevertheless, whilst it could probably fight and win short campaigns, sustained operations still posed huge challenges for the Red Army.

With the dissolution of *Ober Ost* and the departure of German troops, there was an opportunity for Russia to regain some of its lost territories. From the point of view of the Russians, this was essential. Prior to the First World War, the Russian capital had been safe from foreign invasion, but the loss of Finland and the Baltic States suddenly created a substantial threat. From Narva in northeast Estonia to Petrograd was a mere 81 miles (130km), and the presence of Yudenich's troops was therefore a significant threat to the Bolsheviks, particularly as the White forces in the Caucasus, Siberia and Ukraine had already drawn the attention of much of the Red Army. Even though the capital was now Moscow, the loss of such a major city would be a huge – possibly irrecoverable – blow to the prestige of any Russian government.

Lenin, Trotsky and other leading Bolsheviks had every reason to feel beleaguered. White Russian forces were threatening from the east and south, while the western fringe of the Russian Empire had been torn away by the Germans. Throughout 1917, British, French and American ships had brought a steady stream of war materiel to Archangelsk in the north, but the growing disruption of the Russian railways after the February Revolution resulted in large stockpiles building up around the port. When Goltz and the Baltic Division were landed in Finland, there were concerns that the Germans might be able to capture the stockpiles in northern Russia; rather more realistically, the Western Powers had no intention of allowing the stockpiles of modern armaments to fall into the hands of the Bolsheviks, who had made no secret of their intention to export their revolution to the rest of the world. There had been widespread agreement that the troops of the Czechoslovak Legion should be enabled to reach Western Europe, but now that they were embroiled in the Russian Civil War, the presence of western troops in Archangelsk might provide an opportunity for concerted action to overthrow the Bolsheviks. To that end, a mixed force of British, Australian, French, American, and even Serbian and Polish troops was dispatched to Archangelsk. Many of the British contingent were marines who had little experience of war; some were very young, and others were former prisoners of war who had recently been released by the Germans. In some cases, they were denied home leave and were dispatched to northern Russia at short notice, resulting in widespread morale problems. Once there, they found themselves slowly drawn into combat against the Bolsheviks. They succeeded in advancing about 100 miles (160km) south along the railway line leading to the Russian interior before a decision was made to pull back to a tighter perimeter and ultimately to evacuate the expedition entirely; after suffering losses in an attack on a Russian village, one British company of marines mutinied and refused to attack again. Several men were court-martialled and condemned to death, but after intervention by British politicians the sentences were not carried out.[433]

The opportunity to strike a potentially decisive blow against one of these hostile powers encircling Russia was therefore most attractive to the Bolsheviks. Although this has been described as the Soviet Westward Offensive, and according to one source was given the codename 'Target Vistula', it seems that there was no central planned offensive.[434] Rather, a series of uncoordinated movements occurred in the same region, with little if any overall coordination. However, the animosity of the Soviet leadership towards the Baltic States certainly played a part in the development of events. Lenin told his staff:

> Cross the frontier somewhere, even if only to the depth of a kilometre, and hang 100-1000 of their civil servants and rich people.[435]

As with so many wars, the geography of the region dictated the course of the campaigns. The border between Estonia and Russia is dominated by Lake Peipus, with the result that land routes for combat operations are either north or south of the lake. To the north, the confrontation would be across the River Narva, with the city of Narva itself forming part of the battlefield. This area offered the most direct route for a Russian advance towards the Estonian capital, Tallinn (previously known to both the Russians and Germans as Reval), but the northern flank of any such operation would be exposed unless the sea was controlled by the Russian Navy. Consequently, naval operations would play a major role in the fighting. To the south of Lake Peipus, any Russian advance to the Baltic coast, roughly along the border between Latvia and Estonia, could conceivably come under pressure from either flank. As a result of these geographic constraints the conflict in the northern part of the Baltic region, which became known as the Estonian War of Independence, saw repeated thrusts by either side north of Lake Peipus, and although the same territory changed hands on several occasions to the south of the lake, the fighting tended to follow the same pattern: a Bolshevik advance, and an Estonian counterattack against its flanks.

The most northerly Soviet formation involved in the offensive was the Seventh Red Army under the command of the Latvian Jukums Vācietis, who attacked towards Narva with 6th Red Rifle Division. The experienced core of the old Russian Army was gone; many of its troops, sick of the war, had returned to their homes and had no desire to take part in further fighting, and few officers of the old army were regarded as acceptable by the Bolsheviks. The division was made up of volunteers, many of them from the Narva region, with just a sprinkling of veterans. Opposing them were elements of the Estonian Defence League and the German Infantry Regiment 405, originally part of 203rd Infantry Division and the only organised German formation left in northeast Estonia. After a brief battle on 28 November 1918, in which the Soviet armoured cruiser *Oleg* and two destroyers supported the main attack, the Germans and Estonians retreated from Narva, leaving the city in Russian hands. A few days later, the 6th Red Rifle Division pushed on towards Tallinn, and though the newly created units of the Estonian Army, ill-equipped and poorly trained, were dispatched to the front as they became available, the Russians seized Rakvere on 15 December and Koeru ten days later, finally reaching a point only 21 miles (34km) from the Estonian capital by the end of the year.

At the same time, a second Soviet advance developed from south of Lake Peipus. The Soviet 2nd Novgorod Division began to attack westward on 25 November, and made good progress in the face of weak resistance by the White Russian Northern Corps. The 49th Red Latvian Rifle Regiment, part of the 2nd Novgorod Division, took Tartu on 24 December, leaving more than half of Estonia in Russian hands by 1919, but this success was to mark the high-water mark of the Russian advance. Heavy snow, poor roads, and a chaotic supply situation made the prospect of further gains very unlikely without major reinforcements.

In the areas occupied by the Bolsheviks, there was widespread repression of anyone suspected as being a nationalist. In addition, the Bolshevik policy of targeting the 'bourgeois classes' resulted in a variety of individuals, from clergy to teachers, being arrested and shot. It has been estimated that over 500 people lost their lives as a result; not a huge number in the context of the deaths in the First World War, but sufficient to encourage a growth in partisan activity, which further disrupted Russian supply lines.[436]

The reduction of territory controlled by the Estonian nationalists worked in favour of the defenders, who now contended with much shorter supply lines. Colonel Johan Laidoner, who like most Baltic officers of his generation had served in the tsar's armies, had commanded the Estonian Army's first formations, hastily grouped together into an infantry division, and on 23 December was appointed commander of the entire army. He used the lull in fighting to good effect, creating a second infantry division and the staff of a third. In addition, the country's German community raised a Baltic Battalion of volunteers, a welcome boost both in military and symbolic terms: Estonia's Baltic Germans were explicitly supporting the Estonian government, rather than seeking to secure control themselves, as the Germans had originally intended. Almost immediately, the Baltic Battalion was deployed in the front facing towards Narva. The dockyards and railway works of Tallinn improvised a variety of armoured cars for the Estonian Army, which despite their limited mobility – they were badly underpowered and became bogged down in even slightly soft ground – proved to be effective weapons, not least because of the fear with which they were regarded by many in the Red Army.[437] Whilst the old Russian Army had possessed large numbers of armoured cars – mainly supplied by Britain and France – and Bolshevik units elsewhere, even in Latvia, still operated many of these vehicles, they were conspicuously absent from Red Army units in the far north.

Help for Estonia also arrived from the west. Even as the war in the west came to an end, British officials were discussing how to further the cause of anti-Bolshevik forces. Lord Balfour, the British foreign secretary, wrote a memorandum in November, concluding:

> For us no alternative is open at present than to use such troops as we possess to the best advantage; where we have no troops, to supply arms and money; and in the case of the Baltic provinces, to protect, as far as we can, the nascent nationalities with our fleet.[438]

As the Red Army pressed into Estonia, a delegation arrived in London to seek support. British diplomats responded that it would not be possible to send troops, but warships and armaments might be available, leading immediately to objections from the navy; the Baltic area was heavily mined and it was unwise to dispatch warships before the mines had been cleared. Nevertheless, the political necessity to intervene in the Baltic overruled purely naval concerns and on 22 November, after escorting the German High Seas Fleet into British waters where it was to be interned, the light cruiser HMS *Cardiff* and four other cruisers of the 6th Light Cruiser Squadron set off for the Baltic, accompanied by nine destroyers and seven minesweepers, under the collective command of Rear-Admiral Edwyn Alexander-Sinclair. The orders issued to him were a masterpiece of vagueness: he was to proceed to Libau (now Liepāja) and thence to Tallinn, 'to show the British flag and support British policy as circumstances dictate'. He took with him a substantial store of weapons and ammunition and was to advise the governments of both Estonia and Latvia that they had to be responsible for their own defence. In the event of interference by Bolshevik warships, he would be able to call on the support of British battleships, which would soon deploy to Copenhagen.[439]

Problems in obtaining sufficient fuel supplies – the minesweepers of Alexander-Sinclair's force were coal-fired – led to the warships proceeding beyond

Denmark without the minesweeper force. Late at night on 5 December, as they sailed past the Estonian island archipelago that had been the scene of fighting in 1917, the warships found themselves in a previously unsuspected German minefield. HMS *Cassandra* struck a mine and rapidly sank; all but 11 of her crew were rescued. Two accompanying sloops were also lost to mines. A second cruiser, HMS *Calypso*, had been damaged after striking a submerged wreck, and two destroyers sustained light damage when they collided with each other; the rescued crew of *Cassandra* was placed aboard these three ships, which returned to Britain.

The somewhat diminished British force arrived in Tallinn on 7 December, where it received an enthusiastic welcome. With Russian forces close to his capital, the increasingly desperate Päts suggested that Estonia should become a British protectorate and that Britain should immediately deploy troops in the Baltic region. This was clearly contrary to the intentions of the British, who nevertheless reassured Päts that guns and ammunition were en route (they were being carried by the minesweepers, which were still awaiting coal in Copenhagen). Unwilling to allow the Bolsheviks a free hand, Alexander-Sinclair decided to interpret his instructions as loosely as possible and on 13 December dispatched two cruisers and five destroyers east along the coastline to a point near Narva, where they brought the coastal road under shellfire and destroyed a vital bridge, further disrupting the supply lines of the Seventh Red Army. A few days later, the British ships helped land a force of Estonians on the coast to operate in the rear of the Bolshevik troops. At about the same time, as if to confirm the upswing in the fortunes of Estonia, the first of 2,000 Finnish volunteers began to disembark from ships in Tallinn.[440]

The Russian naval authorities suspected the presence of British warships from interception of wireless traffic but were uncertain of their strength. The fleet in Kronstadt was in poor shape following the October Revolution, and attempts to carry out a reconnaissance of Tallinn by submarine were unsuccessful, with repeated mechanical problems; as will be seen, this was a recurrent issue. Many ships had been poorly maintained during the First World War, and spare parts for the vessels – most of which had been built outside Russia – were hard to obtain. Even when they were available, the Bolsheviks often lacked skilled engineers to carry out repairs.

After the British bombardment that disrupted supply lines between Narva and the front line, Vācietis asked for naval support for his Seventh Army. On 24 December, a task force consisting of the battleship *Andrei Pervozvanni*, the cruiser *Oleg* and three destroyers was assembled under the command of Fyodor Fyodorovich Raskolnikov, the commissar of the Baltic Fleet, with orders to carry out an armed reconnaissance and to destroy the British warships – but only if the balance of power was strongly in favour of the Russian force. It is likely that this group of vessels represented a very large proportion of all the warships in Kronstadt that were seaworthy. A plan was drawn up for the destroyers *Spartak* and *Avtroil* to penetrate into Tallinn harbour, where, in addition to looking for British warships, they would shell two small islands to determine whether any defensive batteries had been positioned there. Should they encounter British forces, they were to withdraw towards the island of Gogland, where *Oleg* would be waiting; if a further withdrawal were required, the three ships would pull back towards Kronstadt, in order to bring the pursuing British ships within range of *Andrei Pervozvanni* and her 12-inch guns.

Raskolnikov had played an important part in the Kronstadt Mutiny of 1917, and had held a variety of posts since the October Revolution. He arrived in Kronstadt on 25 December to discover that the destroyer *Avtroil* had developed mechanical problems. Rather than delay the operation, he decided to proceed with only *Spartak*. As *Spartak* set off, Raskolnikov received a signal that the destroyer *Azard*, which had been patrolling the area and therefore might have been available to him as a replacement for the *Avtroil*, was unable to accompany the mission due to a shortage of coal. Towards dusk, *Spartak* encountered the Russian submarine *Pantera*, which was returning from a reconnaissance of Tallinn. The submarine reported no sign of any smoke rising from ships in the Estonian port, but a later account suggested that, like other Soviet submarines, the *Pantera* probably didn't enter the port at all due to major mechanical problems and was forced to make its observations from some distance. *Spartak* and *Oleg* dropped anchor and spent the night near Gogland. The following morning, they waited in vain for *Avtroil* to join them, and when they received a signal informing Raskolnikov that the destroyer's mechanical problems showed no sign of resolution, the commissar decided to press on with just *Spartak*; *Oleg* would wait near Gogland to provide support should the destroyer make a hasty withdrawal.

Alexander-Sinclair's force had undergone further changes. As will be described later, the situation in Latvia required urgent intervention and he dispatched two of his cruisers and half his destroyers to Liepāja; the return of *Calypso* and the much-delayed arrival of the minesweepers was therefore greatly welcomed, not least by the Estonians who took possession of the 5,000 rifles and other weapons that had been brought to equip their army. The crews of the British warships had been invited to a civic reception on 26 December and the enthusiasm of the sailors was probably considerably enhanced by the promise of a dance after the dinner, for which women would be 'hired'. While preparations for the event were under way, there was the sound of distant naval gunfire. Reports arrived swiftly that a Russian vessel had been spotted in Tallinn Bay, attempting to bombard coastal positions. The British personnel hastily returned to their ships and began to prepare for action. As smoke began to rise from the funnels of the two British cruisers and four destroyers, Raskolnikov ordered *Spartak* to reverse its course in order to draw the British onto the guns of *Oleg*.

Raskolnikov's plan had always been ambitious: his destroyer was nearly 90 miles (145km) from Gogland, and even at maximum speed it would take nearly three hours to reach the *Oleg*. Although the British cruisers had a similar maximum speed to the *Spartak*, the accompanying destroyers were faster, and any mishap aboard the Soviet destroyer – mechanical problems, or damage from British shellfire – might prove fatal. Like *Avtroil*, *Spartak* was not in perfect condition and almost inevitably developed engine problems as she attempted a sustained period of maximum speed. As the British destroyers closed in, *Spartak*'s bow gun tried to fire on the pursuing vessels. To do this, the turret had to be traversed until it was pointing back past the bridge, and when the gun was fired, its blast demolished *Spartak*'s charthouse and damaged both her bridge and helm.[441] Shortly after, the destroyer ran aground on the Kuradimuna sandbank. Attempts to scuttle the destroyer failed when the seacocks jammed, and British sailors from the destroyer HMS *Wakeful* came aboard to seize the ship. Raskolnikov attempted to hide in the hold under several sacks of potatoes, but was taken prisoner together with the rest of the crew.

One of the officers aboard HMS *Caradoc* later wrote an account describing the state of *Spartak* and her crew:

> The crew themselves, very dirty and in a dreadfully dirty ship, appeared pleased at being captured. Many of them had articles of various sorts, such as cameras and furs, obviously looted from shops and houses, which they sold to our crew at ridiculous prices, some even offering the things gratis, possibly fearing to be caught by Russians with them in their possession. Much valuable information was found in the ship; also an amusing signal which had been dispatched: 'All is lost. I am chased by English'.[442]

Raskolnikov's despairing signal was not the only piece of intelligence gained with the capture of *Spartak*. There was also a message from Trotsky instructing Raskolnikov that the British warships must be destroyed and confirming the plan to lure them onto the guns of *Oleg*. The two British cruisers promptly set sail in order to locate and destroy the Russian cruiser. To their disappointment, they found the coast of Gogland deserted and returned to Tallinn. On their outward voyage, they had spotted a ship, presumed to be another Russian destroyer, cautiously sailing west, and had decided not to engage it, but now they signalled the British destroyers in Tallinn to put to sea with the intention of trying to capture the Russian ship. Raskolnikov, who was still being held aboard *Wakeful*, described what transpired:

> Then, from above our heads, there was a sudden, deafening sound of gunfire, and after it that soft noise made by the compression of the recoil-absorber which always follows the firing of a gun. There could be no doubt about it: the shot had been fired from the destroyer in which we were held captive. We eagerly rushed to the portholes, but we were so far down in the hold that the field of vision from any of these portholes was small. We could not see anything except the other British destroyers which were sailing near us. The firing ceased as suddenly as it had started. The engine also suddenly stopped. There was a strange silence. The destroyer *Wakeful* had come to a halt. We were taken up to the top deck for exercise. A sad spectacle met our eyes. Right next to us lay the destroyer *Avtroil*, with her topmast awry. She had just been taken by the British, but the red flag still flew over her. The British squadron had come round her from behind and, cutting her off from Kronstadt, had driven her westward, into the open sea. The British commander had ordered us to be let out for exercise at the very moment when *Avtroil* surrendered, so as to wound our revolutionary self-esteem and mock this defeat suffered by the Red Navy.[443]

The two captured destroyers were handed over to the Estonians, who renamed them and put them to use in their new navy. With the exception of Raskolnikov and *Avtroil*'s commissar, the crews were also handed over; despite British protests, about 40 were later executed.

Raskolnikov and his fellow commissar were eventually exchanged for 18 British personnel being held prisoner by the Bolsheviks. Unfortunately for Raskolnikov, a grim fate awaited him. He served as Soviet ambassador to Estonia, Denmark and Bulgaria, but in 1937 was recalled to Moscow. He delayed his return until the following year, but then learned that he had been dismissed. Fearing that he would be a victim of Stalin's purges, he published an open letter to Stalin in which he acknowledged that he had been a friend of Trotsky, and went on to denounce the purges. Shortly after, he died in Nice, either as the result of an unexplained fall from a window, or possibly from poisoning.

With some 13,000 men ready for action, the Estonian Army began a counteroffensive in January 1919. British ships were now in firm control of the sea, and on 4 January the two light cruisers, accompanied by the destroyer *Wakeful*, subjected several Russian positions near Narva to a heavy bombardment. A detachment of Finnish and Estonian troops was landed in the rear of the 6th Red Rifle Division at Kunda late on 10 January; the following day, Rakvere was retaken, and the Estonians advanced steadily towards Narva. A further seaborne operation was carried out on 18 January at Udria, and this contingent moved swiftly into the northern part of Narva. The rest of the city was liberated the following day.[444] Leon Trotsky, who was personally directing the defence of the city, narrowly escaped being captured.[445]

With the northern part of the country free of Soviet forces, attention turned south. Several armoured trains had been created to provide the Estonian Army with much-needed fire support. Mounting a variety of weapons, ranging from machine-guns to 6-inch artillery, the trains were a potent asset, though of course their deployment was dictated by the rail network. Another of the new formations raised during the winter was the Tartumaa Partisan Battalion, created by Lieutenant Julius Kuperjanov; the battalion's young, energetic personnel rapidly gained a reputation for aggression and daring, and the unit liberated the town of Tartu on 14 January, attacking from aboard armoured trains that broke through the Bolshevik lines and entered the town before Estonian infantry disembarked. From here, it was possible to plan an attack to retake Valga, which was astride the only rail link to Riga and the south. The main approach to Valga from the north ran past Paju Manor, and this now became the focus of fierce fighting. Estonian partisans seized the manor on 30 January, but were swiftly driven back by a battalion of Red Latvian Rifles.

The Estonians found themselves at a disadvantage. Retreating Russian units had destroyed the railway bridge at Sangaste, a little to the north, preventing the Estonians from deploying their armoured train. By contrast, the Latvian Rifles had fire support from their own armoured train, in addition to several armoured cars. Undaunted, Kuperjanov led his battalion in an attack on the manor on 31 January across open ground. Along with many of his men, he was cut down by the withering fire of the defenders, but towards the end of the day a body of Finnish volunteers, in a battalion named the 'Sons of the North', arrived as reinforcements. The combined body of Finns and Estonians penetrated into the grounds of the manor, clearing it of Bolshevik defenders in bitter fighting. The following day, the Latvian Rifles withdrew from the area, allowing the Estonians to take Valga without further fighting.[446]

With the railway line from Latvia now in Estonian hands, it became increasingly difficult for the Soviet forces in central Estonia to coordinate their movements, and they were forced to withdraw east. By the end of February 1919, all Estonian territory had been liberated by the nationalist forces. In addition, the Estonians captured 35 field guns, several dismounted naval guns, and thousands of small arms, together with copious stocks of ammunition. The need to rebuild Bolshevik positions in the north forced the Russians to divert troops from Latvia, where they had been enjoying considerable success. The Estonians now drew up a mutual defence agreement with the Latvian government, and began to prepare for an attack against Bolshevik forces in northeast Latvia.

Meanwhile, in the north the battered Seventh Red Army had received substantial reinforcements, and launched a major assault on Narva on 18 February. The Estonian 1st Division, reinforced by the White Russian Northern Corps, successfully beat off the attacks that continued until late April, though the city suffered considerable damage from artillery fire. To the south, a renewed Soviet attack overran southeast Estonia in the first half of March and a gap began to open between the Estonian 1st and 2nd Divisions. To counter this, the Estonian Army deployed its new 3rd Division in the gap and launched a counterattack, recapturing Petseri at the end of the month. Confused fighting in the marshy area continued for several weeks before the Estonians were able to secure their positions, with support from more new military formations: Latvians who had fled to Estonia were formed into a new brigade, and a further 7,000 anti-Bolshevik Russians and Ingrians (from Ingermanland, the region of Russia immediately to the east of Estonia) served alongside the existing Estonian and Finnish units.[447] Throughout this phase of the fighting, the Estonians were able to make efficient use of their limited forces as a consequence of well-organised logistical support. By contrast, the Red Army's supply system was chaotic, and its medical services almost non-existent.[448]

The Estonians had fought off two invasions, and it appeared that the Bolsheviks were interested in peace negotiations. The Hungarian Communists offered themselves as mediators, but Estonia came under pressure from its western supporters, particularly the British, who threatened to withdraw their support; there was still hope that Estonia might be used as a base for an attempt to overthrow the Bolsheviks, and this would clearly be impossible if Estonia and Russia were to agree terms for peace. After a period of preparation, the Estonians and their allies decided to launch an attack of their own. Estonian accounts describe the operation that followed as an attempt to push the Bolsheviks as far as possible from Estonian territory, but the major role played by White Russian forces suggests that there was at least a hope that such an attack towards Petrograd might destabilise the Soviet regime and perhaps give a non-Bolshevik party a chance of seizing power.[449]

On 13 May, Yudenich ordered Rodzianko to commence an operation named 'White Sword'. His 3,000-strong corps attacked at Narva, surprising and overwhelming the 6th Red Rifle Division. Supported by naval units off the coast, the White Russians advanced swiftly and, in anticipation of their arrival, the garrison of the Krasnaya Gorka fortress mutinied. This was a devastating development for the Bolsheviks, as the presence of White Russian forces in this fortress – on the Baltic coast, perhaps two thirds of the way from the Estonian frontier to Petrograd – would effectively make it impossible to defend Petrograd. Despite being aware of the mutiny, the Estonian authorities took several days to pass the information to Rodzianko and Yudenich; instead, they encouraged the Ingrian detachment within their forces to try to reach the area, perhaps preferring that the lands to their east should come under the control of the friendly Ingrians rather than the White Russians. The Ingrian force proved too weak to reach the mutineers, and eventually the Estonians informed Rodzianko, nearly two days after the mutiny had commenced.

Before either the White Russians or the Royal Navy warships operating in the Gulf of Finland could come to the aid of the mutineers, Josef Stalin – who had been given the task of defending the Russian capital – intervened. Born Josef Vissarionovich Dzhugashvili in his native Georgia, he was educated at first for the priesthood but became an atheist and was involved in revoutionary groups before he had finished his studies. He was an early adherent of Lenin and proved adept at organising Bolshevik groups in the early years of the 20th century, resorting to criminal means to secure funds and showing the first signs of the ruthlessness that was to become his hallmark. Like Trotsky, he was arrested and exiled to Siberia, but travelled to Petrograd after the February Revolution, supporting Kerensky at first but then playing a leading role in the work of the Bolshevik Central Committee during the October Revolution. He was appointed People's Commissar for Nationalities' Affairs but like many leading Bolsheviks was required to take command of the formations of the fledgling Red Army against White Russian forces; he soon became known for his uncompromising policies towards White Russian officers, ordering the execution of many, as well as taking draconian measures against Bolshevik deserters and peasants who showed any reluctance to support the Bolsheviks.

Outside Petrograd, Stalin acted with characteristic resolution and force. Two of the large warships in Kronstadt were ordered to commence a bombardment of the fortress, while a force of naval volunteers assembled as an infantry formation to storm the position. After two days of rebellion, even as Rodzianko, finally aware of developments, was ordering his troops to try to reach the mutineers, the ruins of Krasnaya Gorka were back in Bolshevik hands. In another characteristic act, Stalin ordered the execution of nearly 70 Russian naval officers from the Kronstadt base, on the basis that they had been planning a similar revolt. Although Stalin claimed to have documentary evidence of this, including proof that the British had financed the planned mutiny, no such document was ever produced.[450]

A second Estonian offensive took place south of Lake Peipus, and a combined Estonian and White Russian force known as the Petseri Battle Group crossed into Russia and seized Pskov on 25 May. Almost immediately, the White Russians appeared to lose interest in fighting against the Red Army, turning their attention against those that they regarded as Bolshevik sympathisers and supporters. Given the prejudices of the region at that time, it was almost inevitable that all Jews were automatically regarded as being in this group, and there was widespread looting, murder and imprisonment.[451] From Pskov, the Estonians pushed on to the Velikaya River, but it became increasingly clear to the Estonians that their advance was unsustainable, not least due to the growing resentment of the local population towards the behaviour of Rodzianko's troops. The Estonians removed the White Russians from their own line of command, and the Northern Corps reorganised itself into the Northwestern Army. The Bolsheviks counterattacked on 19 June with the reorganised 6th Division, reinforced by the 2nd Division, and rapidly eliminated most of the gains made by the Northern Corps.

Meanwhile, Alexander-Sinclair had been relieved by Admiral Sir Walter Cowan and the British 1st Light Cruiser Squadron. Whilst Cowan's warships were able to control the Estonian coastline, the presence of Russian warships in Kronstadt continued to pose at least a theoretical threat. Fortunately for Cowan, he found himself working alongside a British naval officer, Augustus Agar, who was operating coastal motor boats on behalf of the British Foreign Office, attempting to maintain links with British spies inside Russia. One of them, codenamed ST-25, was the last important agent still on Bolshevik soil, but arranging a rendezvous to collect him seemed almost impossible. Frustrated in his attempts, Agar contacted Cowan and offered to use his motor boats to attack the Russian battleships that had been used to bombard Krasnaya Gorka. There was an exchange of signals with London, as a result of which Cowan was advised that the motor boats were to be used for intelligence purposes only, unless specially directed by an officer of flag rank. Cowan was determined to get his ships into action, and decided to stretch his orders to the limit; he advised Agar that he could not specifically order the motor boats to attack the Russian battleships, but if they did Agar could count on Cowan's support.

On 17 June, Agar set off with two boats. One turned back after developing mechanical problems and news arrived that the Russian battleships had withdrawn and been replaced by the cruiser *Oleg*, which had been part of Raskolnikov's disastrous foray against Tallinn, but Agar pressed on undaunted and made his approach to Kronstadt during the short hours of the summer night. After a fierce exchange of fire with Soviet destroyers, he approached the Tolbukin lighthouse where he was forced to run his boat aground on a breakwater to make repairs. Still under constant fire, he and his men patched up the boat, and then launched a torpedo at *Oleg* before turning and running for the Finnish coast. The 7,000-ton cruiser, which had fought in the Russian Navy's battle with the Japanese fleet at Tsushima in 1905, was struck by the torpedo and sank. Agar and his crew made good their escape in the resultant confusion, still under fire. For this mission, he was awarded the Victoria Cross and promoted to lieutenant commander.[452]

Agar wasn't finished. Cowan wished to eliminate any further threat from the battleships of the Russian Baltic Fleet and planned a new raid on Kronstadt. This operation was codenamed 'RK' in honour of Cowan's friend Admiral Roger Keyes, who led the raid on Zeebrugge in April 1918. On 18 August, Agar led a group of seven small boats towards Kronstadt. On this occasion, he stayed outside the port while the other six boats, led by Commander Claude Dobson, made an attack at night, while British aircraft carried out an air raid to distract the defenders. Cowan's destroyers and cruisers waited a short distance away, ready to intervene if the Russian warships attempted to pursue Agar's force.

The attack achieved complete surprise; the small flotilla passed the silent Russian guardship at the entrance to the harbour and made their attack, and the first that the Russians knew of the presence of the British was an explosion as a torpedo struck the submarine depot ship *Pamiat Azova*, which swiftly sank. Lieutenant Gordon Steele was aboard a boat commanded by Lieutenant Archibald Dayrell-Reed, with orders to attack the battleship *Andrei Pervozvanni*:

> As Dayrell-Reed's boat entered the harbour, fire was opened on us, first from the direction of the dry dock and afterwards from both sides. We headed for the corner where our objectives, the battleships, were berthed. Almost simultaneously we received bursts of fire from the batteries and splashes appeared on both sides. Instinctively I ducked as the bullets whistled past. I turned round and was about to remark to Dayrell-Reed, 'Where are you heading?' as we were making straight for a hospital ship, when I noticed that his head was resting on the wooden conning tower top in front of him. He had been shot through the head. Despite his considerable weight, I was able to lower him into the cockpit. At the same

> time I put the wheel hard over and righted the boat on her proper course. We were now quite close to *Andrei Pervozvanni*. Throttling back as far as possible, I fired both torpedoes at her, after which I stopped one engine to help the boat turn quickly. As I did this we saw two columns of water rise up from the side of *Petropavlovsk* [the second Russian battleship] and heard two crashes. I knew they must be Dobson's torpedoes which had found their target. Then there was another terrific explosion nearby. We received a great shock and a douche of water. I realised that the cause of it was one of our torpedoes exploding on the side of the battleship [*Andrei Pervozvanni*]. We were so close to her that a shower of picric acid from the warhead of our torpedo was thrown over the stern of the boat, staining us a yellow colour which we had some difficulty in removing afterwards. [Missing] a lighter by a few feet [we] followed Dobson out of the basin. I had just time to take another look back and see the result of our second torpedo. A high column of flame from the battleship lit up the whole basin. We passed the guardship at anchor again. Morley [the mechanic aboard the boat] gave her a burst of machine-gun fire as a parting present and afterwards went to see what he could do for Reed.[453]

Three of the British boats were sunk by Russian gunfire, with the loss of 15 crew killed, including Dayrell-Reed, and nine captured from the sinking boats; the Russian account states that the guardship actually spotted the boats as they penetrated the harbour, but chose not to fire for fear of hitting friendly vessels beyond the boats. This does not of course explain why the guardship failed to raise the alarm.[454] For their part in this action, both Dobson and Steele were awarded the Victoria Cross.

Agar had intended to use the attack as cover for another attempt to reach agent ST-25, but was unable to do so. The agent's real name was Paul Dukes, and he had worked for many years as a concert pianist in the Petrograd Conservatoire, gathering intelligence and helping White Russians to escape to Finland. It was a remarkable achievement for a man without any training before he was sent to Russia – he was merely told to establish contact with the agents of his predecessor, the naval officer Francis Crombie, who had been killed by the Cheka, the Soviet secret police. Without knowing even the names of these agents, he succeeded in re-establishing and even building on the network. He wore many disguises and adopted a variety of aliases, infiltrating the Russian communist party, the Comintern (the international organisation dedicated to worldwide revolution) and even the Cheka – he had a forged document that stated that he was a member of the Cheka, allowing him to pass most checkpoints without question. For a while, he adopted the role of a poor Russian, growing his beard and hair, but when he heard that the Cheka were seeking him he shaved and smartened his appearance, taking pride that many of his acquaintances no longer recognised him. Not long after, he was aboard a tram, disguised as a Russian soldier, when he saw a known Cheka and realised he had been spotted by a known informer:

> I did not wait to make sure ... Passing the Tsarskoselsky station I jumped off the car while it was still in motion, stooped beneath its side till it passed, and boarded another in the opposite direction. At the station I jumped off, entered the building and sat amongst the massed herds ... till dusk.[455]

Under his guise as an ordinary Russian, he was conscripted into the Red Army. His observations of the causes of the failure of the various White forces are interesting:

> The complete absence of an acceptable programme alternative to Bolshevism, the audibly whispered threats of landlords that in the event of a White victory the land seized by the peasants would be restored to its former rulers, and the lamentable failure to understand that in the anti-Bolshevist war politics and not military strategy must play the dominant role, were the chief causes of the White defeats. This theory is borne out by all the various White adventures ... the course of each being, broadly speaking, the same. First the Whites advanced triumphantly, and until the character of their regime was realised they were hailed as deliverers from the Red yoke. The Red soldiers deserted to them in hordes and the Red command was thrown into consternation ... Then came a halt, due to incipient disaffection amongst the civil population in the rear. Requisitioning, mobilisation, internecine strife, and corruption amongst officials, differing but little from the regime of the Reds, rapidly alienated the sympathies of the peasantry, who revolted against the Whites as they had against the Reds, and the position of the White armies was made untenable. The first sign of yielding at the front was the signal for a complete reversal of fortune.[456]

Taking advantage of his army unit being dispatched to the front line in September, Duke managed to persuade his commanding officer – who was a tsarist – to allow him to travel to Russian-occupied Latvia with two other soldiers rather than the rest of the regiment. When they reached Latvia, they jumped from their train and disappeared into the forest, joining thousands of other 'Greens' – soldiers who chose to be neither Red nor White, but avoided both factions by hiding in the forests. With secret documents concealed about his person, copied onto sheets of toilet paper, Duke finally reached safety.[457]

Meanwhile, the Russians were making progress against the White Russian and Estonian forces in and around Pskov, and on 10 August the Bolsheviks tentatively offered to recognise Estonian independence in return for a voluntary evacuation of Russian territory by the Estonian forces. This was, of course a welcome development for Estonia, but both the White Russians and the British opposed such a development. The British military attaché in Tallinn, Brigadier Frank Marsh, summoned both Estonian and White Russian officials to the British Embassy in an attempt to push through an agreement that would satisfy British support of both an independent Estonia and the White Russians. He informed the Russians that it was imperative that they formed a Northwest Russian government; this would then have to recognise Estonian independence – unless they did so, the Western Powers would no longer support them.[458] Yudenich had little choice but to agree. However, it appeared that Marsh – and his superior, General Sir Hubert Gough, head of the Western Powers' military mission to the Baltic – had greatly exceeded their authority in forcing such a recognition of Estonia; Kolchak was still refusing any such recognition, and many officials in London were furious about the developments in Tallinn. Meanwhile, Russian troops recaptured Pskov on 8 September.

Politicians from all three Baltic States met in Tallinn on 14 September, where they agreed that they would negotiate for a collective peace with Russia. Formal talks with the Estonian government began on 16 September in Pskov, but were broken off after two days.[459] Part of the reason for this was that the Baltic States had attended a conference in Riga on 26 August, where they met representatives of the Entente Powers. Here, they were urged to support a planned attack by General Yudenich; clearly, supporting such an attack would not be possible if they were actively negotiating a peace settlement.[460] But, given what had been agreed in Riga, it seems odd that there was any point in meeting the Bolsheviks in Pskov. Perhaps it was intended to mislead the Russians; perhaps it was an indication of different factions within the Baltic States pursuing different agendas.

On 10 October, Yudenich launched his Northwestern Army in an attack towards Petrograd. He had spent the months since his previous attack increasing the size of his force; it now numbered over 18,000, with artillery support and two armoured trains. His force even included six British tanks, crewed by British volunteers. The forces opposing him were numerically greater, but were severely handicapped by poor supplies and chaotic organisation.[461] He had tried to secure Finnish support for the attack, but although Mannerheim was in favour, the

Finnish president, Kaarlo Ståhlberg, refused permission. Admiral Kolchak, who was nominally the leader of the White Russian cause, had previously refused to recognise Finnish independence from Russia, and Yudenich's somewhat belated assurances that he would ensure recognition of Finland were in vain.

At first, the attack of the Northwestern Army enjoyed considerable success. The Bolshevik forces were now under the command of Trotsky, Stalin having returned to Moscow. The contrast between the leadership of the two sides could not be greater; Trotsky, the great orator of the revolution, inspired his fellow citizens to take up arms for the defence of the Russian capital, while Yudenich and Rodzianko squabbled about who should command the army in the field. From the moment they crossed the frontier, White Russian soldiers began to desert, even when they were advancing and winning battles. Some joined the Reds, but most were simply taking advantage of being on Russian territory to try to make their way to their homes. Kingisepp fell on 12 October, and, the following day, 1,600 Estonian troops came ashore near the fortress of Krasnaya Gorka. Despite fire support from Estonian and British warships, the attempt to capture the fortress failed, though fighting continued until the end of the month before the Estonians withdrew. On 20 October, the leading elements of Yudenich's force reached and captured Pavlovsk and Tsarskoe Selo, on the southern outskirts of Petrograd.

At approximately the same time, the White Russian forces under Denikin in southern Russia were making good progress and it seemed as if the Bolsheviks might be overthrown. Yudenich was aware of the fragility of his army and the numbers of desertions it was suffering and was anxious to reach Petrograd as soon as possible; however, he was also aware that if he were to reach and capture the Russian capital, he would then inherit a huge problem. The city was close to starvation, and whoever controlled it would be responsible for finding sufficient food supplies to prevent a mass uprising. Hoping that the British and others would be able and willing to come to his aid, he ordered his troops to press on as rapidly as they could. Even Lenin began to consider abandoning Petrograd, but Trotsky had no intention of allowing any such thing. He insisted that the cradle of the revolution could be turned into a fortress, in which every house would be a strongpoint and the White forces would be bled to death. Critically, the rush by Yudenich's troops to reach Petrograd included a division that had actually been ordered to march to the southeast of the city in order to cut the railway line from Moscow. With this vital supply route intact, the Bolsheviks were able to bring up substantial supplies. On 21 October, a Bolshevik counterattack recaptured the southern suburbs of Petrograd. The Fifteenth Red Army drove up from the southeast and attacked towards Volosovo, threatening the supply lines of the Northwest Army. Heavily outnumbered, Yudenich had no option but to withdraw towards Estonia. On 15 November, his troops retreated from Kingisepp, abandoning their last major possession inside Russia. As they fell back, they encountered villages and towns full of White Russian supporters, who had intended to follow them into Petrograd:

> Every village, every house and every shelter of any sort were literally overflowing with miserable, hungry, freezing people. There was not a single sheltered corner where the retreating soldiers could warm themselves and rest. The fighting men therefore had to live without shelter during days and nights when the temperature was 10–18 degrees below zero.[462]

Yudenich intended to withdraw to Estonia and regroup, but the Estonian government had no intention of allowing this. As the White Russians reached the border, most were disarmed. The official reason was that Estonia did not wish to allow such a large well-armed body of demoralised men to wander within Estonia; another explanation is that the Bolsheviks had offered to recognise Estonian independence in return for bringing the war to an end.

For Yudenich, this was the end of his attempts on behalf of the White Russian cause. He was placed under arrest by the Estonians but was released after pressure from Britain and France. He left the region and made his home in France, where he avoided involvement in White Russian circles. He died near Nice, in 1933. He left behind him the disarmed men of the Northwest Army who spent a terrible winter finding whatever shelter they could. Thousands died of starvation and disease; a few of their officers managed to travel to join White forces elsewhere, but for most it was enough to find a way out of their predicament. Many drifted back across the border into Russia and made their peace with the Bolsheviks, returning to the homes they had left many years before. Others made new homes in other parts of the world; few were allowed to settle in Estonia.

The Soviet forces that had pursued Yudenich's retreating army now attacked towards Narva in an attempt to seize the city as a final bargaining chip in the peace negotiations. The Seventh Red Army made some initial gains, but was forced to halt at the end of November to regroup. Peace talks opened on 5 December in Tartu, and, hoping to exert leverage in these negotiations, the Bolsheviks renewed their attack on 7 December, with the Fifteenth Red Army joining the assault nine days later. After breaking through the Estonian lines, the Russians crossed the frozen River Narva south of the city, but the following day the reinforced Estonian

1st Division counterattacked, slowly driving the Bolsheviks back despite suffering heavy losses. In the peace negotiations, the Bolsheviks suddenly made a surprise demand for a strip on either side of the Narva to be kept free of fortifications; when the Estonians refused, they made a final attack on 28 December. By the end of the year, exhaustion and snow brought all combat operations to an end, and the Bolsheviks dropped their demand.

A ceasefire came into effect on 3 January 1920, and the Treaty of Tartu was signed on 2 February. The treaty specified the border between the two nations, with a strip of land to the east of Narva remaining in Estonian control, and allowed for movement of displaced Russians and Estonians to their homelands. It also included a renunciation of any Russian claim to Estonian territory and a transfer of gold from Russia to Estonia, representing Estonia's share of the gold reserves of the Tsarist Russian Empire. For both sides, this treaty represented a significant landmark. For Estonia, it amounted to a 'birth certificate' for the nation, while for Lenin's Russia, it was the first treaty agreed with a foreign power. Estonia had gained her independence, but at a substantial cost: military casualties in the war were estimated at over 3,500 dead and nearly 14,000 wounded. In addition, Narva had suffered substantial damage, with many civilians killed or wounded. Nevertheless, the nation could look forward to a new future.[463]

CHAPTER 15

THE PYGMY WARS: LATVIA

Latvia had been one of the most industrialised parts of the Russian Empire; Riga alone had a population of over 800,000, with most workers employed in industry. When the war began, many Latvians volunteered to join the army while others were conscripted, often in a heavy-handed manner that provoked unrest, even riots. Nevertheless, Latvians featured in large numbers in the ranks of the Russian Army in the early phases of the war, with the Russian XX Corps being 80 per cent Latvian. This corps was effectively destroyed during the Second Battle of the Masurian Lakes in 1915, and over 20,000 Latvians were killed, wounded or taken prisoner.

The origins of the Latvian Rifles have already been described. Recruited largely from the industrialised parts of Riga, where Bolshevik activists had been energetically at work for much of the war, most of their personnel rapidly sided with the Bolsheviks after the October Revolution, though some of these soldiers fought for the Bolsheviks as a result of Lenin's promise that he would grant Latvia independence.[464] The Latvian Riflemen took an active part in suppressing anti-Bolshevik risings in Moscow and Yaroslavl in 1918, and were some of the Revolution's most reliable troops. In Latvia itself, the industrial heartland of Riga remained fertile ground for Bolshevik ideology, and there had been many recruits in the dying months of Imperial Russian rule and during Kerensky's regime. Accustomed to leading an underground existence, these communist cells remained in existence when the Germans occupied the city and waited for their moment.

Latvia itself was almost completely under German control by the end of the war with Russia. As part of the Treaty of Brest-Litovsk, the Russians ceded any claim to the Baltic region, and from the autumn of 1917 Baltic German communities began to form local councils, which they dominated. In April 1918 a Provincial Assembly consisting of 35 Baltic Germans, 13 Estonians and 11 Latvians called upon the kaiser to recognise the region as a German protectorate. They declared the existence of the Duchy of Courland and the Baltic State Duchy, the latter covering the rest of Latvia and all of Estonia, but the kaiser did not afford them recognition until September 1918. Shortly afterwards, a regency council based in Riga was formed to administer the two duchies. This council, headed by Baron Adolf Pilar von Pilchau, elected Adolf Friedrich, Duke of Mecklenburg-Schwerin as head of state, a post that he never took up; originally, the regency council had intended for the kaiser to become head of state, but his abdication brought any such proposal to an end.

Other parts of the Baltic German community had doubts that Germany would be able to offer meaningful support on her own, and Baron Heinrich von Stryk was sent to Sweden to seek Swedish support for a pro-German Baltic state. Anatol von Lieven, the son of a prominent local family, started work on raising a combat unit composed of White Russians. It is a measure of the longevity of the German involvement in the Baltic that Alexis von der Pahlen, who became Lieven's chief of staff, was a descendant of Johannes de Pala, one of the first governors of Riga in 1120. Another notable recruit was the 16-year-old Heinrich von Behr who would see service as a senior officer in the Wehrmacht during the Second World War.[465]

At the same time as these moves by the Baltic Germans, Latvian nationalists established the People's Council of Latvia and issued a declaration of Latvian independence with Kārlis Ulmanis as Prime Minister. Ulmanis had been a participant in the 1905 Revolution and after serving a spell in prison in Pskov he fled to the USA, from where he returned to Latvia in 1913. With Germany engulfed in increasing turmoil, the Baltic Duchy's regency council was dissolved, leaving the Ulmanis administration as the only effective government of the region. This proved to be short-lived, as Bolshevik forces – led by units of the Latvian Rifles – invaded Latvia almost at the moment that independence was declared. The nationalist government announced the creation of a new nationalist army, commanded by Lieutenant Colonel Oskars Kalpaks and began to mobilise manpower, but was severely hindered by a shortage of weapons.

Many of the German units in the area had been badly affected by desertion. Like German regiments elsewhere, they contained within their ranks large numbers of men who were strongly affected by the new socialist ideology. Most units had created soldiers' councils in deliberate emulation of what had happened in the Russian Army; these councils effectively controlled their deployment, and

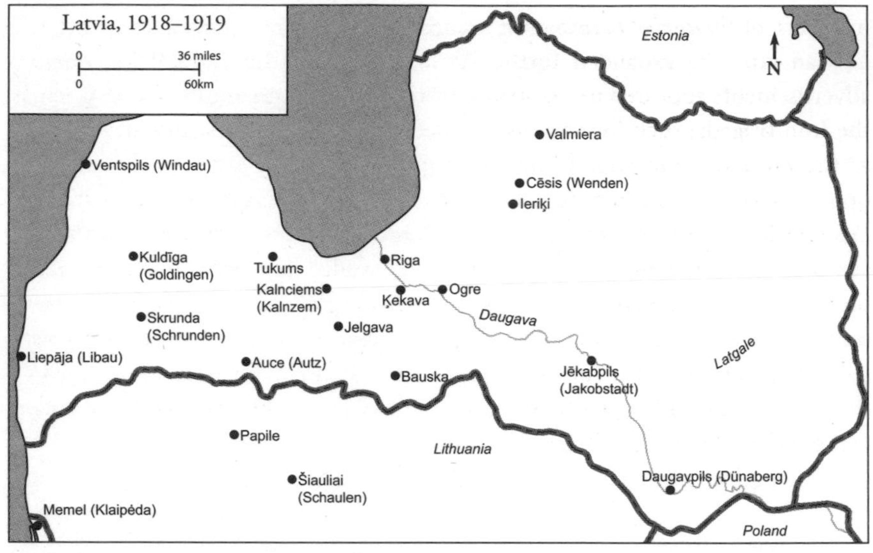

in many cases in Latvia they were in contact with the advancing Bolsheviks. Consequently, as Russian forces approached west, the councils ensured that their units simply withdrew rather than fight. Desertion was widespread, further reducing the fighting strength of the German regiments and divisions. Major Josef Bischoff, who had served as a soldier in the German genocide of the Herero in Namibia and had been awarded Germany's highest decoration, the *Pour le Mérite*, for his conduct on the Western Front in 1918, scraped together a few combat-worthy elements into a formation that he named the Iron Brigade. This was one of the few significant anti-Bolshevik units in the field around Riga.

The Latvian nationalist government was desperately short of troops. With no prospect of aid from any other quarter, Ulmanis turned to the Germans. August Winnig, the German Baltic plenipotentiary, was fully aware of Ulmanis' weakness and took advantage of this late in 1918 to secure two agreements with the Latvian government. According to these agreements, Latvia would grant citizenship to any foreign soldiers who had fought for Latvia for at least four weeks. Baltic Germans would have the right to join any German volunteer units, and Germany would be able to provide officers and NCOs to the newly formed Baltic German militia, the *Baltische Landeswehr*. The *Landeswehr* would consist of seven companies of infantry supported by two artillery batteries, while the Latvians would raise 18 companies themselves, plus a company of Baltic Russians; the numbers of *Baltische Landeswehr* companies would be increased should the Latvian army be expanded further in keeping with this ratio.[466] Meanwhile, advertisements appeared in Germany for recruits to join volunteer units such as the Iron Brigade; such formations became part of the formations widely known as the *Freikorps*, and were ultimately deployed in many parts of Germany to oppose communists and others perceived as hostile to 'traditional' German rule. Posters calling for recruits to serve in the Baltic States appeared all over Germany, stressing that the new volunteer units were needed to defend both the Baltic States and Germany from Bolshevik Russia and listed several conditions of service. These included favourable settlement opportunities for soldiers who were still serving at the end of hostilities, and similar concessions would be offered to those wounded during the fighting, or the families of soldiers who were killed while serving against the Bolsheviks.

Other advertisements made promises in a more lavish style:

> Wonderful Settlement Opportunity! Anyone who wants to own his own estate in the beautiful Baltic, report to one of the following recruitment offices ...[467]

For many German soldiers and officers newly discharged from the army who were struggling to settle into civilian life, the lure of returning to military service with the promise of huge rewards was an attractive one. The *Freikorps* grew rapidly, with tacit – and sometimes overt – support from figures like Gustav Noske, the new German defence minister. Despite every attempt to conduct an orderly 'revolution from above' in which politicians led the way and thus avoided civil unrest, several 'Soviet republics' came into being in Germany in 1919; the largest of these was in Bavaria in April and May, and all were suppressed, many violently. In the case of the Bavarian Soviet Republic, a force of about 10,000 regular troops supported by 30,000 men of *Freikorps Epp* and *Marinebrigade Ehrhardt* entered Munich in early May and forcibly deposed the Bolsheviks, killing at least 1,000 in street-fighting; nearly as many were subsequently killed without trial.

The promise of land in the Baltic region for volunteers would prove to be a source of considerable dispute. The defunct regency council had intended to provide land for large numbers of German soldiers after the war in order to boost the German population and the Ulmanis government had already committed itself to land reform, including the offer of land grants to landless Latvians who served in the new army that was being raised, and it seems that August Winnig – without seeking confirmation from the Latvians – assumed that a similar offer would apply to Germans. The poster-writers in Germany then exaggerated matters further. It is questionable whether the offer of land made much difference to recruitment, but the suggestion that Germans might be given land in Latvia, where so much land was already in the hands of the Baltic German nobility, did cause considerable anti-German sentiment in Latvian circles.

France and Britain had mixed feelings about the presence of German combatants in the region and made unsuccessful attempts to encourage Sweden to take an active part in matters. Finally, the Entente Powers accepted that the Germans were the only force likely to prevent a Bolshevik victory and invoked Article 12 of the Armistice Agreement, which allowed German units to remain outside German territory if the Entente Powers judged that this was desirable in view of local circumstances.

On 17 December the Bolsheviks announced the creation of the Latvian Soviet Socialist Republic headed by Pēteris Stučka, and pressed on towards Riga. There was insufficient time for the nationalists to organise a proper defence: German units continued to withdraw, many after discussions between their soldiers' councils and the advancing Bolsheviks, and British warships departed from the harbour on 1 January 1919. Riga fell three days later, and Ulmanis' government was forced to flee, first to Jelgava and then to the Baltic coast and the port of Liepāja. It has been suggested that the German units in and around Riga may have deliberately pulled back rather than fight to hold Riga on the grounds that a brief period of Bolshevik occupation might make the population more receptive to future German hegemony, but it seems likely that the remnants of the German Army in the area were simply in no condition to put up prolonged resistance.[468] The total number of soldiers fighting for the nationalist cause in December has been estimated as amounting to only 400 Latvians, 500 men in the *Baltische Landeswehr*, and 200 Germans in the Iron Brigade.[469] Bolshevik forces in the region have been estimated as being as many as 45,000, partly through mobilisation of men in the areas controlled by them, but in reality the number of combatants at this stage was probably closer to 10,000.[470]

With the arrival of the Bolsheviks in Riga, the local communist cells that had been in hiding for many years came into the open. Many peasants at first welcomed the new regime, hoping that it would bring with it a redistribution of land, but one of the first policy announcements of the new regime was the nationalisation of agrarian land. This, combined with compulsory central purchasing of all agricultural produce – at prices that the peasants regarded as too low to be financially viable – resulted almost immediately in widespread food shortages. In the cities and towns, the food shortage rapidly brought illness, increasing the unpopularity of the Stučka regime, but a far greater source of anger was the widespread wave of repression. The clergy were particular targets, and many were executed in the most summary fashion. Several thousand people were shot or hanged in a few short weeks and many families had their property confiscated. The breakdown of normal commerce with the surrounding countryside brought not only food shortages but also a lack of firewood. In the middle of the Baltic winter, this added hugely to the hardships of ordinary people and the unpopularity of the Bolshevik regime.

By the end of January 1919, a small segment of Latvia on the Estonian border was under the control of Estonian forces, and Liepāja and much of the western coastal area remained under Latvian nationalist control; the rest of the country had fallen to the Bolsheviks. At the end of the month, the Bolsheviks attacked the isolated port of Ventspils, or Windau, in northern Courland. The Baltic German garrison of about 100 men beat off the first attack but realised that it was too small to put up prolonged resistance and entered into negotiations with the besieging Bolsheviks. In exchange for a guarantee of safe passage, the Germans laid down their arms; with the exception of two badly wounded men, the garrison was locked in a barn and then massacred. However, a general drive by the Bolsheviks to destroy the rest of the nationalist remnants along the Baltic coast failed to develop. Many of the soldiers of the Red Latvian Rifles had deserted to return to their homes, and Soviet supply lines were unable to support both the Latvian and Estonian offensives at the same time. Nevertheless, in the small enclave around Liepāja, there were fears that the German units in the area, disillusioned and war-weary like their comrades elsewhere, might desert, and there was considerable pro-Bolshevik feeling in the town itself. Three garrison battalions had been raised to prevent an uprising, but two were effectively under the control of their soldiers' councils rather than the garrison commander. The pro-German community was hugely relieved when Generalmajor Rüdiger von der Goltz was sent to take command of the German elements, collectively organised as VI Reserve Corps.

After his successes in Finland, Goltz had been posted to Silesia, where he experienced first hand the breakdown in order and discipline in the German Army:

> When he wanted to dismiss a battalion commander who was completely under the control of his men, General von Kessel was arrested and only released after several hours. Every attempt to establish order there, or to discharge surplus, troublesome men, came up against strong resistance. They no longer recognised

> the external foe, who threatened the Homeland, only the internal foe, who wished to restore the State's authority there.[471]

Goltz now took command of what remained of the German Eighth Army, reduced to the forces grouped around Liepāja. He arrived in the port by train from East Prussia on 1 February 1919. One day later, Major Alfred Fletcher, a German artillery officer whose ancestors hailed from Scotland, arrived to take command of the *Landeswehr*.

In his memoirs, written less than two years later, Goltz's disdain for the Latvian government is clear, as are his own prejudices:

> The Latvian government that had been established in Riga in November 1918 was strongly anti-German, [and] had many members who preferred the Bolsheviks to the Germans, but at first out of fear for their own lives and their ministerial posts appeared fairly subdued. Many of the important personalities were outspokenly slavish, fawning and friendly to your face, for example when they needed me, [but] deceitful, false, and always ready to defraud my staff and me and to do the opposite of what they had agreed to do.[472]

However, he also showed some insight into the poor relationship between Latvians and Germans, as he recorded in his diary:

> Mishandling of the Latvians during four years of occupation, the cruelty of the revolutionised hordes of the Eighth Army, the ongoing plundering by [*Freikorps*] volunteers who wish to make themselves comfortable here, and centuries of old hatred against the Balts has resulted in groups who are allegedly not Bolshevik, but who look upon the Bolsheviks more favourably than upon the Germans.[473]

Goltz concluded that he was facing four enemies: the Bolsheviks; the soldiers' council in Liepāja; the anti-German government of Latvia; and the Entente Powers. He decided that it would be best to deal with them one at a time. Two days after arriving in Latvia, he had a meeting with the soldiers' council. The council had played a part in the dismissal of his predecessor, but Goltz made clear his intention to proceed how he saw fit, and to fight any who attempted to obstruct him. According to his own account, his forceful manner played a major part in bringing matters under control; it is likely that the ever-present threat of a renewed Bolshevik attack was also an important factor in concentrating the minds of the leaders of the council.[474] There continued to be friction between

Goltz and the council and between both parties and the local police, but Goltz gradually achieved control. In the meantime, Major Fletcher mounted a surprise night attack on the town of Kuldīga, or Goldingen, and retook it. His men then held the town in the face of several Bolshevik counterattacks. Although the victory was a minor one, it was an important psychological boost for the Germans and Latvians in their little enclave. For the Baltic Germans, from whose families the *Baltische Landeswehr* was recruited, this first victory was particularly welcome.

By the second week of February, reinforcements were arriving in a steady stream from Germany, as volunteers swelled the ranks of the *Freikorps*. Bischoff's Iron Brigade was expanded into an Iron Division, and elements of the 1st Guards Reserve Division – a new *Freikorps* formation, based on the original division of the same name that had served in the war – began to disembark in Liepāja. This was a powerful additional asset for Goltz, numbering about 5,000 men, and consisted of an infantry brigade, a cavalry regiment, an artillery regiment, and even its own combat aircraft. Using a combination of his *Landeswehr* and the newly arrived reinforcements, Fletcher advanced to Ventspils at the end of February and retook the town after a brisk fight. Lacking warships, Goltz nevertheless arranged naval support in the form of merchant ships with field guns deployed on their decks.[475] An Estonian warship arrived shortly after the recapture of Ventspils, too late to take part in the fighting; however, it was clear to both the Estonians and the Latvians that they had common interests, and the two countries entered into a mutual assistance agreement. Colonel Jorģis Zemitāns took command of Latvian troops raised in Estonia, forming them into the North Latvian Brigade.

During this operation, Goltz was in Skrunda, or Schrunden, and took advantage of the opportunity to visit a Latvian battalion in the town, personally led by Oskars Kalpaks, the commander of the fledgling Latvian army. He was favourably impressed by the rank and file, whose attitude and demeanour more than compensated for their lack of combat experience. As ever, his comments give insight into his own views:

> Well-built, straight-backed, from mainly from the upper and lower middle classes, filled with pride and self-confidence, they were ready to risk life and well-being for their Fatherland … one saw grey-haired men and half-grown youths doing their duty side by side. There was a self-imposed, voluntary discipline … which can only exist in a people with minimal party and class differences, with a longstanding love of their country.[476]

At almost the same moment, Heinrich von Stryk returned from his mission to Sweden aboard the freighter *Runeborg*. He was accompanied by both German and Swedish officers, and documents in the possession of the Swedish Lieutenant-Colonel Eklund were confiscated by the Latvian authorities. Examination of these documents revealed details of a proposal to move some or all of the *Baltische Landeswehr* to Sweden where it would be re-equipped and enlarged prior to returning to Latvia, reinforced by Swedish volunteers, in order to establish a pro-German state incorporating Latvia and Estonia.

Goltz later recorded that he had been warned about Stryk's unrealistic views but knew nothing about Stryk's plans prior to being told about them by Stryk himself, shortly after the incriminating documents had been seized. He then learned that a company of Baltic Germans intended to return to Liepāja to prevent any arrest of Stryk and his fellow conspirators. Goltz recorded that he told his informer, 'a prominent, formerly reserved and careful personage', that this company of Baltic Germans would not be able to prevail against the Latvians in Liepāja, and that the proposed pro-German state would never receive the approval of the Entente Powers, nor indeed the support of the current German government, which would in all likelihood withdraw all German troops from the area.[477]

As rumours and messages crossed the town, Goltz issued orders that troops could return to Liepāja from the front only with his express permission. He also placed a detachment from 1st Guards Division on standby and issued an arrest warrant for Stryk. He then offered a German guard to the Latvian government; given the suspicions that must have been circulating, it was hardly surprising that Ulmanis rejected this offer, though Goltz expressed irritation that his gesture had been spurned. Stryk was placed under arrest, but Hans von Manteuffel – a leading member of the Baltic German community who could trace his ancestry back to the Livonian Knights – used his *Landeswehr* unit to 'liberate' him from prison.[478]

After the success at Ventspils, Goltz felt ready to advance on a broader front. The newly arrived 1st Guards Reserve Division began to deploy to the south of the Iron Division on 28 February with orders to push forward towards Šiauliai (Schaulen) in Lithuania; this would secure the southern flank of the operation. The Iron Division, now concentrated on a narrower front, would advance directly towards Jelgava, while the *Landeswehr*, with a single battalion of Latvian soldiers on its southern flank, would attack towards Tukums, and from there would turn south towards Jelgava, cutting the Jelgava–Riga road to prevent the Bolsheviks from retreating. The operation was divided into three phases, *Tauwetter* ('Thaw'),

Eisgang ('Ice melt') and *Frühlingswind* ('Spring wind'). At first there was concern that the operation might be hindered by the imminent warmer weather, which normally brought muddy conditions that made many roads almost unusable. This year, however, there had been little snow, so there was correspondingly little melt water to hinder movement.

The assault began on 3 March. Wherever possible, the German advance avoided frontal attacks against strongpoints, preferring to bypass them. A serious mishap occurred on 6 March when the Latvian battalion of the *Landeswehr* was involved in a 'friendly fire' incident with a German unit. There were casualties on both sides, but the most notable was the death of Oskars Kalpaks, the Latvian commander. In some parts of the battlefield, the conduct of the *Freikorps* and *Landeswehr* on the battlefield strained relations with the Latvians. The nationalist government was keen to recruit disillusioned members of the Red Latvian Rifles into its new army, but in most cases, the *Freikorps* and *Landeswehr* simply shot any prisoners who fell into their hands.[479]

The extreme right flank of the 1st Guards Division reached Papile on 8 March, achieving the objectives of *Tauwetter*. Within two days, two companies of the 2nd Guards Reserve Regiment reached and captured Šiauliai, supported by an armoured train. The next day, the Iron Division took Auce (Autz), opening the way for an advance directly towards Jelgava. Farther north, the *Landeswehr* made steady progress, reaching Tukums on 15 March. Resistance, weak at first, grew steadily stronger as the advance proceeded. The final phase of the operation, *Frühlingswind*, involved an advance on Jelgava simultaneously from the south, west and north, with the intention of encircling the Bolshevik forces fighting to the west of Jelgava before they could retreat into the town. Fletcher's *Landeswehr* moved to cut the road to Riga to prevent any escape in that direction, but heavy resistance along the River Aa at Kalnciems (Kalnzem) stopped the Baltic Germans in their tracks. Nevertheless, other elements of the *Landeswehr* reached Jelgava from the west on 18 March and seized the town.

As the regional capital, Jelgava had seen much activity by the Bolshevik authorities. About 70 of its citizens, mainly clergy, teachers and landowners, had been executed. Others were rounded up and forced to accompany the retreating Bolshevik forces towards Riga.[480] Goltz interpreted these events as further proof of the unacceptability of Bolshevism, particularly their arbitrary nature. Unfortunately for the inhabitants of Jelgava, the arrival of the Germans unleashed a new wave of executions. About 500 Latvians were killed without trial as Bolshevik sympathisers, and a further 200 were killed in Tukums.[481] Goltz's memoirs make no mention of these deaths.

With almost all of Courland in German hands, the advance came to a halt. Soviet counterattacks occurred at several points and even succeeded in temporarily recapturing Tukums. The garrison in Jelgava too came under pressure, but was able to hold out until reinforcements arrived to stabilise the situation.

Goltz's VI Reserve Corps was, nominally at least, under the command of the German *Armee Oberkommando Nord* (*AOK Nord*, or Army High Command North), which now ordered him to stop, declaring that the objectives assigned to the corps had been achieved. Goltz regarded his operations as essential to prevent an ultimate Bolshevik advance into East Prussia and felt that the liberation of Courland should help restore pride and self-confidence in Germany in general and the army in particular. He was therefore disappointed by the belittling of his achievements in the German press, and that he was regarded in some circles as little more than an adventurer. He blamed several agencies for this. The soldiers' council, he believed, feared a decline in its influence if there were military successes and was in regular contact with socialist groups in Berlin, including the press. The Latvians and their nationalist government under Ulmanis showed no gratitude for the deeds of German soldiers, dismissing them – with considerable justification –as merely replacing Bolshevik domination with German domination. Goltz had little time for Latvian aspirations of independence; without German support, he felt, neither Latvia nor Estonia had any realistic prospect of holding out against Russia. He believed that the British encouragement of Ulmanis raised expectations unreasonably; the British would not risk the lives of their soldiers to preserve the independence of the Baltic States, and consequently Latvia and Estonia ultimately would have to choose between Russia and Germany.[482] Relations between Goltz and the Ulmanis government, already strained by the Stryk affair, grew steadily worse. The German general's protestations that there was a difference between Germany as an occupying power, as had been the case during the First World War, and her current role as an 'aiding power' fell on deaf ears. The growing friendliness between Ulmanis and representatives of the British government probably did not please Goltz either.

Another source of friction was the new Latvian army. The agreements of December between Ulmanis and Winnig had called for the creation of 18 Latvian infantry companies, but fewer than half of these had been created by mid-March 1919. The Latvians accused the Germans of blocking their attempts to acquire sufficient weaponry, and made progress only when they were given several thousand rifles by the British, while Goltz maintained that the number of Latvians volunteering for service was low, and any attempt to enforce conscription was tantamount to arming Bolshevik sympathisers – somewhat at odds with his previous comments about the Latvian troops he had met during the winter.[483] He attempted to stop the British-supplied weapons from being unloaded, claiming that they would find their way into the hands of those who would mount a pro-Bolshevik rising.[484] It was, of course, of great advantage to Goltz for the Latvians to remain almost entirely dependent upon German and Baltic German military power.

Goltz also resented the demands of the Latvian government, supported by the British, for control over the civilian police. When the area free from Bolshevik occupation was relatively small, with the ever-present threat of a further Soviet attack, it had made perfect sense for the entire area to be under military control but now, with nearly half of Latvia liberated, Ulmanis' government demanded that it take over the police, particularly in Liepāja. Once more, Goltz refused to cooperate. Relations with the British and French authorities in Liepāja plummeted to new lows. Aware that German *Freikorps* reinforcements continued to arrive in Latvia, the British imposed a partial naval blockade. This had only a limited result, as Goltz's gains in Latvia and northern Lithuania had opened the rail link to East Prussia. Nevertheless, it added to Goltz's growing sense of grievance.

The civilian government and the British were not the only parties growing increasingly hostile to Goltz. He stirred up further antagonism from the Liepāja garrison soldiers' council when he placed the three garrison battalions under the command of Major Götze, a tough disciplinarian. When the soldiers' council tried to interfere with Götze's orders, the major had several men placed under arrest. Anticipating trouble, Goltz ordered a detachment of reliable soldiers to return to Liepāja from the front line, and when the soldiers' council tried to enforce its will Goltz was able to face down its mutinous members. He then used the affair to justify the dissolution of the soldiers' council, thus removing one of his perceived enemies. It is not clear whether he deliberately provoked this showdown, or whether he simply took advantage of events.

With the front line relatively quiet, the German command established a series of troop rotations to allow units to be withdrawn to the rear area for rest and replenishment. One such rotation involved the replacement of the German unit that Goltz had used to overcome the soldiers' council by a *Landeswehr* unit. According to Goltz, Major Fletcher suggested that Hans von Manteuffel's *Stosstrupp* ('shock troop') should move to Liepāja. These troops were therefore close to the centre of matters when constitutional issues were discussed on 15 April. A proposal – suggested by the Americans, in Goltz's account – was put forward that would allow the Baltic Germans autonomy within the new Latvian state, though all legal matters would remain within the jurisdiction of the central government. Although this was less than Goltz and his Baltic German allies wanted, he later recorded that he would have found this an acceptable compromise, but the Latvian government refused to accept it. The following day Ulmanis met Goltz and complained about trouble caused by a newly arrived *Freikorps* unit commanded by Hauptmann von Pfeffer. Goltz replied that he had heard rumours of a pro-Bolshevik rebellion being planned by Latvian dockers for 17 April, and that he therefore needed additional troops in Liepāja to prevent this, hence the prolonged stay of Pfeffer's unit in the town. The meeting ended with angry exchanges.

It transpired that the problems with the *Freikorps* unit were due to the arrest of a German officer by the Latvian authorities. The officer was freed by Pfeffer's men, who then went on to disarm several hundred Latvian soldiers on the grounds that two of their own number were missing, presumed either to be in Latvian custody or to have been killed. While Goltz was investigating the matter, he learned that Manteuffel's *Stosstrupp* was deploying near the shore. Further enquiries revealed that the *Landeswehr* unit had moved against Ulmanis' government and had attempted to arrest officials, an act made easier by the disarming of Latvian troops by Pfeffer's men. Goltz maintained that these events were unconnected and that Manteuffel's attempt to arrest the nationalist government was not preceded by any detailed planning. In any event, Ulmanis and the majority of his ministers escaped; Ulmanis himself sought refuge aboard the steamer *Saratov*, which had brought British arms to Liepāja for the new Latvian army. The presence of ships and personnel from the British naval squadron in the Baltic prevented Manteuffel's men from pursuing Ulmanis and his ministers.

Ulmanis attempted to write to Goltz but the latter refused to intervene, claiming that his task was to keep order throughout the area of military control, and the exact nature of the Latvian government was no concern of his. As unrest spread through the countryside, spilling over into exchanges of fire between German and Latvian troops, Goltz felt it necessary on 24 April to issue a proclamation confirming that he remained the sole military authority and that he would not tolerate any unrest.[485] As he admitted in his memoirs, it could be argued that this was not consistent with his failure to order Manteuffel's *Stosstrupp* to release the government officials that it had arrested. His justification that the overriding imperative was to prevent civil war and a Bolshevik victory seems unconvincing. However, Manteuffel was removed from his command, and when the *Stosstrupp* threatened to restore him to his post by force, Goltz made clear his intention to enforce his order regarding discipline, if necessary by ordering German troops to fire on the *Stosstrupp*, and the dangerous moment passed.

There are other accounts of the coup, suggesting that the disarming of Latvian troops by Pfeffer's *Freikorps* unit on the same day as Manteuffel's move against the Ulmanis government was not a coincidence, and that Goltz's dismissal of the soldiers' council was a prelude to the coup, as it removed an agency that had in the past sided with the Ulmanis government against Goltz.[486] Given that the overwhelming balance of military power in Latvia lay with Goltz and the close relationship between senior members of the *Landeswehr* and the German commander, it seems inconceivable that the Baltic Germans would have made any move without knowing where he stood. On 25 April, the Entente Powers demanded the restoration of the Ulmanis government and Goltz met senior members of the Baltic German community. He wrote that he advised them that 'a new administration must be established by midday the following day, or the entire Baltic game is over'.[487] This does not sound like the statement of a man trying to stay neutral in political matters.

The following morning, the Baltic Germans met once more with Goltz. They advised him that they had formed a new government, including a number of Latvian ministers. The new head of the government was to be Andrievs Niedra, a Lutheran pastor from Riga. Before becoming a pastor he had enjoyed some success as a poet, and had written extensively on the subject of the relationship between the Baltic Germans and ordinary Latvians. He was strongly opposed to socialism and revolution, arguing that progress could come only through gradual evolution. It was these features that made him an attractive candidate to Goltz and the Baltic Germans. He and the other Latvian members of the new government were, in Goltz's opinion, 'great patriots, who placed love of country above [love of political] party'.[488] Needless to say, there were many in the Latvian community who had a different opinion of Niedra. In mid-May a group of Latvian officers attempted to arrest him, but he escaped and returned to Liepāja five days later. Jānis Balodis, who had replaced Kalpaks as commander of the Latvian army, was offered the role of defence minister in the new government but he refused, saying that his allegiance to Ulmanis remained unchanged. However, in the interests of the war against the Russians, he would continue to cooperate with Goltz and the Baltic Germans.

For the Entente Powers this coup was a deeply unwelcome development, but they knew as well as Goltz that there was little they could do. Goltz countered their demands for restoration of the Ulmanis government by threatening to withdraw all his men from Latvia, which would have resulted in a swift victory for the Russians. The German forces in Latvia were effectively the only means of preventing a Bolshevik takeover, especially as Goltz continued to place obstacles in the path of any attempt to increase the size of the Latvian forces. As was the case in relations between the Western Powers and Estonia, a further complication was that Britain and France actively supported the White Russian cause – and the White Russians had as their goal the complete restoration of the Russian Empire, with no room for independent Baltic States.

Shortly after Niedra took power, Gustav Noske – the German defence minister – visited Liepāja. He expressed the opinion that the new Niedra government was unlikely to prove successful as it did not enjoy the support of the majority of the population. In Goltz's opinion, the same was true of the Ulmanis government, but he was unable to persuade Noske of this. A few days later Goltz travelled to Berlin for further discussions with government officials. He was relieved to learn that the German government had no intention of giving in to demands from the Entente Powers for his removal. When it came to consideration of an evacuation of German troops from Latvia, Goltz responded that many men had volunteered in the expectation of being allowed to settle in Latvia; even if this was undeliverable, he argued, it would be worth allowing troops to remain in Latvia in Latvian service as a means of protecting East Prussia from possible Bolshevik attack.

There were also discussions about Riga, which remained in Soviet hands. The main difficulty was not the Bolshevik defence; rather, there were fears about the reaction of the Western Powers, particularly as the peace negotiations at Versailles had not yet been completed. Goltz declared that the best way to proceed was with an attack on the city by the *Landeswehr*. As this force was composed of Baltic Germans from Latvia, such an attack could be regarded as an internal Latvian matter. Goltz also learned that the Estonians planned to attack south into Latvia, and thus the prospect arose of catching the Soviet forces between two pincers, or at least preventing them from concentrating their forces. The discussions went on to speculate whether, with modest reinforcements, it would then be possible to mount a successful attack towards Petrograd, with a view to overthrowing the Bolshevik regime.[489] This must have been music to the ears of the passionately anti-Bolshevik Goltz; however, shortly afterwards he learned that, far from receiving reinforcements, he was ordered to release the 1st Guards Reserve Division, which would be redeployed within Germany.

This version of events is based upon Goltz's own recollections, and there is little by way of corroborative evidence, particularly regarding the discussion about pushing on to Petrograd. Many in the German government regarded Goltz as a dangerous reactionary, just as he regarded them as suspiciously left wing.

It is therefore quite possible that the discussions with Goltz did not cover these topics, or at least not in this manner. However, minutes of a cabinet meeting suggest that the foreign minister, Ulrich von Brockdorff-Rantzau, was of the opinion that a strong anti-Bolshevik stance by Germany might help in the Versailles negotiations; it seems that he did not persuade many of his fellow ministers.[490] When it came to the possible advance on Petrograd, Goltz recorded that this arose during a discussion with 'a senior person in the Foreign Ministry' – but does not name the person concerned.[491]

When he returned to Latvia, Goltz was briefed by his staff. A signal intercept suggested that a large group of prisoners being held by the Red Army were in a camp to the south of Riga, in an area within striking distance of the 1st Guards Reserve Division. The planned attack to recapture the Latvian capital was modified to allow the *Freikorps* division to move towards the camp before it returned to Germany. The overall plan of attack was the same as the original German assault of 1917: the main thrust would be east from Jelgava to the Daugava valley, before turning north to attack Riga from the south and southeast. Although this was portrayed as a *Landeswehr* operation, the Iron Division was ordered to ensure that it remained in contact with the *Landeswehr*, and would thus provide considerable support.

The attack began on 22 May. The Red Army had feared an attack earlier in the year immediately after the German attack that recaptured Jelgava, but the intervening weeks of calm had reduced their alertness. Goltz had his staff officers distribute instructions for the attack in person to reduce the risk of alerting the Russians by increasing signals traffic. From their start line, which was quite close to Riga, the *Landeswehr* made rapid progress. The swampy front-line area was cleared in a dawn attack by Walter Eberhard von Medem's battalion, which penetrated nearly 18 miles (30km) in its first attack. Without pausing for breath, Medem pushed on into Riga, making the very most of the element of surprise, and reached the Daugava bridge towards midday. With two light field guns and four machine-guns, Medem galloped over the bridge, securing a bridgehead on the east bank. From there, accompanied by Manteuffel and his *Stosstrupp*, Medem moved towards the citadel and the main city prison. As they approached they came under fire, and the 25-year-old Hans von Manteuffel was killed. He was one of only a handful of *Landeswehr* casualties during the entire day. Although Medem was able to seize the prison and a nearby convent that had been used to hold female prisoners, he was too late to save many of those who had originally been held in the prison camp south of Riga. Some of these men, who had been brought to Riga over the last few days, had already been executed.[492]

South of the city, the fighting was more intense. The Iron Division found itself confronted by a Soviet armoured train, which it succeeded in driving off. At the southern end of the advance, near Bauska, to the southeast of Jelgava, Major Graf Yorck's battalion of the 1st Guards Reserve Division came under heavy attack. Fighting lasted all day, but, despite growing short of ammunition, Yorck's men held on. Towards dusk, the Red Army pulled back beyond the Daugava. Yorck's battalion suffered the greatest losses of the entire operation, but official accounts of the battle, as reported in newspapers in the days that followed, attempted to emphasise that the assault had been carried out almost exclusively by the *Landeswehr*. Many *Freikorps* soldiers were angry that their own deeds and losses had been overlooked for political reasons, and Goltz marked this moment as the beginning of the decline in morale of the *Freikorps*.[493]

Another of the casualties in the fighting around Riga was Anatol von Lieven, who had created a small White Russian unit to fight alongside the *Landeswehr*. He was badly wounded, and taken to Jelgava. Amongst his command were elements commanded by Pavel Bermont-Avalov, who would later play an important role in Latvia's struggle for independence. Yudenich, the White Russian commander in the region, ordered Lieven and his men to move to Narva, in Estonia, to take part in the planned White Russian attack towards Petrograd. Lieven was against this move, preferring to remain in Latvia; he hoped that in conjunction with Goltz and the *Landeswehr*, he would be able to strike east into Russia and cut the Moscow-Petrograd railway line, and thus facilitate the advance against Petrograd, but eventually agreed to obey Yudenich's orders, albeit reluctantly. Bermont-Avalov refused to move his men to Narva, claiming they weren't ready for such an operation. Consequently, when Lieven and the rest of the contingent moved north, Bermont-Avalov and his men were left behind.

Much of the population of Riga was starving, so many greeted the arrival of the Baltic Germans and their allies with genuine relief. Also, the Bolshevik occupation of Riga had been marked by a wave of arrests and executions, colloquially known to the population as the 'Red Terror'. The arrival of the *Landeswehr* resulted in a new wave of executions, which were named the 'White Terror'.[494] As had been the case in Jelgava, anyone suspected of being a Bolshevik, or even of having sympathised with them, was liable to arrest, imprisonment, or worse. The French envoy recorded that dozens of prisoners were executed every day in the main prison, having been forced to dig their own graves first.[495] As was the case with Jelgava, Goltz condemned the excesses of the Bolshevik regime, but was silent about the executions that followed the city's 'liberation'. The Latvian brigade under Jānis Balodis took part in the attack towards Riga but played no part in the actual recapture of the city; whether this was purely due to operational reasons, or whether Goltz wished to ensure that the recapture was an entirely Baltic German affair, is impossible to say with any certainty. After the battle Balodis' troops moved through Riga and were deployed to the east of the city. When he became aware of the widespread killings of suspected Bolsheviks, Balodis protested both to Goltz and to the representatives of the Entente Powers. Perhaps as a result of his protests, the 'White Terror' then died down.[496]

Orders now arrived from Germany, setting a strict limit on how far German and Baltic German forces were to advance. Furthermore, Goltz was ordered to remain outside Riga. The senior officer in Riga was the commander of the *Baltische Landeswehr*, Major Fletcher, and he now had to take on all dealings with Latvian civilian authorities and the Entente Powers. Meanwhile, the Estonian 3rd Division, supported by the North Latvian Brigade – raised mainly from Latvians who had fled the Bolsheviks into Estonia, and former members of the Red Latvian Rifles – crossed the border on 24 May and drove the Bolsheviks back on a broad front. On 28 May, a cavalry unit from Balodis' Latvian brigade deployed to the east of Riga, made contact with the advancing Estonians and Latvians and placed itself under the command of the North Latvian Brigade. For the Germans and the *Landeswehr*, this was a most unwelcome development. They were aware that the Estonians continued to regard the Ulmanis government, still protected by the Royal Navy aboard the steamer *Saratov*, as the legitimate government of Latvia.

Goltz was acutely conscious of the mutual mistrust between Berlin and himself and wished to press on with his plans while he still had the ability to do so. He therefore encouraged the *Landeswehr* to start advancing northeast, and on 29 May Fletcher ordered his men to move out. It was a development of huge significance. Much of eastern Latvia was still under Russian occupation, and if the *Landeswehr* had moved east, with or without German support, it could have claimed to be continuing its anti-Bolshevik liberation of Latvia. An advance to the northeast could only be directed against Estonia. Perhaps to quieten any objections, Fletcher told his men, particularly new recruits who had joined the *Landeswehr* in Riga, that the Estonians and Latvians in northeast Latvia were pro-Bolshevik forces.

Fletcher deployed his forces in four columns. One was sent down the Daugava valley, towards Jēkabpils (Jakobstadt), while the other three headed northeast. Of these, the leading *Landeswehr* unit, composed of Medem's battalion, encountered the advancing Estonian forces near Cēsis, or Wenden, which had been liberated by the Estonians on 2 June. At first communication between the two sides

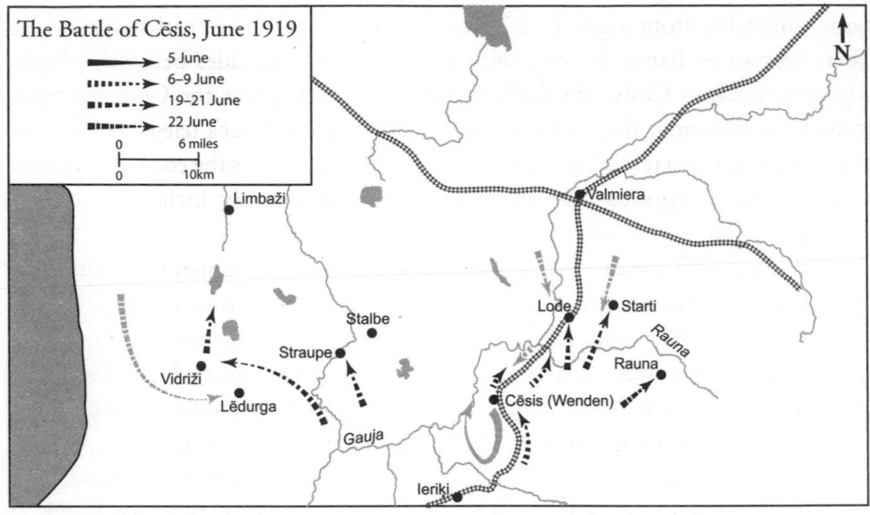

appeared cordial, and Jorģis Zemitāns, commander of the North Latvian Brigade, invited the *Landeswehr* to move east against the Bolsheviks. The Niedra administration, on behalf of the *Landeswehr*, asked the Estonians to withdraw to the linguistic border between the two countries. For the Estonians, this was unacceptable: with their troops operating against Russian forces in the Pskov area, such a withdrawal would leave a potential hostile force almost astride their supply lines, and in any event the Estonian government did not recognise Niedra's authority. The following day, a small *Landeswehr* unit moved into Cēsis, but left when asked to do so. As it became clear that the *Landeswehr* had no intention of moving east to face Russia, Laidoner, the Estonian commander-in-chief, sent a telegram to the Baltic Germans on 4 June, effectively ordering them to withdraw beyond a small river to the southwest of Cēsis. In the absence of such a withdrawal, the Estonians would assume that hostilities had started. No reply was received.

On 5 June two Estonian armoured trains moved forward from Cēsis towards Ieriķi as part of an operation to secure the line of the River Gauja. A message arrived that a *Landeswehr* delegation was on its way from Riga but Lieutenant Colonel Nikolai Reek, chief of staff of the Estonian 2nd Division and commander of this expedition, decided that he would receive the delegation only if Estonian demands for a Baltic German withdrawal had been met. As the first Estonian armoured train approached a bridge midway between the two towns, it slowed while a team checked that the bridge was safe to cross. At this stage, the train came under fire from a group of Baltic German infantry in nearby woodland. There was an exchange of shots with casualties on both sides before the train withdrew back to Cēsis. The Estonians claimed that it was the Germans who started the shooting; the Germans responded that Laidoner's telegram made it clear that a German refusal to withdraw would be regarded as the commencement of hostilities. It appears that neither side was particularly inclined to avoid a confrontation.

The Estonian-Latvian force in Cēsis consisted of an Estonian regiment, two Latvian artillery batteries, and the two armoured trains, a total of about 1,600 men. The *Landeswehr* attacked the town on 6 June with three infantry battalions supported by two cavalry squadrons and four artillery pieces, and fighting raged all day. In mid-afternoon the Estonian commander ordered a withdrawal to the north, and the town's garrison withdrew in some disorder. The following day, reinforced by a further regiment of Estonian infantry, the force advanced back towards Cēsis. A formal assault by two infantry battalions, supported by the armoured car *Estonia* – the Estonian Army had so few armoured cars that they all had individual names – and the armoured trains, as well as artillery batteries, began on 8 June against *Landeswehr* positions immediately to the north of Cēsis. The Baltic Germans had destroyed a small railway bridge, preventing the trains from supporting the attack effectively, and poor coordination prevented the Estonians from bringing all their available forces to bear. During the afternoon the *Landeswehr* counterattacked and the Estonians were driven off. However, their casualties were relatively light, suggesting that their attacks may have been little more than a probing advance.

The following day, the *Landeswehr* advanced farther and briefly seized a railway bridge over the Rauna, a small river to the northeast of Cēsis, effectively cutting off the two armoured trains. An Estonian counterattack succeeded in retaking the bridge, and the trains were able to withdraw behind the river. German attempts to cross the river continued all day and though a small bridgehead was secured, it was soon abandoned when it came under heavy Estonian artillery fire.

On 10 June the American Lieutenant Colonel Warwick Greene, a member of the Allied Military Commission in the Baltic, succeeded in getting both sides to accept a ceasefire. Greene was a relative newcomer to the Baltic region and appears to have been largely sympathetic to the German side, encouraging all forces to turn against the Bolsheviks, with Latvian units – including the North Latvian Brigade, which had been raised in Estonia – coming under the command of the *Landeswehr* and therefore acknowledging the Niedra government. Three days later General Hubert Gough, the British head of the Allied Commission, took over personally with a far less friendly attitude towards the Germans. He ordered that the *Landeswehr* withdraw to a point about midway between Cēsis and Riga. Goltz regarded this as unacceptable – he assumed that the Entente Powers would establish the Ulmanis government in northeast Latvia, from where it would be able to wage war against the Baltic Germans and the Niedra government. Nevertheless he continued to negotiate with Gough, but largely to win time. The *Landeswehr* could turn east, the Germans insisted, only if the Estonians withdrew to the linguistic border first.

Goltz felt that it would be impossible for him to support the *Landeswehr* openly, particularly as the Versailles negotiations were not yet complete:

> On the other hand, the question was put to the commander of the Iron Division, Major Bischoff, if he was willing to transfer his volunteer troops to the service of the Niedra administration. The troops had enlisted for service in Latvia not merely to defend their Fatherland here against the Bolsheviks, but also to seek a new home for themselves here … but it was clear that this would only be possible if a government that was not hostile to Germans honoured Ulmanis' promises, and that Ulmanis, the lackey of the Entente, would never do this. After discussion with their subordinate officers, Major Fletcher and also the commanders of a few other *Freikorps* units agreed.[497]

As has already been discussed, the issue of land and settlement rights for *Freikorps* veterans was a controversial matter and Ulmanis had not made any explicit promise to offer land to German soldiers. But the fundamental policy of Goltz and his *Landeswehr* allies had always been to ensure that the Baltic German aristocracy would continue to hold a pre-eminent position in Latvia, and such a position was unlikely to continue should Ulmanis be able to consolidate power. Therefore, all hinged on a *Landeswehr* victory; it was probable that the Baltic German aristocrats could be persuaded to offer land in Courland for German veterans who wished to settle in the area, and this was the only manner in which this particular promise was likely to be delivered.

And such a victory over Ulmanis was only the first step of Goltz's master plan, which saw no future for independent Baltic nations:

> 'Niedra or Ulmanis' was not the question, rather a pro-German, autonomous Latvia in a modern and orderly Russia, or a vassal state dependent upon England, which could not hold out against Russia, where anarchistic Bolshevik ideals

> triumphed, and due to Bolshevik leanings in part of its population, there remained the danger of it once more becoming Bolshevik.[498]

Finally Gough sent a telegram to Goltz demanding amongst other things that the German troops should withdraw from the front line, that half of Goltz's command should return to Germany, and that Ulmanis should be restored to power. Goltz responded by stating that he rejected Gough's right to issue orders to him and that Gough's demands would be forwarded to higher authorities who would respond via diplomatic channels. It was effectively the end of all prospects of a peaceful resolution to the crisis.

In the fighting that followed, a proportion of the German forces available played no part. Goltz recorded that he had intelligence of an imminent Russian attack along the Daugava valley towards Riga and consequently had to retain forces in reserve, including a proportion of the Iron Division deployed at Ogre. The *Stosstrupp* formerly commanded by Manteuffel, now renamed the 1st Regiment, was also absent; it was in Riga, heavily involved in the ongoing hunt for, and execution of, Bolshevik sympathisers. There was also concern in German circles that the combined Estonian and British control of the sea might allow for landings almost anywhere along the coast. Consequently, Goltz decided on an early assault on the main Estonian forces north of Cēsis in the hope of achieving a swift victory.

Aerial reconnaissance suggested that the area around Limbaži, a little to the west, was relatively clear of Estonian troops, and elements of the Iron Division were ordered to advance in this direction to secure the western flank of the German advance. The bulk of the division under Major von Kleist would attack a little farther east between Limbaži and Cēsis to take Stalbe. The *Landeswehr* would then advance in three groups from Cēsis. The Estonians decided that they would allow the Germans to attack them first, not least because it would allow them to portray the Germans as the aggressors. The bulk of the 6th Regiment was placed astride the road that the Iron Division would use, with the Latvians and the 3rd Regiment extending the front line to the east. The Estonian 9th Regiment would be deployed to the west.

On 19 June the Iron Division's left flank guard under Hauptmann Blankenburg set out for Limbaži. It ran into Estonian forces near Vidriži, and took the town after desultory fighting. The following day Blankenburg was ordered to advance to Limbaži from where he was to turn east and push towards Valmeira. Confused fighting continued all afternoon, and in the early evening the Germans managed to infiltrate forward using the cover of a rye field and surprised the Estonians. Before they could exploit their success they in turn were surprised by an Estonian counterattack, which took advantage of another rye field to turn the German flank. An Estonian attempt to envelop the Germans then failed, but Blankenburg was killed in the fighting and his men withdrew to the south. On the same day, the Iron Division began to advance towards Straupe, and despite capturing the town was unable to advance farther. The following day, further advances were made in the face of determined resistance, but just as the Estonian lines started to look as if they might give way, two Estonian armoured cars – the *Estonia* and *Toonela* – supported by a company of infantry from one of the armoured trains, arrived and restored the front.

The *Landeswehr* attack north of Cēsis was intended to start once the Iron Division had broken through at Straupe. An erroneous aerial reconnaissance report suggested that this had been achieved, and the three columns set off.[499] Fighting became generalised during the morning; in an echo of the First World War, German gunners used gas shells on Estonian artillery positions. A gap began to open between the Latvians on the extreme east wing and the Estonians to their west, and towards the end of the day the *Landeswehr* approached the town of Lode from both the south and east, while the Latvians were driven back through Starti. In heavy fighting, during which the Baltic German gunners once more used gas shells, the Estonians were driven back farther. An Estonian counterattack with the newly arrived Kuperjanov Battalion made little headway, as did a further *Landeswehr* attempt to exploit their modest successes. Late in the day, a small group of Estonian infantry mounted a raid to the outskirts of Cēsis, causing much alarm before they withdrew. The consequence of this raid was out of all proportion to the number of men involved. Fearful that the Estonians might infiltrate into Cēsis, the Germans moved a battalion of infantry from the Iron Division, one of their few reserve formations, into the town as a precaution. Late in the day, the Kuperjanov Battalion managed to recapture some ground, but despite this success, there remained a substantial gap in Estonian lines to the east.

On 22 June, the Estonian units nearest the coast began to move forward. The Iron Division formations facing them put up only sporadic resistance and by the end of the day the Estonians had reached Lēdurga, behind the flank of the Iron Division. Meanwhile, without the battalion that had been ordered to protect Cēsis, the *Freikorps* could make no progress. In the early evening, finally learning that the reserve battalion sent to Cēsis would not be joining him, the German commander made a last attack. Despite inflicting considerable casualties, he was unable to break through to Stalbe and aware that Estonian units in Lēdurga were now behind his flank, he issued orders for a withdrawal.

Farther east, the Estonians attempted to deal with the *Landwehr* salient to the east of Lode. At midday, the armoured car *Vanapagan* led a charge into the village of Starti. After a short, sharp fight, the Germans were driven back. Short of fuel, the armoured car stopped in the village, but the accompanying infantry advanced steadily south. At the same time, the Kuperjanov Battalion attacked Lode directly, completing the elimination of the salient. At the extreme eastern end of the battlefield, Böckelmann attacked the Estonians in the ruins of the old Livonian Order castle at Rauna for two hours before he was forced to give up the attempt.

It was effectively the end of the *Landeswehr* assault. The western flank was badly endangered by the Estonian outflanking move, and with Böckelmann's column blocked and Malmede's driven back, the main Cēsis position was in danger of being outflanked on both sides. Total Estonian and Latvian losses are estimated to be about 500 dead, wounded and missing. By the scale of the battles of the First World War and the fighting that was to come some two decades later, the Battle of Cēsis was a relatively small action, but it was a defining moment in the Latvian War of Independence. It effectively ended any lingering dreams of a pro-German state incorporating Latvia and Lithuania, thus preserving at least some of the gains of the Treaty of Brest-Litovsk. Goltz identified a number of reasons for the German defeat. He was critical of the intelligence reports he received about the numbers and abilities of the Estonian troops, who he felt had not excelled themselves against the Bolsheviks (an odd assessment, given that they had successfully driven the Russians from Estonia), 'but fought against the Baltic Germans and the Germans with passion, had been well-equipped and armed by the English, and were also well-led'.[500] However, he went on to acknowledge failings in his own troops:

> I alone know of four cases of catastrophic panic that forced the higher command to order a retreat. These are therefore signs that there was no longer a universal spirit of fighting for a cause, which gives an invincible will to win, and that there wasn't a good enough spirit to compensate for lack of combat experience and training, and finally that the middle and lower officer ranks failed on several occasions.[501]

He also noted that many of the officers in the *Freikorps* had extensive experience of trench warfare, but little experience of mobile operations. The relative ease of successes against the poorly trained Red Army probably masked such deficiencies. In some cases, it seems that many soldiers in the Iron Division were unhappy that they were fighting Estonians, not Bolsheviks. To an extent Goltz attempted to dismiss such arguments, on the grounds that the men were not fighting 'for the barons, but for their own future against enemies of Germany and half-Bolsheviks'.[502] Whether the soldiers saw it this way is hard to assess. Goltz blamed some of the failure on Bischoff, feeling that the Iron Division commander had not assessed the mood of his men properly when the original plan to 'loan' the Iron Division to the *Landeswehr* was mooted. Unsurprisingly, Bischoff felt otherwise, saying that he had always been unhappy about the arrangement and had doubted its prospect of success.

On 23 June, the Iron Division was ordered to retake Lēdurga but made little effort to do so. The Estonians secured Straupe during the morning, at about the same time that reconnaissance troops cautiously entered Cēsis to find that the *Landeswehr* had withdrawn to the south, leaving considerable amounts of equipment behind in their haste. Between Cēsis and Riga were field positions that had been constructed earlier during the First World War, and the Germans withdrew into these positions. Lieutenant Colonel Reek was anxious to prevent the Germans from digging in, and ordered two of his regiments to attack. One regiment was held up, but the other pressed forward on its own. The Iron Division beat off the attack, but Bischoff decided on a further withdrawal. The following day, the Estonians attacked the *Landeswehr*, which had taken up positions around Inčukalns. Once more, they made little progress, but the Baltic Germans pulled back during the night.

In just a few days, the position of the Baltic Germans had worsened beyond recognition. With morale in the Iron Division collapsing, an attempt was made on 26 June to organise a truce, which the Estonians rejected. The Iron Division and *Landeswehr* withdrew farther to a line that took advantage of the Jugla, Ķīšezers and Baltezers lakes and the lower Gauja valley, immediately to the east of Riga. As reinforcements arrived, the modest numerical advantage the Estonians had enjoyed was eliminated, and the presence of the lakes allowed the Germans to concentrate their forces far better than before. The Estonians probed the defences on 28 June without success, and once more the Germans used gas shells. Two days later Estonian troops crossed the river near Carnikava but fled back in the face of a German counterattack. Finally, on 1 July, the Estonians managed to advance along the coast, turning the flank of the German positions.

Colonel du Parquet, a French member of the Allied Commission, started a series of journeys between the two sides to secure a truce, and the Estonians redoubled their efforts to achieve victory before hostilities came to an end. On 2 July they pressed forward, reaching the Daugava estuary. A truce came into effect on the morning of 3 July, though as Colonel Harold Alexander, one of the

British officers present recorded, it was not easy to get all parties to agree:

> The whole proceedings were very dramatic. We all sat round a table in a bare room with candles flickering in the draught. On our side, Tallents, tremendously alert and business-like; Victor Warrender of the Grenadiers, cool and correct; Harrison, our shorthand typist, rather journalistic; Colonel du Parquet, the Frenchman, obviously not understanding a word of the discussion in English, but looking frightfully formal and severe; Colonel Dawley, the American, making long-winded speeches entirely off the point, and getting rather snubbed by the Germans; the Estonian, frightfully suspicious and not at all anxious to sign an armistice but longing to get at the throat of the Germans.[503]

Under the terms of the truce, the *Landeswehr* would withdraw towards Tukums and the *Freikorps* to Jelgava. Latvian troops moved into Riga on 5 and 6 July. On 8 July, *Saratov* arrived in Riga, and Ulmanis was restored to power. The truce also required the Estonians to withdraw to their border. There had been some tension between Ulmanis and the Estonians in the past few days, and Ulmanis was not enthusiastic about an Estonian advance into Riga itself. The *Freikorps* was to withdraw back to Germany, but for the moment Goltz was able to postpone this, citing transport difficulties.[504] However, he accepted the appointment of a British officer to take command of the *Landeswehr*. The person nominated was Colonel Alexander, who would ultimately rise to the rank of Field Marshal, with an illustrious service record in the Second World War. He took his new command east, and alongside troops from the Latvian and Polish armies, the *Landeswehr* played a prominent role in driving Bolshevik forces from the province of Latgale in eastern Latvia.

There had been looting and plundering by the *Freikorps* since the advance across Courland, but these now worsened with the added demoralisation of defeat. Attempts to restore order via courts martial were only partially successful, mainly within formations that had high-calibre officers. A large part of the blame for this, Goltz, asserted, was the revolution that had swept through Germany, destroying traditional loyalty and discipline. The left-wing press, he wrote, had little interest in reporting the true facts, and merely encouraged the disorder.[505]

With the *Landeswehr* effectively removed from the scene, Goltz desperately sought new allies. He found one in the unlikely form of Pavel Bermont-Avalov. Born in Georgia in 1877, he served as a musical director in a Cossack regiment before serving in a lancer regiment in the First World War. He was an uncompromising royalist and started to recruit like-minded officers into a new body after the fall of the tsar. After refusing to accompany Lieven north to join Yudenich, he enlarged his forces by incorporating Russians formerly held as prisoners of war by the Germans. The small army acquired an unpleasant reputation for indiscipline, something that Goltz blamed upon leftists who he alleged were trying to discredit Bermont-Avalov.[506] The Russian's mistrust of the British was another factor in raising him in Goltz's esteem. In any event, the existence of this body of troops seemed to offer one last opportunity for Goltz to achieve his goals for the Baltic:

> As the German soldiers did not wish to return to their Homeland, but were unable to remain as settlers and had not prevailed against the unfriendly Ulmanis regime by force, the only option for them was to go into Russian service.[507]

Goltz fantasised about a Russian-German drive into Belarus, while at the same time other White Russian forces – Admiral Kolchak in Siberia, and General Denikin in the Ukraine – also advanced into Russia, bringing about the longed-for fall of the Bolshevik government. The threat of a renewal of the Anglo-French blockade of Germany, Goltz speculated, could be sidestepped through the capture of resources in Belarus. Whilst such notions are easily dismissed as mere dreams, they gained some currency amongst the circles of German army officers who felt that they had been betrayed at the end of the First World War and still held out hope for restoration of German pre-eminence in Europe, perhaps as a result of an alliance with a post-Bolshevik Russia. Regardless of the extreme dreams of this fringe, there were others within the German government who were reluctant to see a German withdrawal from the Baltic States. Goltz was therefore given a fairly free hand to prevaricate about a German withdrawal from Latvia. He provided detailed calculations to Gough and the Allied Commission, showing how it would take a minimum of 70 days for a complete evacuation. The Commission grudgingly accepted these delays, which Goltz put to good use trying to secure financial and political support for the transfer of German troops to the Bermont-Avalov force.

In late July, Goltz summoned all German officers from battalion commanders upwards to a conference. He explained to them his reasoning that the only circumstances in which they or their men could remain in Latvia was as part of Bermont-Avalov's corps. He also outlined the difficulties posed by such a plan: the Entente Powers would probably attempt to prevent it, but most important of all, the financial basis for the proposal was not yet established. There was a shortage of winter clothing, making an autumn attack against Russia difficult, if not impossible. He asked his officers to determine how many troops would be willing to stay on in Latvia in such circumstances, even in the absence of adequate financial support. Many men, particularly those with families, chose to return home. However, many others chose to stay, and the remnants were consolidated into fewer formations; as a result, the overall mood and fighting spirit of those who stayed in Latvia was considerably enhanced. Meanwhile, Goltz recorded, he considered the circumstances facing the new Russian-German project. It would be doomed to failure if the Baltic States were hostile to it; therefore, it was particularly important to ensure a friendly regime, particularly in Latvia and Lithuania, before an advance into Russia could be considered. It is arguable that this had always been his primary intention, and that the Russian adventure was little more than an excuse.[508]

Gough and the Entente Commission began to run out of patience. On 2 August Gough informed Goltz that the Commission required the Germans to accelerate their evacuation plans and complete them within 18 days. Goltz stubbornly insisted that this was physically impossible, given the shortage of rolling stock on the railways. Weeks passed with more meetings and discussions. Goltz travelled back to Germany to meet senior government officials, including President Friedrich Ebert. He was advised that the German government would not take action against any Germans who chose to remain in Latvia, as this was a private decision of the individuals concerned. The government also agreed, at least until October, to finance the Bermont-Avalov army – in other words, Germany accepted that German troops would remain in Latvia under the Bermontian flag of convenience, and Germany would continue to pay for them. It was further suggested that, should it become financially impossible for the troops to remain in Latvia, it was possible that they could enter Lithuanian service as there continued to be tension between Lithuania and Poland; such an arrangement, the government felt, would help bind Lithuania to Germany. Clearly, Ebert's administration had not given up hope of retaining substantial influence in the Baltic region.

When Goltz returned to his headquarters in Jelgava, he found that, despite the departure of men who wished to return home, the troops of the Iron Division were in a state of unrest. They demanded that if they were to be returned to Germany, they should be given land within Germany as recognition of their service and the failure of the Latvians to grant them citizenship and land. They also demanded that 30 per cent of the new 100,000-strong *Reichswehr* should be made up of men who had served in the *Freikorps*. In the absence of such assurances, they refused to be sent back to Germany. Goltz told them that he would pass their demands to his superiors, aware that this delay in evacuation, which he could blame upon the soldiers, gave him more time to make progress with Bermont-Avalov.

The vexed question of finance continued to rear its head. For a while, Goltz and like-minded individuals in Berlin, who were in discussion with Major General Neill Malcolm, a British representative in Berlin, appear to have believed that there might be support from the Entente Powers for their proposed anti-Bolshevik war, but it was felt that Goltz and Bermont-Avalov were barriers to such a move. Consequently, Goltz considered trying to persuade Bermont-Avalov to put the entire venture under the command of General Biskupski, a Russian-Polish officer who was nominally serving under Bermont-Avalov, even though the two men had fundamental disagreements. When a further Entente demand for the complete evacuation of Latvia by the Germans arrived, Goltz lost faith in such discussions and felt that the entire episode confirmed his views of the British:

> In the eyes of naïve German politicians, General Malcolm appeared to be a supporter of the beliefs of the inter-allied anti-Bolshevik opposition, but raised only objections … [If he had been genuine] he should long since have asked for his removal given his constant failure, or the British government should have replaced this diplomat who was not carrying out its policies. Instead, these clever British constantly sent us diplomats, politicians and officers who led the most intelligent Germans around by the nose. Britain knew who it was sending to Germany.
>
> I have never trusted these Englishmen, nor will I trust any member of this most callous race until the day of my death.[509]

We do not have Malcolm's version of events, nor is there any documentation to suggest that the British government actively considered supporting such a policy. Whilst having lunch with Ludendorff in 1919, Malcolm discussed the collapse of Germany that resulted in the end of the war, and said to Ludendorff, 'It sounds like you were stabbed in the back, then?' Ludendorff was very taken with this phrase, and it became widely accepted within German army circles. Malcolm was therefore no stranger to making statements that might vary from the policy of his government, and it is therefore possible that he had some rather speculative conversations with German officials whilst in Berlin. It is also possible that some of these officials, desperate to salvage something from what they regarded as the shameful peace settlement at Versailles, heard what they wanted to hear and acted accordingly.

Regardless of the opinion of Goltz's friends in Berlin, the government had to deal with ongoing pressure to comply with all the terms of the Treaty of Versailles. Goltz was ordered to charge Major Bischoff with repeated disobedience for not ordering his men to board trains back to Germany, but he responded that the men had chosen not to return, so their officer was blameless. On 21 September, with growing evidence that Latvian and Estonian troops might be deployed against the remaining German units, and occasional artillery exchanges with the Germans – despite the ceasefire officially still being in force – Goltz sent a signal to Bermont-Avalov, informing him that the Germans who had stayed in Latvia of their free will were now entering Russian service. He also asked Bermont-Avalov to invite the Latvian government to join in their proposed venture against Bolshevik Russia. On 30 September, the German units were ordered to concentrate their forces in preparation of a resumption of hostilities. Meanwhile, in an attempt to resolve his financial problems, Bermont-Avalov had started to print his own money. It was to be redeemed by the value of his future conquests.

Although Goltz had received a signal on 26 September from Berlin granting permission for Germans to join the ranks of Bermont-Avalov's army, new orders arrived on 3 October.[510] The Entente Powers had issued a final ultimatum to Berlin on 27 September, insisting on an immediate withdrawal of Goltz and all German forces – if this was not carried out, Britain and France threatened to re-impose their blockade of Germany.[511] Berlin now ordered the immediate evacuation of all German forces from the Baltic. A further order informed Goltz that he was recalled and would be replaced by General Walter von Eberhardt. A day later came another development: German troops were not permitted to enter Russian service. Why these orders took so long to reach Latvia is unclear, but they allowed Goltz to reason that, as his men who had already entered Russian service were no longer Germans, this order did not apply to them.[512] On 5 October, he wrote to the German general staff:

> There are only Russian citizens at the front now, and all of my efforts can, as before, only be to keep Germany out of the game. On my part, I wrote a letter of resignation to General Burt on 4 October, and must stay in the shadows, as otherwise the troops would become unsettled.[513]

Aware that Latvian forces were about to be reinforced by Estonian troops, Goltz and Bermont-Avalov decided that the die was cast. Bermont-Avalov announced the creation of a West Russian government, and called upon Latvians and Lithuanians to join with him in a war against the Bolsheviks. He and Goltz maintained that their original plan had been to attack east from Daugavpils, or Dünaberg; but with potentially hostile forces massing against them in and around Riga, they decided that they had to deal with securing Latvia first.

Estimates of the strength of the so-called West Russian Volunteer Army, as Bermont-Avalov's force became known, are varied. The highest estimate is 52,000, but this figure probably includes all rear-area units.[514] The true number of combatants is likely to have been closer to 22,000, of whom the majority were German. Many of his men were deployed to secure the rear area in Lithuania, and the number of men available to attack Riga was probably in the region of 8,500, opposed by about 6,500 Latvians.[515]

The plan for the coming campaign was for the Petersdorff battalion and the Riekhoff detachment, both formerly *Freikorps* units, to guard the right flank of the advance. Four battalions of former *Freikorps* troops, grouped together as the 'German Legion', would advance on Ķekava, a little to the southeast of Riga, while the Iron Division launched the main attack on the Latvian capital in three groups. A Russian column would secure the coastal flank – an indication of how small the Russian element of the West Russian Volunteer Army was. The advance began on 8 October and despite heavy resistance reached Ķekava during the early afternoon, in heavy rain and cold wind. Late in the evening, the Iron Division penetrated into the western Rigan suburb of Torņakalns, though a Latvian counterattack during the night drove the Germans back. The following day Bischoff decided against a resumption of the frontal assault on Riga and moved one of his regiments to the southeast to support the advance of the German Legion in an attempt to turn the flank of the defenders. In heavy fighting, the combined force slowly moved forward, reaching Torņakalns late in the day. During 10 October the German grip on the west bank of the Daugava in Riga was secured, and over the two following days the Russian element of the force moved up to the river as far as the estuary. British and French warships moved out into the Gulf of Riga to stay out of range of German artillery, which now subjected Riga to a desultory bombardment; ammunition was in too short supply for a more intensive attack. Bermont-Avalov offered the Latvians a ceasefire, on condition that they agreed to support his plans for an attack on Russia; the Latvians made no reply.[516]

On 14 October, Goltz left the Baltic. He was confident that Bermont-Avalov had achieved as much as he could, and that the Latvians would agree to support a future operation into Russia. As with all hopes for this venture, it was misplaced. Under constant pressure from Britain and France, Germany refused to allow supplies of winter clothing to be sent to the Bermontians, and detained soldiers from the force who had returned to Germany on leave and wished to return to Latvia. British and French warships imposed a complete blockade on German shipping in the Baltic, further reducing the supplies reaching the West Russian Volunteer Army.

On the same day that Goltz left for Germany, the Latvians made their first counterattack across the Daugava. They had detected German troop movements, with elements being sent further upstream and also back into Courland in order to secure more territory there. The attack was largely repulsed, but by the end of the day the Latvians were substantially closer to Ķekava. On 15 October, several British warships moved close to the coast and bombarded Russian positions on the coast, and under cover of their fire Latvian troops crossed the Daugava estuary and secured positions on the west bank.[517] Supplies were now arriving in Riga for the Latvian forces, as well as reinforcements from Estonia. British and French warships continued to bombard coastal positions, though not without consequence; on 17 October, the light cruiser HMS *Dragon* came under fire from a shore battery, and nine sailors were killed. Two days later, the German Legion made its last attempt to cross the Daugava upstream of Riga, and was repulsed.

On 3 November the Latvians had moved sufficient forces across the Daugava estuary to the west bank to allow them to start a major attack. With fire support from Admiral Cowan's cruisers, they made steady progress in driving the Bermontians out of the western suburbs of Riga, clearing the area completely by 11 November. From here they advanced on Jelgava, reaching the town on 16 November. Under pressure from his increasingly rebellious subordinates, Bermont-Avalov resigned as commander of the West Russian Volunteer Army, and the following day both the Iron Division and the German Legion requested that they be re-incorporated into the German Army. Their position on the battlefield was perilous, as they were nearly surrounded in Jelgava, but help arrived just in time. General von Eberhardt, Goltz's successor, was relieved to find that he had at his disposal the 1,000-strong *Freikorps Rossbach*, which had marched from East Prussia across Lithuania despite orders from Berlin not to do so. This unit now counterattacked, allowing the Iron Division to withdraw from near-encirclement.[518]

The fighting was pitiless and brutal. Rudolf Höss, who would later be the commandant of Auschwitz, fought in the ranks of *Freikorps Rossbach*:

> The fighting in the Baltic was more savage and desperate than anything else in all the *Freikorps* fighting I saw before or afterwards. There was no real front to speak

> of; the enemy was everywhere. And whenever there was a clash, it turned into butchery to the extent of total annihilation.[519]

Discipline broke down amongst the demoralised troops, who turned their anger against local civilians:

> The soldiers of the Iron Division and the German Legion unloaded all their despair and fury in one wild power-blow against the Letts. Villages burst into flames, prisoners were trampled underfoot … The leaders were powerless, or else they looked on with grim approval.[520]

The weather worsened with early snow, and Lithuania too joined the war against the Bermontians. Yet another commission was dispatched to the region by Britain and France, led by the French General Henri-Albert Niessel. Having agreed to ceasefires in the past, which failed to result in any final resolution of their problems, the leaders of Latvia were reluctant to allow another such ceasefire, particularly as they felt they had the upper hand on the battlefield. Consequently, Ulmanis rejected a German offer of a ceasefire on 18 November and when Niessel arrived the Latvian prime minister refused to receive him, claiming that he was too ill. On 26 November, the Latvian government announced that a state of war existed between it and Germany, and four days later the Latvian army drove the last remnants of the Iron Division and the German Legion across the border into Lithuania. The Latvians were keen to pursue their defeated foes, particularly as the retreating Germans had stripped the countryside of anything they could take with them, including most of the cattle in Courland, but Niessel managed to persuade the Latvian government to stop its army at the border. Some western officers, such as Admiral Cowan, regarded this as a serious mistake, but the remnants of the *Freikorps* withdrew across Lithuania towards the East Prussian frontier.

Fighting had continued on the eastern frontier too, where Latvian troops and the *Baltische Landeswehr* tried to drive the Red Army from the province of Latgale. The Bolshevik government offered a ceasefire in September, which the Latvians rejected, but they made little progress until Poland dispatched troops to help. Finally, in February 1920, an armistice was agreed. Curiously, the armistice was not made public, resulting in ongoing skirmishes along the frontier. In July, Latvia concluded a peace treaty with Germany, and the Riga Peace Treaty the following month finally brought the war with Soviet Russia to an end. The Latvians received four million roubles in gold, as well as the right to cut timber in Soviet territory, and Russia renounced 'for all time' any right to Latvian territory.[521]

Following his somewhat ignominious departure from Latvia, Goltz returned to Germany, embittered by the outcome of the German intervention in the Baltic. For many Germans, particularly from the old aristocratic families, this episode seemed to mark the end of the *Drang nach Osten* ('drive to the east'), which had become so prominent during the second half of the 19th century. For them, this movement was merely the latest articulation of a long-term move by Germans to spread their influence and culture across Eastern Europe, and just a few short months after the Treaty of Brest-Litovsk seemed to open the door for such an expansion, all their hopes were dashed by – what seemed to them – the vindictive Entente Powers, who they felt failed to recognise the menace of Bolshevism. Like many other disillusioned German officers, Goltz became involved in right-wing politics. In 1920, he was involved in the attempt by Walter von Lüttwitz and Wolfgang Kapp to resist the disbandment of *Freikorps* units; the total strength of the German armed forces was 350,000, with a further 250,000 in the ranks of the *Freikorps*, far in excess of the 100,000 armed forces personnel allowed by the Treaty of Versailles. The 'Kapp putsch' as it became known, was initially successful and the government fled from Berlin, first to Dresden and then to Stuttgart, but a general strike forced the leading conspirators to flee to Sweden. Thereafter, Goltz was a member of the Harzburg Front, a political alliance of the *Deutschnationale Volkspartei* (DNVP, or German National People's Party), the National Socialists, the *Stahlhelm* ('Steel helmet', a right-wing veterans' group) and the *Alldeutscher Verband* (Pan-German League), and in 1934 became leader of the right-wing *Deutsche Staatspartei* (German State Party). He was also in charge of a government department responsible for the military education of German youth. He died in November 1946.

Latvia paid a heavy price for its independence. Compared to the pre-1914 population, the country lost perhaps 700,000 citizens – killed or deported – before independence was achieved; more than a quarter of its population. For Ulmanis and his fellow politicians, the task of rebuilding their nation, and keeping its independence, lay ahead.

CHAPTER 16

THE PYGMY WARS: LITHUANIA AND POLAND

Lithuania, the southernmost of the three Baltic States, has for several centuries been markedly different from its northern neighbours. Unlike Latvia and Estonia, it enjoyed a period during the medieval era when it was an independent state; in the late 14th century, shortly after Christianity spread through the area, it controlled a large area of what is now Russia, Belarus and Ukraine. Following a defeat inflicted by the Golden Horde – the northwest part of the Mongol Empire after it broke away in 1239 – at the Battle of the Vorskla River in 1399, Lithuania became increasingly linked to Poland, and ultimately the two nations formed the Polish-Lithuanian Commonwealth in 1569. Due to the close links between the two countries, Lithuania remained Catholic when the rest of the Baltic region embraced Lutheran Christianity, creating another area of difference with Latvians and Estonians in the north.

After Lithuania and parts of Poland became part of the tsar's empire in 1795, the Russians were keen to exploit tensions between the Poles and Lithuanians as part of their policy of Russification of the region. They granted special fellowships to Lithuanians to study in St Petersburg and Moscow, a privilege not granted to Poles. One graduate of the medical school in Moscow, Jonas Basanavičius, is often regarded as being at the heart of the growing sense of national identity amongst Lithuanians. In 1883, he published a Lithuanian-language newspaper entitled *Auszra* ('The Dawn') in which he promoted the concept of Lithuanian independence, and though the newspaper ran to only six issues – the circulation of which was banned by the Russian authorities – it had a widespread impact. Not long after, another newspaper, *Varpas* ('The Bell') appeared, followed in

1896 by *Tėvynės Sargas* ('The Patriotic Guard'). In an attempt to defeat the Russian censors, these newspapers were printed in East Prussia, where there was a large Lithuanian community. In the same year that *Tėvynės Sargas* appeared, Lithuanians combined with Jews, Poles and Russians to found the Lithuanian Social Democrat Party. However, like almost all nationalist activity, this remained a largely urban movement, with little relevance to the rural population. In the countryside, people often thought about themselves in a different way:

> Ask a peasant or a woman in any mixed area if he or she is a Pole, and the affirmative answer will usually be, 'I am a Catholic'.[522]

This was a significant barrier to nationalist awakening; unlike Latvia, Lithuania remained a largely rural economy during the Industrial Revolution, and urban movements like the Social Democrats therefore represented a minority view. As the population of the country grew in the 19th century, many young people chose to migrate to the New World in search of jobs and prosperity, creating a large expatriate Lithuanian community.

An additional limitation to Lithuanian nationalism was the country's shared history with Poland. There were strong links between the aristocratic families of the two countries, and most regarded the era of the Polish-Lithuanian Commonwealth as being the past for which they yearned; it is striking how many of the key leaders in Poland's independence movement originated from Lithuania. Perhaps it was the preservation of Lithuanian as a distinct language that ensured that, despite all the links with Poland, Lithuania was still able to articulate a genuine desire for independence from all other nations that claimed its territory, regardless of whether they were Russian, Polish or German.

The Germans entered Lithuania in 1915 after driving the Russians from East Prussia. Despite repeated demands from *Ober Ost*, Falkenhayn refused to sanction further major operations in the area, though what were intended to be diversionary attacks prior to Mackensen's major offensive in southern Poland in the spring of 1915 resulted in substantial parts of Lithuania and southern Latvia coming under German control. Freed from the restraints of Russian rule, Lithuanian political thinkers began to articulate their views, and at the time were divided into two broad groups. The conservatives were inclined towards an evolutionary approach to the future, and many were close to the Polish-Lithuanian aristocracy; the radicals favoured more wide-reaching change, including social reform. At first, many members of both groups, including Basanavičius, still favoured the Russians, in the hope that a Russian victory might see the creation of at least an autonomous Lithuania, perhaps with the inclusion of East Prussia, but such hopes were swiftly dashed. After the arrival of the Germans, there was hope that Germany might support a new independent Lithuania, but the Germans seemed more inclined to accept the viewpoint of the Poles and regarded Lithuania as an integral part of Poland; and saw Polish independence only within overall German control. When Lithuanians complained about this, Ludendorff made a remarkably frank confession about the level of ignorance in German circles:

> Because of the lack of publications in German we knew very little of the land and its people; we felt as if in a new world.[523]

Germany's policy towards a post-war Europe developed after the beginning of the war, often in a haphazard manner. The early successes against France and Russia resulted in the autumn of 1914 in the drafting of the September Programme, and Lithuania was expected to play its part in the new world that would arise after a German victory.[524] Within the overall scheme of *Mitteleuropa*, Lithuania would be one of the 'client states' that would be created; it would gradually become more German as a result of settlement, forming part of the great German-dominated hinterland that would provide Germany with a lasting and unassailable counterweight to the British Empire. Together with Estonia and Latvia, Lithuania would be semi-autonomous, with almost complete control of government functions by Germany. Even this semi-autonomous status was not expected to last for a prolonged period; once the area had become 'Germanified' by settlers, it would voluntarily opt to become part of the German Empire.[525] While the war continued, the country remained under the firm control of the German military authorities who requisitioned whatever they needed with little regard for the locals, repeatedly showing short-term greed rather than attempting to establish long-term links and stability. There was also heavy-handed intervention into the network of Lithuanian-language schools, with many Catholic teachers being dismissed in favour of German Lutherans. In some cases, classes were taken by German soldiers.

With the coming of the Russian Revolution, Lithuanian émigrés in Russia formed a Lithuanian *Seimas* (congress) in Petrograd. They saw the future of Lithuania as an independent state within a federated Russia, which immediately put them in conflict with nationalists within Lithuania. Sentiment turned sharply away from such a federal solution after the October Revolution; there was little appetite in Lithuanian circles for Bolshevism, which given the largely rural Catholic population was unsurprising. In Lithuania itself, in an attempt to encourage the

Lithuanians to adopt policies in accordance with German policy, Germany gave permission for the Vilnius Conference to be convened on 18 September 1917. The conference consisted of 20 individuals from a variety of backgrounds. Their first meeting took place six days after the conference was created and its first act was to select Antanas Smetona as its chairman. A law graduate of the University of St Petersburg, he had been involved in Lithuanian nationalist politics for most of his life; he even served a short spell in a Russian prison as a result. A year before the conference, he was one of a group of Lithuanians who presented the German authorities with a demand for Lithuanian independence. *Ober Ost* ignored the memorandum and didn't even make a response.

As the German government opened peace negotiations with Russia, it also made an offer to Lithuania: Germany would recognise Lithuania's independence in return for permanent federation with Germany, with matters such as defence and currency remaining the responsibility of Berlin – very much in keeping with the vision of *Mitteleuropa*. The Vilnius Conference, which was now increasingly known as the Vilnius Council in an attempt to define it as more than a discussion body, considered this offer and responded that it would accept it, provided that Lithuania could retain autonomy over its internal affairs and foreign policy. This latter point was incompatible with the German requirement for alignment on military issues, and the Germans rejected the proposal; nevertheless on 11 December, the Vilnius Council voted to accept the German offer subject to the conditions it had already stipulated, and accordingly made what amounted to a limited declaration of independence. This proved to be a controversial move and was criticised by Lithuanians both at home and in exile. It also attracted the ire of the Entente Powers, who were still at war with Germany. In January 1918 the Vilnius Council attempted to modify its announcement, adding an additional stipulation that Lithuania should be granted a national assembly of regional constituents. The Germans, who had already made clear their opposition to the council's previous stipulations, rejected this latest requirement. The council now found itself facing hostility from all quarters, and many of its members threatened to resign. On 16 February it agreed to issue a new announcement of Lithuanian independence, but this time without any reference to a permanent alliance with Germany. The German occupying forces prevented any publication of this announcement within Lithuania, though it was widely reported in the German press.

In March 1918, following the signing of the Treaty of Brest-Litovsk, Germany announced that it recognised Lithuanian independence on the terms that the Vilnius Council had announced on 11 December, the limited declaration of independence that was subsequently modified. Wrangling over the precise nature of this independence continued, and in June the council invited Wilhelm, Count of Württemberg to become monarch of Lithuania. Whilst this was seen by some as an attempt to steer Lithuania to independence without alienating the Germans, others regarded it as overly subservient to Germany and several members of the council resigned in protest. In any event, the German government refused to accept this arrangement, and prevented Wilhelm, who would have ruled as King Mindaugas II, from travelling to his new country.[526] The frustrated members of the Vilnius Council found that Germany blocked almost every attempt they made to formulate policy, a deadlock that continued until the collapse of Germany in November. At this stage, the council revoked its now largely irrelevant invitation to the Count of Württemberg. It also expanded its membership to include Jewish and Belarusian members; at first, the Jewish community was offered two seats, but this was declined, with the Jewish leaders demanding that their membership should be proportional to the Jewish population within Lithuania. Consequently, they were offered a third seat. A new Lithuanian government was proclaimed, with Augustinas Voldemaras as prime minister. Smetona, who had chaired the council when it first formed, became president.

As German control collapsed, Lithuania found itself in an increasingly chaotic state. During the fighting on the Western Front in 1918, the German Army had transferred almost all its best units to the west, leaving the east garrisoned largely by *Landwehr* and other reservist formations, and these now headed home, crossing Lithuania in a steady stream; whilst some units remained under the firm control of their officers, many did not. Some had formed soldiers' committees in direct emulation of the Russians, while others were simply disorganised gatherings of war-weary men desperate to get home. The new Lithuanian government had no means of collecting taxes and consequently was unable to carry out any significant functions. In an act both of naivety and desperation, Voldemaras announced that Lithuania did not intend to threaten its neighbours, and therefore concluded that there was no urgency to create an army.

Since 1915, the entire region had been firmly under German control, but the unravelling of German power brought widespread instability both to Lithuania and the neighbouring areas. Józef Piłsudski, the former commander of the Polish Legions that had served against Russia as part of the *k.u.k.* Army, had been arrested and detained in Magdeburg in 1917 when the men of his legions refused to declare allegiance to Germany; he arrived in Warsaw on the day that the armistice came into force in the west and immediately renewed his contacts with Polish patriots. It is indicative of the close links between Lithuania and Poland that he was born in Lithuania, the son of a family with ties to the aristocracy of both countries. He grew up steeped in the history and legends of the great days of the Polish-Lithuanian Commonwealth and worked relentlessly for Polish independence; his involvement with the Polish Legions was explicitly intended to ensure that the Poles had a trained, powerful force of troops available in the event of the nation having to fight for its survival. Three days after arriving in Warsaw, he was appointed both president of the new Polish republic and the commander-in-chief of its forces. It was a significant moment – he was the first ruler of an independent Poland since the 18th century.[527]

Poland might have achieved independence, but its precise state was confused, to say the least. Like Lithuania, the Polish government lacked the means to raise taxes, and had almost no fixed borders in the east and west. In the south too, there were disputes with the Czechs and Ukrainians, both of which spilled over into fighting. The western border of 'Congress Poland' – the part of Poland that had been within the Russian Empire – did not take account of the predominantly Polish region around the German city of Posen (Poznań to the Poles), and to the east there was even greater confusion. A large strip of land between the new Polish state and Bolshevik Russia was still under the control of Hoffmann's *Ober Ost*, and the German forces in this region now began to head home, many of them not waiting for orders. Whilst the Entente Powers had specified that Germany should evacuate the territories it had occupied, it was clear to everyone that the German Army was the only organised, disciplined force in the entire region, its own internal problems notwithstanding, and many in the western camp wished the Germans to remain in the east as a barrier against the Bolsheviks; others, like the French, demanded an early withdrawal. Detailed discussions began within days of the armistice and the first troops began to come home a few weeks later; whatever the plans of adventurers like Goltz, Hoffmann had no intention of getting caught up in fantastic schemes to carve out pro-German states in the east. He merely wished to get his men home safely, and deferred all important decisions to Berlin. His relations with the Poles were not good; the German troops in Warsaw had been forcibly disarmed by the Poles when the armistice came into force, and attempts to disarm German forces to the northeast of Warsaw led to violence and the deaths of many Polish civilians. As his men began to leave the strip of land between Piłsudski's Poland and Lenin's Russia, both countries tried to take advantage of the German withdrawal to secure the territory for themselves. For the Poles, this represented the ancient eastern borders of the Polish-Lithuanian Commonwealth; for the Russians, the region had long been part of the empire of the tsars, whose successors now regarded it

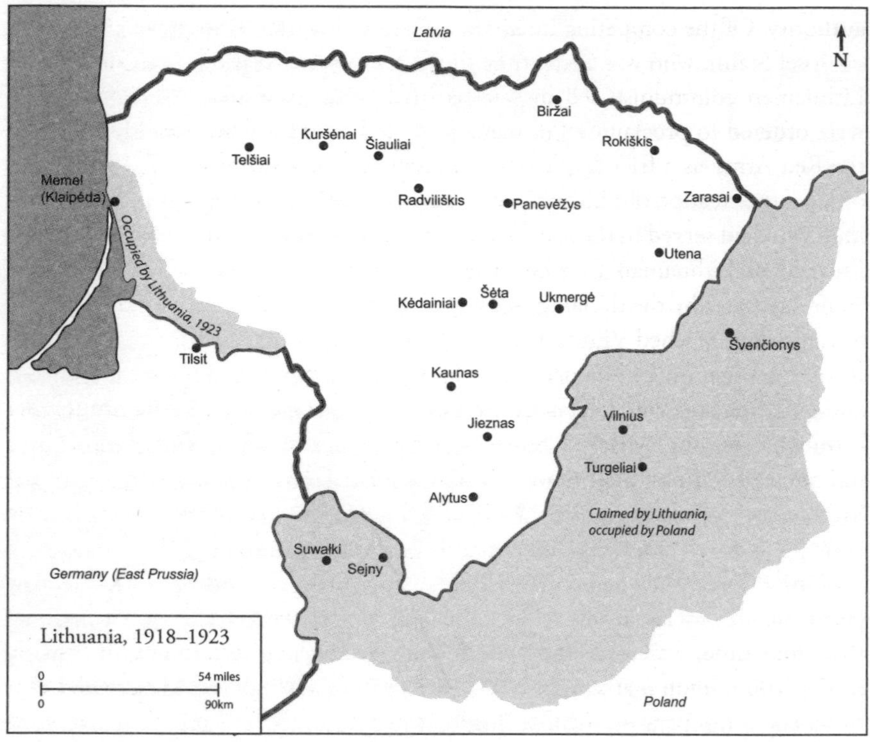

as theirs by right. Furthermore, Bolshevik doctrine insisted that the revolution in Russia would be preserved – and brought to its ultimate fruition – only by the spread of revolution to the west. It was inevitable that this would be through Poland. The Bolshevik government renounced the Treaty of Brest-Litovsk on 13 November 1918, and as the Germans left and both Polish and Russian troops entered the area, a clash was only a matter of time.

In a region of great forests and swampy lowlands, the few cities were of great strategic importance, not least because they were the nodes of the railways that would be vital in any military operation. One of the most important cities was known to the Russians as Vilna; Wilna to the Poles, Wilno to the many Jews who inhabited it, and Vilnius to the Lithuanians who regarded it as their historic capital. Despite this claim by Lithuania, the Poles viewed Vilnius as part of their state on account of it having been such an important part of the Polish-Lithuanian Commonwealth and having a large Polish population, and by the Russians who wished to ensure that at the very least it would be in the hands of a Bolshevik authority. Of the competing interests, it was the Russians who moved first.

Josef Stalin, who was at the time the Commissar of Nationalities, dispatched Lithuanian communists led by Vincas Mickevičius-Kapsukas to Vilnius. They were ordered to proclaim a Lithuanian Soviet Republic, which could then greet the Red Army as a friendly force rather than as invaders. Belatedly, Voldemaras ordered the creation of a Lithuanian army on 23 November, starting by mobilising men who had served in the tsar's armies. Kapsukas proclaimed the creation of the Provisional Lithuanian Revolutionary Government on 8 December, followed eight days later by the declaration of a Soviet state; however, he had to wait until Soviet troops reached Vilnius before he could move into the Lithuanian capital. It was clear that the Lithuanians lacked the military power to oppose the Russians and Smetona and Voldemaras left for Germany on a mission to raise support for Lithuania, leaving Mykolas Sleževičius to head the government, which had relocated to Kaunas. Sleževičius, a Russian-trained lawyer and a member of the Lithuanian Socialists Peasants Party, now found himself prime minister of a country that was rapidly being overrun.

On 29 December, Sleževičius expanded the call-up of personnel for the army and issued a proclamation calling for volunteers to defend the motherland. At the same time, Smetona and Voldemaras signed loan agreements in Berlin, raising 100 million marks to pay for German troops to fight for Lithuania. Large numbers of troops from the German Tenth Army were in Lithuania at the time, but few were tempted by the offer of pay. The most fertile recruiting ground was Saxony, and throughout January Germans arrived in Kaunas; by the end of the month, about 4,000 had been assembled into the 46th Saxon Volunteer Division, though many had to be sent back as they were clearly unfit for combat duty.

In Vilnius, the Polish population tried to take advantage of the lack of any authoritative power. On the first day of 1919, a group of Polish officers declared the creation of the *Samoobrona*, an expression used to describe both the city administration and the self-defence militia that they now attempted to raise. Their first objective was to strike down Kapsukas' Provisional Government and they immediately attacked the headquarters of the communists, killing four and arresting the rest. Their success was short-lived, with Red Army troops now beginning to arrive in support of the Lithuanian communists.

The Russian units that entered Lithuania, grouped together as the Western Army, were from several different divisions. The Pskov Division, later renamed the Lithuanian Division, was accompanied by the International Division, also to have its name changed to the 2nd Red Latvian Rifles Division, and the 17th Division, which would be renamed the Western Division. Formed largely from

Poles in the Red Army, this latter unit first saw action early in 1919 against the *Samoobrona*. It proved to be one of the better Red Army units, though it steadily lost its Polish identity over the following months. The commander of the Western Army was Andrei Yevgenyevich Snesarev, who had risen to the rank of lieutenant general before the October Revolution. He took part in the fighting around Tsaritsyn against the White Russians at the beginning of the Russian Civil War before being appointed to command in the west; this may partly have been due to a strong difference of opinion with Josef Stalin and Kliment Yefremovich Voroshilov, a former head of the Petrograd police who now commanded the Bolshevik First Cavalry Army, a force known as much for its propensity for anti-Semitic violence as its combat capabilities. Voroshilov may have wished to be rid of Snesarev, and therefore put up no obstacles when Stalin – who had also fought near Tsaritsyn, the city that would later bear his name – was therefore able to send Snesarev west.

Though Snesarev was the nominal commander of the Western Army, its units often behaved with little regard to what few instructions they received from his headquarters, and their logistic services were almost non-existent. The level of equipment and training within the units, with the possible exception of the Red Latvian Rifles, was also poor, but they were easily more powerful than the scratch forces opposing them. The eastern town of Švenčionys fell on 22 December, as did Zarasai, near the Latvian border. The following day, the Red Army took Utena, and the units that had seized Zarasai moved west to Rokiškis. The advance reached Vilnius on 5 January 1919, where the only significant resistance – which continued for several days after the Red Army took the city – came from the *Samoobrona*. Emboldened by their early successes, the Russian command ordered the Western Army to advance as far as the rivers Niemen and Szczara. Ukmergė and Panevėžys fell a few days later, and from here the main Russian thrust moved along the road towards the Baltic coast, reaching Telšiai on 25 January; there was still no organised resistance, and the advance was authorised to continue to the River Bug. But despite what appeared to be a series of triumphant advances, several factors were working against the Russians. The simultaneous pursuit of wars against all three Baltic States and Poland was far beyond the minimal logistic capabilities of the Red Army, and, combined with the winter weather and poor roads, this took its inevitable toll. Nevertheless, the Lithuanian nationalist government in Kaunas feared that the Soviet forces that had taken Vilnius would advance swiftly to take the rest of the country before defences could be organised. Between the two cities were several withdrawing German units, and, anxious to avoid unnecessary clashes with the Red Army, the Germans signed an agreement with Russia on 19 January agreeing a demarcation line between the two nations, running roughly midway between Kaunas and Vilnius and extending to the south. As well as allowing the Germans to withdraw unmolested, this served to prevent a direct assault towards Kaunas; instead, the Red Army would have to use the smaller road that it had secured in the north of the country, running towards Telšiai. Crucially, this significantly slowed down the rate at which forces could be assembled, and the Lithuanians gained just enough time to organise their defences.

In the occupied areas, the new Lithuanian Soviet Socialist Republic began to make changes. In an attempt to widen the appeal of the new regime, no fewer than five official languages were adopted: Lithuanian, Polish, Russian, Yiddish and Belarusian. Unfortunately, this policy backfired; few people spoke all of these languages, or even two of them, with the result that Russian rapidly became the preferred language of the regime, alienating much of the increasingly nationalistic Lithuanian population.[528] As was the case within Bolshevik Russia, the Communist Party attempted to harness urban workers to its cause, but the relatively minor impact of industrialisation on Lithuania worked against them. The Pskov Division was renamed the Lithuanian Division; in the absence of any other source of supplies, the division requisitioned whatever it needed. Any lingering sympathy towards the communists in the countryside was further reduced by this policy, which coincided with the forcible shipment of foodstuffs from Lithuania to Russia, creating widespread food shortages. But the final blow was the failure to enact land reform in a way that was acceptable to the peasantry. Instead of breaking up the large estates and giving the land to the peasants, it was official policy to create collective farms, which were hugely unpopular and were interpreted by the Lithuanian peasants as merely replacing one exploitative landlord with another. Given the widespread resentment of the regime, little attempt was made to recruit Lithuanians into the Red Army: a message from Moscow to Vilnius on 9 February warned that conscription of such a hostile population would be counter-productive, and would simply encourage people to join the nationalist army.

The Red Army made its first attempt to advance towards Kaunas on 7 February. The Lithuanian Division's 2nd Rifle Regiment attacked Kėdainiai, north of Kaunas, which was held by a mixture of Lithuanians and German troops from the 46th Saxon Volunteer Division. The attack failed, giving the Lithuanian nationalists a much-needed morale boost: it was their first success against the Red Army, and came at a time when over 60 per cent of the country was in Russian hands. Three days later, the German-Lithuanian force counterattacked and took Šėta, securing the northern approaches to Kaunas.

At the same time, the Bolshevik Lithuanian Division's 7th Rifle Regiment attempted to close on Kaunas from the southeast, taking advantage of the withdrawal of German forces to the west. The town of Jieznas became the focus of heavy fighting, which continued until the Lithuanians and Germans secured it on 13 February. Two further Russian regiments attacked a little to the south and reached the River Niemen at Alytus, but a counterattack late on 14 February retook the town. It was the last major attempt by the Russians to seize Kaunas.

Even as the Saxon division became involved in fighting around Kaunas, the other German formations in the region continued their steady withdrawal towards their homeland. The Russians followed as best they could, given their logistic difficulties, and the Poles decided to take advantage of the opportunity to move their troops into the border regions. The first advances were authorised in early February, and on 14 February the leading Polish troops ran into Bolshevik forces at Bereza Kartuska (now Biaroza in Belarus), some distance to the east of Brest-Litovsk. The Poles rapidly seized the town; at a time when the borders of Poland were still to be settled, there was every incentive to seize as much territory as possible. This was as much a clash of cultures as a battle for territory: the Bolsheviks were intent upon establishing the dictatorship of the proletariat with the abolition of everything that defined Polish society – religion, private property, and a landed class that used its pre-eminence to exert considerable influence on the Polish government.[529] The brief battle for the town is often regarded as the first action of the Polish-Soviet War.

Despite having considerable men under arms, the Poles were struggling to catch up in terms of organising higher military organisations. The legal basis for the army was belatedly formalised in late February, by which time it had 110,000 personnel; they had been boosted by large numbers of German army personnel from regiments raised in and around Posen (now Poznań) who declared their loyalty to Poland in late 1918. Local loyalties remained perhaps stronger than national sentiment, as exemplified by the 1st Cavalry Division. Of its six component regiments, one was from Galicia and remained strongly *k.u.k.* in character; another originated as a Galician reservist formation; two were from the most eastern parts of Poland and had Russian as their predominant language; and one was a former Polish Legion formation. Kazimierz Sosnkowski, the 34-year-old Deputy Minister for Military Affairs, had been imprisoned in Magdeburg with Piłsudski, and he became the more diplomatic face of the Polish military, dealing skilfully with the government in Warsaw and leaving military matters to the abrasive Piłsudski.

On 27 February, there was a new political development: the Soviet Socialist Republics of Lithuania and Belarus announced that they were merging to create the Lithuanian-Belarusian Soviet Socialist Republic, or 'Lit-Bel'. The chairman of the Central Executive Committee of the new merged Communist Party of Lit-Bel and simultaneously commissar of finance was Kazimierz Cichowski, who had grown up in Poland, a further sign of the tangled links between these countries.[530] Kapsukas, who had been the head of the communist regime in Lithuania, remained as the head of state, but the power lay with the party executive committee, and hence with its chairman. There was no significant consequence for the predominantly rural population of the area of Lithuania under communist control; in a further move that only served to alienate the people, the government insisted on all villages, towns and cities making substantial financial contributions.[531] Widespread arrests of those suspected of being hostile to the Bolsheviks compounded the growing unrest and unpopularity of the communists.

Despite their different views on the shape of future independence, Poland and Lithuania were now deeply embroiled in wars with a common enemy. Piłsudski showed an adroit touch, persuading many of the German units retreating through Poland to leave behind much of their equipment. His relationship with the Entente Powers was often difficult, and whilst the French were willing to promise him military aid, the British were far more cautious – they were investing heavily in the cause of the White Russians, who were not inclined to support Polish independence. Piłsudski's pragmatic attitude to all measures that could help Poland achieve independence is shown in a reply he made to an old acquaintance who addressed him as 'Comrade':

> Comrades, I took the red streetcar of socialism to the stop called Independence, and that's where I got off. You may keep on to the final stop if you wish, but from now on let's address each other as 'Mister!'[532]

Piłsudski regarded the unsettled eastern border of Poland as an opportunity. The western borders were dependent upon what concessions the Entente Powers extracted from Germany, but he saw the east as an open door, and he intended to push through it as far as he could.[533] Poland had visions of creating *Międzymorze*, a constellation of nations separating Russia from the rest of Europe, not dissimilar to the German notion of *Mitteleuropa*, though with the important difference that these nations would be tied to Poland, not Germany; it was hoped that this would give Poland sufficient strength to be able to survive between its more powerful neighbours. He was not enthusiastic about supporting the cause of Denikin and other anti-Bolshevik White Russians; they intended to restore the Russian Empire in full, and therefore were hostile to Polish independence and to Poland's hopes of creating separate states stretching from the Baltic to the Black Sea. Therefore, Piłsudski was prepared to wage war against Bolshevik Russia, but only to secure territory for Poland and *Międzymorze*, not to defeat the communists and pave the way for a White Russian victory.

The capabilities of the fledgling Polish Army were limited more by the lack of military infrastructure – logistic and other support services – than innate fighting ability. Nevertheless, there was scope for a limited campaign, and Piłsudski planned for an advance to expel the Bolsheviks from all the territories claimed by Poland and Lithuania as soon as the spring thaw had passed and large-scale movement was once more possible. Planning the operation with his customary meticulous attention to detail, Piłsudski launched diversionary attacks on Lida, Navahrudak and Baranovichi; his main objective, though, was Vilnius, with a force of 800 cavalry, 2,500 infantry, and artillery assigned to the task. On 15 April, he visited the front line to oversee matters personally.

The spearhead of the drive was the cavalry force, accompanied by a few light guns. Setting off at first light the following day, the Polish cavalry commander, Colonel Wladyslaw Belina-Prazmowski, moved forward in the face of almost no resistance, at last partly due to the success of the diversionary attacks. The sectors chosen for these attacks were defended by the Bolshevik Western Division and it was widely assumed by the Russians that Piłsudski had deliberately attacked them either to punish them or in the expectation that they would change sides. Belina continued his advance the following day, moving past Vilnius to the south and stopping at Turgeliai. On 18 April, he spent the day anticipating a Bolshevik counterattack and the arrival of his supporting infantry; deciding further delay benefited only his enemies, he gave orders for his cavalry to enter Vilnius the following morning. Surging into the urban area from the east and southeast, his troops took the few defenders completely by surprise, and as soon as they captured the railway station, they dispatched a captured train down the track towards the west with a small group of men aboard to meet up with the advancing Polish infantry and to ferry them to Vilnius. As the Bolshevik forces rallied, the cavalry kept them off balance, striking seemingly at will wherever they chose, and towards the evening the train returned with the first contingent of Polish infantry. The Bolshevik garrison, largely made up of the Pskov Division, fell back into the northern part of the city, harassed by Belina's cavalry, the newly arrived infantry, and Polish partisans. By 21 April, all of Vilnius was in Polish hands and Piłsudski made a triumphant entry.[534] As was the case in Riga and Jelgava, the expulsion of the Bolsheviks was followed by a wave of arrests and shootings of those believed to be sympathetic to the Bolshevik regime.

Immediately, Piłsudski issued a proclamation stating that the Polish Army had come to liberate the region. He continued:

> I wish to create an opportunity for settling your nationality problems and religious affairs in a manner that you yourselves will determine, without any force or pressure from Poland.
>
> For this reason, although military action and bloodshed continue in the area, I am introducing a civil administration, not a military one, to which in due course I shall call local people.[535]

The Lit-Bel government fled from Vilnius, moving to Minsk; some Bolsheviks attempted to dismiss the loss of Vilnius as being due to treachery, but Kapsukas was more realistic. He wrote a substantial article that was later published in *Izvestia*, in which he described how poor logistics meant that the troops in Vilnius had to resort to requisitioning supplies locally, which alienated the population. Many Russian troops deserted from the poorly supplied units and local antipathy to the Bolsheviks ensured that they could not be replaced with local recruits, even if uniforms, boots and weapons had been available.[536] Lenin demanded urgent action to recover Vilnius, but the local troops were far too weak to do so. The Polish majority in the city rejoiced, restoring the Polish University that had been forced to close a century earlier; the Jews, the second-largest population, were also broadly supportive. Whilst there had been numerous anti-Semitic incidents due to Polish forces, these were greatly outnumbered by those inflicted by Russians, both before and after the fall of the tsar.

The Polish offensive roughly coincided with Rüdiger von der Goltz's advance from the Latvian coast to Jelgava, which also secured parts of northern Lithuania. Local communists, led by Feliksas Baltušis-Žemaitis, had formed a Samogitian Regiment in and around Šiauliai, but they were swiftly driven out by the advancing Germans. Taking advantage of growing demoralisation in the ranks of the Red Army, Lithuania's fledgling army also attacked, trying to push on from southern Lithuania towards Vilnius, but made little progress. However, the Polish advance to Vilnius meant that Lithuanian and Polish units were now facing each other across a common border. At first, the two sides appeared to cooperate, but the first exchange of fire occurred on 26 April.[537] Despite this, there remained a degree of coordination on the battlefield, and as the Poles continued to advance towards the northeast, the Lithuanians added their own attacks on their left flank. Ukmergė was taken on 3 May by a combination of the Lithuanian Panevėžys Volunteer Regiment and 18th Saxon Volunteer Regiment, and 500 Russian soldiers were captured. From here, the combined Lithuanian and Saxon forces continued to push both northeast and east. Whenever the Red Army counterattacked, the Lithuanians found their relatively small numbers and limited equipment and training counted against them, but aided by partisan groups behind Russian lines they steadily advanced, taking Panevėžys and Utena after several attacks and counterattacks. By the end of June, the Bolsheviks had been almost completely driven out of Lithuania. Limited Russian counterattacks late in June stabilised the front, leaving only Zarasai in Soviet hands. Lenin urged his army to retake Vilnius as soon as possible, but his commanders had other more pressing problems. Bolshevik troops that had penetrated into Ukraine and had occupied Kiev were now threatened by the growing power of Denikin's forces, and Kolchak seemed about to cross the Urals from Siberia. For the moment at least, Vilnius would have to wait.

It was now time for the Saxon volunteers to leave, and over the next few weeks their units gradually disbanded. Some went back to Germany, but others were drawn to the growing band of men being gathered by Bermont-Avalov in Latvia. Meanwhile, negotiations had begun between Lithuania and Poland about the territory that both claimed. The main bone of contention was Vilnius, but in addition there were disputes about a smaller area around the town of Suwałki, which was also occupied by Poland. Negotiations were difficult, not least because the Poles refused to recognise Lithuania as an independent country and continued to press for a Polish-Lithuanian commonwealth. The demands around Vilnius were particularly complex. A German census in 1916 suggested that half of the city's population was Polish, and a substantial part of the remaining population was Jewish, leaving the Lithuanians in a very small minority; however, other surveys suggested that the population of the surrounding countryside was predominantly Lithuanian.[538] There was thus ample room for interpretation and argument, and unsurprisingly neither side was prepared to give ground. The Poles insisted that they were acting on behalf of the majority of Vilnius' citizens, while the Lithuanians claimed a majority in the entire territory, and also that Vilnius was historically the capital of Lithuania. Unable to resolve matters, the Lithuanian government appealed to the Conference of Ambassadors, a body set up by the Entente Powers towards the end of the First World War, which would ultimately evolve into the League of Nations. Here, Lithuania was confronted by the disparity in the diplomatic standing of the two countries. Poland had been recognised by the Entente Powers, and was even specifically mentioned in one of Woodrow Wilson's famous Fourteen Points:

> An independent Polish state should be erected which should include the territories inhabited by indisputably Polish populations, which should be assured a free and secure access to the sea, and whose political and economic independence and territorial integrity should be guaranteed by international covenant.[539]

By contrast, Lithuania had not yet received international recognition, and it appeared that Wilson's proclamation regarding Poland seemed to take precedence over his insistence on the rights of the peoples of Europe to self-determination. In many circles, particularly those that favoured a restoration of the Russian Empire, Lithuania's independence was unacceptable. It can therefore have been of little surprise to anyone when the Conference of Ambassadors chose not to return Vilnius and the surrounding area to Lithuania. It suggested a demarcation line running about 3 miles (5km) west of the Warsaw-Petrograd railway line. This suggestion was rejected by the Poles, who actually controlled territory to the west of this line, and would have to retreat to it. With Lithuania's limited army still busy in the northeast, Polish troops advanced from their existing positions, taking advantage of the withdrawal of the Saxon Volunteers, and penetrated farther into Lithuanian territory.

On 18 July, the French Marshal Ferdinand Foch proposed a new boundary between Lithuania and Poland, and his proposals were approved by the Entente Powers a week later. The new line was far more in Poland's favour than the previous demarcation line, granting the province of Suwałki to Poland and moving the main line farther west. Although the Foch Line was even more unfavourable to Lithuania – it was a sign of the different attitudes to the two countries that the Entente Powers showed the new boundary to the Lithuanian government on 3 August, several days after the Poles had already seen it – the Lithuanians had to accept that they had little military ability to resist the Poles, and began a slow withdrawal from Suwałki, perhaps consoling themselves that Foch had stated that his line was only a temporary demarcation rather than a permanent frontier.

There were still substantial German forces in the region, and there was therefore a complex three-way dance between the withdrawing Germans, the Lithuanians, and the Poles in the Suwałki province. As the Germans withdrew, it became clear that the Lithuanians did not intend to leave the town of Sejny, which had been assigned to Poland. There was no question that southern parts of the province were predominantly Polish, while northern parts were strongly

Lithuanian, but there was complete disagreement on where the boundaries lay. Census data was often unreliable or out of date, but the small local Lithuanian force of perhaps 300 men decided that it would hold the town, regardless of where it lay in relation to the Foch Line. The Polish population of the area was understandably unhappy with this. The local branches of the widespread Polish paramilitary organisations created by Piłsudski in 1914 took matters into their own hands, and decided to mount an insurrection.

This was not welcome news for the Polish government. Piłsudski remained convinced that it was in the best interests of both Poland and Lithuania for the two countries to be united and continued to regard the Lithuanian government in Kaunas as something approaching a German puppet. Nevertheless, he could see that there was little prospect of his hopes for union being fulfilled if the Lithuanians became increasingly anti-Polish. Piłsudski and a close colleague, Leon Wasilewski, travelled to Vilnius late in July 1919 where they met Mykolas Biržiška, one of the signatories of Lithuania's declaration of independence. They asked him for his views on a union between the two countries, and from there Wasilewski travelled on alone to Kaunas. Here he met Sleževičius and proposed that the disputed territories should be settled on the basis of a plebiscite. The Lithuanians rejected this, claiming historical rights to all of the Suwałki and Vilnius provinces, and Wasilewski left on 7 August. But, in addition to the public talks, there had been other discussions, both in Vilnius and Kaunas: Wasilewski met Polish and 'friendly' Lithuanian representatives, and sounded them out on the possibility of a coup to topple the Lithuanian government.[540] Whilst Piłsudski wished to have a cordial and constructive relationship with the Lithuanians, he was perfectly prepared to ensure that the government was made up of individuals who would be more amenable to his own long-term plans.

Planning for a coup now entered a more detailed stage, and when rumours of a pro-Polish uprising in Sejny began to circulate, the timing was particularly inopportune – such a move might upset the timing of the coup being planned in Vilnius and Kaunas, and raise anti-Polish sentiment throughout Lithuania. Despite discouragement from Piłsudski and others, the uprising took place on 23 August. The Lithuanians were driven from the town, but retook it two days later. This proved to be short-lived as Polish troops moved to aid the insurgents, and the Lithuanians left Sejny on 26 August.

The main coup to overthrow the Lithuanian government was planned for the night of 28/29 August. In the aftermath of the Sejny rising, attempts were made to postpone it until 1 September, but the message did not reach all participants and some Polish paramilitaries started work to disrupt telephone lines a day before the original coup date. Lithuanian intelligence intercepted messages advising of a delay in the plan, and moved swiftly. The Lithuanian government authorised a small unit of handpicked officers to take countermeasures; unaware of precisely who the coup planners were, they arrested large numbers of Poles and Polish sympathisers in Kaunas. Only a minority of these were coup plotters, and this made it easy for the Polish press to portray the Lithuanian move as merely an act of anti-Polish repression. Lithuanian accusations of a planned coup were rejected out of hand, though Wasilewski later admitted organising the coup.[541] He maintained that he did so without the knowledge of the Polish government, though evidence later emerged confirming Piłsudski's involvement.[542] The main leaders of the coup had escaped arrest, and made plans for a second attempt later in September. This too was detected by the Lithuanians, who were also aided by the acquisition of a list of members of the Polish paramilitary organisations.[543] As a result, the authorities were able to make better-targeted arrests. The only outcome of the entire affair was a further strengthening of Lithuanian demands for recognition of their independence, and increasing distrust of the Poles.

At the same time, fighting flared up against Russia. In an attempt to destroy the hated Bolshevik Western Division and to capture another strategically useful city, Piłsudski decided to mount an attack to capture Minsk. As well as being the capital of Belarus, the city was a key railway node and its loss would deny the Russians the ability to use lateral railway lines. The formerly German formations from the Poznań region were sent to the sector as reinforcements. The local Polish commander, General Stanisław Szeptycki, deployed his forces for a strong cavalry thrust to the north of Minsk while the Poznań contingent would turn the flank of the Russian defences and advance on the city from the south. A smaller force would launch a frontal attack in the centre to try to fix the Russian defences and to stop them redeploying to cover the threatened flanks. The attack began at the beginning of August and the Polish cavalry swept past the northern outskirts of Minsk, swiftly cutting all communications first with the north and then with the east. Although fighting continued for a week, the outcome was inevitable and the Red Army was forced back in disarray. All along the front, Russian troops pulled back; by the end of the month, all territory to which the Poles had an arguable claim was in their hands. With the prospect of the autumn rains imminent, Piłsudski ordered his forces to stop.

There were no other worthwhile objectives within reach, and the Poles opted to try to secure a negotiated settlement with the Bolsheviks. The Poles faced a difficult balance. They had demonstrated that their forces were more than a match for the Red Army, particularly while the Bolsheviks remained involved in a life-and-death struggle with the White Russian factions within Russia. The Russian Civil War complicated matters considerably for Poland; whilst the Poles and White Russians shared a common enemy in the Bolsheviks, none of the White Russian leaders seemed inclined to recognise Polish independence, making cooperation between the two sides almost inconceivable. Nor were matters much easier for the Russians. The collapse of their protégé state of Lit-Bel was a major setback in their long-term ambitions to export their revolution to the west, and this triggered a debate on how to proceed. Many Bolsheviks – particularly those who had spent the last years of Romanov rule in exile in the west – believed that without exporting the revolution to the rest of Europe, Bolshevism within Russia would probably not survive. Therefore, it was vital to resume attempts to spread Bolshevik influence westwards as soon as possible. Others, led by Bolsheviks who had played a leading role in the revolution and the preceding years, wished to consolidate their hold on Russia before considering further foreign adventures. Finally, a third group believed that Russia should strike against colonial assets in the east in order to bring the western empires to their knees. Much as Hindenburg had insisted that the way to defeat France was by defeating Russia, Trotsky stated emphatically that the road to London and Paris was via Calcutta.[544]

Regardless of any desire to resume hostilities with Poland, the Red Army was in no state to do so. It was in the interests of both sides to seek a ceasefire and in November 1919 discussions reached the stage of detailed discussions of demarcation lines, but failure to agree on extending the ceasefire to cover the anti-Bolshevik Directorate of the Ukraine, which was loosely allied to the Poles, proved to be the issue over which the talks unravelled. Neither side trusted the intentions of the other, interpreting internal disagreements as duplicity; the advance of Denikin's White Russian forces brought the Directorate of the Ukraine effectively to an end, with its leader Symon Vasylyovych Petliura and his remaining troops moving into Polish-held territory, where they now came under Polish control. At the end of November, Piłsudski authorised a limited operation against Denikin that drove the White Russians back, and a month later agreed to launch a joint operation with the Latvians to capture Daugavpils; in early January, the Poles moved against the city, isolating and capturing it from the east. The garrison, forced to retreat to the west, was captured by the Latvians. Aware of the need to ensure good relations wherever possible with the new Baltic States, Piłsudski handed the city over to the Latvians almost immediately.

With its tiny army facing both the Bolsheviks in the east and the Poles to the south, Lithuania found itself dealing with another threat. In June 1919, Pavel Bermont-Avalov's ragtag West Russian Volunteer Army crossed the border from

Latvia and seized Kuršėnai. There was little that Lithuania could do, and the Bermontians steadily increased their hold on the area, expanding the territory they controlled to include Šiauliai, Radviliškis and Biržai. Composed mainly of the last remnants of White Russian forces in the region and the defeated *Freikorps* formerly commanded by Goltz in Latvia, the Volunteer Army was not a major military threat, not least because it had no source of logistical support. Its commander had served in II Caucasian Corps of the Russian Army during the First World War, being wounded seven times. After the February Revolution, he commanded a lancer regiment in Petrograd and was extensively involved in plots of varying credibility to overthrow the Provisional Government. He was in Ukraine in the aftermath of the October Revolution and took part in the defence of Kiev against Ukrainian socialist nationalists; he was imprisoned, but then allowed to travel to Germany with other officers. Entering Latvia in 1919, he refused to join the White Russian advance on Petrograd from Estonia, as has already been described. In the autumn, accompanied by perhaps 20,000 men, he entered Lithuania where his troops continued to behave with the same indiscipline and random violence to civilians that they had shown during their march south across Latvia from Riga. Many Lithuanian civilians responded by forming partisan groups that harassed the Bermontians while Lithuanian troops began to concentrate against them, but before major fighting could break out the French General Niessel intervened again, rapidly negotiating a ceasefire. The Lithuanians simply wanted to be rid of this unwelcome and undisciplined force, and raised no objections to Niessel's proposal that they be allowed to continue to the German border. They crossed into East Prussia through Tilsit; many of the relatively few Russians in the force were interned. Bermont-Avalov took up residence in Germany where he had a medal created for the veterans of his Volunteer Army and wrote his memoirs; he became involved in right-wing politics and was deported in 1936 after a brief period of internment. He died in New York in 1974.

The Polish Army survived a difficult winter facing the Russians. Short of all manner of supplies, its troops suffered through the long months of cold weather; the British were unwilling to support Piłsudski's Poland due to its ongoing difficulties with the White Russians, and the change of government in France in early 1920 reduced the enthusiasm in Paris for the Polish cause. Despite his successes to date, Piłsudski had no illusions about the ability of his forces to prevail if the Russians were able to concentrate all their resources against him, and this played a large part in his decision to try to strike first. Although peace negotiations dragged on for several months, there was little prospect of success and, as spring approached, both sides began to prepare for war. Piłsudski had hoped for support from neighbouring countries in the coming conflict, but relations between Poland and the Baltic States remained complicated. Estonia was content with its recent peace treaty, and though the Latvians remained friendly – not least after Daugavpils was handed to them in January – there was ongoing hostility from Lithuania as a result of the loss of Vilnius. Indeed, given the 'privileged' status of Poland on account of its specific recognition in Woodrow Wilson's Fourteen Points, the Lithuanians were increasingly minded to seek Russian support to try to recover their lost capital. The only foreign government Piłsudski could persuade to join him was that of Symon Petliura's Ukrainian People's Republic, and in April the Polish Army moved against Bolshevik forces in Ukraine. These Russian troops were organised into the Twelfth and Fourteenth Armies, but their collective fighting strength was perhaps only a little over 28,000 – barely the strength of a single army corps during the First World War. The Poles had a substantial numerical advantage, enhanced further by a mutiny in the Russian Fourteenth Army. In addition, the Russians were plagued by anti-Bolshevik partisans operating in their rear zones, attacking isolated units and supply columns and destroying bridges.

On 25 April, Piłsudski unleashed his forces, advancing over 50 miles (80km) and reaching Zhitomir in just one day. The Russian formations disintegrated almost immediately, losing much of their artillery and many men; the survivors fell back in disorder. But despite their setbacks, most of the Red Army troops managed to escape, and the Poles learned the same lesson that the Central Powers had learned during earlier years; gaining territory in the east was rarely difficult, but unless it was accompanied by the destruction of the defending Russian forces, the gains were almost meaningless. After a pause to regroup, the Poles resumed their advance, reaching Kiev on 3 May and taking control of the city four days later as the Russians fell back without a fight, leaving all of Ukraine west of the Dnieper in Polish control.

Piłsudski had no intention of staying in the region indefinitely, and encouraged Petliura to establish a civil administration. At no stage in his career to date had Petliura demonstrated the degree of support and skill that the situation now demanded, and it cannot have been a surprise to anyone when he failed completely. But the campaign was merely a distraction: the real struggle would come farther north. Once they overcame their initial surprise and dismay at their speedy setback, the Bolsheviks were quite relaxed about the situation, seeing that sizeable Polish forces had been diverted away from the main battlefield between Russia and Poland, where the issue would ultimately be decided. Gradually, the Red Army built up its strength along the Dnieper and the vastness of the terrain ensured that the Poles simply couldn't defend all of the ground that they had seized. The arrival of the First Cavalry Army – a force of only 16,000 mounted troops, a relatively small force by the standards of the First World War but a potent mobile strike force in the current circumstances – proved decisive. On 27 May, the force moved forward towards the Polish lines, engaging in a series of increasingly fierce skirmishes over the next few days that achieved little. Changing tactics, the Russians abandoned mounted attacks on the entrenched Poles and advanced on foot on 5 June; several elements of the attacking force managed to advance and outflank the main Polish defences. In confused fighting over the next two days, some of the Russian cavalry reached and briefly captured Zhitomir, slaughtering wounded Poles and liberating several thousand Red Army soldiers who had been captured in the Polish advance.

The Russian forces might have enjoyed a substantial success, but they lacked the reserves or supplies for sustained operations. In any event, the main front farther to the north had become active over the preceding weeks. The Poles withdrew from Kiev to the northwest and, by 10 July, the front line in this sector was broadly where it had been a year earlier. Perhaps the only lasting legacy was the growing prominence of the commander of the First Cavalry Army, Semyon Mikhailovich Budyonny. He had served as a non-commissioned cavalry officer on the Turkish Front during the First World War, becoming well known both for courage and clashes with superiors; after the fall of Tsar Nicholas, he was a natural candidate for the regimental and divisional soldiers' committees. His cavalry fought with growing distinction against the White Russian forces of Denikin, and he became a personal friend of both Stalin and Kliment Voroshilov, a relationship that would save him from arrest during Stalin's purges in the 1930s.

Those purges would see the arrest, show trial and execution of another man who now became a prominent figure in the Russian-Polish War: Mikhail Nikolayevich Tukhachevsky. He was a junior officer in the Russian Guards in 1914 and was taken prisoner, but repeatedly attempted to escape captivity. He finally succeeded, returning to Russia via Switzerland in 1917. He joined the Bolsheviks immediately after the October Revolution and played a large part in the defeat of White Russian forces in both Siberia and Ukraine. He acquired a reputation for ruthlessness, frequently executing prisoners and hostages. His views on the war with Poland were typically uncompromising:

> The fate of world revolution is being decided in the west: the way leads over the corpse of Poland to a universal conflagration.[545]

Aware that the Poles were considering a pre-emptive attack to seize the important rail hub of Mogilev, the Russians attacked first on 15 May and forced Piłsudski to abandon his plans. For the first time, the Red Army was able to concentrate fighting men on something approaching the scale of the armies of the tsar and on 4 July they commenced a heavy artillery bombardment. A Russian cavalry corps in Tukhachevsky's army exploited the inevitable gaps that existed in the Polish lines – there simply weren't enough men to man a continuous front – and on 11 July the Bolsheviks recaptured Minsk. From there, the Russian cavalry turned its attention towards Vilnius; learning that the city had a modest garrison, the Russians contacted the Lithuanians to seek their cooperation in a joint operation against the city. Taking advantage of the general confusion, the Russian cavalry pressed on towards Vilnius without waiting to hear whether the Lithuanians would join the attack. The initial frontal assaults on the defensive positions were beaten off, but small groups of horsemen infiltrated past the defenders and turned their positions. On 14 July, the city was in Russian hands. In a gesture that mirrored that of Piłsudski after the fall of Daugavpils, the Russians agreed to assign the city and surrounding area to Lithuanian control.

From Vilnius, the Russians pressed on to Grodno, capturing the city in a surprise advance that triggered major Polish counterattacks. From there, it seemed that their momentum might take them to Warsaw. In an action reminiscent of the wars of previous centuries, Polish Uhlans – armed with traditional lances – engaged a Cossack regiment on 25 July, clashing in an anachronistic cavalry charge of steel and horseflesh. The Poles triumphed, buying sufficient time for their infantry to fall back farther. As had been the case in 1914, the Russians were hindered by the difficult terrain of the Pripet Marshes, with their forces massed to the north and south, and it was intended for the Russian armies in the south to advance towards the northwest on converging axes with Tukhachevsky's army, so that all the attacking troops would concentrate their strength prior to a drive on Warsaw, but the Polish forces proved highly effective in delaying them; the valleys of the Styr and Stochod, where so much blood was spilled in the fighting of 1915, 1916 and 1917 were now the scenes of further loss of life. Soldiers occupied and attacked the same trenches and fortifications that had featured in earlier battles, with broadly the same outcome – the gains and losses were modest compared to the price.

Farther north, Tukhachevsky continued to press forward towards the Polish capital. Alarmed by what appeared to be the imminent arrival of the Bolsheviks, western diplomats left Warsaw on 13 August and moved west to Poznań, which was increasingly the location of those within Poland who opposed Piłsudski; many believed the imminent fall of Warsaw would allow them to declare a new state of their own, and they welcomed the arrival of the representatives of the Western Powers, many of whom were suspicious of Piłsudski and his intentions. In turn, Piłsudski had little time for what he regarded as the high-handed attitude

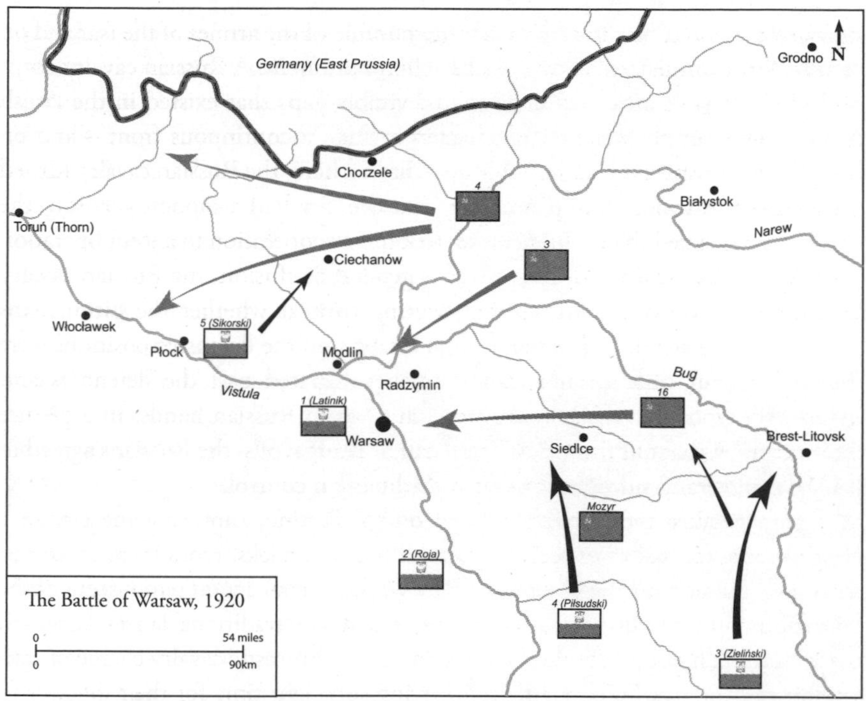

The Battle of Warsaw, 1920

of western diplomats. He had no expectations that they would provide succour, and had taken steps to try to ensure the survival of Poland without outside help. What little money had been promised – mainly by the French – had already been spent, but supplies that had been purchased in preceding months arrived in a steady stream, and patriotic calls for volunteers resulted in a flood of recruits for Poland's armies. Many had seen service in the First World War, and, both numerically and in terms of firepower, the two sides were now evenly matched. On 8 August, Tukhachevsky issued orders for his final assault.

Two days before, the Poles had decided to change their dispositions. To date, defensive actions against Tukhachevsky's forces had proved to be of limited value; given the size of the field of campaign and the relatively modest armies available, it was always possible for an attacker to outflank a defensive line. Most of the Polish successes – even along the Styr and Stochod – were through determined counterattacks, and Piłsudski and his lieutenants decided to opt for a counterthrust from south of Warsaw. Three armies in Józef Haller's Northern Front defended the line to the north of the city, while two further armies defended Warsaw itself, supported by a central reserve under the command of Lucjan Żeligowski. The counterthrust would be led by Edward Rydz-Śmygły. Moving the forces to their positions for the battle was a huge undertaking, especially as many were in contact with Tukhachevsky's advancing units; through a mixture of good fortune, tireless staff work and exhausting marches, most of the Polish formations succeeded in redeploying as planned.

The Poles held a large bridgehead to the east of Warsaw, extending about 13 miles (20km) from the Vistula. Its defenders included many of the Polish 'Blue Army' that had fought on the Western Front, but the first Russian attack late on 12 August resulted in the capture of the town of Radzymin. Fearful that this was the prelude to a major Russian thrust against Warsaw, Haller demanded urgent reinforcements and was assigned Żeligowski's reserves; these succeeded in recapturing Radzymin three days later. To the north, Władysław Sikorski, who had helped recruit and train troops for the Polish Legion during the First World War, launched a surprise attack and captured Ciechanów, and it rapidly became clear that the Russians were concentrating their main attack in this sector rather than the initial probing attack at Radzymin. Despite being outnumbered, Sikorski pressed on, making good use of two armoured trains, eight armoured cars and a small group of tanks. The Russian Fourth Army, advancing to the west, was now isolated and unaware that Sikorski was threatening its rear.

When Piłsudski unleashed the troops he had concentrated south of Warsaw for his counterthrust, he had little clear knowledge of events farther north. He would lead the attack himself, and fearing that defeat might lead to death or capture, he took the precaution of resigning from all non-military posts, so that his personal disappearance would not paralyse the Polish state. Early on 16 August, the advance began. Had Tukhachevsky's original plans been followed, the Poles would have encountered Budyonny's First Cavalry Army, but, instead of marching northwest to support the attack on Warsaw, Budyonny turned west towards Lwów – the former Austro-Hungarian city of Lemberg – and the sector was covered by the so-called Mozyr Group, made up of a variety of badly degraded units that amounted to less than two divisions and covered a front of 90 miles (145km). For the first two days, the Poles encountered almost no resistance and advanced a remarkable 55 miles (88km). With his forces badly strung out and unable to coordinate their strength, Tukhachevsky had no choice but to order a retreat. Most of his forces managed to escape before Piłsudski's strike force could envelop them from the rear, but the Russian Fourth Army was too far to the west. Its infantry was dispersed and overrun, and only its cavalry succeeded in breaking out of the Polish encirclement. However, it was unable to escape and although it caught up with other elements of Tukhachevsky's armies, it was driven over the frontier into German Prussia where it was interned. Through a mixture of good fortune, patriotic fervour and energetic action, the Poles had won a great victory. Tukhachevsky had gambled on being able to turn the northern flank of the Warsaw defences and strike against the Polish capital before the Poles could take advantage of his exposed southern flank; he overestimated the speed at which he could execute his plan, and underestimated the speed at which the Poles could deploy their troops for their counterthrust. Ultimately, the Polish success was due to the failure of the Russian forces in the southwest to cooperate with Tukhachevsky, as Trotsky later wrote:

> If Stalin and Voroshilov and the illiterate Budyonny had not had their own war in Galicia and the Red Cavalry [Army] had been in Lublin in time, the Red Army would not have suffered the disaster.[546]

The Russian invasion of Poland had indeed turned into a disaster. Tukhachevsky's units had already been badly degraded by illness, stragglers and desertion even before the Battle of Warsaw, and the losses in the fighting around the Vistula left Tukhachevsky with perhaps only one third of the men with whom he had launched the invasion. The Poles pursued him into the autumn until exhaustion on both sides and the onset of the muddy season made further fighting impossible. Under pressure from the Western Powers, the Poles agreed to a ceasefire. A peace treaty was signed in March 1921.

Lithuanian troops had taken possession of Vilnius in accordance with the agreement between Lithuania and Russia, but the Poles refused to recognise the territory that had been assigned to Lithuania by the Russians. The grumbling hostility between Lithuania and Poland turned into open conflict, and the new League of Nations pressured both sides into the Suwałki Agreement of October 1920, which attempted to create a demarcation line between Poland and Lithuania; but it did not settle the question of Vilnius. However, there was an implication in the agreement that the region would be part of Lithuania. This was unacceptable to the Poles, and Piłsudski decided to initiate an elaborate plan to return the region to Polish control. On 6 October, Lucjan Żeligowski – acting in accordance with Piłsudski's intentions – told officers of his infantry division that he intended to march to Vilnius and to seize it, with the intention of creating a new Republic of Central Lithuania. At first, many of his men refused to join him, and he advised Piłsudski that he would not be able to execute his plan. However, by 8 October he had sufficient support to risk the venture.

The Lithuanian forces in Vilnius were barely adequate to deal with potential unrest in the city from the Polish majority, still less to defeat Żeligowski's battle-hardened division, and made little attempt to resist. The Poles marched into Vilnius on 9 October to a jubilant reception. Three days later, Żeligowski declared the creation of his new republic. He was joined by more Polish 'mutineers' and fighting continued with the Lithuanians into November. A ceasefire came into effect at the end of the month, establishing the border that would exist between the two countries until 1939. Żeligowski handed over control to a new civilian government, which voted in 1922 to unite with Poland, an event that duly took place the following year. Piłsudski's wish to ensure that the area remained part of Poland had been fulfilled, but the price was considerable. There would be hostility between Poland and Lithuania for decades, and any lingering hope of a Poland-led confederation in the region was gone.

Although its independence wars were over, Lithuania experienced one last moment of political and diplomatic drama. On the Baltic coast was the city of Memel, known to Lithuanians as Klaipėda. The bulk of the city population was German, but the surrounding area was predominantly populated by Lithuanians. After the end of the First World War, the entire region, known as Memelland to the Germans, was separated from East Prussia and placed under the control of the League of Nations until an unspecified time when the people of the region would be able to express a choice about their future. Memel itself was the only significant deepwater port available to Lithuania, and in January 1923 a revolt by Lithuanians in the territory was instigated. The League of Nations, represented by a small French garrison, did little to interfere and the local Lithuanian population petitioned to join with Lithuania. Germany made protests, but opted to take no military action; the German government had decided that Memelland was unlikely to be returned to German control in any event, and continued to fear that Lithuania might prove too weak to resist being incorporated into Poland. If Memelland was to be lost, the Germans reasoned, it was best that it should be granted to Lithuania – at a future date, Germany would be more likely to succeed in persuading Lithuania to return the region to German control than if the territory were in the hands of Poland.

The lands that had seen so much fighting since 1914 now settled down to an uneasy peace. The three empires that had controlled the region at the beginning of the war were greatly diminished, and from their splinters a whole myriad of new nation states had been born. Some like Poland and Lithuania had existed in the past; others like Estonia had never known independence. Only time would tell whether these new alignments would prove durable.

CHAPTER 17

THE IMPERFECT PEACE

The First World War was begun with great expectations of rapid victory. Although many military thinkers feared that a major war between the Great Powers might prove to be a drawn-out affair, they were outnumbered by those who believed that offensive tactics would allow for a swift victory. Instead, the continent was condemned to a drawn-out war of attrition that ended with the three great empires that dominated Central and Eastern Europe – Germany, Austria-Hungary and Russia – all being destroyed and replaced by republics. From their peripheral fragments were born the states that formed complex new patterns and alliances. As has been described, many of these found themselves at each other's throats as they struggled with competing claims and expectations.

The exhausted Western Powers were in no mood to allow the disputes between the new states of Europe to erupt into wars that might plunge the continent back into general conflict. Although France, Britain and the United States continued to maintain powerful navies and the capacity to field large armies, there was no appetite whatsoever for war, not least because there remained fears that Bolshevism might spread beyond Russia. The remaining Great Powers were acutely aware that the Russian Revolution had grown out of Russia's disastrous performance in the war, and no nation wished to risk finding itself drawn into a conflict that might end in the same manner. Instead, the nations of Western Europe all hoped that fear of a future world conflict and the intervention of the new League of Nations would be sufficient to ensure at least a generation of peace.

Ethnicities and nationalities had played a large part in the conflict between the three empires. The spark that ignited Europe – the assassination of Franz Ferdinand and his wife Sophie – was the result of tensions in the Balkans, where the Serbs aspired to create a South Slav state under their control. The entire

Austro-Hungarian Empire struggled in vain to keep its multitudinous nationalities under control, and the lack of any collective sense of identity or loyalty ensured that it was the first empire where centrifugal forces combined with war-weariness to create widespread unrest. Nevertheless, despite these internal pressures and widespread expectation that the Dual Monarchy was an institution with no future, Habsburg rule actually outlasted that of the Romanovs in Russia and the Hohenzollerns in Germany.

As Europe settled down to its new national structures, it was inevitable that many people would find themselves on the wrong side of the new borders that were often created in haste, or with no regard for the realities on the ground. Whatever high-minded principles might have led to Wilson's insistence on the rights of the peoples of Europe to self-determination, the reality was far untidier than he might have expected. The decades of imperial rule had not required different nationalities within any individual empire to live apart, and whilst there had clearly been friction between the different groups, their new status within the new nations of Europe raised this to new levels.

The greatest territorial loser in the rearrangement of Europe was the Austro-Hungarian Empire, which ceased to exist completely. The Italians were awarded territories along their border, completing their long-held dreams of uniting all the lands that they regarded as Italian; the Balkan parts of the empire were largely incorporated into the new Yugoslavia; Hungary was forced to concede Transylvania to Romania; Bohemia and the Carpathian region broke away as the new state of Czechoslovakia; and much of Galicia was absorbed by Poland. Hungary and Austria became separate states, and in a remarkably short period of time Vienna was changed from the centre of a sprawling empire that stretched from the Swiss border as far as the Ukrainian steppes, into the capital of a relatively small nation in Central Europe. It is a measure of how inevitable the end of Habsburg rule had seemed for many years that few Austrians showed any sense of hankering after past glories.

Russia entered the war under the control of the tsars, and ended it under Bolshevik rule. In absolute terms, its loss of territory – Finland, the Baltic States, and Poland – was modest, but these regions included some of its most important economic and industrial centres, particularly Riga. Although exhaustion brought the series of wars that followed the withdrawal of German forces to an end, few in the region believed that the Russians had genuinely accepted the loss of these territories. The Baltic States in particular were fearful that small nations would prove no match for their larger neighbours, but it proved impossible for Estonia, Latvia and Lithuania to agree to cooperate militarily in any meaningful manner.

Their vulnerability would be exposed fully in a future conflict. In the aftermath of the Battle of Warsaw, the Polish Army managed to seize substantial territory to the east, but this created its own difficulties. Much of the land that now formed eastern Poland had a large non-Polish population, and just as it was clear that Russia retained ambitions about recovering its Baltic provinces, there could be no question that, if the opportunity were to arise, the Russian population of eastern Poland might provide a pretext for the Russians to attempt to re-enter this region. Piłsudski had hoped that he might be able to create a Polish-led alliance that would be strong enough to prevail against both Russia and any future resurgent Germany, but the continuing enmity of the Lithuanians over the status of Vilnius effectively prevented this from becoming a reality. For the moment, the military and economic weakness of Germany and the Soviet Union allowed the new states to develop unhindered, but this was no guarantee of long-term survival. Indeed, the status of the Vilnius region would be used expertly by the Soviet Union in the manner in which it absorbed Lithuania.[547]

The former empire that harboured the greatest sense of grievance about the peace that was imposed upon Europe was Germany. Many Germans felt that their nation had been unfairly treated in the negotiations that led to the Treaty of Versailles; they did not accept that Germany was primarily to blame for the war, and resented the territorial losses that were imposed by the victorious Western Powers. There was an arguable case for Alsace and Lorraine being returned to French control, but it should be pointed out that this region was not as unequivocally French as has generally been stated – by the beginning of the 20th century, less than 12 per cent of the population spoke French as their first language.[548] Even at the time of the Franco-Prussian War, Francophones made up less than half of the overall population. However, the anger in Germany at the loss of these territories was far less than the resentment at French occupation of the Saar region of Germany. The French had demanded this area as a territorial acquisition during the abortive peace talks between Vienna and Paris, and there was considerable concern in Germany that the French occupation of the Saar might become permanent.

The loss of territory in the east was also the source of great resentment. Two Baltic cities – Memel, to the north of East Prussia, and Danzig, to its west – were removed from German control, even though the majority of their population was unequivocally German. In both cases, the surrounding countryside was predominantly non-German, and as has already been described, the Lithuanians took advantage of this to seize the entire Memelland region and gain access to the Baltic. The Poles were keen to secure control of Danzig, but although Woodrow

Wilson had assured the Poles that he supported the right of the new Poland to have a Baltic port, it is likely that he had intended this to be by union with Lithuania. Instead, Danzig was declared a free city and the Poles were given control of a corridor of land running past Danzig to the coast immediately to the north. Here, they rapidly developed the minor port of Gdynia into a new maritime centre. The existence of this corridor resulted in East Prussia being left isolated from the rest of Germany. This region, undeniably German in its history, culture and population, had always been a predominantly agricultural area, and there were constant doubts that it would be able to survive in its new isolated state without one day becoming prey for an expansionist Poland. However, when the southern part of East Prussia – the Masurian region, where there was heavy fighting in 1914 and 1915 – was offered a plebiscite in 1920 to decide whether it would be part of Poland or Germany, the result was overwhelmingly in favour of the latter. The Poles protested that there had been widespread intimidation by German police and paramilitary groups, and that results had been falsified, but it seems that many Poles genuinely preferred to be part of Germany rather than Poland; the vote took place in July, when there was a very real threat of Tukhachevsky's armies reaching Warsaw, and many may have felt that they would be safer under German control rather than potentially once more being under the Russian yoke.

All along the eastern fringes of the new Germany, there were substantial German-speaking communities in the new nations of Europe – in Poland, the Baltic States, the Sudetenland, and Bohemia. Even in Transylvania, there were tens of thousands of descendants of Saxon settlers who had lived in the region for hundreds of years. The status of Danzig was unsatisfactory to its citizens, to Poland, and to Germany. Once memories of the terrible cost of the war began to fade and were no longer strong enough to be offset against the continued perceived grievances of the Treaty of Versailles, it was almost inevitable that many in Germany would seek opportunities to put right what they regarded as abiding injustices. The willingness of a future generation to exploit grievances both real and imagined made a second all-engulfing war inevitable. The Austro-Hungarian diplomat Czernin summed up events with considerable prescience in 1919:

> The Council of Four at Versailles [France, Britain, Italy and the United States] tried for some time to make the world believe that they possessed the power to rebuild Europe according to their own ideas ... That signified, to begin with, four utterly different ideas, for four different worlds were comprised in Rome, Paris, London and Washington ...

> Wilson has been scoffed at and cursed because he deserted his programme; certainly, there is not the slightest similarity between the Fourteen Points and the Peace of Versailles ... Clemenceau, too, the direct opposite of Wilson, was not quite open in his dealings. Undoubtedly this old man, who now at the close of his life was able to satisfy his hatred of the Germans of 1870, gloried in the triumph; but, apart from that, if he had tried to conclude a 'Wilson peace', all the private citizens of France, great and small, would have risen against him, for they had been told for the past five years, *que les boches payeront tout* ['that the Germans will pay for everything']. What he did, he enjoyed doing; but he was forced to do it or France would have dismissed him.
>
> ... And thus there came about what is now a fact. A dictated peace of the most terrible nature was concluded and a foundation laid for a continuance of unimaginable disturbances, complications, and wars ...
>
> The Entente, who would not allow the war to end and kept up the blockade for months after the cessation of hostilities, has made Bolshevism a danger to the world. War is its father, famine its mother, despair its godfather. The poison of Bolshevism will course in the veins of Europe for many a long year.
>
> Versailles is not the end of the war; it is only a phase of it. The war goes on, though in another form. I think that the coming generation will not call the great drama of the last five years the World War, but the World Revolution, which it will realise began with the World War.[549]

The closing comments highlight the widespread preoccupation in Europe with the threat of Bolshevism. Lenin, Trotsky and others had always made clear their intent to export their revolution to the rest of the world, and whilst the war between Russia and Poland brought the first, forcible attempt to do this to an abrupt halt, Soviet doctrine remained unchanged. Even if the threat gradually became more ideological than military, the fear of Bolshevism was exploited by those who wished to play upon the fears of the 'bourgeoisie' who had the most to lose from communist government. Whilst the National Socialists in Germany were amongst the leading exponents of exploiting such fears, they were by no means alone. Both the Nazis and the Italian fascists demanded antidemocratic powers as a necessary means of holding back socialism, and such sentiment spread to non-fascist countries such as the Baltic States and Poland. The post-war legacy of ethnic minorities on the wrong sides of Europe's new borders became intermingled with pre-war thinking about social Darwinism and racial superiority; not only was it important to reunite the lost populations with their homelands, it was also vital to save them from oppression by races that were seen as inferior. Even within Bolshevik Russia, there was widespread prejudice against certain nationalities. After coming to power, Stalin – who was a Georgian – rapidly implemented a policy of enforcing Russification, classifying some communities within Russia as 'enemy nations'. Once assigned this title, members of these communities – Poles, Germans, Koreans, Chinese, Kurds, Iranians, Finns, Estonians, Latvians and Lithuanians by ethnicity – were subject to forcible relocation, arbitrary arrest, and even summary execution.[550]

For many in Germany, there was an additional factor: the tantalising sense that German domination of Eastern Europe almost became a reality after the Treaty of Brest-Litovsk. Whilst there was a case for saying that the German Army had been defeated in the west, it was unarguable that it had prevailed in the east. In addition, the soldiers who served with Goltz in Latvia returned home feeling that they had been promised land in return for their service; there was a widespread sense of entitlement, which combined with the notion of German superiority to the Slav people of the region to make many believe that the Western Powers had cheated Germany of its rightful gains in the east. If the opportunity arose, Germany would attempt to make the territorial gains that were snatched away at the end of the war, not least because the spectre of blockade and starvation had to be avoided in a future conflict; given British control of the seas, this was possible only if Germany controlled a large land-based empire in the east.

Inevitably, many in Germany attempted to analyse why their mighty army had failed to win the war. The legend of the invincible army, stabbed in the back by treacherous politicians and left-wing agitators, was popular with the officer corps in particular, not least because it absolved them of all blame. Writing many years later, Hermann Balck gave a rather more sophisticated analysis. There was no question of Germany continuing the war in the context of the loss of the Romanian oilfields and the collapse of the *k.u.k.* Army; even if Austria-Hungary had been propped up, the vast resources of the United States would have brought defeat. Like all the Great Powers, Germany entered the war with considerable unity and enthusiasm, but as Balck pointed out, this was unlikely to last, and the political leadership of Germany – the civilian politicians and the kaiser – did not do enough to ensure that the nation remained united in its pursuit of victory. Decisions about democratic reforms were postponed until after the successful conclusion of the war, an error that merely led to disaffection and growing demands for immediate change. Nevertheless, Balck also concluded that the German Army was not blameless. The extravagance and glitter of the early years of Kaiser Wilhelm's reign alienated many of the Prussian officer corps, who increasingly turned their backs on politics and concentrated on purely military matters, a tendency that would cost them dearly in the Second World War. Balck felt that if Germany was to win the war, victory had to be achieved in the opening years of the war, but despite the constant talk of conflict in the first years of the 20th century, Germany was ill prepared for a war that would find it pitched against multiple opponents. The huge expenditure on the German Navy achieved nothing other than alienating Britain, and diverted precious resources and manpower from the German Army. Once the war began, there were repeated errors: Balck was particularly critical of Falkenhayn's strategy, and felt that Hindenburg and Ludendorff were sidelined for too long.[551]

Like many reviews written in the decades that followed, Balck's opinions are not without merit, but are also selective. There can be no question that the war was lost by early 1918, and there was almost no possibility of the great offensive launched in the west bringing about a decisive victory before the immense power of the United States intervened. But to point out the mistakes that Germany made in the years before the war and once the conflict began is to ignore similar mistakes made by Germany's opponents. Whilst Falkenhayn might have made errors, the commanders of other armies also miscalculated repeatedly. Ultimately, the war was lost because Germany and its allies simply did not have the resources of their enemies. The disintegration of the national sense of unity that took Germany to war was more due to the huge pressures placed upon Germany by its enemies than due to negligence by domestic politicians.

Even in the first months after the Treaty of Versailles was signed, there were clear differences of opinion about whether it had achieved its aims. The British view was that the destruction of Germany's fleet had largely achieved its war aims, but despite Czernin's condemnation of Clemenceau, there was considerable dismay in France that the terms were not harsh enough. The Italians had explicitly entered the war with considerable territorial gains as the price, and although they achieved some of these, others – particularly the Dalmatian coast – were not granted to them. In the years that followed, Germany proved incapable of paying reparations on the scale demanded, leading first to military occupation of the Ruhr and then to the cancellation of payments entirely. David Lloyd George, who played a major part in the negotiations on behalf of Britain, later wrote an evaluation of the treaty in which he concluded that it had not removed permanently the military threat from Germany, and was critical of the manner in which Germany was treated.[552]

The issue of reparations had dominated thinking about the shape of a peace treaty during the war, not least because of the manner in which Germany had imposed reparations on France in 1871. The Germans blamed the collapse of their economy on the punishing payments that were demanded by the French and Belgians, and whilst it would be wrong to blame the period of hyper-inflation entirely on reparations, they certainly contributed to the problems of Germany as it attempted to recover from the war. John Maynard Keynes, the British economist, criticised the treaty as being fundamentally unfair almost as soon as it came into force:

> I believe that the campaign for securing out of Germany the general costs of the war was one of the most serious acts of political unwisdom for which our statesmen have ever been responsible … the financial problems which were about to exercise Europe could not be solved by greed. The possibility of their cure lay in magnanimity.
>
> Europe, if she is to survive her troubles, will need so much magnanimity from America, that she must herself practice it. It is useless for the Allies, hot from stripping Germany and one another, to turn for help to the United States to put the states of Europe, including Germany, on their feet again. If the general election of December 1918 [in Britain] had been fought on lines of prudent generosity instead of imbecile greed, how much better the financial prospect for Europe might be.[553]

Others took a different view. A leading French economist suggested that by restricting Germany to a small army, the treaty allowed Germany to divert funding towards reparations in an affordable manner; others pointed out that the terms were far more lenient than those that Germany had intended to impose upon its enemies in the event of a German victory.[554] Regardless of whether the financial terms were too severe, it is difficult to imagine a peace settlement that would have satisfied French and Belgian demands for reparations and the general desire to weaken Germany militarily, and at the same time would not have left Germany with a great sense of grievance that could then be exploited by German politicians for their own ends. In a letter to a friend written in 1920, Balck mused on the failings of different parts of German society and made a prophetic statement:

> Just like the German *Bürgertum* [bourgeoisie], we too unfortunately must strike our Christian religion, at least in its current state, from the list of factors that can rebuild Germany. The church too has failed. The powerful force of Christian teachings has been watered down and is heading in the wrong direction. Our times are screaming for a reformer or a new religion. Socialism is really nothing but the dissatisfaction of the masses on a religious level.[555]

For a nation with little experience of democratic government, it was almost inevitable that enthusiasm for such new concepts would soon be replaced by disillusionment, especially in the context of a nation humiliated by defeat and struggling with worsening financial circumstances. The lure of a strong man with dreams of reborn nationalism was almost irresistible, and, for a generation brutalised both at home and in the front line by a terrible conflict, the associated violence and racism did not raise the concerns and outrage that might otherwise have prevailed.

It is unarguable that the roots of the Second World War lay in the imperfect peace that was established in Europe after the First World War. But such a simple statement ignores many other factors. Many nationalities were given the opportunity to establish their own states, and Europe was simply too exhausted to continue fighting until German military power was unequivocally destroyed – in the absence of such a conclusive defeat, the terms imposed resulted in perhaps the 'least worst' outcome. The world would have to wait for another war with all its attendant horrors before the imbalances created in the wake of the First World War were resolved, but whilst the Second World War settled some issues, it created many more, leaving Europe divided into two armed camps in a stand-off that would last for over 40 years. Whilst some nations are dragged unwillingly into conflict, those that enter it in the hope of resolving their problems find that they have merely exchanged one set of issues for another – and at enormous cost.

In some respects, the First World War belongs more to the 19th century than the 20th century. It was a conflict with imperial monarchs, the widespread use of cavalry, and statesmen who believed that they could arbitrarily redraw the maps of the world. The events that triggered the outbreak of war show a disastrous failure of deterrence; yet decades later, when Europe was once more armed to the teeth and divided into two hostile, mutually suspicious camps, deterrence proved to be effective at preventing war. Perhaps the cultural memory of the vast waste of the First World War helped the nations of the world, even if only to a limited extent, from making similar miscalculations during the nuclear age.

BIBLIOGRAPHY

Research Institutes

Allgemeines Verwaltungsarchiv (Vienna)
Brigham Young University Online Documents Archive (Provo, Utah)
Bundesarchiv (Berlin)
Bundesarchiv-Militärarchiv (Freiburg)
Geheimes Staatsarchiv Preussischer Kulturbesitz (Berlin)
Heeresgeschichtliches Museum (Vienna)
Hoover Institution Archives (Stanford, CA)
Krasnyi Archiv (Leningrad)
Kriegsarchiv (Vienna)
Liddell Hart Centre for Military Archives (King's College, London)
Soviet History Archive (www.marxists.org)
Tsentral'nyy Voyenno-Istoricheskiy Arkhiv (Moscow)
United States National Archives (Washington)

Journals

Baltic Security and Defence Review (Baltic Defence College, Tartu)
Delo Naroda (Petrograd)
The Historical Journal (Cambridge University Press)
Izvestia (Petrograd)
Journal of Modern History (University of Chicago Press) *Krasnaia Letopis* (Leningradskii Institut Istorii)
La Revue de Genève (Geneva)
New York Times (New York)
Novoye Vremya (Petrograd)
Rabochy I Soldat (Petrograd)
Russian Review (University of Kansas)

Slavonic and East European Review (University College London)
Sõdur (Riigi Trükikoda, Tallinn)
Virginia Quarterly Review (Charlottesville, VA)

PRIMARY SOURCES

Agreement Between France, Russia, Great Britain and Italy, April 1915 (HM Stationery Office, London)

Dokumenty Vneshnei Politiki SSSR (Izd-vo Polit. Litry, Moscow 1957)

Foreign Relations of the United States 1918: Supplement I, The World War (US Government Printing Office, Washington DC 1933)

Historia Polski (Państwowe Wydawn Naukowe, Warsaw 1966)

Letters of the Tsaritsa to the Tsar 1914–1916 (Hyperion, New York 1987)

Proceedings of the Brest-Litovsk Peace Conference (Washington Government Printing Office, 1918)

Protocol of the Proceedings of the Potsdam Conference, 1 August 1945 (US Government Printing Office 1950)

Sbornik Dokumentov Mirovoy Imperialisticheskoy Voyny na Russkom Fronte 1914–1917gg (Moscow, 1939)

SECONDARY SOURCES

Agar, A., *Footprints in the Sea* (Evans, London 1959)

Ahto, S., *Sotaretkillä* in Manninen, O. (ed.) *Itselnäistymisen Vuodet 1917–1920* (Valtion, Helsinki 1993)

Amiguet, P., *La Vie du Prince Sixte de Bourbon* (Editions de France, Paris 1936)

Antonov-Ovseyenko, V., *V Semnadtsatom Godu* (Gosudarstvennoe Izd-vo Khudozhestvennoi Lit-ry, Moscow 1933)

Ascher, A., *The Revolution of 1905* (Stanford University Press, 1988)

Baden, M. von and Mann, G., *Erinnerungen und Dokumente* (Klett, Stuttgart 1968)

Balck, H., trans. D. Zabecki and D. Biederkarten, (*Order in Chaos: The Memoirs of General of Panzer Troops Hermann Balck* (University Press of Kentucky, 2015)

Barnett, C., *The Sword-Bearers: Supreme Command in the First World War* (Faber & Faber, London 2010)

Barrett, M., *Operation Albion: The German Conquest of the Baltic Islands* (Indiana University Press, 2008)

Baumgart, W., *Deutsche Ostpolitik 1918. Von Brest-Litowsk bis zum Ende des Ersten Weltkrieges* (Oldenbourg, Vienna 1966)

Bazanov, S., *Pravo Umeret' za Rodinu. 'Batalony Smerti' v Russkoy Armii v 1917 godu*

(Pervoye Sentyabrya, Moscow 2008)

Beéche, A., *The Other Grand Dukes (Sons and Grandsons of Russia's Tsars and Grand Dukes)* (Eurohistory, Richmond CA 2013)

Benckendorff, P., trans. M. Benckendorff, *Last Days at Tsarskoe Selo: Being the Personal Notes and Memories of Count Paul Benckendorff Telling of the Last Sojourn of the Emperor and Empress of Russia at Tsarskoe Selo from March 1 to August 1 1917* (Heinemann, London 1927)

Bennett, G., *Cowan's War: The Story of British Naval Operations in the Baltic, 1918–1920* (Collins, London 1964)

Berdiaev, N., Bulgakov, S., Gershenzon, M., Izgoev, I.S., Kistiakovskii, B., Struve, P., and Frank, S., trans. and ed., M. Schatz and J. Zimmerman, *Vekhi* (Routledge, Milton 1994)

Biden, J., *The Baltic States and Weimar Ostpolitik* (Cambridge University Press, 2002)

Bihl, W., *Deutsche Quellen zur Geschichte des Ersten Weltkrieges* (Wissenschaftliche Buchgesellschaft, Darmstadt 1991)

Bilmanis, A., *A History of Latvia* (Princeton University Press, 1951)

Blagonravov, G., *The Fortress of Peter and Paul* in McIlhone, R. (ed. and trans.), *Petrograd, October 1917: Reminiscences of Active Participants in the Armed Uprising* (Foreign Languages Publishing House, Moscow 1957)

Blom, P., *The Vertigo Years: Europe* (Basic Books, New York 2008)

Bonch-Bruyevich, M., *Vsia Vlast' Sovietam* (Voenno Isd-vo, Moscow 1964)

Bonch-Bruyevich, V., *Na Boevykh Postackh Fevralskoi I Oktiabrskoi Revoliutsii* (Izdateltsvo Federatsiia, Moscow 1931)

Bourbon-Parma, S., *L'Offre de Paix Séparée de l'Autriche* (Plon-Nourrit, Paris 1920)

Bradley, J., *The Czechoslovak Legion in Russia 1914–1920* (East European Monographs, Boulder 1990)

Brailsford, H., *Across the Blockade: A Record of travels in Enemy Europe* (Allen & Unwin, London 1919)

Brooke, R., *1914 and Other Poems* (Sidgwick & Jackson, London 1915)

Browder, R. and Kerensky, A., *The Russian Provisional Government 1917* (Stanford University Press, 1961)

Bruchmüller, G., *Die Deutsche Artillerie in den Durchbruchsschlachten des Weltkrieges* (Mittler, Berlin 1921)

Brusilov, A., *Moi Vospominaniia* (Voenizdat, Moscow 1967)

Buchanan, G., *My Mission to Russia and Other Diplomatic Memories* (Cassell, London 1923)

Bujac, E., *Campagnes de l'Armée Roumaine 1916–1919* (Charles-Lavauzelle, Paris 1933)

Burdzhalov, E., *Vtoraia Russkaia Revoliutsiia* (Nauka, Moscow 1967)

Bushnell, J., *Mutiny Amid Repression: Russian Soldiers of the Revolution 1905–1906* (University of Indiana, 1985)

Buttar, P., *Between Giants: The Battle for the Baltics in World War II* (Osprey, Oxford 2013)

Buttar, P., *Collision of Empires: The War on the Eastern Front in 1914* (Osprey, Oxford 2014)

Buttar, P., *Germany Ascendant: The Eastern Front in 1915* (Osprey, Oxford 2015)

Buttar, P., *Russia's Last Gasp: The Eastern Front 1916–1917* (Osprey, Oxford 2016)

Cerf, B., *Alsace-Lorraine Since 1870* (MacMillan, New York 1919)

Chaadaeva, O. (ed.), *Soldatskie Pis'ma v Gody Mirovoi Voiny 1914–1917* in Krasnyi Arkhiv (Moscow 1934) Chamberlin, W., *The Russian Revolution* (Princeton University Press, 1987)

Cornwall, M., *The Undermining of Austria-Hungary: The Battle for Hearts and Minds* (Palgrave MacMillan, New York 2000)

Cornwall, M. and Newman, J. (eds.), *Sacrifice and Rebirth: the Legacy of the Last Habsburg War* (Berghahn, New York 2016)

Czegka, E., Heydendorff, W., Kiszling, R., Klumpner, C., Wisshaupt, E. and Zöbl, G., *Österreich-Ungarns Letzter Krieg 1914–1918* (Verlag der Militärwissenschaftlichen Mitteilungen, Vienna 1936)

Czernin von und zu Chudenitz, O. Graf, *In the World War* (Harper & Collins, New York 1920)

Dabija, G., *România în războiul mondial 1916–1919* (Monitorul Oficial și Imprimeriile Statului, Bucharest 1936)

Daniels, R., *Red October: The Bolshevik Revolution of 1917* (Scribner, New York 1967)

Danilov, Y., *La Russie Dans La Guerre Mondiale* (Payot, Paris 1927)

Davies, N., *White Eagle, Red Star: the Polish-Soviet War, 1919–20* (Pimlico, London 2003)

Dehn, L., *The Real Tsaritsa* (Little, Brown & Co, Boston 1922)

De Launay, J., *Major Controversies of Contemporary History* (Pergamon, Oxford 1965)

Denikin, A., *The Russian Turmoil* (Hutchinson, London 1922)

Deutscher, L., *The Prophet Armed: Trotsky, 1879–1921* (Oxford University Press, 1954)

Duke, P., *Red Dusk and the Morrow: Adventures and Investigations in Red Russia* (Doubleday, Page & Co, New York 1922)

Eidintas, A., 'Restoration of the State' in Eidintas, A., Zalys, V. and Senn, A., *Lithuania in European Politics: The Years of the First Republic, 1918–1940* (Donnelley & Sons, Harrisonburg 1997)

Eksteins, M., *Walking Since Daybreak: a Story of Eastern Europe, World War II and the Heart of our Century* (Mariner, New York 2000)

Emmerson, C., *1913: The World Before the Great War* (Bodley Head, London 2013)

Figes, O., *A People's Tragedy: The Russian Revolution 1891–1824* (Pimlico, London 1996)

Fink, C., *Defending the Rights of Others: The Great Powers, the Jews, and International Minority Protection 1878–1938* (Cambridge University Press, 2004)

Fischer, F., *Griff nach der Weltmacht. Die Kriegszielpolitik des kaiserlichen Deutschland 1914/18* (Droste, Düsseldorf 1961)

Fraiman, A. (ed.), *Oktiabr'skoe Vooruzhennoe Vosstanie: Semnadtsatyi God v Petrograde* (Institut Istorii, Leningrad 1967)

Galantai, J., trans. E. Grusz and J. Pokoly, *Hungary in the First World War* (Akademiai Kiado, Budapest 1990)

Gaponenko, L. (ed.), *Revoliutsionnoe Dvizhenie v Rossii Sverzheniia Samoderzhaviia* (Izdat. Akad. Nauk, Moscow 1957)

Garande, J., *The Cost of Freedom* (Authorhouse, Bloomington 2011)

Çērmanis, U., *Oberst Vācietis und die Lettischen Schützen im Weltkrieg und in der Oktoberrevolution* (Almqvist & Wiksell, Stockholm 1974)

Gerutis, A., 'Independent Lithuania' in Gerutis A. (ed.), trans. Algirdas Budreckis, *Lithuania: 700 Years*, 6th edn (Manyland, New York 1984)

Gessen, I. (ed.), *Arkhiv Russkoi Revoliutsii* (Slovo, Berlin 1922–1925)

Gippius, Z., *Sinaia Kniga: Peterburgski Dnevnik 1914–1918* (Tipografija Radenkoviča, Belgrade 1929)

Golder, F. (ed.), *Documents of Russian History 1914–1917* (Century, New York 1927)

Goltz, R. von der, *Meine Sendung in Finnland und Baltikum* (Koehler, Leipzig 1920)

Gordienko, I., *Iz Boevogo Proshlogo 1914–1918gg* (Gos Isd-Vo Polit Lit-Ry, Moscow 1957)

Graber, G., *History of the SS* (D. McKay, New York 1978)

Groener, W., *Lebenserinnerungen: Jugend – Generalstab – Weltkrieg* (Vendenhoeck & Ruprecht, Göttingen 1957)

Gurko, V., *War and Revolution in Russia 1914–1917* (Macmillan, New York 1919)

Hafner, S., *Die Deutsche Revolution 1918–1919* (Rowohlt, Reinbek 2002)

Halpern, P., *A Naval History of World War I* (Naval Institute Press, Annapolis 1995)

Harcave, S., *The Russian Revolution* (Collier, London 1970)

Harris, J. and Barr, N., *Amiens to the Armistice: The BEF in the Hundred Days' Campaign 8 August–November 1918* (Brassey, London 1999)

Hasegawa, T., *The February Revolution: Petrograd 1917* (University of Washington Press, Seattle 1981)

Heenan, L., *Russian Democracy's Fatal Blunder: The Summer Offensive of 1917* (Praeger, Westport CT 1987)

Herwig, H., *The First World War: Germany and Austria-Hungary 1914–1918* (Arnold, London 1997)

Herwig, H., *Luxury Fleet: The Imperial German Navy 1888–1918* (Routledge, London 2014)

Hindenburg, P. von, trans. F. Holt, *Out of my Life* (Cassell, London 1920)

Hoffmann, M., trans. A. Charnot, *The War of Lost Opportunities* (Paul, French, Trubner & Co, London 1924)

Hoffmann, M. and Nowak, K., *Die Aufzeichnungen des Generalmajors Max Hoffmann* (Verlag für Kulturpolitik, Berlin 1929)

Holborn, H., *A History of Modern Germany* (Princeton University Press, 1982)

Hoppu, T. and Haapala, P., *Tampere 1918: A Town in the Civil War* (Tampere Museum, Tampere 2010)

Howarth, D., *The Dreadnoughts* (Time-Life, Fairfax VA 1980)

Ioaniţiu, A., *Războiul României (1916–1919)* (Typografia Geniului, Bucharest 1929)

Jones, S., *Russia in Revolution; Being the Experiences of an Englishman in Russia During the Upheaval* (McBride, Nast & Co, New York 1917)

'Józef Piłsudski (1867–1935)' available at http://en.poland.gov.pl/Jozef,Pilsudski,%281867-1935%29,1972.html

Joseph August (Archduke), *A Világháború Okai: a Hármasszövetség Története* (Róna Nyomda, Budapest 1942)

Judson, P., *The Habsburg Empire: A New History* (Belknap, Cambridge Mass. 2016)

Kakurin, N. (ed.), *Razloshenie Armii v 1917 godu* (Gosudarstvennoi Izd-vo, Moscow 1925)

Kalvoda, J., *The Genesis of Czechoslovakia* (East European Monographs, Boulder 1986)

Kann, R., *Die Sixtusaffäre und die Geheimen Friedensverhandlungen Österreich-Ungarns im Ersten Weltkrieg* (Oldenbourg, Munich 1966)

Katkov, G., *Russia 1917: The February Revolution* (Greenwood, Westport CT 1979)

Kerensky, A., *The Prelude to Bolshevism: The Kornilov Rebellion* (Dodd, Mead & Co, New York 1919)

Kerensky, A., *The Catastrophe: Kerensky's Own Story of the Russian Revolution* (Dodd, Mead & Co, New York 1927)

Kerensky, A., *Russia's and History's Turning Point* (Duell, Sloan & Peirce, New York 1965)

Ketola, E., *Kansalliseen Kansanvaltaan. Suomen Itsenäisyys, Sosiaalidemokraatit ja Venäjän Vallankumous 1917* (Tammi, Helsinki 1987)

Keynes, J., *The Economic Consequences of the Peace* (Harcourt, Brace & Howe, New York 1920)

Kinvig, C., *Churchill's Crusade: The British Invasion of Russia 1918–1920* (Hambledon Continuum, London 2006)

Kiritzesco, C., *La Roumanie dans la Guerre Mondiale 1916–1919* (Payot, Paris 1934)

Klecanda, V., *Bitva u Zborova* (Vojensky Archiv, Prague 1927)

Knox, A., *With the Russian Army 1914–1917* (Hutchinson, London 1921)

Kramer, A., *Dynamic of Destruction: Culture and Mass Killing in the First World War* (Oxford University Press 2008)

Krist, G., *Pascholl Plenny!* (Seidel & Sohn, Vienna 1936)

Kroders, A., *Atmiņas* (Imanta, Copenhagen 1968)

Kuhl, H. von, *Der Weltkrieg 1914–1918: Dem Deutschen Volke Dargestellt* (Weller, Berlin 1935)

Kulikov, S., *Imperator Nikolai II v Gody Pervoy Mirovoy Voyny* (SPB, St Petersburg 2000)

Lappalainen, J., *Punakaartin Sota* (Valtion Painatuskeskus, Helsinki 1981)

Lapin, N., (ed.), *Progressivni Blok v 1915–1977gg* (Krasnyi Archiv, Moscow 1932)

Lenin, V., *Collected Works* (Progress Publishers, Moscow 1964)

Lesčius, V., *Lietuvos kariuomenė nepriklausomybės kovose 1918–1920* (General Jonas Žemaitis Military Academy of Lithuania, Vilnius 2004)

Lichnewsky, M. (trans.), *Lettres des Grands-Ducs à Nicholas II* (Payot, Paris 1926)

Lincoln, W., *Red Victory: A History of the Russian Civil War* (Sphere, London 1991)

Lincoln, W., *Passage Through Armageddon: The Russians in War and Revolution* (Oxford University Press, 1994)

Link, A. (ed.), *The Papers of Woodrow Wilson* (Princeton University Press, Princeton NJ 1985)

Litzmann, K., *Lebenserinnerungen* (Eisenschmidt, Berlin 1928)

Lloyd George, D., *The Truth about the Peace Treaties* (Gollancz, London 1938)

Ludendorff, E., *Meine Kriegserinnerungen 1914–1918* (Mittler, Berlin 1919)

Lukomsky, A., *Vospominaniia Generala A S Lukomskago* (Otto Kirchner, Berlin 1922)

Lyandres, S., *The Fall of Tsarism: Untold Stories of the February 1917 Revolution* (Oxford University Press, 2013)

Mack, K., 'Galizien um die Jahrhundertwende: Politische, Soziale und Kulturelle Verbindungen mit Österreich' in *Schriftenreihe des Österreichischen Ost- und Südosteuropa-Instituts* (Verlag für Geschichte und Politik, Vienna 1990)

Mackensen, A. von, *Briefe und Auszeichnungen des Generalfeldmarschalls aus Krieg und Frieden* (Bibliographisches Institut, Leipzig 1938)

MacMillan, M., *Paris 1919: Six Months That Changed the World* (Random House, New York 2002)

Madajczyk, C., *Generalna Gubernia w Planach Hitlerowskich. Studia* (Wydawnictwo Naukowe PWN, Warsaw 1961)

Maide, J., *Estonian War of Independence 1918–1920* (Graphic House, Washington, reprinted 1968)

Maksakov, V. and Turunov, A., *Khronika Grazhdanskoi Voiny v Sibiri 1917–1918* (Gosizdat, Moscow 1926)

Mangulis, V., *Latvia in the Wars of the 20th Century* (Cognition Books, Princeton 1983)

Mann, T., *Gedanken im Kriege* (Fischer E-Books, Frankfurt am Main 2009)

Mannerheim, C., trans. E. Lewenhaupt, *The Memoirs of Marshal Mannerheim* (Dutton, New York 1954)

Mantoux, E., *Carthaginian Peace, or The Economic Consequences of Mr Keynes* (Scribner, New York 1952)

Martin, T., *The Affirmative Action Empire: Nations and Nationalism in the Soviet Union 1923–1939* (Cornell University Press, Ithaca 2001)

Martynov, E., *Kornilov: Popytka Voennogo Perevorota* (Izdanie Voennoi Tipografii Upravleniya Delami Narkomvoenmor, Leningrad 1927)

Massie, R., *Nicholas and Alexandra* (Dell, New York 1967)

May, A., *The Passing of the Habsburg Monarchy 1914–1918* (University of Pennsylvania Press, Philadelphia 1996)

McIlhone, R. (ed. and trans.), *Petrograd, October 1917: Reminiscences of Active Participants in the Armed Uprising* (Foreign Languages Publishing House, Moscow 1957)

Melgunov, S., Pushkarev, S., Pushkarev, B. and Beaver, J., *The Bolshevik Seizure of Power* (ABC Clio, Oxford 1972)

Michaelis, H. and Schraepler, E., (eds.), *Ursachen und Folgen. Vom Deutschen Zusammenbruch 1918 und 1945 bis zur Staatlichen Neuordnung Deutschlands in der Gegenwart. Eine Urkunden- und Dokumentensammlung zur Zeitgeschichte* (Dokumenten-Verlag, Berlin 1958)

Mikhutina, I., *Ukrainskiy Brestskiy Mir. Put' Vykhoda Rossii iz Pervoy Morovoy Voyni I Anatomiya Konflikta Mezhdu Sovnarkomom RSFSR I Prvatel'strom Ukrainskoy Tsentral'noy Rady* (Books on Demand, Stoughton 2015)

Miliukov, P., Seignobos, C. and Eisenmann, L., *History of Russia* (Funk & Wagnalls, New York 1969)

Mints, I., *Istoriia Velikogo Oktiabria* (Nauka, Moscow 1967)

Mitelman, M., Bistriansky, V., Glebov, B. and Uliansky, A., *Istoriia Putilovskogo Zavoda* (Institut Istori Partii, Leningrad 1939)

Molisch, P., *Vom Kampf der Tschechen um ihren Staat* (Braumüller, Vienna 1929)

Morgen, C. von, *Meiner Truppen Heldenkämpfe* (Mittler, Berlin 1920)

Moritz, V. and Leidinger, H. (eds.), *Die Nacht des Kirpitschnikow. Eine Andere Geschichte des Ersten Weltkriegs* (Deutike im Paul Szolnay, Vienna 2006)

New York Times Current History: The European War from the Beginning to March 1915. Who Began the War, and Why? (New York, 1915)

Nicholas II, *Journal Intime de Nicholas II (Juillet 1914–Juillet 1918)* (Payot, Paris 1934)

Nicholson, N., *Alex* (Weidenfeld & Nicolson, London 1973)

Niessel, H., *Le Triomphe des Bolchéviks et la Paix de Brest-Litovsk: Souvenirs 1917–1918* (Plon, Paris 1940)

Paléologue, M., trans. F. Holt, *An Ambassador's Memoirs* (Doran, New York 1923)

Pares, B., *My Russian Memoirs* (Cape, London 1931)

Plensners, A., *Divdesmitā Gadsimta Pārvērtības* (Grāmatu Draugs, Brooklyn 1978)

Podorozhny, N., *Russkaya Armiya v Velikoy Voyne: Narochskaya Operatsiya v Marte 1916 g* (Voenizdat, Moscow 1938)

Polner, T., *Zhiznennyi put' Kniazia Georgiia Evgenievicha L'vova: Lichnost', Vzgliady, Usloviia Dieiatel'nosti* (Payot, Paris 1932)

Portisch H., *Österreich. Die unterschätzte Republik* (Verlag Kremayr & Scheriau, Vienna 1989)

Rabinowitch, A., *The Bolsheviks Come to Power: the Revolution of 1917 in Petrograd* (Norton, New York 1976)

Rademacher, M., *Reichsland Elsaß-Lothringen 1871–1919* (Osnabrück University, 2006)
Raskolnikov, F., *Raskazy Michmana Il'ina* (Sovetskaia Literatura, Moscow 1934)
Rauchensteiner, M., *Der Erste Weltkrieg und das Ende der Habsburger-Monarchie* (Böhlau, Vienna 2013)
Rei, A., *The Drama of the Baltic Peoples* (Kirjastus Vaba Eesti, Stockholm 1970)
Robien, Comte L. de, trans. C. Sykes, *The Diary of a Diplomat in Russia 1917–1918* (Joseph, London 1969)
Rodzianko, M., *Zapiska M. V. Rodzianko* in Pokrovsky, M. (ed.), *Ekonomicheskoe Polozhenie Rossii Pered Revoliutsiei* (Krasnyi Archiv, Petrograd 1925)
Ronge, M., *Kriegs- und Industrie-Spionage* (Amalthea, Vienna 1930)
Rozenšteins, H. (ed.), *Latvijas Armija 20 Gados*, reprinted from a 1939 Latvian Army publication (Raven, Grand Haven, Mi. 1974)
Roth, A., *Die Juden im Heere: Eine Statistische Untersuchung Nach Amtlichen Quellen* (Deutscher Volks-Verlag, Munich 1919)
Rupprecht von Bayern, *Mein Kriegstagebuch* (Deutscher National Verlag, Munich 1929)
Sablinsky, W., *The Road to Bloody Sunday: Father Gapon and the St. Petersburg Massacre of 1905* (Princeton University Press, 1976)
Sabsay, N., *A Moment in History: A Russian Soldier in the First World War* (self-published, Caldwell, ID 1960)
Samsons, V. (ed.), *Latvijas PSR Mazā Enciklopēdija* (Zinātne, Riga 1967)
Savinkov, B., *K Dielu Kornilova* (Union, Paris 1919)
Scheidemann, P., *Der Zusammenbruch* (Verlag für Sozialwissenschaft, Berlin 1921)
Screen, J., *Mannerheim: The Finnish Years* (Hurst, London 2000)
Senn, A., *The Great Powers, Lithuania and the Vilna Question* (Brill, Leiden 1966)
Shchegolev, P. (ed.), *Padenie Tsarskogo Rezhima: Stenograficheskiy Otchety Doprosov i Pokazanii, Dannykh v 1917gv* (Gosudararstvennoe Isdateltsvo, Moscow 1926)
Shchegolev, P. (ed.), *Otrechenie Nikolaia II: Vospoinaniia Ochevidtsev, Documenty* (Sovyetskiy Pisatel, Moscow 1990)
Singer, L., *Ottokar Graf Czernin: Staatsmann einer Zeitenwende* (Verlag Styria, Graz 1965)
Skocpol, S., *States and Social Revolutions* (Cambridge University Press, 1979)
Smele, J., *Historical Dictionary of the Russian Civil Wars* (Rowman & Littlefield, Lanham MD 2015)
Smilg-Benario, M., *Von Kerenski zu Lenin: Die Geschichte der Zweiter Russischen Revolution* (Amalthea, Zurich 1929)
Smith, C., *Finland and the Russian Revolution 1918–1922* (University of Georgia Press, Athens GA 1958)
Snyder, J., *The Ideology of the Offensive: Military Decision-Making and the Disasters of 1914* (Cornell, Ithaca 1984)
Snyder, T., *The Red Prince: The Secret Lives of a Habsburg Archduke* (Basic Books, New York 2008)

Stachelbeck, C., *Militärische Effektivität im Ersten Weltkrieg: Die 11. Bayerische Infanteriedivision 1915 bis 1918* (Ferdinand Schöningh, Paderborn 2010)

Staff, G., *German Battlecruisers 1914–1918* (Osprey, Oxford 2006)

Staff, G., *Battle for the Baltic Islands 1917: Triumph of the Imperial German Navy* (Pen & Sword Maritime, Barnsley 2008)

Stepun, F., *Byvshee i Nesbyvsheesia* (Chekhova, New York 1956)

Stevenson, D., *With Our Backs to the Wall: Victory and Defeat in 1918* (Penguin, London 2011)

Stockdale, M., *Paul Miliukov and the Quest for a Liberal Russia, 1880–1918* (Cornell University Press, New York 1996)

Strakhovsky, L., *Was There a Kornilov Rebellion? A Reappraisal of the Evidence* in *Slavonic and East European Review* (University College London 1955)

Suhrmann, W., *Geschichte des Landwehr-Infanterie-Regiments Nr. 31* (Stalling, Oldenburg 1928)

Sukhanov, N., trans. J. Carmichael, *The Russian Revolution: A Personal Record* (Oxford University Press, 1955)

Tallents, S., *Man and Boy* (Faber & Faber, London 1943)

Thaer, A. von, *Generalstabsdienst an der Front und in der OHL. Aus Briefen und Tagebuchaufzeichnungen* (Vendenhoeck & Ruprecht, Göttingen 1958)

Tomilov, P., *Severno-Zapadnyi Front Grazhdanskoi Voiny v Rossii 1919g* (Tomilov Collection, Hoover Institution Archives, Stanford CA)

Traksmaa, A., *Lühike Vabadussõja Ajalugu* (Olion, Tallinn 1992)

Trotsky, L., *History of the Russian Revolution* (trans. M. Eastman, 1932, republished Haymarket, London 2008)

Trotsky, L., *Stalin* (Hollis & Carter, London 1947)

Tsereteli, I., *Reminiscences of the February Revolution: The April Crisis* in *Russian Review* (University of Kansas, 1955)

Upton, A., *The Finnish Revolution 1917–1918* (University of Minnesota Press 1980)

Vladimirovich, Andrei, *Iz Dnevnika A. V. Romanova za 1916–1917gg* in Krasnyi Archiv XXVI (Leningrad, 1928)

Volkogonov, D., *Lenin: Life and Legacy* (Harper Collins, London 1994)

Volobuev, P., *Proletariat I Burzhuaziia Rossii v 1917g* (Izdvo Sotsialno-Ekonomicheskoi Litry Mysl, Moscow 1964)

Wade, R., *Red Guards and Workers' Militias* (Stanford University Press, Stanford 1984)

Waite, R., *Vanguard of Nazism* (W. W. Norton & Co, London 1969)

Wasilewski, L., *Józef Piłsudski Jakim Go Znałem* (Rój, Warsaw 1935)

Watt, R., *Bitter Glory: Poland and its Fate 1918–1939* (Simon & Schuster, New York 1979)

Watson, A., *Enduring the Great War: Combat, Morale and Collapse in the German and British Armies 1914–1918* (Cambridge University Press 2008)

Watson, A., *Ring of Steel: Germany and Austria-Hungary at War, 1914–1918* (Allen Lane, London 2014)

Wildman, K., *The End of the Russian Imperial Army* (Princeton University Press, 1980)

Woodward, D., *Mutiny at Cattaro, 1918* in *History Today* (London 1976) 26 (12)

Woodward, D., *World War I Almanac* (Facts on File, New York 2009)

Ylikangas, H., *Tie Tampereelle: Dokumentoitu Kuvaus Tampereen Antautumiseen Johtaneista Sotatapahtumista Suomen Sisällissodassa* (WSOY, Porvoo 1994)

Zayonchkovsky, A., *Strategicheskiy Ocherk Voyny 1914–1918gg* (Vysshiy Voyennyy Redaktsionnyy Sovet, Moscow 1923)

Zayonchkovsky, A., *Perveya Mirovaya Voyna* (Polygon, Moscow 2002)

Zoffe, V., *Pyat' Let Krasnogo Flota* (Narodnyy Komissariat po Morskim Delam, Petrograd 1922)

NOTES

INTRODUCTION

1 Snyder, J., *The Ideology of the Offensive: Military Decision-Making and the Disasters of 1914* (Cornell, Ithaca 1984), p. 153
2 Quoted in Barnett, C., *The Sword-Bearers: Supreme Command in the First World War* (Faber & Faber, London 2010), p. 34
3 Mann, T., *Gedanken im Kriege* (Fischer E-Books, Frankfurt am Main 2009)
4 Brooke, R., *1914 and Other Poems* (Sidgwick & Jackson, London 1915), p. 7
5 *Letters of the Tsaritsa to the Tsar 1914–1916* (Hyperion, New York 1987), p. 9
6 Harcave, S., *The Russian Revolution* (Collier, London 1970), p. 21
7 Skocpol, S., *States and Social Revolutions* (Cambridge University Press, 1979), p. 92
8 Sablinsky, W., *The Road to Bloody Sunday: Father Gapon and the St. Petersburg Massacre of 1905* (Princeton University Press, 1976), p. 344
9 Blom, P., *The Vertigo Years: Europe* (Basic Books, New York 2008), p. 140
10 Ascher, A., *The Revolution of 1905* (Stanford University Press, 1988), p. 91
11 Figes, O., *A People's Tragedy: The Russian Revolution 1891–1824* (Pimlico, London 1996), p. 178
12 Deutscher, L., *The Prophet Armed: Trotsky, 1879–1921* (Oxford University Press, 1954), p. 168
13 Figes (1996), p. 57
14 Bushnell, J., *Mutiny Amid Repression: Russian Soldiers of the Revolution 1905–1906* (University of Indiana, 1985), pp. 15–21
15 Berdiaev, N., Bulgakov, S., Gershenzon, M., Izgoev, I.S., Kistiakovskii, B., Struve, P. and Frank, S., trans. and ed., M. Schatz and J. Zimmerman, *Vekhi* (Routledge, Milton 1994), p. 89
16 Durnovo Memorandum, recovered from archives of Northern Virginia Community College, available at www.novaonline.nvcc.edu
17 Molisch, P., *Vom Kampf der Tschechen um ihrer Staat* (Braumüller, Vienna, 1929), p. 33
18 Chaadaeva, O. (ed.), *Soldatskie Pis'ma v Gody Mirovoi Voiny 1914–1917* in *Krasnyi Arkhiv* (1934), pp. 127–128

CHAPTER 1

21 Figes (1996), pp. 267–268
20 See Buttar, P., *Germany Ascendant: The Eastern Front, 1915* (Osprey, Oxford 2015), pp. 157–328
21 *Letters of the Tsaritsa to the Tsar 1914–1916* (Hyperion, New York 1987), p. 114
22 Danilov, Y., *La Russie Dans La Guerre Mondiale* (Payot, Paris 1927), p. 475
23 Katkov, G., *Russia 1917: The February Revolution* (Greenwood, Westport CT, 1979), p. 218
24 Lincoln, W., *Passage Through Armageddon: The Russians in War and Revolution* (Oxford University Press, 1994), p. 179
25 Tsentral'nyy Voyenno-Istoricheskiy Arkhiv Moscow, 442, pp. 78–79
26 Podorozhny, N., *Russkaya Armiya v Velikoy Voyne: Narochskaya Operatsiya v Marte 1916 g* (Voenizdat, Moscow 1938), pp. 32–33
27 Buttar, P. (2015), pp. 82–118; for casualty figures, see Tsentral'nyy Voyenno-Istoricheskiy Arkhiv Moscow, 278, p. 53, 969, p. 116, also Podorozhny,(1938), pp. 149–150
28 Lapin, N., (ed.), *Progressivni Blok v 1915–1977gg* (Krasnyi Archiv, Moscow 1932), p. 153
29 Knox, A., *With the Russian Army 1914–1917*, (Hutchinson, London 1921), p. 488
30 Paléologue, M., trans. F. Holt, *An Ambassador's Memoirs* (Doran, New York 1923), Vol. III, p. 213
31 Buchanan, G., *My Mission to Russia and Other Diplomatic Memories* (Cassell, London 1923), Vol. II, p. 28
32 Buchanan (1923), Vol. II, pp. 31–32
33 Ibid., Vol. II, p. 41
34 Ibid., Vol. II, pp. 46–50
35 Stockdale, M., *Paul Miliukov and the Quest for a Liberal Russia, 1880–1918* (Cornell University Press, New York 1996), p. 234
36 Hasegawa, T., *The February Revolution: Petrograd 1917* (University of Washington Press, Seattle 1981), p. 182
37 Bundesarchiv-Militärarchiv Freiburg, RM 5/2971
38 Brunauer, E., *The Peace Proposals of December 1916–January 1917* in *Journal of Modern History* (University of Chicago Press, 1932), Vol. IV (4), pp. 544–571
39 Ludendorff, E., *Meine Kriegerinnerungen 1914–1918* (Mittler, Berlin 1919), p. 258

CHAPTER 2

40 Lyandres, S., *The Fall of Tsarism: Untold Stories of the February 1917 Revolution* (Oxford University Press 2013), pp. 273–275
41 Figes (1996), pp. 288–289

42 Andrei Vladimirovich, *Iz Dnevnika A. V. Romanova za 1916–1917gg* in Krasnyi Archiv XXVI (Leningrad 1928), p. 188
43 Massie, R., *Nicholas and Alexandra* (Dell, New York 1967), p. 389
44 Beéche, A., *The Other Grand Dukes (Sons and Grandsons of Russia's Tsars and Grand Dukes)* (Eurohistory, Richmond CA 2013), p. 27
45 Lichnewsky, M. (trans.), *Lettres des Grands-Ducs à Nicholas II* (Payot, Paris 1926), p. 212
46 Hasegawa (1981), p. 200
47 Quoted in Lincoln (1994), p. 315
48 Shchegolev, P. (ed.), *Padenie Tsarskogo Rezhima: Stenograficheskiy Otchety Doprosov i Pokazanii, Dannykh v 1917gv* (Gosudararstvennoe Isdateltsvo, Moscow 1926), Vol. I, p. 21
49 Rodzianko, M., *Zapiska M. V. Rodzianko* in Pokrovsky, M. (ed.), *Ekonomicheskoe Polozhenie Rossii Pered Revoliutsiei* (Krasnyi Archiv, Petrograd 1925), p. 88
50 Hasegawa (1981), p. 210
51 Burdzhalov, E., *Vtoraia Russkaia Revoliutsiia* (Nauka, Moscow 1967), Vol. I, pp. 108–109
52 *Letters of the Tsaritsa to the Tsar*, p. 440
53 Buchanan (1923), Vol. II, p. 52–54; Paléologue (1923), Vol. III, p. 218
54 Shchegolev (1926), Vol. I, pp. 184–186
55 Gordienko, I., *Iz Boevogo Proshlogo 1914–1918gg* (Gos Isd-Vo Polit Lit-Ry, Moscow 1957), p. 57
56 Lincoln (1994), p. 325
57 Trotsky, L., *History of the Russian Revolution* (trans. M. Eastman, 1932, republished Haymarket, London 2008), Vol. I, p. 108; Burdzhalov (1967), Vol. I, pp. 146–147
58 Shchegolev (1926), Vol. I, p. 190
59 Burdzhalov (1967), Vol. I, p. 179
60 Woodward, D., *World War I Almanac* (Facts on File, New York 2009), p. 175
61 Lincoln (1994), pp. 334–335
62 Mints, I., *Istoriia Velikogo Oktiabria* (Nauka, Moscow 1967), Vol. I, p. 534
63 Knox (1921), Vol. II, pp. 553–555
64 Jones, S., *Russia in Revolution; Being the Experiences of an Englishman in Russia During the Upheaval* (McBride, Nast & Co, New York 1917), pp. 119–121
65 *Fevralskaia Revoliutsiya 1917 Goda* in Krasnyi Archiv (1927), Vol. XXI, p. 5
66 Benckendorff, P., trans. M. Benckendorff, *Last Days at Tsarskoe Selo: Being the Personal Notes and Memories of Count Paul Benckendorff Telling of the Last Sojourn of the Emperor and Empress of Russia at Tsarskoe Selo from March 1 to August 1 1917* (Heinemann, London 1927), p. 21
67 Benckendorff (1927), p. 67
68 Brusilov, A., *Moi Vospominaniia* (Voenizdat, Moscow 1967), p. 73
69 Ibid., p. 76
70 Lincoln (1994), p. 340

71 Shchegolev, P. (ed.), *Otrechenie Nikolaia II: Vospoinaniia Ochevidtsev, Documenty* (Sovyetskiy Pisatel, Moscow 1990), pp. 154–155
72 Translated from a copy of the abdication manifesto in the online documents archive of Brigham Young University, Provo, Utah
73 Nicholas II, *Journal Intime de Nicholas II (Juillet 1914–Juillet 1918)* (Payot, Paris 1934), p. 93
74 Translated from a copy of the abdication manifesto in the online documents archive of Brigham Young University, Provo, Utah
75 Available online from the Soviet History Archive at www.marxists.org
76 Brusilov, (1967), p. 77
77 Benckendorff (1927), pp. 28–29
78 Dehn, L., *The Real Tsaritsa* (Little, Brown & Co, Boston 1922), p. 185
79 Benckendorff (1927), pp. 66–67
80 Ibid., p. 73
81 Quoted in Paléologue (1923), Vol. III, p. 235
82 Benckendorff (1927), pp. 74–76
83 Knox (1921), p. 564

CHAPTER 3

84 Jones (1917), pp. 123–125
85 Buchanan (1923), Vol. II, pp. 91–92
86 Ludendorff (1919), pp. 326–228
87 Bruchmüller, G., *Die Deutsche Artillerie in den Durchbruchsschlachten des Weltkrieges* (Mittler, Berlin 1921), pp. 53–56; Suhrmann, W., *Geschichte des Landwehr-Infanterie-Regiments Nr. 31* (Stalling, Oldenburg 1928), pp. 273–278
88 Hoffmann, M. and Nowak, K., *Die Aufzeichnungen des Generalmajors Max Hoffmann* (Verlag für Kulturpolitik, Berlin 1929), p. 159
89 Knox (1921), Vol. II, pp. 585–586
90 Ibid., Vol. II, pp. 586–588
91 Lenin, V., *Collected Works* (Progress Publishers, Moscow 1964), Vol. XXI, pp. 215–216
92 Bonch-Bruyevich, V., *Na Boevykh Postackh Fevralskoi I Oktiabrskoi Revoliutsii* (Izdateltsvo Federatsiia, Moscow 1931), p. 15
93 Lenin (1964), Vol. XXIV, pp. 21–22
94 Trotsky (2008), Vol. II, pp. 136–137
95 Sabsay, N., *A Moment in History: A Russian Soldier in the First World War* (self-published, Caldwell, ID 1960), pp. 259–261
96 Gurko, V., *War and Revolution in Russia 1914–1917* (Macmillan, New York 1919), pp. 326–327
97 Ibid., p. 328
98 Brusilov (1967), p. 77
99 Cornwall, M., *The Undermining of Austria-Hungary: The Battle for Hearts and*

Minds (Palgrave MacMillan, New York 2000), pp. 40–59
100 Buchanan (1923), Vol. II, p. 117
101 Quoted in Figes (1996), p. 379
102 Paléologue (1923), Vol. III, p. 249
103 Knox (1921), pp. 595–596
104 Gaponenko, L. (ed.), *Revoliutsionnoe Dvizhenie v Rossii Sverzheniia Samoderzhaviia* (Izdat. Akad. Nauk, Moscow 1957), pp. 429–430
105 Browder, R. and Kerensky, A., *The Russian Provincial Government 1917* (Stanford University Press, 1961), Vol. II, p. 1045
106 Tsereteli, I., *Reminiscences of the February Revolution: The April Crisis* in *Russian Review* (University of Kansas, 1955), Vol.XIV, no.2, p. 184
107 Knox (1921), Vol. II, pp. 613–614
108 Miliukov, P., Seignobos, C. and Eisenmann, L., *History of Russia* (Funk & Wagnalls, New York 1969), Vol. II, p. 369
109 Kerensky, A., *The Catastrophe: Kerensky's Own Story of the Russian Revolution* (Dodd, Mead & Co, New York 1927), p. 75
110 Quoted in Chamberlin, W., *The Russian Revolution* (Princeton University Press, 1987), Vol. I, p. 150
111 Quoted in ibid., Vol. I, p. 151
112 Knox (1921), Vol. II, p. 598
113 Ibid., Vol. II, pp. 581–582
114 Paléologue (1923), Vol. III, p. 252
115 Volobuev, P., *Proletariat I Burzhuaziia Rossii v 1917g* (Izdvo Sotsialno-Ekonomicheskoi Litry Mysl, Moscow 1964), p. 153
116 Lincoln (1994), p. 383
117 Heenan, L., *Russian Democracy's Fatal Blunder: The Summer Offensive of 1917* (Praeger, Westport CT 1987), p. 44
118 Gurko (1919), pp. 356–359
119 Quoted in Lincoln (1994), p. 402
120 Brusilov (1967), p. 75
121 Gurko (1919), pp. 371–372
122 Denikin, A., *The Russian Turmoil* (Hutchinson, London 1922), pp. 184–185
123 Ibid., p. 186
124 Gurko (1919), p. 377
125 Knox (1921), Vol. II, pp. 628–629
126 Hoffmann, M., trans. A. Charnot, *The War of Lost Opportunities* (Paul, French, Trubner & Co, London 1924), p. 183

CHAPTER 4

127 Balck, H., trans. D. Zabecki and D. Biederkarten, *Order in Chaos: The Memoirs of General of Panzer Troops Hermann Balck* (University Press of Kentucky, 2015), pp. 72–73

128 Czernin von und zu Chudenitz, O. Graf, *In the World War* (Harper & Collins, New York 1920), pp.151–153
129 Bourbon-Parma, S., *L'Offre de Paix Séparée de l'Autriche* (Plon-Nourrit, Paris 1920), pp. 20–34
130 Ibid., pp. 39–40
131 Amiguet, P., *La Vie du Prince Sixte de Bourbon* (Editions de France, Paris 1936), p. 109
132 Bourbon-Parma (1920), pp. 42–43
133 Ibid., pp. 58–60
134 Ibid., pp. 60–62
135 Watson, A., *Ring of Steel: Germany and Austria-Hungary at War, 1914–1918* (Allen Lane, London 2014), p. 449
136 Fischer, F., *Griff nach der Weltmacht. Die Kriegszielpolitik des kaiserlichen Deutschland 1914/18* (Droste, Düsseldorf 1961), pp. 346–351
137 Cerf, B., *Alsace-Lorraine Since 1870* (MacMillan, New York 1919), p. 32
138 Bourbon-Parma (1920), pp. 76–77
139 Ibid., p. 84
140 Ibid., p. 124
141 Singer, L., *Ottokar Graf Czernin: Staatsmann einer Zeitenwende* (Verlag Styria, Graz 1965), p. 132
142 Czernin (1920), p. 163
143 Ibid., pp. 164–168
144 Ibid., pp. 161–163
145 Ibid., p. 172
146 Herwig, H., *The First World War: Germany and Austria-Hungary 1914–1918* (Arnold, London 1997), p. 315
147 Bourbon-Parma (1920), pp. 150–151
148 Ibid., p. 153
149 Ibid., pp. 172–173
150 Ibid., p. 222
151 *Agreement Between France, Russia, Great Britain and Italy, April 1915* (HM Stationery Office, London)
152 *Minister des Innern 12 July 1917*, Geheimes Staatsarchiv Preussischer Kulturbesitz, Berlin XIV.HA.181,31389
153 Michaelis, H. and Schraepler, E., (eds.), *Ursachen und Folgen. Vom Deutschen Zusammenbruch 1918 und 1945 bis zur Staatlichen Neuordnung Deutschlands in der Gegenwart. Eine Urkunden- und Dokumentensammlung zur Zeitgeschichte* (Dokumenten-Verlag, Berlin 1958), Vol. II, p. 37
154 De Launay, J., *Major Controversies of Contemporary History* (Pergamon, Oxford 1965), pp. 66–73
155 Czernin (1920), pp. 207–208

CHAPTER 5

156 Denikin (1922), pp. 211–212
157 Browder and Kerensky (1961), Vol. I, pp. 880–883
158 Ibid., p. 883
159 Brusilov (1967), p. 78
160 Denikin (1922), pp. 212–214
161 Sukhanov, N., trans. J. Carmichael, *The Russian Revolution: A Personal Record* (Oxford University Press, 1955), p. 227
162 Knox (1921), Vol. II, p. 627
163 Quoted in Bazanov, S., *Pravo Umeret' za Rodinu. 'Batalony Smerti' v Russkoy Armii v 1917 godu* (Pervoye Sentyabrya, Moscow 2008), no. 21
164 Kakurin, N. (ed.), *Razloshenie Armii v 1917 godu* (Gosudarstvennoi Izd-vo, Moscow 1925), p. 181
165 Knox (1921), Vol. II, p. 629
166 Knox (1921), Vol. II, p. 633
167 Denikin (1922), p. 260
168 Gurko (1919), pp. 379–380
169 Denikin (1922), pp. 267–268
170 Ronge, M., *Kriegs- und Industrie-Spionage* (Amalthea, Vienna 1930), pp. 273–275
171 Ibid., p. 273
172 Kakurin (1925), pp. 37–38
173 Lenin (1964), Vol. XX, pp. 13–14
174 *Izvestia*, 2 May 1917, p. 2
175 Czegka, E., Heydendorff, W., Kiszling, R., Klumpner, C., Wisshaupt, E. and Zöbl, G., *Österreich-Ungarns Letzter Krieg 1914–1918* (Verlag der Militärwissenschaftlichen Mitteilungen, Vienna 1936) (hereafter cited as *ÖULK*), Vol. VI, p. 46
176 Ibid., Vol. VI, pp. 53–55, 85–87
177 Browder and Kerensky (1961), pp. 924–925
178 Zayonchkovsky, A., *Perveya Mirovaya Voyna* (Polygon, Moscow 2002), p. 44
179 *ÖULK*, Vol. VI, pp. 224–225
180 Kuhl, H. von, *Der Weltkrieg 1914–1918: Dem Deutschen Volke Dargestellt* (Weller, Berlin 1935), Vol. II, p. 106
181 Smilg-Benario, M., *Von Kerenski zu Lenin: Die Geschichte der Zweiter Russischen Revolution* (Amalthea, Zurich 1929), p. 115; Knox (1921), Vol. II, p. 641
182 Much of the detail in the account that follows is from *ÖULK*, Vol. VI, pp. 228–260
183 Knox (1921), Vol. II, pp. 642–643
184 Browder and Kerensky (1961), Vol. II, p. 943
185 Knox (1921), Vol. II, pp. 643–645
186 Kerensky, A., *Russia's and History's Turning Point* (Duell, Sloan & Peirce, New York 1965), p. 286

187 Knox (1921), Vol. II, p. 646
188 Klecanda, V., *Bitva u Zborówa* (Vojensky Archiv, Prague 1927), pp. 31–32
189 Hoffmann and Nowak (1929), p. 171
190 Knox (1921), Vol. II, p. 649
191 *ÖULK*, Vol. VI, p. 252
192 Quoted in Cornwall, M. and Newman, J. (eds.), *Sacrifice and Rebirth: the Legacy of the Last Habsburg War* (Berghahn, New York 2016), p. 165

CHAPTER 6

193 Much of the detail in the account that follows is from *ÖULK*, Vol. VI, p. 262ff
194 Hindenburg, P. von, trans. F. Holt, *Out of my Life* (Cassell, London 1920), p. 275
195 Litzmann, K., *Lebenserinnerungen* (Eisenschmidt, Berlin 1928), Vol. II, p. 156
196 Ibid., Vol. II, pp. 157–158
197 Buttar, P., *Russia's Last Gasp* (Osprey, Oxford 2016), p. 340
198 Litzmann (1928), Vol. II, pp. 158–159
199 Ibid., Vol. II, pp. 159–160
200 Heenan (1987), pp. 114–117
201 Denikin (1922), pp. 286–287
202 Ibid., pp. 287–288
203 Ibid., pp. 288–289
204 Wildman, K., *The End of the Russian Imperial Army* (Princeton University Press, 1980), Vol. II, pp. 46–54; Mangulis, V., *Latvia in the Wars of the 20th Century* (Cognition Books, Princeton), pp. 20–22
205 Wildman (1980), Vol. II, pp. 116–120
206 Quoted in Zayonchkovsky, A., *Strategicheskiy Ocherk Voyny 1914–1918gg* (Vysshiy Voyennyy Redaktsionnyy Sovet, Moscow 1923), Vol. VII, p. 77
207 *Sbornik Dokumentov Mirovoy Imperialisticheskoy Voyny na Russkom Fronte 1914–1917gg* (Moscow, 1939) 24/IV 1613
208 Browder and Kerensky (1961), Vol. II, p. 967
209 Golder, F. (ed.), *Documents of Russian History 1914–1917* (Century, New York 1927), p. 433
210 Litzmann (1928), Vol. II, p. 163
211 Ludendorff (1919), pp. 379–380
212 Hoffmann (1927), p. 174
213 Litzmann (1928), Vol. II, p. 165
214 Quoted in Knox (1921), Vol. II, p. 666
215 Litzmann (1928), Vol. II, p. 170
216 Figes (1996), p. 408
217 Strakhovsky, L., *Was There a Kornilov Rebellion? A Reappraisal of the Evidence* in *Slavonic and East European Review* (University College London, 1955), Vol. 33, No. 81, p. 375

218 Gurko (1919), pp. 386–391
219 Denikin (1922), p. 293
220 Buchbinder, N. (ed.), *Na Fronte v Predoktiabr'skie Dni – Po Sekretnym Materialam Stavki* in *Krasnaia Letopis* (Leningradskii Institut Istorii, 1923), No. 6, pp. 21–49
221 Denikin (1922), p. 298
222 Rabinowitch, A., *The Bolsheviks Come to Power – the Revolution of 1917 in Petrograd* (Norton, New York 1976), p. 97

CHAPTER 7

223 Knox (1921), Vol. II, p. 657
224 Pares, B., *My Russian Memoirs* (Cape, London 1931), p. 465
225 Knox (1921), Vol. II, p. 657
226 Ibid., Vol. II, p. 659
227 Quoted in Figes (1996), pp. 428–429
228 Kulikov, S., *Imperator Nikolai II v Gody Pervoy Mirovoy Voyny* (SPB, St Petersburg 2000), p. 285
229 Polner, T., *Zhiznennyi put' Kniazia Georgiia Evgenievicha L'vova: Lichnost', Vzgliady, Usloviia Dieiatel'nosti* (Payot, Paris 1932), p. 258
230 Martynov, E., *Kornilov: Popytka Voennogo Perevorota* (Izd. Voennoi Tip. Upr. Delami Nkvm, Leningrad 1927), p. 20
231 Denikin (1922), pp. 306–307
232 Martynov (1927), p. 33
233 Savinkov, B., *K Dielu Kornilova* (Union, Paris 1919), p. 14
234 Trotsky (2008), p. 833
235 Knox (1921), Vol. II, p. 680
236 Quoted in Rabinowich (1976), p. 114
237 Stepun, F., *Byvshee i Nesbyvsheesia* (Chekhova, New York 1956), Vol. II, pp. 162–163
238 Halpern, P., *A Naval History of World War I* (Naval Institute Press, Annapolis 1995), pp. 196–198; Staff, G., *German Battlecruisers 1914–1918* (Osprey, Oxford 2006), p. 15
239 Hoffmann and Nowak (1929), p. 177
240 Hoffmann and Nowak (1929), p. 178
241 *Novoye Vremya*, 25 August 1917 [old calendar], p. 3
242 *Izvestiya*, 26 August 1917 [old calendar], p. 3
243 *Delo Naroda*, 25 August 1917 [old calendar], p. 1
244 Gippius, Z., *Sinaia Kniga: Peterburgski Dnevnik 1914–1918* (Tipografija Radenkoviča Belgrade 1929), p. 164
245 Denikin (1922), pp. 304–305
246 Kerensky, A., *The Prelude to Bolshevism: The Kornilov Rebellion* (Dodd, Mead & Co, New York 1919), p. 128

247 Lukomsky, A., *Vospominaniia Generala A S Lukomskago* (Otto Kirchner, Berlin 1922), Vol. I, pp. 239–240
248 Knox (1921), Vol. II, p. 682
249 Denikin (1922), pp. 316–317
250 Ibid., pp. 318–319
251 Martynov (1927), pp. 110–111
252 Denikin (1922), p. 319
253 Ibid., p. 321
254 Ibid., pp. 322–323
255 Rabinowitch (1976), p. 149
256 Gurko (1919), pp. 391–298
257 Knox (1921), Vol. II, pp. 688–689
258 Barrett, M., *Operation Albion: The German Conquest of the Baltic Islands* (Indiana University Press, 2008), p. 84
259 Staff, G., *Battle for the Baltic Islands 1917: Triumph of the Imperial German Navy* (Pen & Sword Maritime, Barnsley 2008), pp. 11–12
260 Barrett (2008), pp. 63–65
261 Staff (2008), pp. 17–20
262 Ibid., p. 34
263 Barrett (2008), pp. 168–170
264 Staff (2008), pp. 89–94
265 Ibid., pp. 112–117
266 Hoffmann and Nowak (1929), p. 182

CHAPTER 8

267 Buchanan, A, pp. 191–194
268 Lenin (1964), Vol. XXVI, pp. 19–21
269 Ibid., Vol. XXVI, pp. 22–27
270 Trotsky (2008), pp. 709–710
271 Rabinowitch (1976), p. 202
272 Trotsky (2008), p. 1265
273 Ibid., p. 1271
274 Ibid., pp. 1199–1200
275 Ibid., pp. 1314–1316
276 Mitelman, M., Bistriansky, V., Glebov, B. and Uliansky, A., *Istoriia Putilovskogo Zavoda* (Institut Istori Partii, Leningrad 1939), Vol. I, p. 569; Wade, R., *Red Guards and Workers' Militias* (Stanford University Press, Stanford 1984), p. 167
277 Trotsky (2008), p. 1319
278 Ibid., p. 1322
279 Knox (1921), Vol. II, p. 702–703
280 Quoted in Trotsky (2008), pp. 1325–1326

281 Lenin (1964), Vol. XXVI, pp. 234–235
282 Knox (1921), Vol. II, pp. 706–707
283 Melgunov, S., Pushkarev, S., Pushkarev, B. and Beaver, J., *The Bolshevik Seizure of Power* (ABC Clio, Oxford 1972), p. 81
284 Daniels, R., *Red October: The Bolshevik Revolution of 1917* (Scribner, New York 1967), p. 160
285 Knox (1921), pp. 709–711
286 Buchanan, A, pp. 207–208
287 Fraiman, A. (ed.), *Oktiabr'skoe Vooruzhennoe Vosstanie: Semnadtsatyi God v Petrograde* (Institut Istorii, Leningrad 1967), Vol. II, pp. 346–347
288 Trotsky (2008), pp. 1414–1415
289 Blagonravov, G., *The Fortress of Peter and Paul* in McIlhone, R. (ed. and trans.), *Petrograd, October 1917: Reminiscences of Active Participants in the Armed Uprising* (Foreign Languages Publishing House, Moscow 1957), p. 206
290 Antonov-Ovseyenko, V., *V Semnadtsatom Godu* (Gosudarstvennoe Izd-vo Khudozhestvennoi Lit-ry, Moscow 1933), p. 319
291 Robien, Comte L. de, trans. C. Sykes, *The Diary of a Diplomat in Russia 1917–1918* (Joseph, London 1969), p. 164
292 Knox (1921), pp. 712–713
293 Knox (1921), p. 717
294 Quoted in Figes (1996), p. 499
295 *Rabochy I Soldat* No. 9, Petrograd, 26 October 1917 [old calendar]
296 Mikhutina, I., *Ukrainskiy Brestskiy Mir. Put' Vykhoda Rossii iz Pervoy Morovoy Voyni I Anatomiya Konflikta Mezhdu Sovnarkomom RSFSR I Prvatel'strom Ukrainskoy Tsentral'noy Rady* (Books on Demand, Stoughton 2015), pp. 180–188
297 Niessel, H., *Le Triomphe des Bolchéviks et la Paix de Brest-Litovsk: Souvenirs 1917–1918* (Plon, Paris 1940), p. 110

CHAPTER 9

298 Ludendorff (1919), p. 409
299 Hoffmann (1924), p. 201
300 *Proceedings of the Brest-Litovsk Peace Conference* (Washington Government Printing Officer, 1918), pp. 17–20
301 Buchanan (1923), p. 225
302 Bonch-Bruyevich, M., *Vsia Vlast' Sovietam* (Voenno Isd-vo, Moscow, 1964), p. 231
303 Quoted in Figes (1996), p. 539
304 Czernin (1920), pp. 217–219
305 Ibid., pp. 241–242
306 Hoffmann (1924), p. 204
307 Czernin (1920), p. 246
308 *Brest-Litovsk Peace Conference* (1918), pp. 38–39

309 Czernin (1920), pp. 250–251
310 Hoffmann (1924), pp. 209–210
311 Czernin (1920), pp. 253–354
312 Hoffmann (1924), p. 211
313 *Obrashchenie Narodnogo Komissariata Inostrannykh Del k Narodam I Pravitel'stvam Soyuznykh Stran* 30 December 1917 in *Dokumenty Vneshnei Politiki SSSR* (Izd-vo Polit. Litry, Moscow 1957), Vol. I, pp. 69–70
314 Hoffmann (1924), p. 213
315 Ibid., p. 214
316 Czernin (1920), p. 256
317 Ibid., p. 258
318 Ibid., p. 259
319 Ibid., pp. 264–266
320 Lenin (1964), Vol. 36, p. 468
321 Gessen, I. (ed.), *Arkhiv Russkoi Revoliutsii* (Slovo, Berlin 1922–1925), Vol. XX, pp. 205–206
322 Bundesarchiv Koblenz, Nachlass Schwertfeger 119, Vol. II, pp. 73–75
323 Hoffmann and Nowak (1929), p. 186
324 Lenin (1964), Vol. 26, pp. 522–524
325 Ibid., Vol. 26, p. 525
326 Hoffmann and Nowak (1929), pp. 186–187
327 Lenin (1964), Vol. 27, pp. 30–33
328 Hoffmann and Nowak (1929), p. 187
329 Lenin (1964), Vol. 27, pp. 36–39
330 *Brest-Litovsk Peace Conference* (1918), pp. 185–187
331 Snyder, T., *The Red Prince: The Secret Lives of a Habsburg Archduke* (Basic Books, New York 2008), p. 42
332 Ibid., p. 100
333 Baumgart, W., *Deutsche Ostpolitik 1918. Von Brest-Litowsk bis zum Ende des Ersten Weltkrieges* (Oldenbourg, Vienna 1966), pp. 132–136
334 For further details see Hoffmann, M., *An Allen Enden Moskau – Das Problem des Bolschewismus in Seinen Jüngsten Auswirkungen* (Verlag für Kulturpolitik, Berlin 1925)

CHAPTER 10

335 Ioaniţiu, A., *Războiul României (1916–1919)* (Typografia Geniului, Bucharest 1929), Vol. II, p. 283
336 Balck (2015), p. 74
337 Bujac, E., *Campagnes de l'Armée Roumaine 1916–1919* (Charles-Lavauzelle, Paris 1933), pp. 100–102
338 *ÖULK*, Vol. VI, Annex A, p. 12

339 Ibid., Vol. VI, Annex A, pp. 3–4
340 Ibid., Vol. VI, p. 104
341 Mackensen, A. von, *Briefe und Auszeichnungen des Generalfeldmarschalls aus Krieg und Frieden* (Bibliographisches Institut, Leipzig 1938), p. 334
342 Joseph August (Archduke), *A Világháború Okai: a Hármasszövetség Története* (Róna Nyomda, Budapest 1942), Vol. V, pp. 70–72
343 Kiritzesco, C., *La Roumanie dans la Guerre Mondiale 1916–1919* (Payot, Paris 1934), p. 308
344 *ÖULK*, Vol. VI, p. 348
345 Dabija, G., *România în războiul mondial 1916–1919* (Monitorul Oficial şi Imprimeriile Statului, Bucharest 1936), pp. 45–58
346 Morgen, C. von, *Meiner Truppen Heldenkämpfe* (Mittler, Berlin 1920), pp. 123–124
347 Ibid., pp. 125–126
348 Balck (2015), pp. 80–81
349 Ibid., p. 83
350 Mackensen (1938), pp. 337–338
351 Morgen (1920), pp. 127–128
352 Ibid., p. 129
353 Mackensen (1938), p. 344
354 Czernin (1920), pp. 288–289
355 Ibid., p. 291
356 Mackensen (1938), p. 345
357 Czernin (1920), pp. 295–296
358 Mackensen (1938), pp. 352–353
359 Bundesarchiv-Militärarchiv Freiburg, H08-39/314, Nachlass Mackensen

CHAPTER 11

360 Garande, J., *The Cost of Freedom* (Authorhouse, Bloomington 2011), p. 33
361 Ketola, E., *Kansalliseen Kansanvaltaan. Suomen Itsenäisyys, Sosiaalidemokraatit ja Venäjän Vallankumous 1917* (Tammi, Helsinki 1987), pp. 368–384
362 Upton, A., *The Finnish Revolution 1917–1918* (University of Minnesota Press 1980), Vol. I, pp. 321–342
363 Goltz, R. von der, *Meine Sendung in Finnland und Baltikum* (Koehler, Leipzig 1920), p. 47
364 Screen, J., *Mannerheim: The Finnish Years* (Hurst, London 2000), pp. 43–49
365 Goltz (1920), p. 44
366 Ahto, S., *Sotaretkillä* in Manninen, O (ed.), *Itselnäistymisen Vuodet 1917–1920* (Valtion, Helsinki 1993), pp. 180–198
367 Goltz (1920), pp. 50–52
368 Hoppu, T. and Haapala, P., *Tampere 1918: A Town in the Civil War* (Tampere Museum, Tampere 2010), pp. 181–201

369 Ylikangas, H., *Tie Tampereelle: Dokumentoitu Kuvaus Tampereen Antautumiseen Johtaneista Sotatapahtumista Suomen Sisällissodassa* (WSOY, Porvoo 1994), pp. 249–250
370 Lappalainen, J., *Punakaartin Sota* (Valtion Painatuskeskus, Helsinki 1981), p. 137
371 Hoppu and Haapala (2010), p. 203
372 Ibid., pp. 204–206
373 Ibid., p. 157
374 Goltz (1920), pp. 59–60
375 Ibid., p. 103

CHAPTER 12

376 For a summary of the proposals for unrestricted submarine warfare, see Bundesarchiv-Militärarchiv Freiburg, R 5/2791
377 Ludendorff (1919), p. 261
378 Scheidemann, P., *Der Zusammenbruch* (Verlag für Sozialwissenschaft, Berlin 1921), pp. 40–42
379 Ludendorff (1919), p. 358
380 Michaelis and Schraepler (1958), pp. 37–38
381 Ludendorff (1919), p. 365
382 Herwig (1997), p. 395; Thaer, A. von, *Generalstabsdienst an der Front und in der OHL. Aus Briefen und Tagebuchaufzeichnungen* (Vendenhoeck & Ruprecht, Göttingen 1958), pp. 163–170
383 Rupprecht von Bayern, *Mein Kriegstagebuch* (Deutscher National Verlag, Munich 1929), Vol. II, p. 387
384 *Talk with Colonel C. Allanson* 19 August 1937 in Liddell Hart Centre for Military Archives (King's College, London) 11/1937/69
385 For a detailed discussion, see Woodward, D., 'Did Lloyd George Starve the British Army of Men Prior to the German Offensive of 21March 1918?' in *The Historical Journal* (Cambridge University Press, 1984), Vol. XXVII, pp. 241–252
386 Stevenson, D., *With Our Backs to the Wall: Victory and Defeat in 1918* (Penguin, London 2011), p.75
387 Hindenburg (1920), pp. 364–366
388 Watson, A., *Enduring the Great War: Combat, Morale and Collapse in the German and British Armies 1914–1918* (Cambridge University Press 2008), pp.196–197, 205–206, 212
389 Ludendorff (1919), p. 518
390 Ludendorff (1919), pp. 550–551
391 Stachelbeck, C., *Militärische Effektivität im Ersten Weltkrieg: Die 11. Bayerische Infanteriedivision 1915 bis 1918* (Ferdinand Schöningh, Paderborn 2010), pp. 346–347
392 Harris, J. and Barr, N., *Amiens to the Armistice: The BEF in the Hundred Days' Campaign 8 August–November 1918* (Brassey, London 1999), p. 291

393 Groener, W., *Lebenserinnerungen: Jugend – Generalstab – Weltkrieg* (Vendenhoeck & Ruprecht, Göttingen 1957), p. 347
394 Buttar, P., *Collision of Empires: The War on the Eastern Front in 1914* (Osprey, Oxford 2014), p. 171
395 Bihl, W., *Deutsche Quellen zur Geschichte des Ersten Weltkrieges* (Wissenschaftliche Buchgesellschaft, Darmstadt 1991), p. 475
396 Link, A. (ed.), *The Papers of Woodrow Wilson* (Princeton University Press, Princeton NJ 1985), Vol. LI, pp. 333–334
397 *Foreign Relations of the United States 1918: Supplement I, The World War* (US Government Printing Office, Washington DC 1933), pp. 380–381
398 Link (1985), Vol. LI, pp. 417–419
399 Ludendorff (1919), pp. 614–615
400 Ludendorff (1919), pp. 616–617
401 Wheeler-Bennett, J., *Ludendorff: The Soldier and the Politician* in *Virginia Quarterly Review* (Charlottesville, VA 1938), 14 (2), pp. 187–202
402 Roth, A., *Die Juden im Heere: Eine Statistische Untersuchung Nach Amtlichen Quellen* (Deutscher Volks-Verlag, Munich 1919)
403 Herwig, H., *Luxury Fleet: The Imperial German Navy 1888–1918* (Routledge, London 2014), p. 245
404 Ibid., p. 245
405 Howarth, D., *The Dreadnoughts* (Time-Life, Fairfax VA 1980), pp. 158–159
406 Moritz, V. and Leidinger, H. (eds.), *Die Nacht des Kirpitschnikow. Eine Andere Geschichte des Ersten Weltkriegs* (Deutike im Paul Szolnay, Vienna 2006), pp. 228–230
407 Hafner, S., *Die Deutsche Revolution 1918–1919* (Rowohlt, Reinbek 2002), p. 65
408 Baden, M. von and Mann, G., *Erinnerungen und Dokumente* (Klett, Stuttgart 1968), p. 599
409 Herwig (1997), p. 445

CHAPTER 13

410 May, A., *The Passing of the Habsburg Monarchy 1914–1918* (University of Pennsylvania Press, Philadelphia 1996), p. 199
411 Quoted in Emmerson, C., *1913: The World Before the Great War* (Bodley Head, London 2013), p. 98
412 Krist, G., *Pascholl Plenny!* (Seidel & Sohn, Vienna 1936), p. 6
413 Kriegsarchiv Vienna, Nachlass Schwestek B/89
414 Mack, K., *Galizien um die Jahrhundertwende: Politische, Soziale und Kulturelle Verbindungen mit Österreich* in *Schriftenreihe des Österreichischen Ost- und Südosteuropa-Instituts* (Verlag für Geschichte und Politik, Vienna 1990), Vol. XVI, p. 14
415 Allgemeines Verwaltungsarchiv Vienna, 22/Galizien K2118 No 14672
416 Rauchensteiner, M., *Der Erste Weltkrieg und das Ende der Habsburger-Monarchie* (Böhlau, Vienna 2013), pp. 734–737

417 Judson, P., *The Habsburg Empire: A New History* (Belknap, Cambridge Mass. 2016), p. 422
418 Kalvoda, J., *The Genesis of Czechoslovakia* (East European Monographs, Boulder 1986), pp. 62–63
419 Maksakov, V. and Turunov, A., *Khronika Grazhdanskoi Voiny v Sibiri 1917–1918* (Gosizdat, Moscow 1926), p. 168
420 For a good summary of the history of the Czechoslovak Legion, see Bradley, J., *The Czechoslovak Legion in Russia 1914–1920* (East European Monographs, Boulder 1990)
421 Woodward, D., *Mutiny at Cattaro, 1918* in *History Today* (London 1976), 26 (12), pp. 804–810
422 Galantai, J. trans. E. Grusz and J. Pokoly, *Hungary in the First World War* (Akademiai Kiado, Budapest 1990), pp. 224–226
423 Kann, R., *Die Sixtusaffäre und die Geheimen Friedensverhandlungen Österreich-Ungarns im Ersten Weltkrieg* (Oldenbourg, Munich 1966), p. 41
424 *ÖULK*, Vol. VII, pp. 497–499
425 Ibid., Vol. VII, p. 561
426 Heeresgeschichtliches Museum Vienna, *Verzichtserklärung von Kaiser Karl I. von Österreich 11 November 1918*
427 Fink, C., *Defending the Rights of Others: The Great Powers, the Jews, and International Minority Protection 1878–1938* (Cambridge University Press, 2004), pp. 110–112
428 Portisch, H., *Österreich. Die unterschätzte Republik* (Verlag Kremayr & Scheriau, Vienna 1989), p. 117

CHAPTER 14

429 The full declaration of independence is available at www.president.ee
430 Biden, J., *The Baltic States and Weimar Ostpolitik* (Cambridge University Press, 2002), p. 10
431 Sibul, E., *Logistical aspects of the Estonian War of Independence 1918–1920,* in *Baltic Security and Defence Review* (Baltic Defence College, Tartu 2010), Vol. 12, no. 2, pp. 109–110
432 Mannerheim, C., trans. E. Lewenhaupt, *The Memoirs of Marshal Mannerheim* (Dutton, New York 1954), p. 221
433 Kinvig, C., *Churchill's Crusade: The British Invasion of Russia 1918–1920* (Hambledon Continuum, London 2006), pp. 259–263
434 Davies, N., *White Eagle, Red Star: the Polish-Soviet War, 1919–20* (Pimlico, London 2003)
435 Volkogonov, D., *Lenin: Life and Legacy* (Harper Collins, London 1994), p. 482
436 Maide, J., *Estonian War of Independence 1918–1920* (Graphic House, Washington, reprinted 1968), p. 23
437 Reek, N., 'Lemsalu – Roopa – Võnnu – Ronneburgi Lahing 19 – 23 VI 1919 a' in *Sõdur* (Riigi Trükikoda, Tallinn 1922), no. 6, p. 158

438 Quoted in Bennett, G., *Cowan's War: The Story of British Naval Operations in the Baltic, 1918–1920* (Collins, London 1964), p. 31
439 Ibid., pp. 34–35
440 Maide (1968), p. 21
441 Zoffe, V., *Pyat' Let Krasnogo Flota* (Narodnyy Komissariat po Morskim Delam, Petrograd 1922), pp. 53–54
442 Quoted in Bennett (1964), p. 41
443 Raskolnikov, F., *Raskazy Michmana Il'ina* (Sovetskaia Literatura, Moscow 1934), p. 76
444 Maide (1968), pp. 21–23
445 Reported in the *New York Times* (22 January 1919)
446 Traksmaa, A., *Lühike Vabadussõja Ajalugu* (Olion, Tallinn 1992), p. 109
447 Ibid., p. 111
448 Sibul (2010), p. 117
449 Maide (1968), p. 31
450 Lincoln, W., *Red Victory: A History of the Russian Civil War* (Sphere, London 1991), pp. 290–291
451 Smith, C., *Finland and the Russian Revolution 1918–1922* (University of Georgia Press, Athens GA 1958), p. 142
452 Bennett (1964), pp. 125–126; see also Agar, A., *Footprints in the Sea* (Evans, London 1959), pp. 110–115
453 Ibid., pp. 324–325
454 Zoffe 91922), p. 118
455 Duke, P., *Red Dusk and the Morrow: Adventures and Investigations in Red Russia* (Doubleday, Page & Co., New York 1922), p. 215
456 Ibid., pp. 235–236
457 Ibid., pp. 298–306
458 Lincoln (1991), p. 292
459 Maide (1968), p. 37
460 Ibid., p. 39
461 Ibid., p. 39
462 Tomilov, P., *Severno-Zapadnyi Front Grazhdanskoi Voiny v Rossii 1919g* (Tomilov Collection, Hoover Institution Archives, Stanford CA), pp. 437–438
463 Sibul (2010), p. 126

CHAPTER 15

464 Ģērmanis, U., *Oberst Vācietis und die Lettischen Schützen im Weltkrieg und in der Oktoberrevolution* (Almqvist & Wiksell, Stockholm 1974), pp. 290–293
465 Eksteins, M., *Walking Since Daybreak: a Story of Eastern Europe, World War II and the Heart of our Century* (Mariner, New York 2000), p. 62
466 Rozenšteins, H. (ed.), *Latvijas Armija 20 Gados* (reprinted from a 1939 Latvian Army publication by Raven Printing, Inc., Grand Haven Mich. 1974), p. 66

467 Waite, R., *Vanguard of Nazism* (W. W. Norton and Company, London 1969), p. 105
468 Bilmanis, A., *A History of Latvia* (Princeton University Press, 1951), p. 310
469 Plensners, A., *Divdesmitā Gadsimta Pārvērtības* (Grāmatu Draugs, Brooklyn 1978), p. 203
470 Samsons, V. (ed.), *Latvijas PSR Mazā Enciklopēdija* (Zinātne, Rīga 1967), p. 690
471 Goltz (1920), p. 120
472 Ibid., p. 125
473 Ibid., p. 126
474 Ibid., pp. 129–130
475 Ibid., pp. 136–137
476 Ibid., p. 137
477 Ibid., p. 169
478 Kroders, A., *Atmiņas* (Imanta Copenhagen 1968), pp. 305–312; see also Goltz (1920), pp. 170–171
479 Plensners (1978), pp. 50–51
480 Chappey, J., *Au Pays des Porte-Glaives* in *La Revue de Genève 7* (Publicitas, Geneva 1928), pp. 194–195
481 Waite (1969), p. 118
482 Goltz (1920), pp. 149–151
483 Rozenšteins (1974), pp. 80–82
484 Goltz (1920), p. 154
485 Ibid., p. 182
486 Mangulis (1983), p. 50; see also Kroders (1968), pp. 314–325, Plensners (1978), pp. 358–366
487 Goltz (1920), p. 184
488 Ibid., p. 185
489 Ibid., pp. 189–190
490 Bundesarchiv Berlin, *Akten der Reichskanzlei, Kabinett Schneidemann*, pp. 209–225
491 Goltz (1920), p. 190
492 Medem, W. E. von, *Riga Himmelfahrt*, in Goltz (1920), pp. 296–299
493 Goltz (1920), p. 195
494 Bilmanis (1951), p. 322
495 Tallents, S., *Man and Boy* (Faber & Faber, London 1943), p. 310
496 Rozenšteins (1974), pp. 113–114
497 Goltz (1920), p. 200
498 Ibid., p. 201
499 Ibid., p. 205
500 Ibid., pp. 211–112
501 Ibid., p. 212
502 Ibid., p. 213
503 Nicholson, N., *Alex* (Weidenfeld & Nicolson, London 1973), p. 44

504 Rozenšteins (1974), p. 173, see also Goltz (1920), p. 210
505 Ibid., pp. 215–216
506 Ibid., p. 222
507 Ibid., p. 225
508 Ibid., pp. 237–239, see also Eksteins (2000), pp. 78–79
509 Goltz (1920), p. 257
510 Ibid., p. 270
511 Rei, A., *The Drama of the Baltic Peoples* (Kirjastus Vaba Eesti, Stockholm 1970), p. 101
512 Goltz (1920), p. 272
513 Ibid., p. 273
514 Rozenšteins (1974), pp. 176–177
515 Rei (1970), p. 103
516 Ibid., p. 105. For details of German troop movements, see Goltz (1920), pp. 277–280
517 Rozenšteins (1974), p. 187
518 Ibid., p. 193
519 Kramer, A., *Dynamic of Destruction: Culture and Mass Killing in the First World War* (Oxford University Press 2008), p. 308
520 Graber, G., *History of the SS* (D. McKay, New York 1978), p. 29
521 Bilmanis (1951), p. 329, Rei (1970), p. 116

CHAPTER 16

522 Brailsford, H., *Across the Blockade: A Record of travels in Enemy Europe* (Allen & Unwin, London 1919), p. 80
523 Eidintas, A., 'Restoration of the State' in Eidintas, A., Zalys, V. and Senn, A., *Lithuania in European Politics: The Years of the First Republic, 1918–1940* (Donnelley & Sons, Harrisonburg 1997), p. 21
524 Gerutis, A., 'Independent Lithuania' in Gerutis A. (ed.), trans. Algirdas Budreckis, *Lithuania: 700 Years*, 6th edn (Manyland, New York 1984), pp. 151–162
525 Madajczyk, C., *Generalna Gubernia w Planach Hitlerowskich. Studia* (Wydawnictwo Naukowe PWN, Warsaw 1961), pp. 88–89
526 Holborn, H., *A History of Modern Germany* (Princeton University Press, 1982), p. 429
527 Davies (2003), p. 10
528 Eidintas (1997), p. 36
529 Davies (2003), p. 19
530 Smele, J., *Historical Dictionary of the Russian Civil Wars* (Rowman & Littlefield, Lanham MD 2015), p. 284
531 Lesčius, V., *Lietuvos kariuomenė nepriklausomybės kovose 1918–1920* (General Jonas Žemaitis Military Academy of Lithuania, Vilnius 2004), p. 34

532 'Józef Piłsudski (1867–1935)' available at http://en.poland.gov.pl/Jozef,Pilsudski,%281867-1935%29,1972.html
533 MacMillan, M., *Paris 1919: Six Months That Changed the World* (Random House, New York 2002), p. 211
534 Davies (2003), p. 50
535 *Historia Polski* (Państwowe Wydawn Naukowe, Warsaw 1966), Vol. IV, p. 258
536 Davies (2003), pp. 51–52
537 Lesčius(2004), p. 252
538 Eidintas (1997), pp. 220–221
539 President Wilson's Message to Congress, January 8, 1918; Records of the United States Senate, Record Group 46, United States National Archives
540 Senn, A., *The Great Powers, Lithuania and the Vilna Question* (Brill, Leiden 1966), p. 20
541 Wasilewski, L., *Józef Piłsudski Jakim Go Znałem* (Rój, Warsaw 1935), pp. 205–206
542 Senn (1966), p. 21
543 Lesčius (2004), pp. 259–278
544 Davies (2003), p. 61
545 Watt, R., *Bitter Glory: Poland and its Fate 1918–1939* (Simon & Schuster, New York 1979), p. 126
546 Trotsky, L., *Stalin* (Hollis & Carter, London 1947), p. 332

CHAPTER 17

547 Buttar, P., *Between Giants: The Battle for the Baltics in World War II* (Osprey, Oxford 2013), pp. 40–45
548 Rademacher, M., *Reichsland Elsaß-Lothringen 1871–1919* (Osnabrück University, 2006) University thesis available online
549 Czernin (1920), pp. 302–305
550 Martin, T., *The Affirmative Action Empire: Nations and Nationalism in the Soviet Union 1923–1939* (Cornell University Press, Ithaca 2001), p. 311
551 Balck (2015), pp. 128–133
552 Lloyd George, D., *The Truth about the Peace Treaties* (Gollancz, London 1938)
553 Keynes, J., *The Economic Consequences of the Peace* (Harcourt, Brace & Howe, New York 1920), pp. 90–91
554 Mantoux, E., *Carthaginian Peace, or The Economic Consequences of Mr Keynes* (Scribner, New York 1952)
555 Balck (2015), p. 137

INDEX